MAKERS OF AMERICAN DIPLOMACY

From BENJAMIN FRANKLIN to HENRY KISSINGER

MAKERS OF AMERICAN DIPLOMACY

From BENJAMIN FRANKLIN to HENRY KISSINGER

Edited by
FRANK J. MERLI
and
THEODORE A. WILSON

CHARLES SCRIBNER'S SONS, NEW YORK

Library of Congress Cataloging in Publication Data
Merli, Frank J.   1929–
    Makers of American diplomacy.
    Includes bibliographies.
    1. Diplomats—United States. 2. United States—
Foreign relations. I. Wilson, Theodore A., 1940–
joint author. II. Title.
E183.7.M472   327'.2'0922[B]   73-1321
ISBN 0-684-13786-0
ISBN 0-684-13797-6 Vol I (pbk.)
ISBN 0-684-13798-4 Vol II (pbk.)

1 3 5 7 9 11 13 15 17 19 c/c 20 18 16 14 12 10 8 6 4 2

Printed in the United States of America

To All Our Children

CONTENTS

PREFACE

These biographical essays—all especially commissioned for this collection—encompass a wide range of interpretive viewpoints and represent a significant dimension of the nation's international experience, stretching from the revolutionary war experiences of Benjamin Franklin to the cold war detente of Henry Kissinger. The figures we have chosen include the obvious presidents and secretaries of state, but to give the reader an idea of the variety and depth of American involvement in foreign affairs, we have also included a representative sample of second-echelon makers of diplomacy. In the selection of contributors we have attempted a balance, geographical as well as generational; but our emphasis has been on the new generation of diplomatic historians trained in the late 1950s and the 1960s. By allowing the contributors the widest possible range of interpretive freedom, encouraging them to find their own ways to illuminate the nature and significance of their subjects, and refraining from any attempt to reconcile opposing interpretations, we intended to avoid the dangers of a facile "consensus" approach and the pitfalls of a "problems" reader. We hope that the collection represents a fair cross section of the debate on the meaning of American diplomacy and the contributions of the men who have molded it.

Because the thrust of this collection is interpretive rather than monographic—and because we hoped to keep the book within manageable bounds—the citations and the scholarly apparatus that a more technical compilation might be expected to contain have been reduced. Omissions should not be difficult to rectify, however; in nearly every case the contributors have derived their essays from works in progress or recently completed in which full documentation can be found.

In the preparation of this volume we received the cooperation of many experts who read the essays for accuracy of information and validity of viewpoint and made helpful, perceptive comments on early drafts. To identify them might imply support for views they do not hold; so we have elected to thank them anonymously but publicly. In addition, Alexander DeConde of the University of California at Santa Barbara, Walter LaFeber of Cornell University, and Richard Leopold of Northwestern University offered helpful suggestions about contributors and the format of the book. Robert Beisner of American University played a key role in the planning stages of the project and has supported it throughout. Without in any way implicating these men in the imperfections this work may contain, we thank them sincerely for the generosity that prompted their responses to our requests for help.

The staff at Scribners, especially Elsie Kearns and Barbara Wood, have been cooperative throughout; their careful attention to detail has saved us from many errors. Mrs. Joan Jander of Dyer, Indiana, compiled the index.

Above all others, one person requires public thanks for his part in bringing this work to fruition. In addition to training both editors and a number of contributors (and coauthoring an essay), Robert H. Ferrell of Indiana University has read all the selections, offering incisive criticism. When the mechanics of the project and the difficulty of keeping so many historians in harness threatened to overwhelm us, his calm and judicious advice brought order and a measure of sanity to the operation. At every stage of the project he has been a wise and sympathetic counselor, and for his contributions we are deeply grateful.

The real heroes of the project are the authors, who struggled against an almost impossible deadline, who cooperated so fully in the task of putting the pieces together—and who so cheerfully suffered our sometimes heavy-handed commentary. For the merits of the work they deserve full credit. They have demonstrated that diplomatic history can deal imaginatively with ideas, that it can incorporate and refine new methodological insights from other branches of history and from other disciplines. Their efforts reveal that historians of divergent backgrounds, ideological commitments, and convictions can move beyond the partisanship and acrimony that have so crippled our field in recent years, that they can meet on common ground and cooperate in the search for a meaningful, verifiable past.

Thanksgiving Day, 1973   Frank J. Merli
                                                    Theodore A. Wilson

INTRODUCTION

To choose the few men who form the subjects of these essays as pivotal figures—as the "makers of American diplomacy"—from the throng who have influenced the nation's foreign relations is certain to provoke displeasure at the selection of some or the omission of others. To attempt to assign responsibility for any idea or decision in foreign policy to a single individual is an equally thankless task. Even in the early days of the Republic, diplomacy was a product of the actions of numerous persons and groups; in the twentieth century, as the international responsibilities of the United States have expanded, so have the constituencies affecting the conduct of diplomacy. The creation of policy in a democracy derives from a complicated interaction of domestic concerns, political calculations, popular attitudes, seemingly irrational assumptions and beliefs—in short, from assorted, ill-defined, and often contradictory purposes. In such circumstances, designating certain men as personifications of the national will or agents of history may indeed appear a naïve approach to a complex problem.

History, in a sense, remains a composite of innumerable biographies, however, so such a task seemed worth undertaking; but it poses once again the eternal conundrum of free will versus determinism. To what extent, if any, does the act of an individual affect the course of events? Even if responsibility for a decision or a general policy could be clearly attributed to a single person, would not the problem of relating it to subsequent decisions and policies be almost insurmountable? Cause and effect relationships do exist, of course; but normally they are so amorphous and intertwined that attempts to unravel them lead more often to ambiguity than to certitude.

It often seems, to paraphrase one of our contributors, that the evil diplomats do lives after them, but that the good is often interred in the archives. Any attempt to find underlying congruities in the work of American diplomats confronts the problem of contemporary animosity and the biases of historians toward past efforts to manage the nation's affairs. The record suggests, superficially at least, that much of the work of American diplomats has been devoted to tearing down, in word if not in fact, the policies of predecessors. It would appear, therefore, that continuity has not been a dominant feature of United States diplomacy. Further, the special concerns of particular diplomats do not always seem directly related to the larger issues of national policy that transcend presidential administrations, the tenure of a particular secretary of state, or the effective influence of powerful pressure groups.

Such warnings merely restate the obvious: that the contributions of individuals, whether twenty-five, fifty, or five thousand, do not and cannot comprise the total of the American diplomatic experience. The essays in this collection suggest another observation, perhaps also self-evident: that those who have created and conducted America's foreign affairs have often responded to forces outside their control; their decisions have furthered aims and aspirations that they understood little and that interested them less. Statesmen must confront the crises of the moment without leisure to analyze the consequences of their acts. The limits these underlying factors place on the conduct of diplomacy have sometimes been more important than personal initiatives. Whether they know it or not, men are prisoners of the milieu in which they live and function and, with some rare exceptions, are constrained by the dictates of their own experience and the conventional wisdom of their age. Few transcend such limits; fewer still build lastingly or institutionalize their insights.

The following essays suggest at the same time that the participation in diplomacy of human beings, each bringing unique beliefs, patterns of behavior, principles, and ambitions to the-common task of directing the country's international business, remains an absolutely essential factor in the diplomatic equation. Men, not abstractions such as Wall Street, the Eastern Establishment, or the United States, "make" diplomacy. These essays treat individuals who are in some ways representative, in some ways atypical, of the men who have conducted foreign relations throughout the nation's history. They suggest the extent to which elements of personality (even idiosyncratic behavior and personal foibles) have affected events. Issues of foreign policy and the forces that produce them transcend the purposes and preoccupations of individual statesmen; nevertheless, they can only find expression through the marvelously unpredictable, chaotic realm of human motivation and the decisions of fallible men. "No matter how 'ripe' the time," as David Brion Davis has said so well in, another context, "there would be no coalescing of . . . opinion until specific decisions and commitments were taken by individual men. . . . Yet when all allowances are made for . . . trends and climates of opinion, one must ultimately come down to the men who precipitated change."[1] Understanding this fact, so obvious yet so often ignored, is a necessary beginning to any re-creation of the context of American diplomacy.

◇◇◇

These essays on men who in some way have contributed to the making or implementation of American diplomacy were originally envisioned as informative but disparate pieces that would form a gallery of diplomatic portraits, reflecting internal meaning but perhaps offering little to assist the reader's grasp of the relationships that cut across eras and styles of diplomacy. Surprisingly, a process of selection that because of circumstance contained an element of randomness and guidelines that offered the contributors considerable flexibility produced something more than a mere "collection." The result demonstrates far greater continuity in the outlooks and actions of these diplomats than anyone had anticipated.

1. David Brion Davis, *The Problem of Slavery in Western Culture* (Ithaca, 1966), p. 489. Professor Davis is discussing the rise of antislavery sentiment and John Woolman's part in precipitating it; but his point about individual responsibility applies as well to the diplomatic realm.

Two hundred years have wrought amazingly few changes in the essentials of foreign affairs—a surprising statement unless one reflects on the basic components of the world views of Alexander Hamilton or Henry Kissinger. Survival in a hostile international environment has remained the touchstone, and the options by which survival is to be ensured appear to be as restricted and fraught with peril today as in the nation's formative years. Power—its definition, articulation, and believability—stands at the center of the agonizing choices with which all American diplomats have struggled.

Certainly the problems that beset the Committee of Correspondence of the Continental Congress differed in degree, and to some extent in kind, from the issues the Department of State faced at the end of the nineteenth century when the United States emerged as a great power. Still, the common themes—from the search of Franklin, Hamilton, Jefferson, Madison, and their peers for a diplomatic strategy that would protect the national interest, assure independence, ward off threats to domestic stability, provide for expansion, and ensure a maximum of commercial opportunity in world markets, and to do all these things while satisfying deep-seated convictions about America's moral superiority, to the formulation of similar goals by Fish, Blaine, and Mahan—are notable and amazingly consistent. The imprint of the early lessons of the 1790s has proved remarkably durable. The international arena at the nation's birth reeked of violence, corruption, and hostility toward the innovative (and therefore threatening) institutions and ideas fostered by the American experiment. That arena, however, was also a marketplace in which commodities, both actual and abstract, necessary for America's survival and growth were traded. Thus, from its inception, American involvement in the world remained ambivalent: diplomatic engagements were restricted to matters that were essential to the nation's well-being and safety; but on the other hand, it was considered permissible, even desirable, to exploit opportunities offered by Old World conflicts and by the disintegration of its political and economic systems. The means by which American objectives were to be realized—isolation (in its peculiar nineteenth-century sense), neutrality, hemispheric domination, reliance on a higher law, exploitation of Manifest Destiny, territorial and commercial expansion, and a quite remarkable talent for fishing in troubled waters—remained constant in importance throughout the nineteenth century.

Although the Founding Fathers might have been surprised by the transformation, over the course of the nineteenth century, of some of these diplomatic techniques (such as isolation and neutrality) into goals in themselves, they shared with later generations of American leaders certain convictions about an appropriate "style" for the nation's diplomacy. The circumstances in which the United States became ensnared varied greatly during this period, but the manner and overall direction of diplomacy changed little. These essays reveal much about such matters as the responsiveness to public opinion of those who made foreign policy, the impact of pressure groups and elites, and assumptions about America's role in the world; indeed, they suggest that a broader definition of diplomacy is needed. Throughout these assessments of public careers winds the theme of the American people's preoccupation with internal growth, with a consequent influence on diplomacy. Deeply intertwined with this theme was another major one, that of America's mission: the belief in the United States as the agent of providential purpose, the repository of a sacred trust, the New Jerusalem. Those who sought to guide the nation's destiny believed that it should teach right precepts, the virtues of liberty and of republican government, to less enlightened peoples. Much of the proselytizing was rhetorical and remained so; but there was an almost irresistible pressure to convert rhetoric into reality, and on an ever larger scale. Whether or not the new diplomacy of Seward, Fish, Blaine, and Mahan constituted a break with tradition remains a moot point. After all, America began its national existence with an attempt to implement a new order of things—a new order, it should be noted, of universal applicability. The empire of liberty was by definition expansionist; creation of that empire surely constituted a key concern of the makers of American diplomacy in the nineteenth century.

In the twentieth century convulsive and repeated changes in both the structure and underlying assumptions of American society and the environment of global politics have occurred. The resulting impact on American diplomacy seems to mark a basic shift in the purposes and methods of United States foreign policy, thus mocking any argument for continuity. Nonetheless, the objectives of American diplomats, as the essays on such apparently diverse personalities as Theodore Roosevelt, Willard Straight, Harry S. Truman, John Foster Dulles, and Henry Kissinger indicate, reflect a deep and abiding commonalty of interest among those who have shaped foreign affairs in this century. One common theme is, again, concern with power and awareness of America's significant role, because of its vast and expanding economic strength, in any tabulation of the global power balance. Allied with this concern has been persistent uncertainty about the nature and extent of America's responsibility, because of its great and growing power, for the melioration of conditions inhibiting lasting peace and universal prosperity. Except for a special few, the judgment of American leaders in the twentieth century has been to proceed with great caution in this strange new situation, to apply the nationalistic precepts of an earlier age, and to conclude that unilateralism, with all its limitations, is preferable to efforts to create some global community requiring the sacrifice of national sovereignty and freedom of action. In fact, it is possible to argue that the imprint of earlier views, especially the moral superiority of American aims, has combined with consciousness of America's staggering power to generate faith in America's ability to establish and maintain world order by unilateral action. Still, American diplomacy in the 1970s in many ways goes back to a less ambitious time and seems to differ little from the foreign policy goals of TR or Willard Straight. The following essays suggest that the ambivalence and widespread ignorance about the world that characterized popular attitudes and the views of most American statesmen in 1900 still prevail.

In other ways, of course, the twentieth century has witnessed an incredible transformation of America's role in the world. This shift in status and involvement has brought along with it equally striking changes in the process by which decisions regarding foreign policy are made. It may not be unfair to suggest that the manner in which TR and his Department of State (some few hundred souls, including Secretary Hay and all American representatives) reached and implemented decisions differed in no important respect from the way in which Thomas Jefferson, his chief clerk, and the handful of American diplomats in foreign missions conducted foreign affairs. As the twentieth century has unfolded, however, the number of persons and organizations participating directly in the making of foreign policy has increased enormously, and the activities with which they have dealt have become more complex and specialized. That circumstance has spawned a huge foreign affairs bureaucracy and has resulted in its emergence as an independent, seemingly uncontrollable force in the decision-making process. In recent decades, presidents have chosen (or have been impelled) to conduct diplomacy themselves, purposefully bypassing a swollen, inert State Department. Ironically, one effect has been to reemphasize the central role of the personal dimension in diplomacy, the absolute necessity for diplomatic initiatives to be backed by the credibility and authority of the individual negotiator. *Plus ça change, plus c'est la même chose.*

Benjamin Franklin *by Joseph Sifrede Duplessis, Henry E. Huntington Library and Art Gallery. Photo courtesy of Robert Merli*

BEN FRANKLIN

in France:
A Maker of American Diplomacy

Cecil B. Currey

Had someone inquired of Ben Franklin, during his service to the Continental Congress in 1775 and 1776, the number of jobs, requests, and committees to which he gave his time, surely the old man's memory would have failed him. The period between his return from England on 5 May 1775 and his departure for France on 25 October 1776 was undoubtedly the busiest of Franklin's public life. Committee meetings filled his days; dozens of official and semiofficial tasks faced him as he served both the nation and Pennsylvania, kept up a heavy correspondence on public and private matters, and met with an endless stream of callers.

It was no wonder that Franklin was usually tired and often sick. Sixty-nine years old when the Pennsylvania House of Assembly chose him as a delegate to the Second Continental Congress, Franklin was both one of the older and one of the better-known men in that body. He was one of the few living Americans with a

1

thoroughly established international reputation, achieved in part because of his prominent service as colonial agent in Britain for four colonies before the war.

Franklin, having spent all the years since 9 December 1764 in England, had sailed from the mother country in late March, and arrived in the American colonies on 5 May 1775. While his ship tossed at sea, the smoking firebrands of discontent, resentment, and resistance finally flared into open war and rebellion. The monumental event began before Franklin landed at Philadelphia. John Pitcairn, major in His Majesty's Royal Army, was ordered to lead a column to Lexington and Concord to seize John Hancock, Sam Adams, and hidden stores of munitions. There a Massachusetts militia captain, John Parker, and his sixty men confronted the British. The militia had earlier heard Parker tell them, "Do not fire unless fired upon, but if they mean to have a war, let it begin here!" Shots rang out and rebellion began. Delegates to the Second Continental Congress hastily assembled in Philadelphia where Franklin joined his colleagues five days after his return from abroad.

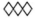

It was proper that Benjamin Franklin should sit among the members of America's nascent government. Born in obscurity, he had carefully nurtured his native talents to their utmost. He had taken a faltering newspaper and made it one of the best known in the colonies and the most lucrative. Although lacking family and status he had become acceptable to even the highest levels of society. His business made him rich but it was his mind that made him well known. He mastered several languages and many of the major sciences of his day, and he became one of the most innovative men of his time. Glorying in relationships with other men, Franklin entered Pennsylvania politics and by the mid-1750s was an acknowledged leader of the legislature. In 1756 and again in 1764, his province chose him as a colonial agent, or lobbyist, before the official boards and agencies of the mother country. As agent, he represented the interests of Pennsylvania on matters of trade, Indian affairs, and various legal issues. He sought to promote in every way possible the well-being of his colony. His adept handling of issues prompted Georgia to commission him as agent in 1768; New Jersey sought him in 1769 and the lower house of the Massachusetts legislature appointed him in 1770. Many colonists regarded him as the most important American in England; the time came when Franklin himself succumbed to that notion.

In later years, Franklin liked to believe that his testimony before the Commons in 1766 had been instrumental in securing repeal of the Stamp Act. In the years after repeal, he was often in the forefront of those counseling resistance to the policies of the mother country. In the vanguard of radical action, he usually held political opinions more advanced than those of many of his countrymen, although in 1765 and 1766, when the colonies adopted nonimportation as a weapon against England, Franklin's letters were generally quiet on the matter. By 1768, however, he also had adopted that policy as the best available economic tool against British taxing programs. In 1767, when he learned of the new Townshend system of excises planned for the colonies, he began a quiet little game with some people that was, in its own way, significant. As deputy assistant postmaster general, it was his privilege to frank his letters. His usual mark was "Free. B. Franklin." Tongue in cheek, he changed it to "B. Free Franklin."

How much colonial resistance Franklin's advice inspired remains a matter of conjecture. Yet General Thomas Cadwalader, Alexander Colden, and General Thomas Gage agreed that his intervention sustained and prolonged American nonimportation during the late 1760s. Franklin's advice to the colonies, however, caused him to lose favor with many members of the imperial government. In earlier years a friend described him as "forever with one Member of Parliament or other." Radical advice, quarrels with cabinet members, and other questionable activities so changed attitudes that a friend later wrote Franklin's son that his father was not only on "bad terms with Lord Hillsborough [but with] the Ministry in General." By the early 1770s, Franklin had acquired several nicknames, including the "Hoary Old Sinner," the "Judas of Craven Street," and "Old Traitor Franklin." He was considered even more a *persona non grata* among British official-dom when he sent to the governor's opponents in the legislature some potentially damaging letters written by Governor Thomas Hutchinson of Massachusetts. Sam Adams got them, edited them to seem much worse than they actually were, and printed them in the newspapers. Many called for the removal of the governor. The British Ministry, taking a dim view of the episode, shortly thereafter dismissed Franklin from his postmaster's position.

Part of the reason for Franklin's headstrong prewar attitudes toward the British government may be found in his long-standing hope of acquiring huge tracts of land in western America. When Franklin retired from business in 1748 he had become convinced that immense riches were to be had through western land investments, and he participated in a number of abortive attempts to exploit land in the West. At the same time, Franklin led a Pennsylvania political movement urging the crown to withdraw proprietary rights from the Penn family. In public he argued against the wisdom of proprietary holdings; privately he sought them for himself.

The Proclamation Act of 1763 prohibited further western settlements. While planning ways to get around the provisions of this law, Franklin bought acreage in Quebec and Nova Scotia and joined a group of speculators, including his Philadelphia friend Samuel Wharton, who thought they could make money in the West in spite of the 1763 law. For two years Franklin and his associates sought permission from the crown for a land grant on the Illinois River. As a result of their efforts, the crown almost issued a charter to the group, but the plan failed when colonial affairs came under the control of the new secretary of state for the American colonies, Lord Hillsborough, who refused to approve a new establishment. Franklin's goal of an Illinois colony was seen to be hopeless early in 1768, so he and his partners abandoned the effort. They then organized the Indiana Company to seek a tract of land near present-day Pittsburgh. This effort also failed.

Samuel Wharton voyaged to England in 1769, and, with Ben Franklin and Thomas Walpole, an English banker, established still another speculative group, which included large numbers of British officials of all ranks and degrees of influence. This enterprise, the Walpole Associates, was established early in 1769 but was soon reorganized as the Grand Ohio Company, which sought a vast charter grant in the vicinity of the present state of West Virginia to be called Vandalia. Franklin and other leaders of the company used many questionable methods in pursuit of their western colony: falsified petitions, secret memberships, code names (Franklin was known as "Moses"), and even lies. Such tactics worked sufficiently well so that by 1773 it appeared that

Franklin and his confederates would soon be proprietors of an American colony; but it was not to be. The Hutchinson letters scandal, the Boston Tea Party, the rapidly disintegrating colonial situation, and Franklin's part in it brought governmental reappraisals, and the ministry shelved the project. To get it moving again, Franklin publicly resigned from the Grand Ohio Company early in 1774 while privately retaining full membership and all his stock shares. The ruse was ineffective; the project was still stalled when Franklin returned to America in 1775.

◇◇◇

Now all this was in the past—but not the dead past, for Franklin still hoped to become a member of the landed rich. Instead of asking permission for the western colony from the crown, he and his partners (including the British ones) turned to the Continental Congress. Again the speculators reorganized. As Samuel Wharton put it, they should "take into the Partnership . . . Members of the Congress" which would create a "Thousand political Reasons" why that body should grant them lands across the mountains. Not willing to wait for official approval the partners met for business in March 1776 at the Indian Queen Tavern in Philadelphia, with Franklin chairing the session. His son, a prominent Tory, who had been a longtime member of these enterprises, was not present, for he was under house arrest at his home in Perth Amboy. Politically divorced from his son, Ben still looked out for his economic interests and that day voted not only his own shares of stock, but his son's as well. After electing officers, the organization authorized the sale of four-hundred-acre tracts of land to all comers. Advertisements appeared in Franklin's old newspaper, the *Pennsylvania Gazette*. It is not clear whether the speculators discussed the fact that they had neither legal title to those lands nor the right to sell even one acre.

In spite of Franklin's best efforts, he gained nothing concrete toward his real estate goal during 1775 and 1776. He had too little time in which to concentrate on his own personal ambitions because of other duties. There were letters to write, people to interview, foreign visitors with whom to talk, committee meetings to attend, including the most important committee on which he sat, the forerunner of our present Department of State, the Secret Committee of Correspondence.

Ben Franklin became chairman of this committee and took an active part in the early diplomacy of the revolutionary war. The committee gathered information from Europe and sent agents there to contact foreign governments and to procure aid, assistance, trade agreements, and military alliances. The day after Franklin's appointment, 29 November 1775, the committee chose its first European agent, a Virginian residing in London named Arthur Lee. Lee and Franklin had been acquainted for years, Lee having for a time served as under-agent for Massachusetts, and the two already disliked each other. The following March of 1776, the Committee of Secret Correspondence sent its first agent to Europe to negotiate with the French government: Silas Deane, who went to France knowing nothing of diplomacy and less of the French language.

By mid-1776, after Franklin's return from a futile effort to persuade the French colonists in Canada to join the American cause, he began considering ways to extricate himself from the complexities and inconveniences of the North American scene. When the Continental Congress decided to send another man to Europe to help Deane, Franklin made the right suggestions and succeeded in being named a commissioner to France. There would now be three men there: Arthur Lee, Silas Deane, and Benjamin Franklin, appointed as coequal members of the American mission. Congress's fetish for committees would nearly prove the undoing of the American cause because of the squabbles, self-seeking, and accusations that would emanate from the scandal-ridden American mission in Paris.

On the basis of recent research, it is at least doubtful whether Franklin decided to go to France so much from a desire to serve the new United States of America as from a need for a more restful and less dangerous environment. France would surely be less hectic, more cosmopolitan and cultured than Philadelphia. In the City of Lights he might be able to return to the leisurely life-style he had earlier pursued in London. Already elderly, he resented the necessarily long hours demanded of him in America that put an undue burden upon his health. In the New World, he was in any case somewhat out of his element. He had been away from the colonies almost continuously since 1757, a total of nineteen years. More oriented toward Europe than America by his long absence, Franklin was a true cosmopolite. As an agent of the Continental Congress, he would have in Paris the prestige that would come with that title. Living abroad, he would share none of the blame if the uprising in the colonies failed. In that eventuality he would be far safer from imperial retribution in France than in the United States. If France joined the war effort in behalf of America, Franklin knew that much of the credit would be his. Yet had he foreseen the troubles ahead of him in France—the ugly rumors that would circulate about him, the near ruin of his reputation and career—he might have changed his mind; for the American mission would become an unequal troika, each of the three pulling in different directions, marching each to the sound of his own drummer.

◇◇◇

Paeans of praise have come from Franklin's biographers as they have told of his wartime diplomatic service. Charles Evans Hughes, an ex–secretary of state and chief justice of the Supreme Court, wrote that Franklin had "for all time set the standards for American diplomacy" and added that he was "the greatest of all the diplomatic representatives of this country and has no superior among those of any time or of other nations." Popularizing historian Helen Augur contended that Franklin became "the most dazzling diplomat in the country's history." Another author has insisted that "due largely to Franklin's adroit diplomacy, the treaty with France was signed." Still another, unaware of Franklin's warning, often repeated, that virgin America should not go suitoring to Europe in search of wartime aid, portrayed Franklin as one of the leading Americans to urge the French toward an alliance with America, repudiating others who were "fearful of sly courtiers and suspicious of alliances." From such authors, a reader would never learn of certain shadowy phases of Franklin's life in Paris that mark heavily the life and career of the oldest of our Founding Fathers during the years he spent abroad in the service of the American Congress.

Even while serving as chairman of the Secret Committee of Correspondence, Franklin had urged Silas Deane to contact Edward Bancroft once he got to France. Bancroft was a British spy who rifled Deane's files at will and who eventually recruited him into membership in the British Secret Service. When Franklin arrived in Paris, he continued to employ Bancroft, defending him from all charges brought against him, including those of Arthur

Lee who quickly identified him as a British spy. Franklin further-more hired other spies for various positions at the American mission, such as William Carmichael (alias Pierre Le Maître) and Jacobus Van Zandt (code name George Lupton). Franklin repeat-edly met with agents sent by the English ministry who sought to disentangle him from his loyalties to America. One was his old comrade from prewar days, the Moravian pastor John Hutton; another was a Franklin acquaintance, Benjamin Vaughan. The chief of the British Secret Service network in France, Paul Wentworth, visited Franklin more than once and offered him huge bribes to change sides. A member of Parliament, William Pulteney, saw Franklin twice in Paris, and his old friend Thomas Walpole sought credentials as an agent of the ministry of Lord North. Refused such legitimacy, he journeyed to Paris anyway. If Beau-marchais's information was correct, this listing does not begin to exhaust the names of those from the British Secret Service with whom Franklin met during 1777, let alone in subsequent years.

Franklin had been in France for but a short time when, with his landlord Chaumont, Robert Morris, the congressional secretary of finance, Silas Deane, and others, he became involved with American merchants in exploiting the rich trade in scarce com-mercial goods. Franklin and Deane named the former's grand-nephew, Jonathan Williams, Jr., as head of the American commer-cial agency at Nantes in order to control the trade at that port city and to profit from the sale of prize ships auctioned there. Williams sold such vessels short, repurchased them, and resold them at a tidy profit, all despite Congress's appointment of William Lee as its agent there! Franklin and Deane worked hard to keep Williams in Nantes and Lee away from it.

In another moneymaking effort, Ben's fellow commissioner Silas Deane, his old speculative partner Samuel Wharton, who was still in London, and Edward Bancroft, secretary for the mission, joined forces to use inside information on war news to play the British stock market. Franklin, who would have had to know what was going on, saw fit to close his eyes.

Franklin's security over personal and state papers was slip-shod. His controls would have made a modern security officer blanch and even in the eighteenth century were something of a scandal. It is difficult to justify such carelessness. He knew the realities of international intrigue as well as anyone. His knowledge was honed during his congressional service from May 1775 to

October 1776. Work on the Secret Committee of Correspondence and the Committee of Secret Correspondence put him in touch with many kinds of intelligence activities. He had appointed secret agents of the United States and had parleyed with French agents sent to contact the American government. He discussed with his colleagues various procedures to follow in obtaining intelligence data. There is little doubt of Franklin's thorough acquaintance with clandestine purposes and methods and of his knowledge of the need for constant security measures to forestall intelligence leaks to the British. He had long used mail drops, ciphers, pen names, false information to mislead others, and other methods of clandestine warfare. Experience in these methods made him as well fitted as any living American for the intrigues of European diplomacy. There are simply no records available, however, to indicate that he ever paid the slightest attention to security measures.

The nature of the assignment given Franklin by Congress necessitated a meticulous regard for security, for some of his duties simply could not be made public nor disseminated on other than a need-to-know basis. Yet when friends faulted him for leaving papers exposed, he laughed at or ignored them. Reminders that he was "surrounded by spies" and advice to keep his papers away from any "prying eye" made little impact.

If Franklin was an astute man, reputed by all who knew him to be keenly aware of what went on about him, he must have known of the duplicity of his associates. Others knew that his headquarters was riddled with security leaks; why did not he? If he did not know his staff was sending information to England, he was less capable than he has been represented by his biographers; if he did know, he was more culpable.

Sent to France to procure military aid and, hopefully, an open alliance, Franklin told his colleague Arthur Lee that "I have never yet chang'd the Opinion I gave in Congress, that a Virgin State should preserve the Virgin Character, and not go about suitoring for Alliances. . . ." Much later, to Arthur's brother, William, "the Doctor replyed that it was a matter to be considered whether it was worth our while to ask any of the Courts of Europe to acknowledge our Independence." William Lee noted that "this, I confess, astonished me greatly." Franklin's lukewarm support of American independence may be seen in the report of Paul Wentworth, the French bureau chief, to William Eden, head of the

British Secret Service. Wentworth and Franklin met for discussions late in 1777 and early in 1778. Wentworth then reported to Eden that "72"—the code number for Franklin—"most particularly Commanded [his affection for England] to be mentioned, & his wishes to stop the progress of war in America." He continued that Franklin hoped "the acknowledgement of the Independency should not be made. . . ." William Carmichael, in a report to England, agreed with Wentworth. He wrote that "our leading man" trembled at the thought that France might soon join America in its war effort. "He wishes no European connection," said Carmichael.

Franklin and Deane both listened to blandishments promising rich rewards if they would help reconcile America and England: governorships, principal secretariats of the cabinet, holders of the privy seal, knighthoods, and baronetcies. Another British agent, William Pulteney, called upon Franklin. Pulteney's brother, George Johnstone, soon to be a member of the ill-fated British Carlisle Peace Commission, later claimed he had information based on those meetings of Pulteney and Franklin. Johnstone asserted that Franklin had suggested that the members of the Carlisle commission offer American leaders seats in Parliament as an inducement for abandoning the war effort. Such a bribe "would be more alluring than any other," Franklin had reputedly said. When the statement was attributed to him he wisely and vehemently denied it, as one would expect him to do; but the claim is still interesting in light of other more demonstrable shadows within which he moved while in Europe.

Franklin met with so many secret visitors from England, many of them members of the British intelligence apparatus, that Beaumarchais warned Vergennes "that secret advances are being made by England to Mr. Franklin, which you are doubtless unaware of. . . ." Between his arrival in France and the end of 1778, Franklin reputedly received no less than twenty English visitors with whom he met secretly. One rendezvous point was an old barge, *Le Pot de Vin,* which had been converted into a bathhouse and was anchored in the Seine not far from Franklin's home at Passy. There, amidst obscuring vapors of steam, an old, balding "Englishman" with long hair who was an excellent swimmer occasionally met unidentified persons. No, the attendants did not know his name, for he had not given it to them, but it is known that Franklin took almost daily swims in the Seine for exercise.

Shortly after Franklin arrived in Europe, he prevailed upon Arthur Lee to undertake a diplomatic mission to Spain in his stead. Lee did so and was successful in gaining some Spanish aid for America. When he returned to Paris, however, he was puzzled to notice that both Franklin and Deane ignored him. They did not inform him of business they had conducted in his absence, nor did they allow him to have keys to locked files, although he was equally credentialed with the other two. Meetings were held, decisions made, and money spent without consulting him. Soon, on Franklin's request, Lee was sent off to Berlin to arrange a treaty with the Prussians. One of the spies in the American headquarters noted the reason for the trip in a letter to England: "There is really some Business, but his Absence is also wanted. We shall now have a clear stage."

After Lee returned from the fruitless trip to Berlin, where his papers had been stolen, copied, and then returned by British agents, he began his first open criticisms of Franklin when he learned that the two colleagues had spent more than five million livres of public money and claimed to owe still more; yet they had no vouchers, receipts, or account books to explain the expenditures. Worried about Lee's suspicions, Franklin tried to weaken any future testimony the Virginian might give by spreading rumors that he was mentally ill. He spoke of Lee's "Sick Mind" full of "Jealousies, Suspicions & Fancies" which were the "Symptomatick Forerunner" of insanity. Deane also took up the cudgels against Lee and the two were so effective that one embassy employee later wrote, "I have heard Dr. Franklin say he thought Arthur Lee was crazy, and I am sure it was current enough at Nantes."

Then Franklin deftly administered the *coup de grâce*. When he learned that Lee needed a private secretary, he recommended a recent arrival from England, John Thornton, whom Lee hired, not knowing he was an army major and a British spy. Franklin reported to Vergennes that the Virginian now had a known British spy working for him and that such naïveté could not be countenanced. Vergennes reported this matter to the French chargé in America, Conrad Alexander Gérard de Rayneval, and at his request the United States Congress recalled the thoroughly burned Lee.

Franklin was also on dangerous ground in his support of a

Maryland sea captain, Joseph Hynson, who had been suborned by
the British Secret Service. Franklin and Deane kept Hynson in
France on the American subsidy list for many months until he
finally had the chance he had been awaiting. Hynson's English
superiors had instructed him to steal American diplomatic dispatches. He did so, substituting blank paper for the original
reports and letters. He thus made off with most of the confidential
correspondence between the French government and the American commissioners from 12 March to 7 October 1777, a real coup
for the British. It was during this period, one author has claimed,
that Franklin came "nearer than ever before in his life to sinking
his fame in an infamy of corruption."

An American Congress made suspicious by the rumors it was
hearing from abroad recalled Silas Deane and replaced him with
John Adams. It did not take Adams long to detect the abysmal
defects in Franklin's financial system. Huge sums had been spent
carelessly, Adams claimed, but no one could remember how. Large
debts remained unpaid, yet no records could be produced to
justify them. Franklin, pressed for an audit of expenditures, called
in Samuel Wharton and Edward Bancroft to review and certify the
accounts. Strangely enough, they found them to be proper and in
order.

Deane returned to Paris from the United States in 1780 and
moved in with Franklin. The two had once calumniated Lee by
describing him as insane. Since John Adams now watched both of
them carefully, they again tried the same tactic; Franklin, Deane,
and Bancroft all claimed Adams to be "actually mad."

Deane wrote a series of letters for the British Secret Service
calling for reconciliation with England. They were later sent to
America and published in New York by James Rivington, a Tory
printer. The incident irrevocably finished Deane's career. Franklin
never condemned him; instead, he loaned money to him and
corresponded with him. Deane continued to use Franklin's home
as a mail drop. As late as 1782, Franklin wrote a certificate of
probity for his ex-colleague, asserting that he had always been
honest and upright in the public service. William Lee claimed that
Franklin had done so for fear that if he did not it might be learned
that he had been as crooked as Deane.

During the negotiations for peace with Britain after 1781, John
Jay and John Adams, the other two principal negotiators with Ben
Franklin, were not terribly impressed with the old gentleman's

help. For a time Franklin supported a peace that would not require Britain's recognition of America's independence. According to some, he seemed to be willing to allow Spain and France to "coop us up within the Allegheny Mountains." He urged his fellow negotiators to accept certain French diplomatic moves inimical to the United States. Far from being the most "dazzling diplomat in America's history," Franklin's colleagues often regarded him quite literally as a "pain in the neck." A rumor then circulated that Franklin "worked secretly against the treaty." Jay, of course, denied it and defended Franklin's role in the negotiations; but the mood around Franklin and attitudes at home led him to ask Jay for a testimonial to his service in behalf of the American cause. Jay gladly complied, thus helping Franklin in his expressed wish to carry his reputation with him intact, at least to the grave.

◇◇◇

Until recently it would have been impossible for a reader to have learned of these darker phases of Franklin's overseas career, for no book or article has discussed them in any detail. When the evidence is in, will our assessment of Franklin's role as a maker of American diplomatic history be affected? In spite of blemishes upon Franklin's career, the traditional picture extolling his service in France is not completely wrong; it is incorrect only in the details from which older, and essentially proper, conclusions have been drawn.

The treaties of 1778 are but one example. The French were not moved to make an alliance with the United States because of America's military victory at Saratoga in 1777 as some have believed. Still less did the government of Louis XVI and Vergennes act because the brilliant, personal diplomacy and argumentation of Ben Franklin persuaded them that the time had come to act. The French ministry decided upon its course of action only when there seemed to be a real possibility of renewed British-American accommodation. On such matters they were remarkably well informed. By late 1777, worried about the possibility of Anglo-American rapprochement, the French ministry announced its intention to sign a treaty with America. It is possible that Franklin may well have had this in mind when he met with emissaries of the English Secret Service; some authors have long thought so. Whether that was or was not his own purpose, the result was the same: France would ally itself with the hard-pressed Americans. The tide of war turned, and Franklin, knowingly or unwittingly, was partly responsible.

In spite of his links with the British Secret Service that would have besmirched his record had they become known to his constituents at home, Franklin made important contributions to the American cause. Perhaps his help came not so much through what he did in France in an official way, for he was often lackadaisical, distracted, diffident, and unwilling to try to push the Vergennes government to an early decision regarding an alliance. This attitude exasperated the younger and more energetic Arthur Lee; yet Franklin was not deterred. He presented his credentials and then turned to other activities, content to wait for the monolithic French regime to act in its own way and time. Until that moment came, Franklin felt free to amuse himself as he pleased. His aplomb in doing nothing captivated the French. They sensed his love of *la dolce vita* and *feminae blandissima.* It was obvious to them that he relished life in France, enjoyed its people, and was taken with their culture and ways. His fascination was infectious and the French gladly returned his interest.

For the French, Franklin was more than simply another diplomat; he was a symbol of all they found fascinating in the New World. He dressed simply, spoke frugally and sparely, but his thoughts came from a mind tempered like steel. For them he was the American Quaker, the constitution maker. It was Franklin who had "snatched the lightning from the heavens and the sceptre from the hands of tyrants." When he met Voltaire at a public theater the two embraced and those who watched cried out that *"Solon et Sophocles"* had met. Courtiers and commoners alike enjoyed Franklin's wit and listened avidly for his latest bon mot. Franklin loved the ladies—so many of them—from his wife, Deborah Read Rogers Franklin in the 1740s, Katherine Ray Greene in the 1750s, his landlady in London, Mrs. Margaret Stevenson, in the 1760s, to the fullness of the 1770s and 1780s in France: Countess d'Houdetot, Madame Brillon de Jouy, and Anne-Catherine de Ligniville Helvétius. This was a trait Frenchmen could understand and they were entranced at the attraction this elderly man had for their womenfolk. They relished gossiping about his latest love interest and drew him to their breast.

Everything that Franklin did became grist for the French mill, whether it was his invention of a new word, *stormonter,* meaning

Benjamin Franklin's reception at the Court of France (1778)

"to lie" and derived from the name of the English ambassador, Lord Stormont, or his latest attack of the gout, or a new broadside from his private printing press in his home at Passy, L'Hôtel des Valentinois. Statuettes of Franklin, called miniatures, were struck by the thousands and Frenchmen, high and low, were not content until they owned one.

This love affair between *le pauvre Richard* and the French nation had repercussions across the Atlantic. For decades France had been the sworn enemy of Americans. Its autocratic monarchy, its Roman Catholicism, its foreign tongue that filled so awkwardly the mouths of Americans trying to speak it, its competing New World colonies, its invading armies and naval dreadnoughts—all had threatened Americans who long before had come to despise the French. England and its New World colonies had fought war after war against that European power. Now in only a few months the Americans' long-formed and time-hardened attitudes began to change; France had opened its arms to one of their own. Suspicions softened—from obvious necessity due to the importance of securing arms from that nation and because of the importance of gaining avowed allies in the struggle with Britain, and because of Old Ben's thorough enjoyment of that Catholic land and its strange people. Franklin was not purposely trying to change the hundred-year-old attitudes of his fellow Americans; he was simply having a good time as only he knew how to do, but his fun had wondrous side effects two thousand miles away. As much as anyone who could be named, Franklin's personal influence helped turn the new United States to a more open attitude toward France.

◇◇◇

Elsewhere in this book, Lawrence Kaplan examines what Thomas Jefferson wanted for America. He analyzes with clarity the goals and accomplishments of the nation's third president within that framework. It would be difficult to fit Franklin's contributions within a similar frame. He was too free a spirit, too unwilling to accept the limitations that bound other men. An example might be his attitude toward money. Whereas Arthur Lee kept careful account of his expenditures in France, and Silas Deane deliberately obscured the dubious ways in which he spent money, Franklin chose a different path. He refused to commit himself to either of his colleagues' methods; as legend would have it, a curious congressional committee questioned his spending when he returned to the United States. The particular question was a mission account deficit of approximately one hundred thousand pounds. Asked of its whereabouts, Franklin loftily replied, "I was taught when a boy to read the scriptures and to attend to them, and it is there said: muzzle not the ox that treadeth out his master's grain." His meaning was clear. Benefits had come to the United States through his service in France; if this service cost America something, if Franklin benefited from that service, then Congress should simply accept that fact and not bother him with mundane accountings.

For Franklin, then, his single-mindedness, his diplomacy— whether in England before the war or in France during the conflict—was devoted to his own purposes rather than to the Revolution. When both interests coincided, he was quite willing to lend his talents to the American cause; when they diverged, he begrudged demands upon him and followed his own inclinations. Today his attitude would be described as "doing his own thing"; that was Franklin's forte. Perhaps more than any other Founding Father, Benjamin Franklin, because of his long stay in England, was aware of the benefits of British government and culture to America. Yet his own temperament was such that in the prewar years, in order to forward his own private goals, he was willing to sacrifice those benefits and work with men seeking independence. In those years some in America suspected Franklin of being willing to ignore their interests for his own; but at least as many thought him to be their voice in the mother country and learned to look to him for the views that would fix and justify their own. Because of overlapping interests, Franklin's personal power struggle coincidentally bolstered colonial seekers of independence and they took him to their bosoms unknowing or uncaring that he was only a practical man working for his own ends and not totally committed, as were they, to the "cause." The question that must be asked about this man is simply, "What did Franklin want for Franklin?"

Examination of Franklin's life reveals a streak of selfishness that guided him and kept him ever mindful of his own goals and purposes no matter what face he showed to the world. His positions were often variable, shifting as the winds, and it is often difficult to know exactly where his sympathies really lay during the war, or how firm was his commitment to the colonial cause.

Perhaps no one will ever know what kind of person was this doughty old man. He was at least far more European than American. His parochial views as a colonist had been tempered in his contacts with the scientists, the literati, the raconteurs of England and the Continent. He received the accolades and memberships of learned societies across Europe. Wherever he traveled, he encountered those who already knew him by reputation and who avidly sought to learn from him. His own views, tempered by acquaintance with European statesmen, scientists, and philosophers, allowed little localism to remain in his ideas. Whether colonist or cosmopolite, he worked first and foremost for Benjamin Franklin. Perhaps this is of little moment; Franklin was no mere mortal even in his own lifetime, and perhaps he who had seen so much and accomplished such great things should not be expected to adhere to the same codes of living that bound lesser men.

Minutiae never fascinated Franklin. He disdained, for the most part, the details of diplomacy; his correspondence was often answered reluctantly and late; papers signifying unfinished work inevitably fouled his desk; his appointment calendar was too seldom clear and was usually a snare dotted with the names of little men waiting to see him about small matters. Such tasks left him drained and bored. His forte was rather the grand display: standing undaunted before the House of Commons in 1766 testifying for the needed repeal of the Stamp Act, a state dinner as guest of George III, suffering in silence before the righteous thunder of Wedderburn in 1774 in the halls of the Privy Council, riotous homecoming to Philadelphia in 1775, festive crowds joyously celebrating his arrival in and procession through France on his way to Paris in 1776, signing of the French treaties as commissioner for America in 1778, presentation to Louis XVI. All such things were the victories upon which Franklin doted and which made lesser things possible to bear.

In his own free time, he sought amusing occupations. He much preferred sitting in England at the Honest Whig Coffee House talking with Burke or Priestley or Canton, or coming home from a party with a "thickened head," or publishing the *Craven Street Gazette* to entertain little Polly Stevenson, or engaging in double entendres in Paris with his favorite lady friends than in pursuing the humdrum but necessary routine of diplomacy. It is not that business was never done so much as that it was done late and without enthusiasm.

Franklin stood in bold relief to his two colleagues in France. Silas Deane, corrupt to the core, concentrated on enriching himself by selling his soul to Robert Morris, Beaumarchais, and the British Secret Service. Arthur Lee, desperate to aid the new nation, agitated himself frenetically and frantically. He traveled to Spain, to Prussia, palavered with his brothers, and sought evidence of corruption to substantiate his suspicions of his two colleagues.

Franklin, only five feet eight inches tall, stood head and shoulders above his co-workers. By pursuing his own ends he provided bountiful but coincidental benefits for America. Old and wise, he knew all there was to know about corruption. He may even have delicately participated in it when he wished, without staining his fingers. Perhaps he made a few dollars. Franklin occasionally flirted with British agents while he pondered the relative advantages of loyalty to America or noble rank in England. Laughing at them all, using them when he could, he turned to his real loves in Paris: printing, chess, jokes, weighty conversations, women, good companions, and better food. When one has recorded the blemishes and acknowledged the peccadilloes, what then may be said of Franklin's service to the nation?

◇◇◇

The coincidental benefits or contributions of Franklin to America include the symbol he became for many Americans, the part he played in bringing Americans and Frenchmen to change their minds about one another; he may well have been instrumental in causing the French government to move toward an American alliance more quickly when it learned through its spies that Franklin was talking rapprochement with British emissaries. These diplomatic victories were real enough even if the thought of them was not always uppermost in Franklin's mind. Yet these coincidental contributions form the base of his historical reputation.

This Talleyrand of the West did not fit conventional molds. He was entirely capable of simultaneously handling and manipulating his own divergent interests and those of the British, the French, and the Americans. One must distinguish between what he really wanted and what he merely talked about, between what he said and what he did, between what he only speculated upon and what he committed himself to accomplish. Gerald Stourzh's remarkable monograph, *Benjamin Franklin and American Foreign Policy*, misses much of that essential nuance. Stourzh did not fully separate what Franklin proposed from what he actively sought, nor was he sufficiently aware of his subject's shortcomings. Consequently Stourzh adopted a too uncritical view of Franklin. His book remains required reading, however, for he properly noted many of the wide-ranging considerations in diplomacy and foreign policy that flowed from Franklin's talented mind. Those ideas usually had to be accepted and acted upon by others, for Franklin, after conceiving them, often turned to new and different matters. It may be that Benjamin Franklin's great contribution in the field of diplomacy was in the realm of ideas rather than on the field of action—not what he did so much as what he suggested. His value lay in his interpretation for others of doctrines already available and in his proposing new concepts in such moderate language that they became persuasive to others. His deeds were often narrow and self-centered; his thoughts, on the other hand, sparked concentrated action by others, and so often became part of the foundation of American foreign policy. No student of nineteenth-century diplomacy should ignore this fact. It is possible that historians, in stressing the virtuosity of Franklin's performance, have missed an important theorist of American diplomacy.

In this respect, we might remember Franklin's advice that new states ought not to go suitoring after alliances, or ponder his warnings against European connections unsupported by mutual interests. Washington's Farewell Address echoes such sentiments, and the first president's "great rule of conduct" in international affairs advised Americans to have "as little *political* connection as possible" with foreign nations. The ideas of John Quincy Adams, as given by James Monroe in his famous message of 1823, also have a Franklinesque ring: the "true policy" of the United States was to abstain from European affairs in the hope that Europe would reciprocate. Even the campaign posters of 1916, proclaiming that Wilson had "kept us out of war," or Franklin Delano Roosevelt who, in September 1940, declared that he had said again and again to the mothers and fathers of America that their sons would not be sent to fight in any European war, are reminiscent of Franklin. Isolation, surely one of the most persistent themes in American foreign policy, extends back to Franklin's attitudes toward entangling alliances; yet historians have seldom connected his name with that theme.

Within that position of isolation and distrust, another strong theme remained, which may well have arisen from Franklin's attitudes regarding Franco-American ties and friendships. From the time of the Sage of Passy's joyful life with his French friends during the Revolution to John J. Pershing's cry of "Lafayette, we are here!" to the GIs of World War II who believed their battles to free France were repayment of an old debt, Americans have held France in particularly high esteem among European nations, for it was France that came to their aid during the War of Independence when America desperately needed help. Thus the "common wisdom" has assessed the historical past.

Franklin conceived another persistent idea in the American approach to foreign affairs: "superparliaments" that might promote harmony and ensure peace. He set forth his Albany Plan of Union as early as 1754 in an effort to establish a new imperial body to oversee affairs of common concern to both the English people and their American colonies. His view has become part of the American Dream and may be seen in the sporadic support of America for justice among its own states, for various European unification efforts, in Wilson's hopes for the League of Nations, in participation in the United Nations, and in support for such partial unions as the European Economic Community. Although by 1775 Franklin opposed a "united nations organization" for the British Empire, he continued to think highly of the concept itself as an answer to many of the ills of warring nations. In 1787, still enthusiastic about the just-completed American Constitutional Convention in Philadelphia, Franklin wrote an old friend, Ferdinand Grant, that Europe should also unite. "I do not see why you might not in Europe carry the Project of good Henry the 4th into Execution, by forming a Federal Union and One Grand Republick of all its different States and Kingdoms, by means of a like Convention, for we had many Interests to reconcile."

Benjamin Franklin could be scathing in his denunciation of the actions of nations that were not bound by concepts of law and justice. To Richard Price, Franklin spoke of his hopes for "the Discovery of a Plan, that would induce & oblige Nations to settle their Disputes without first Cutting one another's Throats." John Baynes reported that Franklin "observed that nothing could be more disgraceful than the scandalous inattention to treaties" demonstrated by various nations. He did, however, think "the world would grow wiser, and wars become less frequent." Most plans to speed that process along were impracticable, Franklin said, for "they supposed a general agreement among the sovereigns of Europe to send delegates to a particular place. Now, though perhaps two or three of them might be willing to come into this measure, it is improbable and next to impossible that all, or even a majority of them would do it." A century or two might allow enough time for all Europe to "agree upon an alliance against all aggressors, and agree to refer all disputes between each other to some third person, or set of men, or power." Such a development was truly important, thought Franklin, because neighboring states required justice as much as neighboring citizens. In his view a robber who plundered in a gang was as despicable as one who acted alone, and a nation that made an unjust war was "only a great Gang." Thus Franklin spoke of this concern, basing his case as was his wont upon pragmatic, practical concerns rather than upon some idealistic concern for liberty or freedom.

During Franklin's term in the Continental Congress he counseled his fellows on two other matters. The first related to American expansion into the trans-Allegheny West and the absorption of Canada, and was born of his hopes for profit in land speculation. This long-standing dedication, when transposed into political terms, became a justification for expansionism for the young nation. Part of his interest in western land stemmed from what has been called "defensive imperialism," the need to oust foreign powers in order to create what Jefferson would call an empire of liberty in the New World. Franklin was as ardent an expansionist as any of the Founding Fathers, and his writings, whether in 1760 or 1776 or 1785, provided a sound rationale for acquiring as much of the West as possible. The American hunger for land broadened with the peace treaty of 1783; that stream became a river with the acquisition of Louisiana in 1803. With Manifest Destiny in the 1840s it became a raging torrent, and the "white man's burden" and overseas involvement changed it into a veritable flood tide of American diplomacy by the 1890s.

Franklin also tried in Congress to broaden the definitions of international law. He hoped that warring nations might ultimately be made to limit their actions to military objectives and to avoid harming neutral nations or individuals engaged in peaceful pursuits of agriculture and trade among enemy populations. Franklin failed to accomplish his goal, but his view of the pacific character of commerce was embodied in the American Plan of 1776 which stated that "free ships make free goods." This doctrine became the cornerstone of the American definition of neutral rights in the nineteenth century and was incorporated into the Treaty of Amity and Commerce signed with France in February 1778.

Two years later, Franklin explained how his idea was gaining currency in Europe: "All the neutral states of Europe seem at present disposed to change what had never before been deemed the law of nations, to wit, that an enemy's property may be taken wherever found, and to establish a rule that free ships shall make free goods. The rule is in itself so reasonable, and of nature so beneficial to mankind, that I can not but wish it may become general." That view did not prevail, and the United States, having fought one war with the mother country to achieve independence, found itself embroiled thirty-four years later in another to maintain it. Mindful of Franklin's contribution to his country's definition of neutral rights, President James Madison said in 1814 that the United States would not continue to honor the doctrine of "free ships, free goods" unless a refinement, almost a new principle, was also observed, "namely, that unarmed merchant vessels, like wagons or ploughs, the property of one belligerent, should be unmolested by the other." That doctrine, he proudly asserted, had "an undisputed American father in Doctor Franklin."

An examination of the extraordinary ideas of Benjamin Franklin remains crucial for an understanding of the development, formulation, and implementation of American foreign policy. Franklin remains one of the chief figures in America's pantheon of greatness, for his ideas, taken up and built upon by others, have become pervasively influential melodies in the hymnody of United States diplomacy.

BIBLIOGRAPHIC NOTE

Extensive documentation for the views expressed in Professor Currey's essay may be found in his two books, *Road to Revolution: Benjamin Franklin in England, 1765–1775* (New York, 1968) and *Code Number 72: Ben Franklin, Patriot or Spy* (Englewood Cliffs, N.J., 1972). To date the best one-volume biography of this distinguished American remains Carl Van Doren's *Benjamin Franklin* (New York, 1938); in some two hundred pages

Verner W. Crane has compressed a wealth of information and shrewd analysis, *Benjamin Franklin and a Rising People* (Boston, 1954), a volume in Oscar Handlin's American Biography series. Both of these biographies are somewhat dated and no doubt as the voluminous Franklin papers are published new biographies will appear. For a firsthand look at Franklin's varied activities the reader should consult Leonard W. Labaree et al., eds., *The Papers of Benjamin Franklin* (New Haven, 1959–), and Labaree's annotated edition of the *Autobiography of Benjamin Franklin* (New Haven, 1964).

Gerald Stourzh's *Benjamin Franklin and American Foreign Policy* (Chicago, 1954) remains a pioneering and indispensable appraisal of Franklin's approach to problems of diplomacy and foreign affairs. It provides, in the words of one reviewer, the first "balanced interpretation of Franklin's ideas in the field of foreign policy."

For extended coverage of the colonial background of the Revolution see the magisterial work by Lawrence H. Gipson, *The British Empire before the American Revolution*, 14 vols. (New York, 1958–69), an impressive monument of American scholarship. See also the same author's volume in the New American Nation series, *The Coming of the Revolution, 1763–1775* (New York, 1954). For the intellectual background of the war one must consult Bernard Bailyn, *The Ideological Origins of the American Revolution* (Cambridge, Mass., 1967).

For the foundations of American statecraft and the colonial experience in international affairs, the book to consult is Max Savelle, *The Origins of American Diplomacy: The International History of Anglo-America, 1492–1763* (New York, 1967), the first volume in the American Diplomatic History series under the general editorship of Armin Rappaport. Also worth consulting are Savelle's "The American Balance of Power and European Diplomacy, 1713–1778," in Richard B. Morris, ed., *The Era of the American Revolution* (New York, 1939); "Colonial Origins of American Diplomatic Principles," in the *Pacific Historical Review* 3 (September 1934), 334–50; and "The Appearance of an American Attitude toward External Affairs, 1750–1775," *American Historical Review* 52 (July 1947), 655–66.

Two recent works that include the nation's early experience with international affairs are Felix Gilbert, *To the Farewell Address: Ideas of Early American Foreign Policy* (Princeton, 1961), and Paul Varg, *Foreign Policies of the Founding Fathers* (East Lansing, Mich., 1963). Both are model studies.

The classic account of revolutionary diplomacy remains Samuel Flagg Bemis, *The Diplomacy of the American Revolution* (New York, 1935), the one book on its subject against which all others are measured. A masterly account of the negotiations for peace at Paris is Richard B. Morris, *The Peacemakers* (New York, 1965); Morris also examines some of the mythology and misunderstanding surrounding the work of American diplomats at Paris in "The Diplomats and the Mythmakers," a chapter in *The American Revolution Reconsidered* (New York, 1968). For an attempt to see the events of the revolutionary era as part of the developing storm in Europe, see Richard Van Alstyne's *Empire and Independence: The International History of the American Revolution* (New York, 1965), a volume in Robert Divine's America in Crisis series. For a provocative and wide-ranging assessment of some of the larger issues of the era see Robert R. Palmer, *The Age of the Democratic Revolution: A Political History of Europe and America, 1760–1800*, 2 vols. (Princeton, 1959–64). William Stinchcombe's *The American Revolution and the French Alliance* (Syracuse, 1969) traces the impact of congressional involvement in foreign affairs and the fate of the alliance in America. For a pioneering effort still worth reading see Edward S. Corwin, *French Policy and the American Alliance of 1778* (Princeton, 1916).

ALEXANDER HAMILTON

and the Diplomacy of Influence

Ian Mugridge

It is presumably no accident that one of the major modern biographies of Alexander Hamilton is subtitled *Portrait in Paradox* or that his reputation, unlike that of some of the other principal American leaders of his time, has undergone great changes since his death in 1804. Hamilton's actions, perhaps more than those of some of his better-known contemporaries, have been subject to widely differing interpretations. Unlike his mentor, George Washington, or his rival, Thomas Jefferson—men apparently blessed with a basic internal consistency and confidence in themselves and their place in society which enabled them to meet challenges and vicissitudes with equanimity and confidence—Hamilton was hardly cast in a heroic mold. Intellectually, of course, he was the

The author gratefully acknowledges a President's Research Grant from Simon Fraser University which facilitated his work on this essay.

undoubted superior of Washington and at least the equal of
Jefferson; but there seemed to be something lacking in him, what
Adrienne Koch has called "a basic defect of character," which
ultimately diminished his standing as a statesman and a national
leader. Professor Koch has also noted that recent interpretations
have been too kind to Hamilton.

It would be an exaggeration to blame Hamilton's origins and
upbringing for his deficiencies, though perhaps the former reinforced the latter. He was born in or about 1757 on the West Indian
island of Nevis, "the bastard brat of a Scotch pedlar" as the much
provoked John Adams once put it, and brought up by his mother
until her death when he was twelve years old. Soon afterward he
set out to make his way in the world. He was blessed with three
basic ingredients for success in that endeavor: brains, ability, and
benefactors, a combination that took him through years of
struggle and hardship until he left for the American mainland in
1772 to embark upon a university career.

In eighteenth-century terms, such origins were dubious;
Hamilton never cared to advertise them, though he never entirely
severed connections with his father and other members of his
family. Other men, however, have come from equally unfavorable
backgrounds and have not exhibited the character traits that
Hamilton repeatedly demonstrated. His background did give him
an almost frantic determination to succeed, to advance to what he
considered his proper place in society, and an equally fierce pride
in his achievements. That these qualities later degenerated into
mere snobbishness, contempt for the lower orders, and a querulous self-defensiveness flowed at least as much from defects in
Hamilton's character as from boyhood deprivations.

When Hamilton arrived in New York City, the series of events
that led to the Revolution and the War of Independence was
already well advanced. He began his studies at King's College,
entering the path that led him to a position of power and authority
in postwar American society. He advanced from a young and
eloquent orator and pamphleteer to an influential and dashing
aide-de-camp to General Washington so that, by the time of the
peace settlement in 1783, he was no longer an obscure and
struggling student, dependent for his survival largely on his own
wits and the generosity of his benefactors. He finished the war as a
colonel, with the friendship and esteem of Washington and a
reputation for dashing if somewhat irresponsible bravery. He then

became, for a short time, a member of the Continental Congress and a lawyer of growing reputation and affluence. Finally, through marriage to Elizabeth Schuyler in which, to quote John C. Miller, "love, money, social prestige and ambition met in happy conjunction," his social and financial status in New York had become secure.

From 1783, until his death over twenty years later, Hamilton remained a major force in American politics, both nationally and locally. His participation in the movement for constitutional reform and in the drafting and adoption of the new Constitution was of undoubted and overwhelming importance. Equally, his work as secretary of the treasury in Washington's two administrations made an enormous contribution to the financial and administrative structure of the new nation as well as to the directions the government took in domestic and foreign policy. After Washington's retirement he remained an acknowledged leader of the Federalist party both in New York and at the national level and was frequently able to affect the policies of the Adams administration. These years, however, were less happy and far less successful; they served as an example of something against which Hamilton warned his countrymen in the *Federalist*: the corrupting influence of being out of power. Alexander Hamilton was then at his worst. Deprived of national office, he used his considerable influence and talent for intrigue to subvert the authority of John Adams whose office he almost certainly wanted for himself. This led to a widening breach with the president, finally made irreparable by the peevish, pointless, and inexcusable attack on him that Hamilton published a month before the election of 1799. His behavior also widened the gap between himself and Jefferson, vice-president under a president with whom he often disagreed and ultimately defeated, but whom he respected and showed no inclination to undermine as Hamilton did. Finally, having fought against the reelection of Adams and against his replacement by Jefferson, Hamilton found himself on the outside, unable to influence in any substantial way the direction of the government, an increasingly querulous and ineffective voice in t'ie political wilderness. Soon afterward, he died as the result of a foolish duel, a ridiculous climax to a fifteen-year feud with a man who was Hamilton's equal only in the enormity of his pretensions.

Hamilton did possess considerable intellectual ability, and he supplemented this with an equal talent for administration. His attention to and grasp of the problems and details of his tasks as an officer in Washington's command, as a lawyer and legislator, and as secretary of the treasury are truly impressive. His talents frequently became liabilities, for he often appeared unable to decide what affairs did not concern him and when he should take no part in them. He tended to make all the business of government, from whatever department, his province; his desire to interfere often helped to negate the constructive nature and good influence of his work. His removal from power only exaggerated this tendency and converted it into plots to influence the Adams cabinet. Later, it led him to play a role in the destruction of the opposition as well as the demise of his own party.

One must add to this catalog of defects an apparently overwhelming desire for self-justification, charitably termed "frankness" by one biographer, which appeared again and again in Hamilton's writings, even during his years of power and influence. Probably his disputes with George Clinton and Thomas Jefferson showed him at his worst in this respect. Writing to Washington about his clashes with Jefferson and Madison, Hamilton loudly justified his own questionable activities by claiming purity of intention and by denouncing what he saw as the sinister machinations of his enemies.

The roots of these many failings were within Hamilton himself. While his background had supplied him with a yearning to advance his status in society, it also narrowed his perspective and restricted effective use of his abilities. Hamilton's times offered challenging opportunities and brought him into contact with unusual men and events, but in the end, despite his intellect and talent, his apparent smoothness and cultivation, he could not survive and flourish in such circumstances. He had not the depth, the confidence, or the grace of, say, Jefferson, who represented much that Hamilton wanted desperately to be and whom, not surprisingly, he grew to dislike intensely. He had not the steadfastness, the soundness, or the assurance of Washington, who dominated the revolutionary and postwar periods. In power, Hamilton achieved much and contributed much of value to the growth of his country; out of power, he lapsed into intrigue and pettiness, and perhaps only an untimely death prevented the ultimate destruction of his career and reputation.

Throughout his public career, between the end of the War of Independence and the end of Washington's second administration, one of Hamilton's prime concerns, if not his principal objective, became the establishment of the United States as a strong and united nation, prepared and equipped to take its place among the great nations of the world. On this question, little disagreement emerged between Hamilton and his most prominent contemporaries during the late eighties and early nineties. Substantial agreement existed between the leaders of the movement for constitutional reform and the new federal government that all energies had to be channeled in the direction of creating a nation that could command respect in the international arena. This was the case even among those who, like Jefferson, Madison, and Hamilton, quarreled so bitterly in later years.

Where Hamilton parted company with his contemporaries—or perhaps merely carried certain ideas further than they—was in the role he assigned to foreign policy in relation to the growth of the nation. Hamilton believed that there could be no realistic division between foreign and domestic policies, for the one supported and augmented the other and both had to be used to move the nation toward self-sufficiency and international influence. If one of these had to be paramount in the national concern, it was foreign relations: the future of the United States as an industrial and commercial power depended largely on the way in which the rest of the world regarded the new nation.[1]

The great English philosopher F. H. Bradley once rather lightheartedly described metaphysics as "the finding of bad reasons for what we believe upon instinct." In this sense, there was something of the metaphysical in Hamilton's approach to questions of national policy. As a poor, ambitious social climber, he had always recognized that the path to success lay in the establishment of his position. As one of the leaders of a poor, divided, and ambitious nation, instinct told him the same thing: that the way to international prominence and respectability lay in establishment of the new nation as honest, fiscally dependable, and firm. In the pursuit of such objectives, the final goal had to be kept clearly in sight and extraneous considerations cast aside.

1. Gerald Stourzh, *Alexander Hamilton and the Idea of Republican Government* (Stanford, 1970), pp. 126–70. See also the essay on Thomas Jefferson in this volume.

National policy had to be designed to ensure domestic unity and strength; then a strong, unified nation might turn its attention to enhancing its prestige abroad. Such was the essence of the Hamiltonian message; it was a theme he repeated throughout his public career.

Although Hamilton's public statements repeatedly expressed faith in the potential of the new nation, he was equally sure that this could only be realized under a form of government different from that of the feeble, nearly impotent Articles of Confederation. Survival in a world filled with actual or potential competitors and on a continent crowded with powerful and potentially hostile neighbors required a government that could give the United States the order, stability, and, through them, the strength and authority to stand confidently on independent ground. Such advantages, such necessities, could never be gained from a government national in name only, whose regulatory power was hopelessly dissipated among thirteen states, whose cohesion in wartime had been precarious and in peacetime virtually nonexistent.

In spite of the progress made by the United States during the 1780s, Hamilton and a growing number of his contemporaries became convinced of the need to jettison the Articles in favor of a stronger constitution. His views of government and national policy, expressed with cogency and consistency in the years between the Treaty of Paris and the Constitutional Convention, later appeared in their most comprehensive form in the *Federalist*, one of the most remarkable exercises in political theory ever produced in the United States. Neither the views of American foreign policy expressed in these papers and the functions of government in formulating and carrying them out, nor Hamilton's work in gaining support for constitutional reform by stressing the baneful effects of America's impotence abroad, have been properly appreciated.

The basic purpose of the *Federalist* was to persuade the people of New York of the virtues of the proposed federal Constitution. Even though these papers were subject to the limitations of propaganda, the evidence of Hamilton's earlier writings as well as of his subsequent words and actions suggests that the opinions presented in the *Federalist* reflected deeply held convictions on these subjects, so that they may therefore be taken as a reasonably accurate guide to his view of the world.

Hamilton believed that the United States, divided and weak,

had cut such a poor figure in the world that even after five years the peace treaty had not yet been fully implemented. This had been the fault partly of Great Britain and partly of individual states. It was also partly the fault of the "nation," for the government of the Articles possessed neither the power nor the authority to compel recalcitrant states to meet their obligations or to ensure that foreign powers met theirs. Congress and its officers were helpless when states, allies, or enemies could not be brought into line. Frequently, requests or representations made to the American government had not been refused; they were simply ignored. In addition to problems over the treaty, all the other major international problems faced by the United States during the eighties remained unresolved: the West remained tenuously attached to the nation; the British still held the western posts; the Spaniards adopted an equivocal attitude toward American rights on the Mississippi River; attempts to enter into a commercial treaty with Great Britain floundered; and efforts to extend American overseas commerce had failed miserably.

To Hamilton, as to his collaborators, a country so threatened and so much at the mercy of external forces could not long survive. John Jay argued that "among the objects to which a wise and free people find it necessary to direct their attention, that of providing for their *safety* seems to be the first." "A cordial Union under an efficient national Government" could best achieve such safety. Hamilton agreed with his colleague that "safety from external danger is the most powerful director of national conduct," and he claimed that the first object of government must be to guarantee such safety, even at the cost of decreased freedom for the people. It followed from these assumptions that a government like that under the Articles, deprived of effective powers of taxation and of ability to act in a unified way at home or abroad, could not—indeed should not—long survive as an independent state. The depressing experience of the postwar period had confirmed the truth of these observations.

Such a situation could not continue under the proposed Constitution, which would give the central government the power, and thus hopefully the effectiveness, denied it by the Articles. Power over taxation, interstate commerce, foreign relations (through the right to make treaties and to undertake direct control over foreign policy), and the army and navy would belong to the federal government rather than to the individual states with

their lamentably particularist record. This newly acquired authority would be the basis for the growth of the United States into the
great nation in which Hamilton had always believed. To him,
power comprised the central fact of political life at any level.
Without it, any kind of government would become ineffective;
with it, the development of a nation to its highest potential could
become a reality.

Such views Hamilton made explicit in his sections of the
Federalist. Later when ideas could be translated into action, when
theories had to stand the test of implementation, the depth of
Hamilton's commitment to such positions became apparent. The
remarkable consistency of his views on the importance of foreign
policy, on the primacy of national strength and security, and on
the necessity for government authority is impressive. Although
specific examples of the ineffectiveness of the Articles, the debility
of the Congress, or the humiliations of the national government
had doubtless reinforced Hamilton's opinions expressed in the
Federalist, he could have written the theoretical sections at almost
any time after 1775.

Hamilton and his collaborators had sought to persuade the
people of New York that the government under the new Constitution would cure the Confederation's ills and would provide the
impetus necessary to push the United States toward greatness; but
in 1789, at President Washington's first inauguration, nothing
changed except the government. The test of theories expounded
in the federal Constitution, in the *Federalist*, and in all that had
been written and spoken about the new government lay in the
future. As in all such cases, the trial of men and their attitudes
toward government and power consisted not in what they said
about them but in what they did with them.

⟨⟨⟨⟩⟩⟩

Any study of the new nation's foreign affairs necessarily
focuses on a consideration of the foreign policy views that
Hamilton recommended to the Washington administrations. The
first president's foreign policy between 1789 and 1796 was, to all
intents and purposes, that of his secretary of the treasury. So
strong was Hamilton's influence, often far exceeding that of the
secretary of state, that he played a key role in determining the
initial American response to the external world. Hamilton's in-

fluence was significant in the Nootka Sound crisis of 1790, the Neutrality Proclamation of 1793, and Jay's Treaty and the debate over its ratification in 1794–95. Moreover, the most characteristic expression of Washington's approach to foreign affairs, the Farewell Address, bears the strong imprint of Hamilton's thinking.

His attitudes toward the foreign relations of the United States from 1789 to 1796 are completely consistent. His words and actions form a remarkable, unified whole, bringing together both his experiences in nation building and his reflections on the nature and uses of national power. His assessment of the position of the United States and his estimate of its future led him to firm conclusions and precise objectives in the international arena that became the goals of his years in power. Felix Gilbert has noted: "Although many Americans looked upon the prospect of participating in power politics only with horror or acknowledged the necessity of such a thing only with reservations and hesitation, eighteenth century power politics had an effective advocate on the American continent. It spoke authoritatively through the voice of Alexander Hamilton." [2]

Convinced that European conceptions about the nature of international relations were accurate and applicable to the New World, Hamilton reasoned that, whether or not the United States wished to withdraw from contact with other nations or to change the nature of international relations, whether or not it wished to impose on the Old World some new order of its own devising, such a course would be impossible until the nation had first established a position of influence among European powers. To move the country toward that goal, the new government first had to strengthen the nation at home by establishing firm control over the country, by placing public credit and national finances on a sound footing, by fostering American industry, and by expanding its commerce. The government might then maneuver more effectively in the international sphere. Hamilton, of course, was keenly aware of the relationship between domestic and international affairs.

Moving the nation to its rightful place in the world arena was a task both delicate and hazardous. The creation of constitutional

2. Felix Gilbert, *To the Farewell Address: Ideas of Early American Foreign Policy* (Princeton, 1961), p. 111.

government in America did not automatically resolve diplomatic problems. Great Britain, while not exactly hostile, was certainly not friendly, and it retained control of the northern frontier of the United States as well as much of the back country in the old Northwest. By refusing to surrender their forts in that region, the British technically contravened the 1783 treaty, but they cited American noncompliance with other terms of the treaty as justification for their violation. Spain, though weak, clung stubbornly to its control of the Mississippi River and New Orleans, thus contributing to dissension in the trans-Allegheny West among Americans who were thereby cut off from a much needed outlet to the sea. The Atlantic remained effectively under British control, and the government at Whitehall, under the influence of men like Hawkesbury and Sheffield, had shown no inclination to liberalize its commercial policies to give American merchants greater access to British ports either at home or in the West Indies. Attempts to open other markets in Europe had been largely unsuccessful, and while American commerce was not foundering, neither was it expanding. In sum, when Washington took office the international situation contained little that was encouraging, and there was small prospect of improvement until the new nation spoke with the firm, united, and effective voice that Hamilton sought to give it.

How Hamilton hoped to strengthen America's international position can be defined by examining his response to the issues of the Nootka Sound crisis of 1790. Great Britain had protested the Spanish seizure of British ships in Nootka Sound on the west coast of Vancouver Island. By the summer of 1790, the British government was actively preparing for war with Spain, and the Washington administration anticipated an attack from Canada on Spanish territory in the Southwest. Apprehensive that the United States might become unnecessarily involved in a war in which it had no real interest, the president asked his cabinet for guidance on an appropriate response in a number of theoretical situations that might arise from an Anglo-Spanish conflict, including a possible British request to move troops across American territory. In the end, settlement of the dispute without war rendered academic both the request and the replies it elicited; but Hamilton's response provides a number of important clues to his general attitude toward America's international position and conduct.

Hamilton divided the question into the theoretical one of the nation's right to refuse consent to the passage of troops and the practical one of the consequences of such an action. He noted the weakness of America and the probable danger of an attempt to stop British troop movements across American territory. While the United States clearly had the right to refuse passage, he maintained, it had neither the financial nor the military resources to prevent the British from doing as they wished. Under the circumstances it seemed to him that cooperation might be wiser than confrontation.

He felt strongly that the government had two primary obligations: to refrain from involvement in the war and to preserve the honor of the United States. It was equally clear that in what might prove to be the first serious test of the new government in international affairs these two obligations might easily conflict. Hamilton concluded that Spain had little reason to expect gratitude or assistance from the United States and that there might be more profit in helping Great Britain, especially if Spain continued to restrict American access to the mouth of the Mississippi. Additionally, refusal to allow passage to the British might mean another war with the former mother country to avoid disgrace, and for a number of compelling reasons that alternative had to be avoided if possible. The British request therefore ought to be honored, for the consequences of refusal—war or disgrace—were worse than the pain of acquiescence. Then, too, cooperation with the British might lead to some advantages. Hamilton finally advised that if the British entered lightly held American territory without permission, a protest should be made to London, though not one strong enough to make war necessary. If, however, British troops in transit forced an American post, then the nation would have to declare war on Britain.

Few pronouncements give a clearer idea of Hamilton's conception of America's role than this one. The Hamiltonian sensitivity to the relationship between means and ends emerges clearly, as does his understanding of the utility of Britain in America's future. The advice reflects also the consonance between his own rise to power and his instincts about the international position of the United States. The country found itself in a weak and friendless position, hemmed in by two more powerful and hostile neighbors, neither of which America could afford to offend. Forced to tread a delicate path between the need for firmness and the prospect of humiliation, any American answer bore the possibility of disaster. Of this Hamilton and Washington were painfully aware.

As has been frequently noted, foreign policy is at best an inexact science, having as its basic ingredient a considerable element of conjecture. Policy makers rarely have full information, and the actions of one nation can seldom be based on exact knowledge of another nation's reaction. Decisions, therefore, must be made according to the government's best estimate of the attitudes and responses of the other parties involved. That assessment must be made in accordance with the answers to a number of questions concerning the nation itself and foreign powers. In calculating a potential foreign response, policy makers ask, "What will happen if we do this?" In formulating policy for the nation, those charged with the responsibility of decision making must ask, "What do we want and how much do we want it?" From such imprecise principles decisions must often be made.

In the situation confronting the United States government in 1790, variants of these questions were asked, but a number of other conditions complicated the search for answers. Apart from Jefferson and Adams, who had served as American representatives abroad during the Confederation period, the cabinet making the decisions had little direct experience in international affairs and no tradition of national policy to guide its actions. In addition, all of Washington's advisers had a somewhat equivocal attitude toward Great Britain; all of them, even Hamilton, had expressed doubts of British trustworthiness during and after the War of Independence. Cabinet members had also become dubious about Spanish intentions. That country, a lukewarm ally in wartime, had given few indications of continuing friendship after the war and had taken some actions that conveyed an opposite impression. Further, Spain's ally, France, a problematical quantity in any case, presented even more uncertainty after the outbreak of its own Revolution.

In such circumstances, the alternatives available to the United States were severely limited, as Hamilton realized perhaps more clearly than any of his cabinet colleagues. At the time and since he has been accused of unseemly haste in acceding to British demands; and in view of some of his subsequent acts, there may be some justice in the charge that Hamilton, the archetypal

Anglophile, used this opportunity, as he did others, to attach his country firmly to the former mother country.

Such an interpretation seems unduly harsh. The Washington cabinet had to estimate the probable consequence of a refusal to allow British troops passage across American territory. Hamilton never doubted the outcome of denial. No good could come from it, and it might well lead to national humiliation, even a threat to independence. While refusal might satisfy national honor or become necessary as a last resort, it would be a futile protest against a powerful neighbor from whose enmity Americans had much to lose and in whose friendship there might be enormous advantage. Rhetorical as he could be on occasion, Hamilton rarely indulged in empty flourishes or refused to accept the consequences of his actions. During the Nootka discussions, he demonstrated both qualities.

It is unfortunate that, since 1938, diplomats and the historians who write about them have been unable to use the word "appeasement" in any but a pejorative sense. Appeasement was often a perfectly reasonable and effective course of action for a weak and vulnerable nation, such as the United States in 1790, in dealing with powerful or predatory neighbors. In his reply to the president, Hamilton was in essence suggesting this course; under the circumstances, it was probably the only realistic one for the United States. Prudence dictated a soft answer to the mistress of the seas, the most powerful country in the world. In his advice during the Nootka crisis, Hamilton seemed moved more by a sense of realism than by any ideological identification with the cause of Britain, though certainly his pragmatic approach to international affairs—and the reliance of his financial system on international trade and capital—did not permit him to forget the possible future utility of a pro-British stance. More importantly, he preferred accommodation to antagonism, and in his discussions of foreign affairs during the Washington years he invariably urged appeasement in the cabinet, perhaps most notably and effectively during the negotiation of Jay's Treaty.

The outbreak of the wars of the French Revolution complicated enormously the search for accommodation with the powers of Europe. Hamilton's response to the problems posed by that cataclysmic event shows another aspect of his approach to international affairs. When general war broke out in Europe in

1793 and France, the nation that had come to America's aid in 1778, once again fought its ancient enemy, a strong party in the United States, both in Congress and outside it, urged on by French agents, loudly proclaimed that gratitude for aid received during the revolutionary war required the nation again to join hands with its erstwhile ally.

In the *Pacificus* papers Hamilton examined the questions raised by these events in Europe and America. Gratitude had no place in international affairs, he said, because it unduly restrained national action and imposed restrictions on it that often worked against the nation's real and enduring interests. In the relations between states, faith and justice were, of course, admirable virtues that could not be "too strongly inculcated nor too highly respected," for they imposed obligations, possessed utility, and were subject to definable rules. The same, however, could not be said of gratitude, and it therefore ought never to be placed on the same level in international relations as in interpersonal ones. Nations should always seek to make their own welfare the primary motive for action. They must never allow gratitude to intrude into the sphere in which the interests of the state, within the limits set by justice and good faith, must predominate. Such sentiments were not intended merely to advance selfish or narrow policies, but to show that a policy regulated by self-interest and bounded by justice and good faith was, and should be, a legitimate objective of the servants of the state. Arguments for a self-denying or self-sacrificing national gratitude for favors received from other nations in the past misconstrued the proper springs of national conduct in the international arena.

Examining the international situation in 1793, Hamilton concluded that the United States had no legal duty to France to enter the war, a conclusion reinforced by a number of other more practical considerations. As in 1790, the dangers of challenging Britain remained: its effective command of the sea, which seemed likely to continue, might ruin American trade; the situation in the Northwest and in the West was still precarious, with British influence there virtually undiminished; and Britain still offered the best prospects for future advantage to America. France, on the other hand, was a more doubtful proposition. Its attitude and policies since the revolutionary change of government were in flux; the activity of its first diplomatic representative in America, Citizen Edmond Genêt, rendered the position of the secretary of state "immensely difficult"; and to many observers like Hamilton its future course, clouded by the horrors and excesses of the Revolution, was impossible to predict.

Under such circumstances, neutrality became the only safe course for the nation while involvement in the war, on either side, was too hazardous; but although there was an administration consensus on the need for neutrality, there was also considerable controversy in the cabinet over the form that neutrality should take. Hamilton wished for a definition that would decrease the aid Americans were obligated to give under the still valid French treaty of 1778, and he sought ways to lessen the impact of neutrality on Britain. Conversely, Jefferson wished a gentler, more indirect expression of neutrality that would allow France to see advantage, or at least the absence of animosity, in America's stance. He hoped to use American policy as a lever for prying concessions from the European powers, in effect forcing them to bid for a beneficent neutrality. "None of the principals involved in the shaping of American foreign policy," Lawrence Kaplan wrote, "wanted involvement in the European war. The sympathies of the president and secretary of state . . . were in full agreement on denying military assistance to the French ally. The secretary of the treasury would not only avoid war but would use the occasion to break the alliance and remove the United States from any obligation to France." The Hamiltonian position was a composite of political, philosophical, and emotional pressures. "France," Professor Kaplan continued, "was an enemy of civilization as long as revolution gripped the nation, while England was the one nation in the world that could protect the world from the French terror as well as the only government that could advance the American political economy."[3] It was perhaps not entirely coincidental that neutrality would enable the United States to reap enormous profits from wartime trade with Europe and the West Indies; not for the last time in American history, profit became the handmaiden of prudence. If the policy of neutrality and the process of strengthening the economy moved America closer to Britain's orbit, Hamilton did not object, for he considered such an arrangement vital to the nation's future.

3. Lawrence S. Kaplan, *Colonies into Nation: American Diplomacy, 1763–1801* (New York, 1972), p. 217. The above paragraph relies heavily on the chapter, "The Hamiltonian Apex, 1793–1796," pp. 216–58.

The negotiations that led to the signing of Jay's Treaty, an agreement that Samuel Flagg Bemis has suggested might more properly be called Hamilton's Treaty, demonstrate the limits of Hamilton's search for accommodation with Britain. In the Anglo-American rapprochement of 1794–95 the secretary of the treasury played a key role. By devising and supporting John Jay's special mission to London, Hamilton defused the ugly clamor for war and in the process thwarted Republican efforts to torpedo his policy by congressional enactment of discriminatory duties on British ships in American ports.

In the months after Washington's decision for neutrality, Britain, instead of appreciating American commercial policy, intensified its sea war against France, seized American goods on the seas, failed to restrain its Indian allies in the West, struck at national sovereignty by impressing American sailors, and by a series of insolent Orders in Council threatened the profitable West Indian provision trade. War might have come from such provocations and the passions they engendered, but, largely because of Hamilton's diplomatic initiative, it did not.

In these negotiations, Hamilton again demonstrated a perhaps too hasty willingness to accommodate the British. In 1794, this haste, if such it was, again went hand in hand with a number of other more pragmatic considerations. First, Hamilton realized that Britain, embroiled in a costly and lengthening war, might be more amenable to American overtures than in the past. It seemed reasonable to suppose that in order to concentrate on the French menace in Europe the British might wish to remove the drain on their resources represented by continuing uncertainty in relations with the United States. This reading of British policy was based in part on a shrewd assessment of the international situation as it might appear to His Majesty's ministers at Whitehall; but it was also based on the requirements of the Hamiltonian financial system for amicable relations with London. The cordial reception that Jay received in London attests to the essential accuracy of these views.

Second, aware as always of the strong interaction between domestic and foreign affairs, Hamilton saw the potential advantages of a settlement with Great Britain. Resolution of some of the touchy problems in the West and the advantages to American commerce and business of an accommodation with the British presented powerful stimulus for opening negotiations. Then, too, the question of war or peace, of ideological commitment to one side or the other—the specters of revolutionary republicanism or reactionary monarchism coming to America—had become emotion-laden issues in domestic politics, splitting both the government and the country into violently opposed factions. Hamilton was not insensitive to the prospects of securing party advantage by concluding a treaty that would confound the pro-French faction and strengthen Federalist influence in the government.

Under no illusions about America's bargaining position vis-à-vis Britain, Hamilton advised Jay to make the best deal he could and to settle as many points at issue as possible. Then, by a series of injudicious conversations with the British minister at Philadelphia, he proceeded to narrow the options open to the American negotiator in London. The inflexibility of the British position, especially on the extremely sensitive question of the interpretation of neutral rights, resulted in large measure from Hamilton's meddling in the negotiations, his overeagerness to indulge the British point of view. Whether he blunted Jay's chief negotiating weapon, an implied threat to join a league of armed European neutrals, by an indiscreet hint to the British minister about America's wish to abstain from European connections remains a matter of historical debate, but there can be little doubt that the British willingness to make concessions lessened as a result of Hamilton's role in the negotiations.

When the treaty came to the United States for ratification and encountered a flood of resentment, Hamilton readily admitted that it was not ideal and in the influential *Camillus* papers defended it on practical grounds: the need for peace, the dependence on revenues generated by trade, the reduction of friction between the two countries. While the treaty left unresolved a number of serious problems between the United States and Great Britain, it did help maintain peace between them; it marked an important milestone on America's road to international respectability; and it marked the apex of Hamilton's diplomatic influence. If the treaty went too far toward appeasement of the British, he regarded the concessions as a necessary part of eighteenth-century diplomacy. "Hamilton's great success," Professor Kaplan noted, "was in understanding the nature of America's link to the Old World and seeking to bend it to the service of the New." He regarded the treaty as an important step in achieving a primary objective of the new federal government:

DEFENCE

OF THE

TREATY

AMITY, COMMERCE, AND NAVIGATION,

ENTERED INTO BETWEEN

THE UNITED STATES OF AMERICA & GREAT BRITAIN,

AS IT HAS APPEARED IN THE PAPERS UNDER THE

SIGNATURE OF

CAMILLUS.

A. Hamilton —

NEW-YORK:

PRINTED AND SOLD BY FRANCIS CHILDS AND Co. AND SOLD BY
JAMES RIVINGTON, AT No. 156, Pearl-street; also, at the other Book
Stores of this City.——1795.

establishing a strong, stable nation with the capacity to take an independent stand in the world. Once again, his instincts and his intelligence served the nation well.

◇◇◇

In his judgments about the position of the United States and in the policies that he recommended Hamilton was consistent, perceptive, and realistic. The course he charted between 1789 and 1796 admirably suited the condition of the United States at that time, a statement that can seldom be made about the policies advocated by his adversaries. On this basis, Hamilton deserves a place in the first rank as a theoretical exponent of American foreign policy. Instinct and reason persuaded him that existing rules must govern the international game, that nations must eschew unrealistic goals, and that the availability of resources and the nation's reputation and influence must temper its aims. It followed that because the former were limited, the latter should also remain strictly limited, at least temporarily. It may be that on this level Hamilton's attitudes toward the international conduct of the United States formed a model that would be hard to fault for any nation, in the eighteenth century or the twentieth.

Unfortunately, however, government policy operates not only on a theoretical level, but also on the more practical level of implementation, and its effectiveness and that of the men who make it and put it into effect must be judged on that level as well. Here, Hamilton's conduct cannot stand close examination. There is—or perhaps there ought to be—a basic distinction between foreign policy and foreign relations.[4] The former is the area in which the discussion of problems and recommendations is undertaken and decisions made. At such a point, in its embryonic stage, foreign policy is often the proper concern of the cabinet as a whole: it is frequently made as the result of discussions in the cabinet and the representations of Congress and other groups. Like many other major policy questions in their early stages, foreign policy remains an affair of the whole government rather than the preserve of a single department or cabinet member.

---

4. For a discussion of this question in a modern context, see William L. Turpin, "Foreign Relations, Yes; Foreign Policy, No," *Foreign Policy* 8 (Fall 1972), 50–61.

Washington's habit of circulating questions on important foreign policy issues to all members of his cabinet seems to suggest his acceptance of such a view. There comes a point, however, at which the theoretical discussion of policy must be translated into action, when decisions must be implemented. At that point, foreign policy, the concern with implementation of policy decisions, passes as it did under the first president into the hands of the Department of State or perhaps even a single person.

In molding foreign policy Hamilton possessed considerable, even paramount, influence, which was, of course, legitimate within the operational context of the Washington administrations. The president apparently accepted and even encouraged it. As noted, the course that Hamilton envisaged for the country and attempted with some success to pursue was a reasonable one in the 1790s. A consideration of his role in the international relations of the United States, however, requires some discussion of his impact on the implementation of policy.

Hamilton had extensive influence over foreign policy because of his personal relationship with the president, because of his mastery of detail, and because he continually urged his opinions strongly and eloquently, in writing and orally, in the cabinet and elsewhere. His authority over implementation was rather more limited, for, theoretically at least, this was the province of the secretary of state. How much this administrative detail restricted Hamilton remains debatable. Washington's most recent biographer, James Thomas Flexner, has argued that the president, who believed himself to be fairly experienced in foreign affairs, allowed his secretary of state a free hand only in the administrative details of his department, and that Washington, basically opposed to many of Hamilton's ideas on foreign policy, allowed the secretary of the treasury as little rope. Washington, in other words, was nobody's tool and at least until early in his second term maintained effective control over his able but warring lieutenants. Others, notably Alexander DeConde, have argued that Hamilton had overwhelming influence at almost every level.[5]

While neither view may be entirely satisfactory, there is little

5. James Thomas Flexner, *George Washington and the New Nation, 1783–1793* (Boston, 1970), pp. 400–415; Alexander DeConde, *Entangling Alliance* (Durham, 1958), pp. 501–11.

doubt that Hamilton attempted to influence American relations, particularly with Great Britain, by conversations outside the cabinet and official channels. Indeed, it has been argued that he took such efforts beyond the bounds of diplomatic propriety, carrying them, in the words of one critic, even "beyond the limits of honorable conduct in public office."[6] Deprived of authority over foreign affairs and restricted largely to running his own department, he used other means to assert influence. During the Nootka Sound crisis, for example, he met regularly with Colonel George Beckwith, an agent of the governor-general of Canada, Lord Dorchester, who in turn reported to the British cabinet. At a time when American policy had not been decided, when the government rightly sought to present a united front to the British, Hamilton frequently assured Beckwith that the Washington administration harbored no ill intentions toward the British, that American policy would ultimately reflect this, and that both he and the president felt that way.

Such devious diplomacy was by no means unusual for Hamilton, for he continued to meet Beckwith whenever the latter visited the United States and he later formed a similar relationship with the first British minister, George Hammond, appointed in 1791. The extent of the information that he supplied to Washington about these discussions cannot be accurately established, but the evidence suggests that it was limited and not entirely accurate; on at least one occasion he gave the president an account of a discussion that was somewhat different from the one that appeared in Beckwith's report to his superiors. So accustomed did Hammond become to receiving inside news from the secretary of the treasury that the British minister could only express amazement when Hamilton refused to show him Jay's instructions. In another conversation with Hammond, Hamilton expressed regret for the intemperance of his cabinet colleague, the secretary of state, in his talks with the British minister.

There has been some debate about the intent and significance of these activities. Hamilton's apologists have maintained that they were relatively unimportant, that at most they indicate a little excessive zeal in furthering the ends of government. His critics, on

6. Julian P. Boyd, *Number 7: Alexander Hamilton's Secret Attempts to Control American Foreign Policy* (Princeton, 1964), p. xiv.

the other hand, assert that his actions represent "a sustained effort" to direct American foreign policy in a pro-British direction, that his conduct in the Beckwith business was "not an isolated instance, but [part of] a consistent and characteristic pattern of behavior," and that in following this course Hamilton committed "almost the gravest offense of which a cabinet officer can be guilty in his role of responsible advisor to the head of state." [7]

It is hard to agree with the apologists. There can be little doubt that Hamilton formed his contacts with Beckwith and Hammond consciously and deliberately. Such conduct was inexcusable and may even have bordered on treason, particularly when, as has often been pointed out, it came from a man who emphasized so loudly and continuously the need for a strong and united government. It meant little that Hamilton's motive was above reproach, that he sought to retain strong, united government by helping to secure the accommodation with Britain that he regarded as vital to the nation's well-being. Nor can his actions be condoned by placing them alongside his unquestioned achievements in other areas, for it was inexcusable for a cabinet member to act in a manner that could only decrease the effectiveness of policies upon which his colleagues had agreed. By acting in such a fashion, by interfering in matters clearly outside his departmental province, Hamilton went far toward reducing his stature as a statesman. Ultimately, a government cannot afford to speak with more than one voice on major issues, and it was fortunate that more unpleasant consequences did not follow from Hamilton's conduct. In pursuit of his policy he entered into private discussions with representatives of a foreign power, gave them information they had no business having, and helped undermine the work of more than one American diplomat. His arrogance and his quest for power led him to irresponsible interference in affairs of state. This was not the conduct of a reliable minister and it may be that the president, too, was partly culpable for such a thoroughly undesirable precedent. [8]

7. Boyd, *Number 7*, pp. xii–xiv.
8. According to Hamilton, his 15 July conversation with Beckwith resulted from the president's instructions, given after Hamilton's report of his 8 July talk with the British agent and relayed to Hamilton with Jefferson's knowledge. Beckwith's version of the conversation, however, contained statements made by Hamilton that were not contained in the secretary's report to Washington.

Still, Hamilton's contribution to the making of American diplomatic history must be accounted a great and lasting one. At the end of Washington's presidency, Hamilton helped draft the document that became the Farewell Address.[9] It contained his own and Washington's political testament. In it, he urged on his countrymen the principles that he had sought to implement for the previous eight years. He advised against "passionate attachment" and permanent alliances with any nation; he advocated as little political connection with other nations as possible. With the French alliance in mind, Hamilton and Washington suggested that foreign entanglements might become impediments rather than aids to securing the national interest. As he had done throughout his years in office, Hamilton again argued that the United States must preserve its freedom of action in the international arena.

Pointing out the weakness of the new nation, he had argued for appeasement of Great Britain in 1790 and for abstention from European wars in 1793, and, recognizing the advantage to be gained from Europe's distress, he had argued for accommodation with the British in 1794–95. To him the important point was always the avoidance of attachments that might become too confining. Thus, he sought to free America from the embrace of the French alliance when his view of the nation's interests dictated that course.

Such ideas formed part of Hamilton's overall conception of national policy. Domestic policy, economic policy in particular, was tied to foreign affairs. The economic health of the nation was essential to the security of the state and to its effective operation in relations with other states. The national policy of Hamilton was designed to achieve strength, stability, and security at home and abroad. In pursuit of that goal the only valid guide to national action was the immediate and long-term interest of the country. Essentially, Hamilton followed a concept of international relations common to eighteenth-century Europe before the French Revolution. It was a view that cast aside considerations of morality, denied the need for international gratitude, and sought short-term alliances that were as unconfining as possible. Hamilton attempted to steer the nation away from firm commitments, toward abstention from European quarrels, and in the direction of

9. Gilbert, *To the Farewell Address*, pp. 123–34.

cooperation with those from whom the greatest advantage could be gained. Always he sought to preserve America's flexibility, its freedom of action in a hostile world, and to avoid burdening the nation with unrealistic and potentially harmful obligations. Flawed though it may be, Hamilton's contribution to the evolution of the nation's stance in international affairs remains a substantial one. A study of his approach remains basic to an understanding of the critical period of the 1790s—and, one may suggest, for the 1970s as well.

BIBLIOGRAPHIC NOTE

The major printed source for future work on Alexander Hamilton must, of course, be the new edition of his papers which has now reached, in time, December 1794, and in volumes, seventeen: Harold C. Syrett and Jacob E. Cooke, eds., *The Papers of Alexander Hamilton* (New York, 1961–). It is a monumental work that, together with the steadily growing number of volumes in the similar editions of the papers of such contemporaries as Jefferson, Madison, and Franklin, provides a solid basis for investigations into Hamilton's life in particular and the revolutionary and early national periods in general. In the category of primary source material, it should also be noted that the best edition of the *Federalist* is now Jacob E. Cooke, ed., *The Federalist* (Middletown, Conn., 1961).

There are two major modern biographies of Hamilton that provide both a comprehensive account of his career and considerable insight into his attitudes and actions. The better is John C. Miller, *Alexander Hamilton: Portrait in Paradox* (New York, 1959). The second is the two-volume work by Broadus Mitchell, *Youth to Maturity, 1755–1788* and *The National Adventure, 1788–1804* (New York, 1957–62). An interesting and important collection of essays on Hamilton is contained in Jacob E. Cooke, ed., *Alexander Hamilton: A Profile* (New York, 1967), which provides discussion of a variety of aspects of Hamilton's life and thought by a group of distinguished scholars. The best treatment of Hamilton's political thought is clearly Gerald Stourzh's brilliant *Alexander Hamilton and the Idea of Republican Government* (Stanford, 1970). Of particular relevance to Hamilton's views on foreign policy is the fourth chapter of this work, "The Foreign Policy of Republican Government," but the whole book is indispensable to future studies of any important aspect of Hamilton's career. Another perceptive and revealing treatment of Hamilton's political thought and career is Adrienne Koch, *Power, Morals and the Founding Fathers* (Ithaca, 1961), in which Professor Koch (who also contributed an important essay on "Hamilton and Power" to Cooke's collection mentioned above) argues persuasively against Broadus Mitchell's view of

Hamilton as "the wise patron of government guidance" with a philosophical and moral basis for his policies.

There are a number of general works on the foreign policy of the early national period and of Washington's administrations in particular. Alexander DeConde, *Entangling Alliance: Politics and Diplomacy under George Washington* (Durham, 1958), the most thorough treatment of Washington's foreign policy, argues the overwhelming influence of Hamilton in this area. Felix Gilbert partly supports this view in an excellent discussion of the intellectual basis of foreign policy under Washington, *To the Farewell Address: Ideas of Early American Foreign Policy* (Princeton, 1961). An opposing view is put forward in a more recent work, James Thomas Flexner, *George Washington and the New Nation, 1783–1793* (Boston, 1972). Another important work, covering the period from the beginning of the War of Independence to the War of 1812, is Paul A. Varg, *Foreign Policies of the Founding Fathers* (East Lansing, Mich., 1963). Perhaps the best survey of American foreign relations in the Washington years, however, is to be found in the relevant sections, particularly the chapter on "The Hamiltonian Apex," of Lawrence S. Kaplan, *Colonies into Nation: American Diplomacy, 1763–1801* (New York, 1972).

On the final and most important achievement in foreign relations of Washington's presidency, Jay's Treaty, three books are worth noting: Samuel Flagg Bemis, *Jay's Treaty*, 2nd ed. (New Haven, 1962), the oldest, most comprehensive and probably still the best discussion of the treaty; Jerald A. Combs, *The Jay Treaty: Political Battleground of the Founding Fathers* (Berkeley, 1970); and Charles R. Ritcheson, *Aftermath of Revolution: British Policy toward the United States, 1783–1795* (Dallas, 1969). The concluding chapter of Ritcheson's volume, "The Preservation of the Peace," includes some provocative ideas about the Jay Treaty and the negotiations surrounding it.

Two recent monographs have dealt specifically with Hamilton's contribution to American foreign policy. Helene Johnson Looze, *Alexander Hamilton and the British Orientation of American Foreign Policy, 1783–1803* (The Hague, 1969), is useful in providing, for the first time, a fairly comprehensive treatment of Hamilton's role as a maker of American foreign policy; but it tends to accept him too uncritically and provides little or nothing that is new or original. A much better work is Gilbert L. Lycan, *Alexander Hamilton and American Foreign Policy: A Design for Greatness* (Norman, Okla., 1970); but this, too, is weakened by too great a willingness to accept Hamilton at face value. Very much opposed to the flattering view of Hamilton in these two books is a brief but illuminating discussion of Hamilton's maneuverings in 1789 and 1790, Julian P. Boyd, *Number 7: Alexander Hamilton's Secret Attempt to Control American Foreign Policy* (Princeton, 1964).

THOMAS JEFFERSON

The Idealist as Realist .

Lawrence S. Kaplan

No statesman of the revolutionary and early national periods made a more substantial contribution to the development of American foreign policy than Thomas Jefferson. From his magnificent synthesis of eighteenth-century political theory in the Declaration of Independence to his death fifty years later, Jefferson's idealism, tempered by pragmatic regard for practical realities, played a key role in defining a distinctively American position toward the external world. No one, it might be said, ever blended the moralistic yearnings of the young Republic for a new international order with the practical pursuit of national self-interest more effectively than he.

Examination of Jefferson's amazingly varied career and multi-

The Kent State Research Committee provided financial assistance for the preparation of this essay.

ple talents highlights the renaissance quality of his mind and work. For another man any one of his accomplishments would have assured the homage of posterity. Over a span of eighty-three years Jefferson pursued an astonishing range of activities: he was largely responsible for founding the University of Virginia; he was an architectural innovator who helped bring classical forms to the New World; he was an agronomist experimenting with transplantations of rice and silk to the South; he was a theologian who attempted to harmonize Christianity with the temper of the Enlightenment. Above all, he was a scholar in the art of government whose ideas spread through the nation as Jeffersonian democracy. The prestige conferred by authorship of the Declaration of Independence and the power of the presidency ensured dissemination of his ideas in a manner rarely available to political theorists. If his virtuosity did not encompass an appreciation for the intricacies of finance, that shortcoming stemmed less from a lack of understanding the techniques of moneymaking than from a taste that placed spending above getting. Against the bankruptcy of his Monticello estate must be weighed the credit of a life-style that warmed guests in the beautiful mansion with their host's hospitality as much as with fine French wines.

This westerner belonged to an aristocratic family, the Randolphs of Virginia. His father had improved his status by a wealthy marriage. As a member of the governing elite of the colony, Jefferson early experienced British and European influences flowing across the ocean to Tidewater and Piedmont Virginia. While there may have been few artists or scientists at the College of William and Mary in the colonial capital, there were sufficient men and books to initiate the youthful Jefferson into the life of the eighteenth-century liberal mind. He enjoyed the best of both the Old and the New World, sharing the excitement of European ideas that ranged from Arthur Young's tracts on scientific farming to the disputed poems of Ossian. Books and papers from European centers found their way to Jefferson's library and to the drawing rooms of Williamsburg and Philadelphia. He was very much a member of the international fraternity of literati that pumped liberal ideas into the courts of Europe and the coffeehouses of America—ideas that ultimately pushed both along the road to revolution. Jefferson's intimacy with such scholarly men as Professor William Small of William and Mary and George Wythe, his law teacher at Williamsburg, and with such sophisticated men of the world as Francis Fauquier, lieutenant governor of Virginia during his student days, were experiences he repeated in Philadelphia and Paris in later years. True, the above names almost exhausted the roster of interesting people in colonial Virginia, but the point is that his circle of acquaintances included some of the broadest intellectual interests there; his six years at the village capital provided him with an extraordinary range of ideas.

At the same time, perhaps more than any contemporary, Jefferson captured the best elements in the transatlantic civilization of the colonies. As an American living close to the frontier he appreciated the richness of his environment and recognized the advantages of a land with few people and abundant resources. The agrarian society he so valued bred equality among its members, fostered self-reliance, and opened opportunities for individual growth that the Old World could never provide; his experiences encompassed facets that Europeans could not share unless they came to America. Jefferson understood what the challenge and opportunity of empty land meant in the life of a man; he could see in a practical way government expressing the will of the body politic. He lived in a society free of most of the oppressive traditions of the Old World. His father had surveyed the lands that became the first political units the son encountered. He understood the strengths and weaknesses of Rousseau's natural man; he knew that the theory of Rousseau and Locke was reality for an American.

Membership in the exclusive group that controlled the colony set Jefferson apart from most of his fellows and conferred special advantages on him. Good fortune allowed him to live a life transcending that of the colonial yeoman, whose scarcity of cash and education limited his freedom to roam physically and intellectually; his appreciation of democracy had an aristocratic base in a deferential society. Granted that class distinctions were slighter than in Europe and lacked philosophical and practical support, Jefferson was, nonetheless, a "gentleman," comfortably fixed in his milieu. He could practice the arts of government as proper and entirely natural functions of his place in society: vestryman in his church, magistrate in the local community, delegate to colonial and national legislatures. Of course, opportunity in the abstract beckoned all men—and it was more than just a pious abstraction in America as compared with other societies—but for men of Jefferson's class there simply was a larger share of opportunity.

Others were similarly endowed; his special distinction lay in his genius, in those qualities of mind and spirit that allowed him to range over the whole experience of mankind and distill its essence in lucid prose.

His public career spanned the period from the conclusion of the French and Indian War in 1763 to the end of his second presidential term in 1809, years in which he turned his talents to the creation and maintenance of independence from Great Britain. Jefferson was not concerned with reordering the internal society of America or with indulging private interests. His greatest satisfactions derived from such contributions to political philosophy as were found in the Declaration of Independence or in political practice, from his part in organizing the Northwest Territories, or from the educational theory he bequeathed to the University of Virginia. His primary work, however, was in public affairs, particularly the relations of America with Europe. It could not have been otherwise.

For him, as for all the Founding Fathers, the central event of life was the creation of a nation out of thirteen disparate British colonies. Every step in making the Revolution and in securing it afterwards involved foreign affairs. In such a context, conventional divisions between domestic and foreign affairs lost meaning. In the first generation of the Republic no national leader could escape awareness of the hostile outside world. Europe intruded in every way, inspiring fear of reconquest by the mother country, offering opportunity along sparsely settled borderlands, arousing uncertainties over the alliance with a great power. Unless the new nation settled for a subsistence economy its prosperity rested upon trade with the Old World; the European market held the American economy captive, and no political theory could alter that fact of economic life. There could be no escape from such concerns, any more than from the language Americans spoke, the customs they followed, or the ideas they circulated.

Anglo-American relations dominated American history in the early years of the Republic. Despite a successful military separation, the economic links of tradition proved more enduring than the political, even though many people, Jefferson included, wished it to be otherwise. If an alternative to a British connection existed, it was not to be achieved by retreating into autarchy but by shifting the economy toward France, the wartime ally; it was to

France that those leaders suspicious or fearful of British designs turned during the administrations of George Washington and John Adams.

Anglophiles and Francophiles alike, however, held a different view of Spain, the third major European nation whose interests impinged on those of America. For most Americans, Spain presented an object of aggrandizement and exploitation, a weak state whose territories might be despoiled, or at least kept out of the control of other European powers. As Americans looked southward and westward at insecurely held Spanish territory they envisaged a future continental empire of liberty that would free them from the superpowers of the day.

The record clearly reveals the Jeffersonian involvement in foreign affairs. His service as delegate to both Continental Congresses, as wartime governor of Virginia, and as commissioner to France at the end of the war were all linked to French and British influences in American life. During the Confederation period he represented the United States in Paris, attempting to mobilize support for its continued independence. Upon return to America he became secretary of state, the first in the revitalized union, absorbed in assuring survival of the nation in a hostile world. The French Revolution and its subsequent wars dominated his years as vice-president and president. The magnificent acquisition of Louisiana, though not wholly his doing, deservedly is credited to him; and the disastrous embargo of 1807, though not wholly his mistake, if mistake it was, appropriately is identified with him. Success or failure, Jefferson the public man was of necessity a maker of diplomacy.

◇◇◇

Jefferson's enemies of every generation make much of what they consider his deficiencies in character. Most dwell on his inconsistency, pointing out that he shifted from one position to another at critical moments out of fear of consequences, instability of judgment, or passion for power. Thus, his movement from strict to loose construction of the Constitution, from agrarianism to support of manufacturing, from fear of executive power to abuse of it in office, from a love of France to distrust and finally to dependence upon that country under Napoleon have all been used by enemies who would dismiss him as weak, cowardly, opportunistic, or worse. His Francophilism has been interpreted as a personality quirk with dire consequences for the country.

Much of the familiar Federalist criticism of Jefferson withers in the face of close examination. A far better case may be made of excessive consistency, of an allegiance to a conception of society long after it had become obvious that the ideal could not be sustained, or of reliance upon economic weapons against Europe after those weapons were turned against him. Jefferson never questioned what he wanted for America; he envisioned a society of cultivated, independent men on terms of equality with one another, keeping government as close to the local level as possible, living on farms rather than in cities because the agrarian life best propagated the good life. Expansionism became part of the plan because an American empire would remove the corrupt and dangerous model of Europe, as it would if the pattern of international commerce could also be reorganized to incorporate the American alternative to mercantilism, free trade. He identified urban commercial society with class conflict, with oligarchic manipulation of politics, and with European financial control over America, most especially Great Britain's economic interests in its former colonies. To combat such dangers, he believed that right reason applied to the right environment would create a society embodying the best blend of the Enlightenment with the frontier.

He never abandoned his vision of the good society. Apparent deviations were responses to external pressures or were expedients, temporary tactical retreats. He shared with other Founding Fathers a belief that alliances with European powers were unnecessary and potentially dangerous to American independence. His musings about a relationship with Europe "precisely on the footing of China," while fanciful, were genuine; and he knew that in an imperfect world less desirable choices sometimes had to be made to attain more desirable ends. Thus, an alliance with France might be made if Britain threatened the nation's independence; the danger of a connection with Europe had to be balanced against the greater damage that defeat or accommodation with Britain might bring. When France took over the Mississippi outlet at New Orleans, Jefferson contemplated a marriage of convenience to the British fleet and nation. Similarly, he recognized that an embargo on trade would require cultivation of manufactures and urban growth in violation of his preference for an agrarian

America; when he saw the alternative as acceptance of British domination, he took the risk. No one celebrated the virtues of limited government more eloquently than Jefferson, but he realized that they had to be subordinated to the need for a national government strong enough to enforce the embargo, just as in earlier years the state governments of the Confederation, though in his view better custodians of freedom than a more centralized union, had to give way to the Constitution when the Republic's survival was at stake. In 1803, Jefferson's firm commitment to strict construction of the Constitution conveniently expanded to avoid loss of a vast empire in the West.

Jefferson's statecraft invited criticisms. His means occasionally distorted his ends and diminished the stature of the man who tolerated the distortions. Indeed, he paid for his concessions by witnessing before he died some of the unfortunate consequences he had always feared would follow from the promotion of an industrial society, and his reliance on economic coercion exacerbated international tensions while it created new domestic ones. If he did not also pay for France's exploitation of his too ardent sympathy, it was only because he refused to confess to any errors of judgment in a pro-French policy.

Part of the explanation of Jefferson's flexibility lies in his early recognition of the importance of the external world in American affairs and in his firm belief in the permanent hostility of Great Britain. Preservation of the new nation from the baneful effects of those realities required statecraft; if Jefferson sometimes overrated the efficacy of diplomacy, he seldom underestimated the danger of involvement in transatlantic affairs. Ultimately, of course, Americans sought a solution in withdrawal from the European arena into their own empire, into a peculiarly American isolationism wherein obligations to Europe did not exist. In one way or another nearly every American statesman worked to free the nation from dependence upon Europe.

◇◇◇

When Jefferson was secretary of state in the 1790s, his countrymen differed violently about the direction of foreign affairs, especially about the American response to the French Revolution and its subsequent wars. The powerful commercial interests of New England and the seaboard towns looked to Great

Britain as a necessary business partner, at least until a viable domestic economy could be created. Many of its leaders equated a pro-British policy with freedom from French ideology and French imperialism. Jefferson and his followers never accepted such views. They believed, at least until after the War of 1812, that Britain intended to reduce America to a position of permanent inferiority in an economic relationship more suffocating than the political connection had been before independence. Like their opponents the Federalists, Jeffersonians responded emotionally to events in France, but they read their import differently. They believed that if the French republic collapsed in its war with monarchical Britain, monarchy if not British rule would return to America.

Jefferson's anti-British animus had deep roots. It grew in part from wartime experiences and received repeated reinforcement during his career. At times his fears approached obsession, but he directed these sentiments more to particular institutions and proponents of policy than to Englishmen per se or to the benign aspects of British culture. However flawed, the British political system surpassed any in Europe; and even when in France desperately seeking help during the Confederation period, Jefferson could in good conscience recommend to French friends that they follow the British political model. If Frenchmen kept in view the example of their cross-Channel neighbor, he told Lafayette, they might advance "step by step towards a good constitution." His feelings for English friends remained as warm as his feelings for Frenchmen. He admired the liberal English reformers whose Anglo-Saxon traditions in law and language he claimed for America—indeed, he who had paraphrased Locke's political philosophy could hardly do otherwise.

In some respects this common heritage exacerbated problems between Britain and America, for the mother country lacked the excuse of ignorance for its abuse of freedom and its threats to liberty. Because Britain had extended its heritage to the New World British behavior became intolerable when it selfishly and abruptly deprived colonists of their right to tax and govern themselves through their own representative bodies. By such actions the ministers of the crown behaved unconstitutionally. In his *Summary View of the Rights of British America*, presented to the First Continental Congress in 1774, Jefferson had observed that emigrants had come to the colonies as free men, voluntarily adopting the mother country's system of law; they wished to continue their union by submitting to a common sovereign, "the central link connecting the several parts of the Empire thus newly multiplied." All that Americans wished from Britain, he argued, was a restoration of lost liberties, a recognition of their rights as Englishmen. In failing to respond to this understanding of Anglo-American relations, the British invited application of the principles of natural right philosophy, which permitted, even demanded, separation from a ruler who had broken the social contract; for as Carl Becker has said, by 1774 such an interpretation had become "familiar doctrine to all men."

Jefferson and his colleagues thought that if the right of revolution was accepted as natural, circumstances justified it and they made their case in the Declaration of Independence. Whether they read history and law accurately, the nature of the charges they brought against their sovereign continued to absorb Jefferson's attention for more than a generation. Throughout his public career he saw British policy as part of a plot to subvert American liberties. That plot ranged from the imposition of taxes and the incitement of Indian massacres to destruction of American trade and suspension of the rights of self-government—all for the "establishment of an absolute tyranny over these states." British policy did not change after independence. As Jefferson left office in 1809, he saw the Orders in Council of 1807 as merely another version of the crown's long-standing attack on "trade with all parts of the world"; impressment was a means of forcing captive Americans "to bear arms against their country"; intrigues among Federalists and Indians were continued royal attempts to excite "domestic insurrections" and to incite "the merciless Indian savages." The hostility that had provoked the Declaration of Independence in 1776 also provided the rationalization for the embargo in 1807.

Of course, experiences in the critical decade after the Treaty of Paris, when he served as minister to France and as secretary of state, had reinforced the Jeffersonian image of Britain as a malevolent force in American affairs. The Orders in Council of 1783, directed against American trade and removing it from imperial preference, corroborated his worst fears. By following the advice of Sheffield rather than the more liberal inclinations of Shelburne the British intended to maintain control over American commerce with minimal reciprocity under their navigation system.

British mercantilists abolished subsidies for critical American exports, denied American ships entry into the West Indies, and accepted American goods in Britain on terms no more favorable than those granted European nations. Such was the price of independence, for British ministers correctly anticipated that the impotent government of the Confederation could not implement retaliation by higher duties on British goods or exclusion of British ships from American ports. To many it seemed that Britain had determined to exploit those structural weaknesses and take advantage of the inability of the states to act in concert.

The first minister in London, John Adams, recognized to his despair that Whitehall's policy would enrich Britons at the expense of Americans, and might destroy the new nation in the process. In a brief visit to London in 1786, Jefferson experienced firsthand the contempt for America that the arrogant British had been demonstrating to Adams. His impressions were even darker than those of his Massachusetts friend, for while the king had at times been civil to Adams, he snubbed Jefferson, moving the latter to rage, "That nation hates us, their ministers hate us, and their king more than all other men."

The French connection, so frequently and so pejoratively identified with Jefferson, derived largely from the foregoing emotion and from the problems that evoked it. To escape the web of British mercantilism and to foil expectations of a collapse of the republican experiment, France became a counterweight to British influence and an instrument of American survival; Jefferson saw opportunity, he thought, to use that country's friendship and alliance as a balance to British power and to build more satisfactory commercial arrangements in international trade. He had not forgotten the enormous service that French arms, supplies, and money had rendered in the revolutionary war; nor had he forgotten the self-interest that had inspired that aid. He hoped to exploit such impulses for further service.

Like Franklin before him, he found the task of winning French friendship a highly congenial one. From his first contacts with Frenchmen during the war he had prized the manners and customs they had brought with them; lengthy and spirited talks with Lafayette and Chastellux in Virginia foreshadowed the pleasure he found in French culture and cuisine. While he may not have been quite the traitor who "abjured his native vittels" for foreign food, as Patrick Henry claimed, he did become a lifelong enthusiast for French food and wine. More importantly, he found in Paris a lively appreciation of the American model of the good society which French reformers wished to use in reshaping their own country. When Jefferson became minister he assumed rightly that he would receive the homage his predecessor had won, and he basked in the veneration of the new American society as he followed a scenario limned by that great diplomatic impresario, Benjamin Franklin. Jefferson, like Franklin, sought to exploit the sympathy of the French intelligentsia for America to bend French political and economic policies to the service of the United States.

These objectives monopolized Jefferson's time in France between 1784 and 1789. Initially, the minister concentrated on securing treaty relations with European powers modeled on the 1778 commercial treaty with France. To the new Republic political recognition was an important mark of international respectability; the psychic value apparently outweighed the practical. Such treaties seemed to confer legitimacy, almost as if the more agreements one made, no matter how little trade resulted from them, the more certain the permanence of the United States became. Sweden and Prussia signed liberal treaties with America, without affording any substantial material advantages. Those contracts reflected the optimism of 1776 when Americans expected, as Thomas Paine's *Common Sense* suggested, that the world would applaud the new nation's challenge to British leadership in international trade and its arbitrary control of the seas. The next step, expansion of the Congressional Treaty Plan of 1776, would be European acceptance of free trade and freedom of the seas, in which the advantage of a small maritime country would be united with the larger conception of a foreign policy following moral law. Philosophes and Physiocrats and their American disciples, among whom were Benjamin Franklin and Thomas Jefferson, tended to imbue free trade with nearly mystical qualities; to them it was a panacea for the world's ills, a cure for wars and international rivalries. It followed, as Felix Gilbert has said, "that in a reformed world, based on reason, foreign policy and diplomacy would be unnecessary, that the new world would be a world without diplomats." It also followed that in such a world Americans would reap enormous economic advantage.

Experiences with the French alliance toned down some of Jefferson's expectations for the implementation of such a new order, but despite his awareness of the limitations of treaties and

THE PROVIDENTIAL DETECTION

of the shortcomings of European altruism, he continued to believe that the words of the philosophes and the sentiments of French liberal circles could be shaped to American advantage. He spoke the language of the Physiocrats when he argued for the removal of trade barriers, pointing out that such barriers on the Continent pushed American commerce into British ports. By appealing to the reformers for support he hoped to serve his country's interests and those of the new international order, the postrevolutionary world that would be governed by the laws of nature. At the same time, while waiting for that new order, he urged upon the ministers in power a full reciprocity of economic policy on the practical ground that all the sacrifices France had made to achieve independence for its ally would be wasted if America returned to the British connection by the back door of economic dependence.

On paper, Jefferson's initial negotiations had some small success. The combined efforts of the Physiocrats and the Anglophobes, particularly those in the foreign ministry, overcame many of the obstacles to direct trade. The French lifted import duties on American whale oil as a result of his pleas, and he made spectacular if insubstantial gains in breaking down exclusive arrangements that Philadelphia entrepreneur Robert Morris had made with the powerful syndicate of financiers, the Farmers-General, who controlled the French tobacco market. New trade opportunities opened to Americans.

Few of them lasted, however. The antiquated economic structure of l'ancien régime could not tolerate the innovations Jefferson advocated. Suspicious from the beginning of the freer access to their domestic market, the Farmers-General found their prejudices confirmed when they observed that American merchants used their French profits to buy more goods from British manufacturers rather than to reinvest in France. Such a turn of events might have been predicted, for the French lacked both goods and credit to replace the British, even if the tug of habit could have been resisted sufficiently to nudge American importers from familiar connections across the Channel.

Appreciating these obstacles, Jefferson hoped to surmount them by having the French compete with the British in products needed in the American market and by having them develop more sophisticated and flexible marketing techniques. That effort failed. For one thing, even his allies in the foreign ministry, Vergennes and his successors, did not support it vigorously; but perhaps more importantly, it soon became apparent that the allies were working at cross-purposes, with the Americans seeking strength and independence through the French, while the latter looked with equanimity on continued American dependence upon France. Vergennes hoped to exploit the uncertainties of America's future, for as long as the United States could not meet its international obligations, France's role as its protector would remain paramount. In the Quai d'Orsay expectations of continued influence over American policy counterbalanced American dependence upon the British economy and inability to pay the French debts. Moreover, the ministers would be making a virtue of necessity, for no diplomat could make permanent constructive change in the rigid economic structure of prerevolutionary France.

◇◇◇

The frustrations engendered by American impotence in foreign affairs and a recognition of the limits on its power of persuasion in the international arena heightened Jefferson's sensitivity to the key events of the last years of his mission to France: the Constitutional Convention in America and the Revolution in France. In his own mind these events were related. Reports from home of dissatisfaction with the Confederation produced conflicting emotions. Suppression of Shays's Rebellion in 1786 and the reputed dominance of Robert Morris's faction in Philadelphia made him despair over the future of the Republic; the avarice of financiers and the anarchy of farmers disturbed him equally, for he saw in both dangerous threats to the safety and security of the nation. Although concerned over the damage demagogues might do to the Republic, he nevertheless retained his sympathy for the complaints of farmers and frontiersmen that stimulated protests against the government.

Rebellion became embarrassing at a time when French reformers looked to the United States as a model. News of transatlantic repression invoked the irony of despotism coming to the New World just as the Old sought to emulate the principles of 1776. In this frame of mind Jefferson reacted to news from Philadelphia. Patrick Henry and James Monroe described the work of the convention as illiberal and aristocratic and fed his initial suspicion of the new Constitution.

Suspicion did not remain the final Jeffersonian position on the federal union contrived at Philadelphia, and he did not return to America in 1790 pessimistic about its future. The views of James Madison and his own recent experiences led him to the conclusion that a stronger government was necessary to assure the nation's survival. Safety in a hostile world required a centralization of power and a unified voice in foreign affairs. He accepted a post as secretary of state in Washington's cabinet on the assumption that the new government would strengthen the nation's hand in international affairs, that it would resolve the problems of diplomacy that the impotence of the Confederation had exposed. Long before the convention assembled at Philadelphia, he had observed that a primary object of his treaty negotiations was to take commerce out of the hands of state governments and to place it under the control of Congress until the states removed the imperfections of the Confederation by a new compact; while the convention deliberated he asserted that the states ought to be "made one as to all foreign, and several as to all domestic matters."

Indeed, one of the unifying forces in Washington's cabinet during much of his first administration was the broad agreement of its members about the need for a strong government and a powerful executive to manage it. Factional antagonisms that later divided the nation—problems of strict vs. loose interpretation, of Anglophilism vs. Francophilism—existed in embryo at the outset of the Washington era, but in 1790 pressures over the immediate course of the nation's foreign policies overwhelmed them.

Although Jefferson returned home with distrust of Britain and admiration for France, he brought with him no illusions about Franco-American relations. His experiences had revealed important qualifications about the nature of French benevolence. Such optimism as he displayed rested not on any agreements between the two governments or decrees that France had made in America's favor, but on expectations about the more liberal regime that appeared in the making after destruction of the Bastille. As he took up his duties France had not yet revealed the full dimensions of change; in 1790, as in 1787, it still closed the West Indies to American ships and retained its monopoly of American products entering France. Jefferson felt that France had not yet seen its self-interest, had not yet recognized the mutual advantages that would flow from the new politico-economic system proposed by America.

To effect a new relationship with France and to break the old one with Britain required a centralized government strong enough to command the respect of its peers in the international arena. In this view Jefferson was at one with John Jay and Alexander Hamilton. Like the former (who had been secretary for foreign affairs under the Confederation) he believed that if Europeans saw an efficient and well-administered national government, with its trade and finances prudently regulated, they would be disposed to cultivate American friendship rather than risk its resentment. This theme, which Jay stressed in the third *Federalist*, found a harmonious response in Jefferson, and he could even join with Hamilton when the New Yorker asserted in the eleventh *Federalist* that "a steady adherence to the Union" might allow the new nation to tip the scales of European competition in the New World for the benefit of Americans. Thus, a commonly recognized impotence in foreign affairs provided a powerful stimulus for strengthening the powers of the central government. The Founding Fathers, even when they could agree on little else, all sought to exploit European disadvantage for America's advantage.

Historians have not always recognized that Hamilton and Jefferson shared belief in a strong executive able to resist congressional encroachments upon its power in foreign affairs. Jefferson earlier had expressed approval of the constitutional device that freed the central government from the interference of state assemblies on matters of taxation; now with the new government in operation, he thought that the federal legislature's natural tendency to interfere with presidential responsibilities must be resisted. In a memorandum to Washington, presented shortly after taking office, the new secretary of state questioned the propriety of presidential consultation with the Senate about diplomatic exchanges. Arguing that there was no constitutional requirement for such solicitation and that the practice would create an unfortunate precedent, Jefferson interpreted senatorial powers as extending no further than approval or disapproval of nominees. Even then, he envisioned the decision as basically presidential—almost exclusively so, "except as to such portions of it as are specially submitted to the Senate. Exceptions are to be construed strictly." Jefferson's rigid construction of the Constitution in 1790 was hardly distinguishable from that of the Hamiltonians around him, including the secretary of the treasury himself.

If the Jeffersonian vision of American foreign policy began

with an executive free of congressional constraints and the shortcomings of the Confederation, it included other elements customarily identified with his great rival, Hamilton: repayment of obligations to foreign creditors through assumption of the debts of previous governments and the promotion of American shipping through an effective navigation system. New England merchants and Philadelphia creditors welcomed these facets of the Hamiltonian program, and, to a point, so did Madison and Jefferson. While it is true that from the outset Jefferson had many reservations about his cabinet colleagues, especially when he suspected them of monarchical tendencies, he could work with them during the early years of Washington's administration. He could tolerate Treasury intrusion into his department by Hamilton's involvement in consular affairs, as long as he believed that Jeffersonian views received a fair hearing. His rivals in the cabinet in those early years were "good men and bold men, and sensible men."

Not even the Nootka Sound affair in the summer of 1790 fully revised that judgment. Although Jefferson strongly opposed Hamilton's wish to grant a British request for the passage of troops through American territory in the event of war between Spain and Britain over the Pacific Northwest, he had no knowledge of Hamilton's intimate connections with British agents. Nor did he adamantly oppose concessions to the British per se. His point simply was that concessions ought to be reciprocal; the United States ought not surrender a bargaining weapon in advance. In their first cabinet debate on foreign affairs Hamilton and Jefferson differed more on tactics than on ideology.

Of course, Hamilton's early hostility to discriminatory legislation against British shipping did evoke criticism from Madison and Jefferson, but not the deep emotional response it was to arouse in 1793–94. Hamilton, after all, had a navigation system, and that was a step in the right direction. It took time before Jefferson's mind converted Hamilton's behavior into a dangerous passion for monarchy and a fatal dependence on Britain.

In part, at least, Jefferson's tolerance for failure of punitive measures against the British may have flowed from the concurrent insensitivity toward America displayed by the liberal regime in France. While the revolutionists had reformed their government under the National Assembly, nothing in those reforms served the interests of the United States. To his chagrin, Jefferson realized that the new bourgeois rulers of France had no more intent than the mercantilists of the old regime to permit liberal terms for American goods in French markets. That realization caught him between anger and embarrassment, for it coincided with a contretemps in relations between the two nations. Madison's navigation law (which failed to discriminate between ships of countries with commercial treaties and those without them) had given rise to a French protest, to which Jefferson normally would have been sympathetic. He recognized that in spirit, if not in letter, it was unfair that British and French ships would receive equal treatment in American ports, and he wished Congress to make special concessions to the French in return for the concessions they had made during his ministry; but French intransigence threatened to undermine support for such an arrangement.

Still, Jefferson sought to exploit the situation. The behavior of the National Assembly freed him from some inhibitions over past French favors and permitted him a degree of flexibility. That France did not see its own advantage in at least removing prerevolutionary restrictions from the West Indian trade seemed incredible to him. His impatience flared into anger when the French consul in New York insisted upon the recall of two consuls whom Congress had sent to the French islands. Jefferson resisted that demand, ultimately winning a minor victory when the American consuls were permitted to remain as "commercial agents." That success signified little and the secretary knew it; he harbored no illusions that an entente had been established between the two countries.

Much of his distress in office, then, stemmed less from the Francophobic character of the Hamiltonians than from the fact that the French refused friendly gestures when they were offered. Neither Madison's persistent attempts in Congress to fashion a navigation system that would benefit French commerce nor Jefferson's illuminating reports on the whale oil and codfish industries (with their clear invitation to France to replace those who had built "their navigation on the ruin of ours") struck responsive chords in Paris. Assuming the impossibility of weaning Americans from British ties, the French middle-class leaders of the Revolution wrote off American commerce. They even revoked the minor concessions that Jefferson had so painfully extracted during his ministry in France. The arrival in 1791 of a new French minister, Jean Baptiste Ternant, did not help matters. Ternant found Hamilton more congenial than Jefferson, so when the latter presented a plan for exchanging with the French full privileges of natives in each other's ports, the negative response did not surprise him. To the minister, free trade seemed to reward Britain at the expense of France.

War in Europe, particularly between France and Britain in 1793, changed the immediate course of Franco-American relations. It revived Jefferson's hopes for a new identity of interests between the two countries, although he recognized the danger of American involvement in the European conflict through obligations incurred in the alliance of 1778. For all his rising anger against Federalists and Britons, Jefferson did not envisage American troops or ships fighting alongside the French in the West Indies or anywhere else any more than did Hamilton. Yet the opportunity for exploiting a new French mood to strike out at British suzerainty over trade and arrogance over maritime claims proved too glittering to resist. The republican government of France opened West Indian ports to American ships and dispatched a more amiable minister to negotiate a liberal commercial treaty based precisely on Jefferson's scheme of mutual naturalization. Small wonder that the secretary's expectations outweighed fears as Europe plunged into the wars of the French Revolution.

◇◇◇

There was a link between the worsening of Jefferson's relations with Hamiltonians at home and improvement of his relations with France. From 1793 to the end of the decade, first as secretary of state and then later as vice-president, he saw the Republic in peril in America and the Republic in peril in Europe. France's part as warrior against British monarchy and imperialism sharpened his antagonism toward British agents in America; increasingly, he saw the Federalist faction as a tool of British interests seeking to restore monarchy to America. Such a goal explained the uses to which Hamiltonian power would be put; it explained the failure of his own efforts to reduce British influence and enhance the interests of American democrats. The whole Hamiltonian program—from funding the national debt and establishing a national bank to Anglo-American reconciliation and a pro-British trade policy—became in his mind part of an enormous invisible conspiracy against the national welfare. The European war unmasked Hamilton's real purpose. Such was the Jeffersonian image of Federalism; of course there was a mirror image of Jeffersonians in the minds of their opponents.

Naturally, this Jeffersonian angle of vision enhanced the importance of France as a counterweight to domestic and foreign enemies. While hardly a new position, its urgency intensified after 1793, and introduced a new and ugly dimension into American debates on foreign affairs and domestic politics. The French republic took on symbolic overtones. According to Jeffersonians, France struggled for more than its own survival—the survival of liberty everywhere was at stake. A British victory would reimpose its rule in America, either directly or through Britain's faithful American servants. Many of Jefferson's friends perished in the struggle for republicanism in France; although he deplored the losses, he endured them stoically, even philosophically, regarding his friends as soldiers fallen in the battle for universal liberty. "My own affections have been deeply wounded by some of the martyrs to this cause," he told William Short on 3 January 1793, "but rather than it should have failed I would have seen half the earth desolated; were there but an Adam to an Eve left in every country. Left free, it would be better than it now is." Written a month before France declared war on Britain, this letter expressed Jefferson's deep commitment to the cause of revolutionary republicanism. Given that predisposition, his fear of counterrevolutionary Britain and its supposed American agents intensified. The mild challenge raised by Britain in the Nootka Sound affair of 1790 had become three years later a matter of the life and death of a society.

The immediate problem for Washington's advisers, however, was the position of the United States toward the belligerents. To resolve that difficulty, Jefferson laid down a precedent for recognition of foreign governments: *de facto* control by the government in power. Possession of domestic power and ability to fulfill international obligations were the tests of legitimacy. Even before Washington raised the question of recognition in the cabinet, Jefferson had spelled out his position in a letter to the American minister in France. "I am sensible," he told Gouverneur Morris on 12 March 1793, "that your situation must have been difficult during the transition from the late form of government to the reestablishment of some other legitimate authority, that you may have been at a loss to determine with whom business might be done. Nevertheless when principles are well understood, their application is less embarrassing. We surely cannot deny to any nation that right whereon our own government is founded, that every one may govern itself according to whatever form it pleases, change these forms at its own will; that it may transact its business with foreign nations through whatever organ it thinks proper, whether King, Convention, Assembly, Committee, President, or anything else it may use. The will of the nation is the only thing essential to be regarded." Jefferson never questioned that the republican government of France should have its minister received, its financial claims honored, and its role as an ally affirmed; when Washington raised these questions after the execution of the French king and the extension of the European war, the secretary of state immediately perceived the mind of Hamilton guiding the president. It outraged him that America seemed more cautious in its support of a republic than it had been in its allegiance to a monarchy. With feeling he asked, "Who is the American who can say with truth that he would not have allied himself to France if she had been a republic?"[1]

In defending the alliance Jefferson marshaled evidence from many authorities on international law of the seventeenth and eighteenth centuries, from Grotius to Vattel. He won his case, at least over recognition and legitimacy of treaties, if not over neutrality. If his position was based on the moral worth of republicans expressing the will of the people rather than on *de facto* control of France by the Girondists, realism needs redefinition. The scholars of international law help little in understanding

---

1. The immediate problem for the Washington administration was the precise posture the United States should strike toward the belligerents when one of them was an ally. It was at this juncture that Jefferson laid down a policy that has been accepted as a precedent for American recognition of foreign powers: a doctrine based on *de facto* control of the society by the government in power. Possession of power and the ability to fulfill obligations to other nations were the appropriate tests of legitimacy. The traditional criteria for recognition deserve scrutiny in light of the periodic practice in the twentieth century of deviating from this approach, of refusing recognition to governments in Mexico, Russia, Manchuria, and China on the grounds that these governments assumed power by force, held it by repression, and displayed hostility to American interests and values. If such were truly deviations from tradition, the contemporary response has been to justify the position by circumventing the Jeffersonian stance and pointing to American concern with government by consent of the governed and the right of rebellion to remove tyranny. In other words, the American outlook on world affairs had always entailed a moral judgment to be rendered against a regime imposed on an unwilling people and disruptive of the proprieties of international conduct.

the Jeffersonian position, for they can be cited either way, as Jefferson himself did when he dismissed that "ill understood scrap in Vattel" that Hamilton had used to deny recognition and then a few months later cited that same Vattel to refute the French minister's demand for a more friendly neutrality. For both Hamiltonians and Jeffersonians the nub of the matter seems to have been the legitimacy of a revolutionary transfer of power. For the former destruction of a hereditary monarchy by revolution stripped from the usurpers all international obligations owed to their predecessors; for the latter, revolutionists merely made legitimate what had been doubtful before by exercising a natural right to alter the form of government.

Neither Hamilton nor Jefferson appeared willing to accept the full implications of *de facto* government as these had been spelled out in Pufendorf's assertion that the actual possessor of sovereignty, however acquired, was entitled to the allegiance of his subjects so long as no claimant appeared with a better, "more legitimate" right. In the absence of such a claimant, Pufendorf asserted, reason dictated that the possessor should continue to hold power. Although this argument fitted nicely into Jefferson's interpretation in 1793, one wonders whether he would have been so solicitous for recognition of a monarchical government if it had come to power by counterrevolution against a republican regime, whether he would have been so insistent upon receiving ministers and authenticating an alliance if the government in question had been British sponsored or Anglophile. It is reasonable to conclude that for reasons of morality and national interest Jefferson would have taken Hamilton's stance in opposition to a *de facto* government if the question turned on the situation of 1814 when a monarchy dependent for survival upon Great Britain replaced Napoleon. Perhaps it was merely fortuitous that the first secretary of state found morality on the side of *de facto* legitimacy in 1793.

Belief in Federalist subversion of America's republican experiment dominated Jefferson's mind for the remainder of the decade. Obsession with Hamiltonian maleficence led him at times to startling judgments couched in picturesque language. Washington appeared elliptically as one of the "Samsons in the field & Solomons in the council . . . who have had their heads shorn by the harlot England." On another occasion he prepared to leave Monticello for a visit to London (which he expected to find under

French occupation) to "hail the dawn of liberty and republicanism in that island." His conviction that the Federalists had accepted a British definition of neutral rights and an inferior position in the British Empire merged with the conviction that they also planned a monarchical government for America. Washington was their captive, and while John Adams resisted Hamiltonian pretensions, the second president was also an adherent of a form of society inimical to Jeffersonian values. So the world seemed to Jefferson, retired in Virginia from 1794 to 1796 and then isolated in the vice-presidency during Adams's administration. A quasi-war with France coupled with assaults upon the liberties of Republicans lent credence to a nearly paranoid view of America that Jefferson did not alter until he became president.

Yet even in his moments of deepest despair over the direction of American policy under the Federalists, Jefferson resisted his natural impulses to expand the relationship with France, for he knew the limits of counterbalance. Even as he tangled with his rival over neutrality in 1793, Jefferson had no wish to bring the United States into the European war. His opponents were far less fastidious on isolation when Britain was involved. What Jefferson wanted was a benevolent neutrality that would assist France rather than Britain; with it he wished to pressure the British for commercial concessions in return for abstention from the conflict. He failed. Once a proclamation of neutrality had been issued, the possibilities for manipulating it to the advantage of Britain passed to Hamilton, and he made the most of them. There is, however, no evidence that for all his unhappiness Jefferson would have risked a war with Britain. He, rather than Adams, might have reaped the unhappy consequences of Jay's Treaty—and he might have handled them less well.

Jefferson's disavowal of Minister Edmond Genêt during his last year in office and subsequent willingness to let the French alliance lapse at the beginning of his presidency provide an appropriate frame for the comment of France's minister in 1796, Pierre Adet, that Jefferson was an "American and, as such, he cannot be sincerely our friend. An American is the born enemy of all the European peoples." Adet recognized a basic Jeffersonian premise, that in the midst of war and revolution he had given his fervent blessings to the French cause—but France essentially was an instrument of policy rather than an object of it. Its society, its people, its culture all evoked a genuine Francophilism. In Jefferson's statecraft with France, however, there were always *arrières pensées.*

In picking up the pieces of the Revolution and making them part of an empire, Napoleon Bonaparte recognized Jefferson's unreliability, though he missed no opportunity to manipulate him. The first consul wisely concealed information about the return of Louisiana to France, anticipating Jeffersonian distress at the prospect of a French neighbor replacing Spain on the Mississippi. More than pressure from westerners or taunts from Federalists moved the president in 1803. France, more than Spain, posed an obstacle to American expansion and had to be removed. With Louisiana safely secured, Jefferson could resume his policy of seeking to balance British power with French. The charges of Francophilism reached their climax in 1807 with the embargo, when the president seemingly fitted his scheme of economic coercion into Napoleon's Continental system. Such an attempted accommodation, however, was hardly a mark of servitude; it was rather a gamble based on the assumption that France posed a lesser threat than Britain. However tyrannical the French emperor might be, his rule would pass away, while the threat of parliamentary tyranny in Britain would remain. Moreover, the British danger hit closer to home by virtue of that nation's control of the sea. "I cannot," as Jefferson phrased it, "with the Anglomen, prefer a certain present evil to a future hypothetical one." The nation's survival required playing one power off against another, while keeping free of entanglements with either. The dismal end of the embargo, and war in 1812, revealed the dangerous defects in that gambit.

◇◇◇

Jefferson's handling of foreign affairs appeared to move from one position to another—from alliance with France in the 1790s, to threat of alliance with Britain in 1803, to collaboration with Napoleonic schemes in 1807; from restrictions upon congressional authority over diplomatic appointments in 1790, to assertions of congressional prerogative over neutrality in 1793, to enlargement of presidential power in the enforcement of the embargo in 1808; from an appeal for a Chinese isolation from the world within an agrarian society, to a concurrent encouragement of trade with

France in the 1780s, to an advocacy of domestic manufactures during his presidency. The exigencies of politics accounted for some of the shifts, but most were more apparent than real.

The primacy of American independence from the Old World remained a constant in Jefferson's thinking. He preferred an agrarian society to an industrial one; but if he had to accept the latter, he wished for an industrial America cut loose from British controls, performing the role France had failed to provide. To ensure insulation from Europe's troubles he pressed for westward and southern expansion to free American borders from the anxieties of war and to make room for the growth of the Republic. Jefferson's early encounters with division and disunity in the Revolution and Confederation had qualified his dedication to states' rights; his major involvement with them was when he felt impotent to control the central government. While he never denied the virtues he had celebrated in limited government, his early advice to Washington and his own behavior during his presidency suggest that when opportunities for vital action by the executive offered themselves the president ought not to be inhibited by excessive deference to congressional or state authority.

The pragmatic strain in Jefferson's management of foreign affairs, which permitted him to accept conditions inhibiting his freedom of action, also permitted him to shape those conditions to his ideas of the needs of the nation. If commercial ties with Europe were indispensable—and they were—he wished them to be conducted with minimal political entanglements as he preached in his first inaugural. He shed no tears for the demise of the French alliance. If developments abroad served the interests of a small maritime power, he could exploit them without surrendering either American interests or principles. Philosophers of the Old World might be enlisted in the American cause, just as the conflicts among European states might serve American trade or territorial advances. Such sentiments marked Jefferson's view of France and his policy toward it.

Whether Europe or America derived more gain from his dalliances remains debatable. What is certain is Jefferson's consistent belief in the justice of his policies; they were moral by virtue of their American character. For all his expediency he never separated national self-interest from morality in the management of foreign affairs. His determination to recognize the French republic in 1793 rested on justice as well as on utility. Recognition appeased his moral sense while it appealed to his practical streak, much as did his ideas on neutral rights and free trade. A characteristic American approach to international relations has been the casting of national interests on a moral base; Jefferson's contribution was to shape this conceit and to seek a relationship with the external world that followed from it.

BIBLIOGRAPHIC NOTE

Any treatment of Jefferson as a diplomatist should begin with Henry Adams, *History of the United States during the Administrations of Jefferson and Madison*, 9 vols. (New York, 1889–91). Adams's biases, particularly his inability to take Jefferson's statesmanship seriously, have affected twentieth-century scholarship. Contemporary studies of diplomacy in the Jeffersonian era either reinforce Adams's charges of Francophilism and insensitivity to the realities of power or react against them. Bradford Perkins, *The First Rapprochement: England and the United States, 1795–1805* (Philadelphia, 1955) and *Prologue to War: England and the United States, 1795–1805* (Berkeley and Los Angeles, 1961), distributes blame for the breakdown of Anglo-American relations on both sides, but allocates a slightly larger share to Jeffersonian statecraft. Alexander DeConde, on the other hand, dealing with the 1790s in *Entangling Alliance: Politics and Diplomacy under George Washington* (Durham, 1958) and *The Quasi-War: The Politics and Diplomacy of the Undeclared War with France, 1797–1801* (New York, 1966), emphasizes Federalist partisanship for Great Britain as a major source of America's difficulties.

Dumas Malone's magisterial but still incomplete biography, *Jefferson and His Time*, particularly volume 2, *Jefferson and the Rights of Man* (New York, 1951), volume 3, *Jefferson and the Ordeal of Liberty* (New York, 1962), and volume 4, *Jefferson the President: First Term, 1801–1805* (New York, 1970), offers a sympathetic and reasonably objective picture of his diplomatic career from his ministry in France to the end of his first administration. Gilbert Chinard, *Thomas Jefferson: The Apostle of Americanism* (Boston, 1929), with its special emphasis on France, and Merrill Peterson, *Thomas Jefferson and the New Nation* (New York, 1970), are the most useful one-volume biographies. Lawrence S. Kaplan, *Jefferson and France: An Essay on Politics and Political Ideas* (New Haven, 1967), shares Chinard's claim that Jefferson's French policy was not under the influence of French ideology but operated consistently under the assumption that Great Britain was the greater threat to American interests. Beckles Willson, *American Ambassadors to France, 1777–1927: A Narrative of Franco-American Diplomatic Relations* (London, 1928), contains a sketch of Jefferson's contributions as minister to France from 1784 to 1789. W. K. Woolery, "The Relations of Thomas Jefferson to American Foreign Policy, 1783–1793," *Johns Hopkins University Studies in Historical and Political Science* 45 (Baltimore, 1927), develops particularly Jefferson's position toward France. Merrill Peterson, "Thomas Jefferson and Commercial Policy, 1783–1793," *William and Mary Quarterly* 12 (3rd series, 1965), 584–611, emphasizes Jefferson's hopes of using France as a counterbalance to Great Britain's economic power over America. Gilbert Chinard, "Jefferson and the Physiocrats," *University of California Chronicle* 33 (1931), 18–31, observes that the differences in the economic ideas of Jefferson and the Physiocrats were greater than the similarities. Robert R. Palmer, "The Dubious Democrat: Thomas Jefferson and Bourbon France," *Political Science Quarterly* 82 (1947), 488–504, notes Jefferson's doubts of French abilities to assimilate a major revolution.

Samuel Flagg Bemis, "Thomas Jefferson," in Bemis, ed., *The American Secretaries and Their Diplomacy*, 10 vols. (New York, 1927–29), has a good capsule account of Jefferson's role as the first secretary of state. Charles M. Thomas, *American Neutrality in 1793: A Study in Cabinet Government* (New York, 1931), presents the dilemma facing the Washington administration as a result of the Anglo-French war. Albert H. Bowman, "Jefferson, Hamilton, and American Foreign Policy, *Political Science Quarterly* 71 (1956), blames Hamilton for most of Jefferson's problems in 1793. Meade Minnegerode, *Jefferson, Friend of France, 1793: The Career of Edmond Charles Genêt* (New York, 1928), is a bitter attack on the secretary by a descendant of the French minister. A more balanced view is offered in Harry Ammon, *The Genêt Mission* (New York, 1973). Philip M. Marsh, "Jefferson's Retirement as Secretary of State," *Pennsylvania Magazine of History* 69 (1945), 220–24, is sympathetic to Jefferson's isolation in a Hamiltonian cabinet.

Adrienne Koch, *Jefferson and Madison: The Great Collaboration* (New York, 1964), deals with the close relationship between the president and his secretary of state. Mary P. Adams, "Jefferson's Reactions to the Treaty of San Ildefonso," *Journal of Southern History* 22 (1955), 173–88, comments on his militant reaction to the Spanish cession of Louisiana to France. Louis M. Sears, *Jefferson and the Embargo* (Durham, 1927), remains the standard treatment on the subject despite the pacifism that he dubiously attributes to Jefferson.

Reproduced from the collections of the Library of Congress

FROM INDEPENDENCE TO WAR:
JAMES
MADISON
and American Foreign Policy

Patrick C. T. White

George Washington's main purpose, he wrote in 1793 as the wars of the French Revolution engulfed Europe, was "to keep our people in peace." That task proved a delicate and challenging one, and if the first president of the United States achieved that goal his successors found it increasingly difficult and finally impossible. The early decades of independence for countries that have thrown off the imperial mantle are seldom easy, as the twentieth century has so clearly demonstrated; what is true today was also true for the thirteen colonies after recognition of their independence in 1783. For more than two decades after that extraordinary event, presidents struggled with the problems of defending American interests overseas, creating a viable economy at home, and

Extensive documentation for the views expressed in this essay may be found in Professor White's *Nation on Trial: America and the War of 1812.*

shaping institutions to govern the new nation. Few men played a more central role in these critical years than James Madison, for he molded the Constitution of 1787, made foreign policy as secretary of state between 1801 and 1809, and as president led the United States into its first foreign war. Wars are the cruelest test for nations, and it was Madison's misfortune to take a divided country into a conflict in 1812. While a majority of his party supported what Calhoun called the second war for liberty, a substantial and purposeful minority passionately believed otherwise.

This deep party division tragically complicated the making of foreign policy, and finally pitched the United States into a war it was ill prepared to fight and not ready to sustain. No president can escape unscathed from the ruinous divisions an unpopular war inflicts upon the nation. When Daniel Webster could cry out in 1814 that the war was being fought to conquer Canada rather than to defend America's national interests, it is obvious how deep the divisions in the country had become. More than a century and a half later Lyndon Johnson suffered the same torments and damage when he involved the United States in a venture in Vietnam that too many of his countrymen believed ill judged, immoral, and harmful to the nation.

◇◇◇

Madison was born on 18 March 1751 in King George County, Virginia. As the son of a well-known planter whose forefathers had settled in that region late in the seventeenth century, he entered a secure and established world. He was related to Edward Pendleton, a distinguished lawyer and revolutionary leader, and to John Taylor, a leading states' rights lawyer. By inheritance and upbringing, then, he naturally viewed property rights as vital to the nation. He did not hold this view narrowly, for his subsequent reading of Locke led him to the same conclusion; the right to acquire property, Madison believed, formed the basis of a just and stable society. Because of his frail health, Madison received his early education at the hands of tutors. For university training he went not to William and Mary College where so many of his contemporaries received their education, but rather to the College of New Jersey at Princeton where the climate better suited his health and where the academic standards were more exacting.

At Princeton Madison read Greek and Roman history and

steeped himself in the writings of Locke, Hume, Addison, and Montesquieu. He absorbed the great English dissenting tradition that was such a vital part of the eighteenth century. His teachers were clerics and so he wedded a deep and lasting Christian ethic to his dissenting thought. The education he received helped shape his political beliefs; from his reading of Livy he discovered the virtues of republican government, from Cicero he learned of the dangers of the military dictatorship of a Caesar. Thucydides warned him of the disasters that fratricidal war might inflict upon a country, and Plutarch stressed the virtues of citizenship. If classical civilization gave Madison an understanding of the state, his reading of Addison, Pope, and Swift gave him a sense of style, manner, and grace. Overriding this, his Protestant ethic instilled in him a conception of man's relation to God. He believed that there were limits to the state's power over the individual, and he accepted Locke's doctrine that men could not be governed without their consent.

When Madison graduated from Princeton in 1771 he was unsure of the profession he wished to pursue. He thought of law, but found politics more fascinating. The principles and forms of government, he once wrote, were too important to be ignored by inquisitive minds. In April 1776, at the age of twenty-six, he was elected a delegate from Orange County to a convention in Williamsburg, Virginia. After a vigorous debate this assembly instructed its delegates to the Continental Congress to call for independence from Great Britain. Madison, who was both young and inexperienced, took no part in the debate but supported the resolution on independence and celebrated its passage. In 1780, he became a delegate to the Continental Congress where he served four years. The experience he gained there shaped his views both of the nature of politics and the extent to which power should be delegated to the individual states. The year Madison entered Congress was a somber one, marked by American defeats at Charleston and Camden and the announced treason of Benedict Arnold. Through these distressing times Congress debated and bickered, showing neither a unity of purpose nor a determination to wage war effectively. Madison shared Washington's fear that one head might gradually turn into thirteen disparate ones, with fearful consequences. The answer to that problem, Madison asserted, lay in greater "authority and vigour in our councils."

At the same time, defining America's future interests concerned him. It was imperative that the government assert its claims to the Mississippi River. Spain and Britain had jointly controlled that river by the 1763 treaty. When Spain entered the war against Britain in 1779 it ignored the United States claim to the area once held by the mother country. Madison composed a state paper laying effective claim to the disputed territory, arguing that the Mississippi was a natural boundary, insisting that America could make more effective use of the territory than Spain, and asserting that to surrender the claims of the individual states to the area would dangerously weaken the war effort. Madison also rejected the Spanish closing of the mouth of the Mississippi to navigation (a right exercised because Spain controlled both banks of the river there) as both harmful to America and its allies and a defiance of natural law. A great tide of American settlers, he suggested, would inevitably settle the West, and it was only right that the future be recognized now. If this was neither Manifest Destiny nor a sense of mission—and it was not—it was nonetheless a clear recognition of the vital importance of the West to the new nation.

By 1782 the defeats that had haunted the United States had turned to victories and Great Britain accepted peace. The negotiations by John Jay, Benjamin Franklin, and John Adams, which culminated in the triumphant Treaty of Paris in 1783, proved the prescience of Madison's view. The agreed terms reflected the skill of the American negotiators and the feelings increasingly voiced in Britain that the attempt to crush colonial aspirations was an unworthy task. The treaty itself recognized the independence of the United States, gave it fishing rights in specified regions of British North American waters, drew a boundary that gave the United States the Mississippi River down to the thirty-first parallel, provided for the evacuation of American territory by British troops, and pledged the United States to work for the restoration of sequestered Loyalist property as well as to create no impediments to the collection of legitimate British debts.

It is an all-too-familiar occurrence that internal disorder follows colonial independence. The United States was no exception to this rule, although its troubles were less turbulent and destructive than most. Nevertheless, the difficulties were real enough to convince Madison that neither internal tranquillity nor foreign relations could be secure until a new and stronger federal authority was created. He observed in 1783 that if the men who had made the Revolution regarded peace with Britain as the end of their labors, if they remained indifferent while anarchy and domestic turmoil dissolved the bonds of government, they would reap the contempt of their fellows and the condemnation of posterity. Peace alone would be insufficient; he demanded that the true purpose of the Revolution be realized: "Let them, by a government adequate to the ends of society, secure those blessings to which the virtues, sacrifices and sufferings of America have undeniable claims."

The years after 1783 demonstrated the truth of Madison's prophecy. State quarreled with state, economic instability threatened the union, and domestic insurrection challenged the central authority. Foreign danger matched this internal tribulation. Great Britain excluded the new nation from the imperial trading system and closed the West Indies to the United States. Even worse, the failure of America to protect both the Loyalists and their property and the inability of the federal authority to prevent individual states from placing impediments in the way of collecting British debts gave London an excuse to keep the Northwest posts. Beyond that, Spain closed the Mississippi River to navigation through Louisiana in 1784. Only the determined opposition of Madison and the stubborn resistance of the southern states prevented the United States from ratifying a proposal that would have accepted that closure for twenty-five years in return for American access to Spanish markets.

With all its risks and consequences this continued instability could not be tolerated. While the nation had violated its treaties with Britain, France, and Holland, those foreign powers had not yet been rigorous in retaliation; but that moderation, Madison warned, should not be taken for "permanent partiality" to American faults. The solution lay at hand: a new framework of constitutional government to replace the discredited Articles of Confederation. For some years Madison had devoted his thoughts and energies to an examination of the means to achieve this. He called for a constitutional convention; when it met in 1787 he was ready to take up the challenge. A shining constellation of talent gathered at Philadelphia—"an assembly of demi-gods," as Jefferson put it. Washington, Jefferson, Franklin, Randolph, and Hamilton were only some of the nation's leaders who attended and lent their gifts to its deliberations. As important as their talent was the commitment of the majority to a nationalist vision of a strong central authority. Madison had observed that the "great desideratum" in government was a modification of the concept of sovereignty to make a centralized government a neutral party between interest groups and factions, to keep one part of society from violating the rights of another, and to prevent the agents of government from becoming interests adverse to society. To reconcile the conflict between those who wished to retain the strength of the individual states and those who wanted a centralized national authority Madison proposed a compromise that would preserve the "due supremacy of the national authority" without excluding local authority where it was "subordinately useful." The result was a "mixed government" that embodied the federal principle, preserved local government, and secured liberty and freedom.

Ratification of the Constitution had to follow its making, and here Madison with Hamilton and Jay excelled. In the *Federalist* papers they produced a defense of the new Constitution that stands as one of the most eloquent tracts on political theory in the English language. It was, as Jefferson observed, "the most authentic exposition" of the federal Constitution, and its clarity of style and force of argument helped convince the nation of its utility.

One of the chief purposes of the new Constitution, wrote Madison, was to act as a bulwark against foreign dangers and serve as the guardian of American commerce. Between 1787 and 1793 he pressed for a foreign policy that would realize these twin goals. Madison's efforts were first directed at the imbalance of American trade with Britain. Since the United States imported from the United Kingdom twice as much as it exported there, America had become dangerously dependent upon British credit and goods. To assure the reality as well as the form of independence it was imperative, Madison argued, to diversify American trade by directing a greater proportion to France. To this end, he introduced a variety of measures in the House of Representatives including preferential duties for the ships of nations that signed trade treaties with the United States. Since Britain had not, and indeed, since it had abruptly rejected a reciprocal trade agreement with the United States in 1784, its ships would suffer discriminatory tonnage duties in American ports. The pro-French nature of this measure, which would additionally have raised the price of goods in the United States, proved too much for Hamilton and Washington, and they rejected it; but an act giving American ships preferences in home ports was enacted. It should be observed that

Hamilton's opposition to these measures did not make him less a nationalist than Madison. The former believed that continuing and developing closer ties with Britain would better serve America's interests. Their increasing divisions on foreign policy when combined with their deepening differences over domestic matters led to the formation of the Federalist and Republican parties, a development that had been neither envisaged in the Constitution nor favored by Washington.

The outbreak of war in Europe placed new pressures upon the United States. In 1793 Britain and France became locked in a savage struggle that did not finally end until the defeat of Napoleon at Waterloo. The distinguished naval historian, G. J. Marcus, turned to Livy's description of the Second Punic War to find a parallel for that exacting struggle. The latter had written in *Historia*, "Never did any other states and peoples of greater strength and resources engage in war against each other; nor were there states of any other times possessed of such resources and power." The war in Europe posed a particular dilemma for the United States, for it enlarged and deepened the divisions between those who argued for the maintenance of closer ties with Britain and those who wanted to encourage a more intimate friendship with France. Some Republicans believed that the treaty of 1778 with France both morally and legally obligated the United States to come to its aid in the likely event that its possessions in the West Indies were attacked. Others, like Jefferson and Madison, felt that American neutrality should be used to extract concessions from the warring powers. Both of these alternatives seemed far too dangerous to Hamilton, for if either led to war with Britain the future of the Republic would be imperiled. The Neutrality Proclamation issued by Washington bore the imprint of Hamilton's views and called only for "conduct friendly and impartial towards the belligerent powers." The cabinet division over policy spilled into public print. In a series of eight newspaper articles, Hamilton defended not only the Neutrality Proclamation but also the general direction of American foreign policy. Madison, who was convinced that Washington's policy wounded national honor and disregarded "stipulated duties to France," answered Hamilton's defense of the proclamation in five tightly reasoned commentaries. Yet he did not criticize the idea of neutrality, for like Jefferson he wanted only to lean toward France. Rather, he challenged the manner in which the policy was decided and announced. He took a legalistic and constitutional view of Washington's actions and drew upon the intentions of the framers of the Constitution in 1787 to shape his criticism. The president's need to act swiftly to protect the nation's interests was, to Madison, a secondary consideration. This was the first debate in the long history of argumentation over executive privilege and the making of foreign policy.

The events that swiftly followed the Neutrality Proclamation further illustrated Madison's determination to pursue a policy sympathetic to France. The first occurred when Secretary of State Jefferson issued a report on the state of American commerce in which he asked that economic coercion be used to compel Britain to lift its restrictive economic policies. In January 1794, Madison introduced a series of resolutions in the House to this end. He proposed that high barriers be placed against British ships and goods until London accepted the principle of reciprocal trade. He admitted that such a mercantilist system would benefit France, but he saw merit rather than disadvantage in that result. To Federalists, however, the Madison plan was a "wild system" that would strike at the foundations of American business and commerce; despite Madison's passionate advocacy of his proposals the House rejected them and instead implemented a temporary trade embargo with Britain.

Following this measure Washington sent John Jay to London to negotiate the differences with Britain. This mission presented Madison with the second opportunity within a year to outline his foreign policy. Jay was instructed to secure the withdrawal of British troops from the Northwest posts, to deal with the vexatious questions of Loyalist debts and boundary disputes, and to soften the blows being struck at neutral rights. It was a mission designed to stop the drift toward war with Britain. When Jay returned to the United States with the treaty, however, he had only secured the first issue, provided for commissions to settle the second, and failed almost completely to reach agreement on the last. That most prized of objects, the complete opening of trade with the West Indies, eluded his grasp, for the concessions on that critical issue were so trifling as to seem an affront rather than an olive branch. The ratification of the treaty proved to be as stormy as the events that had led to its negotiation. Jay was cursed for failing to defend American rights at sea, and for not wringing concessions from Britain over the West Indies trade. He ruefully observed that he could find his way across the country by the light of his burning effigies.

It is not enough to beat the servants of the state; the real question was whether Jay could have secured better terms in the face of British unwillingness to make concessions to a small neutral power—concessions that would, in Britain's judgment, fatally weaken its ability to wage war against France. The alternatives to Jay's Treaty would have been not more favorable terms for America, but war with Britain, and neither Washington nor Hamilton were prepared to take that risk. Madison viewed this posture as self-serving. The treaty was, he insisted, "a ruinous bargain" and could only be explained away by Jay's "blind partiality" for Great Britain. Even worse, he charged, it showed that the Federalists were now a "British party" whose purpose was to secure "an exclusive connection with the British government," sacrificing in the bargain America's commerce and national honor. Beyond that Madison called for the president to submit to the House the papers relative to the treaty, and he boldly asserted the right of the House to pass the legislation necessary to execute its terms. A majority of that body's members felt that such an action would strike at the heart of the treaty-making powers of the president, and rejected Madison's claims.

The election of 1796 followed the ratification of Jay's Treaty. Madison supported Jefferson for the presidency, but he himself decided to retire from public life. He adamantly insisted that he would serve in neither state nor federal offices. His desire on this point, he wrote, was "sincere and inflexible." Certainly his contribution to the nation had been sufficient to justify a withdrawal from the political scene. He, more than any other, had shaped the federal Constitution under which the country lived; he, more than any other, had developed the Republican party, for he, not Jefferson, had organized its structure and led it in the House; and he, more than any other, had formulated a Republican foreign policy as an alternative to the one conceived and practiced by the Federalists.

◇◇◇

If Madison was resolute in his determination to retire from political life, both events and his deep commitment to politics pulled him inexorably back into the mainstream of American life.

The presidency of John Adams with its Alien and Sedition Acts was the immediate occasion for his return to national affairs. The quasi-war with France that had erupted in 1797 distressed him, but the Alien and Sedition Acts, which struck at the heart of American liberty, moved him to profound anger. The Virginia and Kentucky Resolutions were the answers he and Jefferson formulated to this harsh exercise of federal authority. Madison did not claim the right of the state to nullify national legislation; rather he formulated the more intricate doctrine of interposition, the right of the individual state to judge when the federal compact had been broken and its further right to interpose its power between the national authority and the people.

The election of Jefferson to the presidency in 1800 opened a new career for Madison. The president called him to serve as secretary of state; although his health still troubled him, he readily accepted the offer, for he was bound to Jefferson by ties of party, principle, experience, and friendship. Madison brought to his new office both strengths and weaknesses. His powers of advocacy had been admirably illustrated during the debates on the Constitution, but advocacy is not enough in the making of foreign policy. Here the accidents of chance, the interests of other nations, and the recognition of the possible as well as the desirable are critical qualities in decision making. Madison's dispatches had a legalistic, even wooden quality, and too often they read like lawyers' briefs. State documents are not necessarily designed to fire the imagination, but they should reveal a sure and complete grasp of the complexity of world affairs. Madison may have disliked Hamilton's *Realpolitik*, but the latter's grasp of reality frequently served America's interests better than a theoretical defense of abstract principles. Further, the nationalism that had moved Madison to call for the Constitutional Convention and that had shaped his view of America's destiny sometimes blinded him to Britain's dilemma; to survive the dreadful wars of the French Revolution and Napoleonic era England had to utilize every weapon at its command, to exploit its control of the seas, and in so doing had perforce to conflict with American interests in neutral trade. Madison's deeply held conviction that logic and reason shaped men's views fell before the fury of Napoleon's ambitions and the British determination to thwart them.

Men act, Madison had written in his "Vices of the Political System of the United States," from a "prudent regard to their own good, as involved in the general and permanent good of the community." He thought that nations should also act that way. "The wars which afflict mankind are not produced by the intrigues or cupidity of the weaker nations, who wish to retain peace whilst their neighbours are at war." They are rather, he wrote, the "offspring of ambition" or commercial competition. It was in the interest of great powers to act with wisdom and generosity toward lesser powers, for no country remained omnipotent for long, and those that once held the world stage would later become supplicants to the very nations they once mistreated and reviled. Consequently, he concluded, all nations would be best served by supporting a system of international law that dispensed justice evenly to all mankind.

These principles were soon tested. Fortunately, the first year of Madison's tenure as secretary of state was quiet, for the great war in Europe had come to a temporary halt. The Peace of Amiens was signed in 1801 and the issues that had so bedeviled America at sea disappeared. Yet peace was an illusion and the actions of Spain and France soon forced Madison to confront a threat to the security of the United States. The blow fell when Spain transferred Louisiana to France and then shortly thereafter closed the mouth of the Mississippi River to American commerce. Madison reacted swiftly and positively. The Mississippi River, he wrote, was everything to the commerce of the West: "It is the Hudson, the Delaware, the Potomac and all the navigable rivers of the Atlantic States formed into one stream." Furthermore, western states considered navigation on it a "natural and indefeasible right" and would fight to preserve it. An even greater danger loomed, however. Napoleon had sent a powerful army to Santo Domingo with orders to crush a slave revolt there and then establish a great French empire in the Mississippi region. To forestall this dangerous enterprise Madison wanted to secure New Orleans and West Florida. He agreed with Jefferson that if France took possession of New Orleans the security of the United States would depend on the British. The cession of Louisiana to France would change the relationship between that country and America; indeed, he said, "the worst events are to be apprehended." Secretary Madison therefore instructed American representatives in Paris to purchase New Orleans from France and West Florida from Spain. The transfer of territory, he argued, should be made on the supposition that France did not want war with the United States. The claim to

West Florida was less firm. The communication through the rivers of Florida, he observed, was "so natural, so reasonable and so essential" that annexation must eventually take place. For such a diplomatic triumph the United States needed good fortune as well as good management. Fortune smiled upon America, for Napoleon's army at Santo Domingo was decimated, and when the French emperor's grandiose dreams of empire collapsed he hastily sold all of Louisiana to the United States rather than see it fall to Britain. Spain proved more difficult, for the United States had no lever of power to exert upon it. Not until 1810 when Spain was totally occupied with the peninsular war did American forces march in and take that area. Even without Florida, the Louisiana Purchase was victory enough, the one unqualified diplomatic success of Jefferson's presidency. It marked the creation of an American empire that Madison could call an empire of liberty, for its settlers would be Americans cherishing the rights, liberties, and aspirations of the men who had made the Revolution in 1776.

Unhappily, the disaster of war in Europe followed the triumph of the Louisiana Purchase. When Napoleon renewed hostilities with Britain, the United States found itself and its commerce once again cruelly squeezed between the two great powers. Napoleon's swift military victories against the allies in Europe forced Britain to depend upon sea power to fashion a final victory, and in the process neutral rights were summarily ignored. The British reapplied the Rule of 1756 which forbade a nation to trade with European colonies during war if that trade had been prohibited in peacetime; they extended blockades from single ports (the traditional practice) to include entire coastlines; they expanded the definition of contraband from arms and accouterments of war to foodstuffs; and they ended coastal trade in Europe by neutrals. When Napoleon's Berlin and Milan decrees declared the United Kingdom in a state of blockade, Britain retaliated by commanding all ships destined for the Continent to call first at a British port for clearance. Then, when Napoleon decreed that any ship following such instructions would be seized when it reached France, the nature of the American dilemma was clear. Under such circumstances seizure of American ships by either Britain or France was a certainty.

If this were not enough, Britain again began to impress American sailors. The Orders in Council restricted commerce, but impressment affected men. The necessity for maintaining the strength of the Royal Navy lay at the bottom of this British practice. The combination of savage discipline, appalling living conditions, and low wages drove its sailors to desert. Many of them signed onto American ships and Britain was determined to halt the atrophy of the force that was critical to prosecution of the war. Britain therefore stopped and searched neutral vessels on the seas for sailors who had escaped His Majesty's service. More importantly, it seized as its own those who had been born in the United Kingdom but who had become naturalized American citizens. At the time, international law did not recognize the right of people to transfer national allegiance. Once born in a country, one remained a citizen of it always. The practice of naturalization, ruled the law officers of the crown, was "novel" and could not be used to avoid answering the call to service issued by His Majesty's government.

Madison responded to this attack upon American commerce with a scathing denunciation of British practices. In a lengthy pamphlet entitled "Examination of the British Doctrine Which Subjects to Capture a Neutral Trade Not Open in Time of Peace," he scourged Britain for limiting the trade of neutrals during wartime. From Grotius to Vattel, from the practices of the Hansa towns to the treaties with Spain, Madison showed how Britain distorted international law, overthrew accustomed practices, and subverted American interests. "The innovation," he wrote, "which she endeavors to enforce as a right of war, is under that name a mere proposal for extending the field of maritime capture, and multiplying the sources of commercial aggrandizement; a warfare, in fact, against the commerce of her friends, a monopolizing grasp at that of her enemies." He responded with the same anger over impressment. In a series of closely reasoned dispatches to Monroe and Pinckney in London in 1806 Madison denounced the practice as intolerable and demanded that it cease. "Taking reason and justice for the tests of this practice, it is peculiarly indefensible, for it deprives the dearest rights of persons of a regular trial, to which the most inconsiderable article of property captured on the high seas is entitled, and leaves their destiny to the will of an officer, sometimes cruel and generally interested, by his want of mariners, in his own decision." He instructed his representative to bring the British government "more and more to understand their own interests as well as our own"; but it was an error to think that British and American interests coincided. Enlightened self-interest might be much praised, but it was in precious short supply during the Napoleonic Wars. Britain would neither surrender the right to impress nor moderate the conditions that made it necessary.

Matters worsened when a new and more determined government came into office in London. It included Lords Canning and Castlereagh, two of the greatest diplomats in Britain's history; they had resolved to destroy Napoleon. The news of the formation of this new cabinet arrived hard on the heels of fresh intelligence about new restrictive Orders in Council. Then came the *Chesapeake* affair. A British frigate attacked this American vessel on its first cruise in June 1807; four of its crew were killed, eighteen of them wounded, and four alleged deserters seized. This flagrant and unwarranted breach of international law could have led to a complete rupture with Britain. Even Canning, described by John Quincy Adams as that "implacable and rancorous enemy" of the United States, was ready to admit error though less ready to apologize for the incident. The British minister in Washington, David Erskine, saw war as imminent. It might be difficult, he said, to "induce the Nation to determine upon a war with England upon Commercial disputes," but an appeal to national honor could arouse the passions of the people. Jefferson chose to save the nation's honor by other means. The French minister in Washington observed that the president did not want war with Britain and "that Madison dreads it still more."

Jefferson selected an embargo. Madison, who throughout his career had favored the use of economic coercion in diplomacy, supported it. Indeed, the secretary of state drafted the message, which the president sent to Congress with slight alterations. Madison believed that the measure would force Britain and even France to modify their policies. He believed that a secondary benefit would accrue to the United States, for the loss of Europe's markets would stimulate the development of American manufacturing. Unfortunately, Madison overestimated the effect of the embargo abroad and the willingness of Americans to submit to its strictures at home. Britain found alternative markets for its goods in South America; Napoleon refused to lift his decrees; and the United States saw its commerce ruinously damaged. Boston, Savannah, and New Orleans had an air of desolation, and depression gripped the West as agricultural prices plummeted. A great experiment in diplomacy had failed. Conceived as a means to defend America's interests and coerce its enemies, it had impoverished the country, divided the nation's councils, and was held in contempt by Britain and France. John Quincy Adams wrote in 1811 that its only redeeming feature was that it had postponed war. It had; but the problems it had been designed to resolve remained, and it was Madison's ill luck to inherit them.

◇◇◇

Jefferson retired from the presidency exhausted by his efforts but comforted by the belief that history would judge him generously for his unselfish efforts to preserve peace. Madison, whose service and experience made him the natural candidate of the Republican party, succeeded him. He faced formidable problems: the *Chesapeake* affair hung fire, the Orders in Council remained in force, and the embargo lay in ruins. Perhaps a new president could find fresh solutions to old problems; but could Madison rise to the occasion? Certainly Senator Adair of Kentucky thought him "too fearful and too timid to direct the affairs of the nation," although Albert Gallatin found him "firm when the storm arises." The first test came with the formation of the cabinet and here Madison displayed a dangerous weakness. Except for Albert Gallatin as secretary of the treasury he appointed a cabinet bereft of talent and devoid of energy and drive.

Unhappily for America, Congress showed no more unity of purpose or determination of spirit. Some Republicans were ready to arm the nation; others demanded further negotiations; still more Federalists wanted close ties with Britain. Congressional sniping at Gallatin and the incompetent secretary of state's failure to inform the Senate of the president's policy—a procedure, Madison wrote, that was "indispensable to the advantageous conduct of the public business"—did not help matters. The embargo was gone and the remaining nonimportation act was due to expire. Few wished to renew a measure that harmed American commerce more than it hurt Britain or France. As an alternative Nathaniel Macon introduced a bill that permitted American ships to trade overseas, but closed the ports of the United States to the contesting powers in Europe. This was designed to punish those who injured the United States, but when it emerged from a quarrelsome Congress it had been emasculated beyond recognition. Macon's Bill No. 2 simply provided that trade with Britain and France would be renewed—with the proviso that if either of the offending powers rescinded its oppressive decrees the United States would, if the other did not follow suit in ninety days, apply an embargo against the recalcitrant belligerent. This was a mean and dishonorable measure, for it rewarded one guilty party and provided an opportunity for the unscrupulous to blackmail the United States.

That is what happened, for France announced in the duc de Cadore's letter of August 1810 that the Berlin and Milan decrees were repealed, provided that Britain rescind its Orders in Council. It is not difficult to understand Napoleon's motives for this action; he desperately needed American supplies and hoped that by gulling Madison into accepting the Cadore letter he would secure the repeal of the British blockade. He succeeded on the first count but failed on the second. The president grasped at the French move with unseemly haste, but Britain refused to believe that Napoleon had acted in good faith. Even Pinckney, the American minister in London, said that the continued French seizure of American vessels made his efforts to secure Britain's repeal of the blockade impossible. Instructed to argue that the Cadore letter was valid, he privately admitted that he was defending a lie.

If Macon's Bill failed there was little the United States could do. It could continue to negotiate in the hope, however vain, that Britain and France would listen to reason; it could again try economic coercion, although that, too, offered faint promise; it could submit to conditions as they were, although that would be craven; or it could prepare for war. Madison and the Congress opted for the first alternatives. Despite the many grounds of discontent and discouragement, Madison wrote, America was ready to participate in any new experiment for "a cordial and comprehensive adjustment of matters between the two countries." Beyond that a new nonintercourse act was applied to Britain. The embargo as conceived in Macon's Bill was not imposed. Because too many knew that France was still violating American commerce, it was decided simply to prohibit the importation of British goods while allowing American exports to flow anywhere overseas.

Though such halfhearted measures had little merit, the president knew that the nation was not ready for more aggressive moves; but if American action raised the risk of war with Britain, such a course at least had the advantage, as Madison himself observed, of confronting the country with one adversary at a time.

At this juncture two considerations severely restricted presidential maneuverability. In the first place, lack of congressional support justified presidential caution, for the Congress abandoned a pending measure to raise fifty thousand troops and it abolished the Bank of the United States. The lack of men and money dictated prudence, as did presidential involvement in the Florida annexation movement. Madison had long recognized the strategic and commercial importance of that Spanish territory, and he ardently desired to make it a part of the United States. In an exercise of presidential power that would have delighted a Theodore Roosevelt, Madison occupied West Florida, an act that might even have brought war with Spain, Britain's ally. Defensive considerations, the declining stability in the region that might provide a pretext for British occupation to prop up Spanish authority, in part prompted the annexation. The president provided the rationale for the act: the crisis justified unilateral and decisive action, and the act was "understood to be within the authority of the Executive." Such vigorous extensions of presidential power are not usually associated with the author of the Virginia and Kentucky Resolutions.

Great Britain's response to these events in America gave little cause for optimism. The new British minister in Washington, Augustus John Foster, told the president that London would not lift the Orders in Council until it had clear proof that Napoleon's decrees had been absolutely and unconditionally withdrawn. Because that proof could not be provided, England and America moved closer to a final break; but hope was to be found in the Twelfth Congress which met late in 1811, for its members soon showed that they were of a different mettle from their predecessors. Congress was not united in its views, nor did it consistently pursue a clear and coherent policy; but it did show a firmer grasp of reality and a more determined sense of direction. Its nucleus consisted of a group of young activists, the War Hawks: Henry Clay of Kentucky and Felix Grundy of Tennessee were thirty-four years old, John Calhoun of South Carolina was twenty-nine, John Harper of New Hampshire, thirty-two, and Peter Porter of New York, thirty-eight. Defeat of the old members was, said Robert Wright of Maryland, "the sentence of the nation against the doctrine of submission." These new nationalists were determined to see things through to the end. They did not remember the Revolution for most were born just before or during it. War held no terror for them; Jefferson might say that "one war in a lifetime is enough," but they had no patience with such reasoning. They were supremely confident that war with Britain would be short and swift, victory sweet and certain. Clay would take Canada with the Kentucky militia; even Jefferson thought that, at worst, taking Canada would be merely a "matter of marching."

The Hawks dominated Congress and its committees. In addition to making one of their number, Clay, Speaker of the House, they chaired all the major committees: Foreign Affairs, Naval Affairs, Military Affairs, and Ways and Means. Each of these committees contained a substantial number of the young activists. The views of this group were soon expressed in the report of the Foreign Affairs Committee stating that the country could no longer remain indifferent to the wrongs inflicted by Great Britain. Justice and humanity had restrained America from taking up arms, but "forbearance was no longer a virtue." The time had come to put the nation into the "armor and attitude" demanded by events. One of their number later reported that they had "crossed the Rubicon."

The debate that followed the report showed clearly the mood of Congress; one after another, members rose to call for war. The issue, as Senator Robert Wright of Maryland put it, had narrowed down to war or submission—and with the antitemporizers in the ascendancy, sentiment for the latter was fast dissipating. From the last days of 1811 to the middle of 1812, the country drifted toward war.

A number of serious frictions between the two countries prevented reconciliation. Impressment remained a threat to safety and an affront to sovereignty, and it appeared to Americans that British officials were inciting the Indians on the frontier to war. In March 1812, the Henry letters that Madison sent to Congress seemed positive proof of British perfidy: a British agent, John Henry, had been snooping around New England to determine whether, in the event of war, the Federalists there would look to England rather than to Washington for guidance. There was not much in the letters, but they gave rise to outraged cries against British interference in American affairs.

In the early months of 1812, despite the clamor in Congress, Madison, with the assistance of his new secretary of state, James Monroe, continued negotiating for resolution of the points at issue between the United States and Great Britain. It was a hopeless task. The increasing influence of a group in England calling for repeal of the Orders in Council and reconciliation offered some hope, but when the Perceval government rejected a softer line toward America, it pushed the president toward the conclusion that Britain preferred war to repeal of the orders. Ironically, as American patience wore thin, the British government was moving toward a conditional repeal of the hated measures; but the assassination of the prime minister slowed that move until it was too late. Whether repeal alone would have satisfied American demands remains a matter of conjecture. As long as impressment continued, no American was safe at sea, and if the flag could not protect the citizens who sailed under it, America could not be a truly sovereign state.

When combined with western grievances and fears, the cumulative effect of a decade of British actions finally moved the president to call for war, although continued French attacks upon American commerce made his final decision more difficult. A case for war with both Britain and France could be made, as Madison told Jefferson, but such a war would alienate the Federalists, divide the Republicans, and be impossible to fight. So he chose to face Great Britain as the power that had committed the greatest and most unforgivable transgressions. The president waited until the *Hornet* arrived from England in late May with the latest intelligence, and then, after a fruitless last round of talks with the British minister had shown that Britain was still inflexible, he acted. On 1 June 1812 he sent his war message to Congress, citing the just causes for war in order of their importance: impressment, blockades, and the Orders in Council. His choice of priorities was fair and substantial. Impressment struck at the sovereignty of the Republic by challenging its ability to protect its own citizens, while the Orders in Council damaged its economy in a way that became increasingly unbearable with the passage of time.

The president's message set off fierce and protracted congressional debate, but finally, on 18 June, by a vote of nineteen to thirteen in the Senate and seventy-nine to forty-nine in the House, the United States declared war. The nature of this vote revealed a deeply divided nation rather than a united one. Many Federalists felt that by striking at Britain the United States was attacking the last hope of ordered good government in a world gone mad with revolution. Some Republicans thought that the United States was not yet armed for war and that hostilities should be postponed until the needed forces could be recruited. Others believed that republican institutions were still too fragile and untested to stand the shock of war.

"TO THE GRAVE GO SHAM PROTECTORS OF " FREE TRADE AND SAILORS' RIGHTS"—AND ALL THE PEOPLE SAY AMEN !"

Madison was largely responsible for this confusion, for as president he should have carried the nation with him in a spirit of unity and determination. Majority votes are sufficient to pass tax legislation, but not enough for war; for that, near unanimity is required, and Madison's failure was a failure of presidential leadership. On the great issues of war and peace it is the president's duty to unite a quarrelsome and divided Congress and to so address the nation that it places its full support behind his policies. Undoubtedly, presidential eloquence alone would not have persuaded all who doubted the wisdom of Madison's actions, but the lack of it made opposition easier to embrace. The president would have been wise to follow the advice given by Winston Churchill to the British foreign secretary Sir Edward Grey in 1915: "I beseech you at this crisis, not to make the mistake in falling below the level of events. Half-hearted measures will ruin all. . . . You must be bold and violent. You have a right to be."

Circumstances, of course, were against Madison; he was not a man of boldness or of violence. His belief in economic coercion and his hope that reason could overcome ignorance were insufficient to change the policies of great powers involved in a great war. A small, neutral United States had little chance of escaping untouched from the implacable violence of the Napoleonic world war. Chance and fortune had served as Madison's companions in the Louisiana Purchase, but they were unhappy associates in the years of his presidency. There can be little doubt that if it had not been for the Napoleonic Wars there would have been no War of 1812. The issues that led to the latter sprang from the former. The question that bedeviled the United States was how best to protect the national interest in the face of affronts to sovereignty and injury to trade. Madison believed in a system of "perfect freedom" of trade. He had argued for such a system in the formation of the new nation and he called for it as president, but neither Britain nor France shared that view and neither would pursue policies that would lead to it. The tools of economic coercion the United States used to loose Europe from its system were insufficient for the task. The efforts to protect American citizens on the seas proved equally inadequate. Impressment forcibly removed over six thousand American sailors from their ships for service in the Royal Navy. Neither Washington nor Adams, Jefferson nor Madison could design policies to prevent that. When the United States took its place among the nations of the world, Madison asserted, "they assumed and established a common Sovereignty on the high seas, as well as exclusive sovereignty within their territorial water." The declaration of this principle, however, did not establish its practice.

Madison went to war to resolve these dilemmas. His success must be judged, in part, by how he waged war and the terms he secured in peace. In the beginning America suffered disastrous reverses; commanders were weak, troops ill disciplined, and objectives badly chosen. The opposition forces, though small in number, were tightly disciplined regulars brilliantly led by General Isaac Brock. As the war progressed, however, the quality of America's leadership improved and its soldiers acquitted themselves well in battle. By 1814 it was clear to Britain that it could not effectively continue the war except at exorbitant costs. The duke of Wellington, that greatest of soldiers, advised the prime minister, Lord Liverpool, that troops in Canada had held that colony better than he could have hoped and that since a stalemate had been reached the time had come to negotiate a peace. Madison had reached the same conclusion. The United States might, indeed, launch a major invasion of Canada, but the campaign would be bloody and protracted. Furthermore, the Royal Navy, now that Napoleon had been defeated, would devastate the Atlantic seaboard. Finally, the country needed relief, for the swelling tide of domestic opposition to the war threatened national unity.

The peace negotiated at Ghent settled upon a restoration of the situation at the outbreak of war. No mention was made of the maritime issues that had caused the war. This has led some to argue that this was proof the war had been needlessly fought; but by 1814 all the maritime disputes had disappeared with the defeat of France. More importantly, Britain would never again impress American citizens. Daniel Webster warned that to do so would lead to immediate war with the United States, and Britain took this solemn declaration to heart. Beyond that, as Gallatin observed, the war had renewed the spirit of American nationalism and rededicated the nation to its early purpose. While Britain and the United States were to have many dangerous differences later in the nineteenth century they never fell into war again. The lessons of the War of 1812 had not been lost upon them.

Certainly Madison's foreign policy had a distinguishing stamp to it. He believed in domestic freedom based upon personal liberty. He recognized the importance of controlling the Floridas and the Mississippi and he sought to expand American trade overseas. In a violent world he attempted to uphold the nation's rights through economic coercion, but he failed to recognize that it was a frail weapon when used against France and Britain in the era of the Napoleonic Wars. He failed to recognize, too, that a nation without effective armed forces was hardly in a position to extract meaningful concessions from great powers in conflict. Once he had decided upon war he failed to inspire the nation to meet the challenge that lay before it. Yet he did not enter the war for mean or narrow reasons, but rather to preserve the nation whose creation was so much a product of his talent and genius. If he made mistakes in policy and erred in judgment, his work still stands as a monument to his principles.

BIBLIOGRAPHIC NOTE

The War of 1812, one of the most contentious in American history, has captured the attention of historians, partly because it was the first fought by the new Republic and partly because it aroused such domestic opposition. In assessing the war and its causes few historians have been charitable to Madison. Henry Adams, the first and still one of the greatest students of the period, in his multivolume history of the administrations of Jefferson and Madison, damned the president for indecisiveness, weakness, and inability to control events. More recently, both Bradford Perkins, in *Prologue to War* (Berkeley, 1961), and Reginald Horsman, in *The Causes of the War of 1812* (Philadelphia, 1961), have stressed the complicated origins of the war and the importance of European affairs in bringing on the final rupture in Anglo-American relations. Perkins has also drawn attention to the importance of economic matters in relation to the Orders in Council, and he has pointed out Madison's inability to act with determination. Roger Brown, in *The Republic in Peril: 1812* (New York, 1964), has carefully analyzed the part of party division in the coming of the war and has also questioned Madison's qualities of leadership. In *Foreign Policies of the Founding Fathers* (East Lansing, Mich., 1963), Paul Varg suggests that Madison's policies were idealistic but argues that he could use power politics when it suited his interest and that the president inclined toward France as a counterweight to the pro-British proclivities of Hamilton.

A careful study of the period that emphasizes maritime factors in bringing on the war is A. L. Burt, *The United States, Great Britain, and British North America from the Revolution to the Establishment of Peace after the War of 1812* (New Haven, 1940). An interpretation of the war that stresses the role of the West is the old but still provocative work by Julius Pratt, *The Expansionists of 1812* (New York, 1925). This should perhaps be read in conjunction with Warren H. Goodman's introduction to the historiography of the causes of the war, "The Origins of the War of 1812: A Survey of Changing Interpretations," *Mississippi Valley Historical Review* 28 (1941–42), 171–86. An excellent account of the war, its causes, and the diplomacy that ended it appears in Harry L. Coles, *The War of 1812* (Chicago, 1965), a volume in the Chicago History of American Civilization series.

The diplomacy of Ghent is discussed in the following: Fred L. Engelman, *The Peace of Christmas Eve* (New York, 1962), F. A. Updyke, *The Diplomacy of the War of 1812* (Baltimore, 1915), Raymond Walters, Jr., *Albert Gallatin: Jeffersonian Financier and Diplomat* (New York, 1957), and Bradford Perkins, *Castlereagh and Adams: England and the United States, 1812–1823* (Berkeley, 1964).

A nicely written and provocative view of the president's approach to the problem of war or peace appears in Abbot Smith, "Mr. Madison's War," *Political Science Quarterly* 57 (1942), 229–46. In an illuminating essay, Walter LaFeber has argued that Madison worked for the territorial expansion needed by the rapidly growing American population, pressed for mercantile laws to develop manufacturing and agriculture, and saw that domestic faction could be absorbed in an expanding empire on land and sea. LaFeber's views appear in "Foreign Policies of a New Nation," in William Appleman Williams, ed., *From Colony to Empire* (New York, 1972). Irving Brant's multivolume biography of the president, *James Madison*, 6 vols. (Indianapolis, 1941–61), strives—not always successfully —to restore his stature as a statesman. Brant argues that in order for Madison to be effective in diplomacy he needed to deal with men whose understanding matched his own. The absence of such qualities in the president's opponents added to the partisan opposition at home that soon bordered on disloyalty. One of the most recent and distinguished studies of Madison, Marvin Meyers, *The Mind of the Founder: Sources of the Political Thought of James Madison* (Indianapolis, 1973), suggests that Madison's contribution to the founding of America should not be underestimated and that throughout his career he remained the finest and foremost voice of eighteenth-century liberalism. It has been common practice to rank Madison as an "average" president, in the class of Hayes or Hoover, but as Leonard Levy has suggested, the time has come for a reassessment of Madison's extraordinary talents and accomplishments.

JOHN QUINCY ADAMS

Reproduced from the collections of
the Library of Congress

Empiricism and Empire

Norman A. Graebner

John Quincy Adams was born to opportunity. He was scarcely twenty-two years of age when his father took the oath of office as the country's first vice-president. John Adams's earlier diplomatic tours had permitted his son to study in England and Holland and to serve as secretary to the American legation in St. Petersburg. The Adams family heritage, moreover, had prepared him well for the heady intellectual environment of sharp minds and sharper pens that emerged with the new government. Never again would national debate reach those early standards. Thomas Jefferson and James Madison were much in the vanguard, but the younger Adams, by nature and upbringing, preferred the style and thought of the high Federalists, led by Alexander Hamilton. This became especially true after 1793 when national controversy moved into the realm of external policy. Adams learned his lessons well. More than any other American he carried the Federalist tradition in foreign affairs into the subsequent age of the Virginia dynasty.

Historians have judged John Quincy Adams the most accomplished diplomatist in this country's history. Such distinguished performance required above all solid intellectual formulations of policy. That Adams possessed remarkable qualities of mind was evident long before 1817. His unique perceptions of international affairs first emerged when he defended President George Washington's Neutrality Proclamation in April and May 1793. The *Marcellus* papers, which preceded by two months the appearance of Hamilton's noted *Pacificus*, revealed at the outset the fundamentals that would guide Adams's thought and action throughout his diplomatic career. His rejection of the plea that the United States support France dwelt on the importance of interest and power, not good intentions, in the conduct of foreign relations. Having treaties of peace with France, England, Holland, and Prussia, the nation had no corresponding obligation to judge the merits of their respective causes. While men might privately lament the impending bloodshed and misery of the world, a nation far removed from Europe, a nation whose happiness depended upon freedom from all European interests and politics, had a duty to remain "the peaceable and silent, though sorrowful spectators of the sanguinary scene." Neutrality, believed Adams, would serve the interests of American commerce; partisanship would serve no countervailing purpose. Had the king of France remained on his throne and inaugurated the existing war against Europe, the French treaty of alliance—the legal and moral foundation of the pro-French arguments leveled at the Washington administration—could impose no obligation on the United States. No treaty, Adams argued, "can ever oblige one nation to adopt or support the folly or injustice of another." How could the United States aid the French cause when France had declared war on all the naval powers of Europe? To rush to their aid would risk destruction and ruin.

Adams's able defense of Washington's controversial policies propelled him into long periods of service abroad. The president assigned him to the Netherlands in 1794; his father, when he became president, kept him in Berlin from 1797 to 1801. Shortly after his return to the United States, Adams entered the Senate and there defended the troubled foreign policies of Thomas Jefferson and James Madison against the assaults of the New England Federalists, his erstwhile allies. In 1809, Adams again went abroad, this time as Madison's appointed minister to St. Petersburg. Whatever the contribution of Adams's diplomatic experience in Europe to his ability as secretary of state, he himself was not greatly impressed by his early achievements.

In external characteristics Adams scarcely resembled the suave, even-tempered, reassuring diplomatist of the classic mold. He was short and bald, with a belligerent demeanor and a rheumy affliction that caused his eyes to run incessantly. If he at times antagonized his associates, he was scarcely more charitable toward himself. On one occasion he confided in his diary: "I am not satisfied with myself this day, having talked too much at dinner. . . . Yet, in the estimation of others, I pass off on the whole better when I talk freely than when silent and reserved. This sometimes stimulates me to talk more than is wise or proper. . . . Nor can I always (I did not this day) altogether avoid a dogmatical and peremptory tone and manner, always disgusting, and especially offensive in persons to whose age or situation others consider some deference due." On occasion Adams's diary notes were even more pitiless; he saw himself as "a man of reserved, cold, austere, and forbidding manners; my political adversaries say, a gloomy misanthropist, and my personal enemies, an unsocial savage. With a knowledge of the actual defect in my character, I have not the pliability to reform it."

Beyond his dogged convictions that neither time nor circumstance would alter, Adams possessed every other quality essential for diplomatic distinction. His understanding of Europe and its relationship to the New World was profound. He understood with equal precision the limits of effective American diplomacy. For Adams no less than for Washington and Hamilton, United States foreign policy had one major purpose: to serve the interests of this country, defined in commercial and geographical terms. He recognized, as had Hamilton in the *Federalist*, the natural separation of the New World from the Old and the essential advantages the United States enjoyed in its world relationships. Throughout his career Adams denied that a genuine foreign policy could pursue abstract objectives. If he favored liberty, he refused to anchor the nation's foreign policies to its achievement. The means of enforcement, he knew, were not within his control; nor could such an objective be the subject of fruitful negotiations.

European diplomats always found Adams direct, reliable, and realistic. Even when he insisted on the diplomatic equivalent of any concession and refused to surrender any advantage, diplomats found him simple mannered and courteous. On occasion they noted his reserve; but one foreign diplomat in St. Petersburg described him as a bulldog among spaniels.

Adams's residence in St. Petersburg during the closing years of the Napoleonic Wars made him a natural choice to represent the United States in the negotiations with Britain at Ghent after the War of 1812. With the establishment of peace in 1815, Madison transferred him to London where, like his father in 1785, he assumed the task of negotiating issues left unresolved by war.

◇◇◇

In 1817 the third member of the Virginia dynasty, James Monroe, invited Adams to join his cabinet as secretary of state; John Adams advised his son to accept. Jefferson lauded Monroe's choice, noting their complementary characters: "Adams has a pointed pen; Monroe has judgment enough for both and firmness enough to have *his* judgment control." Jefferson's was a Republican view, recognizing differences in personality, not philosophy. Monroe and Adams had occupied opposite poles during the great debates of the Washington years, and Adams's earlier convictions were as firm as ever. "The President, I am sure," he wrote to his mother, "will neither require nor expect from me any sacrifice of principles inconsistent with my sense of right." That the two men functioned as an effective team measured not only the overwhelming conversion of the Republicans in power to the older Federalist notions of proper diplomatic behavior, but also Adams's acceptance of his subordinate role in policy making.

Adams managed the technical aspects of diplomacy with remarkable skill. His diligence compelled him to read all dispatches sent and received by the State Department. Monroe, equally experienced in foreign affairs, maintained a close surveillance over Adams's correspondence. When, on occasion, Adams objected to Monroe's presidential statements or accepted them only after futile argument, it was because the president had again reacted to events abroad from the standard of simple Republican virtue rather than from a clear recognition of the interests and genuine intentions of the United States. Ultimately it was Adams and not Monroe who gave leadership and direction to American foreign relations during the eight years of their close association.

Adams worked independently, often as a minority of one. He

Henry E. Huntington Library and Art Gallery

alone among the nation's leaders knew Europe's leading statesmen personally, especially Czar Alexander, Talleyrand, and Castlereagh. Although Adams believed that his perceptions were keener than those of his less experienced cabinet colleagues, members of Monroe's powerful cabinet opposed him on numerous occasions. Recognizing both the secretary's independence of mind and his refusal to accept views regarded as rash by the diplomatic corps, the French minister, Hyde de Neuville, wrote of Adams, "I know that he has dared to declare himself very strongly on many occasions against indiscreet and purely speculative ideas."

For Adams partisanship was as dangerous as it was inexcusable. Earlier he had lamented the Jeffersonian attacks on Washington's foreign policies as well as the opposition of the New England Federalists to Jefferson and Madison. Of all the wartime deformities in need of elimination, the most disgusting was the "rancorous spirit of faction." To Adams, unrestrained partisanship was rooted in politics and personal ambition; to his critics, therefore, he would seldom attribute sincerity.

Adams believed that his judgments should be measured by recognized standards of propriety, their accuracy in reflecting world conditions, and their possible contribution to the country's welfare. He rebuked the members of the press who criticized him far more savagely than he did those diplomats who sometimes appeared unnecessarily obdurate: "There is not one [editor] whose friendship is worth buying, nor one whose enmity is not formidable. They are a sort of assassins who sit with loaded blunderbusses at the corner of streets and fire them off for hire or for sport at any passenger whom they select." More pointedly Adams passed judgment in his diary on the editors of the *Aurora* and the *Democratic Press*, both of Philadelphia: "They are both men of considerable talents and profligate principles, always for sale to the highest bidder, and always insupportable burdens, by their insatiable rapacity, to the parties they support."

If, as secretary, Adams faced opposition in the cabinet, the Congress, and the press, he towered over the Washington diplomatic corps. Those compelled to negotiate with him never ceased to admire his intelligence and learning, his industry and self-discipline, his unwavering pursuit of his country's interests, which he grasped more surely than any other man of his age. Adversaries questioned only his doggedness and disposition. British Minister Stratford Canning described Adams in his memoirs as "much above par in general ability, but having the air of a scholar rather than statesman, a very uneven temper, a disposition at times well-meaning, a manner somewhat too often domineering. . . ."

The professional respect Adams enjoyed rested in large measure on the essential honesty of his policies. For him the path of virtue was not always clear, nor would it always be crowned with success; but he believed that an otherwise sound policy would be wiser and more enduring if it were essentially virtuous. Perhaps there were occasions, especially in time of war, when deception was justifiable; but fraud was never acceptable when force would not be equally justified. Fraud must be practiced sparingly, he warned, for it "tends when discovered to impair the confidence of mankind in the sincerity and integrity of him who uses it." Stephen Decatur had offered his famous toast, "Our country! . . . may she always be in the right; but our country, right or wrong." Adams would disagree: "I cannot ask of heaven success, even for my country, in a cause where she should be in the wrong. . . . I disclaim as unsound all patriotism incompatible with the principles of eternal justice. But the truth is that the American union, while united, *may* be certain of success in every rightful cause, and may if it pleases never have any but a rightful cause to maintain."

From the beginning Adams recognized the limits of American power and influence in Europe. Toward the Continent, emerging from a quarter-century of war, he urged a posture of strict neutrality. Europe, he wrote in 1815, "consists only of victors and vanquished, between whom no permanent state of social repose can exist. May we persevere in the system of keeping aloof from all their broils, and in that of consolidating and perpetuating our own union." In his noted oration of 4 July 1821, Adams insisted that the United States had conducted its foreign relations in a spirit of friendliness and reciprocity; it had recognized the independence of other countries and maintained its own. America sympathized with the cause of liberty. "Wherever the standard of freedom and Independence has been or shall be unfurled," Adams said, "there will her heart, her benedictions and her prayers be. But she goes not abroad, in search of monsters to destroy. She is the well-wisher to the freedom and independence of all. She is the champion and vindicator only of her own. She will commend the general cause by . . . the benignant sympathy of her example." Any shift from liberty to force, he warned, might make the United

States dictatress of the world and no longer the ruler of its own spirit. To his principle of neutrality Adams added that of nonintervention.

Toward the North American continent Adams was an expansionist, but one who looked to geography, not to war. He believed that the continent was destined to be one nation in language, religion, society, and politics. During November 1819, Secretary of the Treasury William H. Crawford informed him that many British and French citizens regarded the United States as ambitious and encroaching. Adams replied that to argue otherwise would be useless: "Nothing that we could say or do would remove this impression until the world shall be familiarized with the idea of considering our proper dominion to be the continent of North America. From the time when we became an independent people it was as much a law of nature that this should become our pretension as that the Mississippi should flow to the sea." A year later, in conversation with Stratford Canning over the future of Oregon, Adams declared that the London government had certainly concluded that "there would be neither policy nor profit in cavilling with us about territory on this North American continent." When Canning asked if the secretary included Canada in his claims, Adams responded: "No, there the boundary is marked, and we have no disposition to encroach upon it. Keep what is yours, but leave the rest of the continent to us."

To underwrite his hopes for peace and security in a still challenging world, Adams looked to a stronger union, based on centralized government, and to a reasonable level of military preparedness. "No nation can enjoy freedom and independence," he wrote, "without being always prepared to defend them by force of arms." He once reminded Monroe, "We shall have no valuable friends in Europe until we have proved that we can defend ourselves without them." Adequate power—which Adams doubted the country would ever create except in time of war— dared not encourage a mood of belligerency, however. He advised the country to employ every means available to settle disputes amicably and never to enter a war "without a fair prospect of attaining its objects," nor should it remain in a war unless the gains were clearly commensurate with the costs. Such principles and purposes guided him in every diplomatic confrontation of his secretarial years.

◇◇◇

European statesmen recognized the importance of France to the restoration of the European balance of power after the Napoleonic Wars. The allies desired a great and powerful France because French power was "one of the essential foundations of the social structure" of the Continent. The restoration of the Bourbons, as even the British agreed, would serve the interests of all nations in a stable Europe. Despite the later condemnation of the Congress of Vienna for its free assignment of territory, the decisions of that notable international conference underwrote the principle of balance. The Quadruple Alliance that followed in November 1815 represented the efforts of Europe's leading statesmen to carry into peacetime the equilibrium created by the coalition against Napoleon. The later conferences at Troppau (1820), Laibach (1821), and Verona (1822), which adopted interventionist policies toward Italy, Spain, and Portugal, split the great powers. British leaders could detect no threat in liberal uprisings to the allied purpose of maintaining Europe's essential equilibrium. Castlereagh, Britain's greatest foreign minister, broke down in 1822 over his failure to nullify Europe's reactionary policies and took his own life. His brilliant successor, George Canning, withdrew British participation from the affairs of the Quadruple Alliance.

Americans could scarcely approve the principles that guided the Congress of Vienna. Much of the press ridiculed the Vienna settlements because of their apparent disregard for national sovereignty in their high-handed redistribution of territory. American writers were equally distrustful of the principle of legitimacy that restored the monarchs to their thrones. Europe, it seemed, had returned to an age of despotism. Even Czar Alexander's Holy Alliance (formed at Paris in September 1815 by Austria, Russia, and Prussia), with its large standing armies, seemed devoted less to peace and justice than to repression and war. To American observers Europe appeared unstable, harboring ideals far different from those of the United States and filled with combustible materials that any spark could reignite into war. *Niles' Register* in August 1817 warned its readers that the United States could hardly trust the friendship of monarchies. Adams had expressed similar fears: "The Royalists everywhere detest and despise us as Republicans." He later repeated his doubts: "There is already in all governments of Europe a strong prejudice against us as Republicans, and as the primary causes of the propagation of those political principles, which still make the throne of every European monarch rock under him as with the throes of an earthquake. . . ."

Adams recognized the fundamental purpose of Europe's postwar state system: to prevent the resurrection of preponderant power and to restrain threats to the region's stability; but with time he also became critical of the czar's Holy Alliance, complaining that Europe had cast off Napoleon only to return to divine right. Still, through subsequent years the league appeared successful, at least in Europe; in Latin America the challenge to the status quo seemed too distant for the European powers to control. Adams saw clearly that threats to Europe's stability were internal, that tensions endangering the peace centered on relations between peoples and their rulers. He saw clearly why Russia's Alexander patronized the European system: "His territories are the most extensive, his military establishment the most stupendous, his country the most improvable and thriving of them all. . . . his circumstances point his policy to a faithful adherence to the general system, with a strong reprobation of those who would resort to special and partial alliances, from which any one member of the league should be excluded."

Eventually the czar suggested that America concur in the principles of the European league and become a formal member. The compact bound members only to the preservation of peace, and should the United States find itself at odds with one or more members of the Holy Alliance, it could count on the interposition of the czar in its behalf. In precise diplomatic language, Adams instructed Henry Middleton, United States minister in Russia, to reject any such proposal: "As a general declaration of principles, . . . the United States, not only give their hearty assent to the articles of the Holy Alliance, but will be among the most earnest and conscientious in observing them. But . . . for the repose of Europe as well as of America, the European and American political systems should be kept as separate and distinct from each other as possible."

If Europe's great powers desisted, because of predictable costs, from imposing on one another, they scarcely seemed capable of imposing on the New World. Europe's balance served the American interest in achieving a stable and independent hemisphere, but it did not necessarily equalize the capacity of the European powers to influence American affairs or even their intention of doing so. Toward France both the administration and the press expressed indifference. They regarded that power as neither f iend nor enemy. The French government, fearful of British influence in the United States, anticipated considerable benefit from maintaining close and friendly ties with Washington. Shortly after the Congress of Vienna Adams reminded Monroe that Continental powers such as France would attempt to separate the United States from England, but France by itself posed no threat.

Russia, like France, seemed to lack the power or the intention to challenge American interest in the New World. Observant Americans recognized the contrast between the government and society of Russia and of the United States, but they harbored no feelings of fear or distrust. Adams admitted that he trusted Czar Alexander more than any other monarch in Europe. As a Continental power with a large army, Russia wielded major influence in Europe and the Middle East; elsewhere Britain exerted a moderating influence on Russian ambition. Indeed, many Americans, Adams among them, hoped that Anglo-Russian rivalry would restrict the power of both countries outside the Eastern Hemisphere.

The complacency that determined American attitudes toward the Continent did not exist with regard to England, which had the power, and seemingly the interest, to interfere in American affairs. Adams had hoped that Napoleon's retention of power in France might serve as a counterweight to British power. There was little conviction in the United States after 1814, however, that England, having shaken off the restraints of France, would convert the Treaty of Ghent into an instrument of peace. The press freely predicted renewed war, although not necessarily in the immediate future. Adams shared this postwar distrust of England. He wrote to his mother, Abigail, that although British ascendancy in Europe would decline, that country would continue to seek the ruin of the United States. British animosity toward France had been satiated by victory, but, warned Adams, "their feelings against America are keener, more jealous, more envious, more angry than ever."

Believing the United States to be in danger because of Britain, Adams was bitterly critical of the peace societies that not only opposed armaments but also placed enormous faith in the czar's ability to maintain peace. Old John Adams expressed his son's view when he addressed the Masssachusetts Peace Society in July 1816: "Our beloved country, sir, is surrounded by enemies of the most dangerous, because the most powerful and most unprincipled character. Collisions of national interest, of commercial and manufacturing rivalries, are multiplying around us. Instead of discouraging a martial spirit, in my opinion it ought to be excited. We have not enough of it to defend us by sea or land." Similarly, John Quincy later complained that the peace societies, by corresponding with the czar, were endangering the security of the United States. Instead of championing the position of America, these groups were openly endorsing the ideas and leadership of a foreign ruler who had his share of faults and ambitions. Adams believed that it was time for Americans to concentrate on matters at home and devote their energies to more productive enterprises.

⟨⟨⟩⟩

For Adams peace with England was essential for American security and well-being. Britain alone of Europe's leading states had the power to injure the United States. "My special duty at present," Adams wrote from London in May 1816, "is to preach peace. . . . I am deeply convinced that peace is the state best adapted to the interest and happiness of both nations." As secretary a year later he resumed negotiations which he had begun in London on issues still unsettled since Ghent. During the peace negotiations of 1782 his father had sought the dismantling of all fortifications along the Canadian-American frontier. After the War of 1812 the younger Adams had pressed the British for such an agreement, but again without success. Still undaunted, Adams repeated the offer in London during March 1816. The British government, hoping to avoid a naval race with the United States on the Great Lakes, finally accepted Adams's overture. The result was the Rush-Bagot Agreement, signed in Washington during April 1817, which limited British and American naval armaments on the lakes to those required for the enforcement of customs regulations. This treaty, the first reciprocal naval disarmament agreement in modern history, removed a potential source of friction and expense and admirably served the interests of both Britain and the United States.

During the following year Adams achieved the long-standing

American quest for fishing rights off the Labrador and Newfoundland coasts. While in London he insisted that in the original
division of the empire in 1783, Britain had granted the inshore
fisheries on the northern coasts to the United States. The British
agreed to American fishing on the high seas and suspended
trespass proceedings against New England fishermen. Adams later
resumed his conversations on the fisheries question, determined
to eliminate the English use of the word "liberty" when referring
to American access to both the Grand Banks and the open seas.
Privately Adams was opposed to compromise, preferring that the
administration demand full American fishing rights along the
northern coasts and establish them by force if necessary. Over-
ruled by Monroe, Adams proposed that the United States forfeit
the right of drying and curing on the shore and reserve full rights
to fishing. Ultimately Albert Gallatin, who managed the final
negotiations in 1818, achieved more extensive inshore fishing
rights than Adams's instructions had demanded. The new treaty
granted American fishermen permission not only to catch fish
along extensive sections of the northern coasts but also to dry and
cure fish on any of the unsettled coasts of Labrador. The British
resisted the American effort to guarantee these fishing rights even
in time of war, but, as a compromise, they granted Americans
liberty "for ever" to take fish along the northern coasts.

As late as 1815 the United States and Britain had conducted a
flourishing trade without benefit of any formal commercial treaty.
On 3 July of that year Adams signed a commercial convention in
London that, except for the prohibition of discriminatory duties,
merely reaffirmed existing practice. The convention provided for
reciprocal consulates, freedom of commerce between the United
States and British territories in Europe, as well as equality of
treatment of the products, ships, citizens, and subjects of each
country in the ports of the other. The convention permitted
American ships to trade in the British ports of Calcutta, Madras,
Bombay, and Penang in South Asia.

Unfortunately the Anglo-American convention of July 1815
failed to gain full reciprocal arrangements, for Britain refused to
permit American ships in the saltwater ports of British North
America and the British West Indies. These restrictions, by
permitting English traders to engage in a triangle traffic denied to
Americans, canceled the advantages of full reciprocity in direct
United States–British commerce. For Adams this policy was totally

objectionable. The regulation of commerce, he wrote, "should be by arrangements to which both parties consent and in which due regard is paid to the interests of both."

Adams confronted the uncompromising London government with a series of congressional acts in 1817, 1818, and 1820 that imposed special tonnage duties on British ships entering the United States from ports closed to American vessels, and Congress eventually eliminated the importation of all British West Indian goods except those brought directly from the colony where they were grown. These restrictions injured the West Indian economy and prompted Parliament to open some colonial ports to American ships in 1822. At the same time it enumerated American products that might compete with those of Canada. In March 1823, Congress, under Adams's direction, opened United States ports to British ships coming from colonial ports, but only from those ports to which American ships were admitted. At the same time Congress authorized the president to impose a 10 percent discriminatory tariff on colonial goods imported in British vessels until London eliminated all colonial preferences. By 1826 the British had again cut off American trade with their West Indian islands. Adams failed to negotiate conditions of greater reciprocity than those that had existed in 1822.

◇◇◇

Adams's success in defining the boundaries of the Louisiana Purchase demonstrated the breadth of his vision and the virtuosity of his performance. In the Convention of 1818 with England he negotiated the boundary line from the Lake of the Woods westward along the forty-ninth parallel to the Rocky Mountains. West of the Rockies, however, British fur-trading interests were centered south of that parallel, largely along the valley of the Columbia River. London, therefore, demanded the Columbia as the boundary between the mountains and the Pacific. Adams, who would settle for no less than a usable port along the Oregon shore, had been convinced by New England seamen that the Columbia River would never meet that need, largely because of the dangers of the bar that blocked its entrance. He understood also that the Juan de Fuca Strait and Puget Sound (both north of the Columbia but south of 49°) constituted one of the world's best inland waterways. For these reasons Adams demanded no less than the extension of the forty-ninth parallel to the Pacific. When British negotiators proved intractable on this point, Adams agreed to a policy of joint occupancy with Britain in the Oregon country west of the Rockies for a period of ten years, an arrangement that either country could terminate on one year's notice. Thus Adams delayed the final Oregon settlement until a time when the diplomatic advantage would pass to the United States.

Adams's subsequent diplomatic achievement, perhaps his greatest, came in 1819 when in the Adams-Onís Treaty he not only aquired Florida for the United States but also defined the southern boundary of the Louisiana Purchase from the Gulf of Mexico to the Pacific Ocean. Florida in 1817 was still under Spanish rule, but that region had become a problem for the United States government—and for the citizens of Georgia—simply because the Madrid regime was too plagued with political and military disorders elsewhere to maintain order in its colony. British adventurers in Florida periodically armed and incited the Indians to raid north of the boundary. Monroe dispatched General Andrew Jackson to punish the Indians for their destruction of American lives and property. Carrying out his instructions with considerable vigor, Jackson in 1818 pursued a band of marauding Indians into Florida where he captured and executed two British agents as well as two Indian chiefs. Spain protested the action, and Jackson's enemies in Congress demanded his dismissal.

President Monroe and all members of the cabinet, except Adams, agreed. They argued that Jackson had exceeded his instructions and committed an act of war against Spain, which required an official disavowal. Adams reminded the cabinet that Jackson's actions were defensive, that he had entered Florida not to make war on Spain, but to terminate the Indian depredations. Jackson had discretionary powers; to disavow them, believed Adams, was unthinkable. He admitted in his diary that he had pushed his case to the limit; but he added, "If the question was dubious, it was better to err on the side of vigor than of weakness—on the side of our own officer . . . than on the side of our bitterest enemies. . . ." Adams's argument carried. On 23 July 1818 the secretary charged to the complaining Spanish minister, Don Luis de Onís, that Spain had an obligation under treaty to keep order in Florida. The fort at St. Mark would be restored only to a Spanish force strong enough to hold it against an Indian attack. Peace between the United States and Spain, he warned, required that "henceforth the stipulations by Spain to restrain by force her Indians from all hostilities against the United States should be faithfully and effectually fulfilled." If Spain could not control the Indians, then it had no choice but to cede Florida to the United States.

Meanwhile on 10 July 1818 the French minister in Washington, Hyde de Neuville, informed Adams that Spain, recognizing its weakness, would cede Florida to the United States, provided that Washington would assume the claims of American citizens against Spain, estimated at some five million dollars. Onís immediately took up the negotiations, raising the issue of the still undefined southern boundary of the Louisiana Purchase. Spain hoped to push the line eastward and northward as far as possible; Adams sought a boundary that would bring as much of Texas and the Southwest as possible into the United States. Onís, on 11 July, proposed a western boundary that would separate the United States from Spanish Mexico at a line moving northward between Adeas and Natchitoches to the Red River and thence to the Missouri. Adams rejected this outright. So uncompromising was Madrid that in October Adams threatened to break off the negotiations. Then on 31 October the secretary presented a note to Onís outlining what he termed the final United States offer. The boundary was to be a line running from the mouth of the Sabine River to its source, from there north to the Red River and its source in the southern Rockies, up into the mountains to the forty-first parallel, and from there west to the ocean. This was altered slightly by Adams in the course of the negotiation.

By 15 February Onís had agreed to Adams's revised boundary, including the forty-second parallel, but he insisted that the river lines follow the middle rather than the south bank of the streams. Adams countered that Spain would have no settlements near those rivers and that the middle of streams never lent themselves to precise lines of demarcation. He insisted before the cabinet that the United States adhere to the principle of owning the rivers and islands in them. On 20 February Onís capitulated, observing that Adams had given him more trouble than the president. The Spanish minister recalled the words a suitor once addressed to Philip IV: "Sire, your Majesty has no influence with the Minister of Grace and Justice, for he refuses me what you have granted."

On 22 February 1819, Onís and Adams signed the Transcontinental Treaty. "It was, perhaps," he wrote in his diary, "the most important day of my life. . . . May no disappointment embitter the hope which this event warrants us in cherishing, and may its future influence on the destinies of my country be as extensive and as favorable as our warmest anticipations can paint! " Later, members of Congress urged Adams to put the treaty aside and claim the Rio Grande. The secretary reminded one congressman who came to criticize that he and Henry Clay were excellent negotiators in theory. Then he leveled a strong rebuke: "In the negotiations with Spain we had a just claim to the Mississippi and its waters, and our citizens had a fair though very precarious claim to indemnities. We had a mere color of claim to the Rio del Norte, no claim to a line beyond the Rocky Mountains, and none to Florida, which we very much wanted. The treaty . . . barely gives up to Spain the colorable claim from the Sabine to the Rio del Norte. Now, negotiation implies some concession upon both sides. If after obtaining every object of your pursuit but one, and that one weak in principle and of no present value, what would you have offered to Spain to yield that also?" The congressman had no answer.

◇◇◇

Spain's challenge to the United States lay not only in that nation's weakness in Florida but also in its precarious position throughout the Western Hemisphere. Napoleon's invasion of Spain in 1808 had terminated Madrid's effective control of Spanish America. Provisional *juntas* maintained by Spain's ruling classes continued to claim jurisdiction over the empire, but by 1812 their New World influence was purely nominal. Freed of Spain's commercial restrictions, the various regions of Latin America opened their commerce to the world. British and Yankee ships entered South American ports in large numbers. When war broke out between the restored Spanish monarchy and the now rebellious colonies, the struggling South Americans looked to the United States for economic, military, and moral support.

Within the United States, editors, congressmen, and administration officials favored Latin American independence with almost total unanimity; but on the proper national response to Latin America's plight there was no agreement at all. Abbé de Pradt, the prolific European writer, emphasized not only the importance of Latin America to Europe but also the possibility that, inasmuch as

Spanish control was doomed, the great European powers might establish the region's independence on terms that would keep the new nations attached to Europe. Determined to sever Europe's ties with the New World, editors led by William Duane of the *Aurora* demanded United States guardianship of Latin American independence. In Latin America, he argued, this nation would find "the corrective of European jealousy, and the resources with which to defeat and counterplace the intolerant and malignant selfishness of European nations." In Congress the powerful Clay denounced the administration for neglecting American interests and the cause of liberty.

Monroe and Adams would not be stampeded. They recognized the overwhelming preference of their countrymen for Latin American independence, but they refused to commit the United States before the European powers had revealed their intentions or the patriots of South America had demonstrated their capacity to establish their independence and maintain a semblance of order. The open congressional support for Latin America appalled Adams. "There seemed to me," he complained in June 1816, "too much of the warlike humor in the debates of Congress—propositions even to take up the cause of the South Americans; predictions of wars with this country to the end of time, as cool and as causeless, as if they were talking of the expense of building a light house. . . ."

As the public pressure for involvement continued, Adams reminded his father that Latin America had replaced the French Revolution as the great source of discord in the United States: "The republican spirit of our country not only sympathizes with people struggling in a cause, . . . but it is working into indignation against the relapse of Europe into the opposite principle of monkery and despotism. And now, as at the early stage of the French Revolution, we have ardent spirits who are for rushing into the conflict, without looking to the consequences." Because he doubted that the people of South America were capable of self-government, Adams viewed the revolutions with little sympathy. Monroe, who was somewhat more sympathetic, argued that the United States could render Latin Americans no service more useful than to refrain from any action that might provoke direct European intervention. He explained his views in a letter to Jackson in December 1818, although later he omitted the key passage: "By this policy we have lost nothing, as *by keeping the*

Allies out of the quarrel, Florida must soon be ours, and *the Colonies must be independent, for if they cannot beat Spain, they do not deserve to be free.*"

During 1818 the ultimate course of United States policy toward Latin America began to emerge. In March, Monroe requested a congressional appropriation for a commission of inquiry to South America. Hoping to compel the administration to recognize the independence of the Argentine, Clay attached an amendment appropriating eighteen thousand dollars for a United States legation in Buenos Aires, and he even stepped down from the Speaker's rostrum to enter a strong plea for his measure; but the House remained unconvinced and voted down the amendment, 115 to 45. Shortly thereafter Adams expressed his contempt for Congress in his diary: "The present session will stand remarkable in the annals of the Union for showing how a legislature can keep itself employed when having nothing to do. . . ." The proposed appropriation "for a minister to Buenos Ayres has gone the way of other things lost upon earth, like the purchase of oil for light houses in the western country." In July the president's fact-finding commission returned to Washington, hopelessly divided. Still the administration continued to respond to changing conditions both in Europe and in Latin America. By the summer of 1818 Monroe and Adams concluded that the great European states would never agree on measures to restore Spanish sovereignty in South America, especially since Britain clearly favored independence. At the Conference of Aix-la-Chapelle, which opened in September 1818, England opposed the use of force against the Latin Americans; but Castlereagh's rejection of Adams's suggestion for a concerted British-American policy encouraged further caution in Washington.

Throughout 1819 and 1820 Adams moved slowly and deliberately, proclaiming official American neutrality toward the struggles of Latin America though reminding Monroe that any successful revolution eventually reaches a stage when those fighting for independence merit recognition when that recognition no longer constitutes a departure from the obligations of neutrality. He warned the president, however, that the justice of a cause was not in itself "sufficient to justify third parties in siding with it." Finally in February 1821, ratified copies of the Transcontinental Treaty were exchanged in Washington. This eliminated the one remaining international argument against recognition of Latin Amer-

ican independence. That year the striking victories of the revolutionary forces all but destroyed Spain's remaining authority in
South America. Clay secured passage of two resolutions in the
House, one expressing interest in South American independence,
the other encouraging the president to recognize the independence of the new nations whenever he believed it expedient.
Shortly thereafter, in March 1821, Clay and Adams discussed Latin
America at length, each regretting their years of deep disagreement, though Adams still argued the administration's case for
delay. "That the final issue of their present struggle would be their
entire independence of Spain I have never doubted. That it was
our true policy and duty to take no part in the contest I was
equally clear. . . . So far as they were contending for independence, I wished well to their cause; but I had seen and yet see no
prospect that they would establish free or liberal institutions of
government. . . . Arbitrary power, military and ecclesiastical, was
stamped upon their education, upon their habits, and upon all
their institutions. Civil dissension was infused into all their seminal
principles. War and mutual destruction was in every member of
their organization, moral, political, and physical. I had little
expectation of any beneficial result to this country from any future
connection with them, political or commercial."

Monroe recognized the changing conditions in a special
message to Congress on 8 March 1822. He declared that Chile, the
United Provinces of the Plata (Argentina), Peru, Colombia, and
Mexico were fully independent and thus could rightfully claim
recognition by other nations. Congress responded by appropriating funds to meet the expense of "such missions to the independent nations on the American continent as the President might
deem proper." After formal recognition of the five new states,
Latin American representatives added both numbers and variety to
the Washington diplomatic corps.

Further delay, Monroe explained to Madison, would have
produced deep resentment in Latin America and opened the way
for renewed European encroachments. Even as Monroe sought the
exclusion of European influence from the Western Hemisphere he
reassured the European powers that the United States had no
intention of controlling the new governments or of creating a
separate American system. Neither Monroe nor Adams revealed
much concern for the nature of the Latin American regimes; nor
did they favor the immediate assignment of ministers to the new

capitals. No commercial treaties, based on reciprocity, could possibly affect Britain's dominance of Latin America's foreign trade. A race with England for markets or monopolies in the new nations was in Adams's view "neither a wise nor an honest policy."

◇◇◇

Britain made clear its commercial and political preference for Latin American independence at the Conference of Aix-la-Chapelle in 1818. Britain's new foreign minister in 1822, George Canning, refused to follow the American lead out of deference to Spain and the Holy Alliance. So guarded had been Monroe's recognition policy that it produced no break with Spain. British policy, unlike that in Washington, focused on Europe, especially when the Holy Alliance, over London's objection, voted to send a French army into Spain to put down a liberal revolt. In 1822 when the invading French successfully restored Ferdinand VII to his full royal prerogatives in Spain, Canning suspected that France might attempt to restore the Spanish empire as well. Even more threatening was the possibility that France might use its influence in Spain to lay the foundation for another French empire in America. In 1823 Canning warned the Paris government against any move to acquire portions of Spanish America by conquest or cession. When French policy in Spain continued to cause unease in London, Canning in August turned to Richard Rush, the American minister, suggesting that Britain and the United States issue a joint declaration disavowing territorial ambitions in Latin America but warning Europe, except Spain, against intervention.

Rush was highly flattered by Canning's recognition of America's growing importance in the Atlantic world, but insisted on referring the matter to Washington unless Britain recognized the independence of the Latin American nations immediately. This Canning refused to do. Instead, he delivered a secret warning to Paris. The French government responded with the famed "Polignac Memorandum," which assured the British that it had no intention of dispatching an expedition to the New World. Thus Canning, through unilateral action, had resolved the immediate challenge to British policy.

In a long communication of 19 August 1823, Rush relayed Canning's proposal to Washington. Monroe received the dispatch on 9 October. He did not regard Europe as a threat; still he favored Canning's proposition and sought reassurance from his old friend Jefferson, in quiet retirement at Monticello, who in a classic response reiterated his concept of the two spheres which advocated the noninterference of the United States in European affairs and the noninvolvement of Europe in the affairs of the New World. For him it was imperative that this country, if it desired to maintain the status quo in the Western Hemisphere, not take a stand against the existing order in Europe. Only one nation, Britain, could challenge American interests in the New World; it was the part of wisdom, therefore, to enlist that great power in the cause of emancipating the American continents from European influence. Madison likewise endorsed Canning's proposal.

Meanwhile Adams had responded to the French invasion of Spain by reasserting the doctrine of no transfer. France's policy in Spain was not Adams's major concern; what troubled him was the possibility that Spain might cede Cuba to Britain as the price of an Anglo-Spanish alliance. In April 1823, Adams sent a long note to the American minister in Madrid, Hugh Nelson, warning the Spanish government that the United States would oppose the transfer of Cuba to any European power. Such a transfer, wrote Adams, not only would affect Spanish-American relations but would also subvert the rights of the Cuban people and justify the United States in supporting any resulting independence movement. When Canning assured Washington that Britain had no intention of acquiring the island, Monroe suggested to the cabinet that the United States issue a statement of self-denial also. Adams objected; he saw no reason for the United States to bind itself permanently against the possibility that Cuba might one day solicit union with the United States. Monroe assured London informally that the United States had no designs on Cuba.

Russia had also posed a threat to United States interests in the Western Hemisphere and provoked another historic response from Adams. Before the 1820s rumors of Russian encroachment along the Pacific coast of North America as far south as California had produced only indifference in Washington. In Adams's view, Russia lacked both the navy and the merchant marine to establish distant colonies; but in 1821 the Russian emperor issued a ukase that excluded foreigners from trading, fishing, or navigating within one hundred Italian miles of the northwest coast from the Bering Strait to the fifty-first parallel of north latitude. Both Britain and the

United States objected. At a cabinet meeting on 28 June 1823, Adams introduced the question of Russian claims. He believed the United States should contest them, especially since that country had no settlements in the disputed region. On 17 July, Adams informed the Russian minister, Baron Tuyl, that the United States would contest Russia's right to any territorial establishment on this continent and that this nation assumed the principle that "the American continents are no longer subjects for *any* new European colonial establishments." On 22 July he penned a note to Middleton in St. Petersburg: "There can, perhaps, be no better time for saying, frankly and explicitly, to the Russian Government that the future peace of the world, and the interest of Russia herself, can not be promoted by Russian settlements upon any part of the American continent. With the exception of the British establishments north of the United States, the remainder of both the American continents must henceforth be left to the management of American hands." Thus Adams asserted the principle of noncolonization.

When Monroe returned to Washington with the opinions of Jefferson and Madison corroborating his own, Russia had created another crisis. Baron Tuyl warned Adams that the czar would not recognize the new governments of Latin America and that, unless the United States remained neutral, Russia might support a European invasion of the former Spanish empire. This Russian threat merely confirmed convictions in Washington that Canning's proposal should be accepted; but Adams refused to be frightened. He doubted that France intended armed intervention in Latin America; moreover, the British navy was powerful enough to prevent it. The secretary suspected that Canning's overture was aimed less at obtaining unnecessary United States support than in preventing, through a self-denying agreement, future American expansion into Texas and the Caribbean. When the cabinet met on 7 November, Adams proposed that the United States decline the British overture and take its stand against the Holy Alliance unilaterally. "It would be more candid, as well as more dignified," he said, "to avow our principles explicitly to Russia and France, than to come in as a cock-boat in the wake of the British man-of-war."

Adams favored an overall American policy that would combine a letter to Russia with one to France in a single statement of national intent. To this Monroe agreed; but the president still hesitated to reject the British proposal. The news that France had captured Cadiz caused him to despair for the future of South America. Calhoun, equally fearful of Europe, proposed that Rush be given discretionary power to accept Canning's overture, if necessary. Adams argued that Spain had no more power to restore its control in the Western Hemisphere than had Chimborazo to sink to the bottom of the sea. "But if the South Americans were really in a state to be so easily subdued, it would be but a more forcible motive for us to beware of involving ourselves in their fate."

A week later Adams delivered his note to the Russian minister. In moderate language he explained that the United States was a republic and thus was attracted to the Latin American states by the very principles that repelled the czar. He hoped that Russia would nonetheless maintain its policy of neutrality; but Russia quickly created further alarm when another note reminded the United States of the Holy Alliance's success in putting down revolutions in Europe and its obligation to guarantee tranquillity everywhere, including Latin America. As gloom settled over the Potomac, Adams told the cabinet, "My purpose would be in a moderate and conciliatory manner, but with a firm and determined spirit, to declare our dissent from the principles avowed in those communications; to assert those upon which our own Government is founded, and while disclaiming all . . . interference with the political affairs of Europe, to declare our expectation and hope that the European powers will equally abstain from the attempt to spread their principles in the American hemisphere, or to subjugate by force any part of these continents to their will." He thus formulated the principle of "hands off"; Monroe accepted it and decided to proclaim this new American purpose toward the Western Hemisphere in his December message to Congress.

On 21 November, Monroe read a preliminary draft of his forthcoming message to the cabinet. Adams was shocked. "Its introduction," he recorded, "was in a tone of deep solemnity and of high alarm, intimating that his country is menaced by imminent and formidable dangers, such as would probably soon call for their most vigorous energies and the closest union." What distressed Adams especially was Monroe's reversion to his old Republican innocence in taking up the cause of revolution in Spain and Greece, two areas in which he had no intention of acting. He urged the president to reconsider the entire subject: "This message would be a summons to arms—to arms against all Europe, and for objects of policy exclusively European—Greece and Spain. It would be as new, too, in our policy as it would be surprising. For more than thirty years Europe had been in convulsions, . . . and we had looked on safe in our distance beyond an intervening ocean, and avowing a total forbearance to interfere in any of the combinations of European politics. This message would at once buckle on the harness and throw down the gauntlet. It would have the air of open defiance to all Europe. . . . I did not expect that the quiet which we had enjoyed for six or seven years would last much longer. The aspect of things was portentous; but if we must come to an issue with Europe, let us keep it off as long as possible."

Adams was especially disturbed at Monroe's open endorsement of the Greek independence movement, for he had long argued against United States involvement in that cause. The Greek revolutionary movement had slowly gathered strength until by 1821 it posed an immediate threat to Ottoman rule. Sultan Mahmud II retaliated with such violence and destruction that he aroused anti-Turkish sentiment throughout western Europe and the United States. In 1822 *Niles' Register*, dwelling on Turkish barbarities, chided the country for not taking up the cause of Greek liberty and independence. In his annual message of December 1822, Monroe expressed regret that a country that had contributed so much to civilization should live under a gloomy despotism, but concern for the Greek cause still languished. Then in 1823 Edward Everett, professor of Greek literature at Harvard and editor of *The North American Review*, championed Greek independence and enlisted the support of Daniel Webster. Adams remained unimpressed, and he argued strongly against any American meddling in the affairs of Greece and Turkey, especially since the country was not prepared financially or militarily to intervene. When Crawford and Calhoun in the cabinet expressed great enthusiasm for the Greeks, Adams recorded his disgust; he maintained his opposition in the critical cabinet debates on the president's message during late November.

For Adams it was essential that Monroe not antagonize the Holy Alliance needlessly. If the European powers chose to challenge the United States, Washington should meet the issue but not create it. If the Holy Alliance really intended to restore the colonies to Spain, which Adams doubted, the United States had

perhaps been too hasty in acknowledging South American independence. "If they intend now to interpose by force," Adams
warned, "we shall have as much as we can do to prevent them,
without going to bid them defiance in the heart of Europe."
Arguing steadily against any American involvement in European
affairs, Adams summarized his views before the cabinet: "The
ground that I wish to take is that of earnest remonstrance against
the interference of the European powers by force with South
America, but to disclaim all interference on our part with Europe;
to make an American cause, and adhere inflexibly to that." Adams
had added to "hands off" his principle of abstention.

This concept of two worlds Monroe embodied in his cele-
brated message to Congress on 2 December 1823. The so-called
Monroe Doctrine declared specifically that the American conti-
nents were no longer open to European colonization and that the
United States would regard any effort of the European powers to
extend their government to any portion of the Western Hemisphere as a threat to its peace and safety. On the other hand,
Monroe assured the nations of the Old World that the United
States would not interfere with their dependencies in the New
World or involve itself in purely European matters. Meanwhile
Adams prepared documents to Britain and Russia. He assured
Canning that the United States intended to pursue separate but
parallel policies in Latin America. Together Adams and Monroe
had wedded American policies to the status quo in the Atlantic, a
status quo that, if threatened, would have the defense of the
British navy itself. Adams's communication to Russia concluded
with a strong warning against European interference in the affairs
of the Western Hemisphere. The secretary regarded this dispatch,
dated 27 November 1823, as the most important state paper of his
career.

Early in 1824 Adams resolved the conflict with Russia in the
Northwest. New England traders demanded access to the fur seals
and sea otters in the Aleutians far north of 51°. Adams reminded
Stratford Canning in Washington that the United States had no
territorial claims as far north as the fifty-first parallel, and assumed
that British interests would be sufficient to counter Russian
demands. To Russia Adams suggested a boundary at 55° north
latitude. In St. Petersburg the Russian government accepted
Adams's noncolonization principle as well as the American right
of access to unsettled regions north of the line of division. To keep

all of Prince of Wales Island under Russian control, the Russians proposed the boundary of 54°40'. In the Convention of April 1824, Russia gained its preferred boundary but gave up all pretensions to a *mare clausum* in the north Pacific.

Even as the April convention disposed of the Russian threat in the far Northwest Adams's allies laid the Greek issue to rest in Congress. These triumphs for the concept of two worlds as embodied in the Monroe Doctrine were the last of Adams's secretarial years. Through eight years it was his recognition of geographic factors as the foundation of national interests and diplomatic advantage that underlay his varied goals and successes. Adams detected more assuredly than his contemporaries that European influence in the Western Hemisphere was declining. This assumption encouraged his anticipation of Latin American independence, his vision of an expanding republic on the North American continent, and his disinclination to compromise on issues purely American. Recognizing the limits of United States power outside the Western Hemisphere, he argued against all verbal commitments that transcended easily demonstrable national interests or any intention of the government to act. Adams understood that such involvements served no national requirements and ultimately disappointed everyone who took the rhetoric seriously. Rejecting the need of threats of war, he settled for what diplomacy could accomplish. Where he possessed the diplomatic advantage, as in the Rush-Bagot and Adams-Onís treaties, he pursued the American interest as he defined it. Where the nation's advantage was doubtful, as on the questions of Oregon and commercial reciprocity, he either postponed the settlement until the superior interests and advantages of the United States became apparent or simply accepted less than he desired. Where the issue was revolution in Latin America, Greece, or Spain, he abstained from involvement totally. The essence of Adams's statesmanship was his ability to define a clear hierarchy of national interests to be pursued. Adams never permitted his objectives to outrun the means available to him.

Adams's diplomatic achievements were remarkable. What he had contributed to the nation's thought was less tangible but no less impressive; but Adams's ultimate purpose transcended even such triumphs and looked rather to some lasting contribution to the good of the world. Referring to a projected convention for establishing neutral and belligerent rights in wartime, he confided in his diary: "When I think, if it possibly could succeed, what a real and solid blessing it would be to the human race, I can scarcely guard myself from a spirit of enthusiasm, which it becomes me to distrust. I feel that I could die for it with joy, and that if my last moments could be cheered with the consciousness of having contributed to it, I could go before the throne of Omnipotence with a plea for mercy, and with a consciousness of not having lived in vain for the world of mankind."

BIBLIOGRAPHIC NOTE

The mind and the work of America's greatest secretary of state are best approached in his own writings, public and private; nowhere does the new national feeling of the post-Ghent era appear more prominently than in his diary, a classic that reveals the chilling candor and sharp intelligence of an extraordinary mind: Charles Francis Adams, ed., *Memoirs of John Quincy Adams, Comprising Portions of His Diary from 1795 to 1848*, 12 vols. (Philadelphia, 1874–77). The Worthington C. Ford edition of *The Writings of John Quincy Adams*, 7 vols. (New York, 1913–17), remains useful though it stops short of the presidential years. Most of Adams's important public papers are in the series American State Papers, *Foreign Relations*, especially volumes 4 and 5.

In smaller compass, Allan Nevins has compiled a convenient one-volume edition of the *Memoirs* (New York, 1951), and Walter LaFeber collected in paperback a short, sensible selection of excerpts from the letters, speeches, and papers of Adams under the title *John Quincy Adams and American Continental Empire* (Chicago, 1965).

The best biography—definitive and indispensable—remains the two-volume study by Samuel Flagg Bemis, *John Quincy Adams and the Foundations of American Foreign Policy* (New York, 1949) and *John Quincy Adams and the Union* (New York, 1956). The early sketch by Dexter Perkins in volume 4 of the American Secretaries of State and Their Diplomacy series, edited by Samuel Flagg Bemis (New York, 1928), provides a solid appraisal based on multiarchival research. George A. Lipsky's topical approach in *John Quincy Adams: His Theory and Ideas* (New York, 1950) is useful to students. For a contemporary assessment by a self-confessed disciple see William H. Seward, *Life and Public Services of John Quincy Adams* (Auburn, N.Y., 1850).

For the context of Adams's diplomacy, the best introduction is George Dangerfield, *The Era of Good Feelings* (New York, 1952), a masterful, gracefully written account of post-1815 America. The same author's *Awakening of American Nationalism, 1815–1828* (New York, 1965), contains excellent chapters on the Transcontinental Treaty and the

Monroe Doctrine. On the former subject, Philip C. Brooks, *Diplomacy and the Borderlands: The Adams-Onís Treaty of 1819* (Berkeley, 1939), remains definitive; for the latter, Dexter Perkins's monumental three-volume work *The Monroe Doctrine* (Gloucester, Mass., 1927) retains its preeminence. For U.S.–Latin American relations in the Adams era see Arthur P. Whitaker, *The United States and the Independence of Latin America, 1800–1830* (Baltimore, 1941); J. Fred Rippy, *Rivalry of the United States and Great Britain over Latin America, 1808–1830* (Baltimore, 1929); William W. Kaufmann, *British Policy and the Independence of Latin America, 1804–28* (New Haven, 1951); John A. Logan, Jr., *No Transfer: An American Security Principle* (New Haven, 1961); and Charles C. Griffin, *The United States and the Disruption of the Spanish Empire, 1810–1822* (New York, 1937). The president's famous message of December 1823 can be found in many collections, perhaps most conveniently in volume 2 of the widely available Richardson edition of the *Messages and Papers of the Presidents.*

A sophisticated analysis of Adams's diplomacy from the end of the War of 1812 to the enunciation of the Monroe Doctrine in 1823 is the concluding volume of Bradford Perkins's trilogy on Anglo-American relations, *Castlereagh and Adams* (Berkeley, 1964). For the Ghent negotiations see the titles mentioned in the essay on Madison in this volume. For an evaluation of a key theme in Adams's economic diplomacy consult F. Lee Benns, *The American Struggle for the West India Carrying-Trade, 1815–1830* (Bloomington, 1923), a work that George Dangerfield regards as seminal and "quite essential" for an understanding of a complex subject.

Adams's secretarial relations with important American contemporaries are discussed in Harry Ammon, *James Monroe: The Quest for National Identity* (New York, 1971); Raymond Walters, Jr., *Albert Gallatin: Jeffersonian Financier and Diplomat* (New York, 1957); and J. H. Powell, *Richard Rush: Republican Diplomat, 1780–1859* (Philadelphia, 1942). For the views of European diplomats toward Adams see Stanley Lane-Poole, *Life of Stratford Canning*, 2 vols. (London, 1888), and "Correspondence of the Russian Ministers in Washington, 1815–1825," *American Historical Review* 18 (January, April 1913): 309–45, 537–62. Vernon G. Stetser traces Adams's relationship to United States commercial policy in his *The Commercial Reciprocity Policy of the United States, 1774–1829* (Philadelphia, 1937).

*Reproduced from the collections of
the Library of Congress*

CHARLES
WILKES

and the Growth of
American Naval Diplomacy

Geoffrey S. Smith

If mentioned at all by diplomatic historians, Charles Wilkes appears as a cocksure and irresponsible naval officer whose role in the *Trent* affair of 1861 brought the United States and Great Britain to the brink of war. To emphasize that dramatic act to the exclusion of all else, however, obscures two important aspects of diplomacy. Wilkes's prior career suggests that scientific exploration was both a prelude to and a handmaiden of antebellum expansionism; in addition, as Peter Karsten demonstrated in his provocative study of the naval aristocracy, an examination of the careers of American naval officers may clarify neglected dimensions of the nineteenth-century American response to the external world.

This essay is based on the author's forthcoming biography of Wilkes. Professor Smith received financial assistance from the Canada Council.

To appreciate that response and enhance understanding of America's quest for power and prestige in the nineteenth century, one must turn occasionally from such avowed leaders of the period as John Quincy Adams, James K. Polk, and William H. Seward. Then, as now, diplomacy was more than presidential decision, ministerial exchanges, or "what one clerk said to another clerk." Then, if not now, the naval officer often became a diplomat, an initiator and resolver of crises. Even in the era preceding the golden age of Annapolis, it is not surprising that the naval outlook in antebellum America included respect for a proper balance among scientific advancement, commercial expansion, and the advantages of republican government. For much of the nineteenth century Americans did not properly appreciate the increasing need for a strong navy. General sentiment against a peacetime military establishment combined with frugality in government resulted in jeers at Yankee cockboats following in the wake of British men-o'-war. The Atlantic Ocean and the English fleet were thought adequate for coastal defense; but so narrow a view minimized the nonmilitary and diplomatic functions executed by the navy, for during much of the century, and especially in peacetime, it emerged as a sharp cutting edge of American diplomacy. Its explorers were prominent in the diplomatic maneuvers for control of the West, especially the Pacific Northwest.

The manner in which one naval officer—a scientist, explorer, publicist, wartime commander, and self-avowed definer and defender of the national interest—thought about the role of the United States Navy in world affairs suggests that Charles Wilkes deserves a more prominent place among the makers of American diplomatic history than he has been accorded. As one of the first and most important explorer-diplomats, as a representative of mid-century naval interests and outlooks, and as an "embodiment of the wide-ranging energies and aspirations of the American people," Wilkes adds a useful (if usually neglected) dimension to the relationship between navalism and diplomacy in his day. Understanding his part in the acquisition of Oregon heightens awareness of the dynamics of American expansion. His career also coincided with an important period of technological innovation, highlighted by the transition of the navy from wood and sail to iron, steel, and steam. He reached maturity during the reform movement that resulted in the establishment in 1845 of the U.S. Naval Academy at Annapolis. A transitional figure whose sternness and discipline epitomized the "old navy," Wilkes nonetheless exhibited feelings for technological efficiency, scientific exploration, naval strategy during war, and the political and commercial destiny of the United States. In these and other ways, Wilkes foreshadowed the work of post–Civil War navalists Robert W. Shufeldt, Stephen B. Luce, and David D. Porter, those influential but still underestimated precursors of Alfred Thayer Mahan.[1]

Charles Wilkes, a grandnephew of the famous English dissenter John Wilkes, was born 3 April 1798; his early years coincided with America's naval war with France and with the successful demonstration of national sea power during the War of 1812. His death, on 8 February 1877, occurred as American diplomacy entered what historian David Pletcher called "the awkward years," when naval strength touched nadir. Wilkes's father, the son of a Loyalist who returned to America after the revolutionary war, became a New York merchant with commercial connections that directed his family's attention toward the Atlantic. As Charles grew up his interest centered increasingly upon science and the sea. He was an able student with several private tutors, and he concentrated on mathematics, navigation, and draftsmanship. His older brother, a major influence upon him during adolescence, served with the navy in the War of 1812; in his "Autobiography" Wilkes fondly recalled the celebrations held in New York City to honor American naval victories in that war. At the age of seventeen, against his father's wishes, he entered the merchant marine and got his first whiff of salt air on a voyage to Europe. A second voyage placed him under the command of a former officer in the French navy, a contact that led to Wilkes's appointment as a midshipman in the United States Navy on 1 January 1818.

Early in his naval career Wilkes recognized the need for greater national attention to the scientific aspects of navigation and naval technology. From 1824 to 1826, while preparing for his lieutenant's examination, he studied with a Swiss immigrant, Dr. Ferdinand Hassler, who in 1802 had founded what became the United States Coast and Geodetic Survey. From that experience, and from subsequent surveys of Narragansett Bay and St. George's Shoal, Wilkes developed a clear view of the practical importance

1. See the essay in this volume on Mahan.

of hydrography, geodesy, magnetism, and astronomy to navigation. In addition, Hassler's lack of discipline and his primitive surveying instruments provided constant irritation, which strengthened Wilkes's desire for the day when the nation would no longer depend upon European equipment or experts.

The versatile Wilkes put his ideas to work in 1833 when he assumed direction of the Naval Depot of Charts and Instruments. He soon transferred the depot from the western part of Washington, D.C., to Capitol Hill, both to bring his scientific work to the attention of Congress and to facilitate his astronomical experiments; he was the first American to construct an observatory and employ fixed astronomical instruments. He grew stronger in his belief that by expediting the charting of Atlantic ports and coastal waterways, naval surveys and exploration would strengthen developing commercial interests and lead to America's nautical independence.

The idea of a global exploring expedition assumed priority in Wilkes's assessment of the needs of the navy. Such an expedition, initially proposed by John Quincy Adams in 1825 and championed thereafter by Jeremiah N. Reynolds of Ohio, might strengthen the interdependence of science and the navy and augment the reputation of both. Moreover, such an expedition would require a skilled commander, and Wilkes, already a surveyor of ability and an embryonic naval scientist, felt himself uniquely qualified for the post.

Before the navy could become an instrument to further national scientific prestige, shipboard attitudes of both captains and crew had to change fundamentally. Wilkes's introduction to sea life left him disenchanted with naval mores. Although as a navy regular he valued discipline and order as preconditions of nautical efficiency, he recognized that life in the old navy left much to be desired: "No school could have been worse for the morals and none so viciously constituted." Younger men who conceived of the navy as an institution of national prestige were frustrated that older officers, in the absence of a merit system, stood above law and made others "subservient to their pleasures, caprices, and gratifications." "Debauching and drunken blackguards," masquerading as captains, men who often did not acknowledge the existence of scientific aids to navigation, served neither the nation's nor the navy's interests. Hamstrung by the lack of an educated officer corps, troubled by petty bickerings among officers, and debilitated by a lack of pride, the navy needed reform. To redress these shortcomings Wilkes favored creation of a naval academy, but he also stressed the necessity of officers first securing training through a sea cruise; while naval midshipmen were reasonably well educated, their knowledge of shipboard procedures was often abysmal.

Wilkes's attitude toward naval reform affected his feelings about politics in general. A social aristocrat in Jacksonian America, he found the system of political patronage demoralizing and believed that "good men should be above it." He believed that the dictates of party harmony necessitated sacrificing personal integrity; freedom of choice could scarcely exist in the political realm. This antipolitical animus was understandable. Institutional politics had blocked naval reform in the early nineteenth century; sectional and personal politics sabotaged the proposed exploration of the Pacific Ocean and northwest coast in 1825; and soon after Congress created a navy-directed scientific expedition in May 1836, personal jealousies, interdepartmental bickering, and the mismanagement of the navy secretary threatened that project.

Influenced by Wilkes's scientific reputation, Secretary of the Navy Mahlon Dickerson had proposed that he command one of the expedition's smaller vessels; but the commander-designate, Thomas ap Catesby Jones, balked at this suggestion, contending— in unmistakable old navy rhetoric—that Wilkes's attainments were of a "peculiar nature." Seeking a senior officer who would command respect on the quarterdeck, Jones further explained that Wilkes might take charge of instruments and surveying, but that under no circumstances might he be considered "as a commander, or for any other performance of regular navy duty."

Characteristically, Wilkes angrily refused to accept what amounted to a civilian's role in the expedition. Anticipating later navalists who zealously guarded their prerogative over scientific fields related to navigation, he berated Jones's lack of interest in science and ridiculed plans for twenty-one civilian scientists to accompany the expedition. Their presence would make navy regulars (many of whom possessed scientific skills) inconsequential "hewers of wood and drawers of water." To protect his reputation, Wilkes detached himself from the expedition and returned to New York, where he continued his scientific work during the next few months.

While he was away, preparations for the expedition bogged

down. What Congress had planned as a voyage of exploration to aid American whaling interests in the Pacific, to facilitate trade with Latin America, and to augment the status of national science had instead become an acute embarrassment to President Martin Van Buren. Even John Quincy Adams, a staunch advocate of the voyage, remarked that all he wanted to hear about the expedition was that it had sailed. Most of the blame for the delay can be attributed to Dickerson who, after securing from several scientific groups the names of men competent to accompany the voyage, hesitated to convene them, failed to pay them, and proved unable to provide necessary equipment. It seemed to many that the delay might allow rival British and French expeditions, then preparing to put to sea, to steal the thunder of the American navy.

When Captain Jones resigned his command because of poor health in November 1837, and when Secretary Dickerson failed to find a suitable replacement, Van Buren took matters into his own hands by transferring supervision of the project to his capable secretary of war, Joel R. Poinsett. Unwilling to let the prestige of discovery go by default to England and France, the president urged Poinsett to expedite preparations for the voyage. Poinsett, who was an able administrator and an advocate of science, soon settled upon Lieutenant Charles Wilkes to lead the expedition. In Poinsett's view the latter's lack of seniority did not prejudice his qualities as seaman and navigator. In fact, Wilkes's scientific competence made him one of the few officers qualified to command the voyage and to bring it to a successful conclusion.

Wilkes's appointment in April 1838 threatened to disrupt preparations for the expedition. Far from being the first choice, he had served primarily as a shoreside scholar. This fact, plus the two-year delay in mounting the expedition, raised criticism in many quarters. Wilkes's earlier resignation, together with his well-known quick temper and impulsiveness, exacerbated the feelings of colleagues and politicians. Lieutenant C. K. Stribling, who equaled Wilkes in rank, termed the appointment "highly injurious" to the morale of senior officers; a congressman wondered how a junior officer could command respect on so arduous a voyage; another lawmaker proposed that vessels assigned to the expedition be transferred to the coast squadrons for routine duty. Although failing to remove Wilkes from his command, Captain Beverly Kennon, a highly respected officer, succeeded in forcing the administration to divest the expedition of "all military character." By so doing, Kennon hoped to prevent the Wilkes appointment from setting a potentially dangerous precedent; his plan precluded a departure from the usual custom of selecting commanding officers from the senior ranks of the navy. The most bitter criticism of Wilkes, however, came from Lieutenant Matthew Fontaine Maury, whose personal interest in the voyage stemmed from hydrographic abilities equaling his adversary's. Maury scorned Wilkes as "a cunning little Jacob" who had campaigned long and hard for the post. Claiming that his rival had barely enough sea service to familiarize himself with ordinary ship routine, Maury decried the promotion of a shore-bound sinecurist—an armchair admiral—over the heads of many meritorious officers.

Such attacks did not bother Wilkes. With Poinsett's full support he moved swiftly to take charge of the project. He personally supervised the equipping, repairing, and final selection of vessels assigned to the cruise; he reassigned sailors and soothed their dissatisfactions with the move; he named an old Brooklyn friend, William L. Hudson, to be second in command; he reduced the number of civilian scientists assigned to the voyage, arguing that naval personnel were fully qualified for the scientific tasks related to navigation. Finally, he tested and calibrated his instruments at the Naval Observatory in Washington to assure their accuracy. The expedition received a sort of public official blessing in late July when Van Buren, Poinsett, and the new navy secretary, James Kirke Paulding, visited the squadron at Hampton Roads, Virginia.

Despite initial progress and evidence of executive approval, a serious and potentially dangerous problem remained. That problem stemmed from Wilkes's fiery personality, and from his dissatisfaction that promotion had not accompanied his new command. Named to a post of high responsibility, entrusted with a mission of international scientific importance, and representing the nation and the navy before the world, he felt sharply the lack of power and prestige that accompanied professional advancement. Nor did the carping of the crew and their underhand references to the "lieutenant-commodore" mitigate his injured pride. He brought these facts to the president's attention. Speaking for himself and Hudson, he reminded Van Buren that a failure to rectify the existing state of affairs would do "great injustice" to the expedition and its commanding officers. Only patriotism prevented his resignation, he wrote, adding that the failure to promote him might even threaten the success of the mission.

Unwilling or unable to recognize that the administration's failure to raise his rank stemmed at least in part from a desire to avoid further controversy, Wilkes considered it a blow to his *amour propre,* and successful execution of the mission became his obsession. The presumed "slight" (or, more precisely, Wilkes's own sensitivity to it) no doubt contributed to his subsequent transformation into a shipboard martinet. Pique also led to his hiding a commodore's uniform and pennant aboard the flagship *Vincennes* for later use. Characteristically, he planned to resolve the difficulty himself.

◇◇◇

The exploring expedition represented in microcosm the variety of functions executed by naval officers in the 1840s and 1850s. Instructed to "extend the empires of commerce and science; to diminish the hazards of the ocean; and [to] point out to future navigators a course by which they might avoid dangers and find safety," Wilkes took command of a flotilla consisting of 6 ships, 83 officers, and 342 enlisted men. The last global voyage wholly dependent upon sail, the expedition left Hampton Roads on 8 August 1838, only three months after Matthew C. Perry crossed the Atlantic in the *Fulton*—the initial transoceanic voyage by a steam-powered vessel. As one of a number of contemporary episodes matching civilized man against primitive nature, the Wilkes expedition featured human elements of courage, tragedy, and humor as it endured an arduous journey of nearly four years. Ranging from the waters of the Antarctic and South Pacific to the Juan de Fuca Strait, Wilkes and his colleagues surveyed approximately two hundred eighty islands, about eight hundred miles of coastline and contiguous territory in Oregon and Alta California, and some fifteen hundred miles along the Antarctic continent. Although the expedition did not make many new discoveries in the Pacific, the maps and charts resulting from the voyage anticipated Matthew Fontaine Maury's *Physical Geography of the Sea* (1855), providing American merchantmen with new certitude as they plied maritime routes.

Like other expeditions of the 1840s and 1850s, the one led by

Wilkes helped clarify and expand the navy's role in the development of the nation's diplomacy. In the middle years of the century the navy's primary tasks, aside from showing the flag and protecting national interests, centered on commercial, scientific, and political reconnaissance. As gatherers and interpreters of useful information, Wilkes and his colleagues helped construct the foundations upon which the post–Civil War navalists would build a new navy that would become a powerful ally of America's burgeoning network of global trade and commerce.

An important part of Wilkes's work was a series of warnings to the Navy Department about the need to strengthen the American presence in Polynesia and the Pacific Northwest. In addition to surveying oceanic channels, recommending and publicizing points of potential commercial and strategic interest, and informing Washington of the need to augment American power throughout the Pacific region, Wilkes and his colleagues became unofficial diplomats, representing a growing world power in such remote places as Brazil, New South Wales, Manila, and Singapore. The expedition also proved that during the 1840s Manifest Destiny denoted as much a maritime as a territorial force. Indeed, the personnel of the expedition became "maritime frontiersmen," mirror images of the thousands of mountain men, traders, pioneers, adventurers, and army surveyors who trekked westward to the Pacific. Harbingers of an increasingly complex, globally oriented society just beginning to crowd commercial, religious, and technological frontiers, the explorers gathered reams of scientific, economic, and political information at such points of future American interest as the Philippines, Samoa, Hawaii, California, and the Oregon Territory.

The expedition played an important though underrated part in the diplomacy of continental expansion. It enabled Wilkes to emphasize the danger of traversing the bar at the mouth of the Columbia River, and the destruction of one of his ships, the *Peacock*, publicized the inadequacies of Columbia Bay as an ocean harbor. More importantly, he pointed out the strategic importance of the area adjacent to Forts Tacoma and Walla Walla, the commercial potential of the Juan de Fuca Strait and Puget Sound, and the magnificence of the harbor at San Francisco. These descriptions (contained in a special confidential report to the government and in Wilkes's five-volume *Narrative*) influenced various Anglo-American boundary negotiations in the 1840s and stimulated subsequent official interest in California and the Oregon country.

The expedition also coincided with important new developments in transportation and technology; these, in turn, intensified the desire of Americans to subdue what Daniel Boorstin termed a "half-known country." The voyage struck the public mind less as an end in itself than as a means to several specific ends. In seeking reliable geographic data, the expedition created "a public purpose which the democratic society could properly patronize," as George H. Daniels so nicely put it. For the first time in American history civilian scientists utilized the navy to carry out scientific objectives. While the Lewis and Clark expedition of 1804–6 marked the first marriage of science and the military, the Wilkes voyage settled scientific exploration as a province of government, and it fixed the scientists' dependence upon the military for transport and auxiliary services.

An important step in the maturation of American science, this project—a sort of "floating doctoral program"—proved valuable both in training scientists (including some who did not make the journey) and in providing impetus toward the growth of scientific agencies. Yet if this ambitious undertaking in government-sponsored science presented great opportunity, it also posed problems. As a prototype of the close, uneasy alliance of government, science, and the military in the twentieth century, the expedition foreshadowed a patently modern concern: securing and maintaining cooperation between civilians concerned with "pure" science and regular naval personnel, whose scientific interests centered on improvements in naval technology and architecture. Of necessity, Wilkes spent much of his time mediating between civilian demands and the daily requirements of his sailors. Though he did not always succeed in reconciling those differences, he made sure they did not interfere with the objectives of the voyage. To this end, he ordered each officer to keep a journal, refused to become involved in shipboard politics, and sought to prevent the emergence of cliques. Wilkes was an indefatigable worker, and he personally supervised all developments in geodesy, magnetism, physics, meteorology, geography, hydrography, astronomy, and surveying. A hard taskmaster, he drove himself as hard as he drove subordinates.

Among its many other objectives the expedition sought to

protect whalers and traders in the Pacific by regularizing relations with aboriginal tribes through "wood and water" agreements and, when necessary, by punishment. Though usually restrained in his dealings with native peoples, Wilkes could, on occasion, use force; when he believed that power would have salutary effect, he acted decisively. Crew members once imprisoned a native chief implicated in an earlier murder of sailors from an American brig; on another occasion, after natives absconded with supplies pilfered from a disabled cutter, Wilkes destroyed their village; and on the island of Malolo, after the murder of two of his crew, Wilkes ordered two more villages razed. These early instances of gunboat diplomacy marked a step toward law and order and were designed to impress the natives with the consequences of harm to American visitors or vessels.

Wilkes also exercised quasi-diplomatic powers when he appointed agents to represent American whalers and traders at Upolu and the main island of Fiji. The two men earned their posts by aiding negotiations with native chieftains for the protection of visiting ships and crews (and for safeguarding the natives from the sailors), but because few American ships touched at these outposts the agents had little to do. Still, Wilkes's diplomacy, if such it was, represented an early attempt to establish international agreements with native chiefs in Samoa and Fiji. The accords illustrated the growing interest of naval commanders in protecting American overseas property and preserving international order and stability. Foreshadowing similar agreements between army officers and Indians after the Civil War, Wilkes's accords also anticipated executive agreements of the sort that naval commander William T. Truxton concluded with chieftains in the Gilberts, Marianas, and Marshalls in the 1870s.

Several episodes during the expedition, in New Zealand, Hawaii, and Oregon, brought Wilkes in contact with some of the main themes of nineteenth-century diplomacy. Like many of his countrymen, he had a full measure of Anglophobia, and events during the voyage exacerbated that sentiment, furthered his appreciation of the interrelatedness of political sovereignty and economic progress, and revealed him as an ardent advocate of Manifest Destiny.

The first of these incidents occurred in 1840 when Britain established a measure of sovereignty in New Zealand by negotiating the Treaty of Waitangi with approximately five hundred Maori chiefs, an agreement that ceded North Island to the crown. Wilkes, arriving in New Zealand only days after the signing, concluded that James R. Clendon, an Englishman who a year earlier had become the first American consul for the important post of the Bay of Islands, had used his diplomatic post to force the chiefs to agree. More concerned with his substantial landholdings than with defending American interests, Clendon resigned his post in 1841, but not before new import laws and tonnage duties severely damaged a profitable Yankee whaling and shipping trade. Among other things, the new regulations prohibited American whalers from hunting their favorite waters and curing their oil on North Island. In fact, between 1840 and 1841 the number of American vessels calling at the Bay of Islands dropped by 50 percent, and Wilkes estimated that the loss from the annual oil yield would reach three hundred thousand dollars. Terming the Treaty of Waitangi a disaster for the natives that transformed them into prey for "the hosts of adventurers flooding in from all parts," he concluded that Clendon's part in the accord emphasized the need for American citizens to serve as commercial representatives abroad.

Unwilling to involve himself in matters that might jeopardize the expedition, Wilkes adopted a realistic view of his nation's embryonic interests in Polynesia and did not contest the treaty. Nevertheless, Clendon's role in the agreement indicated a deficiency in American diplomacy: commercial connections proved a more powerful motive for becoming a diplomatic representative than either ability or sympathy for United States interests.

The expedition reached Hawaii in late September 1840, and Wilkes lauded the spirit of enterprise and level of civilization there. He also noted with interest the strategic potential of ports at Lahaina and Pearl River and the commercial future of such products as indigo, coffee, cattle, and sugar. The commander expressed surprise at how well local American merchants and missionaries got along with each other. He soon recognized that this cordiality signified less a community of interests than a defensive drawing together in the face of apparent British and French challenges to American commercial and religious interests. The years 1840 and 1841 witnessed a dramatic (though temporary) statistical increase in English commercial contact with the islands. Additionally in the eyes of several Protestant clergymen, France had embarked upon an aggressive Hawaiian policy. In 1837 and

1839, French naval officers forced King Kamehameha III to conclude treaties guaranteeing the diplomatic principle of extraterritoriality to French citizens, the free importation of French wine,
and the toleration and protection of Catholicism. Although subscribing to the Protestant clergy's view that French wine would
accelerate the spiritual and physical decline of sailors and natives
alike, Wilkes did not share the missionaries' anti-Catholicism and
saw no reason to take action beyond dispatching his impressions
to Washington. Lacking specific orders, he did not accede to
Kamehameha's proposal to renew and strengthen an agreement
concluded a decade earlier with Captain Thomas ap Catesby
Jones.

A theoretical devotion to global liberty and equality infused
the rhetoric of many Americans in the mid-nineteenth century,
but navalists did not always share these sentiments. Wilkes's
rejection of a petition for a territorial constitution presented by
American settlers in the Willamette Valley of Oregon seems to
suggest that he responded to pragmatic rather than to ideological
pressures. His demurrer demonstrated an appreciation of the
dangers of premature involvement, which might threaten the
national interest by engaging America in a situation it could not
control. At that time, American interests in New Zealand and
Hawaii did not warrant an active policy, but in the Pacific
Northwest conditions differed. There, the questionable intentions
of Britain's Hudson's Bay Company had made Oregon a contentious issue in Anglo-American relations, a fact reflected in instructions sent Wilkes to accord close attention to the Columbia River,
the northwest coast, and San Francisco Bay.

As members of the expedition carried out scientific and
surveying duties in the Puget Sound area in May 1841, Wilkes and
a party of men journeyed to Astoria, where they encountered the
remnants of the former headquarters of the Hudson's Bay Company. American settlers in the Willamette Valley had charged the
company with "avarice, cruelty, despotism, and bad government,"
but Wilkes found the corporation's representatives, especially Sir
George Simpson and Dr. John McLoughlin, helpful in providing
aid and useful suggestions. Wilkes's praise of McLoughlin's facilities and of the hospitality offered by company officers at Vancouver contributed to the notion that he had succumbed to British
blandishments while ignoring "the wants of the infant settlement
of Oregon." This criticism, popular among Anglophobic settlers

and subsequent local historians, missed its mark. Wilkes could, when necessary, subordinate his own Anglophobia to the demands of mission. In this case he recognized that without the aid of the company his expedition could not proceed as planned, particularly in the northernmost reaches of the Oregon country. Although the committee of five that presented its plans for a territorial constitution claimed to represent the sentiments of all Americans in the region, Wilkes refused to be drawn into the controversy. In fact, he suggested that the committee acted from selfish motives, hoping to induce a flood of new settlement and thus augment the value of their farms and livestock. The settlers, Wilkes concluded, should await a more propitious time when Washington would "throw its mantle over them."

Wilkes's dispassionate view of the Oregon question reflected his skill as a naval diplomat, although his actions belied his true feelings. The removal of the Hudson's Bay Company headquarters to Vancouver struck him as the portent of a glorious American future. Praising the agricultural and commercial potential of the Willamette Valley, he stepped forward as a naval apostle of Manifest Destiny. Sensing that he and his men "were not strangers on the soil," he explained that they "could not but take great interest in relation to its destiny, in the prospect of its one day becoming the abode of our relatives and friends."

Such sentiments, in fact, prevented Wilkes from filing a special report on Oregon until 13 June 1842, three days after he returned to New York. The forty-four-page document remained confidential because Navy Secretary Abel P. Upshur felt its release might threaten concurrent diplomatic negotiations between Secretary of State Daniel Webster and the British diplomat, Lord Ashburton. While Webster and his adversary had hoped to include the Oregon questions in their broad agenda, the return of the exploring expedition prevented its solution. A hint of the report's contents became public on 20 June when Wilkes presented a synopsis of his findings in a lecture at the National Institute in Washington. Scorning the mouth of the Columbia as a potential port, he reported the wreck of one of his vessels as it attempted to enter the river. "Mere description can give little idea of the terrors of the bar of the Columbia," he wrote. "All who have seen it have spoken of the wildness of the scene, and incessant roar of the waters, representing it as one of the most fearful sights that can possibly meet the eye of the sailor." This gloomy description contrasted with his enthusiastic assessment of more northerly harbors, upon which, he suggested, the future security and maritime prosperity of the United States depended. Lauding the safety of the Juan de Fuca Strait, Admiralty Inlet, Puget Sound, and Hood's Canal, he pointed out that no area in the world afforded "finer inland sounds or a greater number of harbors . . . capable of receiving the largest class of vessels, and without a danger in them that is not visible."

Even these views sounded mild when compared with the frankly expansionist tone of the confidential report. Wilkes argued that by surrendering disputed territory north of the Columbia the United States would forfeit a vast storehouse of natural resources that in time would provide "an extensive commerce on advantageous terms with most parts of the Pacific." The report also contained a strong argument favoring a 54°40' boundary. Wilkes noted that a division along the forty-ninth parallel would decrease the value of much territory south of that latitude. Moreover, the nation that commanded northern waterways adjoining the Juan de Fuca Strait would control Vancouver Island and access into the heart of the Oregon country. In addition to pointing out the practical difficulties of locating a boundary along the forty-ninth parallel, Wilkes expressed concern lest the territory then occupied by the Hudson's Bay Company become a staging ground for brigands and Indians to attack Americans in the Willamette Valley.[2]

2. In his confidential report Wilkes sought to dramatize the fact that the Hudson's Bay Company had already moved "to secure permanent settlement in the area" by "asserting its rights to the soil north of the Columbia." In his view American procrastination would allow the company "to obtain such a foothold as will make it impossible to set aside British sovereignty in it." Clearly, Wilkes shared with many Americans a deep-rooted fear of British encirclement. John Quincy Adams, whose dislike of Britain Stratford Canning described as "ravenous," probably best personified this attitude, which was descended from an older New England doctrine of containing French and, later, English strength wherever possible. The need to stave off French Catholic encirclement figured prominently in the external affairs of the Massachusetts Bay Colony, while a subsequent anti-British animus motivated colonial leaders in the decade before the Revolution and influenced Benjamin Franklin's vision of a rising American empire. During the early 1840s, vigilance against what Adams had termed the " 'bastard liberty' of the British, with its inequalities and aristocracy," became an integral facet of America's move to the Pacific. This tendency in American thought, noted by Frederick Merk and Richard W. Van Alstyne, will be considered in greater detail in the author's forthcoming biography of Wilkes.

There is no way to determine the precise effects of the report and other expedition publicity upon subsequent American acquisition of Oregon and California, and certainly no evidence suggests that Wilkes's call for 54° 40′ contributed in any substantial way to the later cry for that boundary. Nevertheless, in late 1842, Navy Secretary Upshur made public the sections of the report setting forth the immense value of the western part of Oregon, stimulating what became a year later the "Oregon fever." Even Webster, who earlier likened Oregon to "a land of deserts, eternal snows, of shifting sands, and sagebrush, fit to be inhabited only by the jack-rabbit and the coyote," admitted that the inland waters adjoining the Juan de Fuca Strait contained all the good harbors between the Russian settlements and California.

Although Wilkes's confidential report did not mention California (an omission reflecting Washington's overriding concern for Oregon), his subsequent *Narrative* offered a glowing description of the strategic importance of San Francisco Bay. Located on a major trade route linking China, Manila, Hawaii, India, and ports in Mexico and South America, the bay promised to become "one of the finest, if not the very best in the world—sufficiently commodious that the combined fleets of all the naval powers of Europe might moor in it." Convinced that the near absence of Mexican authority at Yerba Buena signaled an imminent American windfall, Wilkes suggested that possession of both San Francisco Bay and the harbors of Puget Sound would strengthen American commerce by establishing a transpacific triangle.

While the exploring expedition marked the entrance of the navy into "honorable competition with the navies of the great maritime nations of Europe," the project also denoted an important new chapter in the opening of the West, producing a wealth of reliable information about topography, climate, commercial prospects, and navigational problems. Americans moving westward after 1842 no longer found it necessary to depend for information upon the earlier reports of Lewis and Clark and Lieutenant William Slacum, the fiction of James Fenimore Cooper and Washington Irving, or the sketchy, often contradictory accounts of mountain men and missionaries. Despite shipboard dissension and personal recriminations that led to a court-martial for Wilkes and widespread criticism in the press, the commander's report and *Narrative* must surely be accorded a significant part in transforming the context of the Oregon question.[3]

◇◇◇

Charles Wilkes's Civil War career is too well known to require more than a brief recapitulation here, but during the conflict his definition of the national interest and the tactics he employed to advance it shed useful light on the perils of naval diplomacy at a critical juncture in American history.

His place in American diplomacy centers on the events of 8 November 1861, when on his own initiative he removed two Confederate envoys from the British mail packet *Trent*. Historians have assessed the importance of that event in many ways: from the vantage point of international law, as an example of the way public opinion complicates presidential decision making, as a chapter in Anglo-French diplomacy, as a way of measuring the temperature of British politics during the early Civil War. These and other interpretations have allowed readers to view from more angles than usual one of the most significant crises in American history.[4]

The delicate balance between military necessity and civilian responsibility has, of course, become an issue of vast significance in the twentieth century. In emphasizing this theme as it emerged during the *Trent* affair, historians have failed to stress an unexpected result of the incident. Ostensibly, Wilkes provoked a crisis that brought Great Britain to the verge of war; but the question turned on one variable: whether the Washington government would sanction the seizure. As even the most ardent Anglophobes

3. Frederick Merk, "The Oregon Question in the Webster-Ashburton Negotiations," *Mississippi Valley Historical Review* 42 (December 1956). As William H. Goetzmann demonstrates, however, neither Polk nor Secretary of State James Buchanan evidenced great interest in Wilkes's description of Puget Sound and San Francisco in 1844. See Goetzmann, *Army Exploration in the American West, 1803–1863* (New Haven, 1959), p. 103 and passim.
4. Lincoln and Welles found Wilkes next to impossible to restrain; his capacity to influence national policy resulted from the primitive communications network that left naval officers on their own for weeks at a time. Wilkes's freedom corroborates the observation that throughout the nineteenth century, and well into the twentieth, naval vessels often served perforce as independent, "floating embassies," supplanting distant or nonexistent State Department authority. See also the essay in this volume on Seward.

admitted, that possibility, despite the president's strong inclination to keep the Confederates, was extremely remote.

Many factors, including the problem of defending Canada, the fortuitous advice (and death) of the Prince Consort at the height of the imbroglio, and doubts concerning the motives of Napoleon III of France, militated against Britain entering the conflict. Consequently the martial bluster emanating from both sides of the Atlantic amounted to little more than a rhetorical equivalent of war. In light of these factors, Wilkes's part in the affair was somewhat ironic. What struck many contemporaries (and subsequent historians) as a *casus belli* became a strong force for peace. By establishing earnest diplomatic relations between the United States and Britain early in the war, the *Trent* incident created channels of communication that became invaluable during the ensuing years. Had the incident not occurred when it did, the parameters of Anglo-American relations would have remained uncertain; in November 1861, however, each nation found it necessary to assess publicly and soberly the motives of its adversary.

The *Trent* incident, which featured Wilkes in the combined roles of international lawyer and prize court judge, came at the nadir of Union fortunes and affected Northerners in a way similar to the Battle of Saratoga in 1777 and Jackson's victory at New Orleans in 1815. The overwhelming popular support offered Wilkes as reflected in the unionist denial that his act contravened the principle of maritime neutrality for which the United States fought France in the 1790s and England in 1812 focused attention upon Alexis de Tocqueville's warning, three decades earlier, that "foreign politics demand scarcely any of those qualities which a democracy possesses; and they require, on the contrary, the perfect use of almost all those faculties in which it is deficient." Tocqueville, to be sure, took the position of an alarmist. The nineteenth-century record of American diplomacy reveals a successful balancing of means with ends by leaders who hesitated to extend national interests into areas where the country might prove unable to exercise commensurate power.

The response of President Lincoln and Secretary of State William H. Seward to the *Trent* affair proved no exception to this general rule; yet the incident—and Wilkes's subsequent Civil War career—underlined the ease with which an isolated, impetuous naval officer might involve his country in a crisis. Wilkes's zeal

"POLICEMAN WILKES, noticing by the last Number of *Harper's Weekly*, that the well-known Rogues, MASON and SLIDELL, were about to Pawn some of their late Employer's Property at Messrs. *Bull, Crapaud & Co.'s* Shop, kept a bright look-out for'ard, and nabbed them in the nick of time."

Harper's Weekly, *30 November 1861. Reproduced from the collections of the Library of Congress* during the conflict resulted largely from his own ambition, thwarted during the preceding two decades by a series of frustrating experiences. While other naval explorers carried the flag to North Pacific, Asiatic, and Latin American waters, the commander of the famous exploring expedition had remained on shore, facing the indifference of President John Tyler's Whig administration, enduring a highly publicized court-martial, and waging a ceaseless battle with Congress for appropriations to finance projects connected with the voyage. Meanwhile, another blow fell when a British explorer, Sir James Clarke Ross, denied the validity of Wilkes's greatest accomplishment, proving the continental dimension of Antarctica, by claiming to have sailed directly over the "discovery." Wilkes's survey of California's Sacramento Valley also ended in a bitter dispute, after the famed "pathfinder" of the West, John C. Frémont, located mistakes in Wilkes's map, indicating that he had copied it from a discredited English chart.

Problems like these contributed to Wilkes's aggressive conduct and to his growing tendency to ignore the feelings of individuals and rights of nations with whom he dealt. Unable to accept criticism, he came into continuous conflict with others, including politicians, fellow officers, and enlisted men before and during the expedition; the Tyler administration upon Wilkes's return; fellow scientists and unsympathetic members of the Joint Congressional Committee on the Library as he prepared his *Narrative* and administered scientific collections during the 1840s and 1850s; the Navy Department during the Civil War; and, because of his contempt for international law while intercepting blockade runners and chasing Confederate commerce destroyers in the West Indies, with naval and diplomatic representatives of Britain, France, Spain, Denmark, and Mexico.

Wilkes's derring-do in the *Trent* incident led to his appointment in July 1862 to command the newly formed James River Flotilla, and subsequently, after a nine-day stint in charge of the Potomac River Flotilla, to head the West Indian Flying Squadron. In the first position he earned a reputation as a headstrong commander, on one occasion disobeying Navy Department orders to detach two men from his squadron and on several others entreating the department to allow him to combine his forces with those of General George B. McClellan's Army of the Potomac to storm the Confederate stronghold at Richmond. Even after General Henry W. Halleck ordered McClellan's troops to withdraw to

defend Washington, D.C., Wilkes persisted, informing Navy Secretary Gideon Welles that the mundane tasks of reconnaissance
did not satisfy his desire to turn the tide of conflict.

Wilkes's appointment in September to lead the Flying Squadron represented Lincoln's veiled warning to European nations,
especially the British, to honor the requirements of maritime
neutrality. The president and his advisers could count on Wilkes to
follow an aggressive course; they had a fair idea of the lengths to
which their agent might carry his attempt to capture the *Alabama*,
Florida, and the numerous contraband carriers that slipped past
the Union blockade. Soon, however, it appeared—especially to
the British—that Wilkes had again exceeded instructions; in effect
he had extended the blockade into West Indian waters. Believing,
like Alfred Thayer Mahan, that the navy's major wartime duty
consisted of locating and destroying the enemy, Wilkes disregarded Welles's counsels of caution and acted as though existing
conditions excused breaches of the law or naval etiquette. Wilkes
was convinced that European colonial officials had forfeited their
rights as neutrals by aiding Confederate vessels, and he literally
transformed Havana into a base of American operations as he
searched for the Confederate cruisers. To extend the moderate
capacity of his own vessels, he illegally established and employed
coaling stations on French, Spanish, Danish, and British soil; to
facilitate capture of blockade runners, he allegedly placed "senti-
nels" on British soil and ordered his ships to "hover" in the waters
off the Danish port of St. Thomas; and to strengthen his overall
command, he unilaterally detached vessels from the squadrons of
David G. Farragut and C. H. Baldwin.

Wilkes's failure to capture the Confederate cruisers provoked
widespread criticism of Welles and his department. Antagonism
between the secretary and his ambitious underling increased after
Wilkes charged that the department had discriminated against him
by failing to provide the manpower and vessels required to
execute his mission. Wilkes's assertion that these measures would
have enabled him to capture the *Alabama* or *Florida* contained
some truth; but the Union commander lacked specialized knowledge of the myriad reefs, inlets, and cays dotting Caribbean
waters. This shortcoming, compared with the geographical expertise and nautical skill of his Confederate adversaries, contributed
significantly to the futility of Wilkes's nine-month command.

In Welles's view, Wilkes exhibited less interest in capturing the cruisers than he did in collecting prize money from vessels captured while attempting to trade with the Confederacy. Although its scope made halting the contraband trade virtually impossible, the Flying Squadron upset the continuity of Confederate transactions, forced shifts in the bases of operation, and compelled Southern vessels to ply the Caribbean and Gulf waters with greater circumspection; but Wilkes's arrogant attitude and disrespect for maritime law (epitomized by his frequent use of neutral ports as bases from which to stalk suspected ships) made him a symbol of Anglo-American hostility. His detention of several British ships created legal and diplomatic squalls across the Atlantic, and his heavy-handed pursuit of duty left Englishmen aghast at the actions of a man whom the *Liverpool Mercury* described as "an ill-informed and violent naval officer."

Secretary Welles removed Wilkes from active duty in June 1863 as a diplomatic gesture toward Anglo-American amity that placed the administration in a favorable light. Having demonstrated its toughness by appointing Wilkes, it could now reap the rewards of conciliation by removing him. For Wilkes, however, the recall signaled a bitter end to a stormy career. The *Trent* affair was all but forgotten; Union victories at Vicksburg and Gettysburg would supply a new cadre of military heroes. His reputation tarnished by failure, his zeal unappreciated, Wilkes returned to New York, feeling that he had been sacrificed to Navy Department incompetence and British diplomatic pressure. There remained, however, a denouement, a second court-martial that convened in March 1864. The list of particulars had a familiar ring: Wilkes had disobeyed orders and engaged in conduct unbecoming an officer; by allowing publication of a letter critical of Welles's *Annual Report*, he had displayed insubordination; by falsifying his age and failing to provide a suitable explanation, he had disobeyed a general naval regulation and demonstrated disrespect toward his superiors. Judged guilty on all counts, the "hero of the *Trent*" received a public reprimand and a three-year suspension—a sentence that Lincoln later reduced. In July 1866, as the culmination of a stormy career, Wilkes achieved a lifelong goal when he was named rear admiral, albeit on the retired list.

◇◇◇

Zealous in his execution of duty, imperious toward associates, and single-minded in devotion to God and country, Wilkes exemplified throughout his career attitudes characterizing the old navy. As those who served with him observed, duty addressed Wilkes in severe terms, and he in turn expected as much of subordinates as he did of himself. Like many contemporary navalists, he harbored an enduring faith in America's political, commercial, and spiritual mission—a mission, incidentally, in which he found a major role for himself. This egotism, especially in his later career, led him to make decisions based upon ambition and impulse, to disdain the delicate balance between military means and diplomatic ends, and to ignore naval etiquette when orders or regulations contravened what he defined as a proper course. Wilkes's major weakness lay in impulsive overconfidence. Sincere in believing that he could not err, he defined issues in black-and-white terms. This characteristic often led to disagreements with superiors. Navy Secretary Welles, despairing of Wilkes's contumacy while commanding the James River Flotilla, described the man perfectly as "very exacting toward others, but . . . not himself as obedient as he should be." Possessing ability "but not good judgement in all respects," Wilkes might "rashly assume authority, and do things that might involve himself and the country in difficulty."

His problems during the Civil War leave the impression that Wilkes's significance in diplomatic history lies in his unwarranted assumption of power over the formulation of national policy. Such an interpretation, stressing the danger in a "my country, right or wrong" attitude, is one-sided. As an explorer and scientist he demonstrated courage and ability; as a discoverer, surveyor, and cartographer, he contributed to growing national prestige. Given the primitive technology at his command during the late 1830s, his confirmation of the continental dimensions of Antarctica compares favorably with the complex systems supporting American space efforts during the 1960s. Similarly, rather than ending up in dusty archives, Wilkes's charts of Wake Island, the Makins, and Tarawa endured among the more reliable sources of information employed by the navy during South Pacific operations in 1943.

According to James Dwight Dana, who accompanied the exploring expedition and knew well its commander's acerbic tongue, Wilkes's conceit did not detract from his "wonderful degree of energy." Nor did Dana err when he confided to Professor Asa Gray of Harvard that one could find "no more daring or driving officer" in the navy. As Wilkes's son John stated after his father's death in 1877, the latter impressed acquaintances as "a fearless, energetic, and unflinching officer, never afraid to assume responsibility." Such characteristics, of course, tossed Wilkes into choppy waters as a wartime commander; yet they also contributed to his success as a scientist. His legacy included, quite understandably, the admonition that the national interest depended upon continued government support of scientific research and exploration. Wilkes's participation in organizations such as the American Philosophical Society, his writings on such diverse subjects as the Oregon Territory, meteorology, and the zodiacal light, and the impetus given by the scientific expedition to the development of the Smithsonian Institution and other governmental agencies all advanced the expansionist *Zeitgeist* that permeated the United States in the mid-nineteenth century.

The overall strategic importance of exploration during antebellum America necessitates revision of the diplomatic era traditionally described as dominated by young America. On the one hand, the All of Mexico movement, the Ostend Manifesto, and the ill-fated filibustering expeditions of Narciso López into Cuba and William Walker into Nicaragua illustrate some uncoordinated muscle flexing by an adolescent nation attempting to elbow its way into world politics. Offsetting these episodes in bumptious diplomacy, the government and the navy demonstrated their appreciation of the need to acquire systematic knowledge of the globe and its ports, products, and peoples. Matthew C. Perry's epochal voyage to Japan ranks as the best known of these expeditions; but other voyages, including one led by Lieutenant William F. Lynch to the Dead Sea area in 1847, another led by Lieutenant William L. Herndon and Passed Midshipman Lardner Gibbon to the Amazon River in 1851, and a third in 1853 led by Lieutenant John Rodgers to North Pacific waters off China and Japan, suggest that Manifest Destiny influenced spheres of activity far removed from the domestic emphasis on westward continental expansion.

Apart from his scientific work, Wilkes expressed his greatest concern for the international image of the navy. As his narrative of the scientific expedition made clear, he also appreciated Sir Walter Raleigh's dictum that "whosoever commands the sea, commands

the trade; whosoever commands the trade of the world, commands the riches of the world and consequently the world itself."
Although as commander of the project Wilkes in no way spoke as
a captive of special economic interests, he did conceive of the
Atlantic and especially the Pacific as oceanic highways rather than
barriers. Anticipating the post–1865 vision of Secretary of State
Seward, he believed that knowledge of the seas would consolidate
control over global waterways. Even if the United States could not
wrest maritime supremacy from Great Britain, the navy might
stabilize maritime routes so that American political and commercial interests might profit. Well before Mahan systematically
articulated the strategic variables that comprised global navalism,
Wilkes stressed the continuing necessity of employing sea power
in peacetime as an instrument of scientific, technological, and
economic advancement.

   Although Wilkes favored extending to aboriginal peoples the
benefits of Anglo-Saxon, republican government and Protestant
religion, his Anglophobia precluded kinship with the American
naval aristocracy of the late nineteenth and twentieth centuries.
Although he rejected Rousseau's characterization of the "noble
savage" enjoying an idyllic existence in a Pacific paradise, several
passages in his *Narrative* and "Autobiography" (especially those
dealing with the expedition's transactions with native peoples),
make clear that Wilkes often employed a yardstick of idealized
American cultural values to measure the level of "civilization" of
the aborigines he encountered. He agreed with most navalists
who criticized American missionaries and commercial agents who
failed to execute with sufficient verve their respective moral and
material commissions.

   As an explorer Wilkes exhibited what the historian Richard W.
Van Alstyne has termed "a mariner's sense of distance from the
United States." Wilkes's earnestness in stressing the economic and
strategic potential of Puget Sound and the harbor at San Francisco
presaged an American mercantile empire in the Pacific. In this
sense the naval scientist possessed a "Pacific consciousness" long
before Seward, the first great apostle of that doctrine. Wilkes's
Narrative, although printed in limited number and written in a
turgid style, made him a prophet. Not only in his belief that
Oregon, California, and Hawaii would eventually fall under the
dominion of the United States did he foresee future developments; he also predicted that San Francisco Bay and the Juan de

Fuca Strait possessed "everything to make them increase, and keep up an intercourse with the whole of Polynesia, as well as the countries of South America on the one side, and China, the Philippines, New Holland, and New Zealand on the other." From these sites would come "materials for a beneficial exchange of products and an intercourse that must, in time, become immense, while this western coast," he predicted, "is evidently destined to fill a large space in the world's future history."

While not a first-rate naval officer, nor, for that matter, a maker of American diplomacy in the same sense as Adams, Polk, or Seward, Wilkes certainly qualifies as a builder. Indeed, throughout his career he directed his primary interest toward progress in naval science and other utilitarian ends. His work in the fields of hydrography, geodesy, and meteorology augmented the safety of vessels traversing oceanic routes; his compilation of charts and surveys completed during the expedition facilitated coastal and international commerce; and his maps of California and the Oregon Territory increased the confidence of Americans migrating westward during the late 1840s and 1850s. Wilkes's career suggests, finally, that while the pseudoscience of Social Darwinism contributed heavily to the distinctiveness of the new Manifest Destiny of the 1890s (and to the *raison d'être* of the naval aristocracy), a genuine scientific concern formed a major component of mid-nineteenth-century expansionism.

BIBLIOGRAPHIC NOTE

Like many of his naval contemporaries, Charles Wilkes left scattered records pertaining to his life, which have come to rest in depositories across the United States and in several other countries. Surprisingly, there is only one full-scale biography of this controversial navalist: Daniel Henderson's *The Hidden Coasts: A Biography of Admiral Charles Wilkes* (New York, 1953), a volume that should be retitled "an essay in hagiography." Satisfactory in few areas, its unyielding tone of admiration leaves the impression that Wilkes still awaits his biographer. Wilkes's personal "Autobiography" in the Wilkes papers in the Library of Congress, the major source of primary materials concerning his career, reveals his driving ambition, egotism, and atrocious penmanship. Fortunately, a substantial portion of the manuscript is in typescript.

Turgid and overwritten, yet exhibiting its author's scientific and diplomatic interests, Wilkes's *Narrative of the United States Exploring Expedition during the Years 1838, 1839, 1840, 1841, 1842*, 5 vols. (Philadelphia, 1845), also indicates the ethnocentrism that colored his world view. The only scholarly synthesis of the exploration is David B. Tyler's *The Wilkes Expedition: The First United States Exploring Expedition (1838–1842)* (Philadelphia, 1968), a solid study whose narrow focus nevertheless ignores broad implications of the voyage. An important dissertation suggesting the difficulty in Wilkes's attempt to reconcile his scientific interests with political necessities, John E. Wickman's "Political Aspects of Charles Wilkes' Work and Testimony, 1842–1849," Indiana University, 1964, also assesses the vicissitudes of John Tyler's Whig administration. These sources may be supplemented by Record Group 37 (M-75), a collection of twenty-five rolls of microfilm in the National Archives, containing "Records Relating to the U.S. Exploring Expedition under the Command of Lt. Charles Wilkes, 1836–1842," and a series of articles marking the centennial commemoration by the American Philosophical Society of that voyage. The latter are contained in the Philosophical Society's *Proceedings* 82 (June 1940).

Contemporary accounts of the expedition include "The Exploring Expedition," *North American Review* 56 (April 1843), 258–70; "The United States Exploring Expedition," *North American Review* 61 (July 1845), 54–107; and "The Wilkes Exploring Expedition," *Edinburgh Review* 83 (April 1846), 431–52. Louis N. Feipel, meanwhile, reviews "The Wilkes Exploring Expedition, Its Progress through Half a Century, 1826–1876," in United States Naval Institute *Proceedings* 40 (September–October 1914), 1323–50; and Daniel C. Haskell summarizes the literature resulting from the voyage in *The United States Exploring Expedition, 1838–1842, and its Publications, 1844–1874: A Bibliography* (New York, 1942).

Several authors assess the developing relationship between science and naval exploration during the 1840s. W. Patrick Strauss, "Preparing the Wilkes Expedition: A Study in Disorganization," *Pacific Historical Review* 28 (1959), 221–32, traces the comedy of errors that preceded the voyage. George H. Daniels, *Science in American Society: A Social History* (New York, 1971), A. Hunter Dupree, *Science in the Federal Government: A History of Policies and Activities to 1940* (Cambridge, Mass., 1957), and Dupree, *Asa Gray, 1810–1888* (Cambridge, Mass., 1959), analyze the scientific, social, and political milieu in which the Wilkes expedition occurred. Edward L. Towle stresses the nexus between scientific and commercial objectives in naval planning in "Science, Commerce, and the Navy on the Seafaring Frontier (1842–1861): The Role of Lieutenant M. F. Maury and the U.S. Naval Hydrographic Office in Naval Exploration, Commercial Expansion, and Oceanography before the Civil War," Ph.D. dissertation, University of Rochester, 1966. Three studies that elaborate upon themes related to the Wilkes expedition include John P. Harrison, "Science and Politics: Origins and Objectives of Mid-Nineteenth Century Government Expeditions to Latin America," *Hispanic American Historical*

Review 35 (1955), 175–202; A. Hunter Dupree, "Science vs. the Military: Dr. James Morrow and the Perry Expedition," *Pacific Historical Review* 17 (1953), 29–37; and William H. Goetzmann, *Army Exploration in the American West, 1803–1863* (New Haven, 1959). See also the same author's *Exploration and Empire: The Explorer and the Scientist in the Winning of the American West* (New York, 1966), especially chapter 7.

For accounts of the expedition's work in Pacific waters, readers may consult W. Patrick Strauss, "Pioneer American Diplomats in Polynesia, 1820–1840," *Pacific Historical Review* 31 (1962), 21–30, an article distilled from the same author's "Early American Interest and Activities in Polynesia, 1783–1842," Ph.D. dissertation, Columbia University, 1958. In *The American Frontier in Hawaii: The Pioneers, 1789–1843* (Stanford, 1942), Harold W. Bradley discusses Wilkes's Hawaiian visit against a background of threatening French and British interests.

The importance of maritime and commercial considerations in the expansionism of the 1840s is emphasized in Norman A. Graebner, *Empire on the Pacific: A Study in American Continental Expansion* (New York, 1955); and Richard W. Van Alstyne, *The Rising American Empire* (New York, 1960). Frederick Merk's *The Oregon Question: Essays in Anglo-American Diplomacy and Politics* (Cambridge, Mass., 1967) incorporates many of the author's previously published essays. An early study of Wilkes's importance as a publicist of the strategic and commercial advantages of the waterways of the Oregon Territory and of San Francisco Bay is provided in Helen Ramage, "The Wilkes Exploring Expedition on the Pacific Slope, 1841," master's thesis, University of California, 1916; while Wilkes's confidential report on the Oregon Territory is contained in the *Congressional Record*, 62nd Cong., 1st sess., 15–20 July 1911, 47: 2977–85.

Wilkes's activities during the Civil War have been the subject of two critical studies; the more notable is William W. Jeffries, "The Civil War Career of Charles Wilkes," *Journal of Southern History* 11 (August 1945), 324–48, a distillation of his master's thesis, under the same title, at Vanderbilt University in 1936. Less analytical, though still useful, is John S. Long, "The Wayward Commander: A Study of the Civil War Career of Charles Wilkes," Ph.D. dissertation, University of California, Los Angeles, 1953. The tense relationship between Wilkes and the Navy Department during the war is clearly manifest in Edgar T. Welles, ed., *The Diary of Gideon Welles*, 3 vols. (Boston, 1911). For bibliographic references to the *Trent* affair and related issues, the reader may consult the essay in this volume by Gordon Warren. One book, however, in which the treatment of the incident is perceptive in terms of Wilkes's personal motives, is Jay Monaghan, *Diplomat in Carpet Slippers: Abraham Lincoln Deals with Foreign Affairs* (Indianapolis, 1945). A recent article suggesting a new departure in *Trent* historiography, F. C. Drake, "The Cuban Background of the *Trent* Affair," *Civil War History* 19 (March 1973), 29–49, emphasizes the role of the American consul in Havana, Robert W. Shufeldt, in events preceding the capture of Mason and Slidell.

Important assessments of the navy during Wilkes's lifetime include Peter Karsten's provocative *The Naval Aristocracy: The Golden Age of Annapolis and the Emergence of Modern American Navalism* (New York, 1972), a work that provides the first critical analysis of the affluent Episcopalian milieu that produced the initial generation of modern navalists—officers devoted to Anglo-American rapprochement, the protection of American commerce, and their own professional interests. By stressing Navy Secretary Dickerson's original justification for the Wilkes expedition—as a venture "promoting the great interests of commerce and navigation," with science "an object of great, but comparatively of secondary importance"—Karsten perhaps overemphasizes the primacy of economic motivation behind antebellum naval exploration; and he fails to stress the degree to which science had become a contentious political issue in the years between 1825 and 1836.

Harold D. Langley, *Social Reform in the United States Navy, 1798–1862* (Urbana, Ill., 1967), discusses reform in the pre–Civil War navy. The emergence of the "new navy" in the 1890s should not obscure the importance of earlier developments. See Robert Seager III, "Ten Years before Mahan: The Unofficial Case for the New Navy, 1880–1890," *Mississippi Valley Historical Review* 40 (December 1953), 491–512; Charles O. Paullin, "Beginnings of the United States Naval Academy," United States Naval Institute *Proceedings* 50 (February 1924), 173–94; Harold and Margaret Sprout, *The Rise of American Naval Power, 1776–1918* (Princeton, 1946); Daniel J. Carrison, *The Navy from Wood to Steel, 1860–1890* (New York, 1965); and Bern Anderson, *By Sea and by River: The Naval History of the Civil War* (New York, 1962).

For a critique of "traditional" approaches to diplomatic history, see Alexander DeConde, "What's Wrong with American Diplomatic History?" Society for Historians of American Foreign Relations *Newsletter* 1 (May 1970), 1–16.

*Reproduced from the collections of
the Library of Congress*

JAMES K. POLK

and the Rewards of Rashness

David M. Pletcher

Beyond doubt the one-term president who left the deepest imprint on American foreign relations was James K. Polk. In four years he brought the United States into and out of a major diplomatic crisis with Great Britain and fought a war with Mexico in which the United States did not lose a single major battle. Following his instructions, American diplomats negotiated treaties that added to the national domain the present-day states of Washington, Oregon, California, Nevada, Utah, most of Arizona and New Mexico, and parts of several others. Polk's agents also completed the annexation of Texas, an action that his predecessor John Tyler had initiated. Between 1845 and 1849, while Polk was

This essay is based on the author's *The Diplomacy of Annexation: Texas, Oregon, and the Mexican War*, which was written with the assistance of Fulbright and Social Science Research Council fellowships and research grants from Hamline and Indiana Universities.

165

president, the United States established itself as a second-rank power, one that Europe had to consult or at least consider in any international matters affecting North America, Central America, or the Caribbean.

Despite his importance, historians have treated Polk with remarkable inconsistency. Since he was a narrowly partisan Democrat, it is not surprising that early studies of his administration were mostly party tracts. By the end of the nineteenth century, Clay, Calhoun, and Webster seemed to loom over him so far that J. T. Morse, Jr., failed to include him in his American Statesmen series; but when Theodore Roosevelt began to reassert executive leadership in foreign relations and Woodrow Wilson again drew public attention to Mexico's shortcomings, Polk's tribulations and achievements appeared more relevant than at any time since 1848. In 1919 Justin H. Smith defended the Mexican War in a two-volume history packed with footnotes, which won a Pulitzer Prize and immediately became a classic. After that time no student of America's middle period could ignore Polk. In the early 1960s a poll of historians ranked him eighth in importance among presidents—just below Theodore Roosevelt and above Harry S. Truman.

Polk's manner and personality were partly responsible for his long obscurity. At the age of forty-nine, when he became president (the youngest man until then to hold the office), he was short, spare in frame, with long, grizzled hair brushed back over his neck. His thin face with its high cheekbones and set jaw usually wore a sad expression, sometimes relieved by a stiff smile on his thin lips. The features everyone remembered were his deep-set, piercing gray eyes.

The personality beneath this drab exterior was introverted, intense, narrow, and almost entirely humorless. Self-disciplined and methodical, Polk seldom relaxed; for one period of thirteen months he hardly went outside the city limits of Washington. Some contemporaries thought him devious, for he kept his own counsel more than most other politicians of that easygoing period. A clear and forceful, if not especially inspiring, speaker, he had a sharp memory for names, faces, and interests and was a shrewd but overly suspicious judge of men. Toiling upward through the rough, semifrontier politics of Tennessee, he had hitched his career to Jacksonian Democracy. By 1842 that career seemed to have reached its limits after undistinguished service as Speaker of the U.S. House of Representatives and governor of his state. Then, through energy, careful organization, and good luck at the deadlocked convention of 1844, Polk slipped into the Democratic nomination for the presidency—but only after humbling himself with the promise that he would serve only one term in the White House. Although opponents and some of his own followers belittled him during the campaign, an expansionist program and wavering opposition gave him a narrow victory.

Once elected, Polk was determined to be the master of his own administration. About four months after his inauguration, he started a detailed diary of his actions and thoughts, a remarkably revealing record that clearly shows how he moved toward his goal. Having patterned his career and convictions after his patron, Andrew Jackson, he believed that the president, the only official representing all the people, should dominate the government. More than any other Jacksonian Democrat, he accepted the grinding labor this power involved and mastered the problems and techniques of every executive department. At the same time, however, he was careful to share with Congress the responsibility for every policy that might prove unpopular.

Polk's relations with his cabinet reflected this combination of decision and caution. First, he chose a reasonably able group of professional politicians whom he could control. His secretary of state, James Buchanan, had a reputation as an outspoken Anglophobe and, like Polk, was a shrewd, calculating political manipulator; but he was timid and indecisive in action. While Buchanan's arguments supplied a useful foil in cabinet discussions, his policies did not often prevail over those of the president. Secretary of the Treasury Robert J. Walker affected foreign relations mainly through his low-tariff program, which Polk supported. The only other cabinet member to play a major role in foreign policy decisions was Secretary of the Navy George Bancroft, the New England historian, an ardent Jacksonian and nationalist whose expansionist ambitions exceeded those of Buchanan.

Having chosen his cabinet, Polk exacted of each member the written pledge that he would not campaign for the presidency while in office. At biweekly meetings he sought each man's advice on most important matters, especially on questions of foreign policy, but he made up his own mind. He delegated power reluctantly and demanded frequent and full accountings; Buchanan, for example, called at the White House for consultation nearly every day, bringing the latest dispatches for Polk to examine. When the secretary began his instructions to diplomats with "The President wishes . . . ," he was telling the literal truth.

Polk brought to the conduct of foreign relations no special knowledge or talent. Indeed, he felt little but contempt for diplomatic protocol, especially because he spoke no foreign language.[1] As a nationalist from mid-America, he felt a strong xenophobia, unmitigated by any sophisticated, cosmopolitan appreciation of European culture or institutions. If he entered the White House with any model for relations with Britain or Mexico, it was the one supplied by Jackson in the 1830s: blunt defiance of France for delaying the payment of American claims and the conniving mission to Mexico of Anthony Butler, who sought to obtain the sale of Texas through bribery.

In the midst of the Oregon controversy Polk gave various associates a rationalization of his stern, unbending policy toward Britain, the traditional enemy. This view is most succinctly expressed in a diary account of a conversation with a minor congressman: "I remarked to him that the only way to treat John Bull was to look him straight in the eye; that I considered a bold & firm course on our part the pacific one; that if Congress faultered [sic] or hesitated in their course, John Bull would immediately become arrogant and more grasping in his demands; & that such had been the history of the Brittish [sic] Nation in all their contests with other Powers for the last two hundred years." As he wrote to another man, Britain always took advantage of any nation that approached it for a favor. Polk did not bother to compose a corresponding characterization of Mexico, his other adversary; but his public references to the government and people showed that he held them in contempt, as hardly worthy of nationality. Such feelings could produce only an aggressive policy of bluntness and bluff: Take a bold stand; negotiate from real or apparent strength; assume what you cannot prove; make no concessions that might be interpreted as weakness; and keep your opponent off balance. Ideas of mutual interest and compromise formed little part of his thinking.

1. On one occasion, while receiving a newly arrived diplomat, he delivered a quite acceptable reply without waiting to have the man's presentation speech translated. Later he wrote in his diary that he had guessed in advance what would probably be said.

◇◇◇

When Polk took office, he inherited from John Tyler two major problems of foreign policy, both concerning American territorial expansion. At Tyler's urging, Congress had passed a joint resolution authorizing annexation of the independent Republic of Texas. Most Texans favored annexation, but their government was unsure of its proper course. Agents of Britain and France urged it to remain independent, in order to counterbalance the United States in the international politics of North America; President Anson Jones leaned toward this policy. Mexico, which still claimed Texas as part of its domain even after nine years of *de facto* Texan independence, threatened the United States with war if it went through with annexation. As soon as Congress passed the joint resolution, the Mexican minister called for his passports and departed, thereby breaking diplomatic relations.[2]

An older controversy with Britain had been smoldering for years on the northwestern frontier. Both Britain and the United States claimed title to Oregon, a region between the Continental Divide and the Pacific coast, stretching from 42° of latitude (the northern boundary of California) to 54°40' (the southern boundary of the Alaska panhandle) and including present-day Oregon, Washington, and British Columbia. Treaties of 1818 and 1827 had established joint occupancy of the disputed area, with provision for termination by either party after a year's notice. At first the Hudson's Bay Company dominated Oregon, but by 1845 several well-defined, self-governing American settlements faced the company's trading posts along the line of the Columbia River.

Pressed by Congress, Tyler and his secretary of state John C. Calhoun had opened exploratory negotiations concerning Oregon; but Calhoun, seeing the progress of American migration, favored what he called "masterly inactivity" and let the negotiations lapse. Meanwhile the British foreign secretary, the earl of Aberdeen, had come to the conclusion that the fairest solution to the question would probably be division by a line along 49°, reserving for Britain the whole of Vancouver Island.[3] Aberdeen

2. Tyler's minister to Mexico remained at his post for a time, but he had stopped communicating with the Mexican government after a quarrel, and Polk recalled him as soon as he became president.
3. Vancouver Island extended south of 49° for perhaps one-fourth of its length. The British wanted the whole island for access to the straits south of it, which were

had not determined how to convince his prime minister, Sir Robert Peel, and the rest of the cabinet or how to broach the compromise to the United States without damaging Britain's negotiating position.

In addition to these two western territorial questions, the American desire for Upper California was almost certain to affect foreign relations during Polk's term of office. California was undeniably Mexican territory, to which the United States had no shadow of a claim, but distance and political confusion prevented Mexico from asserting its rightful control. The people of California were a mixture of Mexicans, Indians, Europeans, and Americans; their government was virtually autonomous. Also, New England traders had established firm economic connections between the Pacific ports of California and the east coast of the United States. During the early 1840s a few of the American emigrants to Oregon were straying off into central California; before long they would be establishing independent settlements, as in Oregon. By 1845 the Mexican hold on California had virtually disappeared, and Americans wondered whether the British would intervene there as they were trying to do in Texas.

As Polk was about to assume the presidency, he faced the first decision of his foreign policy: what to say about Texas and Oregon in his inaugural address. He devoted considerable space to Texas, congratulating the country on its approaching annexation and warning foreign powers not to interfere in this purely American problem. He might have passed over Oregon with the remark that delicate negotiations were still pending; but the Democratic campaign platform of 1844 had mentioned the "clear and unquestionable" American title to the whole territory, and westerners expected him to speak out. He therefore declared: "Our title to the country of the Oregon is 'clear and unquestionable,' and already are our people preparing to perfect that title by occupying it with their wives and children. . . . The world beholds the peaceful triumphs of the industry of our emigrants. To us belongs the duty of protecting them adequately wherever they may be upon our soil. The jurisdiction of our laws and the benefits of our republican institutions should be extended over them in the

_____

more easily navigable than those to the north and east. In 1845 the Hudson's Bay Company established its headquarters on the southern tip of the island.

distant regions which they have selected for their homes. The increased facilities of intercourse will easily bring the States, of which the formation in that part of our territory can not be long delayed, within the sphere of our federative Union. In the meantime every obligation imposed by treaty or conventional stipulation should be sacredly respected." Undoubtedly Polk hoped that these assurances would satisfy the West without arousing the British. In the long run, he was wrong on both counts.

After his inauguration, the new president bent his attention to the annexation of Texas. Thinking he would secure Mexican acquiescence, he sent a special diplomatic agent to approach the Mexican government unofficially for a renewal of relations, hinting at possible payment of an indemnity for Texas. Meanwhile, he sent other agents to Texas to join Chargé Andrew Jackson Donelson (nephew of Jackson and Polk's personal friend) in urging the Texan government to accept the terms of the joint resolution. British and French diplomatic agents were also exerting their influence in favor of reconciliation between Texas and Mexico, and the British agent even persuaded the Mexican government to grant Texas formal recognition as an inducement to refuse annexation; but their actions came too late. By May, Texan public opinion was overwhelmingly annexationist; in June and July, the Texan Congress and a special constitutional convention accepted the joint resolution and voted to enter the Union.

The successful campaign of Polk's diplomatic agents in Texas drew the United States measurably closer to war with Mexico. By then Texas was claiming the Rio Grande as its southern and western boundary, on rather dubious grounds; without carefully examining the Texan claim, Polk committed himself to its support. Mexican leaders would recognize neither annexation nor the Rio Grande boundary and threatened to send an army across the river against the Texan frontier. Having promised to protect the Texans, Polk dispatched a naval squadron along the coast, and in mid-June he moved several thousand troops under Zachary Taylor from the Louisiana border to Corpus Christi on the Nueces River, at the northern edge of the disputed zone, with permission to move south if Taylor wished. At the same time, for good measure, he also sent private orders to Commodore John D. Sloat, commander of the Pacific squadron, that if Mexico attacked Texas and war resulted, Sloat should seize the principal ports of California.

Some historians believe that at this point Polk was consciously plotting war with Mexico. To be sure, the commander of the squadron protecting the Texan coast, Commodore Robert F. Stockton, was an ultraexpansionist with powerful political support at home. From certain inconclusive letters of his, it appears that he considered a preventive seizure of Mexican territory south of the Rio Grande, and President Jones of Texas later declared that Stockton proposed provoking a war. Without written orders from Polk or some other equally clear evidence, however, the "plot thesis" rests on surmise. Secretary Bancroft's formal instructions to Stockton were defensive; so were Buchanan's to Donelson; and other factors suggest that at this time Polk neither desired nor expected war with Mexico.

Perhaps the best reason why Polk should have wanted to stabilize the border question was that Anglo-American relations had taken a turn for the worse during April and May, thanks to the blunt passage on Oregon in his inaugural address. British observers failed to notice that the president had carefully respected the sanctity of treaties and that, in proposing to extend legal protection to American settlers, he was only following the example of the British government and the Hudson's Bay Company. They focused instead on his assertion of the "clear and unquestionable" American title, and, smarting at the prospect of defeat in Texas, the British press hurled insults and threats at the overbearing, aggressive Americans, arrogant in words and feeble in deeds. When questions arose in Parliament, Aberdeen passed them off temperately, but Peel bristled and declared that Britain also had "clear and unquestionable" rights in Oregon. Naturally the American press seized these statements and returned them with interest.

Behind the scenes the British government began unobtrusively to check fortifications along the Canadian-American border and also Channel defenses, in case France supported the American cause. At the same time Aberdeen encouraged a few moderates to disparage the value of Oregon in the press and sent instructions to Richard Pakenham, the British minister at Washington, to seek American terms or propose arbitration of the Oregon question. In a private letter Aberdeen suggested that Pakenham draw from the Americans if possible an offer of the 49° line and Vancouver Island, with the right to navigate the Columbia River, so that he might open cabinet discussions in London. Buchanan discouraged talk of arbitration but delayed a further reply for several weeks.

At this point both parties blundered. When Buchanan finally gave Pakenham a formal reply on 12 July, he indeed proposed the 49° line, conceding to Britain all of Vancouver Island although not navigation of the Columbia; but (undoubtedly at Polk's behest) he set forth the ramshackle American claim to the whole area—up to 54°40′—in a manner that made the compromise offer appear to be a gracious American favor. Outraged, Pakenham replied with a strong statement of the British claim and, carried away by his own rhetoric, rejected Buchanan's offer out of hand instead of referring it to London, as he should have done. Polk recoiled, certain that the wily British had tricked him into showing his cards without ever intending to compromise. After brooding over the rejection for several weeks, he had Buchanan withdraw the offer altogether at the end of August and intimated that if the British wished to negotiate, they must assume the initiative with an offer of their own.

Thus, in the first six months of his administration, Polk had widened the breach with both Mexico and Britain and limited his freedom of action in each case. With a little more understanding of diplomacy, he might have realized that Pakenham's behavior had opened the possibility of putting Britain on the defensive by giving Aberdeen a chance to explain and excuse his minister's mistake. The situation called for a Talleyrand's probing pen; instead Polk had used an eraser. The impasse over Oregon continued through the autumn of 1845, for neither Polk nor Aberdeen would move to reopen negotiations for fear of losing face and bargaining leverage. When the American press and public learned of Polk's stand, western expansionists took heart, for the administration now seemed disposed to carry out the party plank of pushing the boundary to 54°40′.

Still, the Mexican issue, at least, did not seem beyond settlement, for Polk's special agent in Mexico City and the American consul there reported throughout the summer that although government and people were furious at the American annexation of Texas, lack of funds and the uncertain loyalty of the army would probably prevent hostilities. Both men thought that the government would receive a special American commissioner to discuss the Texas question (presumably with the idea of granting Mexico a disguised indemnity for its loss). Polk seems to have understood the limited nature of the Mexican concession, but he determined to appoint a full minister plenipotentiary and reestablish formal relations, ignoring the Texas question and hoping that the minister could persuade Mexico to sell California. For this mission he chose John Slidell of Louisiana, a rising young politician with good manners and knowledge of Spanish who had had no previous association with Mexican affairs.

Before Slidell departed in late November 1845, however, news from the Pacific coast suggested that the California question might require more direct action in addition to negotiation for purchase. In mid-October, Buchanan received an alarming dispatch from Thomas O. Larkin, an enterprising American merchant at Monterey whom Tyler had appointed part-time consul to represent American interests. Larkin warned that Britain was apparently preparing to dominate California, for a new British vice-consulate had just been established at Monterey, probably to operate in conjunction with the Hudson's Bay Company. Also, there were rumors that Mexico was sending out troops, paid for by British money, to reassert authority. Larkin's report was three months old, and its contents were exaggerated or downright wrong; but Polk and Buchanan had no way of knowing this.

Without giving up plans for the Slidell mission, Polk added strings to his bow. First he drew up instructions for Larkin to propagandize among the Californians for annexation to the United States and for resistance against any British effort to establish a protectorate, a strategy that Larkin himself had long favored. These instructions Polk sent out with Commodore Stockton in the frigate *Congress*; but since that ship would need several months for the long voyage around Cape Horn, Polk selected a young marine lieutenant, Archibald H. Gillespie, to memorize the instructions and carry them in his head to California by way of a shorter route through central Mexico. At this point the expansionist Senator Thomas Hart Benton of Missouri seems to have suggested that Gillespie should also carry coded orders and private letters to Benton's son-in-law, the army explorer Lieutenant John Charles Frémont, then conducting a reconnaissance in eastern California and Oregon.[4]

---

4. These orders and letters have never come to light. Reports of an earlier Frémont expedition had already publicized the far West. Some historians have regarded the

While Polk stood his ground in the Oregon controversy and drew up instructions for Slidell, Larkin, and Frémont, he was also composing his first annual message to Congress, one of the most important documents of his whole career. In that message Polk said nothing of his hopes and plans for California; but he described the measures he had taken to protect Texas against Mexican aggression, traced the long history of American damage claims against Mexico, and reported that he had sent Slidell to restore diplomatic relations and to obtain Mexican payment of these claims. (The claims had also figured prominently in Slidell's instructions.)[5]

Concerning Oregon, the president described Anglo-American negotiations under Tyler, which he had attempted to continue, and placed the whole blame for their rupture on Britain: "The civilized world will see in these proceedings a spirit of liberal concession on the part of the United States, and this Government will be relieved of all responsibility which may follow the failure to settle the controversy." He called on Congress to provide an armed guard for emigrants to Oregon and make them formal land grants there, and he further suggested that it would be appropriate to give Britain the prescribed year's warning to terminate the joint occupation treaty.

After his discussion of Oregon, Polk reaffirmed "the principle avowed by Mr. Monroe"—the first important invocation of the Monroe Doctrine since its original declaration in 1823. This passage has an interesting history. Apparently Polk intended something like it for his inaugural address but deleted it at the suggestion of some adviser. During the summer he was much irritated to read a statement by the French prime minister, François Guizot, that France must play an active role in North American affairs in order to preserve *"l'équilibre des forces"*—which the American press translated as "the balance of power," a term embodying to Americans all the decadent, deceitful ways of

---

1845 expedition as aggressively intended from the beginning and have suggested that the orders and letters told Frémont to foment revolution in California. Unless the missing papers are found, a final settlement of the question seems unlikely.

5. Most of these claims arose from damage to American property during Mexican revolutions or from arbitrary acts of the Mexican government. A mixed commission (1840–42) had awarded about two million dollars to American claimants, but the Mexican government had stopped payments.

monarchical Europe. Guizot had been referring to Texas, for France had little interest in California and none in Oregon. Polk, however, intended his declaration to reinforce his analysis of the Oregon question and probably also to warn Britain off California.

The purpose of Polk's annual message was twofold, as far as it concerned foreign relations. In it he sought to explain his policy toward Mexico and Britain as favorably as possible, to demonstrate that he was trying to preserve the peace, whatever the adversaries might do in the future. Also, in the case of Oregon, he called on Congress for prompt, decisive action that would show government and country to be united behind him. Britain, he hoped, would then be compelled to break the impasse at a disadvantage and offer new terms, which he could treat as he chose. What he really accomplished was to limit his actions further by revealing too much of his ambitions to the Mexicans and by making Congress his partner in determining policy toward Britain.

Under the political circumstances of the day it was unrealistic to expect prompt, decisive action from Congress. After the bitterly fought election of 1844, a Whig minority sought revenge against the victorious Democrats. What was more important, during the last phases of the Texas question, expansionism had become entangled in the coils of the abolitionist movement; and the resulting confusion of personal ambitions, partisan loyalties, and ideological convictions made it impossible to predict anyone's actions. Dangerous lines of cleavage ran through the Democratic party, separating a group of western expansionists who cried "Fifty-four Forty or Fight!" and a Southern bloc led by Calhoun, who had put his whole heart into the campaign for Texas but now favored delay and compromise in Oregon.

The debate began in December 1845, soon after the reading of the annual message, and dragged on until late April 1846. It was immediately apparent that the critical issue was abrogation of the joint occupation treaty, since this action would remove the only legal safeguard against war over some trivial local incident. Polk wanted a simple, noncommittal statement advising the president to give notice of abrogation; western Democrats, especially in the Senate, wanted to add a shout of rude defiance that would effectively prevent any diplomatic response from Britain; and moderates at first opposed any notice at all. By February, however, Whigs and antiwar Democrats in the House of Representatives managed to pass a mildly worded resolution of notice, virtually inviting Britain to resume negotiations but shifting full responsibility for them to the president. After weeks of thunderous debate, which stirred the country to its depths, the Senate finally accepted the House resolution, as Calhoun and his bloc recognized that some sort of notice was necessary. The innocuous wording infuriated western extremists, who foresaw a compromise settlement and suspected (probably with reason) that Polk had encouraged the moderates in the last weeks of the debate rather than have the Senate adjourn without acting.

Deprived of his demonstration of national unity, Polk made no progress in negotiations with Britain during the winter of 1845–46. Aberdeen was well aware of conciliatory sentiment in the United States through editorials in the antiwar eastern newspapers and roundabout correspondence between businessmen, Whigs, and other Anglo-American moderates. Indeed, the foreign secretary probably underestimated the force of western expansionism pressing on Polk. Since Peel and the rest of the British cabinet insisted on regarding Oregon as a point of honor, Aberdeen continued his campaign of downgrading the area in the press. At first he hoped that Polk might change his mind and either offer terms or accept arbitration. During March and April, however, he reconciled himself to waiting until Congress passed a resolution that would enable Britain to reopen negotiations without loss of face. Meanwhile he dropped hints that Britain might send naval reinforcements to Canada if pressed too hard. (These hints undoubtedly helped induce Polk to favor compromise in the Senate.) Anglo-American diplomatic communications during the impasse were admirably maintained by the two ministers, Louis McLane in London and Richard Pakenham in Washington, who made as much sense as anyone could out of the complex situation.

While Polk's plans for settling the Oregon dispute were going awry, American relations with Mexico were also worsening. Slidell arrived in Mexico City in early December and found nationalists livid at the prospect of selling more territory and a moderate government clinging feebly to power. The foreign minister, unhappy at Slidell's inopportune arrival, refused to receive him on the grounds that his credentials were those of a full minister plenipotentiary rather than a temporary commissioner.[6] At the end

6. This distinction, which seemed like hair-splitting to Polk, actually had some reasonable basis, for if Mexico accepted full renewal of relations before negotiat-

of the month the nationalists had their way in a revolution, and an army leader, General Mariano Paredes y Arrillaga, became president.[7]

Since Paredes hoped for an Anglo-American war over Oregon, he was naturally no more willing to receive Slidell than his predecessor; the continued rejection confronted Polk with a dilemma just as the Oregon debate was approaching its climax in Congress. Undismayed, he advanced his position and took another strong stand. First he ordered Taylor at Corpus Christi to move his forces across the disputed zone and occupy the north bank of the Rio Grande, avoiding any offensive action against the Mexicans. Then, at the end of January he sent Slidell a message that if Paredes would not see him, "nothing can remain but to take the redress of the injuries to our citizens and the insults to our Government into our own hands." Some historians have interpreted the strong language to mean that Polk never expected Slidell to succeed and that the mission was merely an excuse for military attack. At the same time, however, Polk wrote to his brother that Paredes had probably exaggerated his anti-Americanism in order to gain power and that the order to Taylor was merely "a precautionary measure." It is reasonable to believe that he hoped Slidell would sign a treaty but was prepared to increase the pressure if he did not.

During March and April 1846, Polk's relations with both Britain and Mexico reached a turning point. In Texas, after weeks of preparation, Taylor led his army to the bank of the Rio Grande, where the soldiers built a fort within cannon shot of a Mexican border city, Matamoros, and waited to see if the garrison commander there would send troops across the river to challenge them. In Mexico City, Slidell, after reading Buchanan's January instructions, sent a final request for reception, received another refusal, and prepared to leave for home. In London, the British government was clearly waiting for action in Congress on the Oregon question; and in Washington, the congressional debate

---

ing, it would have little chance of any indemnity or other concession in return for the loss of Texas.

7. Slidell reported rumors that Paredes's party intended to establish a Spanish prince on a Mexican throne with British aid. This report was true, except that Spain was actually the instigator. The intrigue lasted from mid-1845 until the first American victories in May 1846.

was splitting the Democratic party and threatening Polk's whole legislative program. (At the beginning of May he told the Speaker of the House that if Congress tried to adjourn prematurely, he would forbid the action and force a showdown.)

Hitherto Polk had regarded war with Mexico as an unlikely possibility. At some time during April 1846, however, he seems to have concluded that a short, limited conflict on the Rio Grande might be the best way to reunite his party and perhaps also to impress Britain while bringing Mexico to terms. During this period he learned of Slidell's final rejection. On 7 April he discussed the whole matter with the cabinet, which agreed that he should send a message to Congress recommending that the United States take matters into its own hands; but he delayed action, first waiting for the end of the Oregon debate, then for Slidell's return to Washington, and finally for some sort of Mexican attack that would arouse congressional patriotism.

The crisis came during the weekend beginning 8 May. On Friday morning Slidell arrived in Washington from Mexico. After talking with him, Polk decided that he must appeal to Congress for action; but on Saturday morning he and the cabinet decided to wait several days longer, hoping for further news from the Rio Grande. Four hours later the adjutant general called at the White House with a dispatch in which Taylor reported that Mexican troops had ambushed one of his reconnaissance parties north of the river, killing or capturing most of its members. Taylor remarked laconically, "Hostilities may now be considered as commenced." Polk agreed; he spent most of Sunday composing a war message, and on Monday morning he sent it to Congress.

A cynic might have guessed that the message had been written on a Sunday, for it combined the self-righteous wrath of the Old Testament with the long-suffering patience of the New. Polk emphasized the "liberal and honorable" terms, the "fair and equitable" principles, that the United States had displayed toward Mexico. He recited American claims and other grievances and elaborately justified Taylor's presence on the Rio Grande. At the end he drew together the strands of his indictment in words that were to serve as the text for a general debate lasting through the whole war: "The cup of forbearance had been exhausted even before the recent information from the frontier of the Del Norte [Rio Grande]. But now, after reiterated menaces, Mexico has passed the boundary of the United States, has invaded our territory and shed American blood upon the American soil. She has proclaimed that hostilities have commenced, and that the two nations are now at war. As war exists, and, notwithstanding all our efforts to avoid it, exists by the act of Mexico herself, we are called upon by every consideration of duty and patriotism to vindicate with decision the honor, the rights, and the interests of our country."

Congress received these stirring words with mixed feelings. Nearly everyone recognized the danger to Taylor's men and favored voting reinforcements and supplies, but the Whigs and Calhoun's bloc of Democrats opposed a formal declaration of war or any statement blaming hostilities on Mexico until they could investigate the circumstances surrounding Taylor's advance and the ambush. Without much difficulty administration forces in the House rushed through the desired war bill. When Calhoun and the Whigs sought delay in the Senate, Polk's supporters outmaneuvered them at every point, and the president pressured Thomas Hart Benton, a key figure, to swallow his doubts. In the end the Senate, too, passed the war bill by an impressive margin, but many Whigs voted for it unwillingly, lest their party incur the stigma of disloyalty to the flag and go to pieces as the Federalist party had done during the War of 1812.

For several months Polk's plans succeeded as never before. On the Rio Grande, Taylor put his troops out of danger by defeating a larger Mexican army in two battles, Palo Alto and Resaca de la Palma. Then he occupied Matamoros and, after receiving reinforcements, moved slowly up the Rio Grande and into northern Mexico. While he was doing this, Americans were carrying through the occupation of California. When Larkin received his new instructions from Lieutenant Gillespie, he set out quietly to propagandize among the inhabitants; but the explorer John Charles Frémont, in the interior, determined on more drastic action. After talking to Gillespie, he marched his band of explorers to a settlement of newly arrived American emigrants near the site of modern Sacramento; within a few days he had assumed the leadership of an independence movement, to found the so-called Bear Flag Republic. At this point Commodore Sloat of the Pacific squadron received news that war had broken out. Moving his ships to Monterey, he cautiously consulted Larkin, and then, seeing the success of the Bear Flag revolt, he occupied Monterey and the bay area. A little later Stockton and the *Congress* arrived;

Polk sent troops overland; and the combined American forces, regular and irregular, completed the occupation.

Meanwhile the United States and Britain were solving the Oregon problem. By early May the conciliatory wording of the congressional resolution on Oregon had made it possible for Aberdeen to renew negotiations. First, the foreign secretary persuaded the rest of the British cabinet to approve the offer of compromise terms—apparently after considerable argument, although no record of the proceedings has been found. Then he proposed to McLane a treaty dividing the disputed territory at 49°, with Vancouver Island reserved to Britain and navigation rights on the Columbia River to the Hudson's Bay Company. When Polk learned of these terms, he balked at the navigation rights but eventually agreed to submit the whole matter to the Senate. Buchanan and Pakenham quickly prepared a treaty, and on 18 June the Senate approved it by a vote of forty-one to fourteen.[8] While the coming of the war undoubtedly made both Polk and Congress more eager for a settlement, it does not seem to have played an important role in forming British policy. During June and July, Britain and the United States further improved their relations by lowering tariffs and thereby increasing their trade.

Success on the Rio Grande, in California, and in Oregon undoubtedly led Polk to expect a short war with Mexico and a quick treaty confirming the annexation of California and some connecting territory. The Mexicans, however, showed unexpected stubbornness and powers of resistance, favored by their formidable geography: a belt of semidesert in the north, mountain ranges in the center, and the fever-ridden Gulf coast. Polk put out peace feelers to Antonio López de Santa Anna, perennial president of Mexico but then exiled in Havana, who had already sent an intermediary to encourage Polk's aggressive policy and offer his help. Santa Anna hinted that he would negotitate if back in power. Polk granted him free passage through the American blockade. Meanwhile he had Buchanan write the government at Mexico City suggesting negotiations. Nothing came of either venture. The government bluntly refused to discuss terms, and when the

8. The treaty granted navigation rights to the Hudson's Bay Company and to those trading with it but specified that these must be entirely subject to United States law on the same basis as the rights of American citizens.

returned Santa Anna gathered his supporters and seized power, he ignored his assurances to Polk. Instead, he issued a call for troops and organized the defense against the Americans. Meanwhile Taylor had advanced beyond the Rio Grande and captured the city of Monterrey, only to see its defenders retreat into the dry lands to the south.

Polk resented these frustrations all the more because several forces were pressing him to make an early end to the war. One was the British government, which had discreetly inquired more than once about the possibility of mediation, an expedient that Polk firmly rejected. More important, the Whig opposition was gaining support for its antiwar campaign in all parts of the country and especially among Northern abolitionists, who were convinced that Polk, a Tennesseean, had started the war to obtain more slaveholding territory. (The fact that Calhoun also opposed the war impressed few abolitionists. By then they thoroughly distrusted him.) Just before Congress adjourned, Polk sought a special appropriation of two million dollars, in order that he might make a cash offer to Santa Anna if the Mexican leader showed any disposition to treat for peace. Abolitionists attached to the bill an amendment (the famous Wilmot Proviso) forbidding slavery in any territory acquired from Mexico, and the resulting debate widened the sectional split. Even though Polk finally obtained his money at the following session of Congress, his opponents had gained an issue and a useful device for harassment.

By the end of 1846, Polk had to choose between alternative strategies for fighting the war and obtaining a peace. One was to occupy all of northern Mexico as far south as Tampico and San Luis Potosí, establish a line of forts, and wait until the Mexicans gave up. The other was to seize Tampico and Veracruz, the principal Gulf ports, send an army west from Veracruz along the old Spanish road through the mountains; and if necessary occupy the central Valley of Mexico and the capital city. The first plan was obviously within American capabilities, for small detached forces had already marched almost at will through New Mexico and Chihuahua. It was the safer and less expensive of the two strategies; but it called for patience from the dynamic American people, already restive at the duration of the war. The second plan was much riskier, for it required a landing and long supply lines of a kind the American army had never before attempted. One lost battle might stimulate the Mexicans to hold out indefinitely, and a

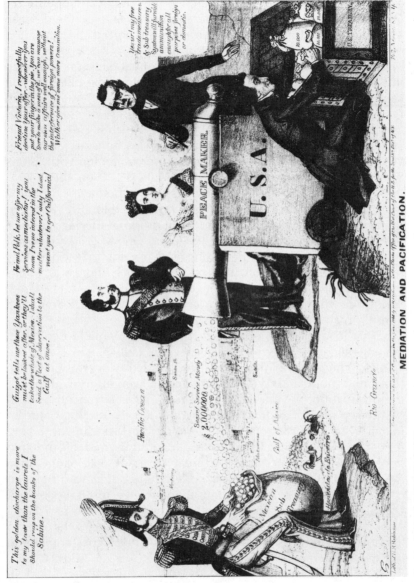

MEDIATION AND PACIFICATION.

series of victories would surely arouse the American appetite for territory. Buchanan and most other moderates favored the defense line. Slidell, Benton (who now ardently supported the war), and other activists called for a central invasion.

For several months Polk postponed a final decision, although in November 1846, he authorized the army to make plans for the capture of Veracruz. (Tampico was occupied without Mexican resistance at the same time.) Meanwhile the president sent special agents into Mexico to inquire about the possibility of peace. In January 1847, a ray of hope appeared, for an emissary arrived at Washington to inquire about American terms, armed with letters from Santa Anna and other Mexican officials. Even today it is impossible to establish the genuineness of this demarche, but Polk must have felt that he had nothing to lose by exploration and sent the agent back to Mexico with a formal proposal for negotiations. The proposal never reached Santa Anna, who was in the north with his army. Instead, the acting government in Mexico City returned a demand to Polk that the Americans withdraw all forces from Mexican territory before negotiations would be considered. Furious at what he considered Mexican trickery, Polk committed himself to an invasion of central Mexico.

This invasion was entrusted to General Winfield Scott, the ranking officer in the army and an excellent choice. Polk suspected Scott's Whiggish political ambitions, but Taylor was a Whig, too—more popular and harder to control. Even after planning for the occupation of Veracruz had begun, Taylor advanced beyond Monterrey against orders and fought a largely useless battle at Buena Vista against Santa Anna, sending the Mexicans on a long retreat to Mexico City. There political conditions had degenerated into virtual civil war; but by a great effort of will, Santa Anna reorganized his battered forces and led them out toward the Gulf coast. By then Scott had landed about twelve thousand troops, bombarded Veracruz, and forced the city's surrender, so Santa Anna took up a strong position in a mountain pass, hoping to thrust the Americans back onto the fever-ridden coastal plain. In the most spectacular victory of the whole war, at Cerro Gordo, Scott managed to outflank the Mexicans and drove them back in disorder; then he occupied the large upland city of Puebla. Beaten for the second time in less than two months, Santa Anna limped back to Mexico City.

Since neither army had enough strength for further fighting, the war again entered a phase of inaction, and Polk decided on another peace feeler. This time he chose an orthodox, if minor, diplomat: Nicholas P. Trist, chief clerk (and *de facto* undersecretary) of the State Department. Trist was a protégé of Buchanan's, a certified Democrat (his wife was Jefferson's granddaughter), and a onetime consul at Havana who spoke fluent Spanish and knew Latin American ways. Trist's instructions concerned the territory to be demanded of Mexico and represented a compromise between expansionists such as Benton and moderates such as Buchanan. Trist was to obtain at least a boundary line up the Rio Grande and across southern New Mexico at about 32° to San Diego on the coast. For this he was to offer fifteen million dollars; but if Mexico would also cede Lower California or other territory, he might raise the price.

After an initial period of jealous bickering, Trist and Scott formed an effective team and tried every conceivable expedient, straightforward or devious, to bring the Mexicans to terms. First, they established a secure line of communications to the Mexican government through the British minister at Mexico City, who was eager to end the fighting. Then, at a hint from Santa Anna, they sent him a "sweetener" of ten thousand dollars and promised immediate payment of one million dollars upon signature of a treaty. When Santa Anna seemed to lose his nerve, Scott led his forces into the Valley of Mexico, defeated the Mexicans in two more battles (Contreras and Churubusco), and encamped just outside Mexico City. Trist then met a commission of Mexicans to discuss terms; but Santa Anna, torn between factions, rejected them. Finally, Scott, seeing no alternative, attacked Mexico City itself, drove out the government, and prepared for indefinite occupation. Santa Anna, thoroughly discredited, resigned and headed for exile again, while the Mexican Congress and the ranking civilian leaders straggled off to a provincial capital to reorganize. The war had reached another impasse.

Back in the United States the news of successive victories and continued Mexican resistance was having a predictable effect on the impatient American public. Opponents of the war continued to cite mounting casualty lists and appropriations, but they faced the arguments of a newly active group of ultraexpansionists, North and South, who proclaimed that the long war and its unexpectedly heavy expenses justified the United States' demand for more territory—even the annexation of all Mexico: "As we shall have no peace until she be annexed, let it come, even though force be necessary, at first, to bring her. Like the Sabine virgins, she will soon learn to love her ravisher." Opponents deplored such ruthless conquest as degrading to the American character and predicted that the "mongrel" Mexican people would corrupt American democracy. Expansionists replied with "Manifest Destiny"—God had provided an opportunity for the United States to regenerate Mexico.

Having undoubtedly learned a few lessons about expansionists during the Oregon debates, Polk reacted to the all-Mexico movement with caution. His cabinet discussions during 1847 show that he was not unalterably opposed to acquiring territory south of the Rio Grande and 32°; but with every Democratic politician jockeying for position in the presidential race of the following year, he did not want to sacrifice control of his party by committing himself prematurely. At first he preferred to leave negotiations to Trist, although the envoy's quarreling with Scott had much displeased him. When Polk learned of the futile dickering at Mexico City, however, he decided to take another strong stand and ordered Trist to abandon his efforts and come home. If the Mexicans decided to discuss terms, they could send a representative to Washington.

By the time this order reached Trist, in mid-November, the situation in Mexico had greatly changed, to the American advantage. The civilian government that had succeeded Santa Anna was moderate and favored negotiation. Although extremists to both right and left invoked patriotism to continue the war, the government gradually brought them under control. When Trist's recall order arrived, he feared that the promising opening for negotiations, if not exploited, might disappear and that Scott's troops would have to occupy central Mexico indefinitely, surrounded by an increasingly hostile population and fighting off guerrilla bands. After several days of hesitation, urged by many American army officers, friendly Mexicans, and Europeans, Trist decided to disobey his orders and stay. Even after that decision, he had to wait two more months for a settlement, since the Mexican commissioners were disposed to argue every point at issue. Finally, on 2 February 1848, they signed the Treaty of Guadalupe Hidalgo, carrying out the most important of Trist's instructions.

Through it the United States obtained Upper California and New Mexico in return for fifteen million dollars.[9]

Trist's courageous insubordination rescued the president from the impossible task of reconciling American and Mexican ultra-nationalists. The news of the treaty arrived just at the height of the all-Mexico movement, and Polk lost little time in submitting it to the Senate. Whatever his feelings about additional annexations, he could not deny that Trist had achieved the original goals of the war, and he had some idea of the dangers to be incurred in continuing it. Except for ultraexpansionists, the country received the treaty with a collective sigh of relief, and when the Senate had taken time to consider the alternatives, it approved nearly all the terms by a vote of thirty-eight to fourteen. The Mexicans accepted its few revisions without difficulty, and the American troops were soon on their way home. The president, however, never forgave Trist for disobeying orders and for a number of tactless comments in his dispatches about presidential actions and policies. He stopped the envoy's salary at the point of his recall, and Trist had to wait over twenty years for full payment—or, indeed, for any other recognition of his accomplishment.

During the last year of his administration Polk briefly considered other ways of acquiring territory on which he mistakenly suspected British designs. It was probably fortunate for the United States that this reconnaissance led to no action, for the southwestern annexations and the sectional arguments they aroused strained the national institutions to their limit. Soon after the war ended, the rebellious Mexican province of Yucatán sought an American protectorate and intervention in a destructive local Indian war. Polk submitted the proposal to Congress, which could not agree on what to do and dismissed the matter. During the summer of 1848 Polk instructed his minister to Spain, Romulus M. Saunders, to explore the possibility of purchasing Cuba, recently racked by rebellion. Saunders, however, bungled the job, and a trial vote in the Senate indicated that Congress would probably have rejected a purchase treaty anyway.

Farther south, in Central America, the influence of Britain was

9. The boundary west of the Rio Grande was drawn along the Gila River to its junction with the Colorado and thence straight to a point on the coast just south of San Diego, which was a bone of contention during the negotiations. The United States also agreed to pay $3.25 million of American claims against Mexico.

more overt; but the Polk administration had little success in countering it. To offset the longtime British consul and chargé d'affaires Frederick Chatfield, Polk sent Elijah Hise as chargé with instructions to encourage the reunion of the weak, feuding Central American states, negotiate commercial treaties, and report on British encroachments. Hise signed two commercial treaties and exceeded his instructions in contracting for perpetual canal rights across Nicaragua, but this treaty was never ratified. The succeeding Whig administration of Zachary Taylor made use of the new prestige the United States enjoyed in the Caribbean after the Mexican War; in 1850 it signed the Clayton-Bulwer Treaty with Britain, thereby somewhat stabilizing the situation in Central America on a basis of Anglo-American equality.

A final act of expansionism by the Polk administration was the treaty of 12 December 1846 with New Granada (Colombia), in which the United States assumed certain responsibilities regarding the Isthmus of Panama. In 1903 Theodore Roosevelt was to use this commitment to justify his intervention and "seizure" of the Canal Zone. The treaty of 1846, however, owed little to Polk's direction. Buchanan had instructed the American chargé d'affaires at Bogotá, Benjamin A. Bidlack, that he should negotiate a commercial treaty and guard against any European effort to obtain sole transit rights across the isthmus. After much pressure from the New Granadan government, Bidlack included in the treaty as Article 35 a long statement in which New Granada guaranteed to the United States that the isthmus would always be open and free to Americans. In return, the United States guaranteed the neutrality of the isthmus and New Granada's sovereignty over it.

When the cabinet saw these provisions, its members remarked doubtfully that the American guarantees seemed to violate the country's tradition against entangling alliances; but Polk submitted Bidlack's Treaty to the Senate. Busy with the Mexican War, that body delayed action for over a year, while New Granada kept a special envoy in Washington to lobby for the treaty. Finally, in June 1848, it was approved with almost no discussion. In this casual manner the United States laid one of the legalistic cornerstones of its future Caribbean policy.

How may one fairly appraise the expansionist policies that Polk followed toward Britain and Mexico? First, it seems clear that he placed too great reliance on bold talk and too little confidence in the possibility of compromise. Suspicious by nature, he was inclined to view each offer by his opponents as a trap or an attempt to exploit American good nature and weakness. Although anxious to negotiate from an appearance of strength, he did not seem to think it necessary to realize that strength by building up the army and navy. As a result, he slipped into the dangerous practice of bluffing. Perhaps he did not appreciate how little respect American military forces inspired abroad; the navy had been in decline since 1815, and the army had struggled to eke out victory over the Seminole Indians in Florida during the early 1840s. More likely he counted on distance, trade, and the vulnerability of Canada to deter Britain from action and despised the Mexicans as strutting boasters, weak and disorganized.

Secondly, beyond these basic attitudes, much of Polk's foreign policy was improvised from month to month in response to events. The statement on Oregon in his inaugural address was a pacifier to the West; Buchanan's offer to Britain, an attempt to draw the fangs of British criticis; and the withdrawal of that offer, a startled and indignant reflex. Similarly, in dealing with Mexico, Polk sought to renew relations in the hope of keeping peace during the annexation of Texas; but as soon as he realized the confusion of affairs in Mexico City, he advanced his goals to the purchase of California. During his first year in office, he regarded war with either adversary as an unlikely last resort. Indeed, he never showed much real concern over Anglo-American hostilities; but in March and April 1846, changed circumstances, especially divisions at home, led him to favor a short tactical war with Mexico. As that war lengthened, he made other political and military decisions required by events.

Thirdly, Polk's largely improvised policies suffered from the phenomenon that twentieth-century analysts have called "escalation." This is a process by which an initial set of decisions starts a chain of causes and effects, each more difficult to control than its predecessor, each widening the area of action and requiring increased forces and money. On inauguration day Polk had a fairly wide range of acceptable policies from which to choose. Some of his early actions and the pressure of circumstances gradually reduced this range. Eventually, when Scott captured Mexico City, Polk found himself boxed in, unable to move, for ultraexpansionists at home would not let him withdraw from central Mexico to a defensive line, and he lacked the resources or the desire to extend the conquest over the whole country. Inaction, too, posed grave problems, for a few small guerrilla victories might have revived the Mexicans' morale and enable them to cut Scott's long supply lines and isolate him in Mexico City.

Finally, one is forced to conclude that Polk's policies were much more hazardous than he realized, thanks to his overbold improvising, the phenomenon of escalation, and the small forces that the United States deployed in the field. Even assuming that Britain had no desire to fight its best customer, Polk could not be certain that a sense of honor over some uncontrollable local conflict in Oregon would not precipitate a general Anglo-American war. Mexico sent a series of appeals to Britain for aid, at one point offering in disguise the cession of California; but fortunately Mexico's revolutions and financial recklessness had so damaged its reputation that the British government showed little interest. Nevertheless, there seems slight doubt that a Mexican victory over Taylor on the Rio Grande would have facilitated a private loan from British bankers. A military stalemate would probably have led to British mediation, and the United States might have had to abandon its hopes for California indefinitely. Fortunately Taylor prevented a stalemate at the outset; but even after more than a year of American victories and Scott's capture of Mexico City, there arose the prospect of an extended occupation—a grave prospect, as we now know, in view of the sectionalism and discord within Polk's United States, not to mention the disastrous French Intervention of the 1860s.[10]

Assuming that Polk was taking long chances as the leader of a tumultuous people and a little-tried army, could he have reduced

10. Between 1861 and 1867 French troops of Napoleon III defeated the Mexican armies of Benito Juárez, occupied most of central Mexico, and tried to establish a puppet empire under Archduke Maximilian of Austria. Juárez had to retreat into far northern Mexico, but his sympathizers kept up constant guerrilla warfare which gradually wore down French strength and made the venture dismayingly expensive. Since the United States would not recognize the puppet empire and European complications demanded attention, Napoleon finally had to withdraw his troops. Juárez retook Mexico City and had Maximilian executed.

these chances through some other line of action? An arguable alternative to bold tactics against either Britain or Mexico was the policy that Calhoun had recommended for Oregon: "masterly inactivity." This policy rested on two assumptions: the continuous, irresistible force of American western migration and the chronic involvement of most of Europe's strength in Old World affairs. At his inauguration, Polk might have refused direct comment on Oregon, while canvassing with Britain the possibilities of a negotiated settlement and carrying through the annexation of Texas. Having offered a compromise line at 49°, Polk should have waited for a formal reply from Aberdeen. If an agreement had been reached during 1845, Polk might have announced it in his annual message, forestalling western resentment with a *fait accompli*; if not, he could still have fallen back on the westerners' arguments.

In any case, Polk should not have proceeded against Mexico before settling the Oregon controversy. There was no need for haste; posting Taylor at Corpus Christi, in the western edge of effective Texan settlement, would have provided sufficient protection with a minimum of provocation to Mexico. As for California, careful analysis of British policy in Europe and the Western Hemisphere should have reassured Polk that Britain had few designs on that prize. Why not allow American settlers to occupy the province, keep American warships cruising off the coast, and see whether or not the Californians would repeat the history of Texas? During some later European crisis (such as the revolutions of 1848 or the Crimean War of the mid-1850s), the United States would have been free to open negotiations with an independent Californian government, which by then might have observed the prosperity of Oregon under American rule.

Perhaps war might have been avoided altogether. At worst, it would have been postponed until a more favorable moment, and, with the United States already occupying Texas and California, any fighting would have been defensive and limited to border areas. Mexicans, of course, would have resented the loss of California under any circumstances, but they had no means of retaining it, and this course would have spared them the humiliation of a foreign army in their capital. Most important to the United States, a policy of more gradual, peaceful expansion would undoubtedly have avoided many of the bitter debates in Congress and the press that widened the alarming gap between North and South.

No one can develop with certainty an argument from "contingent history." Nevertheless, a brief, cautious consideration of Polk's alternatives suggests that his policies, though brilliantly successful, risked too much and aroused hatred and division that gradualism might have minimized. Too impatient to allow time for American migration to take effect, Polk also assigned too small a role to diplomacy—until the last stage of each controversy, when Louis McLane ended the British crisis and Nicholas P. Trist the Mexican War by negotiation.

BIBLIOGRAPHIC NOTE

The principal manuscript sources on which this essay is based are the official foreign affairs archives of the United States, Great Britain, France, Spain, and Mexico; and the private papers of the policy makers involved. The most important private collections are those of James K. Polk, James Buchanan, George Bancroft, Louis McLane, Nicholas P. Trist, Sir Robert Peel, the earl of Aberdeen, and Valentín Gómez Farías.

Among published collections of documents the most important are two sets edited by William R. Manning: vol. 3 of *Diplomatic Correspondence of the United States: Canadian Relations, 1784–1860*, 4 vols. (Washington, D.C., 1940–45), and *Diplomatic Correspondence of the United States: Inter-American Affairs, 1831–1860*, 12 vols. (Washington, D.C., 1932–39), especially vols. 7, 8, and 12. Also useful for the last stages of Texan annexation are George Pierce Garrison, ed., *Diplomatic Correspondence of the Republic of Texas*, Annual Report of the American Historical Association for the Years 1907, 1908, 3 vols. (Washington, D.C., 1908–11); Ephraim Douglass Adams, ed., *British Diplomatic Correspondence Concerning the Republic of Texas, 1838–1846* (Austin, n.d.); and C. T. Neu, "The Annexation of Texas," *New Spain and the Anglo-American West: Historical Contributions Presented to Herbert Eugene Bolton*, 2 vols. (Los Angeles, 1932), 2:71–102. Many valuable documents concerning the negotiation of the Oregon treaty, the Mexican peace treaty, and the New Granadan treaty of 1846, as well as the texts of the treaties, are contained in vol. 5 of David Hunter Miller, ed., *Treaties and Other International Acts of the United States of America*, 8 vols. (Washington, D.C., 1931–48).

Tyler's and Polk's messages to Congress and Polk's inaugural address may be found in vol. 4 of James D. Richardson, ed., *A Compilation of the Messages and Papers of the Presidents, 1789–1897*, 10 vols. (Washington, D.C., 1896–99). Congressional debates are reported in volumes of the *Congressional Globe* for the appropriate sessions and years. A unique and indispensable published source is *The Diary of James K. Polk during His*

Presidency, 1845 to 1849, edited by Milo Milton Quaife, 4 vols. (Chicago, 1910). It is safe to say that no other nineteenth-century president has left such a detailed and revealing record of his thoughts, to say nothing of cabinet meetings and other official actions. Private papers of other major figures have also been published, the most significant being those of James Buchanan, John C. Calhoun, Daniel Webster, Thomas O. Larkin, Zachary Taylor, Antonio López de Santa Anna, and Manuel Crescencio Rejón. Among newspapers consulted the most important are the *New York Herald, Sun,* and *Evening Post;* the *Washington Union* and *National Intelligencer;* the *London Times; Le journal des débats* (Paris); and *El Siglo diez y nueve* (Mexico City).

The most recent secondary account of Polk's diplomacy, from which most of this article is derived, is David M. Pletcher, *The Diplomacy of Annexation: Texas, Oregon, and the Mexican War* (Columbia, Mo., 1973). This contains an amplified bibliography. Charles Grier Sellers is engaged in producing a multivolume biography of Polk, mainly political in emphasis, of which only two volumes were available for this essay: *James K. Polk, Jacksonian: 1795–1843* (Princeton, 1957) and *James K. Polk, Continentalist: 1843–1846* (Princeton, 1966). Frederick Merk has compiled his many articles on Oregon into a convenient book, *The Oregon Question: Essays in Anglo-American Diplomacy and Politics* (Cambridge, Mass., 1967). Other works of his pertinent to Polk's diplomacy (and written in collaboration with Lois Bannister Merk) are *Manifest Destiny and Mission in American History: A Reinterpretation* (New York, 1963) and *The Monroe Doctrine and American Expansionism, 1843–1849* (New York, 1966). These books emphasize press opinion. A shorter survey of the question, attractively written, is Norman A. Graebner, *Empire on the Pacific: A Study in American Continental Expansion* (New York, 1955).

Two older, large-scale secondary works on the subject, longtime classics but now partly superseded, are Justin H. Smith, *The War with Mexico*, 2 vols. (New York, 1919), and George Lockhart Rives, *The United States and Mexico, 1821–1848*, 2 vols. (New York, 1913). Smith's documentation is the more impressive of the two, but Rives has produced a much more balanced narrative. There are no new detailed Mexican monographs worth mentioning. An account by a contemporary of the war which contains some material of value is José María Roa Bárcena, *Recuerdos de la invasión norteamericana (1846–1848)*, 3 vols. (reprint edition, México, 1947). The best study of U.S.-Colombian relations is E. Taylor Parks, *Colombia and the United States, 1765–1934* (Durham, 1935), chap. 12.

The "plot thesis" concerning the annexation of Texas, referred to in this essay, was first advanced with scholarly support in the articles of Richard R. Stenberg, especially "The Failure of Polk's Mexican War Intrigue of 1845," *Pacific Historical Review* 4 (March 1935), 39–68. It has been recently revived with elaborations in Glenn W. Price, *Origins of the*

War with Mexico: The Polk-Stockton Intrigue (Austin, 1967). For fuller comment on this thesis see Pletcher, *Diplomacy of Annexation,* pp. 197–200, 269–71. Concerning the historiographical quarrel over the role of John Charles Frémont see Merk, *Monroe Doctrine and American Expansionism,* pp. 124–30; and Pletcher, *Diplomacy of Annexation,* pp. 285–86. On claims against Mexico see Clayton Charles Kohl, *Claims as a Cause of the Mexican War* (New York, 1914). On the Spanish monarchist plot in Mexico, 1845–46, and Trist's negotiations of 1847–48 see Pletcher, *Diplomacy of Annexation,* pp. 357–60, 362–63, 442–43, 540–50.

Department of State

IMPERIAL DREAMER:

WILLIAM HENRY SEWARD

and American Destiny

Gordon H. Warren

No man faced greater challenges as secretary of state, possessed fewer qualifications for the task, or matured more fully in office than William Henry Seward. Dogged during his first term by the Civil War and the menace of European intervention, then hindered throughout his second by Reconstruction and the executive-congressional struggle, Seward learned to move carefully to save the Union and further his dreams of American empire. The secretary's remarkable success with both goals surprised detractors because nothing in his past had indicated qualties of statesmanship. He was a New York State lawyer unversed in international law, a politician ignorant of the manner of negotiation, and he did not even want to be secretary of state. All his life he reached out for the presidency, but it always eluded him.

Born in a little town in southern New York in 1801, Seward came from English, Irish, and Welsh stock. His paternal grandfather had taken part in revolutionary events and transmitted a faith in republican principles to Seward's father. The latter, a doctor and merchant, had occupied a sort of middle tier of state politics as a postmaster, county judge, and legislator. Encouraged by his father to attend Union College, Seward graduated after acquiring a Phi Beta Kappa key, and proceeded to study law in several firms before accepting a junior partnership in the Auburn office of his future father-in-law, Judge Elijah Miller.

Politics soon attracted the young lawyer whose party mobility—Democratic-Republican to Albany Regency to National Republican to Anti-Mason—reflected a changing set of attitudes as much as local pressure. A keen appreciation of public opinion marked his entire career, and it is sometimes difficult to discern whether principle, practicality, or expediency influenced decisions.

Political groupings in New York tended to follow socioeconomic patterns. Progressives, composed mainly of small farmers, laborers, and skilled craftsmen, supported movements for social justice and democratic reform. Conservatives, usually from the less numerous wealthy mercantile and agrarian interests, relied upon liberal defections to maintain voting power. Seward's professional and social connections often clashed with his republican beliefs, yet he and many conservatives joined the Anti-Masonic movement that swept New York in 1828. As state senator representing the new party, he favored rechartering the Bank of the United States, penal reform, direct election of mayors, and state aid for railroad construction projects. The organization's narrow voter appeal, along with Democratic inroads and new issues, convinced its leaders to dissolve in 1834 and then hammer together an assortment of contradictory elements called the state Whig party. Arm twisting by Thurlow Weed brought Seward the Whig gubernatorial nomination that year. He lost by eleven thousand votes, and promptly retired from politics—always his initial reaction to defeat. For the next four years he kept up a visible practice of law and, maintaining interest in public affairs, supported the Whig dogma of protection, internal improvements, and a national bank. This tactic paid off in an upset election to the governorship in 1838; he became the first non-Democrat to hold that office in forty years. Two terms in Albany marked him as a reformer interested in building a national reputation. By expanding the state's transportation network of canals and roads, advancing education, and taking advantage of popular currents, he hoped to achieve higher office and thus escape the factionalism of New York politics.

While in office he never championed a cause that violated his principles, but he often concealed beliefs that lacked popular support. A characteristic mixture of idealism and opportunism appeared in his treatment of such issues as temperance, immigrant education, and slavery. Thousands of teetotaling converts inspired him to take the pledge, which he broke after leaving office, but his efforts to promote immigrant education arose less from political reasons than from a desire to strengthen the American system. His position on the slavery question perhaps best illustrates his adroit matching of principle to public opinion. He always opposed slavery as a moral and political evil, detrimental to prosperity and America's world image. Still, in the 1838 campaign the candidate declined to endorse black suffrage or jury trial for runaways. Then, as antislavery sentiment quickened, Governor Seward refused to surrender fugitive slaves or extradite alleged slave stealers, and approved British handling of the *Creole* incident.[1] His antislavery stance attracted nationwide attention in the early 1840s, just as the McLeod affair[2] brought foreign notoriety, and revealed an embryonic approach to international relations: firmness in public, conciliation in private.

Seward was a fascinating public character. "I am an enigma, even to myself," he admitted in an unguarded moment, a remark fully supported by contemporary opinion. One observer praised his "ill-disguised contempt both for party obligations and popular applause," while another said he believed in "majorities, and . . . nothing else." His subtlety (critics called him devious) has perhaps been exaggerated. Like any politician he acted artfully at times because indirection served him better. When he spoke his mind it

1. In November 1841 slaves on board the *Creole*, an American vessel en route to New Orleans slave markets, revolted and sailed the ship into the British port of Nassau in the Bahamas. The British refused to surrender the slaves to American officials.

2. In 1840 New York authorities arrested a British subject, Alexander McLeod, for allegedly taking part in the *Caroline* raid (an incident during the 1837 Canadian rebellion when a group of pro-British Canadians destroyed an American vessel for illegally bringing munitions into Canada). London protested to the Tyler administration, which brought pressure on Governor Seward to release McLeod. Upholding New York State prerogatives, he refused; but he assured Washington that he would pardon McLeod if convicted. The court acquitted him.

usually hurt him; and he loved to talk. His conversations, as young Henry Adams marveled, would "inspire a cow with statesmanship." Charming, well read, well traveled, and cosmopolitan, his monologues made commonplace observations sound brilliant. A sociable disposition let him relax at parties where, with a big, black cigar and a drink in hand, he entertained everyone with stories and delightful confidences.

Seward did not seek a third term in 1842 because his devotion to reform and internal improvements had antagonized so many voters. He returned to law and public speaking, determined to forsake office. The governor left the statehouse at a good time; Democratic victories, personal feuds, and philosophical differences among New York Whigs in the 1840s undermined both the party and Seward's career. When not absorbed in cases ranging from homicide to patent rights, he campaigned for Whig candidates and spoke on the popular topics of revolution, war, and, of course, slavery. His support for Ireland's independence struck some people as "impertinent interference," but he thought more of Irish votes than conservative opinion. The outbreak of war with Mexico, supposedly provoked by the Democrats' commitment to southern expansion, persuaded him that slavery had become the overriding issue. Seward was able to oppose Polk's "bastard war" for moral reasons while supporting the president's firm stand on settling the Oregon boundary dispute because he felt it would be popular with voters.

Then office beckoned again; this time it was the Senate. Controversial remarks linking the growth of American empire with expulsion of European colonies from North America nearly prevented his election in 1848. A low profile on some matters helped ensure his political comeback because, as Edwin L. Godkin put it, his safety lay in silence.

Seward's Senate years in Washington coincided with the finale of the great sectional rivalry that had plagued the Union for two generations. The junior senator from New York, unable to keep a freshman's silence, pushed into the battle waged by Calhoun, Webster, and Clay and gained fame overnight for his ability to turn a snappy phrase. As governor he had defended state prerogatives against federal interference; now, upset by Southern attempts to preserve the Mexican cession for slavery, he emphasized Congress's broad constitutional powers of exclusion. Secession threats rarely alarmed him, even during the winter of 1861, when he labeled disunion an "antiquated superstition" fit only to frighten children. He believed that necessity, nature, and mutual benefit had made the Union indestructible.

If delivery of speeches rather than their content determined a senator's influence, Seward might have gone unnoticed. Not even close friends called him an orator. Rasping along in a low monotone, apparently unconcerned whether anyone listened, his opening remarks in 1850 on Clay's compromise plan overwhelmed everyone. Then, as he warmed to the topic, slashing Calhoun, correcting Webster, the senators stirred. They began to sense a moment in history. He attacked all legislative compromise as betrayal of principle and branded Clay's proposals as immoral devices to rescue a temporary institution. Calling for gradual compensated emancipation, he invoked a "higher law" than the Constitution. Providence had chosen the United States to spread the benefits of republican government.

Internal disputes over slavery broke up the Whig party in the mid-fifties and Seward, normally willing to trade party allegiance for personal advancement, drifted into the Republican camp. During the fall of 1858 he gave several speeches including one at Rochester in which he described the free labor–slavery struggle as an "irrepressible conflict." Though nothing distinguished this discourse from previous addresses, "irrepressible conflict," like the catchphrase "higher law," caught public imagination and sounded more sinister than Lincoln's "house divided" speech. The unfortunate words concealed a natural moderation, and people failed to realize, as Major L. Wilson concluded, that "Seward's radicalism was more rhetorical than real." Seward never erased his radical reputation and, notwithstanding efforts by friends to explain his statements at the 1860 Republican convention, "Old Irrepressible" was defeated.

〈XX〉

Seward contemplated retirement until friends, personal ambition, and a flood of speaking invitations dissuaded him. On a western circuit that fall he virtually ignored the Republican platform, speaking instead on slavery and a favorite theme, American expansion. At St. Paul he predicted that Russian fortifications in North America would become outposts of the United States. He had preached the "American gospel" for years and this latest address sounded familiar.

Seward, with a near-mystical belief in Manifest Destiny, had asserted in 1846 that Americans were destined to roll in "resistless waves to the icy barriers of the north, and to encounter Oriental civilization on the shores of the Pacific." He preferred to see America expand peacefully rather than by war (though he did accept the conquered provinces of Mexico). Peace would guarantee domestic prosperity and cultural and economic progress, and would attract adjacent peoples wanting protection of their property and freedom. Subscribing to what might be called the "fruit-drop" theory of expansion—the United States need not fight for land but merely had to wait for contiguous territories and offshore islands to drop like ripened fruit into its lap—Seward relied upon political, physical, and economic laws of gravitation to create an empire. A disciple of John Quincy Adams, he argued that the decay of Spanish power in Latin America and Canadian disputes with Britain presaged absorption of these colonies into the Union. Yet while Adams opposed acquiring territory hospitable to slavery, Seward usually persuaded himself that any new lands would expand, not contract, the area of freedom. Canada appeared "already half-annexed," with Cuba being drawn by "constant gravitation" and Mexico by the influx of American capital and emigrants. A nation must expand "commensurately with its resources and advantages," and the force of attraction exerted by larger bodies upon smaller ones made America's growth unavoidable. The popular application of scientific principles to international politics and the comparison of nations to inorganic matter, according to Albert K. Weinberg, conveniently justified territorial aspirations. The spread-eagle style of oratory came naturally to Seward, who denied that either man or nature could raise a barrier to American expansion.

While he accepted Manifest Destiny he did not trust fate. The federal government had a responsibility to smooth the way for the "three wheels of national greatness": agriculture, industry, trade. It should sponsor internal improvements to speed produce to market and raise tariffs to encourage manufacturing. Above all the nation must advance commerce and "command the empire of the seas, which alone is real empire." He called for a navy to protect American merchant ships, treaties to facilitate overseas invest-

WILLIAM HENRY SEWARD   201

ment, subsidized steamship lines to challenge British maritime
supremacy, surveys of the Arctic and Pacific to broaden trade with
East Asia, and he dreamed of a transcontinental railroad that
would carry immigrants to the unsettled West and commodities to
the Pacific coast. The nation that produced, manufactured, and
sold the most goods would be the greatest power. So "multiply
your ships," he commanded, "and send them forth to the East."
Commerce, the "god of boundaries," would decide upon the
Pacific, its islands, and continents whether the United States or
Europe controlled the world.

Like Jefferson, Seward wanted to create an empire for liberty.
The idea of mission had powerful appeal to generations of
Americans. Since the Puritan migrations they had assumed that the
New World must one day settle accounts with the Old. The
Republic, Seward declared, was "a living offence" to Russia,
Austria, and other despotic powers; Britain's "imperial drumbeat
and the frown of royal battlements" endangered republican
principles. The time of reckoning had come, but there would be
no war. America's destiny, he proclaimed, was to "renovate the
condition of mankind," to carry the spirit of republicanism abroad,
to uplift the degenerate populations of Asia and Europe. The ships
that took American produce to Pacific markets would carry the
democratic creed.

If Seward had intended his expansionist speeches to distract
voters from sectionalism, he failed. After November 1860, extremists on both sides contributed to a postelection constitutional
crisis. Most Republicans, including Lincoln and Seward, doubted
the secessionists' resolution, and overestimated the ability of
Southern unionists to restrain them. Seward attempted to defuse
the situation over the next four months by not opposing the
Crittenden Plan for protecting slavery, preventing enactment of a
"force bill," and encouraging delegates to the Washington Peace
Convention. When conciliatory tactics did not succeed, he proposed that the North try to frighten the South into submission.

The president-elect, according to Seward, adopted a pose of
"masterly inactivity" and supposedly left party leadership to
Seward who soon developed an exaggerated opinion of his own
influence. He feared to leave Washington for even three days lest
the nation disintegrate in his absence. Before the new administration took office he was comparing the president to a hereditary
monarch and telling everyone that Lincoln wanted him to be

prime minister. About a month after officially taking his post as secretary of state, in the well-known memorandum of 1 April 1861, "Some Thoughts for the President's Consideration," he accused Lincoln of having no policy to deal with secession, offered to assume responsibility, and recommended defense measures as well as an aggressive foreign policy to rally the South in defense of the Union. Angry at Spain's annexation of Santo Domingo and the projected conquest of Haiti, he suggested that Lincoln demand explanations from Spain and France, and, if they replied unsatisfactorily, that he convene Congress to declare war. Lincoln should ask Russia and Great Britain to explain what their policies would be during an American civil war, and he should send agents to Canada, Mexico, and Central America. Lincoln filed the memorandum, but its contents leaked. Seward's "foreign war panacea" alarmed diplomats, particularly the British minister to the United States, Lord Lyons, who thought that the New Yorker would be a "dangerous Foreign Minister."

Lyons had all sorts of reasons to worry. Before entering the State Department, Seward had established a reputation among the British for nationalism and opportunism. They could point to the McLeod affair, expansionist speeches aimed at Canada, and a curious episode that occurred during the past campaign when Seward had attended a dinner party at Albany in honor of the Prince of Wales who was then touring America. On this occasion he allegedly remarked to the duke of Newcastle, Britain's colonial secretary and the prince's escort, that he intended to insult Britain to strengthen his own position, but that London should not interpret his remarks as a prelude to war, especially since the British could not afford to fight the United States. Seward denied the conversation, and more incidents followed. In late January, the minister from Bremen, Rudolph Schleiden, hinted that higher tariffs might induce trading nations to favor the South. Rolling his eyes heavenward, Seward stunned the diplomat when he said, "If the Lord would only give the United States an excuse for a war with England, France, or Spain, that would be the best means of re-establishing internal peace." Seward told the British minister early in March that if a European power aided South Carolina, he would "pitch in" to the offending nation and thus heal the Union. Later in the month at the British legation he embarrassed Lyons by denouncing foreign criticism of a new system for collecting customs duties in Southern ports. Then in April came an attack

PUNCH, OR THE LONDON CHARIVARI.—July 6, 1861.

NAUGHTY JONATHAN.

"YOU **SHAN'T** INTERFERE, MOTHER—AND YOU OUGHT TO BE ON MY SIDE—AND IT'S A GREAT SHAME—AND I DON'T CARE—AND YOU **SHALL**
INTERFERE—AND I WON'T HAVE IT."

upon Canada's alleged lack of neutrality. Word of Seward's fulminations spread through Washington, and the chairman of the Foreign Relations Committee, Senator Charles Sumner, decided that the shock of losing the presidential nomination had driven Seward mad.

Seward's motivation, however, was method, not madness. The new secretary of state believed that two factors would deter European intervention in the Civil War; Union victories and a manifest readiness to declare war upon any nation siding with the Confederacy. When Charles Francis Adams, minister to Great Britain, attempted to gloss over Seward's bellicosity, the secretary warned, "You could do no greater harm, than by inducing an opinon that I am less decided in my intercourse with the British Minister than I am reputed to be or less determined to maintain the pride and dignity of our Government." Seward, however, gambled that no government would risk war, that European nations could not submerge their rivalries long enough to act in concert. He cultivated a lunatic image to keep Europe off balance.

Lord Lyons's outward demeanor remained coldly correct toward Seward, who represented the sort of American politician so disgusting to him; inside he was seething. He concluded that the secretary viewed foreign relations as "safe levers" for manipulating public opinion. He recommended to Prime Minister Lord Palmerston that he put Canada in a state of defense, reinforce squadrons in the West Indies, the Atlantic, and the Pacific, and pursue a common policy with France toward American problems. The British government accepted all of his advice.

At about the time Lyons sent these recommendations, Seward drew up a document designed to reinforce his admonitions against interference. Britain and France seemed about to "try to save cotton at the cost of the Union," and the secretary of state sent to Adams in London his Dispatch Number Ten of 21 May 1861. This vigorous instruction, which Seward liked to describe as a "bold remonstrance," contained reckless phrasing. Fortunately for Anglo-American affairs he first showed it to Lincoln, and the president, with Sumner's enthusiastic approval, toned it down. Even if the softened version had been communicated it "might have made a war in five minutes," or so the American minister's son Henry thought. Seward had wanted Adams to indicate that Washington demanded acceptance of the blockade, intended to treat captured privateers as pirates, and considered official or unofficial contacts between the British government and the so-called Confederacy tantamount to a breach of diplomatic relations. Hostilities might ensue between the United States and "one, two, or even more European nations," but Great Britain, not the Union, would be responsible for war. "War in defence of national life is not immoral," he concluded, "and war in defence of independence is an inevitable part of the discipline of nations." At Lincoln's insistence Seward had marked the instruction confidential and not for communication, only to publish it, for all the world to see, in the annual *Diplomatic Correspondence* series[3] he intiated in the autumn.

Unknown to the secretary when he drafted Dispatch Number Ten, Britain already had recognized Confederate belligerency by announcing neutrality the day before the American minister arrived in London. When the news reached Washington Seward did not retaliate, but he commented that the neutrality proclamation questioned the Union's right of self-defense. The administration, he tried to persuade Lyons, harbored no ill will, a statement that diplomat found hard to accept. At this juncture Lyons's dispatches, going beyond criticism of Seward, lacked balance. Page after page carried attacks upon the secretary's character, habits, motives. In the spring of 1861 nothing could sway the British minister's deep conviction that America, with Seward in charge of foreign policy, presented a serious danger to British interests. The secretary learned indirectly of Lyons's attitude from Adams, who wrote that London officials had been stiffened, not frightened, by talk of war. Embarrassed, Seward explained that his "emphatic and sometimes, perhaps, impassioned remonstrances" against Confederate recognition resulted from a "profound solicitude to avert foreign war."

The British and French governments thus could store up unflattering impressions, complicating Seward's problems in the *Trent* affair of late 1861, a situation for which he possessed at least partial responsibility. The affair contained all the ingredients of high melodrama: Caribbean seas and Confederate agents, screaming ladies and gallant officers, the Christmas season and a royal

3. U.S. State Department, comp., *Papers Relating to the Foreign Affairs of the United States, 1861-68*, 19 vols. (Washington, D.C., 1862-69). This was the forerunner of the series now entitled *Foreign Relations of the United States*.

funeral, imperious demands and an eleventh-hour retreat. Throughout the tense weeks of the crisis Seward revealed much about his approach to foreign affairs. No Civil War incident brought more clearly into focus the secretary's abilities and disabilities.

On a dark night in mid-October 1861, James M. Mason and John Slidell, the designated Confederate commissioners to the British and French courts, had slipped past the Federal blockade off Charleston Harbor and steamed toward Cuba where they expected to take passage for Europe. They spent two weeks in Havana before boarding, on 7 November, a British mail packet named the *Trent* which would take them to St. Thomas. The next day Captain Charles Wilkes of the U.S.S. *San Jacinto* stopped the vessel, removed Mason, Slidell, and their secretaries, and allowed the *Trent* to resume its voyage. After a search for precedents, Wilkes had decided that international law justified the arrest of the diplomats as "embodiment of dispatches." He had instructed his first officer, Lieutenant Donald Fairfax, to seize the *Trent*, but Fairfax refused because a seizure would have inconvenienced the passengers, delayed shipment of mail and specie to merchants, and weakened the Union cruiser's part in the anticipated Federal attack on Port Royal, South Carolina. Wilkes thereupon took only the Confederate commissioners and embroiled his government in a controversy of the first magnitude.

The deed raised important questions concerning neutral rights and belligerent obligations: whether Wilkes erred in removing Mason and Slidell, whether he should have taken the *Trent* as a prize, leaving the men aboard, and brought it before an American tribunal to determine if the vessel had violated neutrality by carrying the commissioners. Hardly anyone, including the United States attorney general, seemed to think so. Lincoln kept silent, and Seward, pleading illness, refused public comment, although Secretary of the Navy Gideon Welles reported him to be jubilant. The administration had decided not to risk public disapproval with a premature surrender of the agents and to await London's reaction. The Mason and Slidell affair, Seward predicted in a masterpiece of understatement, "will try the British temper."

If it was a typical Seward move to test British resolution, his adversary refused—perhaps typically also—to back down. The British government, press, and public regarded the *Trent* incident as an insult to the national honor. "The people are frantic with rage," an American living in London wrote Seward, "and were the country polled, I fear 999 men out of 1,000 would declare for immediate war." When Palmerston asked crown law officers for an opinion they responded that international law permitted a belligerent to stop and board a neutral vessel such as the *Trent* and conduct it to the belligerent's port for prize proceedings if there were suspicion of neutrality violations, but the law forbade the removal of any passengers. Wilkes's action was "illegal and unjustifiable." Over the next days the government prohibited export of war materials, began sending eleven thousand troops and tens of thousands of weapons to Canada, drew plans to blockade Union ports, strengthened the North American fleet, and, in a note composed by British Foreign Secretary Lord Russell, demanded that the Lincoln administration apologize and release Mason and Slidell within one week after receiving the protest. This, then, was the harvest of Seward's belligerence; Britain saw the *Trent* affair as his long-desired pretext for war.

At first Seward seemed to continue his usual truculence. Over a month passed after the capture before London papers arrived on 13 December bearing news of war preparation. Peace editorials sprouted, and provocative resolutions lost popularity in Congress. Everyone grew suddenly quiescent—everyone, that is, except Seward. At a cotillion on the sixteenth, where war crisis dominated the conversation, he startled other guests by crying out: "We will wrap the whole world in flames! No power [is] so remote that she will not feel the fire of our battle and be burned by our conflagration."

Then he began to back off. The secretary's defiance accomplished nothing. Three days after the party, Lyons called at the State Department to deliver Russell's ultimatum. Suspecting trouble, Seward persuaded the minister to describe the note's contents informally, give him a copy unofficially, and, when Lyons mentioned the deadline, to postpone formal presentation of the demands until 21 December. Soon after Lyons returned to the legation the secretary rushed over to ask what would happen if, at the end of a week, his answer rejected the ultimatum or proposed further discussion. "I could not accept it," the minister warned. On the twenty-first Seward complained that since other duties had prevented him from studying the note he needed another two days. Lyons agreed, stipulating that he would not accept delay after 23 December.

Lincoln and Seward were at an impasse, and only gradually came out of it. The president had composed a document that called for extensive discussion of the *Trent* and other issues—touching even the British position throughout the Civil War—and submission of the whole affair to arbitration. Knowing that London would never consent to arbitrating a question of national honor, Seward stalled Lyons for four days while he argued with Lincoln. The minister, keeping his promise, finally gave notification on 23 December, thereby setting noon of 30 December as the deadline for a reply. Seward read the dispatch to Lincoln, who remained oblivious to the consequences of keeping Mason and Slidell. "I will never give them up," he said. Seward frowned. "Then I shall be obliged to ask you, Mr. President, to write the reply to Earl Russell for the strength of the argument from our own past policy, so far as I can see, is in favor of a compliance with his demands." On Christmas Eve a cabinet meeting debated the *Trent* crisis. Lincoln continued to push for arbitration and though Seward tried to object he suggested they both draw up answers and compare points. The cabinet met on Christmas morning to hear Seward read Russell's note and a draft reply. Four hours of debate ensued. Members seemed more disposed to surrender Mason and Slidell on the ground of avoiding another war than upon the real issue involving a flagrant violation of neutral rights. They grudgingly approved Seward's reply, and the secretary incorporated their sentiments into the final copy. He polished his draft, read it to the Foreign Relations Committee, and presented the document to Lyons on 27 December, three days before the deadline's expiration.

Seward had functioned as a peace-keeper during the *Trent* crisis once he realized the depth of British anger. He had argued the British case in cabinet, noting that Wilkes's act violated international law and American traditions. Confronted then with the impossible task of satisfying London, salvaging national honor, and preserving his reputation, Seward had written a paper that cheapened the high principles upon which he had urged surrender. He informed the British that Wilkes had a legal right to stop and search the *Trent* and then, quoting an admiralty judge, Sir William Scott, out of context ("You may stop the ambassador of your enemy on his passage"), claimed that the captain could have lawfully captured Mason, Slidell, and their dispatches as contraband of war. Having justified the seizure, Seward groped for an excuse to repudiate it. If Wilkes had involuntarily released the *Trent*, he commented, the United States was entitled to keep the prisoners; yet by voluntarily freeing the vessel he waived any claim. Wilkes's inadvertency constituted an illegal act for which Britain deserved reparation. Seward might well have stopped at this point but he had other purposes and another audience in mind, so he continued. If the Union's security had required the commissioners' detention, he said, they would not have been surrendered despite their illegal capture. Seward surrendered the men for the wrong reasons, indulging in what Lincoln liked to call the "horse-chestnut" style of argument, a "specious and fantastic arrangement of words by which a man can prove a horse-chestnut to be a chestnut horse."

However illogical his note, Seward deserves credit for ending the war crisis at considerable risk to his personal popularity. He also improved his reputation in London. Lyons's dispatches had convinced Russell and Palmerston that he meant to provoke a conflict. When the *Trent* affair, a perfect clash of neutral and belligerent rights, passed without hostilities, they questioned Lyons's interpretation. "I do not believe that Seward has any animosity to this country," Russell declared. "It is all buncom."

Henry Adams best defined Seward's approach. "The foreign policy of Mr. Seward," he wrote, "was, in principle, simple enough, although his expedients were innumerable. His intention was always to avoid war, but always to gain his objects; and he achieved astonishing success." While Seward avoided war over the *Trent*, the tone and phrasing of his note indicated a higher regard for domestic political reaction than for international goodwill.

Before Seward took office his old mentor Thurlow Weed had counseled that since a secretary must be popular with the people to be successful, Seward must cultivate a style that would please the public. Never forgetting that advice, Seward, more than any predecessor, wrote dispatches with an eye to public opinion. He frequently published his instructions in newspapers and, as mentioned, originated the *Diplomatic Correspondence* series. Publication did not endear him to foreign ministers who realized that he worded dispatches to appeal to his own public. "You are I believe aware," Russell wrote Lyons upon receiving the 1861

volume, "that Adams never read me any of those long, vainglo-
rious & insolent dispatches which Seward has laid before Congress."

Contrary to the general belief that Seward became less
volatile as he acquired experience and submitted to Lincoln's
guidance, the secretary's bellicosity persisted for a long period
after the *Trent* affair. The confident, almost cocky tone permeating
his dispatches was designed to bolster the morale of Northerners
at home and abroad. Seward believed that "to betray apprehension would be to betray the Union." When the government's
future seemed darkest he sounded most optimistic. Recognizing
that tidings of military reverses coupled with hostile foreign
judgments depressed American diplomats, the secretary oozed
confidence in his dispatches. To one minister discouraged by a
second defeat at Bull Run, Seward exhorted, "The United States
must demand under all circumstances of their representatives in
foreign countries what the old Romans required of their Generals,
even when defeated, never to despair of the Republic." He did not
despair. Through a series of crises that arose with numbing
regularity—mediation offers, commerce raiders, a French expedition to Mexico—he affirmed his faith in the inevitable triumph of
the Union, "the chief security of nations."

An example is his behavior over the possibility of European
mediation, which issue kept relations between the United States
and Europe in turmoil for two years. From the war's onset the
governments of Great Britain and France had acted jointly upon
the question of deterring Washington from attacking either
power. Both nations recognized Confederate belligerency in 1861,
the British in May, the French in June. Seward ignored their
common policy, hoping that Northern victories and his pungent
language would deter any unpleasant move such as an offer to
reconcile sectional differences by mediation. Fearing that recognition of Confederate belligerency would lead to recognition of
independence, he let it be known that he viewed recognition as
equivalent to an alliance, and therefore a declaration of war.
When France and Britain complained about curtailment of trade
he retorted that the American stake was larger. He rejected the
first offer of mediation in June 1861, warning that foreign
intervention would produce "new and injurious consequences."
He had a special message for Britain. The empire, an "aggregation
of divers communities," might someday undergo strain. "Would it

be wise for her Majesty's government, on this occasion, to set a dangerous precedent or provoke retaliation?" A master of counterattack, he predicted a speedy end to the war if only the European powers withdrew their recognition of belligerency.

Confederate victories nonetheless had fostered a belief in European chancelleries that the American Civil War, so disruptive to international trade and peace, should be humanely resolved by mediation. Lord Russell felt strongly about the matter and, encouraged by that tireless schemer Napoleon III, hatched a plan. He proposed to Palmerston in August 1862 that the British government, in consultation with Russia, Prussia, Austria, and France, should offer mediation to Washington with the intent of recognizing Southern independence if mediation failed. Seward, whose agents had reported an impending change in British policy, fired off a barrage of threatening notes to Adams which were not read to Russell but naturally appeared in the published correspondence for 1862 a few months later. Failure of foreign powers to respect American sovereignty, the secretary wrote, would lead to "a war of continents—a war of the world." It would unite the feuding sections. Fortunately there was to be no mediation. British cabinet members viewed Russian cooperation as essential to the plan's success; but when the enthusiastic French, acting as cosponsors, raised the idea at St. Petersburg in the autumn of 1862, they received a blunt refusal. If Russia and America had antithetical systems of government, they also possessed common enemies, and the czar valued American friendship. Seward's well-known determination to wage war against any power that intervened in behalf of the Confederacy undoubtedly played a part, along with Confederate defeat at Antietam.

The secretary soon ceased to worry about intervention and concentrated on saving the Union merchant marine from foreign-built commerce raiders. Since the Confederacy lacked shipbuilding facilities, it secretly negotiated contracts with British firms to supply vessels and then, obeying the letter of Britain's Foreign Enlistment Act of 1819, armed, equipped, and manned the steamers in the West Indies and elsewhere for careers of destruction. British authorities would not prevent their sailing unless furnished with incontrovertible proof of a belligerent destination. Minister Adams, consular officers, and a company of fumbling spies spent hours securing affidavits of the suspected vessels' destination, but London officials rarely found the evidence overwhelming. Seward accused the British of condoning open piracy and urged Congress to pass a bill authorizing the issuance of letters of marque. Since the Confederacy possessed no maritime commerce, and privateers preyed only on merchant vessels, the proposal was aimed squarely at Britain. Seward wrote in the summer of 1863 that the United States was drifting toward a war with Great Britain, all because its government would not enforce the neutrality law. Why, he asked, did the British insist on setting precedents when one day they might be at war and the United States at peace? Lawyerlike, the secretary prosecuted Britain in the pages of *Diplomatic Correspondence* by publishing scores of Adams's affidavits and intercepted Confederate letters relating to purchase and outfitting of vessels.

The commerce raiders never really endangered the Union war effort, but they did constitute a costly nuisance for which Seward rightly demanded compensation. He pressed for postwar payment of the so-called *Alabama* claims, tying their settlement to negotiation of a naturalization treaty designed to protect Irish-American Fenians from arrest when they visited Ireland. Seward considered canceling the claims in return for cession of Canadian territory, yet he realized that the British government would not accept such terms. The new American minister to London, Reverdy Johnson, finally signed an arbitration convention in early 1869 which incurred the Senate's displeasure for not containing a British apology or reference to indirect claims; however, Charles Sumner, who led the opposition, attacked the treaty because of his dislike of both Britain and the administration rather than because of any objection to the convention's provisions. Unable to arrange a satisfactory agreement, Seward at least laid a solid foundation enabling his successor, Hamilton Fish, to negotiate the 1871 Treaty of Washington.

⟨⟨⟨⟩⟩⟩

Almost throughout his years as secretary, Seward also had difficulty with Napoleon III and devoted valuable time to coaxing French troops out of Mexico. The Maximilian affair originated partly in Mexico's suspension of foreign debt payments in 1861 and the Convention of London of that year in which France, Spain, and Britain agreed to undertake a joint expedition against the Juarez regime to force resumption of financial obligations. Seward had tried to guarantee the Mexican debt by supporting a loan of sufficient proportion to stave off creditors, with Mexico's northern provinces attached as security. The Senate rejected this perhaps bald-faced land grab, and when the powers invited American participation in the joint expedition Seward could only speak of Mexican political and territorial sovereignty. Declining association on these grounds, rather than mentioning the Monroe Doctrine (designed to prevent such invasions), he avoided antagonizing the allies. Seward's Mexican policy, Weed later observed, "breaks no eggs." Having discarded his foreign war idea the secretary saw no point in gasconading about Mexico while locked in a death struggle at home. British and Spanish troops left Mexico early in 1862 but the French, hypnotized by dreams of empire, installed the puppet emperor Maximilian and stayed until 1867. Seward informed Napoleon that popular sympathies toward Mexico made it difficult to enforce American neutrality laws, and that American security depended upon "continuance of free republican institutions" throughout the Americas. Except for occasional perfunctory objections the secretary then let the matter lie.

The State Department's cautious policy toward the Mexican intervention infuriated congressmen mindful of public reaction against a challenge to the Monroe Doctrine. In the spring of 1864 the House resolved that the United States government would not "acknowledge any monarchy erected in America upon the ruins of any republic, under the auspices of any European power." Seward privately described the resolves as passed with "more patriotic zeal than discretion" and assured Paris that the president contemplated no drastic change of policy. Far from adopting a firebrand attitude on every question, Seward thus often served as a brake to popular enthusiasms. Yet increasing public dissatisfaction and Confederate losses led him to publish his dispatches to France— sometimes before they reached Paris. The Civil War ended with almost a million Union soldiers under arms and, although the armies rapidly demobilized, fifty-two thousand troops massed on the Texas border. In September 1865, Seward signified that French evacuation would promote international peace and Franco-American friendship, and in December he induced President Andrew Johnson to warn Napoleon that continued good relations with the United States rested upon his troops taking French leave. The secretary then stated that Americans resented a foreign army overthrowing a republican government and "establishing upon its ruins" a foreign monarchy; significantly, Seward was using virtually the same language as the House resolutions passed two years earlier. Napoleon, perhaps remembering the relationship between discretion and valor, took the hint and agreed to withdraw from Mexico by the spring of 1867, leaving the Hapsburg Archduke Maximilian to his fate.

Seward's handling of the Mexican question typified his cautious approach to matters not directly affecting the Confederacy's status. "This government," he had declared late in the war, "has learned something of the value of concentration of purpose." The specter of Anglo-French mediation had nurtured in him an astonishing respect for the status quo. He maintained strict neutrality during the Italian civil war of 1862, declined to offer mediation of Latin American disputes unless asked, refused to recognize revolutionary governments lacking public acceptance, and condemned "sedition or rebellion against the imperial authority" in China. The man who had praised Hungarian revolutionaries in 1851 later wondered if the great maritime states should form a latter-day Holy Alliance to crush insurrection.

His conservatism appeared in other ways. While he pressed claims at London, he instructed representatives in Italy, Argentina, Santo Domingo, and Brazil to urge no redress of damages collectible only by force. As hostilities between North and South waned, European governments expected the Washington regime to undertake wars of vengeance. Seward's dispatches implied that eventuality, but he repeatedly said that he meant commercial, not political, reprisals. The United States, he wrote, believed in the principle of nonintervention and fielded no armies to wage aggressive war.

To be sure, he liked to keep foreigners uncertain. He suggested international expeditions to chastise Japan and Korea, an inconsistency for someone who defended Mexican sovereignty. His disavowal of postwar territorial ambitions did not impress diplomats acquainted with his desire to restore national prestige. The secretary of state, they thought, was most dangerous when he appeared agreeable.

◇◇◇

Apart from surmounting the problems of foreign relations connected with the Civil War, Seward deserves a prominent place in American history because of his attempt to extend the national boundaries and foster commercial opportunities. Richard Van Alstyne has correctly stated that Seward was "the central figure of nineteenth-century American imperialism." For Africa and Asia, the Antilles and Alaska, he pushed a staggering variety of projects to strengthen his nation in competition with colonial, big-navy powers. A vision of American Manifest Destiny prompted him to rhapsodize:

> Our nation with united interests blest,
>   Not now content to poise, shall sway the rest;
> Abroad over Empire shall no limits know,
>   But like the sea in boundless circles flow.

Mr. Seward, Henry Adams once remarked, "was seldom satisfied with a small policy." All his life he shared the popular conviction that all of North America must fall under American control and worked to achieve that end by peaceful means.

Russian America became part of Seward's grand design. He had long coveted Russian territory, and Confederate raids on Union vessels in the Arctic seas confirmed his feeling that national security made ownership of the region desirable. American warships would secure coaling stations; the merchant marine would compete more effectively in the China trade. The secretary's attitude toward Russia had changed, of course; the alchemy of *Realpolitik* had transformed the czarist government from a "despotic power" in the 1850s to a "good friend" in the 1860s. Delighted at the rapprochement and worried about the unprofitable colony's weakness, the czar instructed his minister in Washington to unload Alaska on the United States. Seward quickly signed a purchase treaty and submitted it to the Senate. When that body appeared more interested in opposing Johnson administration measures than in extending American boundaries, the secretary of state undertook a program of public education, stressing that failure to ratify would insult America's only European friend. The Senate approved, but not for another year did a cantankerous House appropriate over seven million dollars for Seward's Icebox. Acquisition of Alaska fitted nicely into his Pacific policy because it facilitated communications and trade with East Asia, or the "Far West" as he viewed it. Elated at a deal comparable to the Louisiana Purchase, he bragged that if he could live another thirty years he would give to the people "possession of the American Continent and the control of the world."

The secretary spent his last two years in office working to secure territory. He planned to dot the Caribbean and Pacific with a network of ports serving American naval vessels and the merchant marine. He would link the two regions by a canal across the isthmus of Panama (the great American route) to cut transportation costs, strengthen defenses, and blunt British influence in Central America. Tackling the canal project first, the secretary negotiated a right-of-way through Colombia in defiance of the Clayton-Bulwer Treaty and then, believing that the popular mind would have to be conditioned to the idea, insisted on a survey to determine construction costs. Before the survey could begin, however, the Colombian Senate refused to ratify the treaty, setting the stage for a more violent settlement forty years later.

Undaunted by failure, Seward embarked upon a quest for island outposts. His tactics showed ingenuity if nothing else. In the Pacific he attempted to acquire the Hawaiian Islands by signing a generous reciprocity treaty to dispose the residents toward annexation. The Senate tabled it, and the Hawaiian kingdom promptly undertook negotiation of treaties of amity and commerce with Russia and Prussia. Resenting Hawaii's unseemly haste, Seward issued a general confidential circular stating that it would be "incompatible" with American interests to let the islands fall under the "jurisdiction, protection or dominating influence of any foreign power." He thus extended the Monroe Doctrine overseas. Although no minister ever presented Seward's circular, the Hawaiian mission did not succeed.

Closer to home he worked to fulfill an old American desire for Caribbean possessions. The dual problems of chasing down Confederate raiders and transforming the United States into a world power had convinced Seward that his government must acquire harbors in the West Indies or yield maritime supremacy. He experienced heartbreaking defeats. After negotiating a treaty in the autumn of 1867 for purchase of the Virgin Islands he could not persuade the Senate that it would be in the national interest. His standard attempt to rally public opinion failed, and not for another fifty years did title pass into American hands. Paralleling the Danish West Indies negotiations was a long-simmering effort to lease or buy the Bay of Samaná from Santo Domingo, but revolution cut short the lukewarm dickering. By the time the Senate had rejected the project as well as a suggestion to annex the whole island, plans to acquire St. Bartholomew, Culebra, and

Culebrita also had gone aglimmering. During his final days in Washington Seward realized that he would never see the American flag wave over Caribbean territory; yet he could remark with pardonable pride that "the country is not less now, but is larger than I found it when I entered my last public office."

All the while the secretary had been caught in the turmoil of rebuilding a shattered nation, and the failures of the Johnson administration had a good deal to do with the failures of his imperial plans. Intent upon humiliating Johnson, Radical Republican senators voted down nearly every measure originating in the White House or cabinet. Seward wooed key members, but could overcome neither their hatred for President Johnson nor their desire to reassert congressional prerogatives. His efforts to rally public opinion likewise collapsed. After the Civil War people wanted to return to business as usual. Then, too, they found the political struggle in Washington more interesting, Reconstruction problems more demanding, domestic expansion more pressing than Seward's summonses to greatness. Appeals to patriotism, destiny, even avarice scarcely budged a people seeking to avoid new challenges. The public mind, Seward sadly concluded, refused to entertain "the higher but more remote questions of national expansion and aggrandisement." His dreams turned to dust.

◇◇◇

Seward had entered the State Department expecting to use it as a stepping-stone to the presidency. Throughout Lincoln's administration he sought to function as a prime minister, a shadow president, directing the business of government while other cabinet members, in his eyes, served as bothersome if necessary clerks. Cordially disliked by his colleagues, he had the support of both Lincoln and Johnson because they valued his political expertise and popular support. The secretary gradually abandoned his presidential hopes after realizing that, in his preoccupation with foreign relations, he had lost touch with voters and party leaders.

During the years 1861–69 Seward did not make policy in a vacuum, however. Although the flamboyant secretary cultivated the impression that he carried American diplomacy in his coat pocket he always solicited other opinions and weighed domestic and foreign considerations before arriving at a decision. He then ran a gamut of presidential, cabinet, and congressional criticism. Lincoln usually backed the secretary but occasionally, as in the matter of issuing letters of marque, deferred to the informed views of Navy Secretary Gideon Welles. Seward also had to cope with Senator Charles Sumner who, according to David Donald, monitored State Department activities at Lincoln's request and became an indispensable guest at diplomatic dinners. While close supervision affected neither the tone nor content of Seward's dispatches, it sometimes helped him avoid mistaken actions.

The ordeal of conducting diplomatic affairs during the Civil War provided Seward with a lesson in the limits of power. He soon realized that "bold remonstrances" offered scant value if unsupported by force, which was often difficult to apply. In foreign relations, as in politics, Seward knew when to advance and, above all, when to retreat. The *Trent* affair proved to be his most educational experience. In its aftermath, having previously ignored the Royal Navy's awesome firepower, he became almost contrite. He avoided giving offense and to Welles's intense disgust refused to press certain flagrant British violations of neutrality. Seward exercised commendable restraint in handling Britain's failure to detain commerce raiders. Lord Palmerston, himself an expert practitioner of brinkmanship, conceded that he had "acted fairly by us." While his Civil War diplomacy was perhaps not as "masterful" as Alexander DeConde believes, he does merit accolades for steering the nation around the most perilous diplomatic shoals since revolutionary days.

As secretary of state, Seward looked both to the past and the future. A preserver rather than an innovator of foreign policy, he elaborated the hemispheric aims of Thomas Jefferson and John Quincy Adams. Uninterested in solving problems created by the decline of Turkey, the rise of Prussia, and the stagnation of France, he believed his country's interests to be in the Western Hemisphere and Asia. The policies he pursued in these areas revealed a healthy mixture of idealism and realism, as well as a significant amount of opportunism. He had glimpsed the value of a two-ocean navy supported by a system of strategically placed bases in the Caribbean and Pacific to facilitate trade and bolster security. He foresaw the day when East Asia, not Europe, would be the world's theater of rivalries. China with its millions of potential customers had long attracted American entrepreneurs, and Seward by purchasing Alaska hoped to acquire a bridge to Asia. The precursor of late nineteenth-century imperialists, a high priest of expansionism, the secretary anticipated Alfred Thayer Mahan's arguments for a large navy, extensive commerce, and overseas bases. Seward's vision, his aspirations and not his deeds, marked him for greatness. It was his misfortune to head the State Department during the Civil War and, in his second term, an antiexpansionist, antiadministration period. He nonetheless followed policies that led to the emergence of the United States as a world power in the twentieth century.

Over a public career spanning four decades, controversy swirled about William H. Seward. Contemporaries either admired or disliked the man; no one was neutral. Few knew him well enough to see him as history now does; they tended to observe only his loquacity and showmanship. As governor, senator, and secretary of state, he took stands on slavery and sectionalism that made more enemies than friends. A deep respect for public opinion often influenced but never warped his judgment. Surely, despite his unpreparedness for high office, despite his bombast and occasional errors of judgment, despite all that contemporaries found difficult, if not obnoxious, he was, one must say in the retrospect of a century, a great secretary of state.

BIBLIOGRAPHIC NOTE

The most important source of information on William Henry Seward is the collection of his papers in the Rush Rhees Library at the University of Rochester. They comprise one hundred fifty thousand public and personal items, including one hundred thousand letters chronologically arranged and indexed by correspondent. British opinion of Seward and reaction to his policies appear in the papers of Lord Russell and the records of the Foreign Office; both collections are housed in the Public Record Office in London. Lord Palmerston's papers at Broadlands contain thousands of letters, many of which refer to Seward.

Seward's *Autobiography*, 3 vols. (New York, 1877–91), edited by his son Frederick, contains little useful information except on the secretary's early years. George E. Baker, ed., *The Works of William H. Seward*, 5 vols. (Boston, 1884), contains his major speeches and essays. The fullest published documentary record of Seward's diplomacy appears in the volumes for 1861–68 (his successor did not compile a volume for 1869) of *Foreign Affairs of the United States*. Additional information on some diplomatic incidents appears in U.S. War Department, comp., *The War of the Rebellion: A Compilation of the Official Records of the Union and Confederate Armies*, 130 vols. (Washington, D.C., 1880–1901), and U.S. Navy Department, comp., *Official Records of the Union and Confederate Navies in the War of the Rebellion*, 30 vols. (Washington, D.C., 1894–1914). Roy P. Basler, ed., *The Collected Works of Abraham Lincoln*, 9 vols. (New Brunswick, N.J., 1953–55), sheds light upon the relationship between the secretary and the president.

The standard biography of Seward is by Glyndon G. Van Deusen, *William Henry Seward* (New York, 1967). He correctly portrays his subject as a remarkable administrator, a practical statesman, and a dreamer, but perhaps exaggerates Seward's alleged Machiavellianism. In *The American Secretary of State: An Interpretation* (New York, 1962), Alexander DeConde shows how Secretary Seward "expected to govern as a prime minister, to direct the entire government in the President's name." Seward's attitude, as Van Deusen relates in *Thurlow Weed: Wizard of the Lobby* (Boston, 1947), derived partly from the machine politics of New York State where officeholders twitched when party bosses pulled the strings.

Joseph G. Whelan's dissertation, "William Henry Seward, Expansionist," University of Rochester, 1959, is a full account of the philosophy and results of Seward's expansionism. He presents Seward as an economic determinist, political idealist, and international realist. In the prewar years, Seward favored expansion to achieve domestic political balance, while strategic motives explained his post-1861 projects. In a dissertation entitled "William Henry Seward: A Study in Nineteenth Century Politics and Nationalism, 1855–1861," University of Rochester, 1965, Walter G. Sharrow traces Seward's attempt to counter sectionalism with a program of nationalistic legislation. Although Seward was instrumental in making the Republican party a reform movement, according to the author, he cannot be regarded as a radical on slavery.

Seward's views on the nature of the Union and the politician's role in expansion have been explored in several works. Paul C. Nagel, *One Nation Indivisible: The Union in American Thought, 1776–1861* (New York, 1964), illustrates how Seward attempted to "translate reverence for Union into a matter of American morality" and argued that technological advances would cement far western states to the federal government. In "The Repressible Conflict: Seward's Concept of Progress and the Free-Soil Movement," *Journal of Southern History* 37: 533–56, Major L. Wilson points out that Seward conceived of the statesman's task as not to resist but to give orderly expression to the "popular passion" for territorial acquisition. Albert K. Weinberg's *Manifest Destiny* (Baltimore, 1935) places Seward in the mainstream of those Americans who marshaled every conceivable theory to establish a rationale for expansion. Richard W. Van Alstyne, *The Rising American Empire* (New York, 1960), emphasizes the secretary's grasp of the historic directions of American imperialism.

Numerous scholars have examined carefully the policy of the State Department toward Great Britain. Ephraim D. Adams pioneered such research with *Great Britain and the American Civil War*, 2 vols. (New York, 1925), which describes hectic Anglo-American relations, the British response to Seward, and the trials of the American minister. The latter's relationship with Seward is set forth in greater detail in Martin Duberman's *Charles Francis Adams, 1807–1886* (Stanford, 1960). The dangerous issue concerning the construction of Confederate commerce raiders in British ports is treated in Frank J. Merli, *Great Britain and the Confederate Navy, 1861–1865* (Bloomington, 1970). Merli demonstrates that despite the State Department's concern the vessels were a costly nuisance, but no real danger, to the Union war effort. An excellent account of American violations of neutral rights and Seward's twisted interpretations of international law is Stuart L. Bernath, *Squall across the Atlantic: American Civil War Prize Cases and Diplomacy* (Berkeley and Los Angeles, 1970). The difficulties of policing a long border, violations of Canadian neutral rights, and the perils of loosely supervising Confederate activities in Canada emerge in Robin W. Winks, *Canada and the United States: The Civil War Years* (Baltimore, 1960).

An illustration of the impact of personalities and domestic politics upon international affairs appears in David Donald, *Charles Sumner and the Rights of Man* (New York, 1970), which reveals the senator's petty obstructionism and egocentric notions. The Union's relations with France have been examined in two works. Lynn M. Case and Warren F. Spencer, *The United States and France: Civil War Diplomacy* (Philadelphia, 1970), conclude that despite numerous crises, especially the Maximilian affair, Franco-American relations benefited from the Civil War because American power and democratic ideals impressed the common man in France. Daniel B. Carroll's *Henri Mercier and the American Civil War* (Princeton, 1971) treats with admirable understanding the French minister's relationship with Seward and his opinion of the Union.

For an understanding of the complexities of French policy in the Maximilian affair, one must consult the excellent work by Alfred Jackson Hanna and Kathryn Abbey Hanna, *Napoleon III and Mexico: American Triumph over Monarchy* (Chapel Hill, N.C., 1971), a work that incorporates the results of many years of research in numerous archives scattered over the United States, Mexico, and Europe. Calm and judicious, this work fills a long neglected gap in mid-nineteenth-century diplomacy. In smaller compass there is the well-done account of this incident in Henry Blumenthal's *France and the United States: Their Diplomatic Relations, 1789–1914* (Chapel Hill, N.C., 1970).

HAMILTON FISH

and American Expansion

James B. Chapin

As secretary of state, Hamilton Fish should have been an anachronism. At sixty-one, one of the oldest men yet appointed to that office, he came to it a dozen years after the collapse of his political career. His selection by President Grant in 1869 was almost a matter of chance, a sudden grab by an inexperienced president desperate to save face. Contemporaries regarded Fish as an honest if limited man of sound Republican sympathies, but one who was out of touch with the vital concerns of the time. He himself might have agreed with such assessments, for he wrote Charles Sumner

For extended treatment and full documentation of the views expressed in this essay see the author's 1971 doctoral thesis at Cornell University, "Hamilton Fish and American Expansion." A Samuel Fels Fund Dissertation Fellowship provided financial assistance for the research upon which this essay is based. All quotations in this essay, unless otherwise identified, may be assumed to be from the Hamilton Fish collection at the Library of Congress.

that he was going to Washington to "undertake duties for which I have little taste, and less fitness."

Fish's service as head of the State Department was an unexpected climax to a political career otherwise typical of a number of upper-status Whigs whose expectations had been blighted by the political realignments of the 1850s. He had been born early enough to benefit from the lingering politics of deference, but too late for such politics to keep him in office for a lifetime. An unfriendly newspaper summed up the remarkable ease of his life by noting that circumstances, rather than toil or talent, had propelled him forward: "Few men have been more the favorites of the blind goddess than Hamilton Fish."

Born into the upper classes of New York City, Fish was descended from Stuyvesants and Livingstons on his mother's side; his father, Nicholas Fish, attended King's College (Columbia) with Alexander Hamilton and was one of the conservative Whigs who rode the tide of the American Revolution in hopes of taming it. Nicholas Fish served as a lieutenant-colonel under Washington, the first adjutant general of New York, founder of the state branch of the Society of the Cincinnati (the revolutionary officers and their male descendants), a Federalist alderman from New York City, and chairman of the Columbia University Board of Trustees. He was also a major banker, land speculator, and landowner.

He had declined Alexander Hamilton's request to serve as a second in that fatal duel with Aaron Burr; but when Fish had a son in 1808, he named him after his dead friend and endowed him with both wealth and social position. Hamilton Fish graduated from Columbia with highest honors and went on to study and practice law in a series of aristocratic firms. He specialized in legal advice to large property holders and seldom appeared in court. His profession reflected his status, as did his marriage to Julia Kean, descendant of John Kean and Lewis Morris. His father's death in 1833 left him financially secure, and the bequest of his uncle Petrus Stuyvesant in 1847 left him independently wealthy. He never again worked for a living. Throughout his life, Fish belonged to a small group of wealthy New Yorkers, sons of leading Federalists, a bourgeois aristocracy of men who combined wealth, power, prestige, and a unified outlook on social and economic problems; they believed that they were the upper classes of New York City and that the Whigs represented their interests as the Federalists had before.

The New York State Whigs appear to have been a coalition of a rural, liberal group from western New York (which came to the party from the Jeffersonians by way of Anti-Masonry) and a conservative and more urban faction (many of whom were old Federalists). Although the Whigs were the party of the "positive liberal state," to use Lee Benson's phrase, the upper-class city Whigs were less concerned with moral reform than with the power of the state to maintain order and build empire. Many recent historians have stressed the connection of the Whigs with evangelical religious morality, but Fish's group had no such associations. He himself regarded New England as a "nursery of vagaries and fanaticisms," and he hated the "remote philanthropy" of the Yankees, "their booriah-boola-gah enterprises, their frequent fanaticism and pharasaical assumptions."

A dull and dignified man who shared the ideas of his circle and had no desire to transcend them, all his life Fish identified with the principles of his party, desiring no other epithet than Whig. To him that designation implied devotion to the Union and to the great objectives of liberty and stability. Whig principles, he once told George Sumner, were enduring; they did not depend upon transient issues or the vagaries of government. They were, he said, "the principles of law and order, of the rights of persons and property, of personal liberty and social restraint, without which our republican institutions must cease to exist."

As time changed, however, such principles found varied expression. American politicians, then as now, easily slid from conservative to liberal rhetoric and back as occasion demanded; but it seems safe to say that Fish well fitted Louis Hartz's definition of a conservative—he was, after all conserving a liberal world view. In the 1840s and early 1850s Fish defended the right of petition, voted against the gag rule, supported the Wilmot Proviso, expressed his "unequivocal" opposition to the extension of slavery, and thought his generation might fulfill a noble destiny by thwarting oppression, extending freedom of thought, and vindicating personal liberty.

After the collapse of the Whig party, however, Fish looked forward to a new union of the nation's conservative elements, and by the outbreak of war in 1861 was describing himself as a conservative, "the guardian of order, of law, and of *instituted* liberty." Moreover, he felt it necessary to distinguish between that liberty and a natural one. The former was "fixed, established,

appointed, enacted, settled, prescribed"; and by definition it
excluded "that liberty which many claim in a state of nature."

Although Fish's rhetoric changed with his political circumstances, he consistently held to a Whiggish philosophy of the
nature of man and to a Whig version of economic progress that
bordered almost on a technological utopia. To these he joined an
imperial conception of the past and future of America. His
thought was imitative, shaped in the mold of the historical-
minded imperialism of a John Quincy Adams or a William Henry
Seward. Later, his official pronouncements put him squarely in the
Hamiltonian Whig tradition. As a conservative he naturally
thought in historical terms, and many of his state papers began
with an appeal to precedent. He identified a common vision of
society running from the Federalists to the Whigs, and then on to
the Republicans. He recognized and applauded the farsighted
vision of the Founding Fathers, who at the nation's infancy had
predicted its glorious future, seeing that its institutions, authority,
and peaceful influence would one day occupy the entire continent of America. The sense of himself as a natural leader of a
society born to greatness remained with Fish for his entire life.

Raised at a time when upper-class status and involvement in
politics still went together, Fish became politically active immediately upon graduation from college. In the 1830s he worked
behind the scenes; in the next decade he ran for office. Though
checkered with occasional defeat, his career was still remarkably
fortunate: a fluke win of a Democratic congressional seat in 1842,
followed by a crushing defeat in 1844; a race for lieutenant
governor of New York in 1846 and another loss; a second run for
the same office in 1847 and victory; election as governor in 1848,
and then as a United States senator in 1851.

Fish prospered in the political circumstances of the 1840s,
when both parties in his state were badly divided. He gained all of
his electoral victories when the Democrats split. In the Whig party,
he served as a figure capable of avoiding similar splits; he was an
amiable, wealthy, and moderate man who did little while in office,
but who accepted the lead of the Seward-Weed organization.

These qualities served Fish less well in the next decade. The
Kansas-Nebraska Act of 1854 changed the face of politics. Without
the ability to marshal public support either through oratory or
organization and afflicted with timidity and self-doubt in dealings
with politicians and voters, Fish had the wrong kind of abilities for

the politics of the 1850s. In quieter times he might have fitted into the Senate "club" by virtue of wealth, social position, conservative temperament, and amiability. In the politics of mass realignment he was singularly ineffective.

Although he voted some 79 percent of the time with Seward, Fish made a point of defining his views as a conservative alternative to the "radicalism" of his senior colleague. Such definition was left to his correspondence; he failed to speak publicly, and during six years in the Senate never made a formal speech. He was defensive enough on this matter by 1855 to make it clear that his failure to speak owed more to timidity than to reasoned opposition to "agitation." Although he wrote much of riding and controlling the wave of public feeling, he never explained how this could be done by a man without an organization who did not speak to the public. In fact, his naturalistic metaphors of "currents" or "waves" of public opinion seem to have reflected his thought; public opinion was *there,* like the sea, not something shaped, altered, and changed, but only sometimes disturbed by the "winds" of "agitation" before settling down once more to its fixed bed.

When the Seward Whigs went over in a body to the Republicans in 1855, Fish was not informed. He spent a year in futile attempts to revive the old party, for he did not want to join either of its successors, the Americans or the Republicans. In the end, he endorsed the Republican ticket in 1856, listing the chief issues as slavery—not as an abstraction "but as a question of right and of political power"—and the government's foreign policy. "Shall peace and justice, or violence and outrage, be its policy?" he asked.

After the election Fish wrote of the Republicans: "There is not and cannot be much sympathy between them and me. I was compelled to act with them at the late election because there was no other place to go to." He had no chance of reelection to the Senate; in 1851 Weed had wanted to conciliate conservative Whigs by nominating a man acceptable to that wing of the party, but in 1857 the conservatives were Americans, Fish was a laggard and unwilling supporter of the Republicans, and the group that Weed had to conciliate was the ex-Barnburner Democrats.

For a politician, Fish had been a remarkably sheltered man; he had had to do little for his success and rarely moved in circles beyond the class of his birth. Although personally amiable, he never showed any particular empathy for those in less fortunate circumstances. He showed special talent for routine administration. A natural bureaucrat, concerned with the precise discharge of duty and the exact balancing of books, he was a perfect executive, according to the limited Whig conception of what an executive should be: a man who carefully, punctually, and completely handled minor matters.

Fish naturally moved toward the middle of any group in which he found himself. This, indeed, explains the apparent changes in his political views, which tended to shift as the men around him changed—from his conservative New York City set, to the Albany politicians led by Weed, to the Senate, back to New York, and finally to Grant's Washington. He may have seen himself as a great compromiser, but he did not serve that function well. His conception of politics was too rigid, he himself too sheltered and timid, his knowledge of men too limited for him to unite a divided party or a divided country. George Templeton Strong, who always disliked him, once wrote, "If you want to know which way the wind blows, throw up Hamilton Fish." There was an element of truth in that mordant phrase.

After his forced departure from electoral politics, Fish played an active role in attempts to institutionalize his class's claim to status. He served as president of the Society of the Cincinnati, of the St. Nicholas Society, of the Union League Club, of the New York Historical Society, and of the Board of Trustees of Columbia University, and was perhaps the leading lay member of the New York Episcopalian church. He began what appears to have been an attempt to model his life-style on that of the English Whig aristocracy that served as a social and political model for his class, including a two-year tour of continental Europe and building a five-hundred-acre country estate at Glenclyffe. As a member of the most exclusive group in the nation's largest city, Fish stood at the peak of American society.

To Fish, the only important part of the sectional question lay in the destruction of the *political* power of the slave interest. Having no interest in a social reconstruction of the South, he wanted the necessary political climate to put Whig conceptions into practice. (Since these conceptions centered on government support for the development of bourgeois capitalism, they spelled doom for the slave interest in any event.) So he unenthusiastically supported Lincoln in the 1860 election, arguing that the issue of governmental power over slavery in the territories had to be settled once and for all. After Lincoln's victory, Fish advocated compromise with the South; if the new administration were willing "to concede all that the most extreme Southern men ask, (except for the reopening of the Slave trade) Slavery would never again be aggressive in the legislation of affairs of the country."

Fish reacted to the war itself like a panicky conservative. He volunteered his services to the Union, serving as chairman of the New York City Union Defense Committee in 1861–62. He took a soft position on Reconstruction terms but an extreme position on the war itself: "The exemplary punishment of a few disloyal men, the hanging of a few spies, and the shooting of a few deserters would have a most salutary influence." By the end of 1862 he had lost all faith in the national government. ("God protect us—this Administration certainly cannot"), and he spent the rest of the war morosely grumbling about the drift of affairs. Reluctantly and late he adhered to the Lincoln ticket in 1864. After the war, despite his distrust of Seward, he felt that Andrew Johnson was "proving himself to be a first-rate President" and attended a mass meeting supporting his veto of the Freedman's Bureau Bill.

Under pressure of the 1866 elections, Fish backed away from Johnson and eventually endorsed the regular Republican ticket; but by now his political influence was small. In 1868, however, his prospects changed.

After the war Fish had befriended U. S. Grant, who was lionized by New York society as the great hero of the Civil War. The general had visited Fish several times in the years 1865–68. Fish felt that he could support Grant more freely and more consistently than he had any presidential candidate since 1852, and he made substantial financial contributions to the general's campaign. After the election a few people suggested that Fish might become a cabinet member, but most thought that he would receive one of the major diplomatic appointments.

Grant's initial selection of advisers surprised the nation, giving perhaps the first indication that he was not to be a good president. After some ill-considered and unfortunate choices, the cabinet had to be reconstructed. The original selection for secretary of state, Elihu Washburn, a congressman from the president's home district, had no apparent qualifications for the post beyond his early fostering of Grant's military career. The choice for the treasury post raised other difficulties. Grant wanted the millionaire

New York importer A. T. Stewart, who was ineligible for the office
under a 1789 statute that Congress, under Senator Sumner's
leadership, refused to repeal. Washburn served for only five days
and Stewart not at all, so the president had two important
positions that had to be filled on rather short notice. So it came
about that Fish received a sudden and rather offhand letter from
Grant stating, "I have thought it might not be unpleasant for you
to accept the portfolio of the State Department." The appointee's
immediate attempt to decline met with the news that the Senate
had already approved his appointment.

◇◇◇

Fish's career as secretary of state falls naturally into three
periods: the first, lasting some fourteen months, a period of failure
for him and for the administration in general; the second, lasting
nine months, marked by a remarkable reversal of political alliances
that secured Fish a place in power and in history; the third,
covering the remaining six years of his service, showing no
substantial change either in American foreign policy or in Fish's
position within the administration. Thus, the first two years of
Fish's service outweigh in importance the rest of his term.

The key to understanding the changes in this period is the
struggle between two groups in the Republican party. Their nature
is difficult to define precisely, but almost every observer of the
time (and since) recognized their existence. The following tendencies (or self-definitions) might define the spectra of differences:
British or other European role models vs. self-conscious Americanism, educated men vs. practical men, political amateurs vs.
political professionals, respectability and/or honesty vs. success,
old money vs. new money, reformers vs. regulars ("Stalwarts").
Although a cluster of linked attitudes rather than a single clear line
defined the differences, their reality was as obvious (yet as hard to
define) as the reform-regular struggle that has split the Democratic
party in our own time.

Grant's historical identification with the "spoils system" has
tended to obscure the fact that many of his early appointments
went to those identified with the older elite: Fish as secretary of
state, E. R. Hoar as attorney general, Jacob D. Cox as secretary of
the interior, David Wells as special commissioner of revenue, John
Motley as minister to England, Moses Grinnell as collector of the

New York port. Grant made a crucial decision during 1870, abandoning his original appointees and casting his lot with the "Stalwarts." Hoar, Cox, Wells, Motley, and Grinnell all lost their jobs; only Fish survived.

This abrupt—and often overlooked—change in Grant's policy clearly resulted from the failure of the president's attempt to annex the Dominican Republic, which was thwarted by the strong opposition of the chairman of the Foreign Relations Committee, Senator Charles Sumner, and many others of the old elite. Faced with the choice between his old friend Sumner and the president, Fish survived by using his position to help destroy Sumner. In doing so, he not only survived, but turned his defeats into victories; he took advantage of the split with Sumner to settle the greatest foreign policy crisis facing him, the *Alabama* claims controversy, and made himself an indispensable figure in the administration.

Fish's reputation as secretary of state rests largely on the *Alabama* claims settlement.[1] The other aspects of his tenure—the attempt to annex Santo Domingo, the inglorious policy toward the Ten Years' War in Cuba, the policy of drift punctuated by failure in the Far East—are hardly the stuff of which reputations are made. The one expansionist triumph of Fish's term, the Hawaiian

---

1. During the American Civil War, the Confederate States of America succeeded in building a number of naval cruisers in British shipyards. Subsequently armed outside crown jurisdiction, these ships did tremendous damage to Northern commerce. The most famous of these raiders, the *Alabama*, in a twenty-two-month cruise after its escape from Liverpool in 1862, destroyed over sixty American ships and drove many more to the safety of foreign registry. Union diplomats always claimed that the failure to prevent the building and dispatch of such ships—Sumner liked to call them "pirates"—constituted a breach of proper neutral conduct on the part of the queen's ministers, and as the war in America wound down, efforts to force Her Majesty's government to admit culpability and pay damages intensified, and the efforts dragged on for years. Americans found the Johnson-Clarendon Convention of 1869 unsatisfactory because it lacked an apology and an admission of guilt by the British; the Senate rejected it by an overwhelming vote. Before the final adjudication of the claims by the Geneva arbitration of 1872 (provided for in the Treaty of Washington negotiated by Fish in 1870–71) both the United States and Great Britain felt it necessary to revise the rules of neutrality and to incorporate three rules of proper neutral conduct into the Treaty of Washington that Fish signed on 8 May 1871. For a recent extended discussion of the British response to Southern shipbuilding, see Frank J. Merli, *Great Britain and the Confederate Navy, 1861–1865* (Bloomington, 1970).

Reciprocity Treaty of 1875, is not treated at all in the massive standard biography of Fish by Allan Nevins.

Uncritical acceptance of Fish's account of his role in the settlement of the *Alabama* business and of the reasons for his split with Sumner has obscured the important question of what terms Fish himself originally set for settlement. Until September 1870 his terms included a British withdrawal from Canada. In later years this stipulation was laid at Sumner's door, and he was blamed for all the difficulties of Anglo-American relations in 1869–70. Indeed, Fish cleverly shifted the grounds of his split with Sumner from the inglorious question of Dominican annexation to the higher ground of peace with England. Almost every major American political figure in the post–Civil War period shared Sumner's desire for Canadian annexation, however.

When Fish came to power, the Dominion of Canada was less than two years old. Its mere existence challenged the long-standing American dream of continental empire, but there was much evidence that the jerry-built Canadian union might not survive. The new government had not yet established control of any area west of Ontario, and it faced widespread opposition inside areas already incorporated. The Canadian economy had suffered badly from America's refusal to renew reciprocity, with exports to the United States dropping from a duty-free $48.5 million in 1866 to $25 million in 1867, on which duties of some $3.5 million had to be paid. The Maritime Provinces, already least favorable to the confederation, suffered worst of all. The new government took half their revenues to Ottawa, and returned little, while the new Dominion tariff wiped out their chief source of income and reduced imports. Anti-Confederationists swept the Nova Scotia elections in 1867, and despite the defection of their leader Joseph Howe, a series of by-elections in early 1869 showed that they retained considerable strength. This anticonfederation sentiment was concentrated in the economic elite of Nova Scotia and New Brunswick, who were most closely tied to the United States economy.

Under these pressures, the Canadian government was desperate for reciprocity. Since the Americans were unresponsive to their demands, they directed pressure against the weak point in the United States, the fisheries.[2] Canada doubled the license fee for

---

2. In the peace treaty of 1783, Americans had received the right to fish off the coasts of Canada and Newfoundland, and throughout the nineteenth century this

U.S. fishing in 1867 and again in 1868; in 1870 it abolished all licenses and took active steps against American fishermen. Ironically, these moves financially injured groups in America who were favorable to the Canadian position, but did not affect those hostile to reciprocity.

The connection between the *Alabama* claims and Canada was not obvious, and the British steadfastly resisted linking the two questions. Charles Sumner brought the idea of trading the claims for Canada to center stage in a speech on the Johnson-Clarendon Convention in April 1869. This convention, a last-minute stab by the unpopular outgoing administration at solving the claims issue, was doomed in any event (the Senate rejected it by a vote of fifty-four to one). Sumner's speech did not directly mention the exchange of Canada for the claims; the Massachusetts senator rather gave a huge assessment of the damages owed to America, the so-called indirect claims, charging Britain with the entire cost of two years of the Civil War, more than a billion dollars—a sum that by implication could be met only by the cession of Canada.

Contrary to popular belief, Sumner did not originate the idea of trading the claims for Canada; indeed, such an arrangement had already been formally proposed by the Minnesota legislature, and six days before Sumner's speech, John Hamilton (son of Washington's secretary of the treasury and a close friend of both Fish and Grant) had already written Fish that, following the expected rejection of the Johnson-Clarendon Convention, the best American course would be a simple statement of American claims, after which "the territorial acquisition [could] be brought in as an ultimate relief for the difficulties."

"right"—an economic prize of considerable importance—became a frequent source of friction as the United States sought to extend it and the British and Canadians to restrict it. The Reciprocity Treaty of 1854 had given Americans extensive privileges in Canadian waters, but when that treaty lapsed an earlier, more restrictive convention of 1818 again became operative, and Canadian efforts to impose restrictions on American fishing vessels stirred up considerable animosity, especially in New England. The dispute over fishing rights, reciprocity, and the San Juan boundary in the Pacific Northwest were all intertwined with the negotiations over the claims for damage done by Confederate ships, and are usually given the generic title of *Alabama* claims or the Treaty of Washington negotiations. That treaty extended American rights in exchange for a cash award to the Canadians. A three-man commission, after much dickering, awarded Canada $5.5 million in 1877.

Fish's reply to Hamilton showed that his mind ran along similar lines. He wrote that the difficulty lay in the instructions to be presented by the new minister to England (Sumner's man, John Motley, who was to replace the discredited Reverdy Johnson). The private claims were not large but were hard to handle separately; America's real grievance, the national claim, was difficult to specify: the hasty British recognition of the Confederacy's belligerency and other hostile acts had prolonged the war by at least a year, but the bill for such offenses would be difficult to draw up. "The value can never be paid in *money*. It may be compensated by a territorial concession, but *to suggest this to Great Britain is to assure* its refusal." Perhaps accepting Hamilton's idea, Fish decided to let the problem lie, planning later to resume negotiations in Washington. This decision was followed by the cabinet as well; the United States would do nothing to settle the issue, and hope that economic pressure (refusal to grant reciprocity) combined with dissent inside the Dominion and British desire to withdraw troops from Canada would resolve the situation in America's favor.

In the first of his articles entitled "The Session" for the *North American Review* in April 1869, Henry Adams expressed confidence that an American consensus had emerged, noting that the conviction that the "whole continent of North America" would eventually fall under control of the United States was "absolutely ingrained in our people." He further asserted that a British offer to cede Canada in exchange for the claims would find immediate assent in the Senate and that the senators would give their consent "without giving a second thought to international law or establishing any new principle whatever." An impartial observer watching the actions of the senators and reflecting upon their behavior might well conclude that "territorial aggrandizement" lay at the back of their minds, "that these claims were to be reserved and used to lead or force England into a cession of territory." The acute Adams hinted that a prudently managed foreign policy might achieve the desired result, for an independent Canada would be "safer from violence" than it had been under British rule.[3]

3. In the postwar period a group of extreme Irish-American nationalists, the Fenians, conducted a numer of raids on Canadian territory and by their efforts created serious Anglo-American friction, for the British believed that these raids had the connivance, if not the direct support, of American officials. Since many of the Fenians were protesting British policy in Ireland, an independent Canada would presumably eliminate the border raids.

Keenly aware of their weakness in North America, the British recognized that their vulnerability hampered negotiations with Washington. On one occasion, in late March 1869, Prime Minister Gladstone told his foreign secretary, Lord Clarendon, that the "indefensible" Canadian border "made poor John Bull content to exhibit to Americans a submissiveness such as he has never to my knowledge shewn to any other people upon earth." That weakness made the British eager for settlement, especially as the prospect of a Franco-Prussian war came closer—but they were not prepared to give up Canada as the price of settlement with America.

In July, the Canadian minister of finance, Sir John Rose, passed through Washington en route to London and had several days of discussion with Fish. Though Rose wanted a new reciprocity treaty between America and Canada, the secretary of state told him that the time was not ripe either for reciprocity or for settlement of the claims. Although Sumner's speech denouncing the Johnson-Clarendon Convention was not to be interpreted as a demand for damages, Fish described it as a "fair expression" of the American sense of grievance; the next step, he said, would be up to Her Majesty's government.

Consensus on Canada did not prevent disagreement in the American camp. Fish later claimed these differences showed that Motley and Sumner wanted war with England, while he struggled for peace. The evidence does not support his claim. The first disagreement came over a memoir that Motley had presented to Fish as a suggestion for the instructions that would accompany him to London. (The two men later disagreed about how this memoir came to be written, and they could never subsequently agree about who had asked whom for it.) Fish rejected Motley's memoir, but not because of its strong position of indirect claims (a principle fully accepted by Fish and advanced three years later in the American case at Geneva) or because of his hostility to England, but rather because of a disagreement over the right of nations to recognize belligerency. Sumner and Motley felt that the hasty British recognition of Confederate belligerency in May 1861 was the key event justifying the large American claims. At that juncture, however, Grant and Fish were wrestling with the problem of whether or not to recognize Cuban belligerency in the revolt against Spanish rule; they did not wish to inhibit their own maneuverability by any broad statements that might later constrict their freedom of action.

The instructions eventually entrusted to Motley were a compromise between the views of Fish and Sumner, written by that jack-of-all-diplomatic-trades, Caleb Cushing. When Motley first presented the American position to Clarendon in June 1869, however, he used language that followed Sumner's view rather more closely than it did that of Grant or Fish. Though he had technically exceeded his instructions—a rather serious diplomatic fault—at the time he received only a mild rebuke, and nothing more was heard of the matter until a year later, when the administration dredged it up to justify its abrupt dismissal of Motley.

At this time, the summer of 1869, Fish's muted criticism of Motley did not affect his relations with Sumner; but the two men did have a disagreement: Fish did not want to make any further statement of the American position, while Sumner argued that America should make a statement of its case *"so that England may see its extent."* Only then, when Great Britain had seen the enormity of its crime, when it had recognized the extent of America's "massive grievance," would it be "ready for the remedy": departure from North America. Finally, Fish agreed to a restatement of the American position and asked Sumner to draft it, but the latter, pleading overwork, declined and suggested that the task be entrusted to Cushing. The new instruction, Number 70, was sent at the end of September. Later, after breaking with Sumner, Fish argued that there were "wide differences and broad distinctions between those instructions and Mr. Motley's paper." Few contemporaries agreed.

When Number 70 was published at the end of the year it led to a breach between Fish and Clarendon. Despite a formal protest by the British minister in Washington, Sir Edward Thornton, Fish refused to publish the foreign secretary's "observations" on Number 70. Clarendon, who had responded so softly to what the administration later called Motley's "warmongering," was deeply wounded by the September dispatch, considering it "offensive." American refusal to publish his observations sealed his break with the secretary of state.

Earlier, on 6 November, Clarendon had written Fish that the British regretted the absence of concrete suggestions for settlement in Number 70. Her Majesty's government could not "make any new proposition or run the risk of another unsuccessful negotiation" without some definite proposal from America. Fish would make no such overtures; he wanted Canada. He told cabinet colleagues that the British might part with the Dominion if the Canadians so requested, but they would not surrender the province "as satisfaction for any claim." Fish wanted to keep Canada a private matter to avoid stiffening British backs. For example, on 23 December 1869, when Thornton again asked for American terms for a settlement of the claims, Fish declined to give any. The subject then turned to the threat of a new Fenian invasion of Canada, and Fish suggested that a British withdrawal from there would "remove the pretext" for the Fenian threats, while permitting immediate settlement of the *Alabama* claims.

Two days earlier, Fish had told a delegation of midwestern Republican representatives that "the pressure of the existing commercial relations is increasing the feeling for annexation. . . . England is believed willing to allow the Provinces to separate from the mother country. . . . We wish not to retard the growing feeling in favor of annexation." Fish had two new reasons to anticipate annexation: the rebellion of the *métis* (French-Indian half-breeds) in the Red River (the Riel Rebellion) and a petition from British Columbia requesting it. On 6 January 1870, Fish discussed the petition and the rebellion with Thornton, suggesting that these matters presented an opportunity for Great Britain to separate itself from Canada. He hinted heavily that "the removal of the British flag would render easy the settlement of all other questions between the two governments."

By the spring of 1870 Fish had made clear to the British that settlement of the claims depended upon withdrawal from Canada. Though not formally expressed this position was repeated many times in private communications between the two governments. For instance, on 12 March, Fish's assistant secretary, J. C. Bancroft Davis, wrote Sir Curtis Lampson, deputy governor of the Hudson's Bay Company, to propose that the British grant Canadian independence, adding the none-too-subtle hint, "Why could not this change be accompanied by a settlement of differences which now appear too far apart to settle any other way?" Fish later stated the matter even more clearly; on 14 June he told Thornton, "You may depend upon it that twenty-four hours after Canada is independent, you and I will be able to settle the *Alabama* question as easily as possible." Two weeks later he wrote Horace Greeley asking him to devote some space to the idea of Canadian independence, adding that "annexation must follow independence very soon."

Fish based his policy on several misapprehensions. He thought a policy of delay would lead to a settlement; instead it led to trouble. He entertained what Thornton once called the "delusive expectation" that the British would grant Canadian independence. He believed that a policy of pinpricks (ranging from refusing Canadian reciprocity to denying the use of Sault Sainte Marie to British troops on their way to the Red River would speed withdrawal. By the fall of 1870, however, American hopes foundered on the rock of British and Canadian resistance, a resistance that could have been overcome only by a willingness on the part of the United States to bluff, to use its own forces, or to support the use of force by Red River rebels or Fenians. Such willingness might not have meant war, but it would have required steely nerves and a gambler's temperament. Fish had neither, and never thought Canada worth a split with England. (Indeed, he once wrote that the *Alabama* dispute was unfortunate because it weakened England's power in world affairs.)

It is possible to pinpoint within a week Fish's change of policy. As late as 18 September he was still suggesting that "the best solution would be independence," only to meet with Thornton's standard response: "It is impossible to connect the question of Canadian independence with the settlement of the *Alabama* claims." Eight days later, the two men had another conference. Fish began in his usual way, by complaining about the fisheries, but then he suddenly shifted his tone: "Disclaiming any official character or purport in the suggestion, I asked whether Great Britain would settle all the questions pending between the countries at once. . . . That if the United States abandoned their opposition to arbitrating the *Alabama* claims, Great Britain might agree to the American claim of the San Juan boundary line. All commercial claims to be referred to arbitration. The inshore fisheries to be opened to American vessels, and in return a more free trade be allowed in certain articles between the United States and its [Great Britain's] colonies." Fish had suddenly dropped Canadian independence as a requirement of settlement, as well as abandoned his long-standing position that the next gesture must come from the English.

He had received two important communications in the week

between these two conferences with Thornton. On 19 September a letter from the American consul at Vancouver told him that annexationist sentiment in British Columbia had passed, and that the province was about to join the Dominion. A second letter from Representative Benjamin Butler, dated 25 September, complained bitterly of Canadian policy on the fisheries and hinted that his constituents might take matters into their own hands: "The Springfield rifle, loaded at the breech, is the only negotiator." These letters indicated not only that there was little chance of picking off any portion of the Dominion, but also that continued postponement of agreement might lead to war.

Four other factors pushed Fish toward a settlement. First, the death of Lord Clarendon at the end of June 1870 removed from office one of Fish's enemies and replaced him with the amiable "Pussy" Granville. Secondly, pressure for settlement of Civil War damages was mounting. The claim holders included many important economic and political figures who were becoming impatient with the continued postponement of settlement. The "new" Grant administration being created in the fall of 1870 was especially vulnerable to interest group pressure, and when Fish brought his new idea before the cabinet in October he began by mentioning "the desire of many parties interested in the *Alabama* Claims to have that question settled."

A third important influence on the course of Anglo-American relations was the great American war debt. During 1870, the administration decided to refund this massive amount at a lower rate of interest; any refunding would necessitate the cooperation of the English financial community, and this militated against any trouble with England. Sir John Rose listed the American debt first among factors pushing the United States toward settlement. Immediately after Fish told the cabinet of his January 1871 discussions with Rose, Secretary of the Treasury George Boutwell announced that refunding the debt could begin.

The fourth and most important factor—the split between Grant and Sumner—was somewhat fortuitous. Enraged by the defeat of his treaty for Dominican annexation, and feeling betrayed by Sumner's part in senatorial rejection of the treaty, Grant fired Motley as minister to England; this in turn enraged Sumner, who began to pressure Fish to take his side. Fish took exactly the opposite course, answering Motley's complaints by publishing the so-called Moran letter in which he blamed Motley's disobedience of orders (rather than Sumner's opposition to the Dominican treaty) for his dismissal and attacked Sumner by calling him "one who uses the words and assurances of friendship to cover a secret and determined purpose of hostility." This letter ended a twenty-year friendship.

As a result of his speech on the Johnson-Clarendon Convention, everyone identified Sumner with the idea that Canada was a fair exchange for the claims. This identification was sealed in the eyes of the British by a private memorandum that Sumner wrote for Fish on 17 January 1871 repeating the idea that settlement should wait until the British withdrew from the continent; Fish immediately showed the memorandum to Rose. He was able to use Sumner as a universal bogeyman, scaring Grant on the one side and the British on the other.

Most importantly, by joining in the assault on Sumner, Fish allied with the Stalwarts. His conference of 14 January with Senator Zachariah Chandler showed that both men knew what they were doing. Chandler, who had played a leading role in the removal of Fish's erstwhile friends, Cox, Motley, and Hoar, and who just six months earlier had fiercely attacked Fish, now stated that he no longer sought war with England or annexation of Canada, and that he no longer opposed Fish's retention of his post. In other words, in return for Fish's attack on Sumner and for his toleration of the activities of Chandler's friends within the administration, Chandler would support Fish on foreign policy, an area that was not for him of first importance. Fish would lend a touch of respectability to the otherwise raffish new administration, while Anglo-American reconciliation would strengthen Grant among the "independent" voters most likely to defect in 1872.

Settlement of the *Alabama* claims prevented the last real attempt of the United States to absorb Canada. On almost every other issue, however, Canadian interests were sacrificed to Anglo-American reconciliation. Fish did not impose his will on the claims problem. The events of 1869–70 narrowed and defined the alternatives, and suggested the shape of the 1871 settlement. The United States demanded a settlement of the claims and of the fisheries, and would not concede reciprocity; the British would give in at all points except the independence of Canada, and so compromise terms were reached. The American government nearly threw away even this victory by the inclusion of the "indirect claims" in the American case at Geneva, and Fish's later

THE APPLE OF DISCORD AT THE GENEVA TRIBUNAL.

THE LAST SCENE OF THE WILLIAM TELL TRAGEDY.

Harper's Weekly, 5 October 1872

willingness to accept an unfavorable arbitrator in the fisheries dispute and to allow the three rules of neutrality to be abandoned leaves it a moot point whether his earlier course had been a result of cleverness or of weakness. In either event Fish's importance in 1870 was simply that he was realistic. While Sumner and Grant tore each other to pieces over annexation of the Dominican Republic, Fish kept his eye on Canada and Great Britain. Sumner and Grant weakened themselves politically and damaged their historical reputations, while Fish secured a place in power and in history.

◇◇◇

Fish's career was overshadowed by that of Seward. As in the case of his predecessor, the rise of the Whig party in New York in the 1830s had shaped his politics. Influenced by many of the same men, they shared a belief in Whig expansionism. At every step of his career, however, Fish proclaimed that he differed from Seward. In practice these proclaimed differences often turned out to be temperamental rather than ideological. Both believed in the Whig creed of orderly progress, though Fish perhaps stressed the order a bit more than the progress. A genial, expansive, and optimistic man, Seward had made his own way up; Fish, on the other hand, was born at the top of American society, never felt at ease with those who were not at his own level, and spent much of his life defending an established social position.

The relative success of Fish's service in the State Department demands explanation. The change in type of job alone explains part of the difference. He had always been a better bureaucrat than a legislator and worked better in small groups than in large ones. His success was not simply a matter of changing position or adapting to circumstances, but of adapting to a different time in American life. His term of office coincided with the Reconstruction Era. The Civil War, which in many areas had less impact than is commonly assumed, crucially affected the foreign policy and self-image of America. Before the war, Southern interests had always greatly influenced foreign policy. Afterward, foreign affairs became the private preserve of the northeastern metropolitan elite. Fish himself was one of the first representatives of this new breed. In a sense, he marked the beginning of the "establishment" in foreign policy, of the old-family, Ivy League–educated men who were to dominate this area of American life for the next century.

The effect of the Civil War on America's self-image can hardly be overstressed. It seems clearly to have marked the change from a revolutionary to a conservative power. Revolutions directed at the American state had no appeal, and in the face of such a revolution, the state became a positive moral good. It was no coincidence that the reputation of Hamilton began to rise, and that of Jefferson to fall, after 1860.

Meanwhile, important areas in the rest of the world were moving toward the left. The United States had welcomed the 1848 revolutions in Europe, and men like Fish and Calhoun who had opposed them had been a small minority. The Paris Commune of 1870–71 called up a far different reaction. Fish was not alone in his abhorrence of this social movement; almost every opinion maker and politician in the country shared it. Even more striking was the lack of enthusiasm of many Americans for the Cuban revolution. The Spanish revolutions of 1868 and 1873 won greater support because they seemed in the tradition of bourgeois democracy rather than radical revolution. It was now acceptable for a Caleb Cushing to express doubts about even this kind of revolution. If it was impossible to introduce capitalist parliamentarianism into backward nations, and if the only choice was between revolution and reaction, there was no question which the new American leaders would choose.

Fish, who in the 1850s had seemed so out of date, was in the 1870s far more relevant to the new realities of an increasingly conservative America. In a cabinet discussion early in 1870, he even expressed hostility to the principle of asylum. It helped revolution, he argued, and tended to encourage and convert into revolution "every change of political power, [and it] retards civilization and the establishment of a recognized stable government." It is difficult to think of an earlier secretary of state who might have said the same thing. Ironically, Fish's apparently outmoded conservatism made him more relevant to later American history than the "advanced liberals" of his own day.

In stressing the anachronistic aspect of Fish, his biographer Nevins saw him as a magnificent monument from the American past, whose essential world view was cast aside by the men of 1898. One might argue instead that the men of 1898 carried out many of Fish's ideas more effectively than he ever could have. The failure of Nevins and other historians such as Ernest May to see the continuity between Fish and the 1890s has resulted from their tendency to see the history of 1865–1900 as a consistent struggle between imperialists, and anti-imperialists, with one side triumphing in the 1870s and the other victorious in the 1890s. A close study of congressional roll calls and speeches during the years 1865–75 shows that no imperialist–anti-imperialist dichotomy existed at that time; positions on one expansionist issue did not predict positions on other such issues.

Certainly Fish himself could not qualify as a member of either side of this simple dichotomy. He continued the American pattern of expansion into new areas before there was immediate economic or social reason for possessing them, anticipating the future needs of the American political economy. A mere list of places where America intervened militarily during his tenure would serve as an outline of future theaters of American action: Hawaii, Korea, Mexico, Panama, the Dominican Republic.

The American empire, so far from being "accidental," was a conscious intellectual creation. Throughout his public life Fish thought in terms of past and future expansion, and was heavily influenced by the English model. His personal life-style closely resembled that of the English aristocracy, and like other Whigs he was keenly aware of English "free-trade imperialism." He wrote enviously on how the English could gain empire without responsibility, and then proposed steps by which the United States could achieve the same end.

For instance, in his 1870 message to the Senate on Latin American trade, intended as a major statement of policy, he praised the Senate for stating that "close relations of geographical continuity and political friendship" justly entitled the United States to a share of Latin American trade, and for regarding "the commercial and the political relations of the United States with the American states of Spanish origin as necessarily dependent upon each other." After a discourse that traced America's rise to greatness (with particular praise for John Quincy Adams and Henry Clay), he tied the no-transfer principle[4] to the Monroe

4. In his first annual message to Congress on 6 December 1869, the president (in a passage furnished by Fish) said that the United States had no disposition to interfere with the relations between Spain and its colonial dependencies in the New World, believing that Spain and other European powers holding colonies in the Western Hemisphere would find it in their own interests to establish such

Doctrine: "It looks hopefully to the time when, by voluntary departure of European governments from this continent and adjacent islands, America shall be wholly American." Toward the end, in a cool statement, he presaged the more famous Olney Fiat:[5] "The United States . . . occupy of necessity a prominent position on this continent, which they neither can nor should abdicate, which entitles them to a leading voice, and which imposes on them duties of right and of honor regarding American questions, whether those questions affect emancipated colonies, or colonies still subject to European domination."

Fish set forth many of his ideas on the Caribbean policy of the United States in a letter to Colonel Alexander Hamilton, Jr., on 13 March 1870. Beginning with an acid portrayal of British colonialism—which he saw as selfish but successful—Fish noted that the British system nonetheless created benefits for the mother country by securing self-sustaining colonies that were forced to pay tribute to British trade and help fight Britain's wars. He then elaborated his own views. While favoring the independence of Cuba he did not think its people fit to become citizens of the United States, especially since adoption of the constitutional amendments giving blacks equal rights. (He thought the Negroes in Cuba "less educated, less civilized than those who were lately slaves in our Southern States.") The protectorate was his chosen tool for expansion: "My plan looked to independence with a certain guardianship or trusteeship over the Cuban duties, which [would] have enabled a certain training to be extended to the people." He argued that Santo Domingo—"the key to the Gulf"—would be a better acquisition than Cuba because it had equal potential for cultivation, fewer people, and provided a needed "harbor *outside* our Coast line" to protect the proposed transisthmian canal.

---

colonies as independent members of the family of nations. He then went on to say, "These dependencies are no longer regarded as subject to transfer from one European power to another."

5. During the course of an Anglo-American dispute over the boundary of Venezuela in 1895, Secretary of State Richard Olney made a famous—and much quoted—statement of America's position in Latin American affairs: "Today the United States is practically sovereign on this continent, and its fiat is law upon the subjects to which it confines its interposition. Why? . . . It is because, in addition to all other grounds, its infinite resources combined with its isolated position render it master of the situation and practically invulnerable as against any or all other powers."

Annexation of the island would also compel an early Spanish surrender of its "insular possessions on the Gulf."

Fish would have liked an autonomous Cuba under terms that would have guaranteed American control of the island. Spanish unwillingness to leave the island prevented such a settlement, but the Platt Amendment achieved it three decades later.

Fish proposed a similar solution to the Dominican crisis in May 1870, but Grant's obsession with annexation and his unwillingness to compromise with Senators Sumner and Carl Schurz defeated that plan. The latter two equally supported American domination of the Caribbean, but wanted a West Indian confederation under the protection of the United States.[6] This liberal paternalism matched the pattern that Sumner had already tried to establish for the American Negro.

Fish's failures in Canada and Cuba resulted from control of those areas by powers that would not sacrifice their interests to the United States. In the Dominican Republic, American policy failed because the question of annexation became embroiled in domestic struggles within the Republican party. Fish faced no such problem in Hawaii, however; there his plan of American economic control of the island succeeded. In the Pacific, Americans had more options and fewer restrictions on their maneuverability than in the Caribbean. In the Hawaiian Islands no other power was prepared for an open confrontation, and no powerful, concerted, domestic opposition existed to the expansion of American influence there. In such circumstances the United States could keep a warship on permanent station at Honolulu, indulge in direct military action to prop up a friendly regime, and even contemplate a military occupation to protect the citizens and interests of America. Hawaii was so far removed from American concerns that a policy of military intervention in the islands (much like the

---

6. Schurz's own vision of American empire was shown in his praise for the German settlements in eastern Europe: "Colonies not political, but colonies commercial, which protect themselves, regulate themselves and feed German commerce of their own motion, without imposing upon the mother country the remotest political responsibility." (*Speeches, Correspondence and Political Papers of Carl Schurz*, vol. 2, edited by Frederic Bancroft [New York, 1913] p. 117.) Here was the clearest imaginable statement of an old American liberal chimera: the invisible hand translated into international affairs; a self-regulating system in which every other nation would of its own volition serve American national interests.

administration's support of Baez in the Dominican Republic) aroused no significant public or congressional protest.

In the 1870s a majority of Congress opposed both annexation and establishment of protectorates, but was more willing to consider the former than the latter. Fish knew that the greater sophistication of "informal empire" would not win for it any popular support, recognized that protectorates violated the sacred principle of "no entangling alliances," and understood that existing political alignments and attitudes would make it difficult to conduct any subtle policy. Indeed, he knew that it would be extraordinarily difficult to conduct any policy requiring congressional approval.

The beauty of a reciprocity treaty with Hawaii was that an economic negotiation could cover political motives. Fish saw a future that "might extend the jurisdiction and limits" of the nation, one that would require "a resting spot" on the ocean between the Pacific Coast and the "vast domains in Asia, which are now opening to Commerce and Christian Civilization." Like his minister in the islands Fish believed that reciprocity would "bind these islands to the United States with hoops of steel." He negotiated a treaty that provided free entry of Hawaiian sugar into the United States in exchange for the reciprocal free importation of virtually all American products, an arrangement that on balance quite naturally worked to America's advantage.

Fish told the president that he would not negotiate a treaty unless assured of all-out administration support; then, armed with that assurance, he set about getting the treaty through Congress. The Senate Committee on Foreign Relations was informed of the danger that Hawaii's entire sugar crop might go to British possessions and that in the future the islands might look to New Zealand, Australia, and Canada for economic and political support. The secretary's spokesman hinted—and given the prevailing Anglophobia of many Americans it was a clever ploy, well calculated to touch a responsive chord—that the island kingdom might well become an appendage of the British Empire. Senators were reminded of the "grave importance" of reciprocity and that "political supremacy in the islands must inevitably follow commerce." After the addition of a new article forbidding Hawaii to lease bases to other powers or to sign reciprocity treaties with them, the Senate passed the treaty on 18 March 1875 by a vote of 51 to 12. Even more difficult was the task of getting the enabling legislation through the House (which traditionally opposed such treaties as an infringement upon its prerogatives). It took nearly a year of lobbying, support of House leaders from both parties, threats that England might take over the islands, and timely financial inducement to get a 115–101 vote from the House in 1876.

The effect of the treaty was to make the islands dependent upon a sugar monoculture, controlled by large American capitalists, and dependent upon the American market for an outlet for its only product. "The reciprocity treaty of 1875 was a perfect example of a commercial and economic negotiation dictated by political motives. It was designed primarily to extend American influence over the islands and only secondarily to secure economic benefits. The annexationist-minded Grant administration was aware of the prevailing anti-annexationist feeling in the Congress. Hence, there was achieved through the execution of a commercial instrument the substance of a policy that would have been defeated if brought to an open fight on the floor of the Senate. This convention prevented any European power from gaining a political foothold in Hawaii, and at the same time—from the commercial point of view—rendered the archipelago a significant appendage of the United States."[7] That triumph in Hawaii was the only real expansionist success of an administration that had been forced to abandon plans for expansion in the Caribbean and in Canada. For the success of the Pacific venture Fish deserves much credit.

Henry Adams wrote that Fish's reputation was the only one not ruined by association with Grant. The separation of the secretary from the "mess in Washington" has probably been overstressed. Involved on the periphery of several unsavory episodes, he proved himself neither moral enough nor strong enough to do much about them. Although he often complained to Grant, he could not even control patronage in his own department. A sign of the administration's decay after 1872 was that Fish came to be thought of as the "strong man" of the government. Whatever his faults, he was one of the few men left aboard the sinking ship who cared more for policy than for plunder. Fish had

7. Merze Tate, *The United States and the Hawaiian Kingdom* (New Haven, 1965), p. 42 and passim.

convictions, but only rarely carried them into practice. His timidity and lack of strength in enforcing his beliefs often limited his control of foreign policy and generally rendered his policies ineffective. However clearly he defined his principles, in practice he often seemed the plaything of stronger forces and stronger men.

In any survey of American policy during the period, it rapidly becomes clear that the most characteristic feature of American policy under Fish was inconsistency. Purposes were not clearly defined, ends and means were not matched, government lacked the personnel and organization to follow consistent lines of policy toward other nations. Many monographs treating the relations of the United States with other countries during this period stress the weakness of American policy, but almost all, influenced by Nevins, absolve Fish.

All politicians blame their blunders and mistakes on outside forces but few have had their claims so fully accepted by historians as Fish. Grant, Sumner, and Congress have absorbed the blame for the wavering policies of the United States. All deserve criticism, but it is still clear that Fish dominated most areas of foreign policy, and that American policy in many areas under his control showed the same weaknesses as policy in more contested areas.

Fish's historical importance was not that of a man who made history, but of one who responded to it. His main political assets were durability and adaptability. He was not an original man, but reflected the prevailing ideas of the American elite of his time. Although as secretary he might be judged "good in planning, poor in execution," he was not out of date. He had the ability of the true conservative to move with change without abandoning the past. With his roots in the old Federalism of his namesake, he lived long enough to see the beginnings of the new Federalism of the age of William McKinley. Fish's career benefited from the increasing conservatism of bourgeois liberalism, as it became less a triumphant march to the future and more a defense of existing institutions and arrangements of power. He was perhaps the first American secretary of state to define himself as an antirevolutionary, but he was not the last.

BIBLIOGRAPHIC NOTE

The central source for study of Fish is, of course, the massive collection of Fish manuscripts in the Library of Congress, particularly the manuscript diary he kept for his eight years in the State Department. Indeed, the very amplitude of Fish documentation, particularly of the inner affairs of the Grant administration, has somewhat naturally tilted the history books in his favor; most events are seen through his eyes. The Grant papers do not tell us much of this enigmatic man, who still remains one of our more mysterious presidents. The Library of Congress also contains the papers of most of the other significant politicians of the Grant era, with the major exception of Charles Sumner, whose papers can be found in the Houghton Library at Harvard.

No volume of *Foreign Relations* was published for 1869, and the volumes published for the other years of Fish's term are of low quality. Most of the significant published documents having to do with American foreign policy under Fish can be found in the *Executive Documents* of either the House or the Senate (some, on Cuba, were not published until the 1890s).

Just as the Fish diary dominates manuscript materials of Fish's life, so Allan Nevins's massive Pulitzer Prize–winning biography, *Hamilton Fish* (New York, 1936), has dominated secondary materials for nearly forty years. It remains what Matthew Josephson called it: a "literary monument raised by pious hands." With appendices, it comes to more than nine hundred pages. It is a remarkable work with one flaw: too-close identification with the subject. This is particularly obvious in the treatment of Fish's break with Sumner. This impressive work dominated other secondary works until recently. Thus, although C. C. Tansill, in *The United States and Santo Domingo, 1798–1873* (Baltimore, 1938), carefully redressed the balance as to Fish and Sumner, few historians seemed to note it. Sumner's side of the story seemed to reach historians only with David Donald's equally impressive *Charles Sumner and the Rights of Man* (New York, 1970).

There has yet been no book published on Grant's political career to replace William B. Hesseltine's *U. S. Grant: Politician* (New York, 1935), which is somewhat out of date. In some ways the book that still best describes Grant's Washington (as it struck a young aristocrat who knew its leaders) is *The Education of Henry Adams* (Boston, 1918).

The chapter on "Conservatives and Moderates," in Eric Foner's *Free Soil, Free Labor and Free Men* (Oxford, 1970), is an excellent account of Fish and those like him in the years before the Civil War. Modern historians have been keenly aware of the postwar cleavage in the Republican party. Ernest May, in *American Imperialism: A Speculative Essay* (New York, 1968), speaks of division between "cosmopolitans" and "non-cosmopolitans," and uses this division to explain the debate on American policy toward the Dominican Republic and indeed the whole course of American foreign policy from 1865 to 1900. Irwin Unger, in *Greenback Era* (Princeton, 1962), writes of a "hard-money elite," which closely resembles in its membership May's cosmopolitans. Ari Hoogenboom, *Outlawing the Spoils* (Urbana, Ill., 1968), writes of the "better sort" who were thrown out of power in 1870–71 and as a result became civil service reformers. (Hoogenboom is one of the few historians to realize the importance of Grant's new tack in 1870.) Each of these historians seems to be attempting to define the same cultural and political division.

There are numerous books covering America's relations with one country or another during this period. Some recent books treating various aspects of American-Canadian relations are P. B. Waite, *The Life and Times of Confederacy* (Toronto, 1962), a good account of the perilous early years of Canada; Donald Warner, *The Idea of Continental Union* (Lexington, Ky., 1960), detailing nineteenth-century plans for the union of Canada and the United States; Brian Jenkins, *Fenians and Anglo-American Relations during Reconstruction* (Ithaca, 1969), which is stronger on the Seward period than on Fish; and Alvin Gluek, Jr., *Minnesota and the Manifest Destiny of the Canadian Northwest* (Toronto, 1965), a nice little work detailing American designs on the Canadian Northwest.

In a recent article Doris W. Dashew treats the connection between the claims and territorial expansion: "The Story of an Illusion: The Plan to Trade the *Alabama* Claims for Canada," *Civil War History* 15 (December 1969), 332–48. Sumner's part in the claims has been superlatively examined in David Donald's recent biography, cited previously. The *Alabama* claims are a vast subject in themselves, but there is really no recent satisfactory work on them. [Frank J. Merli has work in progress on this subject.—EDITOR]

Department of State

JAMES GILLESPIE BLAINE

The Ideologue as Diplomatist

Lester D. Langley

The world in which James G. Blaine died in 1893 and the world into which he had been born in 1830 were profoundly different. In the sixty-three years of his life, the American people had rounded out the continental domain and fought a civil war. The America of his youth was principally an agrarian society, and its political leadership, dominated by Andrew Jackson, Henry Clay, John C. Calhoun, and Daniel Webster, dealt largely, though not altogether, with domestic issues. At the time of his death America possessed political magnates less intellectually imposing but no less motivated by awareness of domestic tensions and prospects of American greatness in world affairs. Their society was as much industrial as agricultural, and their analyses of foreign policy and

This essay is based in part on Professor Langley's study of U.S-European rivalry in the Caribbean.

253

prescriptions for America's role in the world were products of the political and economic stresses of the preceding thirty years.

In shaping the principles of American foreign policy James G. Blaine played a large role, both as ideologue and practitioner. The sectional stresses that led to the creation of the Republican party and to the Civil War had molded his mind. He dominated the postwar political scene as no other presidential candidate since the era of Clay, Calhoun, and Webster. A later generation of textbook writers would rate Blaine as just another Gilded Age politician, identifying him with unsavory political maneuverings. Yet, in his own way, Blaine contributed more to the shaping of American foreign policy than any individual of his generation, with the exception of William H. Seward.

Like Seward, Blaine felt strongly about America's place among the great powers. Both men proposed far-reaching policies for the advancement of United States economic and political influence in the Western Hemisphere, Seward with plans for acquisition of the Danish West Indies, Blaine by efforts in the Pan-American movement. In both minds the intellectual justification for American hegemony in the hemisphere stemmed from the moral and political "superiority" of the Anglo-Saxon peoples. Seward found it natural to expand his "higher law" antislavery arguments of the 1850s by applying such precepts to the ills of Latin America; Blaine shared his predecessor's assumptions and coupled them with an often expressed pity for the degradation of the Latin American polities, with their backward societies and bickering governments. Both secretaries of state encountered an obstinate Congress that momentarily thwarted their Latin American policies.

In the Pacific and Far East, too, the parallels between the strivings of Seward and Blaine are remarkable. Though never accomplishing so awesome a territorial acquisition as Alaska, Blaine nevertheless continued Seward's basic Pacific policies. Seward tried to bring Hawaii closer to American annexation in his 1867 proposals for a reciprocity treaty, and in 1881 Blaine brought the islands within the scope of the Monroe Doctrine, contending that, for moral and economic reasons, Hawaii's future was tied to that of the United States. Seward and Blaine anticipated John Hay's Open Door notes in their belief that the western Pacific was a gateway to the Asian market. Like Seward, Blaine was a transitional figure in American diplomacy, articulating an imperial plan but never accomplishing the grand task.

◇◇◇

Like other Americans during the Age of Jackson, Blaine was a migrant, though he migrated east, or more precisely northeast, from southwestern Pennsylvania to Maine. At the age of ten, his family sent him to the home of Ohio relatives, where he was tutored by William Lyons, uncle of Queen Victoria's minister to the Lincoln government. He returned to Pennsylvania and entered Washington College. In 1847, at age seventeen, he graduated, sharing highest honors in his class of thirty students, an indication of Blaine's intellectual talents (and, of course, the limitations of the curriculum). For the next six years he taught, first in the Western Military Institute near Lexington, Kentucky, then at the Pennsylvania Institute for the Blind. In his spare time he studied law, often the chosen profession for a young man who wanted to advance; but he soon gave it up. On the last day of June 1850, he married Harriet Stanwood, descendant of a well-known Massachusetts family. One branch of the Stanwood family had established roots in Maine, and this connection provided the opportunity for Blaine to begin his journalistic ventures in that state in 1854.

In Maine, Blaine served with two newspapers, the *Kennebec Journal*, which he partly owned, and the *Portland Advertiser*. There was little in Blaine's journalism career that could be called preparation for the secretaryship of state or any diplomatic post, though as newspaper editor he soon displayed a literary and political interest that the successful newspaperman should cultivate. He also possessed a remarkably retentive mind, capable of recalling many names and much information. In an age when most people intimately associated public speaking with political popularity, his oratorical skills were an obvious asset. (Years later, Blaine could work crowds into a frenzy with his "perfidious Albion" orations yet still charm his dinner guests, who sometimes were British diplomats, with his discourses on literature, history, and culture.)

During these years—years of sectional antagonism and political realignments—Blaine's political attitudes developed and matured. His family voted Whig. Blaine idolized Clay, whose American System with its emphasis on nationalism and national growth had deeply impressed him as a teenager. Thus Blaine naturally identified with the concepts of nation and union. In 1854, during the storm over the Kansas-Nebraska Bill, he urged his readers to reject the Whig title and adopt the new one of Republican. As delegate and secretary to the first Republican convention in 1856, he was in a real sense one of the founders of that party. Later, he served as chairman of Maine's Republican state committee, a post he held until 1881 and from which he virtually dictated the appointments, platforms, and orientation of the state's Republican politics.

In 1863, in the midst of the Civil War, he entered Congress. For the next seventeen years he was caught up in the politics of Capitol Hill, as a member of the House until 1876, then as senator to 1881. In these years Blaine became a national figure, impressing his colleagues with his oratorical abilities and forming political friendships with an emerging group of young western Republican leaders, one of whom was James Abram Garfield. Blaine saw himself as a participant and a witness to a series of momentous events, a horrible war and a grand victory, which culminated in nationhood and unity. Unlike his Maine colleagues who preferred William H. Seward, Blaine supported Lincoln in 1860. Where the president articulated the concepts of union from the White House, Blaine nurtured a similar impulse in the House of Representatives. Elected Speaker of the House, Blaine promoted partisan measures with such zeal that observers compared his leadership with Clay's. (Occasionally his rhetorical abilities made enemies. Roscoe Conkling never forgave Blaine for a spirited verbal assault, and his home district in New York in 1884 went for Cleveland— who won the state and the election.)

On most Civil War issues Blaine faithfully adhered to Republican party dogma, though he never approached Reconstruction issues with the intractability of Thaddeus Stevens or the moral fervor of Charles Sumner and never held a central place in the tightly knit band of Radicals. A decade earlier, when Blaine matured in his politics, slavery had been for him the central issue in a great debate, and thus he matter-of-factly accepted emancipation and ultimately the enfranchisement of the black man. He voted for military reconstruction as a necessary concomitant to the salvation of the South and the uplifting of the ex-slave. When Republican policies moderated in the 1870s Blaine supported them, but he always believed abandonment of Southern Republicanism to be a mistake.

Blaine's first love was politics. Caught up in the presidential fever that affected Republicans in the seventies and eighties, his powers of leadership seemingly unmatched in Congress, Blaine appeared a logical choice for the kingmakers. His ablest biographer, David S. Muzzey, contends that Blaine really sought the nomination only once, in 1876, and that in subsequent conventions he merely deferred to movements in his behalf. His friendship with Garfield matured in the Grant years, and, as Garfield moved steadily from a solitary vote to the nomination in 1880, he did not forget Blaine's support. The president-elect spent four months dealing with the nerve-racking assignment of dispensing jobs to loyal Republicans. When Blaine got the nod for the State Department, the wheelhorses in Conkling's stable of Stalwarts called it a political payoff. It was, though Garfield had more choice in the matter than is commonly acknowledged.

The State Department of 1881 was not by any stretch of the imagination a hotbed of activism. Abroad the United States carried out its diplomatic missions through two dozen ministers plenipotentiary and resident, five chargés d'affaires, and about three hundred consuls. The schooling of most had been in politics and business, not international affairs. Of the regular ministers, the large majority were political appointees like Lew Wallace. (Garfield moved Wallace from Paraguay to Turkey because he had enjoyed reading *Ben Hur* and believed Wallace might follow with another work in a Near Eastern setting.) There were ministers of genuine ability, such as James Russell Lowell and Andrew D. White, sent to London and Berlin respectively, whose reputations had been acquired in literary or scholarly pursuits.

If 1881 represented the "nadir of American diplomacy," as later historians described the era, Blaine was certainly no example of the lethargic party faithful content to mark time as secretary of state. It is true that he and the president had not spent much time discussing foreign policy matters and that Blaine began his assignment with no detailed script for settling individual problems. Instead, he brought to the task only a sense of unflagging determination to make America respected by the other powers and to advance American interests in Latin America.

In Blaine's approach to foreign affairs in 1881 one can find numerous examples of the kind of thinking that Walter LaFeber has analyzed in detail in his prize-winning work, *The New Empire*. Blaine easily grasped the fundamental arguments used by Seward and other foreign policy activists that the emergence of an industrial America dictated the pursuit of commerce and the extension of American interests southward into Latin America and westward across the Pacific. To Blaine, commercial expansion constituted only a part of the grand task; it must be matched with skilled diplomacy to bring peace to the Western Hemisphere, to assert American influence in the isthmian region, to block European intrusion in the hemisphere, and to advance American policies in the Pacific. Collectively these diplomatic efforts—partly economic, partly political—constituted Blaine's plan for demonstrating the strength of American nationality. The nation, having been tested in the Civil War, could now assert itself more vigorously in the Western Hemisphere. More than anything else, Blaine sought to prove to others, particularly to European governments, that the United States had arrived on the world scene and should be taken seriously. He challenged the British for Latin American markets, though he failed to convince Latin America that it should look to the United States, not Europe, for political and economic leadership.

Unfortunately, Garfield's death terminated Blaine's first tenure as secretary of state (he remained on under Arthur until December 1881), and subsequent investigations into his attempts to settle the War of the Pacific between Chile and Peru-Bolivia precipitated public criticism of his Latin American policies. Too much identified with intense partisan politics, Blaine was not yet taken seriously as an innovative and imaginative statesman.

While his friends promoted his candidacy for president in 1884, Blaine began work on his two-volume memoir, *Twenty Years of Congress*, the first volume of which appeared during the presidential campaign year. Though it will never rank with *The Diary of John Quincy Adams* or the *Memoirs of Cordell Hull*—one reason is that Blaine said little about foreign policy—*Twenty Years of Congress* reveals a remarkable mind at work and reflects Blaine's nationalism. If one dismisses those portions of the work that are frankly sustained Republican eulogies, one finds a superior intellect explaining the vitality and strength of the country.

In the 1884 campaign, haunted by vicious stories of political skullduggery and by charges of diplomatic ineptitude during his brief tenure as secretary of state, Blaine avoided foreign policy issues. The public had not embraced his ideas on the subject, and indeed regarded his 1881 foray into Latin America with apprehension and suspicion.

Appointed secretary for the second time in the Benjamin Harrison administration in 1889, Blaine found himself with aggressive associates, particularly Harrison and Secretary of the Navy Benjamin Tracy. Ironically, in his second term Blaine turned out to be somewhat out of touch with the rising tide of spread-eagle diplomacy. In the Chilean imbroglio of 1891, he became the man of moderation, so much so that Harrison himself seized the issue and nearly took the country to war. The Pan-American Conference—planned for Blaine's first term but canceled by his successor, Frederick Frelinghuysen—convened in 1889, but Blaine got little of what he wanted. In subsequent foreign policy matters he seemed more restrained, more cautious, less certain of promoting American interests than he had been in 1881. His failing health and the loss of three children within a year contributed in part to this decline in enthusiasm for a vigorous foreign policy.

◇◇◇

The Blaine "style" in foreign policy was probably most controversial in his dealings with Latin American problems. Remembered principally for his efforts to call an international American conference, Blaine saw in his Latin American involvements an unusual opportunity to bring peace to the southern half of the hemisphere and to promote American political and economic interests. Perhaps no other Latin American venture of these years precipitated more controversy than Blaine's interference in the War of the Pacific (1879–83), a conflict between Chile on one side and Peru and Bolivia on the other.

The war resulted from alleged Bolivian violations of the Chilean-Bolivian settlement of a boundary dispute. In 1874 the two countries had drawn up a treaty stipulating the division of territory on the Pacific coast, in a desolate area called the Atacama Desert. Chile, more economically aggressive than its neighbor, began to develop the nitrate deposits of the Atacama. The 1874 treaty had stipulated that for twenty-five years neither government could increase taxation rates in the region, but four years later, as Chileans increased their exports of nitrate from the Atacama, the Bolivian legislature authorized a new tax, to be paid into the

Bolivian treasury, on nitrates exported by Chile. The Chilean government not only refused to pay but unilaterally abrogated the treaty, landed troops in an area claimed by Bolivia, and seized control of the nitrate fields. Tensions erupted into hostilities, and Bolivia invoked its 1873 alliance with Peru.

Blaine viewed the Chilean-Bolivian-Peruvian conflict as potentially the most serious in a long list of Latin American boundary disputes. Other hemispheric nations looked for some kind of mediation by a friendly power, perhaps the United States or even a European government. In 1880 England, Italy, and France offered their services. Chile agreed, stipulating that Peru cede Tarapacá, also a nitrate province. When Peru and Bolivia objected and asked for United States mediation, the three European governments consented. The conferees met aboard a U.S. warship in October 1880, and agreed on nothing, principally because victorious Chile sought destruction of the Bolivian-Peruvian alliance and refused arbitral solutions.

The following March, Blaine became secretary of state. Though not the initiator of American efforts to end the war, he did go far beyond the policies of his predecessor William M. Evarts. In early 1881, Chile improved its military position, and by the time Blaine took office Chilean troops had occupied the Peruvian capital, Lima, and had installed a more pro-Chilean administration, headed by Francisco García Calderón. When Blaine received Calderón's representative in Washington, the Chileans must have believed that the United States had accepted Chile's basic demands.

Blaine had no such intention, however. He appointed new ministers to Lima and Santiago; to Peru he sent Stephen A. Hurlbut, formerly a Union officer and Illinois congressman whose most recent assignment was the command of the Grand Army of the Republic. Charges of financial mismanagement in the Union occupation of Louisiana had tainted Hurlbut's reputation, but those charges had not impeded his political advancement. To Chile, Blaine sent another ex-officer, Judson Kilpatrick, who had marched with Sherman and who had earlier served in Chile (1865–68) and had married a Chilean with important family connections in the church.

Blaine's instructions to both men showed that peace constituted his paramount consideration. Though recognizing that Chile deserved some form of territorial concession, he believed that the

Chileans should not make cession of territory a *sine qua non* for peace discussions and should, rather, honorably avoid popular pressures for territorial aggrandizement. Peru had a right to "orderly government" and national sovereignty in the provinces occupied by enemy troops that would allow the Peruvians to achieve a "just and reasonable" disposition of their case.[1]

Blaine saw in the Peruvian-Chilean dispute an excellent opportunity to convey to South American nations that a territorial cession wrung from one nation by another in war created continental strife and exacerbated efforts to achieve a general and lasting peace. As he explained in his instructions to the American minister in Santiago, Chile might have some claim to territory by reason of military conquest, but acquisitions obtained by force could never lead to permanent peace. In order to benefit all parties in the conflict, Chilean authorities should accept the referral of territorial questions to mediators. The first task, Blaine continued, was the restoration of a stable Peruvian government free of Chilean interference and military occupation.

Both the content and tone of Blaine's suggestion seem, in retrospect, reasonable, just, and fair; but two issues hampered any settlement along the lines he suggested. The first was the tremendous enthusiasm of the Chileans as their small army (2,400 troops against 13,200 Peruvian and 3,232 Bolivian soldiers) routed and humiliated the enemy. Moreover, the war furnished Chile with the opportunity to overcome the economic doldrums of the late seventies. The opening up of the nitrate fields to Chilean exploitation (financed in large part by English capital) offered to many Chileans the opportunity to modernize their society. To relinquish the grip over the northern lands just because an

---

1. Blaine was in effect asking Chile to repudiate territorial rights won by military conquest and he argued that international justice would be better served without Chilean interference in Peruvian affairs, even though Chilean troops were occupying key provinces and the capital of Peru. The issues, claims, and counterclaims in the dispute were extremely complex; they remained unresolved until 1929 when a treaty between Peru and Chile achieved a diplomatic solution. During the War of the Pacific, Chilean troops had occupied the provinces of Tacna and Arica in southern Peru, as well as its capital, Lima, and its principal port city, Callao. In 1882 Chile voluntarily withdrew from Lima and Callao but remained in the two provinces. After Blaine's repudiation in America, the two Latin American states negotiated an interim settlement that called for a plebiscite in the disputed provinces.

American secretary of state believed that Chilean expansionism hampered inter-American harmony seemed not only unacceptable but ludicrous. Secondly, Hurlbut and Kilpatrick interpreted their instructions loosely, almost working at cross-purposes.

Of the two, Hurlbut played the more crucial role, because he enjoyed Blaine's confidence and could act as intermediary between both Peruvian and Chilean officials in Lima. He advised Calderón to resist Chilean demands for territory and suggested a financial indemnity as the price for Chilean withdrawal. Hurlbut thought the United States must end the war. When the French broached the idea of a Franco-American statement on the war in the summer of 1881, Hurlbut killed the plan, knowing of course that Blaine feared European diplomatic intervention as much as a continuation of the conflict. Later, Hurlbut peremptorily notified the commander of Chile's occupation army that other countries would interpret the seizure of Peruvian territory as the initial step in a campaign of aggression. In Santiago, Kilpatrick adopted a pro-Chilean posture. The differing positions taken by the two American ministers led to a series of mutually acrimonious notes between Lima and Santiago. In November the exasperated Chileans finally arrested the Peruvian chief of state, Calderón, because, as Hurlbut wrote, he had refused Chile's peace terms. To both Hurlbut and Kilpatrick Blaine now sent reprimands, wording Kilpatrick's more strongly since he had misled the Chilean government by his misrepresentation of American policy.[2]

Besides the frustrations caused by the bunglings of his ministers, Blaine involved American policy in the affairs of foreign businesses in Peru. One of these, the Société Générale de Crédit Industriel et Commercial, distracted him from the Chilean-Peruvian settlement. The society was actually a holding company for European owners of Peruvian bonds whose management wanted to move into the nitrate and guano fields, using receipts to reimburse Chile, subsidize Peru, enhance the value of Peruvian

---

2. It should be remembered that by this time Blaine's days in the department were numbered. He had agreed to remain on after Garfield's death in September as a gesture of continuity, but he knew that Arthur wanted his own man. Blaine realized that he had only minimal time to salvage his entire Latin American program: the inter-American conference, the solution of boundary disputes, and the settlement of conflict. If he failed to mediate the War of the Pacific, he would fail everywhere in Latin America.

bonds, and enrich itself. Its president and lobbyist, Jacob Shipherd, a New York promoter, raised an old claim against Peru brought by Alexandre Cochet, a man who had allegedly discovered a scientific means of improving the commercial value of Peruvian guano. Shipherd estimated the Cochet claim at the stupendous price of one billion dollars. Another claimant was that of a U.S. citizen whose brother, Théophile Landreau, contended that Peru had wrongfully annulled a valid contract to exploit certain guano deposits. Blaine inherited the Landreau claim from the previous administration and gave it a nominal bureaucratic interest though he remained suspicious of both claims. Blaine had little respect for Shipherd, but in a series of widely publicized charges the latter convinced many people that he had received support from high officials in the Garfield administration. Naturally, Blaine's political enemies inferred the worst from such charges, though in 1882, during the congressional investigations of American involvement in the War of the Pacific, Blaine presented a spirited defense of his policies. As for Landreau, Blaine sought only to obtain for an American citizen a full and fair hearing in a Peruvian court. There is no evidence that Blaine gave these economic interests anything more than the attention they deserved; yet the cloud of suspicion —that Blaine supported Peru because of American economic activities there—never disappeared, and Blaine suffered some ignominy in life and in death by the unforgettable sobriquet, the practitioner of "guano diplomacy."

Blaine's determination to salvage his Latin American policy, particularly his plans for the inter-American conference, before he left office prompted him to send a special envoy to South America. The new appointee, William Trescot, had assisted Blaine in developing a general Latin American policy earlier in the year. To assist Trescot, Blaine sent along his own son, Walker, third assistant secretary of state. On reaching his destination, Trescot was to convey to the Chilean government Blaine's belief that the Chilean-Peruvian imbroglio had been partly the fault of Hurlbut's indiscretions. If Chile remained recalcitrant, Trescot could suspend (not sever) diplomatic relations in hopes of bringing the Chilean government around to American reasoning. If that failed, then Trescot should tell the Santiago authorities that its policies of territorial acquisition would be discredited by the other American republics, whose governments would be asked to join the United States in an effort to preserve peace in the Western Hemisphere.

TRYING TO BULLY AND BROWBEAT EACH OTHER.

Mr. BLAINE (to Mr. BADGER BELMONT). "I hope you will treat me as a gentleman. I am not in a police court to be BADGERED."

Blaine's allusion to some form of multilateral intervention referred, of course, to his announced plans for the inter-American conference, though he denied that the proposed conference and the War of the Pacific were intimately related. As Russell H. Bastert demonstrated in his analysis of Blaine's Latin American policy, however, the timing of the Pan-American invitations (late November 1881) and the instructions to Trescot (early December) *were* closely related. In addition, Blaine sent most of the invitations to the neutral governments but allowed his envoy to carry the invitations for Chile, Peru, and Bolivia. Trescot's instructions had also included an unsubtle threat of American intentions to appeal to the other republics unless Chile moderated its demands.

Trescot's mission could not succeed, however. While he and Walker Blaine were en route to South America, the secretary of state resigned (19 December 1881); in Panama, the envoys learned of Kilpatrick's sudden death in Santiago; and soon found that Hurlbut was still promoting his own virulent anti-Chilean views among Peruvian officials. These men, assuming that such views were official policy, welcomed the new American envoys as heroes upon their arrival in Callao and Lima. In Chile, however, the Americans found an aroused and angry public, for in early January the new secretary of state, Frederick T. Frelinghuysen, had sent instructions that gave little hint of any softening of the American position vis-à-vis Chile. The envoys went to Santiago unaware that the Arthur administration was in the process of revising its approach to mediation efforts. In private conversations with Chilean authorities, Trescot conveyed the impression that the United States wanted only a peaceful solution fair to both sides (though he held in reserve Blaine's authorization to warn Chile that the United States was prepared to take its case to the other hemispheric governments).

Meanwhile, Frelinghuysen had publicized the diplomatic correspondence by sending it to the House Foreign Affairs Committee. While Trescot continued his negotiations with the Chileans, he privately expressed doubts about the possibility of an easy solution and thought a resort to force or an appeal to the other nations of the hemisphere might be necessary. For a time he debated withholding Chile's invitation to the conference, but learned that Hurlbut had already delivered an invitation to Peru (despite Blaine's instructions that only Trescot should give the invitations to Peru, Chile, and Bolivia). Trescot immediately decided to send the invitation to Chile, and at the same time he authorized the American minister in Bolivia to invite that country to the conference. When Trescot and Walker Blaine interviewed the Chilean foreign minister, Jorge Balamaceda, they were shocked to learn that the Chileans already knew of Frelinghuysen's revised instructions, which, while still blaming Chile for its unjust claims, vetoed any threats against the Santiago government. When, on 22 February 1882, the Chilean government finally received its invitation to the conference, it knew well that nothing would be done there to threaten its territorial claims. It had never officially accepted the invitation when the Arthur administration indefinitely postponed the proposed conference.

Trescot and his aide remained in Chile until late March, then returned to Peru. Before arriving there they learned of Hurlbut's death, and, because Trescot still hoped for a peace settlement under his guidance, when a modified peace proposal surfaced he personally carried it on a pack mule into the inhospitable interior to seek out the Peruvian vice-president's response. All efforts failed, however, and in April the secretary of state recalled his envoys.

Thus terminated ignominiously Blaine's dream of bringing peace to the western coast of South America. Forced to defend his policies in the 1882 congressional investigations of the affair, he never quite surmounted charges of "guano diplomacy." The young Democrat Perry Belmont, who left his account of these affairs in *An American Democrat*, occupied a principal role in the congressional hearings; he handled Blaine roughly in cross-examination. Blaine's defense of his policies never satisfied Belmont (and a later generation of textbook writers) because, for one reason, the former secretary spent much of his time portraying the war as a conspiracy of English capital, with Chile as the instrument of British commercial interests. The personal antagonism between Belmont and Blaine—the conflict between the chairman of the House Foreign Affairs Committee and the seasoned diplomatist— naturally generated public attention all the more, to the detriment of Blaine, whose support of the Landreau claim led inevitably to charges that economic motives explained his instructions to Hurlbut, Kilpatrick, and Trescot.

Blaine did defend the Landreau claim and he certainly displayed anti-English sentiments in his public utterances and in the congressional hearings; but for Blaine and a host of other late nineteenth-century politicians, a public wringing of the lion's tail was instinctive. In the privacy of his home, Blaine could lavish praise upon English culture and charm even the most skeptical English guest. Moreover, he did not neatly catalog separate issues. The prospect of unending conflict on the western coast of South America concerned him as much as the furtherance of American markets in Latin America. Economic expansionism was the hand-maiden of moral regeneration, and Latin Americans should look naturally to the United States for moral and economic leadership. To Blaine, the settlement of the War of the Pacific under United States auspices opened the way to stability, peace, and prosperity.

◇◇◇

In his approach to the War of the Pacific, Blaine set a style that later policy makers sometimes followed. His appeal to the Peruvi-ans and especially to the Chileans rested on the notion that the United States possessed a special mission to settle intra–Latin American disputes. Though not the first secretary of state to mark out Latin America for special consideration, Blaine's meddling went beyond that of any of his predecessors.

In his first term, for example, he also involved American diplomacy in a controversial boundary dispute between Guate-mala and Mexico. Though he never became as irritated with Mexican demands for territorial concessions from Guatemala as he had with Chilean demands on Peru, Blaine encouraged the Guatemalan government to apply to Washington for a hearing. Rumors from Central America that Mexico planned a border war in order to make good its claim circulated in the State Department. Blaine saw in Guatemala the weaker disputant, and he involved American power to the point of preventing by diplomatic means an aggressive Mexican move. When the United States formally broached the idea of arbitration, both Guatemala and Mexico declined and later denounced Blaine's interference. The dispu-tants settled the problem in 1883, almost two years after Blaine left the Arthur cabinet. Mexico obtained a portion of the territory it had claimed, but neither country was satisfied completely with the outcome and neither appreciated Blaine's proposals.

Blaine really feared two related problems: an attempt by Mexico or Guatemala to use force to accomplish its goals and the possibility of European, particularly British, interference in the territorial quarrel. Such apprehensions were consistent with Blaine's approach to Latin American issues. As he had decried the threat to peace posed by the Chilean-Peruvian-Bolivian contest, so he condemned the harmful effects of the Guatemalan-Mexican quarrel. His meddling in that problem was, of course, less intensive than in the War of the Pacific, but he saw in it no less the potential for endless bickering and conflict. Blaine sincerely believed that the United States had a special mission to mediate disputes of this kind by the pursuit of a vigorous foreign policy short of armed intervention. Moreover, a more positive approach to the solution of intra–Latin American disputes would offer an opportunity for the United State to thwart European diplomatic interference in the hemisphere.

In some respects Blaine's participation in the Mexican-Guatemalan affair anticipated Elihu Root's Central American policies of 1906–7, which resulted in the 1907 treaties for the "normalization" of the often violent Central American political scene. Root's dilemma, of course, involved much more than territorial disputes; the Central American situation in 1906 displayed a chronic instability that endangered American interests (military and economic) and upset orderly political processes. Like Blaine, Root saw himself as a benevolent interventionist sincerely striving to show Central Americans how to model their political system on that of the United States. Blaine's intervention did not go as far as Root's because the United States established no Central American protectorates in Blaine's day, but his thinking led ultimately to such a conclusion. Like Root, Blaine also viewed himself as the champion of Latin America against European intrusion.

In his commitment to a more determined American policy in the hemisphere, Blaine laid the foundation for later policies, particularly the Olney and Roosevelt corollaries to the Monroe Doctrine. These amplifications of Monroe's principles rested squarely on moral and strategic doctrines. In the first Venezuelan boundary dispute of 1895, Secretary of State Olney proclaimed the Monroe Doctrine as hemispheric public law and challenged European powers to deal with Latin American nations according to American rules. Theodore Roosevelt's later proclamation of a hemispheric police power for the United States embodied prevailing assumptions that Latin Americans were culturally backward and incapable of straightening out their difficulties with European powers. This kind of reasoning had prompted Blaine to carry his mission of peacemaking to the western coast of South America and to Central America. He never contemplated a resort to "gunboat diplomacy"; yet his assessment of intra–Latin American conflicts led him logically to the idea that American policy had a special role in the hemisphere. Such an assessment constituted a fateful precedent.

Blaine's brusque rejection of a European guarantee for an isthmian canal is an example. After Ferdinand de Lesseps had initiated operations on the Panamanian isthmus, Colombia proposed a multilateral treaty guaranteeing the future canal's neutrality. To Blaine, such a treaty violated the special commitment the United States had made in the 1846 Bidlack Treaty with Bogotá to guarantee Colombian sovereignty and the right of free transit across Panama; it also challenged what Blaine considered to be American primacy in the isthmian region. The Colombian diplomatic venture prompted a note to the American minister in London, James Russell Lowell, stating that a multilateral guarantee of canal neutrality might lead to *political* dominance. Blaine not only decried the proposed scheme but broadened his diplomatic attack to a denunciation of the Clayton-Bulwer Treaty. Like most nineteenth-century politicians, he had learned well the art of baiting the British and thus joined numerous colleagues in his public outcries against the 1850 Anglo-American isthmian agreement, condemning specifically its provisions for the neutrality of any future transisthmian route. He wanted the British to agree to the modification of the treaty allowing American political and military supervision over a future canal. In return, he pledged no American territorial acquisitions in Central America and, if the British wished, Blaine would acquiesce in the designation of free ports at each end of the canal. Such demands anticipated the concessions later obtained in the second Hay-Pauncefote Treaty of 1901, which freed the United States from the neutrality provisions of the Clayton-Bulwer Treaty and virtually assured American domination of any isthmian canal.

Blaine's most remembered contribution to Latin American affairs was his sponsorship of the first Pan-American Conference in 1889. In the eight-year interim between his abrupt departure from the Arthur cabinet and his return to the secretaryship of state in 1889, the idea of calling an international conference of the American states was not scrapped but merely shelved, and the Cleveland administration later played an important role in calling the conference. Blaine claimed that it would promote peace, rebuff European interference in the hemisphere, and advance American commerce in Latin America. The promotion of peace and furthering of commerce were in his mind distinct but related phenomena, each beneficial to the general attainment of a hemispheric harmony and the gradual rise of United States prestige in Latin America. During the Cleveland presidency, when Congress finally enacted enabling legislation, it followed closely Blaine's prescription, but with more emphasis on the economic benefits to be derived from a Pan-American meeting. Blaine in 1881 had given the attainment of peace high priority. In 1888, when Secretary of State Thomas Bayard dispatched the invitations, he followed the congressional mandate that the first business of the conference should be a discussion of measures to advance inter-American prosperity, to establish a customs union, to promote transportation and communication, and to provide a means of arbitration for disputes.

A later generation of diplomatic historians, analyzing the search for late nineteenth-century markets for America's industrial and agricultural surpluses, concluded that Blaine's economic expansionism inspired his Pan-Americanism. Blaine vigorously supported a search for markets, as did many of his contemporaries, and he perceived the close relationship between foreign policy and trade and investments; yet he was not single-minded in his approach. Recognizing the opportunity for promoting American commerce that the inter-American movement offered, he also saw in it an unprecedented chance to enhance American political prestige at the expense of Europe. Blaine was acutely conscious of the American-European rivalry in the hemisphere. At times the battle would be joined on commercial grounds, on other occasions, on political or diplomatic grounds; but always the end was the same: the enhancement of American prestige in the hemisphere. The conferees of 1889 did not adopt a customs union or the arbitral system Blaine had championed, though they did establish the International Bureau of American Republics, forerunner of the Pan-American Union.[3]

So much attention has been given to the economic aspects of

3. Since 1948 the union has become the permanent Secretariat for the Organization of American States.

Blaine's proposals that other, equally important results of the 1889 meeting have been deemphasized. In the first place, the fact that the conference finally met when Blaine was again secretary of state stood as symbolic testimony that his 1881 ideas had found more favorable public reception. In his first term, Blaine had to contend with the animosity stemming from his interference in the War of the Pacific. Public suspicion over the implications of his Latin American policies had done much to undermine what he had considered the principal goal of a Pan-American movement, the creation of a multilateral organization to settle intra–Latin American wars and boundary conflicts. Secondly, the fact that the first conference in the so-called new Pan-Americanism met in Washington had an important political legacy. It virtually assured that the United States would play the principal role in the Pan-American movement in later years; it meant that Washington could set the agenda for the meetings and be assured that no embarrassing criticisms of American policies in the hemisphere would be publicly aired in the conference sessions. In the first two decades of the twentieth century, when the United States became heavily involved in the internal affairs of a number of Latin American governments, Blaine's determination to preserve U.S. domination in the hemispheric system proved to be of immense political value to Washington. It prevented for years what American policy makers feared: a grand debate in the inter-American system on the Latin American policy of the United States. It should be noted, as did Alice Felt Tyler in her study of Blaine's foreign policy, that Blaine did not advance American control over Pan-American conferences to the exclusion of debate. He sincerely believed that Latin America deteriorated because of constant bickering and disputes and that the hemispheric nations might do well to follow his prescription for peaceful settlement of conflicts. The building blocks of true Pan-Americanism were goodwill and the recognition of common political and economic interests; but Blaine seemed not to realize that his presumptions of American cultural superiority, his grand design for the hemisphere, were interpreted by many Latin Americans as just another example of insufferable Yankee meddling. It was ironic, for Blaine saw in himself the true Pan-Americanist; yet his interference did much to advance the interests of one state over twenty others in a system that was ideally a partnership of equals, and it logically led to a

Pan-Americanism that two generations of Latin Americans would condemn as a front for American imperialism.

As he had done in Latin America, Blaine pursued assertive policies in the Pacific and the Far East. His policies were a logical continuation of the post–Civil War commercial expansionism typified by the foreign policies of William H. Seward; Blaine's approach constituted an important link in the evolution of Asian policy from Seward to John Hay. As Garfield's secretary of state, Blaine wrote the instructions to Commodore Robert Shufeldt, who opened Korea to American economic penetration. In his second term, Blaine encouraged the increasing Korean isolationism from China. New York investors interested in exploiting Korean mineral resources looked to Blaine for diplomatic assistance. He accepted matter-of-factly the 1878 treaty arrangement whereby the United States acquired rights to Pago Pago in Samoa and agreed to intercede in its behalf in disputes with other powers. When British and German interests began their encroachments into the islands, the American government interpreted their actions as a threat to Samoan autonomy. To ease tensions, Bayard called a conference in Washington in 1887, but it produced nothing more than a German suggestion that Samoa be transformed into a protectorate; Bayard insisted upon Samoan autonomy.

Harrison and Blaine inherited the unresolved dispute in March 1889. Already there had been trouble in the islands when German agents, rebuffed by the Samoan king, declared war and deported him. Their makeshift government fared no better at the hands of Samoan natives, and, in retaliation for an attack on German seamen, German ships shelled villages and proclaimed martial law. After these incidents, German, American, and British ships anchored in Apia harbor. News of the Samoan incidents, particularly the German counteroffensive against the native rebellion, filtered back to the United States. Journalistic embellishments of German wrongdoing inflamed American opinion against Germany, whose discriminatory decrees against allegedly diseased American pork exported to Europe had already aroused many people. In mid-March, Harrison named three commissioners, including John A. Kasson, to the Berlin Conference, called to settle the Samoan imbroglio. In a belligerent mood, Congress appropriated five hundred thousand dollars for protecting Americans in Samoa and another one hundred thousand for improving the harbor at Pago Pago. Before the conferees began their discussions, a hurricane slammed into Samoa, wrecking or sinking three American and three German ships in the harbor. The British fleet fared better. Most diplomatic historians point to the hurricane as a major factor in the peaceful resolution of the dispute, on the presumably unassailable grounds that it prevented any resort to force at the scene of action; but there is much evidence that neither Chancellor Bismarck nor the American government wanted to press the issue. Blaine wanted to preserve Samoan autonomy, a plan unsatisfactory to the British and Germans; Kasson tended to be pro-German, one of the other American commissioners, intensely anti-German. In the midst of such divided opinion it became difficult to achieve autonomy for Samoa. When the idea of a tripartite protectorate surfaced, no one found it very satisfactory but all accepted it as better than no agreement. Had Blaine been less insistent on autonomy, the British and Germans would have accepted the division of the islands on almost the same basis as the final settlement of 1899.

In the Samoan squabble Blaine revealed another trait in his approach to foreign policy: a suspicion of European power. In this he was of course very much in the tradition of the nineteenth century, where it was *de rigueur* to expatiate endlessly on the dangers of European embroilments. Where Samoa was concerned, he was not really expansionist but a man determined to preserve Samoan autonomy against European encroachment. When antagonisms with European countries involved areas closer to the Western Hemisphere, Blaine became much more assertive, invoking that spirited foreign policy with which his diplomacy has become associated. In his brief tenure in 1881, he had penned some thoughts on Hawaii that demonstrated clearly his belief that the islands were within the scope of the Monroe Doctrine. Later, in his post-1881 commentary on diplomatic and political affairs, Blaine revealed his deeper reflections on the future of the islands. Though Hawaii lay thousands of miles from the United States, it bore economic resemblance to Cuba, which controlled the Gulf trade, for the islands were the "key to the maritime dominion of the Pacific States." The United States rejected Cuban and Hawaiian annexation but forbade their acquisition by another European power lest they be "cut adrift from the American system, whereto they both indispensably belong." Blaine's analysis went beyond economic factors to incorporate his views of the destructive elements in Hawaiian society, by which he meant Oriental influence. The gradual rise of "Mongolian supremacy" he linked with Hawaii's future degradation. In the annexation crisis of 1893, for instance, some of the sugar planters were torn between the arguments against American absorption, which might mean the end of cheap Oriental labor, and the proposals for annexation, which among other things would thwart the antiforeign cultural nationalism of Queen Liliuokalani.

Blaine believed that ultimately Hawaii would be annexed. In 1889–90, he tried and failed to work out new treaty arrangements, sought as much by Hawaii as by the United States, that would have resolved the matter of reciprocity with the islands and, at the same time, laid the basis for a protectorate. In 1891, Queen Liliuokalani ascended the Hawaiian throne and launched her reactionary anti-American policies. John L. Stevens, Harrison's appointee to the Hawaiian post, was an avid annexationist. In the troublesome politics of the islands, Stevens encouraged and abetted the movement to overthrow the queen. He played a crucial role in the January 1893 revolution and in the drafting of an annexation treaty. Critics presumed that Stevens's precipitate maneuvers represented Blaine's policies. Both were annexationists; both feared the undermining of American influence in the islands; both sought to protect the interests of the sugar growers. Stevens and Blaine had known each other since their newspaper days in Maine in the 1850s; yet Blaine had never sent Stevens definite instructions, and there is no reason to believe that the resourceful Stevens required Blaine's inspiration to promote the usurpation of power. Had he lived, Blaine probably would have approved the annexation treaty, despite the embarrassing circumstances of its birth, but this is not sufficient evidence to argue that he plotted Hawaiian annexation.

Blaine tried to resolve a number of other disputes: the Bering Sea controversy over pelagic sealing, the Chilean war crisis of 1891–92, the lynching of Italians in New Orleans in 1891. In one, the matter of pelagic sealing, Blaine assumed an intensely uncompromising stance; in the others, he symbolized the model statesman, striving to moderate the bellicose sentiments of his associates and at the same time to represent the position of his government.

◇◇◇

Among the principal liabilities in studying Blaine's diplomacy is the problem of coping with several major interpretations of the man. Blaine's political career, stormy and controversial, confuses matters because he obviously sought the presidency and he aroused a loyal and dedicated following. Though lacking the moral firmness of Cleveland, Blaine operated by a higher code of ethics than most Gilded Age politicians; certainly he displayed more intellectual creativity and innovation than other late nineteenth-century secretaries of state.

In some respects, Blaine's intellectual energy hampered American policy and did his reputation no good. He brought to the Department of State no previous diplomatic experience, save journalistic and congressional discussions of foreign affairs. Though not unique in this matter, his lack of prior training was a hindrance, particularly in learning to deal with the day-to-day problems a policy maker encounters. Most of the other late nineteenth-century secretaries were men of meager preparation in diplomacy, but at least they did not attempt to chart crusading courses in foreign policy. Blaine did not suffer from that kind of self-doubt.

In the historiography of the period there exist several "Blaines." The first is the intellectual, the righteous Republican, the cultivated gentleman who appears in the biographies by Edwin Stanwood and Mary Abigail Dodge (Gail Hamilton). Except for the fact that both were intimates of the Blaine family, their accounts could be written off as campaign pieces; but the paucity of Blaine letters has compelled later historians to rely heavily on the two for details of Blaine's private life.

Then, there is Blaine the misunderstood thinker and diplomatic innovator and, if one stretches the logic sufficiently, the founder of the Good Neighbor policy. This Blaine was to a great extent the work of Alice Felt Tyler and David S. Muzzey, who wrote scholarly but sympathetic accounts of him. Tyler's study, originally published in 1927 but still the basic work on Blaine's foreign policy, portrays Blaine as a statesman striving to bring peace to the republics of Latin America by refurbishing the Pan-American dream of Simón Bolívar. Muzzey devotes more space to Blaine's life, particularly trying to defend his subject against the many charges of political and financial malfeasance. Blaine as the founder of the Good Neighbor policy is an interpretation derived by inference from the standard surveys of the period. Obviously, he performed a critical role in the inter-American conference of 1889; but the Good Neighbor policy of the 1930s stood essentially for noninterference, nonintervention, and a practical cooperation between the United States and the republics of Latin America. Blaine's contributions to inter-Americanism promoted meddling, interference, and intervention, and in the twentieth century gained few scholarly adherents north of the Rio Grande and certainly none south of it. The value of the "Blaine inter-Americanism," Luis Quintanilla wrote in *A Latin American Speaks*, may be summed up in the phrase "Blah Blah Pan Americanism." At least this view offers some alternative to the diplomatic-history-text interpretation of Blaine who, according to Thomas A. Bailey, was strong on oratory and short on common sense. Even Samuel Flagg Bemis, ordinarily favorably inclined to the more nationalistic secretaries of state, does not come to grips with Blaine the thinker and innovator.

Actually, Blaine the thinker has been more the subject of the less sympathetic accounts, particularly the revisionist diplomatic studies focusing on the "new American empire" of the nineteenth century. Walter LaFeber in his prize-winning *The New Empire* and William Appleman Williams in *The Roots of the Modern American Empire* depict Blaine as a major architect in the search for industrial and agricultural markets. Both focus on Blaine's role in the reciprocity debates of the Harrison years, wherein Blaine apparently converted the staunchly protectionist McKinley to the idea of lowering duties in order to expand agricultural markets. Such an interpretation lends credence to the theory that a "marketplace consensus" existed among politicians of the period; but, as Paul Holbo has demonstrated in a recent essay, the revisionist interpretations fail to take into account the bitter emotional and political rivalries, particularly the Democratic determination to lower the tariff, that affected economic aspects of foreign policy. Moreover, revisionist students are inclined to believe that nearly all policies dovetail into the economic. In Blaine's case, this view sometimes illuminates, sometimes confuses. For instance, Blaine did promote American economic expansionism in Latin America, in part because he correctly observed a rising glut of agricultural and industrial products without outside markets, but also in part because he believed that the American and not the European political and economic system was a better standard for Latin Americans.

Finally, there is Blaine the transitional figure. Too partisan to forget the antagonisms generated in the fifties and sixties, Blaine identified the destiny of the nation with that of Republicanism. Yet, in his intellectual repertory and in the policies of his two brief terms in the State Department, he displayed an imaginative and creative mind explaining the role of America in global affairs. He carried out, as far as possible, the foreign policy goals of Seward, and his Latin American ventures foreshadowed in intent if not execution the protectorate philosophy of the twentieth century.

BIBLIOGRAPHIC NOTE

Blaine was careless with his letters. There is a small collection of Blaine manuscripts in the Georgetown University archives, and three volumes and thirteen boxes are found in the Library of Congress Manuscripts Division. The letters of Garfield and Harrison contain numerous pieces to and from Blaine. Albert T. Volwiler has edited *The Correspondence between Benjamin Harrison and James G. Blaine, 1882–1893* (Philadelphia, 1940).

Blaine wrote a great deal. Among his many articles and several books the best insights into his thinking are *Twenty Years of Congress: From Lincoln to Garfield*, 2 vols. (Norwich, Conn., 1884–86), and *Political Discussions: Legislative, Diplomatic, and Popular, 1856–1886* (New York, 1887). For Blaine's official correspondence, of course, the interested student should consult the relevant *Foreign Relations* volumes for 1881 and 1889–92. The full State Department correspondence for these years is available on microfilm.

There are several biographies, mostly campaign pieces or works written by friends or distant relatives (for example, by Edwin Stanwood and Gail Hamilton). A sympathetic but scholarly treatment is David S. Muzzey, *James G. Blaine: A Political Idol of Other Days* (New York, 1934).

Still the best account of Blaine's foreign policy is Alice Felt Tyler, *The Foreign Policy of James G. Blaine* (Hamden, Conn., 1965; originally published in 1927), though it should be supplemented with more recent works, particularly Russell H. Bastert, "A New Approach to the Origins of Blaine's Pan American Policy," *Hispanic American Historical Review* 39 (August 1959), 375–412, David M. Pletcher, *The Awkward Years: American Foreign Relations under Garfield and Arthur* (Columbia, Mo., 1962), Walter LaFeber, *The New Empire: An Interpretation of American Expansionism, 1860–1898* (Ithaca, 1962), and Milton Plesur, *America's Outward Thrust: Approaches to Foreign Affairs, 1865–1890* (De Kalb, Ill., 1971). H. Wayne Morgan offers a synthesis of Gilded Age politics in *From Hayes to McKinley: National Party Politics, 1877–1893* (Syracuse, 1969).

LESTER D. LANGLEY

Blaine has become more and more the subject of revisionist studies focusing on the economic background of late nineteenth-century foreign policy. For Blaine's role in these matters, see LaFeber, *The New Empire*, and William Appleman Williams, *The Roots of the Modern American Empire: A Study of the Growth and Shaping of Social Consciousness in a Marketplace Society* (New York, 1969). Recent dissertations that deal with Blaine's ideology are Richard C. Winchester, "James G. Blaine and the Ideology of American Expansionism," University of Rochester, 1966, who argues that Blaine's support for a rapidly expanding domestic economy before 1881 was transmuted logically into a vision of global empire; Allan B. Spetter, "Harrison and Blaine: Foreign Policy, 1889–1893," Rutgers University, 1967, who contends that Harrison and Secretary of the Navy Benjamin Tracy played the dominant roles in the Harrison administration's foreign policy; and Edward P. Crapol, " 'America for Americans': Economic Nationalism and Anglophobia, 1876–1896," University of Wisconsin, 1968, who shows that the nineteenth-century anti-English attitudes of Americans stemmed in large part from the power of English capital in the domestic economy, in Latin America, and in the Orient.

*General Research and Humanities Division,
The New York Public Library, Astor, Lenox
and Tilden Foundations*

ALFRED THAYER MAHAN

Turning America Back to the Sea

Kenneth J. Hagan

Alfred Thayer Mahan, a naval officer who died in 1914, enjoys today a reputation and prominence unmatched by any other officer of the United States Navy. His most famous book, *The Influence of Sea Power upon History, 1660–1783*, was first published in 1890. In the introduction to the edition that is still in print Louis M. Hacker, a distinguished historian, compared Mahan to Darwin, noting that Mahan's book, "in its way and its place," had "as profound an effect on the world" as Darwin's *Origin of Species*. He found the lessons of Mahan still relevant and believed that the strategy of sea power enunciated in the book remained the key to American security and world peace, just as it was the secret of world peace while Britain was mistress of the seas.

Naval officers have joined historians in perpetuating Mahan's fame. Rear Admiral Stephen B. Luce, the founder of the Naval War College who convinced Mahan to join its first faculty, set the tone.

Deeply impressed by Mahan's lectures at the college, Luce hailed his colleague as a modern naval Jomini, a philosopher and strategist who at last had codified the principles of naval warfare and strategy. A half-century later, Captain William D. Puleston, U.S.N., repeated the theme in his biography of Mahan. He found his predecessor "an extraordinarily successful naval historian, naval biographer, and essayist. His historical studies were profound, his biographies illuminating, his essays timely and suggestive." Writing on the eve of World War II and in the midst of a hot debate over the relative merits of battleships, aircraft carriers, and submarines, Puleston attributed great influence to Mahan: "It is no exaggeration to assert that today, in the American Navy, every officer who prepares for or discusses war, follows the methods and invokes the ideas of Mahan." Much more recently, in October 1972, the president of the Naval War College justified sweeping changes in the curriculum of that institution with the observation: "There may be another Alfred Thayer Mahan in this year's class or the next. We cannot afford to miss him."

◇◇◇

The man who has been the object of so much eulogy was in 1884 an obscure officer commanding the U.S.S. *Wachusett* off the west coast of South America. The United States was attempting to protect the investments of certain American corporations during a series of revolutions in 1884 and 1885, and the *Wachusett* was part of the minuscule but persuasive show of naval force used to dissuade revolutionaries from destroying American property. Mahan was bored with the assignment; sea duty generally had bored him throughout his career. Unexpected respite came in the form of a letter from Rear Admiral Stephen Luce, offering Mahan an appointment to the faculty of the newly formed Naval War College at Newport, Rhode Island.

Notwithstanding the tedium of shipboard life, Mahan expressed trepidation. He would "like the position, like it probably very much," but he thought Luce mistakenly gave him credit for knowing more than he did, and for "having given a special attention to the subject." Although Mahan had already written a study of the Civil War navy, *The Gulf and Inland Waters*, he otherwise had not displayed creative prowess. Many other officers by 1884 had contributed a great deal to the evolution of strategic and technological theory through the medium of the U.S. Naval Institute *Proceedings*, first published in 1874; Mahan had written only a single essay on naval education for that journal. Thus he had reason to doubt Luce's judgment in selecting him as the officer who could deliver decidedly didactic lectures on naval history to the classes at Newport. Unfortunately, Luce remained silent on the source of his inspiration, and all that is known is that the two officers had an acquaintanceship dating back more than twenty years to duty together at the U.S. Naval Academy and aboard the *Macedonian* during the Civil War.

Despite his initial doubts, Mahan proved equal to the task. Between 1885 and 1889 he composed the lectures that would be published in 1890 as *The Influence of Sea Power*, which contained the essence of all Mahan ever said on the subject of naval strategy.

The comments of Luce, Puleston, and Hacker suggest that there were at least two facets to Mahan's writing: history and propaganda. In the preface to his great work, Mahan readily admitted that he was "a naval officer in full sympathy with his profession." He was writing naval history because he believed "the study of the sea history of the past will be found instructive, by its illustration of the general principles of maritime war, notwithstanding the great changes that have been brought about in naval weapons by the scientific advances of the past half century, and by the introduction of steam as the motive power [of ships]."

Mahan was making a subtle but fundamental distinction that he repeated throughout the book. Naval history illustrates general, immutable principles of international relations and warfare at sea that are affected very little, if at all, by technological changes in weapons systems; put in other terms, Mahan distinguished between strategy and tactics. He contended that history illustrates unalterable strategic principles while tactical conditions vary to some extent with technology. The warrior's milieu is strategic before "hostile armies or fleets are brought into *contact*." Thereafter the environment is tactical; while history remains useful, it is a far less trustworthy guide.

Mahan's distinction is significant for two reasons. The first is that he clearly allowed for changes in naval warfare brought about by technological developments; thus those critics who have criticized Mahan's specifications for the ideal battleship have dealt with peripheral issues. More to the point is Puleston's argument

that Mahan would have welcomed aircraft carriers and submarines, but even here the essence is missed. Mahan was simply not
deeply concerned with—perhaps one ought to say he was
uninterested in—naval technology. The cursory manner in which
he passed over the millennial changes from oar to sail to steam
reflects this. "The best-planned schemes might fail through stress
of weather in the days of the galley and the sailing-ship; but this
difficulty has almost disappeared. The principles which should
direct great naval combinations have been applicable to all ages,
and are deducible from history; but the power to carry them out
with little regard to the weather is a recent gain."

The second significant aspect of Mahan's distinction between
strategy and tactics is its determinism. Mahan exposed himself as a
creature of the late nineteenth century, accepting change as
inevitable but believing that in every instance "deducible" laws
both limit and guide that transformation. War has unalterable
principles; "their existence is detected by the study of the past,
which reveals them in successes and in failures, the same from age
to age." Aware of the intellectual climate of his era, Mahan
concluded that the principles shaping strategy belonged "to the
Order of Nature, of whose stability so much is heard in our day;
whereas tactics, using as its instruments the weapons made by
man, shares in the change and progress of the race from
generation to generation."

Mahan's determinism was not limited to warfare; on the
contrary, it embraced the study of what today would be called
international relations. For Mahan the entering wedge was maritime trade. "The profound influence of sea commerce upon the
wealth and strength of countries was clearly seen long before the
true principles which governed its growth and prosperity were
detected." The enlightened age of the late nineteenth century had
mastered the underlying principles of national prosperity, which
Mahan set down in *The Influence of Sea Power*. "In these three
things—production, with the necessity of exchanging products,
shipping, whereby the exchange is carried on, and colonies, which
facilitate and enlarge the operations of shipping and tend to
protect it by multiplying points of safety—is to be found the key to
much of the history, as well as of the policy, of nations bordering
upon the sea."

The nation that continually increased its production, shipping, and colonies would maximize "its sea power in the broad

sense, which includes not only the military strength afloat, that rules the sea or any part of it by force of arms, but also the peaceful commerce and shipping from which alone a military fleet naturally and healthfully springs, and on which it securely rests." Regardless of their shrewdness and ambition, however, statesmen have less effect on the growth of a nation's sea power, and hence prosperity, than certain "natural conditions." Mahan enumerated these as geographical position, physical conformation, extent of territory, size of population, character of the people, and character of the government.

A favorable geographic position meant separation by sea from other nations, so that a country was "neither forced to defend itself by land nor induced to seek extension of its territory by way of land." The favorable geographic complement to isolation by sea was a series of deep harbors, especially if they were "outlets of navigable streams, which facilitate the concentration in them of a country's internal trade." The depth and quality of those harbors, together with the length of a nation's coastline, were more important to Mahan's calculation of sea power than the total area of a country. Likewise, the number of people in a nation was not nearly as important as "the number following the sea, or at least readily available for employment on ship-board and for the creation of naval material."

Aside from these physical and quantitative ingredients, Mahan stressed national and governmental character as determinants of a nation's maritime greatness. "If sea power be really based upon a peaceful and extensive commerce, aptitude for commercial pursuits must be a distinguishing feature of the nations that have at one time or another been great upon the sea." A taste for the sea and a benevolent geographic environment destined a people for "the most brilliant successes," so long as there was "intelligent direction" of their affairs "by a government fully embued with the spirit of the people and conscious of its true general bent."

For Mahan, the ideal sea power was Great Britain, which had in profusion all of his essential "natural conditions." Alone among the powers of Europe, Britain was insulated from invasion by the all-encircling ocean; but what really made Britain a great sea power was the character of its people. Like the Dutch, the English "were by nature businessmen, traders, producers, negotiators." They surpassed the Dutch, however, in their ability to colonize.

"Successful colonization, with its consequent effect upon commerce and sea power, depends essentially upon national character; because colonies grow best when they grow of themselves." To an unparalleled degree, Englishmen had been successful colonizers because those who went abroad thoroughly identified themselves with the colony where they resided, and they worked for its economic development within the imperial system. Unlike other colonists, Englishmen did not seek short-term, highly exploitative gains from their colonies.

Mahan was not perfectly lucid about what precisely made colonies so valuable to the mother country. Certainly there was an economic factor—colonies meant trade, and trade meant wealth—but the naval aspect predominated in his extensive discussion of the need to maintain "suitable naval stations, in those distant parts of the world to which the armed shipping must follow the peaceful vessels of commerce." He worried about protecting far-off naval bases and concluded that the greatest security lay in "a surrounding friendly population. . . . Such friendly surroundings and backing, joined to a reasonable military provision, are the best defences, and when combined with decided preponderance at sea, make a scattered and extensive empire, like that of England, secure." Colonies, then, were shields of naval bases.

The United States, the real object of Mahan's interest, fared less well. His own nation had enormous potential in each of the "natural conditions," but that promise had yet to be realized. As for geographical location, "the position of the United States upon the two oceans would be either a source of weakness or a cause of enormous expense, had it a large sea commerce on both coasts." In other words, while the United States enjoyed internal lines of communication, it suffered from inability to concentrate its naval force because of its extended coastline.

Even more significant to Mahan was the distance of the United States from the great trading centers of Europe. This separation meant that the United States in the future could not successfully employ its most popular form of naval warfare, commerce raiding, "unless she finds bases in the ports of an ally." Mahan saw one ray of hope to diminish American separation from Europe: construction of an interoceanic canal in Central America. Should that long-awaited event occur, the commerce of Europe would be attracted to the Caribbean, which would then become "one of the great highways of the world." European nations would have interests "close along our shores, as they never have before." The United States would no longer be able "to stand aloof from international complications. The position of the United States with reference to this route will resemble that of England to the Channel, and of the Mediterranean countries to the Suez route." Then the geographical conditions would be perfect; the mainland would provide permanent primary bases of naval operations, and to guarantee complete American hegemony in those waters the United States would simply have to obtain secondary bases of operations in the Caribbean.

Should the canal not be constructed, Mahan saw little hope for realization of the American potential for maritime greatness. The people of the United States had the national character suitable for creation of power at sea—"The instinct for commerce, bold enterprise in the pursuit of gain, and a keen scent for the trails that lead to it, all exist"—but popular attention had been drawn inland, toward development of the continental resources. The government had contributed to the decline of a once prosperous merchant marine by refusing to subsidize domestic shipbuilding and by maintaining tariffs preventing American shippers from purchasing vessels built in European yards. Thus, of the three activities reflecting proper utilization of the "natural conditions," the United States had manifested genius only in production. Shipping continued to deteriorate as American goods were carried in foreign-owned ships, and colonies "the United States has not and is not likely to have." The only hope for creation of commercial and naval sea power lay in an isthmian canal that would rekindle the American mercantile spirit by competition close to home. It would also force the construction of a navy to defend those renewed interests.

◇◇◇

Mahan wrote *The Influence of Sea Power* with full knowledge that reconstruction of the United States Navy in fact had already begun. In 1883 Congress had appropriated funds for new ship construction for the first time since the Civil War; thereafter appropriations came regularly. The "new navy" of steam power, steel hulls, and rifled breech-loading cannon was a reality before 1890.

It is true that no battleships had been constructed at the time

SHIPWRECKED PATRIOTISM.

UNCLE SAM AT SEA:—"It's Washington's Birthday, and I want to decorate, but—ahem—well—just lend me the loan of your mast, will you?"

Puck, 22 February 1882. Prints Division, The New York Public Library, Astor, Lenox and Tilden Foundations

Mahan wrote, but there were two excellent reasons for this failure. One was the technological immaturity of the American steel industry. Capacity to roll armor plate and forge heavy guns was only created during the 1880s as a result of experience gained by building small, very lightly armored warships. The United States could not have built a battleship in 1883. Secondly, when naval officers initially planned the vessels of the "new navy" they concluded that battleships did not meet "the necessities of *the present time.*" Rear Admiral John Rodgers and his fellow officers on the Naval Advisory Board of 1881 believed battleships would be *"absolutely necessary for the defense of the country in time of war,"* but they thought war unlikely. In time of peace, they contended, the squadrons of the American navy were used for "surveying, deep sea sounding, the protection and advancement of American commerce, exploration, the protection of American life and property endangered by wars between foreign countries, and service in support of American policy in matters where foreign governments are concerned." Should the United States unexpectedly find itself at war, a fleet of cruisers and smaller ships could temporarily defend the American coast, carry out unspecified "offensive measures of possible vital importance, and hold a naval enemy in check until armored vessels can be supplied to perfect the defense and undertake offensive operations."

Rear Admiral Rodgers's statement demonstrates that some American naval officers had contemplated building battleships and had conceived a strategy of offensive warfare at sea before Mahan. In these crucial respects, and in several others, Mahan's thinking was not original; indeed, the keystone to his scheme of sea power, the interrelationship of production and shipping, previously had been described in great detail.

Before Mahan, the most eloquent naval spokesman for an American national policy of vigorous commercial expansion was Robert W. Shufeldt, the officer who commanded the U.S.S. *Ticonderoga* on a global cruise from 1878 to 1880. Shufeldt's purpose in making that voyage was to find new markets for American manufactured goods, especially cheap cotton fabrics. On the eve of departure Shufeldt explained his conception of the relationship between the navy and American commerce to Congressman Leopold Morse of the House Naval Affairs Committee.

Shufeldt advised Morse that commerce was important to a nation for two reasons. First, it served as an index of national

greatness. Secondly, foreign markets could absorb surplus industrial and agricultural production. China was an object lesson to be
studied. The absence of a substantial trade meant that even with a
population of four hundred million, China was "simply an
aggregation of people without external force." The United States
must take heed, for the American republic was recklessly abandoning to rivals its share of the transoceanic carrying trade. Such a
policy was "courting the contempt of nations and cultivating our
own insignificance." Before long this neglect would render the
United States "as formidable beyond her limits as China or as a
turtle in a shell."

Shufeldt used American history to document the proper
relationship of the navy and commerce. He reminded Congressman Morse that American naval operations historically had
been "interwoven with commercial enterprise upon the sea and
linked to every act which has made the nation great." Soon after
the birth of the United States the navy had eradicated piracy in the
Mediterranean Sea and West Indies. In the War of 1812 the navy
vindicated "the motto of 'free trade and sailor's rights.'" During
that war, said Shufeldt, Captain David Porter had "opened the
trade of the Pacific Ocean to the whaling fleet of America, and
incidentally to general American commerce." In mid-century
California was conquered, Japan awakened, South America pene-
trated, and the vast areas of ocean stretching from the equator to
the North Pole explored. "All this, while acting as the police of
every sea, the Navy has done in the aid and for the aggrandizement of American commerce."

Shufeldt advanced a naval-commercial argument that had all
the trappings of Mahan's thesis of sea power. He did not believe
that the interdependence of the navy and merchant marine was
restricted to periods of hostilities, either past or future; the
relationship was also that of protector and protected in time of
peace. "The Navy is, indeed, the pioneer of commerce." In his
search for new markets around the world, the merchant of every
Western nation needed "the constant protection of the flag and
the gun. He deals with barbarous tribes—with men who appreciate only the argument of physical force." Navies were the means
by which the searching trader could best be protected, and
Shufeldt even conceived of the naval role as one of pathfinder.
"The man-of-war precedes the merchantman and impresses rude

people with the sense of the power of the flag which covers the one and the other."

In addition to rebuilding the navy, Shufeldt advocated establishment of a worldwide network of American steamship lines to ensure access to foreign markets. Virtually every American naval officer of the 1870s and 1880s agreed with Shufeldt that the United States merchant marine must be revived; they disagreed on how to effect that revival. Some favored subsidies to American shipping companies carrying mail overseas. Others advocated reduction of the tariff to permit purchase of merchantmen built in Europe. Still others favored federal subsidies to domestic shipbuilders. Unable to agree and faced with congressional indifference toward the merchant marine, naval officers could only lament its decline and worry, as did Shufeldt and Mahan, that naval and national greatness might consequently escape the American grasp.

Some officers cut the Gordian knot by advocating naval construction regardless of the state of the merchant marine, and here they were bolder than Mahan. As Lieutenant Frederick Collins observed in the Naval Institute *Proceedings* of 1879, a recognition of the intimacy of commerce and the navy "should impel any nation discovering its commerce on the wane to redoubled efforts to maintain an efficient navy as one of the most important aids to its resuscitation." In other words, a nation should first build a great navy; a merchant marine and national greatness would then necessarily follow.

As noted previously, despite Mahan's citation of production and shipping as indexes of national strength, he discounted the historic American reliance on commerce raiding in time of war. Here again he was not breaking new ground. As early as 1874 Commodore Foxhall A. Parker had hinted that the United States should plan a strategy for the "encountering of a hostile force at sea." Parker would have exercised different classes of vessels— large gunships, torpedo boats, and rams—as units. "For at sea, as on land, 'war is nothing more than the art of concentrating a greater force than the enemy upon a given point.' " The commodore sensed the futility of discussing "the assembling of fleets when our flag scarcely floats from the mast-head of a merchantman upon the sea"; but he was looking to the future when "the great Republic will awaken from her lethargy . . . and once more put forth her strength upon the deep." If American mer-

chantmen again roamed the "remotest corners of the earth,"
Parker believed "that a navy will be created for its protection
worthy of a great people."

Half a decade later, Lieutenant Frederick Collins applauded
Parker's "perspicuity" which represented "in a general way, the
views of most of our officers" at that time. Collins wished to
augment the American "power of acting on the offensive." To do
so, he would build "as quickly as possible a fair number of
powerful ships, sufficiently alike in size, speed and armament to
form a homogeneous fleet." By 1890 senior flag officers like
Admiral David Dixon Porter and Rear Admiral Stephen B. Luce had
publicly espoused creation of a battleship fleet competent to
engage an enemy on the open seas.

Whether operating singly or in fleets, steam-driven warships
must refuel. Mahan had admired Great Britain because it had
woven a network of colonies to shelter the naval bases supporting
the global fleets and squadrons of the Royal Navy; in 1890 Mahan
could envy the British their colonial system, but he could not
believe the United States would acquire overseas colonies. Thus
he satisfied himself with a rather ill-defined hope that his country
at least would "provide resting places" for its warships, "where
they can coal and repair." In this modest expectation also he had
been anticipated.

In 1883 Secretary of the Navy William E. Chandler recommended establishment of "coaling and naval stations" in the
Caribbean, Brazil, the Strait of Magellan, El Salvador or Honduras,
Madagascar, the island of Fernando Po off the west coast of Africa,
the coastal islands of Korea, and on both sides of the Panamanian
isthmus. During war, Chandler believed, American cruisers would
"require frequent supplies of coal at distant points. If they
attempt, in default of the necessary coaling stations, to cruise
under sail alone, their offensive power will be reduced to the
lowest limit." They would "become the prey of vessels one-third
their size, approaching under steam." Despite this strongly
worded recommendation, by 1889 the United States Navy had
stacks of coal only at Honolulu, Samoa, and Pichilinque in Lower
California, and an old hulk, the *Monongahela*, had been outfitted
to store one thousand tons of coal at Callao, Peru.

The hesitancy of naval officers to dispute the traditional
American reluctance to expand overseas accounts in part for the
absence of coaling stations. Before 1889 only a handful of officers

counseled a break with the past. In 1880 Lieutenant Charles Belknap hoped that the question of coaling stations would be studied at the highest levels. His essay on naval policy was awarded the Naval Institute's first prize by the judges, Secretary of State William M. Evarts and Secretary of the Navy Richard W. Thompson. Six years later, when nothing had come of Secretary Chandler's proposal, Lieutenant Commander F. M. Barber angrily complained that "general usefulness in *time of war,* for a *man-of-war* . . . is a question of coal-piles and not of canvas . . . for no man-of-war would dare go to sea in time of war under sail with any expectation of reaching port, let alone of capturing or protecting anything." He thought naval officers should make Congress aware of what American warships would have to do if deployed "away from home when a war broke out and coal is still contraband of war—viz. *Stay in port,* and in case of a long war dismantle ships and send crew and officers home."

Belknap and Barber were lonely voices in a wilderness of complacency and might have remained so had there not been a crisis over Samoa in 1888 and 1889. At issue was control of the fine natural harbor of Pago Pago. Britain was nominally a participant in the dispute, but Germany and the United States were the principal contenders. In the late fall of 1888 and early months of 1889 each of the three countries gradually increased the number of its warships in Samoan waters while the diplomats devised arguments to justify exclusive rights over the islands. Berlin and Washington made the strongest claims against each other, and the diplomatic gulf widened ominously. Fortunately for international peace, a hurricane struck Samoa in March of 1889, blowing several ships ashore and figuratively cooling the tempers of statesmen half a world away, who hastily negotiated a tripartite sharing of Samoa.

American naval officers drew their own conclusions from this first real brush with a determined European power in an area long thought to be an American preserve. Some, such as Rear Admiral Stephen Luce, simply reaffirmed their dedication to battleships without altering their conviction that cruisers must have sails. Others, notably Commander T. F. Jewell, reassessed American naval strategy in light of the new technological and political environments. Jewell was willing to keep some sailing vessels as training ships because indoctrination aboard square-riggers produced officers with quick wits and seamen with strong bodies; but he did not think the United States Navy should "take a step backward in order to develop the muscles of our men." He advocated removing all sails from every class of warship, and he preferred the most direct solution to the lack of overseas refueling depots: "Our country should establish coaling stations abroad." It might not be possible to acquire them "peacefully to any great extent, but it certainly could be done in the Pacific, and not improbably in the West Indies, without resort to force." Jewell thought Hawaii the best location in the Pacific, and he urged the government to establish a regular naval station there and to stop "wasting a golden opportunity" to ensure American hegemony in the Pacific.

The Pacific Ocean, an isthmian canal, the Caribbean Sea, and commerce were all interrelated in the minds of Mahan's predecessors. Writing in the *Journal of the American Geographical Society of New York* in 1886, Commander Henry C. Taylor pointed to the Caribbean and Gulf of Mexico as natural destinations for the industrial and agricultural products of the Mississippi Valley. The United States must dominate both bodies of water. "It is more than a consequent [*sic*] of greatness, it is greatness itself; it is part of the definition—we cannot be a nation of the first rank while lacking control of the seas and coasts immediately south of us."

Lieutenant Commander Charles H. Stockton chose to elaborate on the implications of a canal for trade with the Pacific. No island or country bordering that ocean would be immune to accelerated economic growth once a canal cut Central America. As an example of the potential of Pacific commerce, Stockton referred to New Zealand. Geographically analogous to the British Isles, it was peculiarly fitted "for colonization by whites of Anglo-Saxon origin." It was endowed with abundant coal deposits, splendid agricultural resources, and spacious harbors, and was already a leading producer of wheat and wool. In time it should become as well "a maritime and manufacturing country, and an important element in the commerce of the world." Without question, Stockton asserted, "New Zealand belongs to the domain of the American canal, both with regards to the United States and Europe."

Naval officers of the generation before Mahan also agreed on the strategic significance of the Caribbean Sea. Toward the end of the 1880s, in a confidential letter to Secretary of the Navy William C. Whitney, Rear Admiral Stephen Luce assumed a posture that Commander Taylor and others writing for publication could not then hold. Luce predicted early completion of an isthmian canal, "and those maritime people who have the gift of foresight are making timely provision to protect and control the stream of ocean commerce that must pour through one or more of the openings in the cordon of islands that enclose the Caribbean Sea." Specifically, he espied French plans for a protectorate over Haiti. If successful, "St. Domingo will certainly follow, when the whole island [of Hispaniola] will become French to the discomfiture of the English." Even if France governed the island, however, England still would have Jamaica and Bermuda. "The latter is at our very front door, as it were; a standing menace to any complications that might arise between this country and Great Britain." From a naval viewpoint, Bermuda was second in strength only to Malta "in the long line of England's outposts."

Luce understood American repugnance to overseas territorial aggrandizement. To prevent European encirclement of the eastern access to a canal, he proposed an American protectorate over the Virgin Islands. Denmark should be induced "for a consideration . . . to surrender her claim to the islands." Local autonomy should be preserved, while the people could "decide to pass under the protection of the American flag" by plebiscite. Luce hoped thereby to acquire a strategic toehold in the eastern Caribbean without entailing "certain embarrassing features inseparable from actual possession."

Mahan was strangely quiet about Hawaii in *The Influence of Sea Power*, but other officers were quite vociferous. In 1876 Admiral of the Navy David Dixon Porter raised the specter of English domination of the Hawaiian Islands. Congressman Fernando Wood of the Ways and Means Committee had charge of a bill to implement the Hawaiian Reciprocity Treaty of 1875, and he had asked Porter's opinion. The admiral warned that the islands were geographically analogous to Bermuda. Porter brooded that the British "have long had their eyes upon them" as "a principal outpost on our coast where they could launch forth their ships of war upon us with perfect impunity." Bases on the North American continent were always vulnerable to attack by the American army, but islands were relatively secure. To Porter it almost seemed as if Her Majesty's government had a grand design for Pacific power. The British had recently acquired a base in the Fiji Islands, an action that could only be viewed as "the preparatory step to the occupation of Hawaii." Porter did not fear territorial or cultural alienation of Hawaii from America; his concern was mercantile. Believing that acquisition of Hawaii would enable England to complete a chain of naval stations across the Pacific, he saw danger in such an arrangement, for it would allow a foreign power to dominate American commerce in that ocean.

Behind Britain loomed another dangerous power with similar ambitions. Writing thirteen years before the Samoan crisis of 1889, Porter noted that Germany had quickly risen as a naval power and in a decade would be "second only to England and France." Berlin sought island bases in the West Indies and in the Pacific "for the same reason as England, namely, the extension of her commerce." Porter was convinced that other European powers also eyed Hawaii avariciously, and growth of "the foreign element in the population of the islands" meant that in fifteen years they would easily fall "into the hands of some other power." The remedy was simple: tie the islands to the United States through reciprocal trade and reiterate the Tyler Doctrine of 1842 which denounced European acquisition of the islands as inimical to the interests of the United States.

Congressman Wood accepted the navalist's emphasis on commerce when reporting the bill. He concluded that the Hawaiian Islands could "do but little in promoting their prosperity, without more intimate relations with this or some other commercial authority." Observing briefly that Hawaiian civilization and religion were "modeled after our own," he passed on to the heart of the matter. "The Pacific Ocean is an American Ocean, destined to hold a far higher place in the future history of the world than the Atlantic." Significantly, he placed the commercial consideration first when describing the Pacific as "the future great highway between ourselves and the hundreds of millions of Asiatics who look to us for commerce, civilization, and Christianity." The Hawaiian Islands lay "midway between us and them as the necessary post provided by the Great Ruler of the universe as points of observation, rest, supply, military strategy, and command, to enable each other to unite in protecting both hemispheres from European assault, aggression, and avarice."

◇◇◇

Mahan caught up with Porter and Wood in 1893, when the *Forum* published his article "Hawaii and Our Future Sea Power."

The Hawaiian revolution of that year posed the question of American annexation of the islands in unmistakable terms, and Mahan elaborated on his "natural conditions" in arguing for acquisition. Geography determined the islands' significance and the American responsibility. Hawaii was twenty-one hundred miles from San Francisco and from the archipelagoes of the western Pacific. An enemy warship could not reach the west coast of the United States and return home without refueling at Hawaii. Equally important was the commercially central position the islands would occupy once an isthmian canal was opened. China and Japan, regarded by Americans of the late nineteenth century as highly promising outlets for their industrial goods, would be most directly reached from the canal by a route passing near Hawaii. The islands would be at a crossroads of trade between the consuming Orient and the producing east coast of the United States.

As always, Mahan dealt in absolutes when contending that for naval and commercial reasons Hawaii must be under the domination of the United States. "Let us start from the fundamental truth, warranted by history, that the control of the seas, and especially along the great lines drawn by national interest or national commerce, is the chief among the merely material elements in the power and prosperity of nations." From that axiom "necessarily follows the principle that, as subsidiary to such control, it is imperative to take possession, when it can be done righteously, of such maritime positions as contribute to secure command." This principle "has its application also to the present case of Hawaii."

If the Hawaiian revolution seemed to have created that "golden opportunity" of which Commander Jewell dreamed, other events in the Pacific during the last decade of the century added the negative impetus of threat. The Samoan crisis of 1889 marked the beginning, as Mahan tersely observed in the *Atlantic Monthly* of December 1890. "The incident of the Samoa Islands, trivial apparently, was nevertheless eminently suggestive of European ambitions. America then roused from sleep as to interests concerning her future." Mahan interpreted the dispute as symbolic of "the conflict between German control and American interests in the islands of the western Pacific," and he brooded over "the alleged progress of German influence in Central and South America."

What made German-American competition especially explosive was the character of the two peoples. While Germany's moves into the Pacific were "sustained with the aggressive military spirit characteristic of the German Empire," Mahan thought the expansion arose "from the national temper more than from the deliberate policy of the government, which in this matter does not lead, but follows, the feeling of the people,—a condition much more formidable." The American people, especially those on the west coast, were assured, energetic, and determined in assertion of United States preeminence in the Pacific. Mahan's nation was "by far the greatest, in numbers, interests, and power, of the communities bordering upon the eastern shores of the North Pacific."

Other nations, notably Japan, were manifesting expansionist tendencies in the 1890s. Japan's ambitions were directed largely against China, which seemed helpless; yet Mahan did not rule out the possibility that the "racially homogeneous" and rapidly multiplying Chinese might somehow "obtain the organization by which alone potential force receives adequate military development." If the "teeming multitudes of central and northern Asia" should expand, there was no doubt in Mahan's mind that their direction would be eastward to the islands of the Pacific and perhaps even to the North American continent itself. In that case, "the only barrier will be the warlike spirit of the representatives of civilization." Then naval power would play "the leading part which it has in all history, and the United States by her geographical position must be one of the frontiers from which, as from a base of operations, the Sea Power of the civilized world will energize."

As the decade of the 1890s advanced, Mahan became increasingly insistent that the large standing armies of Europe would be indispensable in any future conflict between Christian European civilization and the barbarism of the East. Moreover, he found in the armies of Europe a testament to the superiority of Western civilization. Informed by the Social Darwinism of the era, Mahan could write in seriousness: "Conflict is the condition of all life, material and spiritual; and it is to the soldier's experience that the spiritual life goes for its most vivid metaphors and loftiest inspirations. Whatever else the twentieth century may bring us, it will not, from anything now current in the thought of the nineteenth, receive a nobler ideal."

Such a militaristic conclusion stamped Mahan's outlook as

decidedly more aggressive than that of his naval predecessors; yet his definitions of civilization and barbarism differed very little from those held by the officers of the 1870s and 1880s. Mahan concisely defined "our not unjustly vaunted European and American civilization" in the *North American Review* of November 1894. It was an "oasis set in the midst of a desert of barbarism, rent with many intestine troubles, and ultimately dependent, not upon its mere elaboration of organization, but upon the power of that organization to express itself in a menacing and efficient attitude of physical force sufficient to resist the numerically overwhelming, but inadequately organized hosts of outsiders." The only difference between this definition and the descriptions of the world accepted by officers like Luce, Porter, and Shufeldt was a slight one of tone. Mahan apparently felt threatened by the possible expansion of Asian peoples, whereas his forerunners conceived only of the use of naval and military force for the extension of American commerce.

Mahan had composed a conundrum he could not solve. Germany in Samoa in 1889 and Britain in Venezuela in 1895 showed that European policies impinged on American interests. The civilized nations were obviously divided among themselves. Still, if Asia should awaken, European and American interests would be equally threatened. As the decade wore on, Mahan warned against both dangers without ever questioning the ostensible superiority of Western civilization. "The seat and scene of the loftiest culture, of the highest intellectual activities, it is not in them so much that it has exceeded the rest of the world as in the political development and material prosperity which it has owed to the virile energies of its sons, alike in commerce and in war."

A variety of forces determined the expression of this manly vigor, and in Mahan's explanation of late nineteenth-century European expansion several themes neatly intermingled and reinforced one another. Manifest Destiny, racism, and Darwinism blended smoothly with a pre-Hobsonian analysis of the results of industrial surpluses. "It is because so much of the world still remains in the possession of the savage, or of states whose imperfect development, political or economical, does not enable them to realize for the general use nearly the result of which the territory is capable, while at the same time the redundant energies of civilized states, both government and peoples, are finding lack of openings and scantiness of livelihood at home, that there now obtains a condition of aggressive restlessness with which all have to reckon."

It was "entirely evident" to Mahan that the United States did "not now share this tendency"; but by the Monroe Doctrine the United States had long before accepted "the necessity, recognized with practical unanimity by her people, of insuring to the weaker states of America, although of racial and political antecedents different from her own, freedom to develop politically along their own lines and according to their own capacities, without interference from governments foreign to these continents." The United States had voluntarily assumed this duty. Since it rested "not upon political philanthropy, but simply upon our own proximate interests as affected by such foreign interference, [it] has towards others rather the nature of a right than a duty."

Nowhere was the duty of the United States more clearly defined by history and interest than in the Gulf of Mexico and Caribbean, and as the 1890s closed Mahan again embroidered the theme of necessary American domination of those waters. He compared them with the Mediterranean, and he drew conclusions from the analogy of Suez. "Wherever situated, whether at Panama or at Nicaragua, the fundamental meaning of the canal will be that it advances by thousands of miles the frontiers of European civilization in general, and of the United States in particular; that it knits together the whole system of American states enjoying that civilization as in no other way they can be bound." The Caribbean was "the very domain of sea power . . . and centre of those influences by which such a maritime highway as a canal must be controlled, even as control of the Suez Canal rests in the Mediterranean."

There were two ways by which to dominate the canal itself. One was to exercise political and military power in and around the isthmus. Mahan preferred indirect control by means of "a distinctly preponderant navy." He believed the mobility of naval force always gave it an advantage over fixed installations. To be truly preponderant in the Caribbean and Gulf of Mexico, however, and thus to be certain of controlling the canal's eastern approaches, a naval power ought to secure certain outlying geographical points. By 1897 Mahan was willing to be quite specific, and in an article published in the October issue of *Harper's* he forecast the direction American imperialism would take in the

Caribbean within the next three years. He observed that "the phenomenon of the long, narrow peninsula of Florida, with its strait, is reproduced successively in Cuba, Haiti, and Puerto Rico, with the passages dividing them. The whole together forms one long barrier, the strategic significance of which cannot be overlooked in its effect upon the Caribbean; while the Gulf of Mexico is assigned to absolute seclusion by it, if the passages are in hostile control." One result of the Spanish-American War was that the United States acquired the right to naval bases in two of the three critical islands Mahan named, thereby ensuring that the adjacent waterways would never be "in hostile control."

Neither the outcome of that war, nor its inception, nor any major American diplomatic event of the late nineteenth or early twentieth centuries can be directly attributed to Mahan. He was not a Richard Olney, who as secretary of state in 1895 bluntly informed the British government that in matters concerning the Western Hemisphere the decree of the United States was "law." He was not a John Hay, whose Open Door notes moved the United States to center stage in the dramatic confrontation of Western powers over helpless China. In fact, he was not even the independent commanding officer of a ship whose men might precipitate a war scare between Chile and the United States by brawling in Valparaiso or ensure the triumph of Hawaiian revolution by landing in Honolulu.

In 1890, at the time of publication of *The Influence of Sea Power upon History*, Alfred Mahan was merely a captain in the United States Navy with thirty-four years of continuous service. His senior status was primarily a function of longevity. In the navy of that era a line officer could reasonably expect to advance to rear admiral if he lived long enough. Mahan was on his way to flag rank, which was customarily followed by retirement and oblivion. Instead, seven years later, Captain Mahan was an international celebrity who had discussed naval strategy with Queen Victoria and received honorary degrees from Oxford, Cambridge, Harvard, and Yale. He published almost a book a year, and his articles in such popular journals as the *North American Review, Atlantic Monthly*, and *Harper's* earned five hundred dollars apiece.

With the exception of a short stint on the Naval War Board

during the Spanish-American War and membership in the American delegation to the first Hague Peace Conference of 1899, Mahan had no direct formal access to American policy makers in the 1890s. He spent the first two years of the decade awaiting reconvening of classes at the Naval War College and writing his second major interpretive history, *The Influence of Sea Power upon the French Revolution and Empire, 1793–1812.* In 1893 he was ordered to sea as commanding officer of the U.S.S. *Chicago,* much against his will and over the protests of influential friends like Theodore Roosevelt and Henry Cabot Lodge. His extended cruise in European waters was both gratifying and frustrating. During stops in England in 1893 and 1894 the British lionized him, but the rear admiral aboard the *Chicago* found public adulation of his flag captain increasingly distasteful and irksome. He used pettifogging irritants, those timeless and ineffectual remedies of minor tyrants, to make Mahan pay the piper, but he did not drive him to insubordination.

When the *Chicago* returned to the United States, Mahan retired from active duty in order to devote all his energy to writing. He soon produced *The Life of Nelson,* which was extremely well received in England. Mahan's immortality was assured, and for the rest of his life he enjoyed the delightful *fin de siècle* existence of a gentleman of letters. He kept in touch with the powerful men of his times through essays, letters, and conversations and with the great men of history through research and books.

William D. Puleston, Mahan's biographer, believed that as a member of the Naval War Board Mahan's "direct responsibility for the major decisions of the war was scarcely less than McKinley's." There is little if any evidence to support this conclusion, and Puleston's very next sentence is a far more accurate appraisal. "But it was through his writings that he exerted the greatest influence on the course of events." Lodge, Roosevelt, and other expansionists on this side of the Atlantic imbibed Mahan along with Strong, Fiske, and Burgess. On the other side of the ocean, British commentators credited Mahan's works with greatly facilitating parliamentary approval of appropriations for the naval expansion of the 1890s. In a Nelson Day editorial of 1893 the *Times* of London took the broadest view by comparing Mahan to the great scientific lawmakers of history. "By his pregnant conception of sea-power and his masterly exposition of its influence upon the history of the

British Isles, Captain Mahan may almost be said to have effected a revolution in the study of naval history similar in kind to that effected by Copernicus in the domain of astronomy."

The comparison with Copernicus is suggestive. In his brilliant historical novel, *The French Lieutenant's Woman*, John Fowles vividly depicted the foundation of Victorian thought as science, particularly the Darwinian hypothesis. By the close of the century British and American thinkers had converted Darwin's biological analysis into a scheme of social theory known as Social Darwinism. Liberal reformers and die-hard conservatives alike accepted the postulates of this interpretation. Basically it held that competition in the marketplace resulted in the triumph of the men most fit to hold wealth and exercise power as trustees for the less well-endowed mass of mankind. With a few exceptions, Social Darwinists believed that governmental interference with the economy must be at an absolute minimum if the competitive process was to function properly. Ignoring the embarrassing contradictions of imperial preferences and protective tariffs, they concluded that by virtue of their efficient industrial production Great Britain and the United States had proven themselves most in harmony with natural law. The British and American economic, political, and social systems therefore represented the highest step thus far attained on the evolutionary ladder. To these theorists, Anglo-American civilization should envelop the world, and most of them were willing to help spread the gospel.

Alfred Thayer Mahan fitted perfectly into this environment. He stressed the importance of industrial production and commerce to the United States and any nation seeking greatness. He very obviously believed that Anglo-American civilization was superior to all others, and he was anxious to extend that culture into regions of barbarism. In these respects, however, he differed little if any from a host of other American naval officers.

What made Mahan's writing unique and so thoroughly harmonious with the intellectual milieu of his time was his injection of science into history. Stephen Luce had described naval warfare as a science and had hoped to find someone who could deduce principles of naval strategy from history; Mahan did precisely that. Nowhere is his success more evident than in the first chapter of *The Influence of Sea Power*, where he discussed with apparent detachment five elements, or "natural conditions," that had "determined" the "history of seaboard nations." In all of his subsequent narratives he never abandoned those determinants, and in his topical, analytical essays on contemporary events he artfully employed them to enhance the case for American naval and political expansion overseas.

It was Mahan's great fortune to be writing in a decade when certain changes in national and international conditions made imperialism increasingly popular with large numbers of Americans. Domestically, beginning in 1893, there was a serious depression that did not moderate and revert to a period of boom in the usual cyclical manner. The depression of 1877 had first given rise to serious consideration of the need for overseas outlets for surplus American industrial products by politicians like Secretary of State William M. Evarts and Secretary of the Navy Richard W. Thompson, as well as by naval officers like Robert W. Shufeldt. Increased exports would mean fuller employment of factory workers at home and thus reduction of social discontent and the chances of upheaval and revolution. With the more extended and far more serious depression of the 1890s these ideas were revived, but markets were less accessible abroad. In the 1880s and increasingly in the 1890s the European powers colonized Africa and Asia and levied heavy or prohibitive duties upon importation of American goods into the new dependencies. Thus the United States seemed to have two choices: increase its exports to those areas not yet closed or acquire protected markets of its own. In both cases colonies would be essential, either as bases from which the navy could protect the lives and property of American merchants in distant places, or as markets.

The colonies and overseas naval bases Mahan desired came with the Spanish-American War. Almost simultaneously Mahan's friend Theodore Roosevelt was elevated to the presidency. That vigorous exponent of American expansion built the canal in Central America that Mahan and other navalists had long expected. Through energetic use of naval power Roosevelt assured American hegemony in the Caribbean, as the naval officers of the last decades of the nineteenth century had insisted would be necessary once the canal became a reality. By showing the fleet to countries as far away as Australia and Japan Roosevelt thrust the American naval frontier far into the Pacific, something naval officers had been urging for a quarter of a century. The former assistant secretary of the navy did not neglect shipbuilding when president. He consistently urged and won congressional approval for bigger warships with greater range, heavier guns, and thicker armor.

In most aspects, Roosevelt's naval and diplomatic policies represented fruition for the naval officers of the late nineteenth century. Mahan was one of those men, and it was his writing that most forcefully and effectively summarized their position. In present-day terms, he was a highly successful propagandist for a policy of "realism" by which American statesmen pursued power through judicious use of the stupendous geopolitical resources of the United States.

BIBLIOGRAPHIC NOTE

Any study of nineteenth-century American naval history must begin with Harold and Margaret Sprout, *The Rise of American Naval Power, 1776–1918* (Princeton, 1939), who roundly praise Mahan. A recent dissenter is Peter Karsten, *The Naval Aristocracy: The Golden Age of Annapolis and the Emergence of Modern American Navalism* (New York, 1972), who concludes that Mahan's views were outdated when first expressed. The most well-balanced biography is still [Captain] William D. Puleston, *Mahan: The Life and Work of Captain Alfred Thayer Mahan, U.S.N.* (New Haven, 1939).

Robert Seager II analyzes the ideas of navalists in Congress and in uniform during the decade preceding Mahan in "Ten Years before Mahan: The Unofficial Case for the New Navy, 1880–1890," *Mississippi Valley Historical Review* 40 (December 1953), as does Kenneth J. Hagan in *American Gunboat Diplomacy and the Old Navy, 1877–1889* (Westport, Conn., 1973). Benjamin Franklin Cooling, *Benjamin Franklin Tracy: Father of the American Fighting Navy* (Hamden, Conn. 1973), carefully reassesses Mahan's immediate impact on American naval policy and concludes that it was less than believed by Walter R. Herrick, Jr., *The American Naval Revolution* (Baton Rouge, 1967). John A. S. Grenville and George B. Young, *Politics, Strategy, and American Diplomacy: Studies in Foreign Policy, 1873–1917* (New Haven, 1966), argue that Luce was the great innovator and Mahan the popularizer.

The final answer to the riddle of whether Luce or Mahan more heavily influenced Secretary of the Navy Tracy and his successors must be sought in the annual reports of the secretaries of the navy, the *Congressional Record*, and the hearings of the Senate and House appropriations and naval committees. The indispensable guide to the documentary history of the nineteenth-century American navy is Robert W. Neeser, *Statistical and Chronological History of the United States Navy, 1775–1907* (New York, 1909).

Walter LaFeber, *The New Empire: An Interpretation of American Expansion, 1860–1898* (Ithaca, 1963), deftly sketches the intellectual, political, and economic environment that shaped Mahan's "strategic formulation." Harold U. Faulkner discusses the domestic and international turmoil of the 1890s in *Politics, Reform, and Expansion, 1890–1900* (New York, 1959); but the essay by Marilyn B. Young in Barton J. Bernstein, ed., *Towards a New Past: Dissenting Essays in American History* (New York, 1968), most succinctly captures the flavor of disruptive imperialism that made Mahan's ideas popular after 1893.

Charles C. Taylor, *The Life of Admiral Mahan* (London, 1920), reflects Mahan's continuing popularity in England. William E. Livezey, *Mahan on Sea Power* (Norman, Okla., 1947), catalogs the effect of Mahan's thinking on American domestic and foreign policy. More limited in chronological scope, but deeply researched and finely balanced, is Richard D. Challener, *Admirals, Generals, and American Foreign Policy, 1898–1914* (Princeton, 1973). Harold and Margaret Sprout describe an apparent decline in the influence of Mahan's ideas after 1918 in *Toward a New Order of Sea Power* (Princeton, 1940). During the interwar period Louis Hacker condemned nineteenth-century imperialism by exaggerating Mahan's influence and criticizing his views in "The Incendiary Mahan," *Scribner's Magazine* (April 1934).

The U.S. Naval Institute *Proceedings* and the *Naval War College Review*, the two most prestigious professional American naval journals, frequently carry articles extolling Mahan and arguing that his work remains relevant to contemporary American policies. The most intelligent of these is [Commander] James A. Barber, "Mahan and Naval Strategy in the Nuclear Age," *Naval War College Review* 24 (March 1972). Other examples are [Captain] Carl H. Amme, "Seapower and the Superpowers," U.S. Naval Institute *Proceedings* 95 (October 1968), and [Captain] Jack E. Godfrey, "Mahan: The Man, His Writings and Philosophy," *Naval War College Review* 21 (March 1969).

The striking similarity between the analyses of twentieth-century "realists" and Mahan's ideas is evident in Hans J. Morgenthau, *Politics among Nations: The Struggle for Power and Peace* (New York, 1948). George F. Kennan interprets Mahan from the realist's perspective in *American Diplomacy, 1900–1950* (Chicago, 1951).

Mahan's prolific pen made any interpreter's task congenial. His most important works are *The Influence of Sea Power upon History, 1660–1783* (Boston, 1890), *The Life of Nelson: The Embodiment of the Sea Power of Great Britain* (Boston, 1897), and *The Interest of America in Sea Power, Present and Future* (Boston, 1897). The historical method and political viewpoint introduced in these three books were simply amplified in Mahan's other writings.

CAUTIOUS WARRIOR:

THEODORE ROOSEVELT

Reproduced from the collections of the Library of Congress

and the Diplomacy of Activism

Eugene P. Trani

As president and as extraordinary citizen, Theodore Roosevelt created a unique niche for himself in the American political pantheon. Much about TR is familiar, as John Blum reminds us in *The Republican Roosevelt*: "The teeth, the famous intensity, the nervous grimace, impelling leadership, physical courage, moral fervor—sometimes frenzy. . . . There are the busted trusts, the outdoor life, the nature fakirs, simplified spelling, rivers discovered, lions felled." These externals, the personal quirks and enthusiasms of Roosevelt's life, are well remembered; however, understanding of his purposes and policies during the seven years he occupied the White House lags far behind. This imbalance is especially noticeable in studies of TR and foreign affairs, in which

Professor Trani acknowledges the assistance of the Woodrow Wilson International Center for Scholars in the preparation of this essay.

carrying a big stick while speaking softly remains the accepted, if too easy, characterization of his diplomacy.

Of all the functions of the presidency, none fascinated Roosevelt more than foreign affairs. The stimulus of world responsibilities enraptured him, and he went out of his way to undertake tasks for himself and for the United States. TR always acted to promote the national interest, of course, but he relied always on his own perception of America's aims. He seldom consulted Congress on foreign policy, except when a clear legal obligation existed, and he was willing to stretch executive power to the limit and sometimes beyond.

More than any other American of his time, TR assisted in the emergence of the United States as a world power. He also forced the nation to assume some of the responsibilities that derived from its new role, though in this he was only partially successful. He viewed the cautious reaction of his fellow citizens to world affairs, especially the hectic struggle for power and prestige before the First World War, with impatience and often exasperation. As president, Theodore Roosevelt won much recognition for his country and diplomatic achievements crowded his tenure in office. The United States exerted dominant influence in Latin America, pushed into European politics, protected and expanded its interests in the Far East, modernized the army and expanded the battle fleet, and pursued an active and generally enlightened policy toward its new colonial dependencies.

◇◇◇

That the United States would assume a larger role in world politics was predictable when Roosevelt succeeded the assassinated President William McKinley on 12 March 1901. TR's views of foreign policy derived partly from his background and partly from the intellectual currents dominant in America in the latter years of the nineteenth century. He was born in 1858 in New York City to a socially established and moderately wealthy family. He received a typical upper-class education—tutors, Groton, and Harvard—and profited from exposure to the cosmopolitan social milieu to which he belonged by right of birth. As a youth TR traveled through Europe and the Near East and, indeed, except for Thomas Jefferson, the Adams family, and James Monroe, was more traveled than any preceding president. He possessed an inquiring mind and read voluminously on a multitude of subjects from natural history to modern warfare, a catholicism of interests that continued into manhood.

A childhood fraught with illnesses, particularly a serious asthmatic condition, greatly influenced TR's personal development. He determined to overcome his body's weakness and launched in his early teens a strenuous program of walking, riding, and boxing. This struggle for physical vigor, which eventually was totally successful, greatly influenced his outlook on life. It was to be dominant in his style of conducting the duties of the presidency, especially foreign policy. Roosevelt's views also owed much to the influence of his father, whom TR later termed the "best man" he ever knew. The elder Roosevelt, a dedicated philanthropist, possessed a strong sense of *noblesse oblige* that the son inherited.

The young Roosevelt found a philosophical rationale for his inchoate enthusiasm for individual and national self-improvement in doctrines that came into favor after the Civil War, at the time he was reaching adolescence. By the end of the century, these ideas, based in large part on Charles Darwin's epochal treatise, *On the Origin of Species*, had metamorphosed into a new fervor for national expansion. Enthusiasm for America's "Manifest Destiny" swept the country, and Roosevelt found himself at the forefront of its advocates. This renewed expansive frenzy gloried in such phrases, advanced by Darwin and his popularizers, as "natural selection," "survival of the fittest," and the "law of the jungle." Proponents of the new Manifest Destiny believed the United States, as a result of its emergence as a world power, was a fit nation, a chosen nation, qualified to instruct backward countries, and, indeed, required to do so. The "white man's burden" was a reality, and it imposed tasks that could not be shirked.

Those who called for realization of the national destiny asserted that America must have possessions in the Caribbean, Pacific, and Far East. Their ideology was a carbon copy of the European imperialism then burning its way across Asia and Africa. During the administrations of Grover Cleveland, Benjamin Harrison, and William McKinley, the United States became involved in diplomatic crises throughout the world: it challenged Great Britain and Germany in Samoa and obtained the harbor of Pago Pago; it extracted from Chile a $75,000 indemnity and an apology for the killing in Valparaiso of two crewmen and the injuring of sixteen others from the cruiser U.S.S. *Baltimore*; it annexed Hawaii in 1898; and in 1895–96 it forced Lord Salisbury's government to arbitrate the boundary between British Guiana and Venezuela. The century closed with the Spanish-American War and acquisition of an overseas empire. Advocates of a strong foreign policy were well satisfied with the start that had been made; America had come of age and had moved into the mainstream of history.

Further progress could be expected as these men attained positions of authority in Washington and elsewhere. Theodore Roosevelt's advance to prominence was especially swift. While still a young man, he served as commissioner of the civil service, New York police commissioner, assistant secretary of the navy, and as a volunteer lieutenant colonel in the war with Spain. Though playing only a secondary role in the great decisions of the 1890s, TR was influential, serving as an effective publicist for the causes then in favor. He attracted popular attention by vigorously expressing theories of international relations in books, articles, and reviews. In America, such ideas became most closely identified with Roosevelt, because he was able to lend them a special glamor. As David Healy has noted, Roosevelt's views were neither strikingly original nor distinct from contemporary opinion, but they were "frequently and forcefully expressed, formed a coherent whole, and suited the temper of the times." Many resulted from discussions with a circle of friends, gathered over the years, some of whom owed allegiance to other governments, who were to help TR with foreign policy during his presidential tenure. This group included Henry Cabot Lodge; the Adams brothers, Henry and Brooks; William W. Rockhill, an acknowledged expert on Far Eastern affairs; and Captain Alfred Thayer Mahan.

As the century drew to a close, Roosevelt's views about the wisest course for America became more concrete and demonstrated a confident grasp of the complexities of international politics. He urged commercial and territorial expansion, favored the annexation of Hawaii, supported the construction of an isthmian canal, and, of course, championed the creation of a first-class navy. Above all, he advocated policies that would uphold the honor and interests of the United States. "I am not hostile to any European power in the abstract," he once said. "I am simply an American first and last, and therefore hostile to any power which wrongs us." Friendly competition with the nations of

Europe, in particular Great Britain, was acceptable, for TR held as a first principle faith in Anglo-Saxon superiority.

The challenge lay elsewhere. Reviewing Charles H. Pearson's *National Life and Character: A Forecast* in 1894, TR observed that the great task facing mankind was to bring peace to the world's wasted spaces. Lasting peace was not possible, he believed, until the civilized nations achieved some sort of domination over the "barbarous" countries. This was racism raised to the level of principle. He justified the exclusion of Chinese immigrants, for example, by asserting that "the American democracy," demonstrating impressive clearness of vision, had realized that the presence of Chinese would be ruinous to the white race. To be sure, backward races could attain superior qualities, thus deserving and commanding respect. TR admired the Japanese because they had kept only the strongest of their traditions, scrapped the rest, and emulated the civilized nations of the West.

Although he professed to believe only in just wars, any war in which Americans fought was by definition just, and so TR could describe the Spanish-American War as the most righteous conflict of the century. "All the great masterful races have been fighting races," he claimed, "and the minute that a race loses the hard fighting virtues, then . . . no matter how skilled in commerce and finance, in science and art, it has lost its proud right to stand as the equal of the best." In this respect, the author of *The Influence of Sea Power upon History* and well-known promoter of the U.S. Navy, A. T. Mahan, greatly influenced Roosevelt's thinking. His ideas were, in fact, a starting point for almost every conversation Roosevelt had about foreign policy. Mahan forced TR to consider problems in military-strategic terms and to worry a good deal about national security. He soon came to believe the nation's safety required expansion, including construction of a powerful navy as well as territorial acquisitions. Strategic concerns alone do not explain Roosevelt's ardent advocacy of expansion, however. The national character would benefit, for the American people would have to overcome the physical softness and moral slackness that inevitably accompanied the transition from a pioneering country to a wealthy, developed nation. Maintenance of national strength thus became for him one of the central problems of American society.

After the Spanish-American War, Roosevelt's view of the

world became more complex, for he recognized that the great powers could clash with each other as well as with barbarians, realized that power struggles in such places as East Asia affected the balance of power in Europe, and learned that a nation that threatened American interests in one region might share its interests in another. He concluded that America should use its status as a world power to increase its strength and prevent any nation from injuring the United States or its friends, and he warned that America could not renounce its international obligations and avow itself "merely an assemblage of well-to-do hucksters who care nothing for what happens beyond [their borders]." No longer did he gauge events solely in terms of American interests, though these of course were paramount. He still divided the world into a few great civilized powers, purveyors of enlightenment and culture and protectors of law and order; but he admitted that these nations were themselves engaged in a constant conflict for supremacy, though he averred that the conflict would remain peaceful.

In sum, TR's pronouncements on foreign affairs reflected an increasingly shrewd and subtle assessment of world problems, though this is often ignored because of the moral exhortations, the evangelical commentaries that made Roosevelt seem almost an anachronism after he left the presidency. Stripped of their rhetorical embellishment, his thoughts do not now, in the 1970s, appear outdated. If his presidential statements customarily contained moral and ethical appeals, he understood that in the absence of any accepted body of international law and of an agency to enforce its rulings the determinant in world affairs was power, and he believed that as long as nations existed the loftiest ideals were worthless unless backed by force. Thus, a weak America invited attack and ultimately destruction. TR especially feared those he described as "peace demagogues," men who preached disarmament. While nations should be equitable in their dealings, they must possess the capability and determination to defend their own interests. For the United States, this meant ability to ensure its new empire, including supremacy in the Caribbean, extension of power in the Pacific, and construction of a transisthmian canal for rapid movement of the navy from ocean to ocean.

As TR was keenly aware, the changing structure of power elsewhere in the world jeopardized these purposes. Looking abroad, he beheld a British imperium in gradual decline and the rising strength of Germany and Japan. Such shifts of power were unacceptable to TR, a devout Anglophile. It had been with an approving nod that he had observed the rapprochement between the United States and Britain in the last years of the McKinley era, largely because of the work of John Hay, ambassador to the Court of St. James's and later secretary of state. TR believed the two English-speaking countries had to think and act as one. When as president he occasionally scolded the British, he did so not because of any serious disagreement but because contention of any kind had been permitted to arise. TR was dedicated to shoring up British power and was convinced that if England weakened fatally the United States would have to step in to maintain the world balance of power—against any and all contenders.

These sentiments were far in advance of the opinions of the American people. Indeed, TR's active part in world politics while president did not derive, as Raymond Esthus has noted in his study of TR's response to international rivalries, from any belief of the American public that the United States had an important stake in world affairs. Curiously, however, the public's indifference proved advantageous. President Roosevelt became a key figure in the two great power confrontations of his day—the Russo-Japanese War of 1904–5 and the first Moroccan crisis of 1905–6—mainly because the major powers looked to the United States as the one nation with sufficient disinterestedness to mediate these crises fairly. To be sure, the size and potential power of the United States and a growing fear of the likelihood of a general war made America's goodwill and diplomatic support a prize worth cultivating. Although foreign diplomats might believe that the president was able to use the power of the United States as he wished, Roosevelt recognized the limits on his freedom in foreign affairs. He understood the isolationist views of his countrymen and, though never fully reconciled to the cautious policies those attitudes demanded, accepted them as facts of life.

◇◇◇

Perhaps the best example of TR's careful balancing of the American public's feelings and his own concern about the changing balance of power was his mediation of the Russo-Japanese War. This episode was both typical and atypical of his diplomacy: it brought together all of the Rooseveltian beliefs regarding foreign policy, from informal diplomatic contacts to a search for an orderly world ruled by the great powers; but at the same time TR realized that he could not easily intervene in an international conflict of such dimensions and complexity. More often than not, he permitted subordinates to conduct diplomatic negotiations, recognizing that a president has other responsibilities than foreign affairs which, if neglected, will produce domestic pressures inimical to everything he may hope to accomplish.

The period of the Russo-Japanese War, the era of TR's deepest involvement with personal diplomacy, was coincidentally a time when he served in all but title as his own secretary of state. John Hay, who had been in poor health for much of his tenure, died in the summer of 1905. In the spring of that year the president was already writing diplomatic notes that went to the Department of State, next door to the White House, for transmission to envoys abroad. His diplomacy was so personal that at times Mrs. Roosevelt was his principal adviser. In this respect TR emulated the diplomatic style of other leaders of his day: Théophile Delcassé, Bernhard von Bülow, Sir Edward Grey, Wilhelm II, and Edward VII.

One should note parenthetically that the president never had large differences of opinion with Hay, whom he had respected; the contrasts in their diplomacy largely were ones of technique. Roosevelt differed in his manner of obtaining information, for unlike Hay he had little faith in America's regular envoys. He was wont to talk with bureau chiefs, head clerks, anyone he trusted, in or out of the government. TR also disliked diplomatic formalities and especially despised the appellation "excellency" referring to the president, as he saw no need of a title. Procedural details irked him. He told American diplomats abroad to use common sense in dress and to wear whatever would please the sovereigns of the countries in which they served. He enjoyed breaking diplomatic traditions, such as the custom that supposedly prevented him from entertaining people of equal rank. He took a truant boy's delight in forcing dignitaries into horseback rides in Rock Creek Park or walks up and down the wooded hills along the Potomac—Roosevelt's head thrown up to catch sight of birds, looking like a grotesque, burly Peter Pan while his guests huffed and puffed behind. Underlying the levity and seeming lack of decorum, however, were sound purposes and a professional's shrewd assessment of personalities and policies.

When Roosevelt assumed direct control of the State Department in 1904–5, relations with Russia presented difficult problems. One centered on communications between the two countries; the Russian ambassador in Washington, Count Arturo Cassini, had few qualifications for the post and did not fit into the scheme of Rooseveltian diplomacy. Difficult to get along with and, what was worse in TR's view, untruthful, Cassini impeded harmony between the United States and Russia. His own government did not keep him fully informed, and the president sometimes knew St. Petersburg's plans before Ambassador Cassini himself. The channel of communication was no better at the other end. TR considered the American ambassador in St. Petersburg, Robert S. McCormick, politically important but diplomatically useless. In December 1904 he shifted McCormick to Paris and replaced him with George von Lengerke Meyer, then U.S. ambassador in Rome and an old Harvard friend.

With Japan the communication problem was not as severe. The American minister in Tokyo, Lloyd C. Griscom, though experienced, was not an important cog in Roosevelt's diplomatic machine. TR preferred to deal with the Japanese minister in Washington, Kogoro Takahira, who had the double advantage of being fully trusted by his own government and the president. Then, in 1904, the Tokyo regime thoughtfully sent over Baron Kentaro Kaneko, one of TR's schoolmates at Harvard, as director of Japan's publicity effort in America. Kaneko and Takahira monopolized the president's correspondence with the Japanese government, putting Griscom almost out of the picture. The stage was set for a study in contrasts during negotiation of the Peace of Portsmouth in 1905, with Cassini shouting at one and all, and Japanese diplomats supplying TR with reading lists about their country and, upon request, a jujitsu teacher.

The president's arrangement of relations with the Japanese and Russians displayed his liking for congenial envoys, reliance on personal channels of communication, and preference for what a later generation would call "summitry." He also consulted many persons outside government about foreign affairs. Prominent in this group, who collectively were sometimes known as the Tennis Cabinet, were the French and German ambassadors in Washington, Jean Jules Jusserand and Hermann Speck von Sternburg, and Cecil Spring Rice, a British diplomat who in 1905 was an adviser *in absentia*, for he was first secretary of the British embassy in St.

Petersburg. All helped negotiate an end to the Russo-Japanese War, as did William Howard Taft who after 1904 was TR's secretary of war. If between 1901 and 1909 the participants changed, the president's style of conducting foreign affairs varied little. When Roosevelt wanted a message conveyed to another government he would call upon someone he trusted to deliver it, a technique that at times was extremely important in TR's diplomacy. His use of personal envoys and total control of foreign policy—excluding not only Congress but many times the State Department—certainly served as significant precedents for presidents Woodrow Wilson, Franklin D. Roosevelt, and Richard Nixon, among others, and appears to have marked the beginning of an ever-greater concentration of authority over foreign affairs in the White House. Such techniques appear outdated to some in the 1970s when problems of international relations have grown so complex that it is almost impossible for a few individuals to conduct personal diplomacy; eventually they produced irritation in the Congress and discouragement in the State Department. They were necessary, however, at a time when Americans cared little about foreign affairs.

At the *fin de siècle* Roosevelt worried greatly about the Far East. The decline of Great Britain was most apparent in that region where Russians, Japanese, Germans, and French were hastily and, as it turned out, thoughtlessly carving out spheres of commercial and territorial influence. Western interest in China had increased throughout the nineteenth century: Christianizing, civilizing, commercializing. Divided and weak, China remained a nation despite invaders, jackals, and false friends. Roosevelt's view of China included approximately equal parts of religion and economics. He certainly supported the concept of the Open Door—that all nations deserved rough equality of commercial opportunity in the Orient—but his interest principally derived from strategic concerns, from recognition that the struggle over China made up only one part, though a most important one, of a world struggle among the great powers. Roosevelt had come to the conclusion that China could not control its own territory, and thus the China problem would be long-standing.

China's defeat by the Japanese in 1895 had inaugurated a new era, a time of wild scrambling for spheres of interest. The Russians extorted from the feeble government in Peking the right to build a spur of the Trans-Siberian Railway through Manchuria and to construct naval facilities at Port Arthur. The Germans got Kiaochow, the French Kwangchowan, and the British Weihaiwei. These concessions alarmed the then citizen Roosevelt because they seemed to endanger American interests, and because U.S. economic involvement in China, which had become important in the latter part of the nineteenth century, was rapidly increasing when TR assumed the presidency. The work of American missionaries, U.S. economic interests, and, most importantly, strategic considerations such as the need to protect the Philippines and Hawaii appeared threatened by possible turmoil in the Far East.

In the regions surrounding China two nations in addition to the United States—Russia and Japan—had become powerful, and TR's views toward this three-power imbroglio revealed a sophisticated understanding of the nature of international rivalries. Initially, he had not been hostile toward the Russians. Relations had been cordial, and as a student of history TR knew that Russia had shown its friendship during the Civil War. Later, the czar had sold Alaska to the United States. This procession of events led Roosevelt to write in 1898 that "Russia, and Russia alone, of European powers, has been uniformly friendly to us in the past." Shortly before becoming president his view changed. Russia's encroachments in the Far East at the time of the Boxer Rebellion challenged Anglo-American interests. The treaty powers had moved troops into China, and Russia, with its long Chinese border, virtually occupied Manchuria. By 1903 the Russians' failure to withdraw from Manchuria much disturbed Roosevelt, as did another event at this time, an outbreak of violence against Jews in Russia in April 1903. He publicly criticized Czar Nicholas II and the Russian autocracy; some months later he wrote of a strong respect for the Russians but warned: "Unless they change in some marked way they contain the chance of menace to the higher life of the world. . . . Our people have become suspicious of Russia; and I personally share this view."

Toward the Japanese the president's feelings likewise shifted during his tenure. Throughout his public life he was torn between admiration for the efficiency and fighting qualities of the Japanese and fear of their strength and military zeal. When Japan protested the possible annexation of Hawaii by the United States in 1897, then Assistant Secretary of the Navy Roosevelt had declared, "The United States is not in a position which requires her to ask Japan or any other foreign power what territory it shall or shall not acquire." After the Spanish-American War, he worried about

Japanese interest in the Philippine Islands. Then, in the years 1900–1904, admiration overcame fear and he became convinced that the Island Empire did not threaten American interests. Unable to use America's power to stop the Russian advance, the president saw the Japanese as a possible barrier to Russian expansion. He thoroughly approved the alliance between Japan and Britain concluded in 1902; he realized that the American people would not permit any U.S. role in the alliance (which would have been a massive break with the past), but, even without U.S. participation, the alliance offered protection to American interests. When the Japanese protested Russian policy in Manchuria, the president expressed sympathy, looking upon Japan not only as a protector of the Open Door but, even more importantly, of the balance of power in Asia.

From the beginning of the Russo-Japanese War in February 1904, TR's sympathies were with Japan. Two days after the Japanese suddenly attacked the Russian naval base at Port Arthur, the president noted in a letter to his son Kermit that for several years Russia had behaved very badly in the Far East, especially by being grossly overbearing toward Japan. "I was apprehensive lest if she at the outset whipped Japan on the sea she might assume a position well-nigh intolerable toward us." Roosevelt was nonetheless wary of too sweeping a Japanese victory in the conflict, for Japan might become "puffed with pride." He did not want Japan to become a threat to American commercial and territorial interests. The Japanese must not establish themselves in China, though they could have Korea; above all, they must guarantee protection for U.S. interests in East Asia. Such was the reasoning behind TR's desire for peace in 1904–5. He sought a balance of power that guaranteed the interests of the United States as well as those of the other nations concerned.

TR was also anxious to stop war between civilized powers, a conflict he believed bad for the world, and by mediating he assumed he could guarantee Japan the fruits of its victory, preventing another triple intervention. Whether or not Roosevelt wished to mediate the war in order to advance his own reputation as a great statesman, he certainly was eager to play a part in world events. He prided himself on his independence from British activities and may have wished to show the world he could act alone; but there is no evidence to suggest that TR sought personal

"GOOD OFFICES"

Harper's Weekly, *24 June 1905*

advantage from a conflict in which thousands of lives had been expended.

Throughout 1904, if without success, the president used every opportunity to press his good offices on the belligerents. He met with the Japanese minister several times and urged Japan to take advantage of its surprising military successes while he tried to ascertain the Japanese peace terms. He badgered the Russian ambassador so much that, to quote Secretary Hay, "Cassini throws a pink fit at any reference to peace." By late 1904, as Japan's military successes continued, the president decided the best course was not to take a public stand on the issue of mediation until assured that both powers would respond favorably.

The Japanese victory at Mukden in March 1905 further moved world opinion toward expectation of peace. The president warned the Russian ambassador that if peace were not arranged soon, Japanese terms would be much more severe. The Russians had one last chance: the Baltic fleet under Admiral Zinovi Rozhdestvenski, then steaming eastward around the Cape of Good Hope and rapidly nearing the Far East. That hope disappeared when, on 27 and 28 May 1905, Admiral Heihachiro Togo annihilated the Russians in the Tsushima Strait.

Three days after this battle, on 31 May, Foreign Minister Jutaro Komura instructed his representative in Washington to suggest to the president that entirely on "his own motion and initiative" he invite the belligerents to direct negotiations. Details were left to his discretion, but the Japanese government wished to avoid the impression of a direct approach to Russia on the subject of peace. Roosevelt swung into action. To make sure that his views were conveyed directly to the czar, the president instructed his representative in St. Petersburg to inform Nicholas that the contest was "absolutely hopeless" and that if the Russians would consent to negotiations Roosevelt would, on his own initiative and as secretly as possible, seek Japan's consent for preliminary talks. Roosevelt also got the German kaiser to support this effort by appealing to his cousin Nicholas. Roosevelt had reached a commanding position. No objection would come from Britain, Japan's ally; France, the ally of Russia, had internal problems; both Japan and Germany favored the intervention of the president. Only Russia remained to be brought into agreement.

The offensive succeeded. Ambassador Meyer requested an audience and pointed out to the czar the futility of the war, its unpopularity, the threat of revolution, and noted the president's concern, for Meyer had kept TR informed of Russia's internal difficulties. Nicholas agreed to negotiations, provided that Japan consent before the czar's acceptance was made public and that the conference be without intermediaries.

After long discussions and much difficulty, the belligerents chose their delegations, agreed on Washington as the meeting place (later changed because of the summer heat to the naval yard near Portsmouth, New Hampshire), and Roosevelt called the conference.[1] The president felt compelled to ensure that the negotiations did not fail. After the arrival of the plenipotentiaries he entertained them at Oyster Bay, his home on Long Island, the Japanese on one day, the Russians on another. He told both groups that this opportunity for peace must not be missed.

The peace conference began with a formal luncheon for the envoys at Oyster Bay on 5 August 1905. From there the delegates traveled to Portsmouth. By 18 August, after twelve formal sessions as well as several private meetings, it seemed that an impasse over two issues, collection of an indemnity and cession of territories, would deadlock negotiations and perhaps even wreck the conference. Japan demanded the island of Sakhalin, already under military occupation by its forces, as well as an indemnity; the chief Russian delegate, Sergei Witte, refused both demands.

Roosevelt again intervened to urge both sides to compromise, pointing out the advantages to each, and political pressure, more or less subtle, accompanied these exhortations. From the czar he gained for Japan the southern half of Sakhalin. His influence was decisive with the Japanese, to whom he stressed that they had gained what they had fought for: Korea and southern Manchuria. These arguments, plus the financial strains of the war, brought the Japanese to terms, removed the final obstacle to settlement, and led to signature of a peace agreement on 5 September 1905.

The Peace of Portsmouth was a personal triumph for Roosevelt. The conference had assembled on his initiative; he had convinced the Japanese and the Russians of the need for a settlement; his preaching made the powers think of moderate

---

1. At the opening of the conference, there was no armistice between the belligerents. At Japanese insistence an armistice would not be effective until the peace treaty was drafted and only shortly before its final approval.

terms; his influence convinced the Japanese representative, Ko-mura, to modify Japan's demands even before the conference began; and he kept the conference going by constant discussions with the plenipotentiaries and their governments. Although the war would have ended sometime, it seems that peace would have been precious long in coming if TR had not intervened. To be sure, Witte, by disobeying his czar's instruction to break off the conference, aided Roosevelt, but the president's influence brought the final compromise. It was for its day an impressive performance, even if the results were more transitory and less satisfactory than expected.

The Treaty of Portsmouth was the best possible solution for the time, serving the interests of Russia and Japan as well as the United States. Beyond immediate details of the negotiations, the peace greatly enhanced the prestige both of the United States and its chief executive. Portsmouth stands as the last of the personally managed peace conferences and, in effect, it closed the diplomacy of the nineteenth century. TR's success is all the more surprising when one considers that the Russo-Japanese War was one of the first chapters of the major power rivalries that have littered the landscape of international relations in the twentieth century and have proved almost impervious to mediation. TR succeeded where later mediators, such as Woodrow Wilson and Franklin D. Roosevelt, would fail.

The treaty's importance to the United States lessened in the years that followed, as the Rooseveltian power balance in the Far East collapsed, but this was the result of alignments looking toward the world war, Far Eastern instability, and the nature of competing interests in that region. In the Russo-Japanese treaties of 1907 and 1910, the two powers agreed to divide Manchuria through control of the two major Manchurian railways. Immigration policy at this time became an issue of domestic American politics as well, and it, of course, exerted tremendous influence on United States–Japanese relations. Any residual pro-Japanese sentiments had almost disappeared by the time TR left the White House and certainly played no part in the Taft administration's Asian policy. Most important, perhaps, was a change in China, a new nationalistic and antiforeign attitude, which had developed as the nineteenth century closed and became even more powerful in the early twentieth century. Roosevelt had discounted this last factor, since he considered the Chinese a backward people and did not believe that China could soon become a major power; here TR proved dead wrong. Still, much was to happen between 1905 and 1949 and China's performance in world politics between 1894 and 1905 gave Roosevelt little reason to doubt his judgment. Nevertheless, his policy of a balanced antagonism between Russia and Japan, an antagonism that would protect America's interests, eventually failed.

◇◇◇

Seeing that it was no longer possible for the United States to avoid involvement in world affairs and that, contrary to the belief of many Americans, peace might not be a normal condition, Roosevelt spent a good deal of time between 1901 and 1909 insisting that his country recognize its international obligations and have sufficient resources in readiness to honor them. He was aware that revolutions in communication, production, and transportation had created a situation in which available power, not just potential, was necessary, especially because of the heightened nationalism of the early twentieth century. He urged preparedness, but, as John Blum has noted, "this was not simple militarism." Preparedness to TR meant development of natural resources, an increase in industrial productivity, and maintenance of the American people's moral character. It meant changes in the military forces, and during Roosevelt's tenure the army and especially the navy underwent large and, as the world war was to show, vital changes.

Roosevelt understood that the United States did not require a large standing army, but the poor performance of the army during the Spanish-American War had shown vividly the need for drastic reforms. Elihu Root, who had been appointed secretary of war by McKinley, understood the necessity for reform, but it was not until 1902, and then only with TR's support, that Root was able to concentrate on army reorganization.[2] He increased the size of the army, abolished the permanent assignment of officers to staff duties in Washington, and overhauled the educational structure, creating the Army War College. He reformed the antiquated

2. Between 1899 and 1901, Secretary Root had to deal with problems in Cuba, Puerto Rico, and a difficult and embarrassing insurrection in the Philippines.

militia system and, most importantly, introduced the principle of
the general staff. The organization of the army became more
effective, and its capabilities were demonstrated in 1917 when the
United States next entered a major war.

As might be expected, Roosevelt devoted most of his attention to the navy. Applying Mahan's theories, he concluded that
because of its two ocean borders the United States had to develop
a strong navy, second only to that of Great Britain. He conducted a
persistent campaign for more and bigger ships, the global voyage
of the "Great White Fleet" perhaps being the high point of this
effort. Congress responded by greatly increasing the navy between
1901 and 1909. Roosevelt did not always get his way, and his
request for four battleships of the dreadnought class in 1908 was
cut in half. Still, the navy grew and its facilities improved. It
acquired a potential base at Subig Bay in the Philippines, leased a
site (Guantánamo Bay) in Cuba, and obtained funds for a base at
Pearl Harbor.

Sea power lay behind much of Roosevelt's attitude toward
Latin America. Here he sought preservation of the Monroe
Doctrine and protection of American rights. When European
powers, especially Britain and Germany who possessed powerful
navies, seemed to challenge American supremacy in the Caribbean, demanding settlement of debts by the Venezuelan dictator,
Cipriano Castro, Roosevelt readied the U.S. fleet and brought the
issue to the Hague Court. He acted not because he supported
Venezuelan interests, but because he believed that preservation of
order in Latin America, an essential element in United States
strategy, required American initiative. This belief led to the
famous—or infamous—Roosevelt Corollary to the Monroe Doctrine, which claimed an exclusive American right of intervention
in the Western Hemisphere. Of course, TR added that such
intervention would come only as a last resort, but the mere idea,
proof of a double standard of morality, was repugnant to Latin
Americans and many of the president's fellow citizens. In retrospect, it was perhaps not so radical an idea, since a large nation
probably does have certain perquisites in its sphere of influence.
Roosevelt's corollary and the right of intervention were later
abandoned, the latter during the first term of his cousin, FDR; but
events in subsequent years in Guatemala, Cuba, and the Dominican Republic suggest that such simple repudiations of basic
interests are perhaps not really possible.

No single incident tarnished Roosevelt's reputation more than the Panama Canal affair. According to his critics, at the time and since, he was guilty of blatant imperialism, cynically fostering a revolution in order to obtain the rights to a canal. An isthmian canal had been one of his fondest dreams and was necessary in his view because the United States Navy needed to protect the country's increased interests throughout the world. Roosevelt stretched his powers in this affair by showing sympathy to those conspiring to revolt against Colombia, but he did not foment the revolution. The United States quickly recognized the new regime and concluded a treaty obtaining for itself exclusive rights to build a canal. A story (perhaps apocryphal) about his defense of these actions to the cabinet best illustrates the president's trouble. After speaking vigorously about all the criticisms leveled against him, he asked if he had answered the charges. Secretary of War Root, the only person present whose relationship with TR permitted a frank answer, replied: "You certainly have, Mr. President. You have shown that you were accused of seduction and you have conclusively proved that you were guilty of rape." Roosevelt perhaps did proclaim his innocence too loudly.

Once the canal rights were established, the president pushed ahead with construction and after administrative difficulties arose gave the whole job to the army under George W. Goethals, who carried the task to conclusion in 1914. While TR's methods in this episode can be and are properly criticized, they ensured the completion of the isthmian canal at a time when it was needed. The Panama Canal has remained an American enterprise, though it has produced a great residue of animosity. Given the transportation revolution and the lessening strategic importance of the canal in recent years, the time has come for United States internationalization of the Canal Zone, a step one can imagine Roosevelt supporting today, for he understood that various means existed to preserve a nation's interests and that it was necessary to avoid needless friction in international politics.

During Roosevelt's second term he continued to serve as policeman of the Caribbean, but, having established the principles of American policy toward Latin America, he allowed the State Department and Secretary of State Root (appointed after the death of John Hay) to handle day-to-day affairs. The result was improved U.S.–Latin American relations. America had established its determination to prevent European intrusion into the Caribbean, and

Root was now free to lessen difficulties with Latin American countries by treating their diplomats with dignity and by goodwill journeys to the south. The president was content to remain in the background, realizing he was an object of controversy in Latin America. As long as strategic and commercial interests were guaranteed and the duty of bringing order when necessary remained in U.S. hands, he allowed subordinates to carry out policy. Root did this well, earning the title of "the first Good Neighbor" from some historians. One can argue about Roosevelt's Latin American policy but, given more than sixty years of perspective, it does not seem altogether unreasonable, and the Latin American policy of Roosevelt's successors in the White House has not changed perceptibly.

Toward the Orient the president demonstrated flexibility, allowing a series of significant modifications over the years. Before 1905 he strove to erect a balance of power, which he achieved at Portsmouth. While voicing the thoughts of his first secretary of state about the Open Door, TR understood that the American people would not go to war to protect China or American interests in that country. He turned to the Japanese to protect American and world interests, recognizing that Japan would have special rights in China as did the U.S. in Latin America. He even talked to Japanese diplomats about a Monroe Doctrine for Japan in Asia.

After 1905 and the Treaty of Portsmouth the situation in the Far East changed dramatically, and so did the president's views. Japan moved to close the Open Door in Manchuria, and the Sino-Japanese rivalry, later to be one of the dominant events of the century, intensified. Roosevelt showed little interest in the former development and, like most Western politicians, little understanding of the latter. This resulted from his increased attention to European problems; his belief that Japan had special rights in China; his belief that the best protection of American interests in the Pacific, especially the Philippines, was avoidance of controversy with Japan; his realization that the American people would not resort to war to protect the Open Door; and the heating up of the immigration problem with Japan. It is true that Root and some of his subordinates in the State Department, such as Willard Straight, pressed hard for American rights in China and that, with TR's approval, they were able to salvage some guarantees from the Japanese. The president took no part in Straight's fierce anti-Japanese crusade, however, and seems to have had almost no knowledge of it. One fact is certain: there were practical limits to how far the State Department could go in its campaign to preserve Chinese sovereignty; its only useful instrument was negotiation with Japan. Although Root conducted relations toward the East Asian powers after 1905, there is little doubt that the president would have denied him the use of threats to protect China from the Japanese. Of course Taft, Roosevelt's successor, allowed the anti-Japanese prejudices of some State Department officials to become national policy; TR watched with great displeasure as the Taft administration scrapped his policies and blundered into difficulties in Asia.

Part of the difference between Roosevelt's and Taft's policies resulted from changes in the mechanisms for dealing with foreign affairs. As TR's interest in the Far East lessened, the State Department assumed more and more responsibilities. To handle them, Root set up the Division of Far Eastern Affairs in 1908, the first of the geographical divisions of the State Department. This new structure, as Charles Neu has noted, provided "an opportunity for policy to move upward from lower bureaucratic levels." While not particularly significant in the last years of Roosevelt's administration, this change proved decisive in the Taft years, when individuals such as Straight and Philander C. Knox exercised great influence; for, to be kind, President Taft had few definite ideas about foreign policy.

Even more important was TR's belief that the Open Door in China simply was not worth a war with Japan. One of the best expressions of this attitude appeared in a letter written to Secretary of State designate Knox on 8 February 1909, in which Roosevelt noted that relations with Japan were of "great and permanent importance." He said that it was most important for the Taft administration to understand that "Japan is vitally interested in China and on the Asiatic mainland and her wiser statesmen will if possible prevent her getting entangled in a war with us, because whatever its result it would hamper and possibly ruin Japan when she came to deal again with affairs in China." Since the Pacific coast of the United States was relatively defenseless and "we have no army to hold or reconquer the Philippines and Hawaii," war must be avoided.

TR's conclusion was that China and American interests in China were insignificant in the broader context of United States foreign policy; but Taft and Knox, prodded by subordinates and

American businessmen, thought they could isolate China and especially Manchuria from general Far Eastern problems and preserve the Open Door as they perceived it. Historians who have
argued that there is essential continuity between Roosevelt's and
Taft's policies toward the balance of power in East Asia have
emphasized too much the attitudes of certain State Department
officials and business leaders. At the top—TR and Taft—there
existed differences with enormous consequences. As TR told his
successor in late 1910, the Open Door in China was an excellent
idea, "and I hope it will be a good thing in the future, so far as it
can be maintained by general diplomatic agreement; but, as has
been proved by the whole history of Manchuria, alike under
Russia and under Japan, the 'Open Door' policy, as a matter of
fact, completely disappears as soon as a powerful nation determines to disregard it, and is willing to run the risk of war." One
such nation, TR believed, was Japan.

With these thoughts in mind, the Japanese immigration
problem occupied almost all the attention TR gave the Far East
after 1905. Immigration by Orientals had become a political issue
in the United States by 1900. China was too weak to protest
restrictive practices, but Japan, flushed with its magnificent victory
over Russia, a white nation, was not. In 1906 the San Francisco
Board of Education precipitated trouble between the United
States and Japan by ordering Oriental students into a segregated
school. Rhetorical and legislative excesses on the part of Californians irritated the president and weakened his position, revealing
once again the limits domestic attitudes placed upon him. TR
worked for peace with Japan but prepared for the worst. By means
of the Gentlemen's Agreement and other negotiations and as a
result of Japanese action, the flow of immigrants slowed, but not
without a war scare. Japanese, dissatisfied with the Treaty of
Portsmouth and blaming the president for preventing additional
Japanese conquests at Russia's expense (incorrectly as history has
shown), called for action by Japan to protect its citizens residing in
the United States. Roosevelt decided to dispatch the U.S. fleet on
a round-the-world cruise to remind the American people of their
global commitments, strengthen his political position in western
states, and stimulate pronavy sentiment in the Congress. He also
assumed the Great White Fleet would have a sobering influence
on Japan by demonstrating America's ability to defend its interests
in the Pacific. Given these goals, the trip proved a success. More

important was a decision by both governments to prevent the immigration issue from souring relations. When Roosevelt left the White House the two nations had returned to a status of respect, if mutual suspicion.

One area remains to be discussed: Europe. Bitter rivalries occurred there in the early twentieth century, Austro-Russian, Franco-German, and Anglo-German being the most important; but only the latter was of continuing concern to President Roosevelt. One idea dominated his European policy: conviction that Great Britain was a friend and Germany a potential enemy. With that in mind, he set out to clear away standing differences between the United States and Britain. He was disturbed about the Venezuelan crisis of 1902–3, approved the Anglo-Japanese alliance of 1902, was happy about solution of the Alaskan boundary dispute, and determined, after the death of the British ambassador to Washington, Sir Michael Herbert, to ensure good communications by securing the appointment of someone he trusted. During this time Roosevelt also tried to improve relations with Germany, but not at the expense of Britain. The German government never succeeded in gaining equality with the British, even though it enjoyed the advantage of having one of Roosevelt's closest friends, Baron Hermann Speck von Sternburg, as ambassador, and notwithstanding TR's repeated expressions of admiration for Kaiser Wilhelm II. The Germans alarmed TR. Their vigor, military skill, and aggressiveness were all traits he admired, but he considered them a menace to the peace of the world and to American security.

The Moroccan crisis of 1905–6 confirmed these images of Germany and had a lasting effect on Roosevelt's views regarding the European balance of power. After the German ruler's dramatic visit to Tangier, Morocco, in March 1905 challenging French control of that country, the president concluded that Wilhelm was most unreliable and possibly even dangerous. In the negotiations that followed this famous visit, TR, as he had done at Portsmouth, played a large role. The Germans sought support for an international conference on Morocco, hoping to weaken French control there. The French refused and war seemed a possibility. Once more working behind the scenes because of limited American public interest and using his wide contacts, Roosevelt persuaded the French and Germans to agree to a conference, gaining also a pledge from Ambassador Sternburg that Germany would accept whatever TR thought to be a fair solution. As it happened,

Sternburg unwittingly had misrepresented his instructions, giving Roosevelt a veto over German policy. Skillfully exploiting this inadvertent veto, the president moved to defuse an explosive situation.

The principals conferred at Algeciras, Spain, in early 1906 with Henry White representing the United States. After much difficulty Roosevelt brought about a compromise favoring the French, by placing the Moroccan sultan's police force under French and Spanish supervision. The Germans at first opposed this arrangement, but the president threatened to announce publicly that they had broken their word to him, and Berlin's resistance collapsed. Then, since he recognized and appreciated the need of nations to save face, he worked arduously to make the agreement appear to be something other than a great defeat for Germany. Because of TR's efforts, Europe in 1906 retreated from a world war.

By siding with the French, the ally of Great Britain, in the Moroccan crisis, as he had done with the Japanese, another British ally, in the Russo-Japanese War, Roosevelt demonstrated the pro-British orientation of his diplomacy. He continued this policy from 1906 until 1909 and, of course, even after he left the presidency. While some officials in London failed to appreciate the direction of American policy, Foreign Secretary Lord Lansdowne in particular, it was apparent to King Edward VII that friendship with the United States must be an essential part of any British foreign policy. After Sir Edward Grey succeeded Lansdowne, friendship with America indeed became the foundation of London's diplomacy. Throughout this period, Wilhelm struggled to bring Roosevelt over to Germany's side, at one point suggesting a German-Chinese-American alliance. Such schemes only persuaded TR that the kaiser was unpredictable and untrustworthy.

American diplomacy in Europe, except for the Moroccan crisis, was less active than elsewhere, for while American interests in Europe, especially commercial interests, were expanding, the situation there was not nearly as unstable as in Latin America and East Asia. As with other policies, however, TR based his European diplomacy on realism; his faith in Anglo-American cooperation was to characterize American foreign relations in the twentieth century.

The late Howard K. Beale has summarized the many successes of Rooseveltian diplomacy. Yet, after noting TR's extraordinary comprehension of foreign affairs, his ability to look into the future with regard to Russia and Great Britain, his understanding of the influence of internal events on the foreign policies of modern nations, his determination not to take stands he knew the American people would not back, and a host of other achievements, Beale wrote, "In the end, for all his activity, his tremendous influence on foreign policy, his surprising insights and prophecies, Roosevelt failed in his most important objectives." The stable world based on order for which he worked was not realized; Britain declined faster than expected; nationalism grew beyond all predictions. Beale believed TR should have grappled with these issues, that he had an opportunity to choose between "imperialism" and its alternatives; by selecting imperialism he created many of the problems of the present day. This criticism seems too harsh. There were certainly persuasive arguments against expansion; Fred H. Harrington and Robert Beisner have discussed the anti-imperialists, whose ideas Roosevelt dismissed too lightly. To suggest that he could have led America down a path other than that described by Beale as imperialism, however, is to miss an essential point about the nature of U.S. diplomacy. Given the tremendous changes in the United States and the world during his presidency, TR was in most cases either reacting to or anticipating the proclaimed interests of the American people. In some instances, rather than being the instrument of imperialism, he actually slowed the pace of expansion. As he came to understand the necessity and difficulty of defending colonial possessions, he steered clear of further territorial annexation, despite pressure to move in that direction.

Roosevelt never solved the problem of a democracy pursuing a course of expansion and imperialism; he never gave much thought to the subject. He did come to realize that there were great costs in imperialism that were at times not worth the benefits. While his rhetoric was often excessive, caution characterized his actions in foreign affairs, and he appears much less an imperialist than Taft, or perhaps even Wilson. Akira Iriye has suggested that Taft's diplomacy marked "the beginning of a moralistic diplomacy in East Asia." One wonders if that statement can be made more general—after TR left the White House the United States began to use moral arguments more and more to justify its acts and distinguish them from those of other nations; morality was no longer an end in itself. Eventually, American officials would begin to succumb to their own rhetoric and move on to such disasters as Vietnam. Roosevelt's model of foreign relations was that followed by the "most civilized" western European nations; to expect him to have invented another is perhaps to ask too much of one man burdened with the responsibilities of power.

Theodore Roosevelt made a major contribution by preparing his country for the international problems it was sure to face in the years after 1909. This was no easy task, for he had to work against many decades of tradition and apathy. Thus, he was an instrument of change. Almost as important is the fact that he increased the world's awareness of the United States. Because of his colorful personality, the policies he followed, and the successes he attained, America gained international recognition, though not yet concomitant respect. Roosevelt's policy was also one of continuity. In each of the major geographic areas of diplomacy, Asia, Latin America, and Europe, he dealt with existing ideas, refining them, using them to suit a changing world, but generally following long-held American traditions.

TR's stewardship of foreign affairs occurred at a critical time for the United States. Had the nation continued to ignore its relationship to world events perhaps the European war would have come sooner and turned out differently; it might certainly have turned out worse. There are many possibilities as to what might have happened had Roosevelt not been president between 1901 and 1909. There are also some certainties; one is that he served his country well.

BIBLIOGRAPHIC NOTE

A good deal has been written about TR, partly because of the abundance of primary materials. His own manuscript collection, the Roosevelt manuscripts in the Library of Congress, is extensive. An excellent published collection of primary materials is Elting E. Morison, ed., *The Letters of Theodore Roosevelt*, 8 vols. (Cambridge, Mass., 1951–54). The best general accounts of TR's life are John M. Blum, *The Republican Roosevelt* (Cambridge, Mass., 1961), William H. Harbaugh, *Power and Responsibility: The Life and Times of Theodore Roosevelt* (New York, 1961), G. Wallace Chessman, *Theodore Roosevelt* (Boston,

1969), and Henry Pringle, *Theodore Roosevelt* (New York, 1931). The two best general treatments of Roosevelt's diplomacy are Howard K. Beale, *Theodore Roosevelt and the Rise of America to World Power* (Baltimore, 1956), and Raymond Esthus, *Theodore Roosevelt and the International Rivalries* (Waltham, Mass., 1970). See also David H. Burton, *Theodore Roosevelt: Confident Imperialist* (Philadelphia, 1968), George Mowry, *The Era of Theodore Roosevelt* (New York, 1958), and David Healy's excellent "Theodore Roosevelt and the Sturdy Virtues," in his book *U.S. Expansionism* (Madison, 1970). An excellent article on Roosevelt's technique of diplomacy is Nelson M. Blake, "Ambassadors at the Court of Theodore Roosevelt," *Mississippi Valley Historical Review* 42 (1955).

For exact citations for the quotations from Roosevelt's correspondence and for a detailed analysis of the Treaty of Portsmouth and TR's role in it, see Eugene Trani, *The Treaty of Portsmouth: An Adventure in American Diplomacy* (Lexington, Ky., 1969). For a study of Ambassador George Meyer's reaction to Russian internal events during this time, see Eugene Trani, "Russia in 1905: The View from the American Embassy," *Review of Politics* 31 (1969).

A general treatment of TR's Latin American policy is in Samuel Flagg Bemis, *The Latin American Policy of the United States* (New York, 1943). There are a number of specialized studies; two of the best are on the interventions in Cuba. See David Healy, *The United States in Cuba, 1898–1902* (Madison, 1963), and Allan Millett, *The Politics of Intervention: The Military Occupation of Cuba, 1906–1909* (Columbus, 1968). An older account, still of some value, is Howard C. Hill, *Roosevelt and the Caribbean* (Chicago, 1927). There are a number of good recent studies on Roosevelt and the Far East. The best general account is Raymond Esthus, *Theodore Roosevelt and Japan* (Seattle, 1966). See also Charles Neu, *An Uncertain Friendship: Theodore Roosevelt and Japan, 1906–1909* (Cambridge, Mass., 1967). Both of these studies are based on Japanese as well as American sources. More general treatments of America's Far Eastern policy are Akira Iriye, *Across the Pacific: An Inner History of American-East Asian Relations* (New York, 1967), and Ernest May and James C. Thomson, Jr., eds., *American-East Asian Relations: A Survey* (Cambridge, 1972). The latter includes essays by Esthus, covering the period 1901–6, and Neu, covering 1906–13. In addition to some of the more general accounts, one should consult Charles S. Campbell, *Anglo-American Understanding, 1898–1903* (Baltimore, 1957), and Bradford Perkins, *The Great Rapprochement: England and the United States, 1898–1914* (New York, 1968), for treatments of Roosevelt's policy toward Europe.

WILLARD D. STRAIGHT

and the Great Game of Empire

Helen Dodson Kahn

Separating twentieth-century policy makers into "realists" and "idealists" has led to misunderstanding of the men, motives, and policies that have shaped the nation's foreign affairs. Such confusion is especially apparent in analyses of the turn-of-the-century period, the seminal years of United States involvement in the Far East. President Theodore Roosevelt was a "realist," some historians argue, because he appreciated the limits of American power in the Far East and subsequently ended American involvement in Manchuria, recognizing it as a Japanese sphere of investment opportunity. William Howard Taft is depicted, on the

The author gratefully acknowledges the financial assistance of a Herbert H. Lehman Fellowship and an American Association of University Women Fellowship which allowed her to complete this essay. Full documentation can be found in the author's doctoral dissertation, "The Great Game of Empire: Willard D. Straight and American Far Eastern Policy," Cornell University, 1968.

other hand, as pursuing an "idealistic" and "quixotic" Dollar Diplomacy in attempting to dislodge the Japanese from Manchuria, thereby placing the United States and Japan on a collision course. Wilson, according to the traditional analysis, was an "idealist" who, motivated by moralistic concern for the Chinese, withdrew from the international railroad consortium and renounced Dollar Diplomacy.[1]

Such an arbitrary division misses the important continuity of policy from Roosevelt through Taft and even Wilson. These three administrations shared an essential unity of goals. Although tactics shifted several times during those years, they did so mainly in response to changing conditions in the Far East and did not indicate altered goals among policy makers. All three administrations based their policies on a similar understanding of American national interests (regarding which moralistic considerations were not of primary importance), and committed themselves to preserving the Open Door in China.[2] Dedication to keeping China free

1. For this interpretation, see in particular Robert Osgood, *Ideals and Self-Interest in America's Foreign Relations: The Great Transformation of the Twentieth Century* (Chicago, 1953), and George Kennan, *American Diplomacy, 1900–1950* (Chicago, 1951). A. Whitney Griswold, *The Far Eastern Policy of the United States* (New York, 1938), Raymond A. Esthus, *Theodore Roosevelt and Japan* (Seattle, 1966), and Charles Vevier, *The United States and China, 1906–1913: A Study of Finance and Diplomacy* (New Brunswick, N.J., 1955) all draw a sharp dichotomy between the policies of Roosevelt and Taft. Harley Notter, *The Origins of the Foreign Policy of Woodrow Wilson* (Baltimore, 1937), and Li Tien-yi, *Woodrow Wilson's China Policy, 1913–1917* (New York, 1952), make a sharp distinction between the policies of Taft and Wilson.
2. The Open Door doctrine, with roots deep in the nineteenth century, became official American policy in 1899 and 1900 when the great powers were vying for position in China. The Open Door notes, issued by Secretary of State John Hay, announced to the world that the United States was vitally concerned with the future of China. Hay sought the concurrence of the strong Western powers not to challenge the sovereignty and integrity of the Chinese Empire through the establishment of spheres of influence. Instead, China's vast export market should remain open, without special privilege, to all world commerce. Admittedly fragile, this policy needed the agreement of the concerned powers to uphold its tenets, a consensus that never really was achieved. Moreover, the assumption that China would passively accept this Western penetration ignored the nationalistic fervor already stirring within the empire. Thus, in the twentieth century, the Open Door doctrine would face repeated challenges both from within and without China. A penetrating analysis of the formulation of America's Open Door policy is found in Thomas McCormick, *China Market: America's Quest for Informal Empire, 1893–1901* (Chicago, 1967).

from the domination of other powers and open to American trade and influence became the keystone of American Far Eastern policy for much of the twentieth century.

The activities of Willard Straight, a State Department officer whose fascinating career spanned the Roosevelt, Taft, and Wilson administrations, typify the essential concerns of United States diplomacy toward East Asia. Straight was both artist and activist, a dreamer of grandiose dreams and an ambitious achiever. He thought in huge sweeps of time, planning fifty to one hundred years into the future, molding history and shaping empires as the British imperialists had done. Yet, after drafting these far-reaching schemes, dreams that would have done justice to a Rhodes or a Clive, he proved a prodigious worker and an excellent negotiator. He labored long hours over the minutest details, changing words, adding paragraphs, refurbishing and polishing long, detailed arguments designed to effect accord among Peking, Washington, and Wall Street and thereby provide structure and definition to his plans.

◇◇◇

Born in Oswego, New York, in 1880, Straight was the son of two college teachers. Both parents died of tuberculosis before the boy reached ten, leaving him to be raised by two old-maid friends of his family. While enrolled as an architecture student at Cornell University, he became a member of the Kipling Club. This association changed his life. Straight became a disciple of Rudyard Kipling and adopted the British poet's virile code of ethics as his own. Kipling recognized the fragility of man's existence but, unlike the *fin de siècle* authors who anguished over the meaninglessness of civilization, Kipling preached that reality was to be found in the total involvement of man's energies in work. The active life, Kipling explained, was the "bulkhead 'twixt despair and the Edge of Nothing." Like his poet-mentor, Straight conceived of all life as a game, a struggle carried on in a hostile environment with the aim of surpassing or defeating the other contestants. He first applied this grim philosophy to his own situation. Beginning the fight without family, status, or material wealth, Straight decided to use his abilities to gain the "most thought-of things in the world": fame, riches, and position. Quitting or withdrawing from the contest meant retreat from life and resignation to fate, a course that he deemed moral cowardliness.

Kipling's ideology also provided a framework for Straight's early understanding of the purpose of the Western presence in Asia. A self-avowed imperialist, Kipling viewed the British Empire as an engine of progress. The British, carriers of the "white man's burden," imposed civilization on backward peoples who were incapable of improving themselves. Straight wholeheartedly embraced this doctrine of racial superiority; the Anglo-Saxon's special genius for government imposed a duty to take civilization, enlightenment, and progress to those whom the poet called the "lesser breeds without the law." As an advocate of Kipling's view that the most fit should rule, Straight believed firm, orderly, and beneficial government to be more important than self-government. This view, tragically inadequate, later shaped his response to the growing antiforeign movements in China.

After graduation from Cornell University in 1901, Straight seized an opportunity to reach the Far East by accepting a position in the Chinese Customs Service. Having lived in the East briefly as a child, he now intended to study the language, customs, and art of China and to employ his artistic ability as a journalist-illustrator, and hoped in time to become as famous as Kipling. After six months of intensive language training, Straight became the personal aide and private secretary to Sir Robert Hart, inspector general of the customs. Despite this auspicious start to his career, Straight craved a more exciting life than that of a customs official, and in 1904 he resigned to accept a position as a Russo-Japanese War correspondent for Reuters and the Associated Press; then, after the war, he became vice-consul and secretary of the American legation in Seoul, Korea.

Throughout his life, Straight exhibited a rare talent for forming deep, lasting friendships, an ability he consciously developed because he knew that friends could help him move along the road to success. In Peking, Straight became well acquainted with most members of the diplomatic community, with the newspaper correspondents, and with European financial and business agents. In Tokyo during the war he cultivated the friendship of the American minister and his secretary, Huntington Wilson (who would later head the State Department's Far Eastern desk), and many war correspondents. These friendships introduced him to people with wealth, social status, and business and diplomatic importance. By handling the arrangements for the 1905 Korean visits of E. H. Harriman, the railroad magnate, and of Alice Roosevelt and her entourage (and later arranging honeymoon plans for Alice and Nicholas Longworth), Straight established important friendships that led to meetings with President Roosevelt and a 1906 appointment, conferred directly by the president at Harriman's suggestion, as consul general in Mukden, Manchuria.[3] He was then twenty-six.

During these years in the Far East, Straight broadened and modified his views, gaining a new appreciation of American involvement in Asia. He read voraciously, a habit he maintained all his life; he studied in particular the ideology of expansionists such as Josiah Strong, Archibald Colquhoun, Arthur Smith, and Alfred Thayer Mahan. He accepted as accurate William H. Seward's famous prophecy that the Pacific region would be the "chief theatre of events in the world's great hereafter." Civilization had evolved ever westward; indeed, the Far East already had become the scene of a struggle for world power. Straight concluded that an American refusal to participate in this struggle would constitute a confession of its moral cowardliness and decadence.

Moreover, Straight accepted the argument forcefully advanced by Arthur Smith and many progressives that a fortunate coincidence existed between the needs of the United States, then seeking a new economic and perhaps spiritual frontier, and those of an awakening and Westernizing China. Trade and investment there could guarantee the viability of the American system and at the same time bring Western civilization, democracy, and progress to China, thus guiding its renaissance. Like Mahan, Straight was certain that developments in China would determine the future of the world. Within the next hundred years, he noted, China would either be "one of our most dangerous enemies or most powerful friends," depending upon which powers controlled its modernization. Straight wanted America to "reshape the East," an action he deemed "essential to the logical and inevitable growth of the United States into a world power."

At the outbreak of the Russo-Japanese War, Straight agreed

3. Straight's contacts also led to his engagement to Harriman's daughter, broken when her father refused to sanction the marriage. Straight eventually married Dorothy Whitney, daughter of William C. Whitney, Cleveland's secretary of the navy, and heiress to a Standard Oil fortune.

with Secretary of State John Hay, President Roosevelt, and W. W. Rockhill (the president's key adviser on Far Eastern affairs) that the Japanese represented the forces of enlightenment and progress, checking the Muscovite tide that threatened to exclude Western civilization from Manchuria. As a war correspondent, however, Straight found his admiration for the martial qualities of stoicism, bravery, patriotism, and efficiency of the Nipponese tempered by their condescending treatment of Westerners. His dealings with them during and immediately after the war produced in him an intense racial hatred of all things Japanese. Moreover, the discriminatory treatment of American commercial interests Straight witnessed in Korea aroused fear that the Island Empire intended to police the Far East solely for itself. If, after the victories over Russia, Japan determined to exclude Westerners from Korea and Manchuria, as seemed increasingly obvious by 1906, Japanese ambitions posed a dangerous new threat to American commercial interests.

Soon after Straight's arrival in Mukden in 1906, he became involved in a dispute with his superior in Peking, an argument based on a fundamental and irreconcilable difference in outlook on the Far Eastern situation. W. W. Rockhill, the American minister to China, thought that despite Japan's greatly strengthened position resulting from Portsmouth, it would cooperate in maintaining the Open Door in the former war zone. Rockhill had urged full diplomatic support of Japan during the Russo-Japanese War and believed that because of its dependence on foreign capital Japan would continue to respect the integrity of China. In contrast, Straight was convinced that, despite promises to the contrary, Japan's military and civilian administrations in Manchuria were willfully using the period of military occupation to secure a dominant position and extinguish United States trade in southern Manchuria.

Straight believed that Japan already had demonstrated unwillingness to work with American investors in Manchuria. At the close of hostilities, E. H. Harriman had negotiated with Premier Taro Katsura for the establishment of an international syndicate to control Japan's newly acquired South Manchuria Railway. The Komura Agreement of December 1905, however, limited control of the railroad to Chinese and Japanese shareholders, and thus canceled Harriman's plan for cooperative development. The pact also contained a secret pledge by China never to build any railroad prejudicial to the south Manchurian line, a commitment that justified Japan's opposition to any non-Japanese railroad construction in Manchuria and threatened the future of competitive investment in northeast China. Refusing to relinquish his vision of an around-the-world railroad, Harriman asked Straight to watch for an opportunity to secure the missing Manchurian link.

In 1907–9, when he first initiated proposals to secure an American position in north China, Straight was young, enthusiastic, and fully convinced that his country was on the verge of assuming an imperial mantle and fulfilling its mission and spiritual destiny. Manchuria, he thought, would be the "key to all China"; cooperation with the emerging progressive leadership there would enable Americans to mold the "Chinese renaissance." With proper handling the task of empire shaping might fall to the United States—and what a great work it would be! It was a golden age, a time when one might believe he played a part in shaping the destiny of nations. Straight had a "great dream," as his vice-consul later recalled. "He might well have been—indeed he was for the moment—a potential Rhodes or Clive of North China."

From Mukden, Straight proposed what was eventually treated in Washington as an alternative to the bankrupt pro-Japanese policy. Like George F. Kennan's "long telegram" forty years later, Straight's recommendations reached the Department of State at a pivotal juncture. China, he reported, was then engaged in a promising postwar reform movement. In the three eastern provinces, newly appointed, capable, progressive officials, particularly T'ang Shao-yi, the governor of Fengtien province, were fearful of Japanese purposes and wished to secure foreign financial and political support for the development of Manchuria under Chinese auspices. Rather than depend on the questionable goodwill of the Japanese, or expect support from Great Britain or Germany (powers that had omitted Manchuria from their Open Door declarations), the United States should act unilaterally in China. Such a policy would protect future opportunities for American trade and investment in this region, which Straight now viewed as the "new West," a "virgin territory" that needed only American capital to become "one of the most prosperous districts in the world."

In cooperation with T'ang, Straight worked out a proposal for American financiers to fund a Manchurian bank, which as sole fiscal agent of the provincial government would undertake the development of the three eastern provinces. Straight approached

This cartoon aptly portrays the "wait and see" attitude toward China and American involvement there that Willard Straight sought to change.

Harper's Weekly, 5 March 1904

Harriman for support of the bank, but the panic of 1907 rendered the railroad magnate's consideration of the offer impossible. Rather than await an improvement of the economic climate in the private sector, Straight tried to interest Washington in encouraging extensive American investment in Manchuria. At a 1907 meeting with Secretary of War William Howard Taft at Vladivostok, Straight proposed utilization of the Boxer indemnity remission as security for a Manchurian development loan.[4] Apparently, Taft accepted Straight's argument that cooperation with progressive Chinese would enable the United States to block Japan's attempt to control north China, an area that might become a vital frontier for ambitious Americans. Taft formally recommended that Peking seek State Department approval for the use of the Boxer indemnity to develop Manchuria. Buoyed by Taft's encouragement, T'ang made plans to visit Washington.

As the date of T'ang's visit approached, financial conditions in the United States improved enough to permit Harriman to negotiate with the Chinese, and he asked Secretary of State Elihu Root to recall Straight to Washington. The young China expert returned as acting head of the Division of Far Eastern Affairs, instructed by the secretary of state himself to assist Harriman and to interest key eastern businessmen in the commercial development of Manchuria. Straight found Harriman and his financial backers, Jacob Schiff and Otto Kahn of Kuhn, Loeb and Company, prepared to undertake T'ang's proposed Manchurian development bank and a Chinchou to Aigun railroad across Manchuria. Moreover, he secured their agreement to finance China's purchase of the Chinese Eastern Railway, which in the spring of 1908 Russian officials had expressed interest in selling.

In the course of the discussions, Schiff proposed that the purchase of the Chinese Eastern Railway be linked to an overture to the Japanese for sale of the South Manchuria Railway. At the banker's request, Straight drew up a memorandum regarding this purchase, which Schiff presented to an official of the Bank of Japan. He suggested that it would be desirable "if American capital could be made the stakeholder of the main line of communication and transportation both in Southern and Northern

4. The idea favored by many American officials, including Rockhill, was to use the $12.5 million remission for the education of Chinese students in the United States.

Manchuria." Russia intended to sell, he said, and if Japan did not, the possibility would always exist that the Chinese government might build a competing line. This proposal, presented by New York bankers to Japan in 1908 during the closing days of the Roosevelt administration, was essentially the same as the one Taft's secretary of state would present in 1909 as the Knox Neutralization Proposal. Instead of relying on American capital exclusively, however, Knox would advocate international control. In both instances Japan refused to consider the idea.

While Schiff was engaged with the Japanese, T'ang Shao-yi began negotiations in the United States. Officials at State were hopeful that T'ang's proposals might provide the United States the substantial position it required in Manchuria if the Open Door doctrine were to be upheld. When Secretary of State Root met with T'ang in December 1908 he agreed that the Chinese could use the Boxer indemnity remission as security for a Manchurian bank loan. Moreover, Root promised United States support for a second plan, the reform and stabilization of China's currency. Negotiations proceeded well, so well that a friend of Rockhill's, not in sympathy with T'ang's plans, complained to the American minister that Straight had been successfully "running things" from his desk in the State Department and had secured a favorable reception for T'ang's proposals both "in White House and Department circles." Unfortunately for the schemes of these shapers of empire, just as negotiations were nearing completion, events in China—the empress dowager's death and Yüan Shih-kai's subsequent fall from power—brought T'ang's sudden recall.

By authorizing the use of the Boxer indemnity remission as security for a Manchurian bank loan and agreeing to support a currency reform loan, Secretary Root initiated during the Roosevelt administration the policy that during the Taft administration would be derisively labeled "Dollar Diplomacy." Root unofficially supported American financial interests in China, cognizant that the successful implementation of their plans would make Americans codirectors in a bank empowered to oversee all development projects in the three eastern provinces. The vast implications of this project were certainly not lost on the astute secretary: the establishment of the Manchurian bank would create a solid financial interest in Manchuria from which the United States could challenge Japanese expansion. Indeed, if successfully implemented, it would make Manchuria a virtual sphere of investment opportunity for the United States.[5]

T'ang's negotiations with Root, Harriman, and the New York financiers regarding Manchuria occurred in juxtaposition to Root's 1907–8 negotiations with Japanese Foreign Minister Kogoro Takahira, which according to most historians constituted an American recognition of Japanese dominance in Manchuria.[6] If these contradictory negotiations could be attributed to a deep split within the State Department one could accept the interpretation that high officials such as Secretary Root, who supported the Root-Takahira negotiations, overrode lower-ranking staff members, such as Straight, Huntington Wilson, and William Phillips, who supported the T'ang-Harriman negotiations. This explanation is untenable, however, because the evidence indicates that both Secretary of State Root and President Roosevelt supported T'ang's proposal for a Manchurian bank to be financed by the Boxer indemnity. Root's support of T'ang's anti-Japanese proposals is solid evidence that in 1908 the Roosevelt administration had no intention of withdrawing from Manchuria. On the contrary, it saw an opportunity to implant a strong American influence there to end Japanese domination of the region and guarantee the future of the Open Door.

The Root-Takahira Agreement can better be understood within the context of a wide-ranging diplomatic offensive that the United States waged against the Japanese in 1907–8. Washington knew that Japan faced severe domestic economic difficulties and problems related to the prosecution of its postwar policies in Korea and Manchuria. Confident that Tokyo was anxious to avoid war with the United States, the Roosevelt administration attempted to convince Japan of its determination to uphold the

5. Historians have ignored or belittled the significance of Root's discussions with T'ang. Esthus argues that because Roosevelt and Root had recognized Manchuria as Japan's sphere of exclusive investment opportunity, they refused to support the Manchurian bank.
6. Griswold and Vevier state that Roosevelt gave Japan a free hand in Manchuria. Esthus explains that Root recognized Manchuria as a Japanese sphere of exclusive investment opportunity. Charles Neu, *An Uncertain Friendship: Theodore Roosevelt and Japan, 1906–1909* (Cambridge, 1967), goes so far as to argue that Roosevelt and Root also accepted Japan's infringement of China's territorial and administrative integrity, a view with which neither Esthus nor the present author agree.

Open Door in Manchuria. In 1907, TR ordered the fleet to display the "big stick" of United States naval power in the Far East. In another, somewhat puzzling move, he actively encouraged Chinese and German overtures for an entente designed to challenge the Japanese position in Manchuria. Moreover, the State Department quietly but firmly supported China's position in the Manchurian railroad dispute with Russia and Japan, a controversy that Root realized had great consequences for the Open Door and the territorial integrity of China. These American actions, coupled with Taft's Open Door pronouncements made while in the Far East and the support for the T'ang proposals, nourished persistent worldwide rumors of an impending clash between the United States and Japan.

Roosevelt's diplomatic offensive elicited a Japanese proposal for an exchange of notes with the United States concerning their respective Far Eastern policies. Although Washington believed that Japan was retreating from her aggressive policies in north China, Japan had other intentions. Tokyo was seeking to improve relations with the United States and quiet the speculations of war that adversely affected its position on the European financial exchanges. It anticipated turning the potentially threatening visit of the American fleet into a friendly visit by an ally. Most importantly, it hoped to undercut the T'ang Shao-yi mission and forestall the completion of an American-German-Chinese entente. Straight harbored deep reservations about the proposed exchange and expressed concern that the agreement might be misunderstood in China as constituting another in Japan's series of Far Eastern ententes. Indeed, as Straight warned, Tokyo successfully propagandized the completed Root-Takahira Agreement not as a mutual reaffirmation of the Open Door, but as an American recognition of Manchuria as Japan's exclusive sphere of investment opportunity. Straight believed that Tokyo used the agreement to undermine the pro-American progressives in Peking, particularly Yüan and T'ang, and thus defeat the American effort to obtain a financial position in Manchuria. The Root-Takahira Agreement was, Straight maintained, a "terrible diplomatic blunder," and he never forgave Roosevelt for his role in it.

◇◇◇

Although historians generally overlook Straight's impact on Roosevelt's 1908 Dollar Diplomacy, most do recognize him as the principal architect of Taft-Knox Dollar Diplomacy. From the time of their meeting at Vladivostok in 1907, Taft had considered Straight a valuable Far Eastern adviser. President Taft shared Straight's concern for the future of the American position in Asia and believed American investment in Manchuria could thwart an imminent Japanese threat to the Open Door there. Therefore he continued Roosevelt's Far Eastern policy, particularly the support that Root and Roosevelt had given to Harriman and Kuhn, Loeb for the Manchurian bank proposal, the Chinchou-Aigun railroad plans, and the Chinese Eastern Railway purchase. Taft hoped eventually to resume negotiations with T'ang for a currency reform loan. Although after T'ang's recall Straight received routine orders to return to his post at Mukden, the new secretary of state Philander C. Knox canceled them at Harriman's request and kept Straight in the State Department where he might study the possibilities for introduction of American capital into China, particularly Manchuria. Knox was committed to maintaining the Open Door, but it was not, as he noted, "a quixotically altruistic task for China's benefit." Rather, he kept the ultimate purpose of the Open Door clearly in view, "a door open for us equally with all other nations."

The Hukuang Loan provided the first opportunity for the introduction of American capital into China. In May 1909, Straight learned that a new German-French-British syndicate was negotiating with Peking to finance construction of a railroad in the fertile Yangtze Valley. Through the blunt tactic of threatening the discontinuance of the Boxer indemnity remission unless American interests were included, the State Department wedged the newly formed "American group" of bankers into the Tripartite Consortium. The United States demanded, and eventually secured, one-fourth participation in the loan, equal provision for the purchase of construction materials in the United States, and equal consideration in all other particulars.

Knox's demand for equal participation by the United States in the Hukuang Loan constituted an extension of the Open Door doctrine as originally defined by Secretary of State John Hay in 1899, but not a radical departure from existing American policy. According to some historians, Hay recognized spheres of influence with special privileges in railroad and mining concessions, asking only that equality of commercial opportunity be maintained within such spheres. Hay had understood the close relationship existing between investment and commercial opportunities and between investment opportunity and Chinese sovereignty, however. In 1902, therefore, he had opposed Russia's demands for "the exclusive right and privilege of opening mines, establishing railroads, *or in any way* [italics added] industrially developing Manchuria," on the grounds that such a monopoly would jeopardize both the sovereign rights of China and the trading rights of other powers. "The inevitable result" of exclusive investment spheres, Hay informed St. Petersburg, "must be the complete wreck of the policy of absolute equality of treatment of all nations in regard to trade, navigation and commerce within the confines of the Empire." Accepting Hay's argument regarding the interrelatedness of investment opportunity, commercial opportunity, and Chinese integrity, Knox extended Hay's opposition to general and exclusive concessions to include specific contracts. Especially in the case of railroads, which by their very nature were monopolistic, specific as well as general contracts threatened the Open Door for commercial opportunity.

The Taft administration's Dollar Diplomacy did not push apathetic American bankers into China; the initiative lay with the bankers. Harriman and his financial supporters, not the State Department, initiated the Manchurian railroad projects. The International Banking Corporation first brought the Hukuang Loan to the department's attention when it asked support for its threatened interests. The relationship between business and government was, however, understandably close. The bankers were totally dependent upon Washington's diplomatic support to conclude negotiations, while the State Department needed the bankers' financial power to secure a foothold for future American trade. This interdependence was implicitly recognized when the group selected Straight as its Peking agent. Because of his association with Harriman and his backers, his experience with the diplomatic community, and his connections with T'ang and Yüan (the Chinese officials most likely to grant contracts to American interests), Straight was the natural liaison between the government and business leaders. He viewed his new position with the Wall Street financiers as temporary; once the banking group was functioning, Straight intended to return to government service.

Unfortunately for Straight's plans, negotiations did not proceed rapidly. Britain opposed Washington's Open Door strategy of cooperative investment, preferring to keep the Yangtze Valley as a British sphere. American purposes also clashed with a developing antiforeign movement in China demanding recovery of control of Chinese resources. Unlike American leaders, many nationalistic Chinese saw little difference between cooperative and unilateral foreign investment, for both resulted in increased foreign control over China. Opposition to Western imperialism was directed also against the increasingly ineffective central government that granted the concessions. Because Straight believed the Chinese were incapable of developing their resources without the guidance and tutelage of Westerners, he viewed the movement as reactionary. Whatever its ideological basis, rights recovery posed a serious challenge to successful implementation of the American Open Door strategy.

While Straight served as the American group's Peking agent, he disagreed radically with the philosophy underlying Taft's China policy. Washington sought to prevent spheres of interest by securing absolute equality of opportunity vis-à-vis all concessions and contracts. This policy depended upon agreement among the European powers to seek no special rights and privileges from a weak Chinese administration. Rather than conceding the fact of a weak China, Straight desired to strengthen Peking sufficiently to maintain its integrity and thus preserve the Open Door for American trade.[7] For him, the Hukuang Loan was a means to this greater end.

Straight's involvement in the Hukuang negotiations occurred while his attention was still focused primarily on Manchuria. In that region, not troubled by any "rights recovery movement," he believed the opportunities for American investment were great. Harriman, the guiding spirit behind the American group, also was uninterested in the Hukuang Loan and its underlying philosophy of creating an "international financial community of interests." To him, the American group would prove most useful by providing financial support for a unilateral American project in Manchuria.

7. In the back of his mind, Straight wondered if a strong China might refuse to hold the door open, but because that day seemed so remote, that possibility did not seriously concern him.

Even though his attempts in 1905 and 1908 to secure the Manchurian link for his worldwide transportation system had failed, Harriman was not discouraged and embarked on still another effort. In 1909, he proposed that Russia sell the Chinese Eastern Railway and grant him trackage rights over the Trans-Siberian Railroad. This scheme received the apparent approval of the Russian finance minister. At the same time, Straight obtained a preliminary Chinchou-Aigun contract from the Chinese, but at this promising juncture Harriman died, and fate deprived Straight of his major support. The American bankers did not understand the import of Harriman's secret schemes and refused to consider them before completion of the Hukuang negotiations.

Straight assumed total responsibility for the advocacy of the Manchurian proposals. Working zealously all through 1909, he tried to convince New York and Washington to shift their attention from the Hukuang Loan to Manchuria, Mongolia, and Siberia, which he characterized as "the most attractive field for the Group's Far Eastern endeavours." Straight expanded Harriman's neat, uncomplicated project, designed to increase American influence in Manchuria, into a grandiose scheme for rearranging the entire Far Eastern power structure. He linked T'ang's 1908 proposals for a Manchurian bank to direct the development of China's northern provinces (including the construction of the Chinchou-Aigun railroad) with Harriman's 1909 plans for the purchase of the Chinese Eastern Railway from Russia, and then joined them to ideas for British-American-Russian cooperation in Siberian, Mongolian, and Manchurian development projects proposed by J. O. P. Bland, the Peking agent for a British banking firm. To this grand design, he added elements of his own; he proposed, for example, the negotiation of a Russian-American entente to secure Russian support for the Open Door in Manchuria.[8] In addition, Straight advocated judicious manipulation of American and European attitudes toward the war loan conversion and treaty revision sought by Tokyo in exchange for Japanese acceptance of

8. Specifically, Russia would agree to recognize China's sovereignty and administrative rights over the Manchurian railway settlements. Then, under the terms of the 1905 Portsmouth treaty and Komura Convention, which granted Japan the same rights in southern Manchuria as held by Russia in northern Manchuria, Japan would be forced to do likewise. This alone would do much to restore Chinese control over Manchuria.

the Chinchou-Aigun line. If necessary, he recommended American recognition of Japan's ambitions in Korea in exchange for her withdrawal from north China. By ending Japanese domination in Manchuria, this complex plan would effectively neutralize the area and open it to American commercial interests.

Once again, more cautious policies prevailed in Washington. Knox saw Straight's Manchurian proposals, principally the Chinchou-Aigun railroad contract, as tools that might be employed to force American capital into the entire Manchurian railroad system. The secretary of state radically altered the philosophy of Straight's plan; instead of the Russian-American cooperation Straight advocated, Knox based his proposal on the cooperative principle implicit in the Hukuang negotiations. This principle, which he considered a "concrete statement" of the Open Door, meant that whenever China pledged its credit for railway construction, the powers pledged to the Open Door principles of equal trade opportunity in China and the preservation of China's political integrity possessed such a "direct interest" as to be entitled to equal participation in the loans. Knox proposed the purchase of the existing Manchurian railroads and the financing of the Chinchou-Aigun line by an international consortium. The establishment of such a financial community of interest would preclude the establishment by any one power of a sphere of influence.

The two controlling powers promptly rejected the Knox proposal. Japan's rejection did not concern Straight, for after Jacob Schiff's 1908 exchange with Tokyo bankers, Straight had abandoned hope of acquiring control of the South Manchuria Railway. Rather, he intended to countermand Japanese influence by cooperating with Russia to build a competing Chinchou-Aigun Chinese Eastern Railway system and by forcing Japan to relinquish its claims of administrative control over the railroad zones. He further believed that Russia's failure to endorse the Knox policy did not pose a major obstacle, since Straight still assumed that Russian-American cooperation in the Far East was possible.

In spring, 1910, Washington officials agreed to seek Russian support for Straight's neutralization plan. The State Department sent Straight to St. Petersburg in search of a pact that Washington hoped would secure Russian goodwill for future enterprises in Siberia and Mongolia, as well as support for the Open Door in Manchuria. The negotiations, however, demonstrated the extent to which the two countries' Far Eastern policies diverged. Russia refused to support projects inimical to the Japanese position in northeast China; indeed, while Straight talked in St. Petersburg, Russia was completing an agreement with Japan expressly designed to close the Open Door in Manchuria.

Bitterly disappointed, Straight claimed Washington had bungled this opportunity to secure Russian support for the Open Door.[9] His criticisms had point, but many other obstacles precluded Russian-American cooperation in the Far East. The czar's top political council was divided into two groups holding antagonistic views of Russia's Far Eastern interests. One group, headed by Vladimir Kokovtsov, the finance minister, believed Russia should pursue an active expansionist policy and responded favorably to the Straight-Harriman proposals for Russian-American cooperation. The other group, headed by Alexander Isvolsky, the minister of foreign affairs, believed Russia's primary objectives lay in Europe and urged the czar to consolidate Russia's remaining Far Eastern interests through an accord with Japan. Great Britain, whose support Washington needed, refused to press Russia to challenge Japan. Rather, with an eye on the impending European struggle, Britain encouraged a Russo-Japanese entente. Other difficulties arose. Once Japan learned of the Straight-Harriman plans in 1909 (and before Knox announced his proposal), Tokyo officials prepared to offer Russia an agreement that would effectively block American designs in Manchuria. For these reasons, virtually no possibility existed in 1910 for Russian-American cooperation in the Far East.

The Russo-Japanese entente dealt a serious blow to America's Open Door policy. Fearful that continuation of any plans for the Chinchou-Aigun railway might provoke Russo-Japanese reprisals and yet equally worried that retreat would be a complete admission that the Open Door in northern China was dead, State Department officials seemed immobilized, unable to decide on a course of action. A proposal made earlier by the Tripartite Consortium bankers finally suggested a new approach. They had suggested that the interbank cooperation for the still pending

9. Principally, he charged that the decision to combine the bankers' Chinchou-Aigun proposal with the Chinese Eastern–South Manchuria Railway neutralization scheme made it a diplomatic proposal and thus involved the anti-American foreign minister Alexander Isvolsky, rather than a financial proposal involving the more sympathetic finance minister Vladimir Kokovtsov.

Hukuang Loan be extended to include all Chinese business. The State Department hoped that cooperation among members of the proposed quadruple consortium in the Manchurian bank loan and later in the Chinchou-Aigun contract would create that international community of financial interests the administration had sought unsuccessfully via Knox's proposal.[10]

Straight dutifully negotiated formation of the Quadruple Consortium though he still disagreed with the administration's cooperative policy. He preferred unilateral American establishment of a Manchurian bank and construction of the Chinchou-Aigun railroad. In late 1910, however, as he struggled with the four-power negotiations over the Hukuang and currency reform loans, Straight came to understand that Washington lacked the financial power to complete the loans under consideration unilaterally. Because of the limited market in the United States for foreign securities, American financiers could not successfully compete against European banks for Chinese loans. Straight's belated realization of American financial impotence led him to discard all hope for an independent or semi-independent policy and to become a proponent of a cooperative approach to maintaining the Open Door.

◇◇◇

The youthful enthusiasms of 1907–9 had disappeared. Instead, Straight complained that his taut nerves were likely to "snap like a guitar string," and the pressures to which he was subjected brought him close to a nervous breakdown. Two years later, he could still recall the horror and nightmare quality of that period. The deep despair which he experienced arose principally from growing appreciation of the deteriorating framework in which he sought to implement American China policy: the creeping weakness of the Chinese regime; the determination of Russia and Japan

---

10. Former President Roosevelt disapproved the decision to seek a consortium loan in Manchuria. He advised Knox to recognize Japan's paramount influence in Manchuria where American interests were "really unimportant" and where the United States lacked the power to stop Japanese expansion. This disagreement, which has been widely cited as evidence of policy differences between the two administrations that extended back to 1908, occurred not in 1908 but only in 1910, in the wake of the Russo-Japanese entente.

to secure control of Manchuria; the unwillingness of Great Britain and France to support an Open Door policy against their allies; and the financial, political, and military inability of the United States to pursue the Open Door unilaterally.

The Chinese revolution finally caused Straight to abandon all hope of creating a viable native administration that could guarantee the Open Door for American trade and investment in China. Ironically, the Hukuang contract ignited the revolution in Szechuan. To Straight, the Hukuang Loan symbolized his efforts to impose Westernization and progress upon China and provide rational, efficient development under the Manchus. Supporters of the rights recovery movement, however, opposed the railroad as an example of foreign financial domination and the extension of Manchu control over the provinces. Beginning in May 1911, when the central government issued an edict nationalizing some provincial railways as required by the Hukuang contract, a wave of civil disturbances flared in China. In September, when the Peking government attempted to put down the unrest in Szechuan, the outbreak there increased to a full-scale revolt.

In the early stages of the revolution Straight remained optimistic that, although the Manchu dynasty was crumbling, his friend Yüan Shih-k'ai would emerge at the head of a strong constitutional monarchy. Such a regime, for which Straight sought Western support, appeared to him to offer the best hope for "good government," one capable of maintaining conditions conducive to Western trade and investment. When a weak, decentralized republican government emerged in 1912 instead of the strong constitutional monarchy on which he had pinned his hopes, Straight concluded that continued support for Chinese control over Manchuria and Mongolia, which he had consistently advocated since 1906, amounted to "tilting at windmills." Preferring not to think of himself as a "visionary," Straight advocated negotiating an accord with Russia and Japan that would recognize their dominance in Manchuria and Mongolia in exchange for assistance in maintaining the Open Door in China proper. Such an accord might permit some United States participation in the development of Manchuria and, more importantly, the cooperative policy would keep weak China open to "the trade and investment of all powers."

The compromise he proposed never materialized. Straight's next task was to represent the American bankers at the meeting called to admit Russia and Japan to the Four-Power Consortium. Instead of recognizing Russo-Japanese dominance in Manchuria and Mongolia, as he had proposed earlier, Straight had to carry out his assignment of creating a six-power consortium based on absolute equality of participation. The State Department hoped that such an agreement would preclude any monopolization of loans affecting particular sections of China; but the words of the agreement belied reality. Because of its importance to Great Britain and France in the European struggle for power, Russia controlled the consortium and prevented it from functioning while the czar's agents pressed the Chinese for concessions regarding Mongolia.

The inability of Washington officials to dominate the consortium did not, however, cause them to consider withdrawal of the American group. During this critical revolutionary period in China, the threat of Western intervention, imposition of a foreign financial protectorate, or perhaps the long-feared partitioning of China loomed large. As in the critical 1899–1900 period, American policy makers believed the only opportunity for controlling or modifying the action of the other powers and influencing the future direction of China depended on the maintenance of a cooperative policy. Leading Taft administration officials and, with the sole exception of Kuhn, Loeb, all the key Wall Street financiers agreed that the preservation of the consortium, their chosen instrument of international cooperation, was of paramount importance.[11] Despite this consensus, in the opening days of the Wilson administration the new president renounced Taft's cooperative policy and the diplomatic support for the group of Wall Street bankers. Instead, Wilson promised an expanded policy of Dollar Diplomacy, modified by the New Freedom, which he expected would enable smaller financiers to operate independently in China.[12]

11. Griswold, Li Tien-yi, and Roy Watson Curry, *Woodrow Wilson and Far Eastern Policy 1913–1921* (New York, 1957), all argue that by the end of the Taft administration, the American bankers wanted to withdraw from the consortium.
12. Wilson's withdrawal is an ideal example of Jerry Isreal's thesis, in *Progressivism and the Open Door* (Pittsburgh, 1971), that the Open Door strategy debates between competition and cooperation mirrored the domestic debates of the trust versus the competitive tradition, with the same forces and pressures shaping both domestic and foreign policy.

During the Wilson administration, Straight devoted himself primarily to the expansion of American trade and investment in the Far East. Through his connections with Colonel House, the president's closest adviser, Straight tried to secure a position in the State Department. His failure, he believed, was due to his close association with Wall Street. In 1915, after leaving J. P. Morgan, he became vice-president of the American International Corporation in charge of Chinese affairs. The corporation, then being formed under the direction of Frank Vanderlip, president of the National City Bank of New York (one of the members of the American group), was designed to merge a construction company and trading organization with the financial facilities of the National City Bank and the International Banking Corporation. Notably, its corporate structure was identical with the one Straight repeatedly had urged upon the American group of bankers. It provided a broad-based commercial mechanism to coordinate the efforts for acquisition and implementation of development loans. In its initial year of operation, Straight guided the corporation's completion of several contracts in China, principally the Huai River Conservancy Loan and the Siems-Carey Agreement for financing and building fifteen hundred miles of railroad.

Straight undertook these operations in China with the intention of resuming a cooperative approach to the Far East. Convinced that the United States could not successfully compete with the consortium or with Japan, Straight believed President Wilson would eventually be forced to reconsider his opposition to the consortium. In anticipation of a change in policy, Straight sought a position for the American International Corporation in the original American group. He used his friendships with Colonel House, Secretary of State Lansing, and State Department officials William Phillips and Frank Polk to lobby both for renewed American participation in the consortium and negotiation of agreements with Russia and Japan. Such accords would concede Russo-Japanese dominance of Manchuria and Mongolia in exchange for reaffirmation by those powers of the commercial Open Door in those regions and of the "neutralization of the eighteen provinces of China."

In 1916, increasing State Department concern about Japan's opportunistic encroachments on China's sovereignty brought the administration to admit the failure of its unilateral New Freedom policy. In June, the president approved the State Department's proposal, a plan formulated by Straight, for immediately reviving United States participation in the consortium. Although the State Department's efforts to implement this program stalled because of the financial interests' inability to reach an accord, they constituted the first step in the establishment of the Second China Consortium.

◇◇◇

Willard Straight viewed himself as an empire builder, fighting to establish and maintain an American presence in Asia. Unlike Clive or Rhodes, his British counterparts, Straight envisioned an economic empire rather than a formal colonial system based on political control of the native population, for the former secured the advantages while avoiding the responsibilities of political control. He played the "Great Game of Empire," not in the manner of a friendly chess game or sporting contest, but as a deadly serious struggle among the world's great powers for the right to dominate China. Like other key American policy makers of this period, Straight honestly believed that access to foreign markets, in particular the China market, was crucial to the future industrial prosperity and to the political and social health of the United States: that is, to America's position as a world power. Because of the great power rivalry in the Far East, access to the vast China market had to be secured without delay. As Straight explained his objectives, he was staking a claim for the future when American trade in China would be developed. "If we don't make our position secure now," he said, "it will be difficult if not impossible to come back." Imbued with Kiplingesque ideology, Straight constantly talked about America's "great responsibility" to complete the tasks "vital to the regeneration of China." Nonetheless he clearly appreciated that the "white man's burden" had an intensely pragmatic object. China, he once said, must be saved so that the altruists (among whom he counted himself) might "reap the profits of her development." That, he argued, was what Western philanthropy really implied.

Based on his understanding of American national interests, which in this period of industrial growth and consolidation he framed largely in economic terms, Straight accepted the goals of American Far Eastern policy. Perhaps as well as any of his contemporaries, he understood that the problem confronting

American leaders was the conflict among the great powers for control of the undeveloped areas of the world. In any weak country in which the United States sought markets for its nationals, two options existed. It must "either acquire territory or insist on an equality of commercial opportunity. It must either stake out its own claim or induce other interested Powers to preserve the 'open door.'" There was no middle course. Securing a sphere of influence, which would have guaranteed access to part of the China market for the United States, was not a viable alternative. American public opinion, not to mention America's diplomatic, military, and economic weakness, would have prevented the establishment of a colonial regime in China.

During the difficult 1905–17 period, Straight was involved in the dilemma of implementing America's Open Door policy and did much to shape the twists and turns of his country's strategy. At the outbreak of the Russo-Japanese War, Straight agreed with the decision of Washington policy makers to support Japan in its efforts to check the Russian advance into Manchuria. After the war, however, Straight perceived Japan as the greater threat to commercial opportunity in Manchuria. From his position as consul general in Mukden, he devised a new Open Door strategy that gained the support of New York financiers and Washington officials. Building on Straight's proposals, Root reversed the pro-Japanese policy followed by the Roosevelt administration at Portsmouth and, initiating a policy later termed Dollar Diplomacy, attempted to use financial power to secure an American position in Manchuria.

Straight also devised the schemes that became the basis for the Taft administration's efforts to create an international financial community of interest in China. Knox's 1909 proposal of neutralization and the overtures to the czar for the abortive 1910 Russian-American entente were based on plans proposed by Straight. He served effectively during the Taft administration as the agent of the American group of financiers, negotiating the formation of the Quadruple Consortium, the Hukuang Loan, and the Currency Reform and Manchurian Development Loan, and was justly credited by the American minister in Peking as responsible for the success of the negotiations.

Despite his role in the formation of the Taft-Knox cooperative policy, Straight preferred to follow a unilateral American policy to support the Chinese against Japanese expansion in Manchuria.

Such had been the rationale of the Manchurian bank and his proposals to gain control of the Manchurian railroad system. Ironically, by the time Wilson adopted a unilateral Far Eastern policy, Straight had become a leading advocate of cooperation. The United States, he had learned, lacked the financial resources to compete with the European banks for Chinese loans. Furthermore, the revolution critically weakened China and destroyed all possibility of successfully supporting Chinese development, either unilaterally or internationally. Because of the great power rivalries in the Far East, unilateral competitive investment spelled almost certain conflict. An international financial community composed of former competitors offered the promise of rational, peaceful international commerce. Equally important was the fact that international investments, made by a consortium on the principle of equality, might challenge the existence of spheres of influence, reinforce the Open Door, and effectively neutralize China. It should be noted that the consortium structure that Straight helped to create formed the basis of United States economic diplomacy in the Far East in the twenties.

Straight's promising career ended in 1918 when, at the age of thirty-eight, as he was preparing to serve as secretary of the American peace commission at Versailles, he died of pneumonia. At the time of his death, Straight was involved in planning the peace and he foresaw the general course of American Far Eastern policy in the postwar period. Maintenance of an American position in the Far East depended upon reaching an accord with Japan, one that would recognize Japanese supremacy yet preserve the Open Door. Membership in an international financial combination, he still insisted, would provide the economically powerful United States with the opportunity to become preeminent in the Orient. If, however, Japan were to challenge that dominance, American policy makers would confront unfortunate alternatives. They would either have to revise their belief that America's future depended upon access to the China market or be prepared to shed blood for the preservation of the Open Door. The ferocity with which Straight played the "Great Game of Empire" strongly suggests what would have been his answer.

BIBLIOGRAPHIC NOTE

Primary source materials for the study of Willard Straight and

American Far Eastern policy are abundant. The Straight papers housed at Cornell University are a particularly complete collection. Papers of many State Department officials, including Root, Knox, Bryan, Lansing, and lesser figures such as Henry Prather Fletcher and Breckinridge Long are in the Division of Manuscripts, Library of Congress. The State Department records are in the National Archives. Paul Reinsch's papers are at the State Historical Society, Madison, Wisconsin; W. W. Rockhill's, in the Manuscript Division, Houghton Library, Harvard University; Huntington Wilson's, at Ursinus College; Frank L. Polk's, at Yale University.

Griswold's 1938 work, cited previously, laid the basis for the traditionalist interpretation of American Far Eastern policy. The works of Esthus, Vevier, Li Tien-yi, and Roy Watson Curry, all cited previously, offer the best traditionalist accounts of the Taft and Wilson Far Eastern policies. Jerry Israel's book is a contribution to the revisionist interpretation of American foreign policy originally argued by William Appleman Williams in several works including *The Tragedy of American Diplomacy* (Cleveland, 1959), and by Walter LaFeber, *The New Empire: An Interpretation of American Expansion, 1865–1898* (Ithaca, 1962), and Thomas McCormick, *China Market: America's Quest for Informal Empire, 1893–1901* (Chicago, 1967). Herbert Croly's sympathetic biography, *Willard Straight* (New York, 1922), offers insight into the young diplomat's career.

TO DO GOOD IN THE WORLD:
WOODROW WILSON

and America's Mission

Ross Gregory

Seldom in American history has a president of the United States so influenced foreign policy as Woodrow Wilson in the years before, during, and after the First World War. It was a time when impressing personal qualities upon policy, as Wilson did, was a fateful endeavor. His presidency coincided with the greatest war in history up to that time, and its more than four-year course in Europe and throughout the world produced many changes, some good and some extremely bad: the crumbling and collapse of old attitudes and institutions, the upheaval of social and economic activities, and the appearance of new problems that would mark the subsequent event-ridden decades of the twentieth century.

◇◇◇

It has been said that a man never forgets his past. Woodrow Wilson not only did not forget but glorified the experiences of his

359

youth; if there had been defects in his upbringing he was blind to them. He always recalled his childhood with fondness, and drew eagerly upon his parents' teachings. Born in 1856 in Staunton, Virginia, he grew up in a South conditioned by Civil War and Reconstruction. Memory of the great internal conflict produced a dislike of violence so intense as to border on pacifism. Although he never acquired the sectional hatred that plagued many of his fellow southerners, he easily accepted other attitudes characteristic of the South. Jeffersonian individualism provided the basis for his economic thinking; white supremacy so pervaded local—and national—psyche that he scarcely questioned the principle, and as president he found nothing improper in placing nonwhite people beneath the level of other Americans.

Of all the experiences of youth none left a deeper imprint than the religious environment in the Wilson household. His father was a Presbyterian minister, his mother, the daughter of one. The God Wilson came to know was that of John Calvin—and of the Reverend Dr. Wilson—a loving but demanding sovereign who drew a clear line between good and evil and expected the maximum of obedience and service. The Wilsons lived a comfortable, if detached, middle-class existence, enjoying the prestige and respect afforded a minister's family. That he was a preacher's son made the community expect more of young Tommy (he was christened Thomas Woodrow) and his father, a firm disciplinarian, made certain his children reflected the family's religious beliefs and the community's expectations. Hearing God's word each day of the week, the young Wilson moved easily toward the conclusion that he had privileged access to truth and a special obligation to serve God and mankind. This moral tutelage had lasting effect, inspiring him in later years not to intellectual rebellion but to continued obedience to the Presbyterian creed. Many of the features of personality that characterized him as president—detachment, activism, discipline, fondness for order, self-righteousness—originated in a childhood spent in a Presbyterian parsonage in the post–Civil War South.

At a time when ambitious young men of education and social status might have plunged into the industrial expansion of the late nineteenth century, Wilson found a career befitting a minister's son more suitable to his tastes. He wanted no long hours working on a farm or in the factory, no risk of tarnishing his character in the grimy competition of business. Even so, the choice was not instantaneous, not without indecision and surely some self-doubt. He spent several years in study, which produced an undergraduate degree from the College of New Jersey, as Princeton then was known. He took some courses in law (enough to pass the bar) at the University of Virginia and earned a Ph.D. from Johns Hopkins in Baltimore. There followed a successful career in teaching and writing. He spent seventeen years as a college professor, eight more years as president of Princeton; he wrote nine books and many articles, mostly on American history. In the course of this long career Wilson showed exceptional ability as a teacher, a penetrating student of American institutions, and, as Princeton's president, an innovative manager of the university's affairs.

The academic experience also fostered personal tendencies that had appeared earlier. Years of professional study strengthened his qualifications for speaking on politics and government and seemingly confirmed an ability to discover and interpret truth. Wilson's responsibilities as professor and president left him master of his domain; he preferred making decisions with no outside interference and exhibited at times a disturbing intolerance toward individuals brave enough to challenge his will. He became involved in two huge power struggles at Princeton, the last of which (an unsuccessful contest for control of the graduate school) left him embittered and anxious to move on to new fields of endeavor. By that time he had become known in New Jersey as a reformist educator and worthy prospect for political leadership in the Progressive Era. After a two-year political apprenticeship as governor of New Jersey he undertook the campaign for the presidency in 1912.

Swept into office on a wave of Progressive reformism, albeit mainly because Theodore Roosevelt had split the Republican party, Wilson appeared a political novice, the eastern schoolmaster who had come to instruct and discipline. He looked the part: trim and fashionable, standing erect with firm jaw, straight mouth, and eyes staring through pince-nez. He wished to be for the people, not of them, and he never appeared with open collar and shirtsleeves performing tasks beneath presidential dignity. He could be charming and graceful; but he could also be stubborn and inexorable, and political cartoons of the day—perhaps the clearest indication of a politician's image—scarcely ever portrayed him with a smile. He brandished none of the cocksure bantering that Franklin Roosevelt was to perform in the presidential chair, none of the clowning the people had enjoyed with Theodore Roosevelt. Wilson was no pessimist, and he certainly did not lack confidence; he simply handled his office with the same determined seriousness with which he approached life.

The new president could not forget that he was the Reverend Dr. Wilson's son. Still the hard-headed Presbyterian, seeker of truth, doer of God's will, he continued to have trouble dealing with people. "His prejudices are many and often unjust," remarked his friend Edward M. House. "He finds great difficulty in conferring with men against whom, for some reason, he has a prejudice and in whom he can find nothing good." Driven by a disconcerting tendency to talk down, he preferred to communicate through his books or from the comfortable distance of the platform. In speeches he communicated extraordinarily well, and his presidential messages were notable for use of the proper adjective or noun, the memorable phrase, the inspiring urge to some high goal. The same qualities produced other less admirable traits, however. His keen mind and superb powers of analysis left an appearance of intellectual arrogance; he did not take criticism gracefully, and turned small issues into large personal quarrels. Finally, the president's high-mindedness and oratorical talents so influenced his thoughts that he seemed to have trouble separating rhetoric from facts, the ideal from the real.

In his conduct of foreign affairs the president's personal characteristics shone through. He insisted upon taking charge. When large problems arose he not only supervised policy, but also concerned himself with minutiae, often writing dispatches on his portable Hammond typewriter with its wide-spaced letters and blue ribbon. Distrustful of professional diplomats and officials removed from his supervision, he preferred to deal directly with governments, or through unofficial contacts such as Colonel House. He appointed few strong men to advisory positions, and seldom followed their recommendations. Service in Wilson's State Department was no pleasant undertaking. The first secretary of state, William Jennings Bryan, resigned in 1915 in protest of the president's handling of the *Lusitania* crisis, hurt that Wilson had made so little use of his talents. Bryan's successor Robert Lansing fared better; at least he remained in office a remarkable five years, freely gave advice, and appeared as a dignified spokesman of policy. Lansing did not make the policy he articulated, however;

his influence rarely extended beyond opinions on international law, and even in this field he proceeded in gingerly fashion.

The person to whom Wilson turned most for help was his friend House. A quiet little man with a mouselike face ("Colonel Mouse," he sometimes was dubbed), he dabbled in politics and had mastered the art of human manipulation. He gained his greatest success with Wilson—an accomplishment all the more remarkable because the subject was Wilson—and soon became known as the president's "alter ego" and "second self." Wilson conferred regularly with this Texas colonel, confessed problems and frustrations, sent him on special assignments; yet rarely did he allow House to decide large matters. Knowing the president's temperament, House did not try, at least not directly; he catered to Wilson, flattered him, and in this tactful way maintained a remarkable friendship for many years. House surely helped relieve the oppressive loneliness of the presidency, but he did little to lighten the burden of decision making, one that the president showed no inclination to relinquish.

In some ways Wilson contributed timely changes to the conduct of diplomacy. His assertion of executive authority vis-à-vis legislative control was in tune with demands of the twentieth century; only Theodore Roosevelt had done as much. With Wilson in the White House no one doubted who was in charge, and so allocation of praise or blame was a simple matter. He obviously carried the process of presidential domination too far; by limiting diplomacy largely to himself, he narrowed perspective, weakened morale in the State Department and foreign service, and even unknowingly prompted secret efforts at undermining and sometimes lowered consideration of important issues to a level of petty personal rivalry. In all his writings on government Wilson had exalted executive leadership, going so far in one book as to remark that presidential authority in foreign affairs was "virtually the power to control them absolutely." No president would learn better than Wilson the error in that statement.

Other than the emphasis on personal leadership Wilson's academic and political background gave little hint of how he would conduct foreign affairs. Elected on a program almost entirely concerned with domestic problems, he had taken little notice of foreign policy other than to express a vague intention to be honest and just and an even more remote and ill-defined desire to place the United States at the "service of humanity." His scholarly studies had touched upon foreign policy only in passing and he had given recent international developments no more attention than had the average educated American. The haphazard manner with which he approached policy appeared in his appointment of the secretary of state. Bryan had traveled around the world some years before, an experience that should have instructed him in some of the world's ways; but in fact he was more innocent than his chief—which was saying something. Such an attitude had not seemed unusual, given the character of American politics at that time. Had Wilson lived in a settled and peaceful world, he probably would have followed the pattern of most previous presidents: keeping watch on domestic matters and keeping his political house in order.

As it was he came to office during a momentous time in world history. For all the progress in technology—such remarkable new machines as the automobile and airplane had recently been invented—there had been a distressing slowness in development of human institutions. It was a world of kings, colonial empires, exploitation and oppression, class conflict, dreadnoughts and fleet pageantry, and then in 1914, little more than a year after Wilson took office, the rush into a great war. The United States had observed these developments with an air of interested but confused detachment. Half a century of industrial growth had drastically changed the nation, propelling it into first place among economic powers; but Americans still remained puzzled about their place in international affairs. The Spanish-American War and Theodore Roosevelt's zestful diplomacy had thrust the nation into global politics, but many individuals had expressed fear lest the United States come to resemble the greedy, jealous nations of the Old World. The success of Progressive reformism at home seemed all the more reason for America to find a new role in the world appropriate to national strength and yet consistent with American ideals.

Wilson appeared on the world stage when the nation could delay a decision no longer. Lacking a systematic philosophy of foreign relations, he acted in accord with his philosophy of life, and so diplomacy became an application to world problems of the president's thoughts about mankind, the United States, and himself. At the heart of the philosophy were Wilson's belief in man's ability to improve the world and his desire to make the

United States an instrument of global reform. With proper leadership—his leadership, as it developed—nations could find institutions to conquer hunger, oppression, and war and bring to fruition God's plan for an orderly world. Taken together, Wilson's responses, at least his rationale, had such scope and consistency as to comprise a new philosophy of foreign relations.

To many people Wilsonian diplomacy came to represent a typically American approach to foreign policy, for the president's ideas encompassed attitudes and institutions already at work in the United States. First and most important was Wilson's idealized faith in democracy. As with most Americans of his day and class the country's success enthralled him, and he attributed national greatness largely to political institutions that had allowed the United States to grow and prosper while avoiding domestic upheaval and wars of conquest. Wilson attributed most world problems to the existence of colonial masters and autocratic governments led by selfish, powerful men who owed no explanation to the people they governed. Democracy constituted the logical expression of the human will—even God's will—in politics. It replaced conflict with discussion, armies with parliaments; it represented the most promising device for promotion of peace and order. While some areas might require time and enlightened guidance, the president believed democracy to be ultimately within reach of all. "When properly directed," he once said, "there is no people not fitted for self government."

A democratic nation would probably also be capitalistic. While Wilson came to the presidency a spokesman for Progressive economic reform, he was at heart a nineteenth-century liberal who believed that capitalism, despite some minor flaws, constituted the most humane and dynamic economic system. Capitalism represented nothing less than freedom and democracy in economics, a system that allowed all people, not some elite alone, to determine a nation's destiny. What had worked in the United States should function in other nations and in economic relations between states. "Lift your eyes to the horizons of business," he once told some American businessmen. "Let your thoughts and your imagination run abroad throughout the whole world, and with the inspiration of the thought that you are Americans and are meant to carry liberty and justice and the principles of humanity wherever you go, go out and sell goods that will make the world more comfortable and more happy, and convert them to the

principles of America." Even though Wilson understood the value
to the United States, in terms of markets and places for investment, of international capitalism, national self-interest did not
represent his only reason for urging economic expansion, probably not even the most important one. He envisioned a reformist,
humanized capitalism, designed to serve entrepreneur, worker,
and consumer; ably and justly managed, such a system could serve
as the economic arm of democracy.

Above all stood a vision of the United States as a superior
nation, admirably suited to lead. Not burdened with militarism,
unentangled in Old World *Realpolitik* or the dirty competition for
colonies, the United States stood alone as a shining example of
national morality. Under Wilson's humane guidance America
could offer to undeveloped nations capital for economic growth
and tutelage to a high level of social and political development. To
the European states, now busily destroying themselves and each
other, the United States could provide leadership in a new system
of international relations.

For much of Wilson's presidency his ideas reflected more a
vague goal than a concrete plan. He had not come to office
expecting to change the world in his generation, and at first he
attended only to those foreign problems that were brought to him.
He did not propose anything resembling a program until 1918,
when some new structure had become imperative. There did
occur early in his administration one problem, in Mexico, which
gave an indication of the future. Convinced that brigands were
depriving the Mexican people of liberty and jeopardizing the
Western Hemisphere, he intervened, first with diplomatic pressure, later by sending troops, hoping to preserve order and open
the door for stable government. Instead he aroused native
resentment, enmeshed the United States in bewildering Mexican
politics, and nearly brought the two nations to war. Intervention in
Mexico and later in other Latin American states demonstrated the
shortcomings of Wilson's idealism. It exposed the fallacy of
applying a single American solution to vastly different problems,
of one nation's leader purporting to know what was best for
others. The president's policy revealed his ill-concealed feelings of
racial superiority and self-righteous paternalism ("I am going to
teach the Latin American Republics to elect good men," he once
said) and contradicted his stated purpose of making government
the object of popular will. Amid proclamations of goodwill and

high moral purpose, Wilson sponsored military intervention on a scale never seen before in that region.

While idealism—some authors have called it missionary idealism—set the rhetorical tone for Wilson's diplomacy, there was a more traditional and practical side. Whatever he hoped to accomplish in world affairs, he frequently acted in accord with restraints imposed by local conditions or the demands of national interest. He was an internationalist, but he felt a sense of nationalism and an obligation to protect his own nation's interests. His Latin American policy, whatever its stated purpose, sustained American supremacy in the Western Hemisphere. In the Far East he expressed sympathy for Chinese independence and in fact attempted halfheartedly to discourage Japanese encroachment; but he did not commit the United States, and when he left office China was at best a semisovereign state. Even though these and other policies were steeped in practicality, he preferred not to defend them in terms of national interest, for he felt that simple pursuit of national goals, which one might equate with selfishness or greed, was in itself not worthy justification for the actions of a great moral nation. In most cases Wilsonian universalism, the propensity to evaluate problems by American standards, provided easy reconciliation between national interests and the interests of the world.

Even though Wilsonian diplomacy was identified as a new diplomacy, not everything the president proposed was unique. Economic expansion long had been an article of faith to presidents, business, and agricultural interest groups. For many decades spokesmen had expounded the uniqueness of America, its superior political and economic institutions, if not its world mission. The nation's largest foreign venture in nearly a century, the Spanish-American War of 1898, had come about partly because of a widely popular missionary urge to free Cuba from Spanish rule. Wilson did not originate idealist diplomacy; he simply carried it further than any previous American leader. With a deep-seated belief in its merits and his incomparable mastery of language, he gave it articulation such as the nation, and the world, never had heard.

◇◇◇

Wilsonian diplomacy has little meaning unless it is seen in the context of the First World War. Shortly after he came to office, Wilson's world seemed to be falling apart. The Great War of 1914–18 overwhelmed his presidency, occupying his attention during nearly six of eight years in office, causing sleepless nights and presenting problems larger than any president had faced since Abraham Lincoln. By exposing the decadence of the old political system, endangering the United States and American principles, the war was the primary factor in shaping the president's thoughts about Europe, America, and the world. At the end it provided both reason and opportunity for development of his world plan.

It is sobering to observe how the United States moved from a safe, remote position in 1914 when the war started, a nation disclaiming concern about the war's causes and about how it might end, to some two and a half years later when American leaders felt compelled to send young men to die, like millions of Europeans before them, in the muddy trenches of France and Belgium. With hindsight one may argue that if certain decisions had been different the United States could have stayed at peace. Yet there seemed something almost inevitable about American participation, if the war lasted long enough, for it was impossible that a nation as rich and strong as the United States, with broad world interests and such national pride, could remain unaffected by a conflict of such magnitude. While Wilson acted as national leader and spokesman, made all major decisions, and absorbed responsibility for the fateful consequences, his influence appeared less in the decision to enter the war than in the rationalization of intervention and interpretation of a war the United States now had become obliged to fight. Another president probably would have led the nation to war at some time but probably would have explained the cause a different way.

As did the majority of his countrymen, Wilson expected that the United States would take no part in the conflict. Though he experienced a certain sympathy for the Allies, as did House, Lansing, and nearly all his advisers, he had no intention of supporting either group of belligerents, feeling that his responsibilities consisted of preserving neutrality and protecting American rights while holding himself in readiness should the combatants ask for his help as an impartial negotiator. For many months mediation seemed the best way to provide Christian service and assure that the United States would remain at peace. He made repeated overtures, and twice sent House on "peace missions" to Europe, only to conclude sadly that the belligerents wished to end the war their own way.

Meanwhile problems of commerce had begun to show the precarious nature of neutrality. Americans immediately put to sea to resume normal trade with Europe and take up what new business the war might bring. Wilson supported this activity, assuming it to be a legitimate, safe (not to mention profitable) expression of neutral rights. Whatever moral objections the president might have had to the sale of guns and ammunition—he seems to have had remarkably few—became submerged in the emphasis on legalism, and so contraband became an important part of the war traffic. Because of the prewar pattern of trade and Britain's renowned mastery of the sea it seemed only natural, and not at all objectionable, that the bulk of commerce would go to the Allies. What Wilson and everyone else failed to anticipate was the emergence of the submarine as Germany's primary means of economic warfare. The United States became caught between German and British efforts to strike at each other on the seas. Wilson strenuously protested the activity of both nations, but he threatened only Germany, in some measure because of a growing relationship with the Allies, in larger measure because only Germany used submarines, a means of warfare he thought illegitimate and a costly, savage, irreparable infringement of neutral rights.

In the course of the long struggle over submarine warfare, Wilson experienced some of the most trying times of his presidency. Torn between a desire to keep his nation at peace and the need to protect its rights and honor, he personally agonized over the decision regarding each submarine incident, unwilling to trust the judgment of advisers. While critics attacked his policies—almost equally, it seems, for being either too lenient or too harsh with Germany—the majority of the American people chose to follow his leadership. Unfortunately, Wilson alone could not determine America's fate. The nation had become so entwined in international politics and economics that each major disturbance affected its well-being, and any American decision, even a policy of absolute isolation, affected the course of the war. Wilson scored outstanding victories through his protests against submarine warfare, but each German concession further aligned the United States with the Allies, handicapped Germany's war effort, and made demands in Berlin for an unrestricted U-boat campaign more appealing. Given such circumstances, it is remarkable that intervention came so late. Pursuing a delicate middle course between belligerency and outright pacifism, Wilson preserved both peace and prosperity for some two and a half years. He did not keep the United States out of war altogether, but his policies allowed Americans to escape some of the war's most savage encounters and to avoid intervention until the conflict, measured in months of combat, was two-thirds over.

Wilson's style is evident less in his opposition to submarine warfare than in the way he opposed it. He faced impressive practical reasons—public opinion, economic needs, national prestige—for refusing to accept unrestricted submarine warfare. He had no desire to ignore these factors; but he would not justify policy on the ground of practicality, however justifiable, not when national selfishness had been responsible for the war. He much preferred to rest his argument on moral and legal principle. As he wrote in the second *Lusitania* note, 9 June 1915: "The Government of the United States is contending for something much greater than mere rights of property or privileges of commerce. It is contending for nothing less high and sacred than the rights of humanity." By couching policy in terms of international law and principle, lecturing the Germans and the British on their responsibilities as civilized nations, Wilson impressed European belligerents as a phrase-making evangelist who showed little appreciation of their problems.

These same policies produced practical results, however. They enhanced the theme of international economic liberalism, as manifested in Wilson's principle of freedom of the seas, upheld friendly and prosperous American relations with western Europe, particularly Britain, and helped prevent German domination of the European continent. By defining American interests in terms of international law, Wilson gave this policy the universalist tone that had become familiar in Wilsonian diplomacy.

War came to the United States not because Wilson and the American people pursued it—indeed, to the final moment the president searched desperately for a way to avoid intervention—but because events brought the nation to a point where no other choice seemed reasonable. Wilson reluctantly concluded that the United States would suffer less loss of life, property, commerce, national prestige, and influence by going to war than by remaining the victim of submarine warfare. He had become a prisoner of his policies; but perhaps such imprisonment was inevitable because of the nation's increased involvement in global affairs.

In characteristic fashion the president's war message of 2 April 1917 spoke of larger issues. In this most momentous of his presidential performances Wilson could not resist making a rhetorical appeal to truth and principle. He explained that the German government had provoked American intervention as it had promoted war in Europe, but that Germany represented only a recent example of an enduring evil of history: oppressive, aggressive, undemocratic government. Thus the first object of war should be to crush German military autocracy. Once the Allies had accomplished that task they could move on to larger goals. "We shall fight," said the president, "for the thing which we have always carried nearest our hearts—for democracy, for the right of those who submit to authority to have a voice in their own governments, for the rights and liberties of small nations, for . . . concert of free people as shall bring peace and safety to all nations and make the world itself at last free." An eloquent and stirring speech, the address evoked acclaim from liberals over the world. Therein was part of the president's shortcoming; he had been too eloquent and high-minded. He had interpreted the war in remarkably simplistic terms and established objectives that no peace settlement could accomplish. Perhaps there could have been no other way, given the emotion of the time and the way Wilson handled foreign policy; but the war message of 1917 laid the basis for generations of cynicism about the war "to end all wars" and to make the world "safe for democracy."

Events soon showed that Wilson did not intend his speech as mere talk. He prosecuted the war with the peace in mind, making sure that as American military contributions increased political influence, his influence also increased. He insisted on a voice in all major decisions, kept the American army separate from the Allied armies, and in January 1918 outlined in fourteen points his ideas of a just and lasting settlement. He undertook major reponsibility for arranging the armistice, insisting as a precondition that Germany renounce its military government. In choosing a peace commission he paid virtually no attention to politics or public opinion, preferring to select men (such as House and Lansing) that he knew and trusted. To lead the American delegation to the Paris Peace Conference the president, not surprisingly, chose himself.

When the shooting stopped at last in November 1918, Wilson traveled to Europe and appeared before crowds almost wild with enthusiasm. Large portions of Europe lay in rubble; the monarchies, the symbol and much of the substance of the old order, were destroyed; war no longer seemed an acceptable device for settling disputes. The people were hungry and weary, and they longed for someone to lead them. It surely seemed that the president's moment in history had arrived.

Only with the start of serious diplomacy did Wilson understand the difficulty of his task. In Paris he came face to face with men who shared neither his perspective on the European war nor his thoughts about the perfectibility of human institutions. "I really think," wrote British Prime Minister David Lloyd George, "that at first the idealistic president regarded himself as a missionary whose function it was to rescue the poor European heathen from their age-long worship of false and fiery gods." European leaders looked upon Wilson as possessing not superior wisdom, but the wealth and power of the United States, and it was in terms of wealth and power that they wished to deal. There was Georges Clemenceau of France, seventy-seven years old, with droopy eyes and droopy moustache, practitioner of *Realpolitik*, pessimistic about mankind. He wanted reparations and a weakened, if not destroyed, Germany. Lloyd George, the "Welsh Witch," had come to Paris after promising Britain to make Germany pay heavily. Vittorio Orlando, the least prestigious member of the Big Four, demanded for Italy a full share of money and territory. Other national leaders put forth various financial and territorial claims. It became apparent that what Wilson thought to be an opportunity, Europeans thought to be a problem. They acknowledged the need for political change, but wanted no settlement that might further weaken their nations and above all wished to give first attention to immediate concerns. Their proposals represented no more than a fitting end to a long and costly war, practical efforts toward reconstruction and security.

Wilson's trip to Europe marked a culmination of his efforts to change American and world diplomacy. Convinced that isolationism had become obsolete, he was prepared to accept perpetual American involvement in world affairs. He had come to the peace conference asking no indemnity, no territory or other material benefit. While he planned a peace program with American interests in mind, a system in tune with American political and economic institutions, the president regarded participation in the settlement as largely an act of service, one that he could not perform, he believed, if nations reverted to the old political system. Traditional diplomacy had failed and so genuine security could come only through a new system of cooperative relations. The initial step involved creation of a community of democratic states in accord with the principle of self-determination. Wilson did not expect to see such regimes quickly established in all nations; neither did he anticipate immediate dismantling of the colonial empires, the most obvious obstacle to self-rule, however much he wished it. The peace conference could make a proper beginning by stripping the defeated nations, Germany and Austria-Hungary, of territory to which they had no ethnic claim, and by fostering self-government in new states created from liberated areas in central and eastern Europe.

One of the most perplexing problems of the conference grew out of complex and fluid conditions in Russia, where a group of Bolshevik revolutionaries asserted the right to speak for the Russian nation. Neither Allied military intervention nor conciliatory gestures had ousted the Communists or moved them from a radical ideological line. The rise of bolshevism was a shocking development, an indication of what could happen elsewhere unless the nations meeting in Paris could put the world in order. Wilson hoped that the Russian people, no less than any other, could enjoy peace and self-determination, and yet he could not believe that the Communist regime was a fit participant in a partnership of democratic nations. Lacking understanding of the Russian situation, and with no better alternatives, he decided to withhold diplomatic recognition from the regime of V. I. Lenin and await developments, hoping that the Russians in time would see the light.

The second and most important Wilsonian theme at the conference was the proposal of the League of Nations, a grand parliament of the world. American and European liberals had supported similar schemes for many years, though Wilson had not endorsed the idea until 1916. Once committed, however, he gave the league the prestige of his office and his incomparable powers of persistence and oratory. In the peace conference it became the focus of Wilson's plan for world settlement and a new diplomacy. The league symbolized his belief that wars resulted from nationalism, greed, and power politics, conditions fostered by autocratic

OVERWEIGHTED.

President Wilson. "HERE'S YOUR OLIVE BRANCH. NOW GET BUSY."
Dove of Peace. "OF COURSE I WANT TO PLEASE EVERYBODY; BUT ISN'T THIS A
BIT THICK?"

government. Nations had no forum for rational discussion, no device to stop the machines of war. Wilson proposed a council of nations, equipped and willing to deal openly with territorial disputes, commerce, and armaments, or any issue that threatened peace and justice. If balance of power diplomacy had embodied man's evil nature, the new diplomacy appealed to his inherent goodness, for while the league was to have access to collective action against recalcitrant members, as suggested in the controversial Article Ten, its primary instrument was to be discussion. Wilson doubted that force would often, if ever, be needed.

The weakness in Wilson's efforts at peacemaking rested not in his financial and territorial proposals, for most of them were reasonable, but in his belief that the victorious nations would sacrifice immediate national interest to a larger crusade for peace and justice. Success of the League of Nations depended upon uniformity of purpose, a common definition of right and justice, among members. Negotiations at Paris showed that states were most concerned with advancing national interests, and that what might constitute justice for one country was unjust to another. Not entirely opposed to a league, European leaders were practical men who remained convinced that power would continue to be the determining factor in international relations. Understanding Wilson's obsession with the league, they bargained and maneuvered, finally threatening to withhold support unless he yielded on certain issues. Though the president resisted some of the most severe Allied demands, he gave in on others. Most damaging to his prestige were compromises out of harmony with a liberal peace program. He accepted a financial and territorial settlement for Germany likely to incense its people and make it difficult to bring a liberalized Germany into the world community; he approved territorial concessions, such as Japanese retention of the Shantung Peninsula, that infringed upon the principle of self-determination and constituted outright surrender to traditional power politics. Although Wilsonian idealism did not collapse beneath the weight of national demands, the president's program had begun to sag, a poor omen of things to come.

Wilson did not interpret his efforts at Paris as failure. Despite the bickering and need for compromise he felt he had salvaged a workable treaty. Above all he had obtained approval of the League of Nations, and functioning as anticipated—as Wilson anticipated —the league could correct mistakes in the treaty and preside over a world of peace and orderly change. The president returned to the United States in July 1919 convinced he had laid the groundwork for a new era. "The stage is set, the destiny disclosed," he proclaimed in placing the treaty before the Senate. "It has come about by no plan of our conceiving, but by the hand of God who led us into this way."

The struggle for acceptance of the treaty was of course Wilson's last major battle and a sad ending to what in some ways had been an outstanding presidency. Opposition immediately arose among senators who disliked both the form and substance of Wilson's foreign policy. Using every tactic of parliamentary obstruction, Republican critics subjected the treaty to "pitiless publicity," hoping to expose the slightest discrepancy in the long and complicated document. In the course of the extended debate the American popular attitude changed from enthusiasm for the league to confusion, then skepticism, and finally weariness. Americans developed many differing opinions, some favorable, some unfavorable, about the League of Nations; but at the end most seemed disturbed about the obligations implied in Article Ten and the prospect that America could lose control of its foreign policy. Like their counterparts in Europe, Americans placed their national interests first.

For all its shortcomings, the treaty might have passed had Wilson handled his duties differently. He took personal charge of negotiations throughout, in almost total disregard of the Senate, the Republican party, even public opinion. The compromises in Paris had lessened his prestige, particularly with liberals; long absence from the country, nearly six months, had had a bad effect on American opinion. When it became apparent that he could succeed only through compromise, the president refused and allowed the treaty to be defeated. To be sure, Republican critics behaved little better, for such senators as Henry Cabot Lodge were also personal and partisan; but the president had fostered this attitude by making the treaty personal on his part. Politics and personality so muddled the debate as to discourage a rational assessment, at that time or in later years, of Wilson's program, and it is not yet clear to what extent some senators were opposing the league, and to what extent they were resisting Wilson himself. As it was, the president suffered a bitter defeat. He lived on until 1924, nearly five years after his physical collapse; but his spirit died in 1920 with his league.

Perhaps it is better to say that Wilson's league did not die because it never came to life, and that the Senate did not reject an organization as much as an idea. The league survived for a generation without American membership, but it never functioned as Wilson had hoped. Leadership fell to the war-weary nations of western Europe, particularly Britain and France, which looked upon the league as an agency for enforcing the treaty and preserving the status quo. Their idea of justice, which did not mean abandoning empires, was closely related to what suited their national interests. The most one could have expected from the league was prevention, at least delay, of another large war; but the European powers were so weak and disunited that they failed. The league's most memorable legacy seemed the fact that the Second World War came so soon.

Stronger leadership might have preserved the European settlement longer, but the league had little chance of acting as Wilson's parliament of the world. Nations found it difficult to agree on basic rules because they seldom had common interests; they experienced different stages of development, different ideas of fairness and justice. While the league's purpose was to promote peace, order, and justice, the world possessed problems not likely to be solved in an orderly way. Satisfied nations, such as the United States, stressed order while dissatisfied states stressed change. Colonies wanted independence and nations wanted colonies; France wanted reparation and security from Germany, and Germany wanted restoration of lost territory and relief from an intolerable financial burden; Americans were satisfied with the prospect of a capitalist world, which Soviet leadership believed to be the worst of all possible evils. Small wonder the league did not function as Wilson had planned; small wonder its successor has had only slightly more success. The United Nations has experienced longer life than its predecessor and served as a useful sounding board for national grievances, but such large issues as the postwar government of China, the political structure of Europe, the status of Indochina, and even disarmament have been handled outside its chambers. These problems would not vanish in the presence of appeals to man's rationality and sense of justice. Even so, had Wilson returned to life some fifty or sixty years later and surveyed world history since his death and the problems ahead, he probably would have remained convinced of the need for a vastly different method of handling world affairs.

◇◇◇

Wilson's death and the end of the world war inspired an outpouring of books and articles that has continued with little interruption to the present. Scholars continue to show interest in Wilson's complex personality and all aspects of his presidential career, but his foreign policy intrigues them most of all. An obvious reason is that Wilson was president during a time of national and world crisis. He dealt with foreign problems because conditions forced him to do so; many were so complex that any policy undoubtedly would have invited criticism. The president, moreover, was an activist and innovator; he sought to make his office and country agents of change, to give foreign policy a distinct style, to show the way to a peaceful and better world.

After arguing for years the merits of the League of Nations and Wilson's effect on large-power diplomacy, historians during the tumultuous 1960s turned to new areas of concern. The important themes of that decade were not world order and parliamentary procedure but change and social justice. Wilsonian diplomacy seemed out of step with these movements, in view of the president's opposition to revolution and radicalism and his admiration for American capitalism. According to this new outlook, Wilsonian diplomacy did not fail; rather it had been all too successful. The president had provided a rationale for a dubious American policy in coming years; at worst he had encouraged suppression of social change and the construction of an American economic empire, thus contributing to making the United States the most conservative, perhaps the most greedy, nation in the world.

The argument has some measure of truth even though it rests on the questionable practice of applying contemporary values to conditions of another era. Wilson devoted much of his attention to finding order among the powers, to settling one war and preventing another, and not to the undeveloped—what many people then called "backward"—areas, where revolution came to be considered the only effective method of change, where capitalism could mean exploitation more often than economic betterment for the native population. Lacking a sophisticated understanding of the "third world," he viewed these areas with racial and national prejudices, and with belief in the universal acceptability of American institutions.

Wilson had made no secret of his fondness for capitalism. He encouraged American businessmen to seek markets abroad; his resistance to submarine warfare, whatever its tone, had the effect of protecting wartime commerce. He looked upon capitalism as economic reformism, a means of supplying goods and capital to areas without funds, a vast improvement over previous devices of outright colonial control or the old-type foreign concession, through which investors were nearly sovereign within technically independent states. He expected the system to function with advantage to buyer and seller, investor and citizen of the place of investment, and occasionally attacked concessionaires in China and Mexico who exercised excessive power. Wilson dreamed of a community of liberal democratic states willing to practice a system resembling free trade, and while he knew the United States would prosper in such a system he did not anticipate creation of an American order. The world was to have no overlord other than the League of Nations, which was supposed to handle all large matters of trade as well as politics. The flaw in Wilson's economic thinking came not from a desire to control the world, but from concern with the philosophy of capitalism rather than its application to given circumstances, and from his tendency to think in universal terms.

Some of the same observations applied to Wilson's attitude toward revolution and radicalism. An heir to the Civil War's violence, a product of middle-class upbringing (he might have thought differently had he worked, let us say, in Elbert Gary's steel mills), he had enduring faith in evolutionary democracy. In his mind revolution developed when an armed minority, unable to win popular support, sought to seize control. The object in all cases was to suppress the masses. As he told an audience in 1919: "If you have disorder, if you have disquieted population, you are going to have autocracy, because the strongest is going to seize power, as it has seized it in Russia. I want to declare that I am an enemy of the rulership of any minority, however constituted. Minorities often have been right and majorities wrong, but minorities cease to be right when they use the wrong means to make their opinions prevail. We must have peaceful means; we must have discussion." As recent scholars have stressed, Wilson opposed revolutionary socialism, but he also hoped to see the world free of militarism, monarchy, and dictatorship. Most revolutions of his day had been rightist efforts to seize power; until the

Bolshevik Revolution of 1917–18 he faced no major upheaval from the Left. From what he understood that revolution seemed no different, except perhaps in being more oppressive, from dictatorships in Latin America. Wilson's shortcoming was not a desire to prevent change, but a failure to appreciate ways by which change might take place.

Whatever the president's purposes, he left a powerful legacy that future generations might apply in different ways, some admirable, some of dubious wisdom. It is doubtful that Wilson would have approved all the policies the United States was to follow in later years, but his successors, in fighting the Second World War as in establishing global policies during the cold war, could believe they were following the true spirit of Wilsonianism.

No student can read the major expressions of Wilsonian diplomacy—the speeches and proclamations, the private messages to leaders abroad or individuals in the United States—without concluding that here was a well-meaning man promoting the cause of human dignity. He rejoiced at signs of success, brooded over indication of failure. One of his most difficult decisions at the peace conference permitted Japanese concessions in Shantung, an unwanted settlement that fostered imperialism in the Far East. Speaking to a friend a short time afterward, Wilson expressed his feelings: "He said that he had been unable to sleep the night before for thinking of it . . . [but that] the settlement was the best that could be had out of a dirty past. . . . The only hope was to keep the world together, get the League of Nations with Japan in it and then try to secure justice for the Chinese not only as regarding Japan but England, France, Russia, all of whom had concessions in China. . . . He knew his decision would be unpopular in America, . . . that he would be accused of violating his own principles, but nevertheless, he must work for world order and organization, against anarchy and a return to the old militarism." As a result of his efforts to reform world politics, Wilson became the symbol of American diplomatic idealism.

Unfortunately he also helped identify shortcomings of that approach. Good intention and moral purpose are admirable and often necessary in one nation's dealings with another, but alone they are not enough. Good intention lends itself to misinterpretation, can impede more practical if less high-minded efforts, and perhaps can lead to an inflexible self-righteousness. Supported with abundant treasure and an activist temperament, idealism can lead nations to take sides in factional disputes, even to impose one nation's standards on another. Wilson intervened in Latin America to relieve the masses of oppression, and in so doing sponsored oppression of a different sort. Perhaps governments cannot, nor should they always, refrain from moral judgments about their neighbors, but they should act only after careful consideration of what is the nation's business. The lesson applies acutely to large nations, such as the United States, with strength to impose their will. They otherwise stand the risk of justifying on grounds of moral correctness what in fact was only a matter of power.

It is not fair, however, to think of Wilson only in negative terms—the problems he did not solve, his lack of thoroughness in thought. Almost lost amid controversy over his ambitious plan has been the fact that he performed capably in the primary presidential function of protecting the security of the United States. His diplomacy preserved relations with western Europe and helped prevent European encroachment on the Western Hemisphere. He guided the nation through its greatest foreign war at that time, and without that effort Americans might have had to face a Europe dominated by the German army. When he left office the United States was more powerful than when he entered it in 1913. His league failed and its successor fell short of being a true parliament of nations, but the world refused to reject the idea of supranational authority. If it is true that power continues to be central in relations between states, it is no less true that those dealings often have been unsatisfactory to everyone concerned. Should the world advance beyond the nation-state to some higher political order—to, let us say, a federation of nations—the president at the time probably will lay a wreath at the grave of Woodrow Wilson.

BIBLIOGRAPHIC NOTE

Individuals who wish to study the Wilson period will find no shortage of published and unpublished materials. The files of the State Department at the National Archives in Washington are massive, as are Wilson's papers in the Library of Congress. Other valuable manuscript collections include the papers of Edward M. House in the Yale Library, the papers of William Jennings Bryan and Robert Lansing at the Library of Congress, and the papers of Walter Hines Page (the ambassador to Great Britain) at Harvard. One also can find much information about American policy in the records of the British Foreign Office and in private collections of such British officials as Sir Edward Grey, Lord Robert Cecil, Sir Cecil Spring Rice, and Arthur Balfour, all in the Public Record Office in London.

The student fortunately has easy access to many of the important papers through the State Department's excellent published series, *Papers Relating to the Foreign Relations of the United States.* The regular series, one volume per year, deals with normal diplomatic relations; the nine-volume *Supplements* cover the diplomacy of neutrality and war; and the thirteen volume *Paris Peace Conference* deals with peacemaking. A special two-volume supplement, *The Lansing Papers,* includes many private messages passed between members of the American government.

Of the many biographies of Woodrow Wilson the best brief studies are John Morton Blum, *Woodrow Wilson and the Politics of Morality* (Boston, 1956), and John A. Garraty, *Woodrow Wilson* (New York, 1956). Easily the most comprehensive coverage is Arthur S. Link's *Wilson,* 5 vols., (Princeton, 1947–65), a study that has several volumes yet to come having reached only to 1917. Marked by extensive research and scholarly objectivity, Link's work tends to give a balanced yet generally favorable treatment of its subject. Books focusing on Wilsonian diplomacy include Harley Notter's old but still useful *The Origins of the Foreign Policy of Woodrow Wilson* (Baltimore, 1937), Link's series of interpretive essays, *Wilson the Diplomatist: A Look at His Major Foreign Policies* (Baltimore, 1937), and N. Gordon Levin, Jr., *Woodrow Wilson and World Politics* (New York, 1968). Levin's volume is a penetrating and provocative analysis of Wilson's search for a liberal world order. It is questionable, however, whether Wilson would have agreed with the author's conclusion that America's global policies after 1945 constituted a "complete triumph" for "Wilsonian values." The multivolume publication of Wilson's papers, edited by Arthur S. Link, has not yet reached the presidential years.

For Wilson's secretaries of state the best studies are Daniel M. Smith, *Robert Lansing and American Neutrality, 1914–1917* (Berkeley, 1958), and Paolo E. Coletta, *William Jennings Bryan: Progressive Politician and Moral Statesman, 1909–1915* (Lincoln, Nebr., 1969). There is no good biography of Colonel House, but one can follow Wilson's relations with his friend in Alexander I. George and Juliette George, *Woodrow Wilson and Colonel House: A Personality Study* (New York, 1956), and in the important collection edited by Charles Seymour, *The Intimate Papers of Colonel House,* 4 vols. (Boston, 1926–28). A study by Ross Gregory, *Walter Hines Page: Ambassador to the Court of St. James's* (Lexington, Ky., 1970), discusses efforts by Page and Lansing to undermine the president's neutrality policies.

The period of neutrality has attracted a great amount of attention, much of it focusing on whether Wilson's neutrality policies were practical or idealistic. The realist point of view, which questions less the necessity for American intervention than the hopelessly moralistic tone of policy, comes out in George F. Kennan, *American Diplomacy, 1900–1950* (Chicago, 1950), Hans Morgenthau, *In Defense of the National Interest* (New York, 1951), and Robert E. Osgood, *Ideals and Self-Interest in American Foreign Relations* (Chicago, 1953). Recent volumes that have found considerable realism in Wilsonian diplomacy include Ernest R. May, *The World War and American Isolation, 1914–1917* (Cambridge, Mass., 1959), a book that first made extensive use of German documentary materials; and portions of the three most recent volumes of Link's huge biography. Examples of older "revisionist" criticism, a viewpoint that challenges both the tone and purpose of neutrality policy, are Walter Millis, *Road to War, 1914–1917* (Boston, 1935), and Charles C. Tansill, *America Goes to War* (Boston, 1938). Two recent brief accounts that find Wilson moved by multiple factors, some practical, some idealistic, are Daniel M. Smith, *The Great Departure: The United States and World War I, 1914–1920* (New York, 1965), and Ross Gregory, *The Origins of American Intervention in the First World War* (New York, 1971).

Students unfortunately do not yet have a good, up-to-date, single-volume account of Wilson's handling of the Treaty of Versailles and League of Nations. Scholars thus have had to rely on older books, specialized works, or the brief coverage in general studies of Wilson. Still useful are the old books by Thomas A. Bailey, *Woodrow Wilson and the Lost Peace* (New York, 1944), and *Woodrow Wilson and the Great Betrayal* (New York, 1945). Lawrence E. Gelfand in *The Inquiry: American Preparations for Peace, 1917–1919* (New Haven, 1963) has investigated Wilson's extensive preparation for peacemaking. Much recent attention has been devoted to the attitude of the United States toward events in Russia at the end of the war. The volume by Levin and Arno J. Mayer's *Politics and Diplomacy of Peacemaking* (New York, 1967) focus on the conflict between Wilson's liberalism and Lenin's revolutionary socialism at the peace conference and in the world. William Appleman Williams in *American-Russian Relations, 1781–1947* (New York, 1952) has argued that American policies in Russia were concerned most with overthrowing bolshevism, and George F. Kennan, in *Soviet-American Relations, 1917–1920,* 2 vols. (Princeton, 1956–58), has found other factors more important. For the treaty in the United States one should consult Bailey's volume, such specialized studies as Ralph Stone, *The Irreconcilables: The Fight against the League of Nations* (Lexington, Ky., 1970), and general works on Wilson. The last volumes of Link's biography are much needed and awaited.

Courtesy, Carnegie Endowment
for International Peace

PEACE WAS HIS PROFESSION:

JAMES T. SHOTWELL

and American Internationalism

Charles DeBenedetti

The death of James Shotwell in his spacious Manhattan apartment in 1965 at the age of ninety-one set off a flow of tributes that he had seldom known in life. *Time* marked the passing of a "tireless advocate of international political co-operation," while the *New York Times* eulogized "a statesman without portfolio." Certainly Shotwell's career justified both judgments. Though a historian and foundation official by occupation, he was by temperament an indefatigable private diplomat. For some forty years he worked tirelessly to organize peace. Oscillating between government service and private action, Shotwell sought to rationalize international politics by involving the United States and other nations in cooperative ventures for world order. His campaign began in 1917, when Woodrow Wilson initiated America's massive involvement in European politics, and it crested in 1945 when America and its allies established the United Nations. In between, the Canadian-born historian undertook numerous individual actions that in their

entirely embodied a robust definition of the place of internationalism in American diplomacy. Long before the Strategic Air
Command pledged to stand ready to atomize the world for peace,
he and his fellow internationalists struggled to overcome the
irrational impulses within international politics through the creation of an orderly structure that promised peace with change.
Peace was their profession—a profession in faith, and a profession
in common action.

Shotwell's vision of world politics gained its focus from the
American internationalist tradition that evolved in the first two
decades of the twentieth century. Conjuring the dream of a world
order founded on cooperation and comity, assorted aspects of the
internationalist approach to world politics long had appealed to
members of the American policy-making elite. Legalists such as
former Secretary of State Elihu Root favored the extension of
international law in patterns cut by the American judicial experience. Arbitrationists such as William Howard Taft supported
treaties of binding conciliation, while the militant nationalist
followers of Senator Henry Cabot Lodge sought to build a league
to enforce peace. World War I exerted a transforming effect upon
internationalism in America. The shocking sweep of violence,
combined in 1917 with the reality of revolution and President
Wilson's feverish promises of a New Diplomacy, produced a new
internationalist faith evolving from two beliefs: that war was a
social evil vulnerable to planned elimination and that the most
disastrous kind of war—total war—invariably resulted from mal-
function of the unreformed European state system. More Europe-
anist than internationalist, Wilsonian internationalists after 1917
did not seek global activism for the United States so much as
American supervision of Europe's mismanaged politics through
the League of Nations system. Dreading the next war and
confident of the pacifying power of America's influence, progressive internationalists resolved to persuade the American people to
support the great work as independent supervisor of relations
among the European powers. Peace for the world would come
through the pacification of Europe, and that grand aim was
possible—if the great powers accepted the systematization of
their relations under America's independent direction as expressed through the league. Peace need not be enforced; it had
only to be managed.

As the leading exponent of Wilsonian internationalism in

interwar America, James Shotwell led the campaign for a managed peace. During this period he operated in numerous capacities. Trained as a medievalist, he began teaching at Columbia University in 1900. Twenty years later, still a Columbia faculty member, he assumed an official position with the Carnegie Endowment for International Peace. In addition, he acted from time to time as an adviser to governments, an organizer of international committees, a public speaker, a publicist, a poet, and the driving force behind several pressure groups and organizations. Shotwell also served as an observer and occasional participant in the crucial events of his time.

A man of incurable optimism and simple decency, Shotwell worked unceasingly after 1917 to effect the ideology of liberal internationalism that Woodrow Wilson had so rousingly proclaimed but had never defined. More than anyone of his time, Shotwell gave substance to the vision of orderliness, rationality, measured change, expert planning, and free trade through multilateral action that undergirded Wilson's hopes and still remains at the center of the ideal world of American liberalism. Shaken by the revolutionary effects of World War I, Shotwell set out to revive the components of the Wilsonian coalition that had disintegrated during the fight over the League of Nations. He welded internationalist ideology and its followers into a force that exerted strong appeal for those who conducted American foreign relations in the years between 1920 and 1945. Liberal internationalism survived not because of lingering regard for Wilson, but largely because of Shotwell's work.

Shotwell's internationalist vision emerged from concern with what he identified as the most stubborn conflict of his time: the clash of scientific and industrial dynamism against entrenched social habits. Portraying himself as a concerned social scientist, he insisted that the power of scientific discovery constituted "the greatest revolution in all human history from the Ice Age down." He felt, however, that its ramifications were lost among peoples encased in prescientific habits. Although awed by the force of the scientific and industrial revolutions, Shotwell never forgot the frustration of flying from London to Paris in two hours in 1919 and then having to wait for five hours while government officials cleared him through customs. The experience impressed him as a classic example of the enormous cost that resulted from the failure to adapt social practices to scientific advances.

Preoccupation with the conflict between scientific dynamism and social-political *immobilisme* began early in Shotwell's tenure at Columbia. There he taught innovative courses in the history of the industrial revolution and formed close friendships with Charles A. Beard and James Harvey Robinson, two colleagues who shared his interest in the relationships among science, industrialism, and democracy. Before the war, Shotwell gravitated with them toward a group of "scientific progressives," New Yorkers who were united in the belief that the scientific mode of inquiry and planning offered the best hope for liberal democracy in an industrial America. Inspired by the philosopher John Dewey and the journalist Walter Lippmann, Shotwell and his friends held that cadres of experts, spreading the gospel of efficiency through instruments of technology, could guide American democracy through the stresses of spreading industrialization. Their message was gaining a respectable audience when the First World War suddenly intensified the complexity of their task and presented a challenging new forum for their plans. As a result, the dream of constructing a mass democratic order in industrial America expanded to embrace the world.

The formal basis of Shotwell's world view appeared between 1917 and 1920, when he enlisted his faith in the scientific approach to social issues in Wilson's crusade for reform of the international system. His guiding values were unspoken but explicit. Presupposing the existence of a universal moral order, he believed that peace, free trade, individual liberty, and free inquiry were hopes natural to all men. He further assumed that these hopes would flourish best through the global influence of the Anglo-American peoples. Certain that the advent of scientific warfare had finally ended America's isolation from the Old World, Shotwell demanded that the U.S. cooperate with England in pacifying Europe. This was to be accomplished through institutionalized reason, not force; through organized intelligence, not arms. He feared excessive American intervention abroad, and he opposed the idea of peace through deterrence, which meant threats of physical retaliation against aggressively ambitious states. While recognizing that lasting peace rested on material foundations, he pressed for a peace of conciliation that would thrive as people cooperatively sought more rational control over "those questions of economic and social justice which are the fundamental issues behind war."

Organized peace might begin in deterrence, but it could survive only through conciliation.

Beyond these basic assumptions, Shotwell's world view developed in response to practical experiences. In 1917 he proclaimed himself "an academic war casualty" and joined the National Board for Historical Services, a group of historians recruited to justify America's war policies by past precedent. He quit after four months to help Colonel Edward M. House and Walter Lippmann assemble the nation's top social scientists in the Inquiry, an organization intended to arm the president with an objective assessment of world conditions. Shotwell and other Inquiry leaders later assisted American negotiators at the Paris Peace Conference in the formation of the International Labor Organization. Fearful of mounting revolutionary sentiment throughout Europe, the Columbia historian identified the ILO as the liberal capitalist alternative to advancing socialism. Indeed, he characterized the infant organization as the prototype of a new line of functional institutions that would reconcile classes in industrial society and thereby maintain the social basis of international law and order.

The second phase in the development of Shotwell's world view occurred in the 1920s, as he gained fuller comprehension of the interdependence of industrial nations. For the Carnegie Endowment in 1920 he initiated the vast *Economic and Social History of the World War*, an attempt to determine the precise impact of modern war upon advanced societies. With an international staff of cooperating analysts, Shotwell directed the Carnegie project in gathering evidence that pointed toward the inescapable conclusion that war was no longer a viable instrument of national policy. The wizardry of science had transformed war into an enterprise whose incalculable destructiveness ended its historic usefulness as a means of national power. In an interdependent world of science and industry, unilateral violence jeopardized the well-being of every member state. It was imperative, Shotwell told an audience of German military and civilian leaders in 1927, for statesmen to realize "that *Machtpolitik* is no longer *Realpolitik*." The careless romanticism of power politics had to give way to the higher realism of cooperative action.

Shotwell also became convinced in the 1920s that social scientists were formulating a real methodology of international peace. He often compared the expanding science of peace studies with the state of economics in the 1770s, when Scotland's brilliant Adam Smith "transferred the science of Political Economy from the field of vague philosophy to that of an inductive science." In the same way, Shotwell argued, experts were beginning to demonstrate empirically that each nation shared vitally in the health and wealth of the entire international community. Shotwell's recurring references to Adam Smith likewise served as a striking reminder of his tendency to equate the development of "peace science" with the beneficent expansion of American business enterprise. Convinced that Washington officials opposed tributary colonialism, he believed that the American organization of peace depended in large measure upon the ability of other states to consume U.S. products, a problem that carried back "to the original problem of Adam Smith: how can the prosperity of our nation be increased through the increased prosperity of others?" Like Smith, Shotwell believed that the answer to that question lay in greater industrial productivity and free trade. The same forces that were sweeping advanced peoples toward fuller interdependence and shared material prosperity would someday "substitute for the passing armistice of nations an enduring peace."

Shotwell's interest in an operating science of peace subsided in the 1930s as Germany and Japan moved toward aggressive expansion. At first he responded ambiguously, urging America to cooperate with the league but at the same time advising Geneva to act with restraint in meeting threats to peace. Attributing expansionist impulses to economic factors, he called for international agreements on more equitable access for all industrial powers to overseas markets and sources of raw materials. A strong defender of the Open Door, he praised the preferences of Cordell Hull's State Department for free trade and worked closely with Thomas J. Watson, president of the International Business Machines Corporation and treasurer of the Carnegie Endowment, to promote "world peace through world trade." At the same time, Shotwell played a central role in fusing America's polyglot peace movement into a coherent political force. Joining pacifists Kirby Page and Ray Newton in 1935, he organized the Emergency Peace Campaign for the peaceful revision of the international status quo and reform of the world economic system. Increasingly, however, his revulsion against Nazi excesses and Japanese aggressiveness drove him to demand that America align with the Allied cause. By 1939 his attitude of scientific detachment in international politics had given way to a fear that the planet was split between authoritarian aggressors and peaceable Anglo-American democracies. A London-Washington axis became the new core of his liberal internationalism; peace depended on continued preeminence of that axis.

The final phase in the development of Shotwell's world view took place after the outbreak of the Second World War. He and his close friend Clark Eichelberger founded the Commission to Study the Organization of Peace, basically another attempt to mobilize experts in search of a rationalized peace. In addition, he helped the State Department in wartime to plan a postwar international organization. Shotwell functioned in these matters according to his old faith in the beneficence of rationalism, functionalism, organized expertise, expanding free trade, and guarantees of social justice; however, he strikingly emphasized the deterrent power of a peace-keeping agency in moments of urgent crisis. In the early 1940s, for the first time, Shotwell called for an American military commitment to a collective security system and for creation of a genuine international police force. The decade of world crisis left a remarkable imprint upon his approach to world order. The prevention of war had become as important as the preservation of peace.

Shotwell's acceptance of the need for American participation in the enforcement of peace was symptomatic of the larger shift among liberal internationalists late in the 1930s to interventionism. Wilsonians had long tried to straddle the contrary claims of cosmopolitan internationalism and nationalistic interventionism. Most recognized that slight—but profound—differences separated the two approaches to foreign affairs. Where internationalists viewed peace in a social and economic perspective, interventionists defined it as a military enterprise. Where internationalists urged American action through collective agencies, interventionists supported unfettered freedom of action for the U.S. Where internationalists saw the American interest in world order as conditional and specific to certain European developments, interventionists perceived the nation's interest as universal and immutable.

Friction between the two approaches flashed periodically. In 1918 Shotwell and his compatriots had organized the League of

Free Nations Association (parent of the present-day Foreign Policy Association) as a liberal alternative to the interventionist League to Enforce Peace and as the true defender of Wilson's ideals. Nine years later during the Nicaraguan crisis and again in 1931 over the Manchurian question, liberal internationalist forces behind Shotwell (who urged moderation in Washington) further clashed with interventionists such as Henry Stimson who were demanding forceful action by the United States. The violent and rapid crises of the 1930s, however, rallied Wilsonians behind demands for American intervention against the Axis. Confronted with Hitler's ambition, internationalists subordinated their pleas for American support of a collective order to the more immediate necessity of American intervention in the European war. Ironically, their short-term success was a long-term disaster. By pressing for intervention in the European struggle, internationalists converted the Wilsonian vision of America's world role into a new set of images. They began to urge the American people to become the guard and not merely the supervisor, enforcer and not merely manager, of a reconstituted global system. With that shift in emphasis there arose a self-justifying rationale for expansion that carried American physical power across western Europe and throughout former European colonial dominions at an economic and moral cost that may never be fully calculated.

Although his outlook and assumptions were fundamental to his work as a private diplomat, Shotwell's technique was equally important. As a professional peace seeker with solid intellectual credentials, he nonetheless confronted that perennial problem of the man of ideas in the world of politics. He had intellectual independence but no political base, influence but no power; he had attracted the attention of court patrons, but not the ear of the king. Lacking the support of a political party or powerful faction, Shotwell worked indirectly by building extrapolitical pressure groups and by filtering ideas into the policy-making process. This strategy enabled him to pursue three distinct but interrelated tactical approaches. He first organized and directed groups of experts in collecting data and proposing feasible alternatives to the use of force for consideration by policy makers. Secondly, he attempted to affect national policy through contacts with informal

pressure groups and influential political figures. Finally, he assisted
the internationalist wing of American business through groups
such as the Council on Foreign Relations and the International
Chamber of Commerce in forming economic ties across national
boundaries.

A quietly persuasive man, Shotwell liked to lead informal
committees in conducting research, gathering data, writing
memos, formulating draft treaties, and issuing reports. Once his
position was established, he tried to advance it through an
informal network of contacts in Washington, New York, and
foreign capitals. In a parallel way he recognized the importance of
public support and worked assiduously through writings,
speeches, and publicity mechanisms of the organized peace
movement to energize popular sentiment behind the many causes
he supported. Although Shotwell preferred to shape policy
through private means, he remained always mindful of the
imperative of sympathetic public opinion.

Shotwell, along with several groups of experts, gave continuing attention to the effort to form an international body of peace
managers. As noted previously, his first ventures in this direction
took place in 1917, when he collaborated with other scholars in
the Inquiry, and two years later, when he helped establish the
International Labor Organization as a voluntary international
agency where technicians and specialists would propose standards for proper governmental behavior.

While setting up the ILO, Shotwell formed close and valuable
friendships with international experts in other countries. He
expanded this circle of connections between 1920 and 1937, while
he was general editor of the *Economic and Social History of the
World War*. Indeed, he had accepted that post with the intent of
using it to erect a network of foreign policy experts who favored
the League of Nations and more extensive international cooperation. He crisscrossed the Atlantic several times in the twenties to
organize scholars and government officials for the Carnegie study
and to build an embryonic community of peace scientists. His
efforts brought him especially close to figures such as the French
economist Jean Monnet, the German economist Albrecht Men-
delssohn-Bartholdy, the Austrian historian Joseph Redlich, and the
English journalist David Mitrany. Not one of these men exercised
direct, decisive influence on policy within his nation, but all
occupied influential positions within the governing circles of their

respective countries. Further, all were men of rank and distinction within the larger European liberal community from which Shotwell hoped to draw the proponents and shapers of a world order.

Shotwell became director of the Division of Economics and History of the Carnegie endowment in 1924, a position that gave him great mobility and even larger influence. Three years later, he became chairman of the Committee on International Relations of the Social Science Research Council and director of research for the American branch of the nascent Institute of Pacific Relations. He participated in meetings of the institute in Honolulu in 1927 and in Kyoto in 1929, where he maintained that the calm discussion of critical Pacific issues offered new hope that past prejudices among peoples were giving way to a collective "strategy of peace." Though unfolding events mocked that hope, Shotwell refused to abandon his plans to organize the world's peace experts. In 1932 he accepted the chairmanship of the American branch of the Committee for Intellectual Co-operation. Quartered at the League of Nations, the CIC sought to unite scholars and intellectuals in the work of understanding the cultural and ethnic diversity that international organizations must respect. It was a unique, if increasingly isolated, center for rational dialogue in a world that was visibly sinking into a morass of renewed tribal hatreds.

Appalled by nationalistic excesses, Shotwell pursued various political activities in the 1930s that prevented him from engaging in any further organization of peace experts until November 1939, when he and Clark Eichelberger established the Commission to Study the Organization of Peace. Its membership ranged from former league officials such as Huntington Gilchrist and Arthur Sweetser to the financier Thomas Lamont and the historian Henry Steele Commager. Its members all believed that a lasting peace required a new international organization. To be effective and endure, this international agency had to be rational in structure, efficient in operation, resistant to forced change, and responsive to the universal human desire for social justice.

When it came to influencing issues of immediate national policy, Shotwell was not averse to involving himself directly in politics. The Inquiry had exposed him initially to the business of shaping policy at the highest level, and he never forgot its seductive pleasures. In 1924 he reorganized his former Inquiry associates into the American Committee of Disarmament and

Security, an informal effort to help the league powers deal with Europe's two most intractable problems. The committee drafted a formal Treaty of Disarmament and Security for the league's consideration, hoping "to supplant emotion by intelligence where intelligence is most needed." Some of the group's proposals were attached to the abortive Geneva Protocol of 1924, but Europe generally ignored this unofficial exercise in applied intelligence. Undaunted, Shotwell took advantage of the situation to create four cooperating committees of experts overseas. More importantly, the committee experience led him to conclude that U.S. neutrality constituted the largest obstruction to European disarmament. With neither Britain nor France willing to move without at least tacit U.S. support, America's hands-off attitude checked any hope of meeting Europe's overriding need for disarmament through the league system. A neutral and indifferent America, Shotwell concluded, posed the main barrier to organizing European peace and a saner world order.

For the next eight years, Shotwell struggled to revise neutrality and align American power with the league system. The most memorable incident in his campaign for neutrality revision came in March 1927 when he persuaded French Foreign Minister Aristide Briand to call for a Franco-American treaty to "outlaw war." For Briand, a joint renunciation of war with the U.S. promised to bolster French security by discouraging France's enemies. For Shotwell, the French bid provided an opening wedge in the close alignment of American neutrality with France and the league. Neither anticipated the imaginative resilience of hostile Republicans. Instead of rejecting Briand's olive branch openly, a decision sure to be unpopular, the secretary of state, Frank B. Kellogg, shrewdly channeled the French offer into the innocuous Kellogg-Briand Pact of 1928, a peace pact that joined sixty-two nations in a dual pledge to renounce war as an instrument of national policy and to use only pacific means to settle disputes. At Secretary of State Kellogg's insistence, however, it contained no distinction between covenant keeper and covenant breaker and thus no framework for the alignment of America with the league. Still, Shotwell continued the fight. He claimed that America's renunciation of war in the Kellogg pact bound Washington not to abet aggression through neutrality. He worked closely with Republican Senator Arthur Capper of Kansas and the League of Nations Association to convert the peace pact into a usable link between America and the league. That connection would come, he believed, as soon as Washington vowed never to permit its neutral trading position to assist a state that had broken the Kellogg pact by unilateral use of force as an instrument of national policy.

Shotwell's attempts to unite the U.S. and the league through the Kellogg pact persisted until 1933, when the continuing crisis in Manchuria and Hitler's rise to power gave greater immediacy to the management of conflict. While urging American cooperation with the League of Nations, he criticized Geneva for its censorious attitude toward Japan's actions in Asia. "The implication of force to police the world toward agreement will not succeed," he declared. "We must try to find that measure of agreement which substantially coincides with the belief of both parties. That is the basis of permanent peace." He helped organize two successive peace coalitions to generate American support for international economic reform and the collective preservation of order. He attacked the powers for abandoning the league as an organized means of peaceable action, and he urged league leaders to reorganize the Geneva system in a realistic way that reflected the varying interests of the powers in the maintenance of global stability. In order to survive, the league had to recognize that each state held a specific place on the "rim" of concentric circles that encompassed the "abyss" of a new European war.

Throughout the thirties, Shotwell's political activities were conducted at a discreet distance from official Washington. Though known to Secretary of State Cordell Hull and familiar with presidential advisers Norman Davis and Sumner Welles, he did not possess direct access to the corridors of power when President Roosevelt maneuvered warily in the face of powerful isolationist forces. Shotwell's reputation as an outspoken proponent of fuller American responsibility for world order excluded him from a visible place of influence in New Deal Washington. Yet, he did not permit Roosevelt's anxieties to interfere with his private efforts. In 1935 he inspired an unsuccessful attempt by Senator James Pope of Idaho to align America with the league on the condition that Geneva accept the Paris peace pact as the touchstone of its policies. In the same year, he assumed the presidency of the League of Nations Association and for the next four years led the fight to revise American neutrality. In the spring of 1940 he joined the Policy Committee of The Committee to Defena America by Aiding the Allies. Formed by Clark Eichelberger behind the

AN UNFORTUNATE OMISSION AT THE INTERNATIONAL REGATTA.

INTERNATIONAL COOPERATION

Morning Post *(London)*, 1933

nominal leadership of the journalist William Allen White, the committee worked to build public pressure on behalf of U.S. assistance to beleaguered Britain. For Shotwell, the decade that began with a crusade to preserve peace in Europe through American cooperation with the league ended in a battle to propel the United States into a European war.

After Pearl Harbor, Shotwell's respectability rose appreciably in Washington. He was named to the State Department's Advisory Planning Committee which was responsible for planning the postwar organization of international peace keeping, and he contributed substantially to the work of the committee. Then, Shotwell worked toward mobilizing public sentiment behind administration plans for a new international organization. He attended the founding of the United Nations at San Francisco in 1945 and took understandable pride in this confirmation of America's leadership in internationalism. At the same time, he worried about the sincerity of Washington's commitment to the new world organization, for there was little evidence of a true internationalist spirit among top figures in the Truman administration. Shotwell's doubts multiplied in August 1945 when the atomic destruction of Hiroshima and Nagasaki fulfilled his fear of the apocalyptic power of modern science in an immature international system. Within weeks of the dawn of the atomic age, Shotwell was busily organizing new groups of experts in an effort to internationalize America's atomic secrets and make real the UN's potential for global leadership.

From his concern for the power of science and industry, Shotwell fashioned a third tactical approach to influence policy making: cooperation with the internationalist wing of American business. Between 1919 and 1921 he played a central role in forming the Council on Foreign Relations, the dominant private influence on foreign policy for the next half-century. Also in 1921 he figured in the calling of the Porto Rosa Conference, a meeting of those Balkan states concerned with the economic revitalization of southeastern Europe. When the conference began to flounder in ancient animosities, Shotwell arranged with friends in the International Chamber of Commerce to intervene with a plea for economic efficiency in the Danube Basin. The ICC intervened too late with too little to salvage the conference, but its presence highlights Shotwell's multifaceted operations. Convinced that capitalism meant peace, he collaborated with business groups in continuing attempts to advance a world system in which "diplomacy instead of being geared to the army and navy will be linked into the great structure of international business."

Instead of shaking his faith in the existing order, the Great Crash and Depression reinforced Shotwell's belief in the costliness of world war and in the need for fuller trading opportunities for all peoples. He worked closely with Thomas J. Watson and contributed periodically to the IBM journal, *Think*. With Watson's encouragement, Shotwell supported Secretary of State Hull's efforts to negotiate reciprocal trade agreements and headed extensive investigations into the weaknesses and needs of the international trading community. In 1938 he headed a study of "World Economic Co-operation" which detailed the interrelationship of freer world trade and a stable peace. Six years later he wrote a report for the Committee on International Economic Policy, a distinguished group of business leaders, which repeated the demand for a more open world trading community and cooperative planning toward international reconstruction. Like all Wilsonians, Shotwell believed strongly that freedom for business meant freedom from strife.

◇◇◇

To all of his endeavors, James Shotwell brought conviction, enthusiasm, and a determination to build world order because it was necessary and right. He had tremendous appeal within the country's internationalist constituency, a large and potentially powerful group. A smooth writer with a convincing style, he produced several books and scores of articles for journals ranging from *Foreign Affairs* to *The Christian-Evangelist*. Also a popular public speaker, he exerted particular influence among church groups and women's organizations. Informative but not didactic, inspiring but not obscure, he succeeded as an extraordinarily able advocate of the causes he championed. At the same time, he operated as an effective private negotiator and an active force in committee sessions. A master of planning and publicity, organization and agitation, he pursued a dual career: one private, one public; one behind the scenes, one on center stage. This dualism was in practice complementary and vital to the policy alternatives that he so energetically sought. A firm but gentle crusader, he thought carefully before he acted; yet he acted forcefully when necessary.

Shotwell never defined or implemented any one foreign policy decision for the United States. Nonetheless, he contributed richly to the American diplomatic experience. A liberal in the tradition of William Gladstone and Woodrow Wilson, Shotwell was the most active and articulate exponent of the credo—consisting of reason, service, orderliness, benevolent capitalism, and cooperative progress beyond class conflict—that constituted the Wilsonian legacy in post-Versailles America. Wilson had proclaimed the beatitudes of world order and American international activism; it was left to Shotwell and his associates to give strength to the unsteady body of principles that the president had suggested. To a much greater extent than most have appreciated, the internationalism of Woodrow Wilson was more the work of the disciples than of the master.

As Shotwell and others advanced the faith after 1919, Wilsonianism signified the call for an organized peace that was anchored in Anglo-American power, rationalized by scientific experts, and couched in the rhetoric of democratic liberalism. It was thus a liberal prescription for a peace founded on expert knowledge and reasoned reconciliation. Shotwell believed that new techniques of planned cooperative diplomacy had to replace balance of power politicking and was convinced that the productive power of modern industrialism demanded a manageable world order supervised by experts and functioning through "the machinery of discussion." Opposed to European colonialism and military adventures, Shotwell sought an international system that would preserve order with prosperity; he wanted liberalism to function as "an instrument of liberation" instead of "an apology for things as they are." He looked mainly to America to bring about, through rationalization of industrial society at home and abroad, a cooperative international system that would minimize disorder and spread the material basis of a lasting peace.

Shotwell and other liberal internationalists assumed that their model world organization would control the momentum of the two most explosive forces of modern times: egotistic nationalism and interlocking science. As international observers who took pride in their realism, these men understood clearly the attractions offered by modern nationalism. In addition, they were proudly nationalistic in their own right and convinced that the United States had a special responsibility to extend its brand of progress. Wilson's greatest achievement, Shotwell said, was to issue a global challenge "which accepted nationalism but turned it against itself." In the same way, Shotwell and his associates sought to generate from the diversity of nationalism a collective force that defined the common good through calm analysis and rational action. Organized in a consensual structure and linked to advancing science, nationalism would thus become the principal means to attain a liberal, cosmopolitan world of general order, economic stability, and individual freedom. Nationalism and science, joined through the rational adaptability of pragmatic liberalism, would provide twin engines of progress within a new, dynamic, and reliable international order.

Shotwell's continuing fascination with nationalism and science equipped him at once with a sense of realism and a yearning toward idealism. Hardly a befuddled utopian, he perceived science as the most potent force for transforming international politics. Often his perception enabled him to view matters with the kind of striking prescience that he exhibited in the dark spring of 1941, when he declared, "The greatest fact in the world today is not to be found in the European war, vast and portentous as that war is, but in those laboratories where the atom may yield potentialities utterly beyond the control of any master of military powers." Yet, Shotwell's respect for facts and reality was juxtaposed with an abiding faith in the beneficence of science and human reason. Throughout his life he consistently refused to concede that man was bound to distort the power of science for antihuman ends. An irrepressible optimist, he insisted that progress was advancing in his own time as science joined liberalism, democracy, and intelligence in a structure of peace that promised order with justice: "The increasing mastery of time and of space and of human conditions makes us more and more dependent upon each other, and this process will go on increasingly from now until the end of time. With science we are turning a corner on the long road of human evolution. It is the newest thing since the ice age and the most potent. It is intelligence in action. But intelligence cannot achieve its true purposes under the iron compulsions of war; its vital need is freedom, without which it withers and dies no matter what material resources are placed at its command. For this fundamental condition of life, it will sacrifice everything, face all odds. Seen in this light, science is the final, and invincible, ally of peace, and scientific war is destined to be a contradiction in terms." If Shotwell and other internationalists sounded naïve, it was because hope in the future and faith in their fellow men infused their beliefs.

In most ways, Shotwell's hope sprang from his devotion to the tenets of Anglo-American liberalism. He was plainly a reformer, a working pragmatist who proposed to adjust the existing international system to those massive displacements brought about by the collision of war, science, and social change. A tinkerer by temperament, he hoped to establish institutions that would allow for controlled change in the belief that peace flourished in an environment of liberalism (which he defined as "the upbuilding of fair dealing and fair thinking between nations"). Liberalism and liberal institutions offered the best tools for nations' attempts to deal in a scientific and organized way with a world of daily change. Like other internationalists, Shotwell had little confidence in popular control of diplomacy. He clearly preferred expert over democratic direction and feared that popular ignorance of world politics formed the chief breeding ground for mindless jingoism. Only expert analysis by an international "creative scientific mind" could educate the masses to awareness of the world's complexity.

Unfortunately, the power of expert analysis failed Shotwell and his friends when it became necessary to penetrate the fundamental content and direction of American diplomacy. Though he often criticized specific national policies, the Columbia scholar never attacked the American diplomatic establishment or the cluster of ruling groups that establishment represented in world affairs. He and his colleagues much preferred dabbling in institutions of world order to questioning the policy-making process and the distribution of authority within the United States. Satisfied with the domestic structure of power, liberal internationalists were incapable of mounting a fundamental challenge to this system, though to have done so might have compelled American policy makers to forego the politics of unilateralism and to seek the nation's highest interests in international cooperation. Shotwell and his friends elected to work as the servants and not the critics of power; it was a choice that would cost them their distinctive status and ultimately their cause.

The failure of liberal internationalists to analyze the structural deficiencies within American diplomacy reflected their tendency to view the world through the distorting lenses of American liberal nationalism. Shotwell and his associates too often identified the needs of humanity with the interests of the American political economy. Deceived by their own nationalistic and class biases, they badly underestimated the abiding unilateralism of most followers of Wilson and grossly overestimated their commitment to the principle of international organization. This compound error was tolerable in the years to 1938, when the Wilsonian faith was formally excluded from policy considerations that were basically isolationist; but their misjudgment was disastrous after 1938, when Washington grafted the old faith onto a policy of renewed global activism. This Wilsonianism was not the flexible formula that Shotwell had advanced for meeting changing international conditions through a consensual order; rather it represented a stiffening determination to apply the power of the United States unilaterally throughout the world against expansive authoritarian nations. Successive administrations in Washington adopted the Wilsonianism of liberal interventionism, not that of liberal internationalism. This legacy of Woodrow Wilson bespoke the moral universalism of such imperial proconsuls as Henry Stimson, and not the rational interdependency of James Shotwell.

The modern creed of liberal interventionism, which Stimson and his successors have disguised since the late thirties as liberal internationalism, assumed that peace among nations was not interdependent and regionally segmented but rather a fabric that was one and indivisible. Other tenets grew quickly from this central conviction, each rooted in the implicit belief that the Western powers could have prevented the Second World War and consequent Soviet expansion through early cooperation under America's militant direction. By the formula of liberal interventionism, revolutionary states that rejected American influence were authoritarian; authoritarian states consumed with ideological fervor were totalitarian; totalitarian states were aggressive; aggressor states were insatiable, and they inevitably menaced the integrity of peace. The preservation of American security through order therefore depended upon containment or elimination of hostile revolutionary governments anywhere at any time. Although more universalist than internationalist, this reasoning came to appear self-evident to those who matured amid the ugly events of the 1930s. The completion of the circle ironically vitiated the dream of true internationalism, the dream of an organized peace of interdependent powers. Once Washington equated its security with an indivisible global order, "realism" demanded neglect of those interdependent agencies that had already proven their incapacity to maintain order after Versailles. A peace based on cooperation was inadequate to the fears of Wilsonian interventionists, even those who professed to seek such a system. Only an armed America could be relied upon to protect *world* law and order.

Because of his nationalism and pragmatism, Shotwell contributed in some measure to the interventionist credo of the "national security liberals" who have militarized American foreign policy out of a determination to prevent a repetition of the disastrous events of the thirties. Yet the essential spirit of Shotwell's contribution to the American diplomatic tradition was contrary to the unbending unilateralism that successive liberal interventionists, running in a bipartisan line from Henry Stimson to Dean Acheson to Richard Nixon, have tried to disguise as a fulfillment of the nation's commitment to the ideals of collective security and international cooperation. Open, intelligent, sensitive, and cosmopolitan, Shotwell was genuinely concerned with the unity of all the industrial peoples in a commonwealth ensuring freedom, prosperity, and order. He responded energetically to countless challenges, but he believed that the largest question before his generation was whether industrial man could employ organized political intelligence to establish global institutions that could control the awesome physical power uncovered by organized scientific intelligence. James Shotwell approached this question in ways that were often superficial and frequently wrong; nevertheless, he was more successful than any other diplomatist in preatomic America in posing and pursuing what has surely become the paramount problem of our time.

BIBLIOGRAPHIC NOTE

Of available published studies, *The Autobiography of James T. Shotwell* (Indianapolis, 1961) provides the most comprehensive survey of the internationalist's life. Harold Josephson's unpublished dissertation, "James Thomson Shotwell: Historian as Activist," University of Wisconsin, 1968, is a thoughtful and critical work and includes a valuable bibliographical essay on Shotwell's many writings.

Scientific Progressivism is a notion described in Ronald C. Tobey's

The American Ideology of National Science, 1919–1930 (Pittsburgh, 1971). The milieu that shaped this concept is brilliantly analyzed in Morton G. White's *Social Thought in America: The Revolt against Formalism* (New York, 1949) and Charles G. Forcey's *The Crossroads of Liberalism: Croly, Weyl, Lippmann and the Progressive Era, 1900–1925* (New York, 1961). Bernard Crick's *The American Science of Politics: Its Origins and Conditions* (London, 1959) succeeds modestly in examining a topic that deserves much wider consideration.

Internationalist thinking in America before 1920 is surveyed extensively in Warren F. Kuehl's *Seeking World Order: The United States and International Organization to 1920* (Nashville, 1969). Sondra R. Herman has provocatively portrayed varieties of internationalism in *Eleven against War: Studies in American Internationalist Thought, 1898–1921* (Stanford, 1969). N. Gordon Levin's *Woodrow Wilson and World Politics: America's Response to War and Revolution* (New York, 1968) presents an invaluable analysis of the ideology of liberal internationalism, while Robert Divine's *Second Chance: The Triumph of Internationalism in America during World War II* (New York, 1967) engagingly describes the second great internationalist crusade.

The story of the interwar peace movement and the idea of collective security are examined in Robert H. Ferrell's *Peace in Their Time: The Origins of the Kellogg-Briand Pact* (New Haven, 1952) and Roland N. Stromberg's *Collective Security and American Foreign Policy: From the League of Nations to NATO* (New York, 1963). Ferrell expresses the same jaunty skepticism toward the work of peace seekers in "The Peace Movement," an essay that appears with Richard N. Current's helpful "The United States and 'Collective Security': Notes on the History of an Idea" in *Isolation and Security: Ideas and Interests in Twentieth-Century American Foreign Policy*, edited by Alexander DeConde (Durham, 1957). In a more sympathetic spirit, Charles Chatfield, Jr., explores the stark dilemmas faced by peace leaders between the wars in *For Peace and Justice: Pacifism in America, 1914–1941* (Knoxville, 1971). Finally, Richard J. Barnet tracks the formative effect of the years 1937–45 on the national security managers of cold war America in *Intervention and Revolution: The United States in the Third World* (New York, 1968) and *Roots of War* (New York, 1972).

U.S. Office of War Information

HENRY L. STIMSON

Republican Internationalist

William Kamman

When Henry L. Stimson died on 20 October 1950, he believed a lifelong dream had been realized: the United States had accepted the "active duty of world membership." Stimson was confident that most Americans in the ten years after Pearl Harbor understood that the free security so long enjoyed by the United States no longer existed. Isolationists who had misgivings about the League of Nations and World Court and had supported neutrality legislation to circumscribe presidential action in foreign relations were no longer intellectually fashionable. Membership in the United Nations had little opposition in 1945. Congress extended the selective service legislation that Stimson had championed, voted massive aid to Western Europe for economic revival, and in 1949 approved a military alliance to contain Russia's advance. Only a few months before Stimson's death President Truman ordered General MacArthur to defend South Korea with American troops.

Stimson welcomed these developments in United States

407

policy. During his long public career he had urged similar changes
in American foreign relations: acceptance of world responsibility
and United States leadership in preserving order and stability.
How Stimson thought the United States could achieve this role is
seen in his service under seven presidents, spanning some forty
years. He was United States attorney for the Southern District of
New York, secretary of war twice, soldier, special representative of
President Coolidge in Nicaragua, governor-general of the Philippines, and secretary of state. He believed in a strong federal
government with aggressive presidential leadership that would
assert control over contending interests in the country and guide
the nation's domestic and foreign policies. In his younger years he
supported Elihu Root's army reforms, moved to strengthen the
general staff, and infused a feeling of movement in the army.
When the First World War came he sympathized with Britain and
France and was an early advocate of preparedness but not of
intervention, at least not until unrestricted submarine warfare
became German policy. In the quiet years after 1918, dealing with
colonies or small Caribbean republics, Stimson had accepted the
burden of the white man to advise, teach, and direct. As secretary
of state from 1929 to 1933 he came to feel that peace was
indivisible and that aggression should be stopped early, an idea
that dominated the rest of his public career. The United States, he
believed, had an international duty to support the Monroe
Doctrine, the Open Door, and the European balance of power, all
in the name of national safety and democracy. His views on these
questions were not always original, but the positions he held and
the decisions he influenced were important, sometimes determinant, in the foreign policy of his country.

◇◇◇

The long-lived Stimsons, an energetic, middle-class lot, arrived in America in the seventeenth century. They fought in the
French and Indian War and the Revolution, and a great-grand-
mother told young Henry of conversations with George Washington. Stimson's father fought in the Civil War. The family imparted
a sense of history and duty to its members and Henry L. Stimson
was no exception. By the time he was born in 1867 the family was
comfortably established in New York City. Henry spent a few years
in Europe while his father studied medicine. Then his mother

died, leaving a maiden aunt to raise Henry and a younger sister in their grandparents' house in New York. When the city lacked appeal for the boy and his schooling proved unsatisfactory, his father sent him to Phillips Academy at Andover where rigorous training prepared him for Yale. In New Haven he felt his most important educational experience was election to Skull and Bones, a secret society. After college he went to Harvard Law School and eventually with his father's aid entered the prestigious New York law firm of which Elihu Root was senior partner.

Stimson once remarked that as a young boy blessed for some time with four grandparents and four great-grandparents still living, he thought an individual's normal life-span was at least a hundred years. He did not achieve the expected centennial, but his life was long, though not exceptionally so when compared with such contemporaries as Root, Cordell Hull, Herbert Hoover, or Charles Evans Hughes.

Probably more than most of the nation's leaders who spanned the nineteenth and twentieth centuries Stimson had to confront peculiarly twentieth-century problems. He had known the western frontier before the Census Bureau officially declared it closed. He had roamed the wilderness, exploring and mapping portions, and had a mountain named after him. He once witnessed an Indian uprising. The outdoor life appealed to him as it appealed to his older friend, Theodore Roosevelt; this was one of the bonds between the two men. For Stimson a frontier America populated with Indians and cavalrymen was as real as the atomic weapons and mechanized warfare of the mid-twentieth century. The American wilderness left its mark on him as he handled twentieth-century problems; for him the frontier cleared away moral confusions and emphasized "courage, truthfulness, and frankness."

Stimson's early physical and intellectual environment produced a man in many ways similar to the Progressive profile as described by the historian George E. Mowry. As a lawyer, he was economically secure, well educated, and a member of the white-collar class that was "restless, sensitive, and troubled." He once told an audience at a class reunion that the legal profession never completely satisfied him because the ordinary New York lawyer was usually devoted to making money. That was not enough for Stimson, who wanted to work for a good cause. When Roosevelt, with Root's encouragement, offered him such an opportunity, a job defending the public interest, Stimson unhesitatingly accepted. He described service as U.S. attorney for the Southern District of New York, his first public office, as going from a dark place out to where he could see stars and get his bearings once more. He hammered away at wrongdoers until it was clear that their offenses would be consistently punished just as he would later try to hammer away at international aggressors.

Stimson shared with many Progressives an abiding patriotism and love of "rural" values, evident in his frontier and hunting adventures and in his attachment for Highhold, his Long Island estate. Highhold was a place of peace and beauty that provided refreshment and happiness during many trying periods. There Stimson played the role of country squire, taking proprietary interest in the community, associates, and friends. He was of the gentry who supplied the Progressive movement with important leadership, who offered service but were not servants, who sought power as a source of progress and improvement.

Stimson's second opportunity for public service came in 1911 when President William Howard Taft asked him to become secretary of war. The appointment, influenced by the tangled political situation in the Republican party, surprised Stimson. Taft had almost decided on another candidate when Secretary of the Treasury Franklin MacVeagh suggested Stimson. The idea appealed to the president. Stimson accepted after consulting family and friends including Roosevelt, who thought Stimson's future would be better served as an ex–secretary of war than as merely a defeated gubernatorial candidate (he had run unsuccessfully for governor of New York in 1910). Stimson viewed his appointment as a move to lessen Roosevelt's criticisms of the administration.

When Stimson took office the army was not large but it offered opportunities for continuing the modernization begun by his mentor Root. The new secretary of war also gained experience in administering colonies and working with Congress. His service in the War Department and later as a colonel of artillery in the First World War confirmed his natural sympathy with regular army officers.

Before 1914 Stimson's interest in political affairs concerned primarily domestic issues. He aimed at undercutting the machines and bosses, and he worked especially to reform the Republican party and the New York State constitution. He had some success in these areas, but as a vote-getting politician he was a failure. He was not good on the hustings; his speeches were lifeless and his demeanor not such as to instill warmth or devotion. He was a patrician with much ability and a strong moral sense to correct evil. If his America had inequities, if its democracy was deficient, Stimson felt it was his duty to change it through better laws and the election of strong leaders. He had read Herbert Croly's *The Promise of American Life* and accepted the author's faith in America's future; it was a land of promise and he yearned to leave his mark on its development.

In 1914 a century of peace came to a saddening end. For the United States, although this was not clear at the time, it meant that the choice to dabble or not in world politics would be constricted. Stimson's opportunities for public service reflected this change. As he took on new tasks involving diplomatic relations with other countries he may have pondered a passage in Croly's *The Promise of American Life*: "The American nation, just in so far as it believes in its nationality and is ready to become more of a nation, must assume a more definite and a more responsible place in the international system. It will have an increasingly important and an increasingly specific part to play in the political affairs of the world; and, in spite of "old-fashioned democratic" scruples and prejudices, the will to play that part for all it is worth will constitute a beneficial and a necessary stimulus to the better realization of the Promise of our domestic life."

Stimson met these new challenges in much the same way he had met earlier ones: with a sense of propriety and honor, faith in the law, and acceptance of responsibility both for himself and his country. These views along with his admonitions in later years that "gentlemen do not read each other's mail" and that "the surest way to make a man trustworthy is to trust him" were personal convictions and also reflected the code of his class.

◇◇◇

At the beginning of the First World War in 1914, Stimson supported a neutral position for the United States, although his sympathies were with England and France. In 1915 he told a veterans' group that America stood for humanity and justice and that the country would betray its birthright if it went in any direction but toward those goals. He gradually came to believe that his nation's concern in World War I transcended protection of neutral rights; the real enemy was a way of thinking that led to military aggression, what he and his generation called Prussianism.

Early in the war he came out strongly for preparedness, a matter of great concern since his years as secretary of war. Stimson supported preparedness beyond the immediate crisis. He urged defense training in the public schools and later advocated a program of universal military training, which he thought would develop initiative and an understanding of what American citizenship meant. A strong military also had diplomatic benefits. He once asked rhetorically, "Is there a man who doubts that Wilson's note to Germany would receive more attention if it were known that our navy was in readiness and that our 'free people' in the language of Washington were 'disciplined and trained in arms'?" Interestingly he opposed woman suffrage during this period in part because he thought women might very well hinder preparation for self-defense.

When war came in 1917 Stimson hailed the decision and volunteered for service in order to "feel comfortable in his mind." His view of the struggle was idealistic. The future of free institutions was at stake; if the tide of battle went against the Allies "the cause of democracy—even here in far-off America—would go down with them." Czarist Russia confused Stimson's neat delineation of the war as a conflict between democracy and autocracy, but the March Revolution led him to say in the oratory of the hour that "out of the caldron of war has issued another great democracy vindicating its position on the side of freedom. Into such a struggle a man may well go with a lofty faith and burning ardor." Later reflection on these events caused him to recognize that in his zeal he had probably overlooked difficulties in defining the war. Yet the penchant for easy division between right and wrong, which he retained when he faced later problems, in this case had not produced a tragic error, he believed. The tragedy came with peace, when the United States failed to "remain a member of the team."

Stimson's views on the League of Nations paralleled those of his friend Root. Both men favored a world organization with American participation; but they believed that Wilson had gone too far too fast, and that a more general covenant would have allowed a gradual development more acceptable to the American people. Even before the opening of the peace conference Root had told Stimson he opposed any agreement binding a nation to go to war on the order of a league. The world was not ready for such a proposition and it would not win public support. After publication of the league covenant in February 1919, Root and Stimson went over it in detail; later Stimson urged his friend to expound his objections, which Root did. He objected to Article Ten, the clause providing for collective security, because it seemed to perpetuate the status quo as established at Paris. For Senate consent of the treaty he proposed three conditions: Article Ten should be excluded, the United States should have the right to withdraw from the league and determine for itself whether its obligations were fulfilled, and there should be no interference with America's freedom to act in purely American questions. These reservations also expressed Stimson's position. They provided a middle way for American participation, between Wilson and the irreconcilables.

The end of all hope for American participation in the league was slow in coming, for even after adverse votes in the Senate the 1920 election provided opportunity for renewing the debate. During the campaign Stimson was among the thirty-one prominent Americans who signed a statement urging Harding's election as the best way to advance the cause of international cooperation. He thought a Republican president would gain the consent of the Senate with reservations on Article Ten. Looking back in later years he regretted his participation in this effort, recognizing that in 1920 he had been self-deceived.

The years immediately after the election of 1920 were not the happiest of Stimson's life, for he was disappointed with America's role in the peace settlement and was also back in private law practice, which did not satisfy him. Since the Republican administration in Washington dominated (he noted) by westerners was not congenial, he shared, according to his memoirs, an oblivion that overtook many younger eastern Republicans during this period. Yet while he may have fretted about life as a private citizen as he approached threescore years of age, unbeknownst to him the best part of his public career was in the future. President Calvin Coolidge retrieved him from exile and President Herbert Hoover offered him the secretaryship of state.

◇◇◇

Henry L. Stimson's first important work in foreign affairs and in dealing with alien peoples was in a proconsular role, in response to the United States' particular interest in Central America. In 1927 President Coolidge sent him to Nicaragua where he spent a month settling a revolutionary situation that was fast involving U.S. troops. For years Nicaragua had attracted United States attention because of its closeness to the Panama Canal and its own possible canal route, and because one of the nation's dictators, José Santos Zelaya, had disturbed Central American peace early in the century. The first American intervention to stabilize Nicaragua began during Taft's administration and ended in 1925. When the hoped-for peace and stability evaporated a few weeks after the departure of U.S. Marines, Nicaraguan affairs embroiled the United States more than before; when considered in conjunction with Mexican problems in the mid-1920s the situation appeared serious. Stimson's task was to restore order.

The Nicaraguan situation was not untypical for the United States in the Caribbean, particularly just after the turn of the century. A paternalism had developed to which Roosevelt, Root, Taft, Philander C. Knox, and Woodrow Wilson all contributed, and Stimson, greatly influenced by Roosevelt and Root, continued the pattern. It was a tradition in which phrases like "Roosevelt Corollary" and "Dollar Diplomacy" conveyed interest in stable political conditions to ensure safety for foreign lives and property, and concern that economic and financial matters be handled in such a manner that there would be no foreign complaints or intervention. Intertwined with these policies was a belief that the small republics could best fulfill their obligations if their governments were democratic. Watching over everything was the United States, claiming predominant interest in the area and a right to intervene. When Stimson went to Nicaragua, American power was part of his baggage.

The month spent in Nicaragua was a profitable occasion for Stimson, one of the best of his life. In his "pilot biography" published in 1948 he reflected that the big lesson from his work there was that "if a man was frank and friendly, and he treated them as the equals they most certainly were, he could talk turkey with the politicians and other leaders of Latin America as he could with his own colleagues." This view was similar to that of his old friend Root who in trying to improve Latin American relations undertook a campaign of "considerate friendship." While the

Root and Stimson approach was an improvement over all-too-fre-
quent assumptions of superiority by North Americans, there was
still a certain condescension and no small measure of a big-broth-
erly attitude. Stimson described the policy as one of avoiding
Scylla and Charybdis, of sailing between timid aloofness and
selfish exploitation. It was a righteous exercise that did not
recognize these countries as capable of independent existence.
For Stimson the upright course was supervision or intervention,
provided that intervention were based upon the welfare of the
country in question and not upon selfish interests of the United
States. The earlier intervention in Nicaragua had been simply
naked American interference from Stimson's point of view because it had done nothing to promote self-government. His offer
of supervised elections during his mission was the constructive
difference, for it would lead the country nearer to self-government.

The months and years after Stimson's departure revealed
weaknesses in his Nicaraguan proposals. One obscure liberal
officer, Augusto C. Sandino, refused to lay down arms; with a
handful of men in the jungles and mountains of northern
Nicaragua he conducted guerrilla warfare against Nicaraguan and
American forces. While the enigmatic guerrilla leader failed to
disrupt the program of election supervision and formation of a
nonpartisan national guard, he underscored the pitfalls of intervention. In large part because of him, Coolidge's successor Hoover
and Stimson, his secretary of state, had to rethink policy toward
the Caribbean. Stimson believed that the American record in
Nicaragua, Cuba, and the Dominican Republic had been credita-
ble, but that local nationalism made retrenchment necessary.

For Stimson this belated concession to nationalism was not
the chief lesson of the Nicaraguan affair. The important result was
development of a regular procedure for overcoming disorder and
instability for the well-being of all. In his mind international
society was not far different from a community where the
policeman, the sanitary code, and compulsory school had developed to guide and protect those with less knowledge and power.
The same law of evolution worked among nations; Stimson felt
America must be its brother's keeper with an obligation to be
helpful and responsible for the Central American countries in their
progress toward democratic self-government.

When Stimson went to the Philippines as governor-general in

early 1928 he revealed the same willingness to accept the burdens of the white man. For him the Philippines, which resembled Latin America more than its surrounding Asian neighbors, offered an opportunity to develop democracy and self-government but not necessarily independence. The Philippines' connection with America protected the islands from overpopulated adjacent lands with greater industrial and military capacity. When Stimson had first visited the islands in 1926 he had found great progress, under supervision. For people who urged more Philippine autonomy he noted developments during the tenure of Governor-General Francis B. Harrison, which allowed Filipinos greater self-government at the expense of financial and sanitation reforms. He approved a reversal of this trend after General Leonard Wood became the chief administrator of the Philippines, and when he succeeded Wood in that post he continued to think of a long-term role for the United States in the islands.

For Stimson the islands offered more than just a chance to evolve an imperial relationship. They were important as an outpost in the Far East, or as he and Wood said, a "spearhead of the great Christian effort." In addition, many persons who like Stimson approved the Open Door policy believed that United States presence in the islands strengthened America's position in the Far East. When in the 1930s Japan threatened Chinese territorial integrity, Stimson argued against giving up the Philippines; he thought such action would indicate that America was getting out of the western Pacific, thereby encouraging the Japanese and greatly reducing United States prestige in Far Eastern countries. The argument was consistent with his world outlook and acceptance of American responsibility, but if carried out logically it was fraught with danger of war, a danger present in both Nicaragua and the Philippines. In Nicaragua Stimson ignored nationalism and American marines confronted guerrilla combat; in the Far East where Stimson desired to strengthen the Open Door and increase American influence, America confronted Japan in the Philippines.

◇◇◇

Stimson enjoyed his tenure in the Philippines, his "experiment in responsible government," and when word came that President-elect Hoover was considering him for a cabinet post he reacted with mixed feelings. He refused to consider appointment as attorney general but would, if approached, become secretary of state. Hoover, after being refused by his first choices (including Senator William E. Borah and Charles Evans Hughes), offered the post to Stimson, a man who had a reputation for service to his party and country and who was supported by Root, Hughes, and Taft. The new president and his secretary of state had known each other since World War I, though not well. Working together closely from 1929 to 1933 was not always easy for either man. Their work patterns were dissimilar (Hoover worked much harder than Stimson), but perhaps more important was the president's growing preoccupation with economic matters, which may have increased his natural inclination toward cautiousness in foreign policy. For Stimson, disposed toward strong leadership of the Theodore Roosevelt type, the Hoover administration was a disappointment. Hoover thought his secretary of state too militant, and had he been reelected would not have retained Stimson in the cabinet.

It is an interesting commentary on American politics and ideology that Hoover offered the top job at the State Department to both Borah and Stimson, the first an isolationist and anti-imperialist, the other an internationalist and imperialist. Stimson directed many of his efforts in United States foreign policy toward mitigating what he considered to be the mistakes of 1919 and 1920 when the Senate—Senator Borah had been an irreconcilable—refused to approve membership in the League of Nations. After that there was no chance of American acceptance of the league covenant, but Stimson pushed for cooperation. Seeking other ways for international cooperation in the preservation of peace Stimson seized upon the Washington treaties of 1921–22, which supported the status quo in the Far East and gave international recognition to the Open Door, and upon the Kellogg-Briand Pact, a multilateral renunciation of war as an instrument of national policy. For Stimson these pacts became the basis on which to stigmatize aggression and to take some sort of collective action against violators.

The first test of the Kellogg pact was in Manchuria in July 1929. For several months Chinese nationalists had acted to remove Russian influence in Manchuria and particularly to end their control of the Chinese Eastern Railway. When the Soviets broke diplomatic relations and news reports indicated the possibility of an armed clash, Stimson sought a solution by reminding China and Russia, both signatories of the Kellogg treaty, of their obligations.

He also urged other signatories to encourage a peaceful settlement because, as he said, the efficacy of the treaty depended upon
the sincerity of the nations party to it; their attitude would in turn
strengthen world opinion in support of peace. Stimson later
recognized that his use of the Kellogg-Briand Pact might have had
little to do with settlement of the Sino-Russian differences, but he
believed there was at least outward success in this first invocation
of the treaty that encouraged "believers in the new order of
peace." Stimson had faith in marshaling world public opinion, but
in this episode, the Japanese and Russians thought his approach
suspicious. How thoroughly Stimson understood the intricacies of
Far Eastern politics is doubtful; his main concern was that even in
the most difficult portions of the world in which the Kellogg treaty
might be challenged, the United States had acted to organize
public opinion against war makers. Although Stimson had invoked
provisions of the antiwar pact during the Sino-Soviet conflict,
there was no real test of those principles. Russian troops had
evacuated Chinese territory in short order, and, as now seems
clear, Stimson's use of the pact had little positive effect.

Extension of Japanese control in Manchuria beginning with
the Mukden incident provided a greater challenge that allowed
Hoover's secretary of state an opportunity to extend by several
steps his thoughts on the keeping of peace. United States–Japanese relations had been satisfactory for some time when on the
evening of 18 September 1931 an explosion tore up a few feet of
track along the South Manchuria Railway near Mukden. The event
triggered a Japanese occupation of south Manchuria and led to
strained relations between Tokyo and Washington. Stimson
reacted slowly to the Manchurian crisis of 1931 because there was
hope that the Japanese government could regain control of its
Kwantung army which was apparently acting independently, and
he had no desire to make the affair even more difficult by arousing
Japanese nationalism. Hopefully, direct Sino-Japanese negotiations would restore the status quo; if not, Stimson told the
Japanese ambassador, the affair would create a bad impression
and force consideration of treaty obligations.

Meanwhile Stimson looked toward the League of Nations.
Cooperation with the league was a delicate problem for Washington, but he was glad the league had shown interest in the crisis.
The United States could carefully support the league, and if any
controversy arose with Japan it would be against the world rather

The Bird in the Gilded Cage

than the United States. The United States thus could avoid taking the initiative and (as President Hoover put the case in a cabinet meeting) avoid having the baby dropped on its doorstep.

As the Manchurian crisis evolved, Stimson overcame his early reluctance to be actively involved. Through the autumn of 1931 he kept pressure on the Japanese government, for he wanted Tokyo to know it was being watched. What he saw and heard became increasingly distressing. When diplomatic pressure and watchful waiting seemed to have little effect Stimson suggested to Hoover some form of collective sanctions, but Hoover preferred a more cautious approach. Stimson himself was not sold on an embargo; there were so many complications, not least of which was popular support. If the league had imposed sanctions he would have been delighted and would have promised no interference, but there would be no unilateral American sanctions.

After the collapse of Chinese resistance in Manchuria Stimson took another approach to the Far Eastern crisis: nonrecognition. The United States would uphold the Open Door and refuse "to recognize any situation, treaty, or agreement which may be brought about by means contrary to the covenants and obligations of the Pact of Paris." For Stimson, Japan's lack of respect for repeated admonitions to observe the spirit and letter of international promises was a moral outrage. He wanted to record that his government would not recognize these violations and wanted to set a standard to which others might repair. While acting for the United States alone, because he did not want the delay or equivocation that joint action might bring, he hoped for sympathetic, if not similar, responses from other signatories of the Nine-Power Pact, one of the agreements signed at the Washington Conference of 1921–22. In this he was disappointed.

Nonrecognition was a policy that most Americans could support because it voiced revulsion for Japanese aggression but made no promises to the victim. In this respect it reveals the dilemma American leaders faced in the 1930s. Although it was probably the only course open, Stimson was not happy with it, for he wanted the treaties to be more than scraps of paper. Yet the state of American preparedness, the pacific inclination of the president, and the preoccupation of public opinion with the depression made anything more than verbal action impossible. Stimson did not consider his diplomacy of January 1932 the last word. His faith in the treaty structure as a basis on which international law could evolve, as common law had, precluded approval of aggression. Nonrecognition did not roll back the Japanese occupation of Manchuria; it did not prevent the occupation of Shanghai a few weeks later, nor beginning in 1937 would it stop the invasion of China; but it did set a proper if not very forceful precedent.

Thus the lines were drawn in 1931–32 for a conflict with Japan. Stimson had carried on the policies of his predecessors John Hay and Charles Evans Hughes in the Far East. Early in 1933 he passed them on to a receptive Franklin D. Roosevelt and his new secretary of state Cordell Hull. Obsessed with the Open Door and strongly influenced by the arguments of missionaries in China and Chinese students in the United States, Stimson believed that education and Christianity could exert a profound influence on China's progress. Also, the enormous potential for United States commerce dazzled him. He emphasized political and humanitarian idealism, which he compared with the colonial effort in the Philippines to "train an Oriental people in the art of self-government according to the American model."

Japan threatened those concerns, and especially the treaty framework of European and world peace, which Stimson believed would preserve American interests and at the same time prevent another world war. As matters turned out, his goals were contradictory. Preservation of the status quo as supported by the league covenant, the Nine-Power Treaty, and the Kellogg pact was one hope. These agreements, he recognized, were "initiated by Western nations, and especially designed to fit the exigencies of the industrialized world of Europe and America"; while they might not be taken seriously in the Orient, they did exist. As for the other goal of peace, Stimson noted that for better or worse the treaties expressed the "earnest hopes of our part of the world," and if the Western nations gave in and allowed the treaties to be treated as "scraps of paper," then the hope of peaceable development in the world would "receive a blow from which it would not soon recover." The Japanese did not see China as he saw it; conditions there were not satisfactory to Japan. When the military, which had gained greater influence in policy, decided to make changes in China, and when the United States refused to recognize the results of Japanese aggression, Stimson worked, not always successfully, to present a common front against Japan, and the hope for peace, while not impossible, lessened. China remained the stumbling block in Japanese relations; the break came ten years after the Mukden incident. Stimson continued to believe that the issue of right and wrong—by that time in Europe as well as in the Far East—was more important than the choice between peace and war.

◇◇◇

On inauguration day, 1933, Stimson returned to private life. The law took some of his time; he traveled to Europe; he wrote (*The Far Eastern Crisis*); perhaps more importantly, he was an elder statesman who kept abreast with people of influence and power through conversation and correspondence. He had a friendly relationship with President Roosevelt and Secretary Hull whose views on foreign policy were not far from his own.

After seven years as a private citizen Stimson returned to public service. This, his last appointment to office, resulted in large measure from the mounting Eastern challenge to isolationism. Increasing dissatisfaction with Secretary of War Harry Woodring, in part for his opposition to foreign military commitments that might interfere with America's rearmament, culminated in June 1940 when President Roosevelt asked for Woodring's resignation and named Stimson as his successor. Stimson first met Roosevelt during the changeover of administrations in 1933. They had gotten along well and in the following years there were other meetings. Stimson's immediate support came from Grenville Clark, a founder of the Plattsburg Training Camps during World War I and a strong advocate of military conscription in 1940, who arranged for Felix Frankfurter, an associate justice of the Supreme Court, former protégé of Stimson when he was U.S. attorney for the Southern District of New York, and friend of FDR, to propose Stimson's name to the president. The arrangement included Robert P. Patterson as assistant secretary of war, later undersecretary, to serve with Stimson, who was almost seventy-three years old. Patterson was the first of an excellent staff brought together by the new secretary.

Political implications surrounded Stimson's appointment, but his views on foreign affairs had also been attractive to the administration. At the end of the Hoover presidency Stimson's advocacy of collective security and use of economic sanctions against aggressors had intensified. He deemed traditional neutrality no longer appropriate; he wanted to warn aggressors and would-be aggressors that America's moral and material resources would be on the side of their victims. On the eve of his appointment he emphasized the importance of the British fleet to American security and called for compulsory military service. After taking office he did not disappoint those who pushed his nomination. The destroyers-bases deal with England in 1940 and evidence that same year of greater cooperation with Canada and Britain encouraged him. The Lend-Lease Act of 1941 making America the great arsenal of democracy had, of course, his wholehearted approval.

In the Far East Stimson urged the utmost firmness; he assumed that the Japanese did not want a war with the United States, a belief not shared by officials who feared that Japan might move southward while avoiding a direct attack on United States territory. The administration's concern was to maneuver the Japanese "into the position of firing the first shot"—which meant, according to Professor Richard Current, convincing the American people that expansion into Southeast Asia was as great a threat to the vital interests of the United States as an attack on the Philippines, Guam, or Hawaii. This concern became academic on 7 December 1941, and Stimson and others were relieved of their dilemma. Stimson had feared that Americans were not alert to events in Manchuria, Ethiopia, Spain, the Rhineland, Austria, Czechoslovakia, and Poland and had tried to strengthen America's peace and security through neutrality legislation rather than cooperative action. Now there was unity. "The self-imprisoned giant was set free."

As secretary of war, Stimson contributed to major diplomatic and military decisions, but none of the questions arising during the Second World War has led to as much soul-searching and historical analysis as the use of atomic power. Some writers have questioned use of the bomb and have asked whether victory would not have come as quickly through a demonstration, warning, or description of the weapon, especially if the Americans had been explicit about the future status of Emperor Hirohito. Others put the bomb in the context of developing conflict with the Soviet Union and explained its use as an attempt to force Russian acquiescence to American plans for Europe.

For Stimson the decision was a military one and the logical consequence of his thinking for fifteen years. In 1932, when

Japanese forces were having some unexpected difficulties overcoming the Chinese around Shanghai, Stimson pondered whether
the higher the price militarists had to pay the better for the
ultimate reign of law in the world. He hoped that Chinese
resistance would give pause to the Japanese militants and allow
moderates a chance to regain control in Tokyo. Events proved
otherwise, but he saw another chance later when other nations
and eventually his own challenged Axis expansion in Europe as
well as Asia. He accepted the value of power and war; the atomic
bomb gave the United States awesome power in the summer of
1945. At that time Stimson concluded that to gain Japanese
surrender their leaders had to experience "a tremendous shock
which would carry convincing proof of our power to destroy the
Empire." It seemed that only the complete destruction of Japanese
military power would open the way to lasting peace. The United
States after 16 July 1945 had the means to stop what had started at
Mukden on 18 September 1931.

When the Second World War ended in early August 1945 with
the mushroom clouds over Hiroshima and Nagasaki, new military
and diplomatic problems had already arisen. Of these Stimson was
remarkably aware; yet he, like other American leaders, faced them
with some uncertainty. He had misgivings about approaching
Russia with the bomb "rather ostentatiously on our hip," but soon
recognized that his old maxim from Yale days in the 1880s about
"the surest way to make a man trustworthy was to trust him" was
not always appropriate. His advice was patience and firmness.
These were not to be his problems, however. He retired in
September 1945, leaving a legacy of commitment to a world
community in which he hoped his country would be the leader.

◇◇◇

Henry L. Stimson's role in American foreign policy carried on
the tradition of power and responsibility championed at the
beginning of the twentieth century by his friends Theodore
Roosevelt and Elihu Root. His ties to Root were particularly close.
During that statesman's long life (Root died in 1937) Stimson
frequently conferred with him, for, as he once told Justice Oliver
Wendell Holmes, many people depended on Root and his advice
to be the most valuable they could get in the world. Root's
influence was evident in Stimson's attitude toward the League of

Nations, the World Court, development of international law, and Latin American diplomacy. In Far Eastern affairs, although there were some differences, his approach generally followed Root's ideas. During his years in the War Department in 1940–45 Stimson kept in his office a bound set of Root's collected papers, often relying on them to provide the guiding principle for a decision.

Root's views on international law had a particular effect on Stimson. An abiding hope for an evolution of international law had influenced Stimson's thinking increasingly during 1931–41, and was evident in his interpretation of the Kellogg-Briand Pact to which he frequently referred when considering Far Eastern problems. He did not agree with some contemporaries that the pact was only a voluntary and simultaneous declaration of which each nation remained the sole and independent interpreter, and he disputed the claim that the treaty gave no rights and imposed no obligations. He emphasized the phrase in the treaty's preamble stating that powers resorting to war should be denied benefits furnished by the treaty, and, mirroring Root's faith in the world community's interest in violence against one member, Stimson believed that the Kellogg-Briand Pact made international conflicts a legal concern of all nations connected with the treaty. This covenant he believed to be the foundation for a new order. Positive construction of its provisions, expressed and implied, could strengthen the treaty. During the increasingly anarchical decade before Pearl Harbor he urged these views on Americans and in 1939–40 encouraged revision of the neutrality laws to allow this country to support victims of aggression, at least with measures short of war. When the surviving leaders of Germany were tried at Nuremberg in 1945 after the war's end, Stimson likened the proceedings to the common-law tradition. The trials were natural and proper; they were "a great new case in the book of international law."

As the years passed and Stimson, through experience, the precepts of Elihu Root, and the saddening course of human events, sought to gather his ideas, he gradually fastened on a strong president as the key figure in American foreign policy. For a long time, from his days as a Roosevelt Progressive until his last service as FDR's secretary of war, he had argued for greater executive power. In 1913 he had criticized government by congressional committee, which he termed wretched and impossible, prompting selfishness and corruption. He wanted to grant the president power to introduce a budget and proposals for revenue; he proposed forbidding Congress to add items to the budget without presidential consent. At another time he advised that a man or government could not be held responsible for doing wrong unless he were given the power to do right. He once told Root that international relations were different from domestic questions because greater leadership was required. "Americans know pretty well about their domestic affairs but they are ignorant as babies about their foreign relations; therefore, it was a much greater duty to lead and guide public opinion in international relations than in domestic relations and the attitude of the ear-to-the-ground statesman was far less justified in the former than in the latter." He was not satisfied with President Hoover's approach to foreign policy. Hoover was a Quaker and an engineer, which made Stimson believe he did not understand the psychology of combat. One should press ahead, not vacillate or give the appearance of timidity, discouraging followers while encouraging enemies. Stimson the lawyer had found the military maxim "In case of doubt march to the front" effective in law cases and true in other ventures as well. In human affairs requiring joint action one could not foresee or plan very far in advance for what was going to happen; it was not like building a bridge where one could calculate the stress and know mathematically the power and strength of it all. When he was urging modifications in neutrality legislation he inclined toward vesting complete and unlimited discretion in the president. He did not fear that the president would abuse this discretion, for he had observed that in no sphere of political action did the sobering effect of responsibility so affect a man as in relations with other nations. The man who "honestly and fully enjoyed the exercise of power" carried the mark of presidential greatness. The Roosevelts filled the bill.

Bold leadership and willing use of power in the conduct of foreign policy were signs of strength; men would follow a clear demonstration of duty and brush aside those who opposed. Too often, Stimson thought, there were lapses in presidential leadership: in the preparedness movement before entrance into the First World War, in the hesitation to support American participation in the World Court, in the initially weak stand against Japanese and German aggression. Too often presidents, fearing opposition, were timid or moved too gradually. Stimson was a man of action, and when blocked by his chief or the American people he was not happy. His proconsular service in Nicaragua and the Philippines had been agreeable; his years as secretary of state were disappointing; his tenure in the War Department, particularly after Pearl Harbor, was rewarding because hesitation and inaction had ended. Moral condemnation of aggression, as a sufficient policy, was over. The country could face, as he said in the postwar years, the second part of the question: an obligation to catch the criminals, which meant war. Stimson was not as reluctant to accept war as many Americans. He agreed with Theodore Roosevelt, who put peace above everything but righteousness, and believed that the final issue of policy was not peace and war but right and wrong.

In the intellectual milieu of American foreign policy Stimson was not original. He purveyed a traditional sense of destiny and power accompanied by preachments of law and morality. In the interwar period he had participated in one of the great debates of American diplomatic history, and events seemed to vindicate his position. Earlier than most Americans he was aware of the implications of Japanese expansion, and looking back from December 1941, his fellow citizens could well consider whether economic sanctions and closer cooperation with other nations might have nipped Japanese plans and, as he had hoped, prevented war. Perhaps the references to law, righteousness, morality, and the emphasis on Chinese territorial integrity may have made difficult a *modus vivendi* with Japan that would have entailed a compromise on China until a more propitious time for settling Far Eastern affairs. After all, China was lost to communism anyway, after the Second World War. Perhaps Stimson's position on aggression was more appropriate in Europe.

In the longer view of American foreign policy, with retrospect of a generation and more, questions arise about whether an act of war in any part of the world injures the United States, whether it is wrong to set limits to American activity as a member of the world community, whether it is true that the United States has an unlimited liability in the peace and freedom of the world, and how much discretion a president should have in foreign affairs. Stimson's words about peace and war, right and wrong, and his hope for a trumpet call to save freedom throughout the world seem a little jaded in the 1970s; his faith in international law does not have the appeal that it once had for many Americans. Perhaps he did represent a tradition that has brought the United States to the brink of catastrophe; but hopefully the architects of change in United States foreign policy will not exaggerate the virtues of withdrawal, weak executives, and the lack of idealism, thus creating an even more unfortunate condition.

BIBLIOGRAPHIC NOTE

Events during Stimson's public career, spanning almost a half-century and including two world wars, have attracted much commentary. Fortunately for historians Stimson provided an extensive record of his place in American history. The chief source is the large collection of Stimson papers and diary volumes at the Yale University Library, but there is readily available for students a sizable amount of printed material by and about Stimson. Frequently during his career he explained his role in important events. After his retirement Stimson, with the son of an old colleague in the State and War departments, McGeorge Bundy, wrote a "pilot biography," *On Active Service in Peace and War* (New York, 1947), which allowed him to explain and assess his public service. He wanted to forestall, as he said, other volumes that might be written without benefit of his papers or his counsel.

Earlier, after completing his mission in Nicaragua for President Coolidge, Stimson had published a slim volume, *American Policy in Nicaragua* (New York, 1927), in which he outlined his efforts in that nation. American policy, he believed, had a proper regard for Latin American independence although he recognized special geographic interests in Central America that made necessary particular regard for how these countries fulfilled their responsibilities. For him this condition derived from broad principles of self-defense.

Stimson chronicles his Far Eastern policies arising from the Manchurian incident of 1931 in *The Far Eastern Crisis: Recollections and Observations* (New York, 1936). More than a record of his activities during the "crisis" it is the testament of an American who in the mid-1930s strongly urged collective security, world order under law, and greater Anglo-American cooperation. In 1934 he gave the Stafford Little Foundation lectures at Princeton which were published as *Democracy and Nationalism in Europe* (Princeton, 1934). He was hopeful and optimistic about democracy in the face of European problems.

The Council on Foreign Relations and its quarterly *Foreign Affairs* provided a regular outlet for Stimson's views. "Future Philippine Policy under the Jones Act," appeared in *Foreign Affairs* 5 (April 1927), 459–71; "The United States and the Other American Republics," *Foreign Affairs* 9 (April 1931), Special Supplement; "The Pact of Paris: Three Years of Development," *Foreign Affairs* 11 (October 1932), Special Supplement; "Bases of American Foreign Policy during the Past Four Years," *Foreign*

Affairs 11 (April 1933), 383–96; "The Nuremberg Trial: Landmark in Law," *Foreign Affairs* 25 (January 1947), 179–89; and "The Challenge to Americans," *Foreign Affairs* 26 (October 1947), 5–14. One may also trace Stimson's views in news stories of the *New York Times* and particularly in his letters to the *Times*.

The best coverage of Stimson's diplomacy is Robert H. Ferrell's *American Diplomacy in the Great Depression: Hoover-Stimson Foreign Policy, 1929–1933* (New Haven, 1957), and his book on Frank B. Kellogg and Henry L. Stimson, volume 11 of American Secretaries of State and Their Diplomacy series (New York, 1963). Richard N. Current has been critical of Stimson for emphasis on law and morality in diplomacy and for interpretations and applications of policies that could mean a policeman's role for America in the world. See Current's *Secretary Stimson: A Study in Statecraft* (New Brunswick, N.J., 1954), his essay on Stimson in Norman A. Graebner, ed., *An Uncertain Tradition: American Secretaries of State in the Twentieth Century* (New York, 1961), his essay "Consequences of the Kellogg Pact" in George L. Anderson, ed., *Issues and Conflicts: Studies in Twentieth Century American Diplomacy* (Lawrence, Kans., 1959), and his article "The Stimson Doctrine and the Hoover Doctrine," *American Historical Review* 59 (April 1954), 513–42 in which he notes two separate doctrines. In the mind of Hoover nonrecognition was final and sufficient; for Stimson it was the first step toward stronger sanctions. For an explanation of Stimson's remark on maneuvering the Japanese into firing the first shot which does not support the contention that Roosevelt and his advisers were planning for an attack on Pearl Harbor, see Current's "How Stimson Meant to 'Maneuver' the Japanese," *Mississippi Valley Historical Review* 40 (June 1953), 67–74. Elting E. Morison has published an excellent biography of Stimson: *Turmoil and Tradition: A Study of the Life and Times of Henry L. Stimson* (Boston, 1960).

Some "New Left" historians see Stimson as the example in American leadership of the corporate lawyer and supporter of international peace and order who emphasizes American overseas economic expansion; see William Appleman Williams, *The Tragedy of American Diplomacy* (New York, 1962). In *The Contours of American History* (Chicago, 1966), Williams refers to Stimson as a descendant of the old feudal gentry. By the end of Stimson's career in 1945, Williams believes, he had broken with Theodore Roosevelt's conception of world power and come close to abandoning what the author terms the "frontier-expansionist outlook" when he advised greater cooperation with Russia on the atomic bomb. Gar Alperovitz in *Atomic Diplomacy: Hiroshima and Potsdam* (New York, 1967) traces Stimson's part in the decision to use the bomb, noting the dilemma between desiring to use the bomb as an instrument of diplomacy and fearing that such use would be disastrous.

Many writers have given attention to Japanese expansion in China in

the early 1930s and America's response. Students of Stimson may consult
Armin Rappaport, *Henry L. Stimson and Japan, 1931–33* (Chicago, 1963),
who believes that at times Stimson may have acted rashly in handling the
problem, but he ponders whether results would have been different had
Stimson remained silent. Note also Herbert Hoover's *Memoirs*, vol. 2
(New York, 1952). Sara R. Smith, *The Manchurian Crisis, 1931–1932: A
Tragedy in International Relations* (New York, 1948), regrets the failure of
Anglo-American harmony in the affair and lack of greater United States
cooperation with the League of Nations. For an account of New Deal
views on Stimson's Far Eastern policy see Bernard Sternsher, "The Stimson
Doctrine: FDR versus Moley and Tugwell," *Pacific Historical Review* 31
(August 1962), 281–89.

U.S. Office of War Information

THE OPEN DOOR IN PERSPECTIVE:

STANLEY K.
HORNBECK

and American Far Eastern Policy

Russell D. Buhite

During the Second World War, when a Japanese official was asked if he knew of Stanley Hornbeck, he remarked, "Yes, he is the one responsible for war between the United States and Japan." Although that was a simplistic assignment of blame, Hornbeck, as a high State Department official and professional diplomat, did thrust himself into the vanguard of those in the government who opposed Japanese expansion. He was clearly more responsible than any other single individual for the application of economic sanctions against Japan, an act of great consequence in the coming of war. Indeed, beginning in 1928 and continuing for a period of sixteen years, few questions of America's Asian policy

This sketch is based in part on Kenneth G. McCarty, "Stanley K. Hornbeck and the Far East, 1931–1941," Ph.D. dissertation, Duke University, 1970. Professor McCarty is currently working on a full-length study of Hornbeck's career which promises to shed important new light on both Hornbeck and American foreign policy.

escaped his attention and few policy makers exerted such direct influence on the course of affairs. The dominant element in Hornbeck's view of the Far East was that he saw the area essentially in strategic terms and expressed greater concern for the larger picture than for any of its component parts. China was not so much the object of policy as it was one in a row of dominoes, the fall of which would eventually threaten American security. Hornbeck deserves attention especially because his views of the Open Door and of China made him the embodiment of the basic principles, strategy, and tactics of United States Far Eastern policy.

Stanley K. Hornbeck was born on 4 May 1883 in Franklin, Massachusetts, the son of Marquis and Lydia Hornbeck. His father was a Methodist minister just out of seminary. In 1883, not long after Stanley's birth, the family moved to Illinois, where the elder Hornbeck served several churches before accepting the presidency of Chaddock College, a small Methodist school located in Quincy. When Stanley was ten the family moved to Colorado, where he received much of his education. He attended a preparatory school in Boulder, was a student at the University of Colorado for two years, then transferred to the University of Denver, completing his B.A. degree in 1903. A classics major, Hornbeck was a good student and a hard worker but by his own admission no scholar. Notably, he did not acquire grounding in either history or political science. After graduation he accepted a teaching position in Golden, Colorado, but pounding Cicero into the heads of bored high school students quickly palled, and at the end of his first year Hornbeck decided to cast his sights higher.

In 1904 he applied for, and much to his surprise received, a Rhodes Scholarship, the first given to someone from Colorado. That scholarship wrought a major change in young Hornbeck, for the years at Oxford broadened his horizons, helped him develop a world view, and provided him with a sense of confidence about his ability to compete in a larger setting. Moreover, through his Oxford studies in modern European history he developed an interest in scholarship that was to be vitally important later.

Hornbeck returned to the United States in 1907, having decided to enter graduate school, and he enrolled at the University of Wisconsin. In 1909, after intensive study under the direction of Paul Reinsch, a specialist on the Far East and world politics who was later to become President Wilson's minister to China, he earned a Ph.D. in history and political science. During his years at

Wisconsin, Hornbeck came in contact with some of the best minds in the academic world, men like Richard Ely, John Commons, and Frederick J. Turner, though the precise degree of their influence on him is impossible to determine.

After the completion of his graduate study, circumstances led Hornbeck to an assignment that affected his career far more than his academic training. Unable well into the summer after graduation to secure a good teaching position in an American college, he came across a newspaper advertisement for a position in China, which, with the blessing of Professor Reinsch, he ultimately accepted. Later that year, Hornbeck went to China to assume the position as teacher of history and international law at Hangchow Provincial College. If Hornbeck's years at Oxford were critical, those in China were even more so; he spent four years traveling about the country, observing China's politics and learning its history. These were important times there. Hornbeck's stay coincided with the overthrow of the Manchu dynasty and the establishment of the republic. Also during this period he met Nelson T. Johnson, E. T. Williams, and John V. A. MacMurray, who were later to become chiefs of the State Department's Far Eastern Division.

After returning from China in 1913, Hornbeck's career took several turns before he settled into the policy-making structure of the State Department. When Reinsch was appointed United States minister to China he recommended that Hornbeck take his place at the University of Wisconsin, and the young scholar became an instructor in political science. His work in the position was apparently satisfactory, as he published several articles and one book during his tenure; but for reasons of his own, Hornbeck decided to leave teaching in 1917. He accepted an appointment to the U.S. Tariff Commission but he soon resigned, and in 1918 joined the army where he served as a captain in the army ordnance corps. Then he was detailed to the Inquiry,[1] an assignment that lasted until after the war when he became one of Wilson's advisers on Far Eastern questions at the Paris conference. In the twenties Hornbeck was a lecturer at Harvard and sometime

1. The Inquiry was a group of social scientists gathered under the direction of Woodrow Wilson in 1917 for the purposes of keeping him informed of international conditions and making policy recommendations.

adviser to the State Department until, in 1927, Nelson Johnson was promoted to assistant secretary; Johnson recommended his friend Stanley Hornbeck for the vacated departmental post, and in early 1928 Hornbeck became chief of the Far Eastern Division. From 1928 until his assignment in 1944 as minister to the Netherlands Hornbeck dealt primarily with Far Eastern questions, after 1937 as special adviser on political affairs in the State Department and in 1944 as director of the newly created Office of Far Eastern Affairs.

Like a number of men active in United States–Far Eastern relations during the first half of the twentieth century, diplomatic figures such as W. W. Rockhill, E. T. Williams, Paul Reinsch, John V. A. MacMurray, and J. Leighton Stuart, Hornbeck was a scholar-diplomat in the truest sense. He was an excellent lecturer and spoke often on Far Eastern topics before learned and academic societies. He also wrote several books and numerous articles. The University of Wisconsin published Hornbeck's dissertation, *The Most Favored Nation Clause in Commercial Treaties*. In 1916 Appleton published his most successful book, *Contemporary Politics in the Far East*, and his articles appeared in *Foreign Affairs, Annals, Current History*, and other journals. Later as a State Department official he did a good deal of public speaking, and he spent his retirement years after 1947 writing on the China question, sometimes in the editorial pages of the *New York Times*.

Neither Hornbeck's appearance nor his personality would have inspired poets. He was of medium build and height and could not in any sense be termed handsome. Extremely quick intellectually and possessed of a caustic tongue, he was an unwelcome and formidable foe in argument, and he had a scholar's eye for the ill-reasoned memo and poorly drafted dispatch. His precise and colorless demeanor stamped Hornbeck, in the eyes of some of his colleagues, as a kind of "fuddy-duddy." He also possessed the puritan's distaste for indolence. A hard worker who drove himself unmercifully, Hornbeck expected others to measure up; when they failed, he let them know. Accordingly, foreign service officers and subordinates often referred to him as "the old autocrat." Though he could be charming and a generation of scholars remembers him as friendly and helpful, Hornbeck did not have many close friends. The old China hand, Nelson Johnson, was probably the closest, in part because the two men were in substantial agreement and also because of Johnson's amiable spirit.

Personally, politically, and philosophically, Hornbeck was a conservative. Man, he often said, was a selfish, scheming creature and he once remarked to this author that in his view the most gracious act of generosity was simply selfishness turned around. His views on diplomacy accorded well with his view of man. Diplomacy, he once said, was not, as so often described, a game of chess. "Chess is played on an open board, with no chance of deceit or lying; diplomacy is not." Diplomacy was more like "a game of cut-throat auction bridge." This, he often stated, was not the way he wished it to be but the way it was.

At the same time, Hornbeck had no doubt that American statesmen generally followed a superior code of conduct and that both the goals and the methods of American policy transcended those of other states. Similarly, United States policy in the Far East, while of course designed to serve American interests, accorded with the basic principles of fair play to which much of humanity subscribed. Except for brief periods at the beginning and at the end of his career, Hornbeck was as staunch a supporter of that Far Eastern policy as he was a firm adherent of nationalism.

◇◇◇

It was during his first participation in policy formulation at Paris in 1919 that Hornbeck found himself in opposition to established policies, because he believed the United States was needlessly sacrificing its moral and practical position in the Far East. As an adviser at the Versailles conference he worked against a pro-Japanese settlement of the Far Eastern question and opposed President Wilson's final commitment on the matter. The major Versailles discussions on the Far East focused on the interests and aspirations of Japan arising out of its participation in the war against Germany. In fall 1914, Japan had entered World War I on the Allied side and had taken over German possessions, in particular Shantung on the China mainland. Shantung, a northern Chinese province jutting into the Yellow Sea, had become a German-dominated area after the orgy of concession seeking in 1898; the Germans had acquired control of the coastal area of the province, known as Kiaochow, and mining, railroad, and other rights in the interior. Japanese quickly replaced the German officials in the concession and began running it as their own. In the famous Twenty-One Demands of 1915 and again in 1918 by treaty, the Japanese forced Chinese acceptance of the changed status of Shantung. and in a series of secret agreements made to secure Japanese naval assistance against Germany, Japan obligated the British, French, and Italians to support its postwar claim to the region. At Versailles Japan wanted formal recognition of its interests in that province. Tokyo also asked acceptance of two other points: acknowledgment of its right to annex certain formerly German Pacific islands and support for an international declaration of racial equality.

The question of the Pacific islands received much attention at the conference because of Japan's demand for annexation of the Marshalls, Carolines, and Marianas, and the West's fear of Japanese expansion. At length, the conferees devised a mandate system under which the league powers would administer the Pacific islands; the three island groups were placed under Japanese authority. Hornbeck favored American or British control but was willing to accept the mandate system; however, he was thinking ahead, for if the United States made concessions to Japan on this question, the Japanese might be brought to withdraw their claims of a "special position" in Shantung.

The Japanese were also thinking ahead. Hoping to strengthen their position on Shantung by making themselves the injured party on another issue, they pressed for a statement on racial equality, knowing they had little chance of getting it. Although President Wilson personally favored such a declaration, his own advisers and the British warned him of the proposition's political dangers. The British dominions, in particular, were bitterly opposed. Accordingly, the president did not vote for the measure and it was defeated.

Shantung was the major issue. Based on the Twenty-One Demands, the secret treaties, and the agreement of 1918, the Japanese claim to that region was difficult to dispute, and they pushed it vigorously. The Chinese, on the other hand, argued that the agreements were only temporary, that they had been forced upon China, and that in view of China's participation in the war, concessions that Germany had earlier extracted ought in justice to revert to China. The American position, on which Wilson's advisers were in unanimous agreement, was to support China, but because the Allies would not support the American position, and because the Japanese threatened to refuse to sign the treaty and withdraw from the conference unless they got their way on

Shantung, Wilson relented. Italy had already withdrawn over the Fiume issue, and the loss of Japan might imperil the treaty and league. Hornbeck, who had worked hard for the Chinese cause, believed, however, that the Japanese would eventually compromise and were simply using a technique they had learned from the Italians; in short, they were bluffing. He deplored the president's decision as neither just nor wise. It did not conform to "President Wilson's 'fourteen points' nor with the spirit and principles of American Far Eastern policy," the disappointed diplomat complained.

Although Hornbeck took the Chinese side in the Versailles deliberations he possessed little sentimental or romantic attachment to China. The blind sympathy for things Chinese exhibited by some "old China hands" was not what he meant by the "spirit" and "principles" of American Far Eastern policy. His concern about China, though genuine, was directly related to the position of Japan and the matter of present and future American interests. The overriding aim was to check Japanese imperialism, and Hornbeck hoped that China would develop into a stable, unified nation, one to which the United States would have free access. He deplored political chaos and refused to accede to the "whims" of Chinese nationalism if American "rights" were threatened thereby. Thus, when China in the twenties challenged the American position, the limited nature of Hornbeck's sympathy became clear. He supported the status quo in Sino-American relations and emphasized China's obligations as well as its rights.

In the 1920s China experienced the concurrent phenomena of unsettled political conditions and burgeoning national consciousness. The failure on the part of the great powers at both the Versailles and Washington conferences to make more than a gesture toward lifting the burdens of the unequal treaties from China created a sense of outrage in that country. Young Chinese workers and students, who were more aware of the outside world and some of whom were infected with Western Socialist and Communist ideologies, pressured their leaders to expel the foreigner or limit his prerogatives. Anger and frustration stemming from China's submissive role had burst forth in the May Fourth Movement of 1919 and in other antiforeign demonstrations. At the same time, China possessed no unified government for much of the twenties. The Kuomintang or Nationalist party of Sun Yat-sen, revitalized with Russian assistance, became the center of power in south China while the recognized government held power in Peking. In addition, countless warlords exercised more power at the local level than either of the two principal claimants to national authority. Finally, in the spring of 1926 Chiang Kai-shek led a Nationalist military drive northward, expelled the Communists from Kuomintang ranks the following year, and in 1928 secured nominal control of the country.

These conditions brought about direct clashes with the treaty powers. In May 1925, strikes in Japanese-owned cotton mills led to antiforeign marches, to sloganeering, and ultimately to bloodshed as foreign police fired on Chinese demonstrators. The following year, Chinese strike pickets attacked British nationals working at Canton; in November Chinese Nationalists attacked the customhouse at Hankow in an attempt to immobilize the customs administration; and in March 1927, a group of soldiers in Nationalist uniforms attacked foreign nationals living in Nanking, killing several, and inflicted considerable property damage.

American policy makers now tuned the China question into sharper focus than at any time since the Boxer Rebellion. There were two reasons: conditions created great and immediate concern about American lives and property in China, and Chinese demands forced the United States to consider its long-range policy on treaty revision, particularly with regard to the issues of the tariff and extraterritoriality. For years the United States had equated its own interests with those of the Chinese, assuming that the inviolability of Chinese sovereignty would provide the best chance for success of the two main goals of American policy, equal commercial opportunity and the right to carry on missionary activity. When the Chinese began to assert their independence, the United States found itself in an awkward position.

As events transpired, the United States occasionally used force in the defense of lives and property, as in the Nanking incident. Treaty revision posed more of a problem. The United States supported the cooperative policy agreed upon by the powers at the Washington Conference, but cooperation in using force to defend the treaty structure was not possible. Yet to give in to China was to act unilaterally and invite others to contravene the cooperative policy in their own way. In view of China's instability, it also risked damage to American interests.

The United States finally resolved the dilemma by taking a measured step toward meeting China's wishes, though not without considerable debate among State Department officials. Nelson Johnson, as Secretary of State Frank Kellogg's major Far Eastern adviser, desired conciliation to as great an extent as practical. John V. A. MacMurray, the American minister in China, wanted to stand firm because he believed that to give an inch would be to yield a mile, and he also feared the influence of bolshevism in China.

Although not in an official departmental position until 1928, Hornbeck leaned throughout toward support of the status quo. The problem as he saw it was that "none but a politically organized people, a state, can at once enjoy the rights and fulfill the obligations of sovereignty," and China did not meet that test. "There is now in China," he wrote in 1927, "no person or group whom a majority of the Chinese people, or a majority even of the leaders, recognize as having authority to make commitments on China's behalf or to accept commitments made by the Powers in China's favor." More than this, the treaty system had developed "not without cause and reason." Whatever its flaws it rested upon law. "It has been the legal basis upon which many foreigners and more Chinese have ordered their lives, made their investments, created and carried on their business . . . ; it cannot be abolished suddenly. . . ." Hornbeck was, however, willing to discuss extraterritoriality, but only if the United States went slowly and agreed only to a gradual relinquishment of that right, and he disdained the use of force to defend anything but lives and property. As he explained the cooperative policy, when the issue was peculiar to another country and China, when little U.S. interest was involved, or when the use of force was anything but defensive, the United States would not cooperate. While the United States might resist treaty revision, it could not cooperate in "aggression" against China; to do so would violate the principles of the Open Door to which the United States was irrevocably committed. Because Secretary Kellogg was generally predisposed toward a liberal approach, he worked closely with Johnson and in 1928 the United States granted China tariff autonomy and began negotiating on extraterritoriality.

◇◇◇

If Chinese nationalism in the twenties brought American China policy into sharper focus, Japanese actions in the succeeding decade created greater apprehension about the larger questions of America's Far Eastern approach and the future of world peace. Japan's aggression in Manchuria and later in China proper consumed more of Hornbeck's time and that of his colleagues than any other question. American policy makers spent the decade assessing U.S. interests, debating alternative actions, and reacting to Japan's initiatives.

The story of the Manchurian crisis has been told many times. Japan attacked in Manchuria on 18 September 1931, proceeded to occupy strategic points, expelled foreign influences and interests, and in 1932 made it a puppet state called Manchukuo. In the process of securing control of this province Japan also attacked Chinchow, for the first time using air power against innocent civilians, and later waged pitched battles against Chinese troops in Shanghai because of anti-Japanese boycotts and other activities in that city. In spring 1933, Japan signed the Tangku Truce with China, giving the Japanese time to digest the heady potion they had just consumed before resuming the feast.

The Japanese blitz occasioned surprise, uncertainty, and chagrin among American officials. At length, the United States and other interested powers decided to pursue a policy of moral remonstrance and diplomatic pressure. Secretary of State Henry Stimson first tried conciliation, wishing to allow the Japanese civilian government time to rein in the military. When this did not work and the aggression continued, he invoked the Kellogg-Briand Pact, a multinational renunciation of the use of force as an instrument of policy. When this failed, he called his advisers together to consider economic sanctions, but the opposition of President Hoover and depressed economic conditions precluded their use. In January 1932, Stimson revived a policy utilized by Secretary of State William Jennings Bryan in the crisis of 1915 over the Twenty-One Demands: nonrecognition of any agreement between Japan and China contravening U.S. treaty rights in China. In February as the Japanese established "Manchukuo" he sent a letter to Senator William E. Borah pointing out the interrelatedness of the Washington treaties and suggesting invocation of the U.S. right to reject the Five-Power Naval Limitations Agreement.[2] In

2. The Washington Conference of 1921–22 had produced several agreements dealing with naval and political issues in the Pacific. Taken together these treaties could be considered a comprehensive program to sustain the status quo in the Far

parallel action dating back to October 1931, the League of Nations also invoked the Kellogg pact and then in December sent an investigating team known as the Lytton Commission to the Far East. None of these efforts, either American or league, deterred Japan.

No less than others in the State Department, Hornbeck agonized over the proper response to Japan's moves; and the metamorphosis of his thinking in the 1931–32 period is of considerable interest. The day after Japan's initial move in Manchuria he prepared a memorandum for the secretary of state in which he stated that events in Manchuria would intensify the struggle between the civilians and the military in Japan's government. External factors would determine who would win. Therefore, the United States should act to strengthen the hand of Foreign Minister Kijuro Shidehara. American concern, Hornbeck believed, should not be expressed in terms of American interests in Manchuria, nor should the United States at this point invoke the Kellogg pact. The latter option should be left to the World Court. In October when Stimson invoked the pact as a means of acting, Hornbeck acquiesced in the move, though he thought it little but an irritant to Japan and was never very sanguine about its effect.

This did not mean that Hornbeck was not willing to "get tough" with Japan under the proper circumstances. When the State Department discussed the possibility of applying economic sanctions, Hornbeck favored the move if the United States could act in conjunction with the other powers. "If the boycott is not given serious consideration," he wrote in early December, ". . . historians will attribute to the United States no small share of the blame for its failure." Sanctions would cripple Japan and could force an early end to its aggression. Any action, however, must be multilateral. In particular, Hornbeck did not want the British to push the United States into the lead on this matter, because American interests did not warrant such a position. Fear of European deviousness also governed his reaction to the question of American coorperation with the league in fall 1931. Britain and France "controlled" the league and would "use" the United States in the Far East. When the league decided in

_____

East. Successive American administrations accepted this interpretation; the Japanese did not.

December to send the Lytton Commission to the Far East, Hornbeck saw the move as meaningless; moral condemnation would do no good, and unless the powers did something concrete, Japan would stay in Manchuria.

Similar skepticism underlay Hornbeck's position during the discussion of the nonrecognition proposal; consequently he was of two minds about its utility. In this he differed with Secretary Stimson. Aware of the slight effect of Bryan's nonrecognition policy in 1915, Hornbeck saw little chance that the same policy could be any more effective in the thirties. Yet he realized that neither the United States nor the league could use force and that sanctions were out of the question. Nonrecognition was one of the few alternatives open to the United States; it would keep the American legal record clear and had the advantage of flexibility since it could later be canceled. In the fall of 1932 he went so far as to describe nonrecognition as a "positive policy."

Stimson's letter of 23 February 1932 to Senator Borah accorded with Hornbeck's views in that it suggested naval rearmament; in fact, Hornbeck himself had written the first draft of the letter. Actually, by early 1932 his views had begun to crystallize: Japan, he believed, would stay in Manchuria; economic sanctions as well as force were out of the question; the United States did not have sufficient interests at stake to warrant a confrontation with Japan; Japan had violated the Open Door and the treaty structure built up since 1919; the United States ought not to take the lead against Japan in defense of the treaty structure. Hornbeck concluded that the best way to avoid war in the Manchurian affair and the most sagacious course for the United States in its future relations with Japan was for America to look to its broader Far Eastern interests and increase its naval strength in the Pacific.

Once he purged himself of his anger over Japan's action and had time to reflect on the situation, Hornbeck began to see American Far Eastern policy in essentially the same perspective in which it was nearly always viewed. When the powers began dismembering China at the turn of the century the United States responded with the Open Door notes, which comprised a restatement of some long-cherished principles and a formalization of its pre-1900 approach to the Far East. The Open Door represented an attempt to do something about the China situation when the alternative of force was an impossibility. As Japan gained ascendancy in Manchuria during the Theodore Roosevelt

administration, the American response was to call attention to the
Open Door and concentrate on the protection of the Philippines
but to avoid conflict with Japan, since no vital interests were
involved in Manchuria. With the exception of President Taft (who
tried Dollar Diplomacy as an alternative to force in an attempt to
neutralize Japan and promote the Open Door), subsequent
administrations based their actions on rather realistic assessments
of American interests. The basic fact governing American policy
was that the United States had a vital interest in the broader area
of the Far East and Pacific but not in China.[3] Notwithstanding the
Nine-Power Treaty, no administration was willing to go very far to
support China's territorial integrity.

American policy and Hornbeck's own ideas in the 1933–37
period reflected this same "realism." In early 1933 the Far Eastern
situation seemed improved because of the truce signed by Japan
and China. As Nelson Johnson, American minister to China, put it,
the Japanese needed a respite and were simply putting their
diplomatic foot forward; in any case they had additional objectives. Proving the U.S. minister's contentions, a spokesman for the
Japanese Foreign Office in spring 1934 enunciated a doctrine for
eastern Asia that specifically forbade foreign interference in China.
Then in 1935 Japan demanded a wide range of concessions in
north China south of the Great Wall, including the right to
comment on the appointment of Chinese officials in that area, and
by the end of the year had secured the creation of an autonomous
zone in Hopei and Chahar provinces. The Roosevelt administration, largely on the advice of Hornbeck, changed tactics in dealing
with Japanese expansion. It did so not because Stimson's approach
was out of accord with U.S. principles but because concern about
possible war with Japan led to questioning the wisdom of further
protest.

Hornbeck's recommendations in these years hammered at the
point of avoiding friction with Japan, ruling out both irritating
protests and statements of support for China. When the spokesman of the Japanese Foreign Office Eiji Amau issued a statement
on the question of foreign interference in the Sino-Japanese

3. See the essay in this volume on Willard Straight for a contrasting view of United
States policy. It should be noted, however, that three decades, reflecting great
change in the situation and American attitudes, had elapsed since Theodore
Roosevelt and Willard Straight enunciated the goals of American policy.

What About China's Rights in China?

Richmond Times-Dispatch, 1938

quarrel, Hornbeck drafted an exceedingly mild protest which Secretary of State Cordell Hull ultimately issued. The message stated simply that the United States wanted to be a good neighbor but it was the American view that no nation could "rightfully endeavor to make conclusive its will in situations where there are involved the rights, obligations, and legitimate interests of other states."

In response to suggestions that the United States assist China or even mediate the conflict, Hornbeck took a firmly negative position. In the first place it was impossible to work with a nation like China which in its foreign relations spoke "through a multiplicity of mouths." In the second, to get involved was to risk offending Japan over the wrong issue. When the Chinese requested a loan in 1933 Hornbeck, though not averse to a revival of the consortium idea, advised against a United States loan. The Chinese had not "fulfilled past obligations." Later, as other requests came in, he said that China was a "gimme" country and advised telling the Chinese that the United States was tired of "playing the role of Santa Claus; that we want evidence of a real inclination on the part of debtors to meet their obligations." Hornbeck was clearly not prepared to allow China to become the dominant issue in Japanese-American relations, a principle that became the basis of the Roosevelt administration's policy, demonstrated by the paucity of its assistance to China and the mildness of its response to Japan's actions.

In the period from 1937 to 1941 American policy underwent a transformation from passivity to active opposition to Japan, because Japan's actions in extending the conflict beyond the confines of China and related events in Europe brought vital American interests very much into play. Once he perceived the threat to these interests, Hornbeck, who had long believed in naval preparedness and the futility of anything but force in confronting Japan, took the lead in counseling a more vigorous stance.

When the undeclared war between China and Japan erupted in 1937 American policy makers responded with extreme caution. They refused to mediate the conflict; they refused to give the Chinese any aid and cautioned them not to expect any; and they refused to invoke the Nine-Power Treaty. Secretary of State Hull invoked vague principles and attempted a continued "impartial" approach. Hornbeck was not in substantial disagreement with the

American response. The major debate in the early period of the crisis occurred over application of America's neutrality laws, passed in 1935–37. Hornbeck, who had opposed enactment of this legislation in the first place, advised against its use and was pleased when the administration accepted his point of view.

As fighting in China continued, President Roosevelt in October 1937 gave his famous "quarantine" speech, stating that aggression was like a disease requiring isolation. Soon afterward, in mid-October, the United States consented to attend the Brussels Conference; however, the former sentiment was quickly tempered, and the U.S. delegation at Brussels, which included Hornbeck, was not permitted to commit the United States to the use of economic sanctions. Although a constant element in U.S. Far Eastern policy was protection of American lives and property, in September 1937 the State Department warned Americans that they stayed in China at their own risk, and in December the Japanese sinking of the U.S. gunboat *Panay*, a brutal and wholly unwarranted attack, occasioned what was under the circumstances only a mild response from the Roosevelt administration.

Not long after the *Panay* affair, however, the United States began to alter its attitude; Hornbeck perhaps foreshadowed the change. By the time of the Brussels Conference he began to consider the need to take some action with regard to Japan, "not for humanitarian reasons, not for the sake of American property and interest in China, but because she threatens or will in the long run threaten our security." This is an important point in understanding American policy in the interwar period. Beginning in 1938 the United States began to aid China and stiffen resistance to Japan for reasons closely approximating those mentioned by Hornbeck.

Two areas were of primary concern to American officials after 1938: China and Southeast Asia. Because China became so intertwined in the fabric of American diplomacy, historians have concluded that the United States went to war with Japan in defense of the Open Door there. China, however, was important to Hornbeck, allegedly the most pro-Chinese of all of Hull's advisers, because China could tie Japan down, deplete Japanese resources, and exhaust its will to fight. In short, it would be in America's interest for China to fight Japan. While Japan's aggression was limited to China, moreover, the logical way to confront Japan was through assistance to China. "Better to have Chinese soldiers continue to fight Japan and take now the small risk," Hornbeck stated in 1938 in arguing for a loan to China, than for the United States to confront a stronger Japan "using the resources of China in support of her onward march of conquest."

As Japan continued the conquest of China and in November 1938 proclaimed the New Order in East Asia, the United States considered appropriate responses. Hornbeck recommended several related steps. He continued to promote the naval building program. "For us, investment in a strong navy will be an investment for peace. Possessed of a strong navy, our position will be such that no other country will venture to attack us." Reflecting a harsher view of the situation than in 1932, he also advocated stopping the flow of all war materials from the United States to Japan, boycotting Japanese goods, and granting loans and credits to China. In pursuing the course of economic sanctions, the United States should also abrogate its 1911 commercial treaty with Japan. By the end of 1938, in one form or another, most of Hornbeck's suggestions were adopted: the United States began a rearmament program, it purchased Chinese silver in large amounts, and it authorized a Chinese loan of twenty-five million dollars.

In the following year the Japanese made clear what Hornbeck and other American policy makers had already begun to discern: that they planned to extend their aggression beyond the borders of China. In February they occupied Hainan, an island off the coast of Indochina, and in March they took the Spratly Islands. These actions, signaling that a more deliberate southward thrust would follow, acutely alarmed the State Department. Hornbeck by this time firmly believed that an "infantile" expansionism possessed Japan, and no domestic developments would divert Japanese leaders from this course; therefore, nothing would be lost by going ahead with the policy best suited to American interests. He personally favored a program "the opening number of which would be application of economic sanctions," and, if need be, the closing number of which "would be use of armed force."

Events in Europe gave Japan unprecedented opportunities in 1940. As Hitler swept through the Netherlands and defeated France much of the resources-rich Southeast Asian area was opened up for exploitation. Because of its growing interest in the war in Europe and because of economic and strategic facts related to its own existence as an independent nation, the United States could not view with disinterest the fate of Southeast Asia. Hornbeck grasped this immediately. As a scholar who tried to keep abreast of works relevant to the Far East, he read as widely as time would permit and he frequently informed his colleagues of items of interest. In 1940 he circulated an article within the State Department that reflected his own views and revealed the great significance of the Southeast Asian region. The article, written by Professor Robert Burnett Hall of the University of Michigan and published in the April 1940 issue of the *Geographical Review*, stressed two points: that Southeast Asia possessed more than 90 percent of many raw materials vital to the United States, and that it was the one area of the world to which the United States could not be denied access. "Only on the lands west of the Pacific," Hall concluded, "and especially on Southeastern Asia, is our dependence so vital and complete that our very existence as a great industrial power, and perhaps even as an independent state, is threatened if the sources should be cut off." To Hornbeck, this was "the most interesting, incisive, and concise exposition that I have seen anywhere of the tremendous economic importance, especially to the U.S., of the Far Eastern Area."

Whatever the accuracy of this assessment, the threat posed by Japan's move southward in 1940 created great apprehension about U.S. interests, brought about stringent sanctions, and eventually led to war. In the summer of that year Japan sent a military mission to Indochina, closed the Burma Road, and threatened to move into the Netherlands East Indies; in September it signed the Tripartite Pact with Germany and Italy. Throughout the year Hornbeck continued to press for economic sanctions, including the embargoing of oil. Five years earlier, in fact, he had written his friend Nelson Johnson in China that oil "was the weak point in Japan's strategy," suggesting that when the United States chose to respond, cutting off oil would be a good tactic. With regard to the Netherlands Indies, he later pointed out that not only would a Japanese occupation be particularly harmful to American economic interests but it would allow Japan to obtain oil there, thus weakening the ability of the United States to apply pressure on that country through an embargo. While he advocated sanctions, he also fought vigorously to prevent shifting the fleet from Hawaii to the Atlantic. In sum, Hornbeck in 1940 worked extremely hard for an anti-Japanese policy, which included economic sanctions and, if Japan attacked Singapore, the use of force. So militant did

Hornbeck become in fall 1940 that his colleagues sometimes sought to exclude him from their discussions and Assistant Secretary Breckenridge Long called him a "dangerous man." [4]

The history of United States–Japanese relations in 1941 is a record of recrimination, statement and restatement of conflicting positions, and, because Japan's drive for empire did not abate, progressively applied American sanctions. Hornbeck did his part. Believing now that no chance of real peace existed until Japan had either exhausted its resources or was defeated, he actually opposed any further negotiations. He opposed the Hull-Nomura discussions; he rejected the idea of a meeting between Prime Minister Fumimaro Konoye and President Roosevelt; he disdained any attempt at compromise over the Japanese presence in China in late November. The best course, he believed, was to increase aid to China, which would tie Japan down and drain its strength, and add to the American embargo. As one of the first to advocate freezing Japanese assets, Hornbeck believed that these steps, if properly applied, were likely to bring Japan to its knees.

In the meantime Japan would not attack the United States. As late as 27 November 1941, Hornbeck offered five-to-one odds that the United States and Japan would not be at war on or before 15 December, three-to-one odds that the two countries would not be at war on or before 15 January, and even money that there would be no war on or before 1 March. "The undersigned," he wrote further, "does not believe that this country is now on the immediate verge of war in the Pacific." In a rather hastily conceived analogy, he stated that Japan was like an ass grazing in a field full of rocks and thistles. To the north and south of the field were haystacks, but between the ass and the haystacks were barbed wire fences. The animal had a choice of staying where he was or going against the barbed wire toward the haystacks. Japan, thought Hornbeck, would not go against the barbed wire. Unfortunately, as any country boy would have known, he was as wrong about asses as he was about Japan.

Once the United States became involved in World War II, the focus of American Far Eastern policy, for both military and political

4. Though Secretary Hull was not as militant he was willing to embargo some strategic goods, such as aviation gasoline, and to agree to grant China loans and military aircraft.

reasons, again shifted to China. The optimum hope militarily was that China would develop an effective fighting force and inflict heavy casualties on the Japanese; the minimum was that it could at least remain in the war and continue to tie down over a million Japanese troops. In the beginning, the United States also thought that China would be a staging area for bombing and eventually for an invasion of the Japanese home islands. Politically, the United States wanted a strong, united, and democratic postwar China able to take its place as the dominant country in Asia. These objectives led President Roosevelt to include China in major wartime conferences, to refer to Chiang Kai-shek as leader of a world power, and, in short, to assign China a higher status than warranted by the facts. Several conditions prevented the realization of these goals, among them inefficiency and corruption in Chiang's government, the internal struggle between the government and the Communists, and the wartime priorities that allotted most American resources to the war in Europe. The result was that the effort in China contributed only marginally to the winning of the war, and that, once the war ended, conflict between the Communists and Nationalists culminated in a Communist victory.

The tangled situation in China forced consideration of difficult questions in the State Department during the war: how best to aid Chiang, how to pressure him to reform his government and his armies, and to what extent the United States should help compose the differences between his government and the Communists. A basic element in these discussions was the growing strength of the Communists and concern regarding how to fit them into American policy. Some officials argued that the United States ought to support only Chiang's government while encouraging the Communists to cooperate with and accept a place in it. Others suggested that a more flexible policy would be better, including aid to the Communists. The administration opted for the former, though not without some genuine effort at compromise.

As usual, Hornbeck left little doubt where his sympathies lay. He advocated increased and virtually unconditional support of Chiang Kai-shek. To those who argued that Chiang's government was corrupt, he replied that the United States did not scrutinize the internal workings of other Allied governments. Moreover, the Chinese had been fighting Japan alone for years and there were bound to be problems; in any event, support should be given on the basis of China's engagement of Japanese troops and on the logic of aid to the legitimate government in power. To those who argued that Chiang's government was dictatorial, he responded that so was Stalin's.

Hornbeck therefore bristled at reports by American Foreign Service officers that detailed elements of decay in Chiang's regime and extolled the comparative virtues of the Communists. In response to one of these messages, he commented, "Seldom if ever have I seen any document prepared by a responsible officer of the Department or of the Foreign Service, of no matter what age or length of experience, expressive of such complete self assurance on the part of the author that he knew the facts, all of the facts . . . and that he could prescribe the remedy. . . . Never before have I encountered so sweeping a charge that almost everything . . . is wrong with China." He went on to point out that he considered the dispatch "irresponsible" and that he had taken time "to refresh my knowledge of its author," an ominous observation.

As events turned out, a military crisis in China in 1944 prompted President Roosevelt to demand that Chiang accept an American as full commander of his armies and that he carry out needed reforms. In sum, the administration now applied the pressure, though as it developed not terribly successfully, that Hornbeck so long remonstrated against. A simultaneous development in Hornbeck's career, perhaps because of his dogmatic insistence on arguing a contrary view, was his appointment as U.S. ambassador to the Netherlands. This position, which Hornbeck held until his retirement in 1947, took him away from Far Eastern problems for the first time in his career, but it did not eradicate his deep and continuing concern about the region. Indeed, assignment in Europe during the critical postwar years imbued Hornbeck with an even deeper hatred of communism and its portents for Asia. Recurring themes in his later lectures and articles were to be the mistakes in American policy during and after the war and the need to maintain a constant vigil against the Communist threat.

◇◇◇

Until his death in 1966, Hornbeck remained an active observer of world politics and consequently spent most of his retirement in the study of his Washington apartment researching and writing essays on American foreign policy. Hornbeck deplored the Yalta decisions, opposed postwar American China policy, and supported war in Korea and Vietnam. In the case of Roosevelt's Yalta agreements on the Far East, he believed the United States "bought with Chinese coin unneeded Russian action and worthless Russian pledges." Later, American statesmen "caused the Chinese to buy, with their confirmation, a made-in-Moscow trojan horse." U.S. policy, moreover, accounted in part for the success of the Communists. American leaders, he believed, foolishly accepted certain faulty assumptions: that the Communists were agrarian reformers, that Russian pledges would be honored, and that Chiang's government was corrupt and therefore not worth saving. These assumptions, particularly the last, led to the termination of American aid and the Truman administration's verbal condemnation of Chiang Kai-shek.

Hornbeck believed China should have been included in America's effort to contain the Communist menace. What the Nationalists lacked "were the very things which but for the United States the Greeks also would have lacked, the things but for which Greece would have been overrun by the Communists." This failure to respond to the threat in China was the more deplorable because "a Communist China . . . will be a highway by which . . . Soviet influence will move and Communist armed force be able to strike southward and eastward." As one might expect, Hornbeck later defended support of the Nationalists on Taiwan and opposed the recognition of the People's Republic as "inconsistent" and "damaging" to America's effort "to contain Communism and achieve security." In a 1955 article defending nonrecognition he seemed to be reviving the Stimson Doctrine. The United States could not insist that other states do as it wished or subscribe to its principles; often it had to tolerate conduct it disapproved. "It is, however, under no compulsion to give assent to such. It certainly can refuse to authorize, it can decline to sanction, and it can withhold endorsement."

Just as Hornbeck believed the United States should have resisted Communist expansion in China so he also thought it essential that the United States respond in Korea and Vietnam. In the case of Korea, he thought President Truman's decision to intervene was wise (though it would not have been necessary had the United States prevented the fall of China). Although Hornbeck was no longer as certain of the monolithic nature of communism by 1950, the expansion of Chinese power and Communist intrusion into Southeast Asia had to be denied. Because Southeast Asia and the Pacific region constituted vital American interests, it was as important to prevent the domination of the region by a hostile power in the 1960s as it was in the late thirties and early forties. To Hornbeck, therefore, Vietnam, like Korea, was a necessary war.

The focus of Hornbeck's concern with the Far East continued to be its strategic implications. In the years immediately after World War II, he had envisaged the Soviet Union replacing Japan and, using China as an agent, extending its domain in Asia. Later, he perceived Chinese power as an independent threat. While Hornbeck was among the staunchest proponents of the Open Door in public life, he was unwilling to back the principle with force in its specific application to China until after the Second World War and even then thought that assistance to Chiang would achieve U.S. aims. Moreover, in the late forties and fifties Hornbeck became concerned less with the traditional Open Door and more with thwarting Communist expansion and maintaining American access in a broader sense. As an internationalist, he believed (along with most of his generation) that the major lesson of the thirties was that democracies could not allow "aggression" to succeed.

Patrick Gallagher of the *New York World* once said of diplomat Henry White that "his heart beats for the Open Door." He may well have said the same of Hornbeck, though it is doubtful that Hornbeck's perception of the concept would have accorded with Gallagher's. In any event, an assessment of Hornbeck's career offers insight into the real meaning and significance of the Open Door, indicating that it was more an ideal than a policy. As Philip Moseley once observed, "hope divorced from power is not a policy." In its application to China Hornbeck thought the Open Door simply "a declaration of intentions" in support of the principles of equality of commercial opportunity and a necessary corollary, respect for China's territorial integrity. These principles had not been discovered on the spur of the moment. "The doctrine of equality of commercial opportunity had behind it a century and a quarter of American diplomatic expression and effort; it required no explanation to the American people; it was representative of the average American's conception of justice and of his own and other countries' rights." American policy was shaped by the belief that "free states should remain free." In this respect, Hornbeck believed, "the Far Eastern policy of the United States has sprung from the same root in American thought from which sprang the Monroe Doctrine in relation to the Western Hemisphere." The United States opposed "imperial adventure or partition" and possessed the right to make clear its opposition.

As the foregoing suggests, Hornbeck saw the Open Door not only as it related to China, but as the expression of a broader dimension of American foreign policy. The Open Door to him was a perfect reflection of the American system, way of life, and approach to foreign affairs; its roots were deep in the nation's past. "In the realm of formulated effort," he wrote, "the principal major objective of American policy since the earliest days of the Republic has been to ensure for American nationals and for American trade equality of opportunity. . . . The 'open door' doctrine in its two phases, equality of opportunity and the integrity of the state in regard to which it is applied, is the cornerstone of American foreign policy." On another occasion, Hornbeck cited Secretary of State Charles Evans Hughes's statement to the effect that the broadest principles of American foreign policy were simple. The United States did not covet territory, special economic influence, or control of others. "We wish to protect the just and equal rights of Americans everywhere in the world. We wish to maintain equality of commercial opportunity; as we call it, the open door." Because the Open Door policy was an extension of and was so closely tied to America's institutions, moreover, it could not be altered or changed lightly, not even in the face of Japan's thrust in the thirties.

This view of the Open Door is especially interesting in light of a provocative interpretation of that policy currently accepted by some scholars, that the functional needs of the American economic system have forced the United States to pursue an expansionist course, and that this expansionism has been expressed not in the acquisition of colonies or formal empire but through a persistent policy of demanding access to markets and raw materials and freedom of enterprise. Thus, America's twentieth-century world objectives, as manifested in the Open Door, have been hegemonical in nature and are equated with the interests of capitalism. With regard to China and other underdeveloped states, the policy dictated insistence on commercial and investment opportunities and opposition to nationalism and revolution.

There are some similarities and many differences between Hornbeck's Open Door and the one constructed by this interpretation. Clearly, Hornbeck believed that the Open Door had roots deep in the American domestic system. He also considered it a perfect expression of American commercial policy everywhere in the world. Moreover, in terms of policy recommendations, his interest in Southeast Asia and the Pacific in the late thirties and early forties partially reflected a concern for the continuing access and freedom of enterprise on the part of the United States. The same could be said about his postwar response to Communist power in both Europe and Asia. One can find numerous statements in Hornbeck's articles and speeches that reflect his fear of a world closed to American commercial activity; these help explain his support of U.S. actions during the cold war.

Further examination of Hornbeck's views, however, suggests the inadequacy of defining the Open Door simply as an expression of policy growing out of the needs of capitalism. No one was more devoted to the concept than he; yet he was willing to acquiesce in some of the demands of Chinese nationalism in the 1920s. At any rate, other American policy makers did go a considerable distance in implementing a liberal approach to China. In the thirties he refused to consider confronting Japan as long as the Japanese limited their activity to China. In short the Open Door in China was not important enough to warrant a fight. What this suggests is that because he refused a priori to sanction the means necessary to back the principles he so admired, to Hornbeck (and in fact the conclusion extends to nearly all American statesmen) the Open Door in the case of China existed at the level of aspiration rather than policy.

It could be argued that once Japan threatened to move southward Hornbeck counseled the use of force rather than acquiescence in Japanese take-over of a region vital to U.S. economic interests and that after World War II he advocated forceful action for similar reasons. The significant point, however, is not that he proposed to get tough rather than suffer limitations on U.S. access, but rather the reason for his concern. A study of Hornbeck's career reveals only a limited regard for American economic interests. These interests did not lead him to advocate action in China, and they were only partially responsible for his apprehensions about Southeast Asia. There is little evidence that such considerations determined his anticommunism or his post–

World War II demand for an open world. Hornbeck believed open access and a congenial world to be important to the nation's economic well-being, but far more vital was the guarantee of U.S. physical security and the defense of liberal democratic principles.

The basic element in understanding Hornbeck's conception of American foreign relations is national pride. The United States was morally and politically superior to other nations, for its domestic institutions manifested fair play, equity, and the freedom and dignity of the individual. Because the Open Door arose from these ideals, it in fact constituted the alignment of the United States with principles of fairness and equity in international relations. Notwithstanding the sophistication of his specific recommendations or the complex analyses he sometimes presented, Hornbeck's views were essentially simple, they were consistent, and they flowed directly from his deep faith in and love of his country.

BIBLIOGRAPHIC NOTE

The Stanley K. Hornbeck papers are available to scholars at the Hoover Institution, Stanford University. The Nelson T. Johnson papers, Library of Congress, are an important source for a study of Far Eastern policy in the twenties and thirties, as are the Henry Stimson papers at Yale and the Cordell Hull papers at the Library of Congress. All of these have been instrumental in this interpretation of Hornbeck. The *Foreign Relations* volumes are vital to a study of any phase of American foreign relations as are the State Department records located in the National Archives. For the forties, materials from the Franklin D. Roosevelt papers at Hyde Park and the Patrick J. Hurley papers, University of Oklahoma, were also useful. Hornbeck made his views public from time to time through speeches, journal articles, and books, many of which are cited in the text of the essay. These provide a fairly comprehensive statement of his beliefs and concerns.

Because Hornbeck's career coincided with an eventful period in United States–Far Eastern relations, the secondary literature is abundant and continues to grow. For the deliberations at Versailles two of the most substantial studies are Roy Watson Curry, *Woodrow Wilson and Far Eastern Policy, 1913–1921* (New York, 1957), and Russell Fifield, *Woodrow Wilson and the Far East: The Diplomacy of the Shantung Question* (New York, 1952). On the twenties one should consult Thomas Buckley, *The United States and the Washington Conference 1921–1922* (Knoxville, 1970), Dorothy Borg, *American Policy and the Chinese Revolution,*

1925–1928 (New York, 1947), and Akira Iriye, *After Imperialism: The Search for a New Order in the Far East, 1921–1931* (Cambridge, Mass., 1965).

The Manchurian crisis has received considerable scholarly attention. The best books on this phase of United States Far Eastern policy are Robert H. Ferrell, *American Diplomacy in the Great Depression: Hoover-Stimson Foreign Policy, 1929–1933* (New Haven, 1957), Armin Rappaport, *Henry L. Stimson and Japan* (Chicago, 1963), Richard N. Current, *Secretary Stimson: A Study in Statecraft* (New Brunswick, N.J., 1954), and Elting E. Morison, *Turmoil and Tradition: A Study of the Life and Times of Henry L. Stimson* (Boston, 1960). Dorothy Borg's excellent study, *The United States and the Far Eastern Crisis, 1933–1938* (Cambridge, Mass., 1964), is the authoritative book on the mid-thirties.

For Japanese-American relations and the approach of war, two standard works are Herbert Feis, *The Road to Pearl Harbor* (Princeton, 1950), and Paul Schroeder, *The Axis Alliance and Japanese-American Relations* (Ithaca, 1958). Waldo Heinrichs's *American Ambassador: Joseph C. Grew and the Development of the United States Diplomatic Tradition* (Boston, 1966) provides an excellent account of an important figure in American Far Eastern policy during the same period.

There have been several studies of Sino-American relations in the forties. Those dealing most satisfactorily with the complicated aspects of American policy are Tang Tsou, *America's Failure in China, 1941–1950* (Chicago, 1963), and Herbert Feis, *The China Tangle* (Princeton, 1953). Barbara Tuchman's *Stilwell and the American Experience in China* (New York, 1971) is a superb biography of a controversial figure. Russell D. Buhite's *Patrick J. Hurley and American Foreign Policy* (Ithaca, 1973) adds insight into the activities of Hurley in China.

THE MASKS OF POWER:

FRANKLIN D. ROOSEVELT

and the Conduct of
American Diplomacy

Theodore A. Wilson and Richard D. McKinzie

Almost three decades after his death, the personality of Franklin D. Roosevelt still broods, sphinxlike, over the landscape of United States diplomacy. Few contemporary problems and achievements can be explained without recourse to the decisions of America's thirty-second president. During Roosevelt's tenure in the White House from 1933 to 1945, the United States shrugged off traditional restraints of indifference, isolation, and insecurity; by April 1945, when death swept FDR from office, the nation had assumed a stance in world affairs more consonant with its economic, military, and political strength. Franklin Roosevelt himself set in motion some, and presided over all, of the decisions that moved America from a position of relative unimportance in world politics to one approaching global domination.

FDR was a focus of controversy throughout his brilliant career; however, after his death the partisans in an enduring

459

historical debate assigned greater significance to his actions than either admirers or critics attributed to them during his lifetime. Some historians have credited President Roosevelt with almost superhuman abilities, arguing that, had he lived, he would have avoided the errors—of omission, commission, and suspicion—that blighted wartime Allied cooperation and ultimately generated the cold war. Others, equally credulous, have asserted that FDR was solely responsible for divers misguided or evil acts, such as luring Japan into the Pearl Harbor attack and selling out Eastern Europe to the Soviet Union, to cite but two examples.

The intellectual community did not seriously question the view of FDR as a bold, farsighted president for nearly two decades. Only in recent years have scholars attacked the judgment that Roosevelt was a dynamic leader. While asserting that FDR was the principal architect of U.S. policy during his tenure, some have concluded that he was indecisive and excessively cautious, even timid. As Robert Divine has written: "Franklin Roosevelt's claim to greatness must rest on his achievements in domestic affairs. His conduct of foreign policy never equalled his mastery of American politics and his ability to guide the nation through the perils of depression and war." Divine's widely read book emphasizes Roosevelt's flexibility and sense of realism rather than the personal qualities stressed in earlier accounts. Many recent studies (on such topics as neutrality, lend-lease, unconditional surrender, and foreign economic policy) have virtually ignored the factor of presidential influence, because of ideological presumptions or bafflement as to the workings of FDR's mind, "that heavily-forested interior." Even in works with such pervasive themes as American economic expansion and national interests, FDR figures only as an unknown or neutral factor.

It would seem that victory in the long debate has gone, perhaps by default, to proponents of the view that Franklin D. Roosevelt was "an accidental hero." Many years ago, in his brilliant analysis of individual responsibility, *The Hero in History*, Sidney Hook disqualified FDR as a "true" hero. Instead, he was a man whirled to the surface by events, who for a time circled in the vortex of history and whose lasting influence was an accident of time and location rather than an individual reordering of historical forces.

Beyond that insight, a generation of scholarship has left almost untouched the central mystery of FDR's influence. The dominant explanation in foreign affairs—and, to a lesser degree, domestic politics—today is about what it was during Roosevelt's lifetime; the essence of this explanation is dichotomy. FDR was at once "both lion and fox," a man possessing an unclouded, realistic grasp of human weakness and capacity for error, and also a passionate awareness of humanity's potential nobility. In simple terms, FDR was both pragmatist and idealist; he was a remarkably skilled politician and a functioning idealist. To an amazing extent, discussions of Roosevelt's beliefs and actions boil down to a simple equation: $FDR = TR + WW$; that is, he combined the political skills and realism of his cousin Theodore Roosevelt with the visionary idealism of Woodrow Wilson, under whom he had served and whose portrait he kept in the Oval Office in the White House.[1]

FDR's "success" or "failure" in any circumstance thus depends on his "batting average," the number of times he correctly identified a situation as demanding a practical response (and, conversely, the frequency with which he hit away for idealism). Some have judged his batting eye well-nigh perfect. FDR's sense of timing occasionally deserted him, because he misread signals from his manager, public opinion (for example, during the court-packing fight of 1937 and the debate over intervention in 1940–41), because he accepted bad advice from teammates (such as the decisions on unconditional surrender and the second front), or merely because advancing age dimmed his eye and slowed those marvelous reflexes. Still, he remains the "Sultan of Swat" in American diplomacy, and the suspicion persists that, if he had not been abruptly yanked from the game, the United States would have swept the world series of postwar negotiations.

Unhappily, the pragmatist-idealist hypothesis does not contribute much to understanding this complex man and the decisions he managed. Though not a false issue, a Dr. Jekyll–Mr. Hyde explanation (success being assessed in terms of the observer's definition of good and evil) is superficial and misleading.

---

1. This interpretation has been revived and glitteringly refurbished by James McGregor Burns, whose two-volume biography, *Roosevelt: The Lion and the Fox* (New York, 1956) and *Roosevelt: The Soldier of Freedom* (New York, 1970), is the most perceptive study of FDR. For an insightful critique of the Burns thesis, see Robert Dallek, "Franklin Roosevelt as World Leader," *American Historical Review* 76 (December 1971), 1503–13.

In common with the vast majority of human beings, FDR wore not two faces but an infinite variety. These masks reflected good intentions but at the same time obscured and delineated other less rational and amorphous feelings. He changed these masks for reasons he himself may not have understood clearly.

In the case of presidential motivation, James Barbour has written: "Like any person facing extreme uncertainty, the President seeks within himself some ground of continuity, some identity he can recognize as his way of being. That identity is inseparable from his personal history; he senses what he is in large measure by what he was and by what he hopes yet to be. A moment's introspection will confirm that we tend to respond to new challenges with old habits—of belief, of feeling, and of action." Political leaders are extraordinarily skilled at concealing their inner feelings, so disciplined that the masks they wear appear to be and may become reality. This makes analysis of their psychological development necessary; indeed, if it is valid to say that political ambition is grounded in a need for ego gratification so great as to be compulsive, understanding the psychology of men such as Franklin D. Roosevelt is essential.

The screens President Roosevelt erected around his motives have proved remarkably durable, and few historians have endeavored to penetrate the elaborate network of rhetoric, jocular remarks, and obfuscation. Obviously, in common with his generation and his class, he held convictions about the nature of American society and America's proper role in world affairs; however, these beliefs did not comprise a rigid, all-encompassing definition of the limits within which he functioned. If, indeed, FDR possessed a *Weltanschauung,* it was only one of various factors shaping his response to men and events. For him, it seemed that each day brought a new world to conquer; each day a different FDR arose to begin the conquest.

◇◇◇

One could arrange the facts of Franklin Roosevelt's life to conform to a mechanical formula for becoming president and contend that from birth he was destined for the White House. He certainly had numerous advantages: wealth and social position, physical attractiveness, an engaging personality, family influence in national politics, an "Eastern Establishment" education, and a dramatic struggle with disease that earned him sympathy and admiration. Superficially, at least, the progress of his career—New York state senator, assistant secretary of the navy, Democratic vice-presidential nominee, two-term governor of New York, landslide victor in the presidential election of 1932, and subsequent reelection to an unprecedented four terms—bespeaks a rendezvous with destiny. Nonetheless, such a construction is too facile. It misrepresents FDR's personal goals and the manner of his emergence as a figure of national and international importance. Doubtless the ambition for power always existed, but, as Roosevelt himself often admitted, his political successes were largely a matter of accident.[2]

Franklin D. Roosevelt was born 30 January 1882 at the family estate on the east bank of the Hudson just outside the quiet village of Hyde Park, New York. His father James, a comfortably fixed Dutch patrician, was a fifty-two-year-old widower at the time he married Sara Delano. The bride, exactly half his age, had overridden the vehement opposition of her doting father to wed his neighbor and business associate. This late autumn–early summer union, one may speculate, greatly affected the psychological development of FDR, the marriage's only issue.

The Hyde Park Roosevelts were as close to "country gentry" as America could provide, having possessed modest wealth and high social status for several generations. James Roosevelt, a man of stern mien and unimpeachable dignity (muttonchop whiskers, top hat, and cane), considered himself above all else a gentleman farmer. He served as vice-president of the Delaware and Hudson Canal Company, which had investments in anthracite coal, and as director of several other companies. Except for the panic of 1873, speculative ventures might have won him domination of the eastern coal industry. After this reverse, he settled down to be the squire of Hyde Park. He was "wealthy enough to have his own railroad car, eccentric enough to keep five hundred dollars in gold always handy, established enough to refuse an invitation from the *nouveaux riches* Vanderbilts." His was a life of family dinners,

---

2. Biographers have emphasized various factors, but no one as yet has explained how and why FDR aspired to high political office. Notably, James Barbour, whose recent work *Presidential Character* (New York, 1972) contains an interesting essay on Roosevelt, labels him an "active-positive" president but does not attempt to plumb the wellsprings of his ambition.

clubs, quickly consummated business deals, and quiet participation in community and philanthropic projects. Sara Delano Roosevelt, excluded from much of her husband's life, found satisfaction as mistress of the household and in molding the development of her only child. She was a formidable person on many counts, but on none was she more dogmatic than the code of "proper behavior" she imposed on her son.

The environment in which "little Franklin" grew up was that of upper-class Victorian America at its zenith. "In the long shelf of the biographies of American Presidents," a Roosevelt scholar asserted some years ago, "one searches in vain for the story of a childhood so serene and secure." Both James and Sara Roosevelt doted on their only child, though FDR's mother assumed principal responsibility for his welfare. Young Franklin never lacked material things; there were elaborate toys, hobbies, a pony, a twenty-one-foot sailboat on his sixteenth birthday. The Roosevelts kept an apartment in New York City and a summer place on Campobello Island, New Brunswick. FDR first visited Europe as a two-year-old and returned several times before reaching his teens.

By all accounts he was surrounded with love and companionship, but for most of his formative years it was adult love and adult companionship. As a result, he learned early to respond to grown-ups in ways they preferred, to act mature beyond his years. Sara Roosevelt's protectiveness of her "little man" was suffocating. She kept her son in dresses until he was five, shielded him from "common" children, and schooled him at home. FDR's dependence on his mother survived his marriage and even his accession to the presidency. The story is told that when a local politician came to ask thirty-two-year-old Franklin Roosevelt whether he would run for the state assembly, FDR responded with enthusiasm.

"But," he said, "I'd like to talk to my mother about it first."

"Frank," his visitor replied, "there are men back in Poughkeepsie waiting for your answer. They won't like to hear you had to ask your mother."

FDR gulped and said, "I'll do it."

There were, of course, minor and major rebellions—his decision to marry Eleanor Roosevelt, a love affair with his wife's social secretary, Lucy Mercer, reentry into politics after a nearly fatal bout with polio—but they were in a sense irrelevant. FDR was accustomed to having his way; he gained it by adjusting his wishes to the stronger will of others or by persuading others, less determined than he, that satisfying his wishes was what they really wanted. The point is not that FDR possessed a domineering personality (which he did) or that he allowed others to protect and fawn over him (which he did); it is rather that his relationship with Sara Roosevelt (and to a lesser degree his father) conditioned him at an early age to rely upon a unique repertoire of responses and methods with which he dealt with the world. His upbringing seems to have given him no interest in ideas as contrasted with people, extreme flexibility, reliance on indirection and postponement, and tolerance of disorder. Above all, he became accustomed to seeing himself as the center of his universe.

The demands placed on FDR by his parents were social and familial. Beyond good manners and respect for one's elders, little was asked, though much was assumed. "Study law as I did," his father advised. "It prepares a man for a profession." FDR's profession was to be that of gentleman. Anything else was extra. Sara Roosevelt inculcated a sense of *noblesse oblige,* a recognition that "from those to whom much is given, much is expected"; but what this meant was never explained, and the future president apparently interpreted it to mean that he should play the role of plain citizen whenever appropriate. It was certainly a simple part to master, much less challenging than most of the numerous other roles he would be called upon to play.

FDR's childhood passed without apparent trauma in this atmosphere of benevolent authority. The first break came at age fourteen when he left home for Groton, best known of that peculiar New England institution, the "prep" school. Groton's founder and headmaster, the Reverend Endicott Peabody, preached and taught a life of active, responsible Christianity, and he laced the school curriculum with heavy doses of competitive athletics and Episcopalianism. His credo was service to God and mankind, tinged with a genteel brand of Social Darwinism. Peabody set out to make his charges the agents of social betterment. His "was the faith of a man of action, a spiritual athlete, rather than a contemplative scholar, and Roosevelt came to accept it as his own," Frank Freidel has written.

Because Roosevelt was two years older than his classmates (his mother had held him back), he found adjustment difficult. He encountered problems with "interpersonal relationships," which he resolved by trying to become a stereotypical Grotonian, singing in the choir, debating, taking his lumps on the scrub football team, even rejoicing over black marks for deportment. He worked hard at being accepted by his peers, adding yet another role to his repertoire, though this was not his best performance. The courses he took at Groton were dull when not stultifying, and FDR found no reason to achieve above the level of a "gentleman's C."

In 1900 Roosevelt went on to Harvard, where he performed competently in academic work, but devoted more attention to social opportunities and extracurricular activities. "Am doing a little studying, a little riding, and a few party calls," he wrote his mother. It does not appear that Sara Roosevelt cramped her son's style when she took an apartment in Cambridge after James Roosevelt's death during FDR's freshman year. He enrolled in the liberal arts program, but his instructors never fired him with intellectual curiosity. He complained that the curriculum was "like an electric lamp that hasn't any wire," and later remarked, "I took economics courses in college for four years and everything I was taught was wrong." Harvard's defects combined with Roosevelt's lack of interest yielded a mediocre education. To the extent that FDR took away from Harvard any social and political philosophy, it was "a mixture of political conservatism, economic orthodoxy, and anti-imperialism, steeped in a fuzzy altruism and wide ignorance." The same might be said of his views thirty years later, after he became president.

Roosevelt was active in the Harvard Glee Club and worked on the undergraduate daily, *The Crimson*, becoming editor in chief during his junior year. His greatest disappointment, which some biographers identify as the root cause of his political ambition, was not being tapped for Porcellian, the leading social club on campus, to which his famous cousin Theodore Roosevelt had belonged. For once, family connections and geniality failed to smooth the way. Eleanor Roosevelt later stated that this rebuff gave FDR an inferiority complex, and another relative termed it "the bitterest moment of his life." Its effects upon his personality and social views is unclear, though one may speculate that the experience, in combination with the insecurity caused by the difficulties he encountered at Groton and Harvard, drove him to shield his desires and encouraged a habit of not risking his self-esteem except on the safest of bets.

The characteristics of FDR's personality, the "repertoire of habits" with which he dealt with life, were formed by the time of his graduation from Harvard in 1904. He attended Columbia Law School, passed the New York bar in 1907, and joined an old Wall Street law firm. These were years of drifting, during which almost his only independent act was the decision to marry his fifth cousin Eleanor Roosevelt in spite of his mother's outraged and tearful objections. Sara lost this battle for her son's affection, but appears, ultimately, to have won the war.

FDR drifted into politics in 1910, by chance discovering his true vocation. He won election to the state senate from Dutchess County by ignoring partisan issues and playing up his relationship with "Uncle" TR. His swift rise to a position of leadership in Albany, despite his having the appearance of a "political prig," resulted from hard work, humor, lack of concern about issues and party lines, and a large element of luck. He seemed to be auditioning for "dynamic young politician," and since it brought him to center stage, even if in a provincial theater, he enjoyed the part.

In 1913, as payment for his energetic support of Woodrow Wilson's presidential campaign, Secretary of the Navy Josephus Daniels offered Roosevelt the position of assistant secretary. Always fascinated by the sea and aware of the parallels to be drawn with TR's career, he accepted enthusiastically. "I'd like it bully well," he told Daniels. This decision propelled him into a world vastly different from the one he had known, leading to broader perspectives and new challenges.

FDR sought out kindred spirits in Washington, members of old families who were beginning to accept government service as a civic duty, rather than as a function of *noblesse oblige.* The ingrained feeling of superiority natural to a Hyde Park Roosevelt continued to be present. When war broke out in Europe, FDR no longer could control himself. "I am running the real work" of the Navy Department, he wrote his wife, "although Josephus is here! He is bewildered by it all, very sweet, but very sad!" Between 1916 and 1919 he concentrated on improving the navy's efficiency, tinkering with administration but not proposing serious reforms. He was competent, visible, and accessible to the press, which was intrigued by this quotable, photogenic young man, especially since he was a Roosevelt.

When a few voices raised his name as a presidential candidate in 1920, Roosevelt moved to squelch the movement. It was not that he rejected the idea of becoming president, but rather that the possibility of his nomination and election was a long shot. "I can tell you . . . perfectly frankly," he wrote a friend, "that I do not propose to make an early Christian martyr of myself this year." Less stigma attached to a losing vice-presidential candidate and Roosevelt happily accepted the offer of the second place on the ticket when the Democratic party held its convention. During the campaign he proved more popular than the lackluster standard-bearer, James M. Cox. He spoke eloquently for U.S. participation in the League of Nations and for a return to prewar progressivism; but his voter appeal was personal. Reporters described him as "almost the poster type in public life" and "the figure of an idealized football player." They conceded that people were more taken with the man than with anything he said. That the Republicans won the election of 1920 was much less the result of candidates' actions than it was of the actions of President Woodrow Wilson.

In any case, before FDR had much time to brood over his party's defeat or plot his next move, physical catastrophe struck him. Vacationing with Eleanor and their five children at the family retreat on Campobello, FDR was suddenly seized with chills and stiffness. Within hours docors had diagnosed his affliction as poliomyelitis. Roosevelt, who prized physical strength and virility, had lost muscular control of his legs. All his biographers have described his mental and physical agony over the next few years, though they make light of his mother's insistence that he renounce public life and live out his days in genteel seclusion at Hyde Park. Some insist that the tragedy had beneficial results. Frances Perkins, later his secretary of labor, stated: "Franklin Roosevelt underwent a spiritual transformation during the years of his illness. I noticed when he came back that the years of pain and suffering had purged the slightly arrogant attitude. The man emerged completely warmhearted, with humility of spirit and a deeper philosophy. Having been to the depths of trouble he understood the problems of people in trouble." One could as easily argue that the changes others saw in FDR resulted from greater maturity, the adjustment of his public facade to conform to the expectations others had of a cripple, or a calculated appraisal of how he could use his infirmity to further his political career.

Roosevelt never seriously considered a future as a pampered invalid, and he slowly reentered political life. Perhaps the most important effect of his illness, recuperation, and slow return to politics was that the currents of the 1920s passed him by. FDR was preoccupied with his own problems; *The Wasteland*, the KKK's nativism-run-amok, or the vacuous hedonism of flappers and jellybeans never challenged his amorphous beliefs in the old ethics and values. The public demonstration that his handicap would not deter his career came at the Democratic convention in 1924. Clenching the rostrum to support his upper body and relying on eleven pounds of steel bracing to steady his legs, Roosevelt placed in nomination his fellow New Yorker, Alfred E. Smith. By 1928, he was ready to run for governor of New York. Though indebted to Alfred Smith for his victory, FDR set his own course in Albany. In some areas he acted boldly, assembling a "brain trust" to deal with the problems the depression rained on New York in 1929. Yet every decision was made with an eye to its national implications, for FDR and practically everyone else considered his two terms as governor an apprenticeship for the presidency.

FDR won the Democratic nomination on the first ballot in 1932. Running against Herbert Hoover, he took the safest course, giving voters a chance to vote against the man who had failed to end the depression. In large part he relied on his personal magnetism. Arthur M. Schlesinger, Jr., has noted that "people began to look for the Roosevelt characteristics; the upthrust head; the confidential look with eyebrows arched when he let fly a gibe at the opposition, followed by the slow grin as the audience caught on; the sly mockery; the biting scorn; the righteous wrath." Roosevelt promised a "New Deal" to the American people, but he rarely talked about specific changes; these could be criticized. (Another reason for vagueness was that no New Deal reform program existed.) He evaded sensitive questions and sometimes contradicted himself. The champion of the League of Nations in 1920 told an audience in his home state: "American participation in the League would not serve the highest purpose of the prevention of war and a settlement of international difficulties in accordance with fundamental American ideals. . . . I do not favor American participation." Driven frantic by the shifting views of his opponent, Hoover labeled FDR a "chameleon on plaid"; and so, within a limited spectrum of political colors and ethical motifs, he was.

James McGregor Burns has posed the central question about Roosevelt: "Was there then no hard center, no core personality, no final commitment in this man?" Burns concludes that a nexus of deeply held beliefs did exist under that "bright, smooth flow of talk," that President Roosevelt, for all his deviousness, was "basically a moral man. . . . He believed in doing good, in showing other people how to do good, and he assumed that ultimately people would do good. By 'good' he meant the Ten Commandments and the Golden Rule as interpreted by Endicott Peabody." It is possible that when Roosevelt voiced these teachings of his youth he was merely assuming another role, putting on another mask. Even if a compulsion to "do good" lay at the center of his being, was that a sufficient guide for a man faced with a devastating economic depression, the complexities of global politics, a shattering war? FDR was not and did not pretend to be an original thinker. He possessed in abundance a gift for using men and their ideas to his own advantage and for expressing in simple language the complicated arguments of others.

The absence of commitment and of logically derived views was especially apparent in his approach to foreign affairs. FDR, as noted, possessed no "world view," no inner world of ideas and assumptions, except perhaps in the most general sense. His ideas regarding foreign affairs justifiably may be termed unsophisticated, and on some vital issues he had no opinions at all. When he entered the White House, his views on foreign affairs were a mishmash of "family tradition," half-assimilated theories picked up at Harvard and Washington cocktail parties, and conversations with fellow politicians. The touchstone was belief that the United States must take an active role in world affairs. From Theodore Roosevelt he inherited faith in a strong navy and all that implied; yet Democratic forebears instilled in him an emotional rejection of "imperialism" and colonial regimes. Those views he did advocate tenaciously were almost all taken from childhood experiences and impressions. A summer spent in a German *Volksschule,* along with bicycling excursions through the countryside, persuaded FDR that he knew everything required to deal wisely with Germany; during the Second World War, almost every person who raised with the president the thorny problem of Germany's future was subjected to an involved reminiscence about FDR's youthful adventures, capped by a claim of presidential omniscience on the basis of these experiences. Similarly, Roosevelt based his assertion of superior knowledge about Asian policy on recollections of his grandfather Delano's participation in the China trade in the mid-nineteenth century.

Attachment to "internationalism" was another of Roosevelt's convictions, though he refused to define—either for himself or others—what that implied for the nation's foreign policy. Although he much admired the dream of Woodrow Wilson, FDR faulted him for his failure to make the dream reality. Apparently, FDR concluded that the earlier president had tried for too much too fast, had been too trusting, not hard enough, too fuzzy headed. According to one scholar, he believed that "war must still be the touchstone of policy in foreign affairs. At thirty Roosevelt was a worshiping Wilsonian. Into middle age he espoused a world order under a union of nations; but unlike Wilson, the evangelist, while pursuing peace, he never neglected military preparedness." He came to advocate what he termed "realistic" methods of achieving world order, scoffing at the Kellogg-Briand Pact, refusing to support the World Court, and arguing that the United States must go its own way in meeting the Great Depression. Not surprisingly, his attitudes regarding international relations were egocentric, nationalistic, and paternalistic. Other nations should accept the moral leadership of the United States, because it was right, necessary, and "realistic" for them to do so. Internationalism for him, as for many other American leaders in this era, became a justification for U.S. activism in world affairs, and not a program of specific measures to attain lasting peace.

Oddly coexisting with this "realistic approach" were several secondary Wilsonian principles. One was faith in the efficacy of disarmament. As he told Adolf A. Berle, Jr., in June 1941: "Don't forget that the elimination of costly armaments is still the keystone—for the security of all the little nations and for economic solvency. Don't forget what I discovered—that over ninety percent of all national deficits from 1921 to 1939 were caused by payments for past, present, and future wars." He held similar opinions about the theoretical desirability of an economic open world, a return to that "golden age" of free trade invented by classical economists.

One might pile up a list of particulars to prove that the president held opinions on various issues in U.S. foreign policy, that "FDR said X," "FDR supported Y," "FDR read Z" (though that would be more difficult); but it would be a meaningless exercise. His mind essentially was a *tabula rasa*. Compelled to play roles, Roosevelt seems to have been incapable of carrying out prior analyses of problems and taking stands on the basis of his conclusions; nor did he wish to do so. A well-meaning friend once told him that the New Deal was analogous to a great painting; therefore, like a great artist when his best work was almost finished, he should retouch the painting here and there, perfecting it, and then offer the masterpiece to posterity. The president rejected the analogy: "There 'ain't no such thing' as a masterpiece of permanence in the art of living or the art of government. That type of art catches a mood, fits the method of expression into the emotions of the day and mingles oils with watercolors, and steel engraving with dry point." On another occasion Eleanor Roosevelt brought up the question of religious education for their children. FDR replied that they should attend church and learn what he had learned.

"But are you sure you believe in everything you learned?" she asked.

"I really never thought about it," he admitted. "I think it is just as well not to think about things like that."

To analyze his own beliefs might inhibit the flexibility he so valued, and, besides, action resulted from responses to people, not abstractions. Roosevelt trusted his intuition to grasp what others wanted of him, and he was confident of his ability to satisfy their perceptions. He could be TR or Wilson or John Q. Citizen. His enormous versatility and dramatic skill, after all, had brought him to the presidency. Why should he concern himself thereafter with finding and projecting an "authentic" Franklin Roosevelt? Not only would it be a tiresome exercise, it might well flop.

◇◇◇

Had the international scene remained relatively quiet during FDR's presidency, it is possible that isolationism would have characterized American diplomacy. This might have occurred in spite of the deeper forces pushing the United States toward world leadership and despite President Roosevelt's distaste for a less than preeminent role for himself and the country. The incoming president looked out on a world in political and economic disarray. The global depression in some ways had increased the importance of the United States in international affairs. Economic disaster forced the admission in European capitals that American participation was essential in efforts to restore a viable world economy and political stability. Yet the depression also turned the

AND COMPANY ALREADY ARRIVING

J. N. Ding Foundation. First published in Des Moines Register

American public inward and restricted the freedom of action of those responsible for foreign policy.[3]

Lacking a consensus, FDR attempted to ignore foreign affairs for much of his first term. He concentrated on domestic problems, where a consensus did exist, where individuals and groups across the spectrum of American politics were begging him to act boldly. Nothing comparable existed in the realm of foreign affairs. FDR confessed in early 1934: "In the present European situation, I feel very much as if I were groping for a door in a blank wall. The situation may get better and enable us to give some leadership." As a result, the United States swung to and fro between partnership in and boycott of the world community. Decisions such as the Roosevelt-Litvinov Agreements, ending America's paranoid refusal to recognize the existence of Soviet Russia, were in keeping with a sort of passive pragmatism. FDR's own opinion of the Soviet experiment reflected skepticism and disdain, but as always political calculations outweighed his personal views.

In May 1933 the president stepped forward with a plan to assure peace, a forthright appeal to world leaders to sign a nonaggression pact, renounce all weapons of offensive war, and curb arms production. Violent opposition abroad and in the Senate caused him to back down. Concluding that any attempt to realize other Wilsonian dreams, such as American enrollment in organizations for international cooperation, would similarly arouse the isolationist coalition, he opted for another Wilsonian trademark, watchful waiting. He deferred to Congress in the question of war debts, cooperated with the Nye Committee's investigation of arms trade and manufacture, and acquiesced in the passage of neutrality legislation that implicitly blamed Woodrow Wilson for American entry into the First World War. It may be, as Robert Divine has argued, that Roosevelt did these things from conviction and that until 1937 he believed isolationism was the only practical course for the United States. More likely, however, this "foreign policy by makeshift" stemmed from the inability of the public to cue him to any other response and to the fluctuating influence of his ideologically diverse advisers.

3. Whether the situation in foreign affairs would have been susceptible to aggressive leadership is moot. The pressures affecting U.S. diplomacy at this juncture are well described in Robert H. Ferrell, *American Diplomacy in the Great Depression* (New Haven, 1957).

FDR's penchant for indirection and his peculiar style of administration militated against a consistent foreign policy. The president's compulsion to hold power securely in his own hands led to the creation of overlapping administrative empires in competition with each other and with access to information and power linked to Roosevelt's personal survival and authority. FDR apparently thrived in the resulting atmosphere of confusion and Byzantine intrigue. Antagonistic to the rigidity and mechanical processes of bureaucracy, he preferred to act himself or to use personal agents to conduct sensitive negotiations. Though the dispatch of special diplomatic missions was as old as the Republic, FDR institutionalized the practice. He heartily distrusted the "striped-pants boys" in the Department of State and soon wearied of their dignified, hypercautious chief Cordell Hull. After trying various methods of getting around Hull, in 1937 he engineered the appointment of Sumner Welles, a fellow Grotonian and Harvard man who had been a page boy at his wedding, as undersecretary of state. Thereafter, he used Welles as his chief diplomatic counselor and confidant, avoiding any need for boring consultations with his secretary of state. By 1940 the strained relations between Hull and Welles were common gossip, and the secretary was threatening to resign, "because the President very obviously seeks Sumner Welles' advice in preference to his own." Later, the versatile Harry Hopkins assumed a similar function.

Presidential scorn for established procedures served merely to immobilize State, not to purge and restructure the chaotic foreign affairs bureaucracy. Weakened by internal divisions, competition for primacy with other agencies, deep-seated malaise and elitism, and other problems, the department bumbled on, still conducting the great bulk of the nation's diplomacy. Mutual lack of respect and communication between the White House and the inhabitants of the ornate State-War-Navy Building next door was to prove unfortunate, for it inhibited the president's ability to exercise leadership when he chose to do so.

Roosevelt's actions with regard to two issues soon after he assumed office—the Reciprocal Trade Agreements program and the Good Neighbor policy—clearly revealed his style of diplomacy. Democratic administrations traditionally had supported efforts to reduce tariffs and remove barriers to the freer flow of international trade. For some, that effort had become a crusade, which embodied mankind's best hope of achieving prosperity and lasting peace. Cordell Hull, appointed secretary of state largely because of his political standing with Congress, had fought for tariff reform since he delivered his maiden speech in the House of Representatives on the subject in 1905. An assistant once said of the secretary's obsession with trade issues: "Of course that is Hull. That is his . . . *raison d'être*. . . . His trade agreements . . . are the base on which rests his whole foreign activity." Having been assured during the campaign that FDR supported his principles, Hull expected to gain realization of his life's dream.

The route to trade reciprocity proved extremely circuitous. The president, whose understanding of international economics did not extend much beyond glittering generalities learned at Harvard, was captivated by the economic nationalism of his domestic advisers. In late 1933 he appointed a committee to coordinate trade policy and designated George N. Peek, a dogmatic opponent of tariff reductions, as its chairman. Hull was apoplectic. When neither side could amass clear evidence and public support, the president suggested a bastard compromise. He invoked a principle that had served him well in the past: when in doubt, postpone. Hull eventually brought such pressure that Roosevelt sponsored the trade agreements program. Although the Reciprocal Trade Agreements Act proved remarkably effective, it was only a beginning of the economic open world which Hull and a dedicated band in the State Department sought. Hull found himself struggling ever after to maintain FDR's allegiance.

In contrast to the crusade for trade reciprocity, the reordering of relations with Latin America, immortalized by President Roosevelt's reference in his inaugural address to the necessity for the U.S. to be "a good neighbor," was negative in purpose. It was designed to remove from the Roosevelt administration's list of potentially embarrassing issues the always ticklish problem of Latin America. The Good Neighbor policy resulted more from concern for U.S. purposes than from a new recognition of the sovereignty of Latin American nations. Further, Roosevelt only confirmed the trend toward disengagement inaugurated by his Republican predecessors. Hoover had quietly shut down military protectorates in several countries, and the "Clark Memorandum," written in 1928 but not made public until 1930, virtually repudiated the Roosevelt Corollary to the Monroe Doctrine.

Before the Second World War, Good Neighborism proceeded through two stages. The first reflected Washington's almost total concentration on domestic problems. The depression made FDR anxious to avoid awkward and costly entanglements abroad, such as were threatened by intervention in Latin America. Secretary Hull was deputized to work out the details. The U.S. refrained from intervention in Cuba when several revolutions shook the island, long a ward of the United States and land of opportunity for American investors. A year later, in April 1934, the Platt Amendment was abrogated, and soon thereafter the U.S. Marines withdrew from Haiti. Hull had anticipated these decisions by attending the Pan-American Conference at Montevideo. A second stage opened with the Buenos Aires and Lima conferences. It reflected U.S. anxiety about developments in Europe and Asia— and the immediate fear that Nazi Germany might obtain footholds in the Americas.

President Roosevelt's role in these events was that of publicist and conduit for policies conceived in the State Department. He never devoted serious effort to understanding Latin America's problems and always dealt with Latin American affairs, when the subject arose, from a viewpoint of kindly but smug paternalism. Ultimately, the efforts to achieve hemispheric solidarity produced treaties for collective security; but such acts as the Declaration of Lima (1938) and the Rio Pact (1947), milestones on the road to hemispheric cooperation, also derived from negative impulses— the depression, fear of German penetration, and the later obsession with communism—rather than acceptance of the need for mutual assistance. Untouched by these acts were the economic difficulties separating the Americas: the vast disparity in standards of living between North and South, the dependence of much of Latin America on one-crop economies and the power of North American investors and businessmen in many of these countries, the refusal of the United States, because of political calculation and scruples about economic theories, to assist in the diversification and reform of Latin America's economics. In this sense the present is not much different from 1932.

Franklin Roosevelt cannot be blamed for centuries of neglect and deprivation; however, his administration's indifference to the economic and social problems assaulting Latin America (and Asia and, in different ways, Europe as well) and the assignment of responsibility for those matters to a State Department that was backward looking and lacking in direction amounted to an abdication of leadership. FDR believed that the state of public opinion and the critical problems at home dictated a passive role in foreign affairs. Above all else, there impended the absolutely essential goal of his reelection in 1936. As a result, when the president gave serious attention to foreign affairs, the world had changed, and for the worse.

◇◇◇

The president's awakening to the ominous situation in Europe and Asia most often is identified with his Chicago "quarantine" speech of 5 October 1937. This address, which shocked his countrymen and official Washington when delivered and has puzzled historians since, unveiled a new FDR, the statesman who would protect civilization against international lawbreakers. Demonstrating belated concern about conflicts then flaring in Spain and China, the president warned that America could not isolate itself from "a breakdown of international order and law." He then said, "When an epidemic of physical disease starts to spread, the community approves and joins in a quarantine of the patients in order to protect the health of the community against the spread of disease." If he was advocating, via this medical metaphor, collective action against aggressor nations, he soon backed off, even asserting after his return to Washington that the speech was an expansion rather than repudiation of neutrality.

The "quarantine" speech has been interpreted as a "trial balloon," a puff of hot air, the first shot in a battle to convince the American people of the growing threats to their security, and as FDR's public conversion to internationalism. Quite possibly, it represented all or none of these. Roosevelt himself was confused about his motives. Asked by journalist Ernest R. Lindley what he meant by the speech, he said: "I can't give you a clue to it. You will have to invent one." It did reveal that FDR once more was shifting roles. The repertoire of devices and tricks available to him in domestic matters was pretty well exhausted. Although he won reelection in 1936 by an unprecedented margin, this personal victory had not sparked a consensus such as he had enjoyed in 1933–34. The evidence seemed irrefutable. Dr. New Deal had lost his ability to mesmerize. The attempt to pack the Supreme Court, in which he perhaps risked more of his personal prestige than on any other issue, closed out of town to rotten notices. The "Roosevelt Recession," looming over the country when he spoke in Chicago, posed a challenge that a fireside chat and exuberant confidence could not overcome. The Spanish civil war, outbreak of a full-scale conflict between China and Japan, and Hitler's bellicose maneuvers in Europe merged with the president's domestic difficulties to stimulate a search for a new consensus. This time FDR chose foreign affairs as the stage for exercise of his unique talents.

One may argue that the Second World War began in 1931, when Japan manufactured an excuse for sending troops into north China. Then and later the United States had appeared powerless to halt Japan's imperial ambitions. The American response to the Manchurian crisis, the Hoover-Stimson Doctrine, nonrecognition of any forced conquest, relied on the force of American and international public opinion. The Roosevelt administration did little better. There developed a pattern of U.S. moralism and Japanese contempt for American strength of will that took the two nations ultimately to war. By 1937, it may have been too late to reverse course and FDR never seriously tried, leaving the thorny problem of Asia to the legalistic-minded Hull.

The situation was no more encouraging with regard to fresh initiatives elsewhere in the world. The president soon discovered that the consensus that he deemed necessary for forthright leadership would prove more difficult to achieve than a comparable mobilization of opinion on domestic issues. There existed widespread popular indifference to events elsewhere in the world, and bitter hostility about the wisest course divided those who were interested in foreign affairs. His own uncertainties and the conflicting advice of associates militated against aggressive leadership. Furthermore, Neville Chamberlain, Adolf Hitler, and other foreign statesmen proved less malleable than the ward bosses with whom FDR dealt so skillfully.[4]

The period 1938–41 was a frustrating time for FDR. To be sure, it was also an exciting time. The president sent messages of

---

4. Historians differ strongly on the issue of popular attitudes in this period. Polls, newspaper editorials, the White House mail, and other indicators have been invoked to "prove" that the American public adamantly opposed intervention in any form—or to "prove" just the opposite. No one has explained fully how FDR viewed "public opinion," what sorts of information he considered most revealing of the public mood. It is clear that the isolation imposed by the office and his physical limitation had great influence on his reading of popular attitudes.

encouragement, cajolery, and warning to the heads of powerful nations, many of whom accorded him recognition as the leader of world opinion. He moved battleships from one ocean to the other, approved decisions that eventually gave the United States unimaginable military power. He played at strategy and plotted naval engagements. Once it became certain that the American public desired defeat of the Axis powers, the president renounced the spirit of neutrality and, using brilliant dodges to contravene the letter of the law, funneled aid—ships, munitions, raw materials, dollars—to Great Britain and other nations resisting aggression. Such acts as the agreement to trade American destroyers for British bases and lend-lease were stopgaps. They did not confront, and indeed allowed FDR to postpone confronting, the basic issue: whether the nation's security demanded America's participation in the war.

FDR struggled with this conundrum for two years, until Pearl Harbor released him from the paralysis it inflicted. Nothing in his background and grab bag of habits prepared him for this sort of crisis, which required patient self-analysis and leadership amid the din of conflicting views. As James McGregor Burns has observed: "Roosevelt, in a sense, was captive to himself as well as to his political environment. He was captive to his habit of mediating among pressures rather than reshaping them, of responding eclectically to all the people around him, of balancing warring groups and leaders against one another, of improvising with brilliance and gusto. Impatient of theory, insatiably curious about people and their ideas, sensitively attuned to the play of forces around him, he lacked that burning and almost fanatic conviction that great leadership demands." The strongest criticism of Roosevelt's conduct of foreign affairs is that at critical points he failed to provide leadership, to "give the cue the people needed." Those who have offered this criticism assume that FDR, by an effort of will, could throw off his subservience to public opinion and political maneuvering and issue a clarion call for American intervention in the Second World War. A contrary claim is that the president's restraint "showed excellent political sense," that he admitted U.S. entry into the war was necessary but decided only a carefully planned campaign to educate the American people would avoid cataclysmic divisions destructive of this purpose.[5]

5. The claim that FDR was carrying out a shrewd campaign of public education dominated the early literature on his conduct of foreign affairs. See, for example,

The fact is that FDR's outlook did not permit him to respond in ways other than he did respond, and his reaction had little to do with consistency or calculation. The situation was ambivalent; therefore, he had to be ambivalent. Brief examination of one of the many "events" with which Roosevelt dealt in the period before Pearl Harbor exemplifies the degree to which he was entrapped in the contradictions of that "puzzle within an enigma," his personality.

◇◇◇

Only after the startling collapse of France in June 1940 did the American people begin to realize that a Nazi-dominated Europe threatened the security of the United States. At the same time, Japanese adventurism created concern for American interests, real and mythical, in the Pacific. A tidal wave of sentiment for preparedness swept the country, though a thoughtful few asked, "Preparedness for what?" Congress acted to create a two-ocean navy and two months later, in September 1940, approved the Selective Service Act, the first peacetime draft in America's history.

After his reelection in November 1940, FDR proceeded to make material aid available to the Allies, but he resisted pressures for direct involvement in the war. This policy reflected the contradictory opinions of the public: 75 percent approved helping the British, while 85 percent indicated a desire to avoid war at all costs. Roosevelt possibly believed that material aid would suffice and that it would not be necessary to send American boys to die on foreign soil. He knew by early 1941, however, that lend-lease alone would not ensure an Allied victory. The British simply did not have the resources to win the war by themselves. It also became clear that the conversion of the United States, in FDR's words, into "the great arsenal of democracy," could not take place without full-scale mobilization, which required a declaration of war.

These grim calculations plunged the president into a deep

Samuel I. Rosenman, ed., *The Public Papers and Addresses of Franklin D. Roosevelt*, 13 vols. (New York, 1938–50). Careful examination of the president's actions in the controversy over revising the neutrality statutes, the Russo-Finnish War, and the convoying debate suggest that he was not a teacher but a pupil, himself waiting to be educated.

depression. Apparently, he thought his magic touch no longer worked, that he faced a "new ball game" in which his ability to outguess the opposition and stir up his own team had disappeared. An assiduous student of public opinion polls, Roosevelt gained from these indicators in spring 1941 confirmation of the futility and foolhardiness of frank leadership. FDR had a singular perception of the *mésalliance* between the presidency and public opinion. While possessing allegiance to the abstractions of the democratic process, he had rather less confidence in the electorate's ability to reach mature judgments. He was often disturbingly paternalistic, fond of playing the kindly but firm teacher, giving his pupils (the public) precepts for right action. In 1941 his tutorship was in disfavor. FDR's reaction was to withdraw from direction of affairs. He used a series of colds and sinus infections to shut out visitors bringing pleas for deeper American involvement. The key to this period of withdrawal was frustration. Roosevelt concluded that his effort to push through lend-lease had "temporarily exhausted his credit both with Congress and the country," and he must remain passive until the public caught up.

Presidential intimates could not refrain from pleading for action. In May, Secretary of the Interior Harold L. Ickes was despairing: "In every direction I find a growing discontent with the President's lack of leadership. He still has the country if he will take it and lead it. But he won't have it much longer unless he does something. It won't be sufficient for him to make another speech and then go into a state of innocuous desuetude again." Henry Morgenthau noted that the president and his sickly familiar, Harry Hopkins, appeared baffled. "They feel that something has to be done but don't know just what." Hopkins had told him that "the President is loath to get into this war, and he would rather follow public opinion than lead it." FDR's inability to pull the nation along by his assertive self-confidence was a novel and fearsome occurrence, and his advisers did not know what to make of it.

Almost the only project in which the president took an interest in this period was the planning for a conference with the British war leader, Winston Churchill. As he worked on this project he began to grasp its potential for easing the pressures upon him. It seemed a marvelous pedagogical device, and such opportunities—since the Germans and Japanese refused to provoke hostilities—had been nonexistent in recent months. A Roosevelt-

Churchill conference, prefaced by some stirring call for unity in the confrontation between good and evil, could have bombshell effects on attitudes at home and abroad. Perhaps a secret meeting of the democracies' two great leaders was *the* event for which FDR had been longing.

It is testimony to the extent of the president's personal approach to problems that the meeting with Churchill became a means of rescuing him from his malaise. It also embodied most of the techniques that were characteristic of Rooseveltian diplomacy: secrecy, indirection, drama, careful timing, and personal participation. The Atlantic Conference was the first of a series of meetings in which Allied leaders dealt with the strategic issues of the war and sketched the outlines of the peace. This meeting, which took place on U.S. and British warships anchored off Argentia, Newfoundland, from 9 to 14 August 1941, did confirm military aid to Great Britain, produced a short-lived agreement on policy toward Japan, sanctioned that statement of high principle, the Atlantic Charter, and, perhaps most importantly, brought about the first encounter between two leaders of the triumvirate that was to manage the destruction of the Axis.[6]

The decisions reached at Argentia were embryonic and temporary. The conference produced only one formal agreement, a statement of war and peace aims, which survived American entry into the war; the Atlantic Charter, ironically, was one matter to which President Roosevelt gave little importance. The meeting was most revealing about the president's style of diplomacy and established a pattern of behavior that was to dominate wartime negotiations. Demanding that the conference transpire in total secrecy, FDR limited the U.S. delegation to military leaders and members of his personal entourage. He brought along Sumner Welles to handle the details of any diplomatic conversations. Roosevelt excluded Secretary Hull from preparations for the meetings and did not even inform him of its existence until the conference was almost over. One effect of the insistence on haste and secrecy was that the Americans were poorly prepared for substantive discussions with their British counterparts. The president apparently preferred it that way.

6. For a full description of the Atlantic Conference and the issues summarized here, see Theodore A. Wilson, *The First Summit: Roosevelt and Churchill at Placentia Bay* (Boston, 1969).

Released from his imprisonment in the White House, FDR proved a patsy for the large dollops of flattery laid on by the British and for Churchill's sweeping expositions on politics and grand strategy. By meeting's end the president had agreed to a virtual ultimatum to Japan (later emasculated by the State Department), indicated support of the British strategy of bombing, blockade, and subversion, and approved a clause in the Atlantic Charter that subverted the foreign economic policy of his administration. Only on the question of a declaration of war did FDR resist British blandishments; however, Churchill soon learned that presidential commitments were as stable as shifting sand. Roosevelt really had not committed either himself or the country.

In retrospect, the meeting's significance lay in the relationships established (proof that Roosevelt and Churchill, each having gigantic egos, would be able to work together; the introduction of U.S. and British officials) and for the informal alliance between the English-speaking nations that it affirmed. Less clear at the time was the transfer of power that Argentia symbolized. Thenceforth, as America's gigantic industrial and technological resources were applied to the war, the United States became the senior partner, taking from Britain's faltering grasp the glories and obligations of world leadership. FDR came to relish that role more than any he ever played.

The meeting at Argentia did not resolve the immediate problem facing the president. Far from easing his difficulties, the conference pinned FDR tightly between the horns of isolationist denunciation and interventionist outcry. After his return to Washington, he chose to ward off accusations that the meeting meant war. This sacrificed a large part of the impact. How the American people might have responded had Roosevelt confessed that he had met with Churchill to deal with a desperate crisis and then proclaimed that the country must endure whatever sacrifice was required is idle speculation. Such a risky act of leadership was precisely what he hoped to avert; to him it would have been inconsistent with every dictate of experience.

The nation's drift toward war abruptly terminated with the shock of Japan's attack on Pearl Harbor. For Roosevelt, it was as if a great weight had been lifted from his heart. "They have attacked us at Pearl Harbor," he calmly informed a jubilant Churchill. "We are all in the same boat now." A new role, commander in chief, had opened for him. During the next four years, in the guise of Dr.

Win the War, he made brilliant use of all the enormous resources at his command. He led, cajoled, and maneuvered the United States toward the single goal of total victory and, it may be said, sacrificed his life in that cause.

◇◇◇

It is regrettable that the limits President Roosevelt accepted and imposed on this last and greatest role in order to win the war were to destroy much of his achievement in diplomacy. The tragedy of Pearl Harbor, aside from lives lost and ships sunk, was that it did not resolve but merely papered over the debate about America's real interests in the conflict. America was at war, but beyond the motive of survival there was little understanding of why the United States was fighting, what interests were at stake, and what might be gained. Unrealistic hopes about the future blossomed and the American people mistook idealistic rhetoric for national goals. Perhaps even more tragically, they and their leaders miscalculated the nation's ability to achieve both ideals and self-interest.

The president, who now had the undivided attention of his audience, chose not to engage in any further educational efforts about the world and America's place in it. He concentrated on prosecution of the war and shunted aside difficult questions: the nature of the postwar world, the relationship between national sovereignty and a viable world peace-keeping organization, basic conflicts among members of the Allied coalition. Invoking the Wilsonian principle of "no predetermination," FDR refused to engage in political deals, or, indeed, to make any arrangements on postwar political matters. He insisted that such questions as the status of Germany and the future of colonial peoples be left to a "universal peace conference" that would be convened at war's end and over which he intended to preside.

The president did not lack awareness of the antagonisms beneath the surface of Allied cooperation. Nor did he ignore entirely the factors that limited American capacity to overcome these antagonisms. In fact, at times he minimized U.S. ability to influence the course of events. Because of his addiction to "the vice of immediacy" during the first part of the war, American diplomacy reflected a conscious acceptance of *Realpolitik* and *Machtpolitik*. Certainly, no desire to "make the world safe for democracy" was discernible in U.S. dealings with Franco's Spain, the tortured history of American relations with Vichy France, Roosevelt's self-serving treatment of the Nationalist Chinese, and Washington's cynical acceptance of the Badoglio regime after Italy's surrender. Similarly, the unconditional surrender policy, the administration's callous policy toward small nations, especially its cobelligerents in Latin America, and its adoption of "modern" techniques of warfare—population bombing and unrestricted submarine operations—betrayed easy acceptance of the principle that might makes right. President Roosevelt was not directly responsible for all these acts, but he set the tone: winning the war took precedence.

Overshadowed by the emphasis on wartime necessity, American diplomacy was riddled with inconsistency and crippled by lack of understanding about the purposes it was to achieve. The president's administrative style, founded on improvisation, proved inadequate to the demands of wartime diplomacy and postwar planning. FDR retained control over all diplomatic matters affecting strategy, and the confusion as to what was "diplomatic" and "military" ensured that little was done without presidential authority. He dealt with political questions affecting the great powers, mostly at the conferences with Churchill and Stalin. The wartime summits followed the script written at Argentia, often with unfortunate results.

The final meeting between the Big Three—Churchill, Roosevelt, and Stalin—took place at Yalta, a seaside resort in the Russian Crimea, in February 1945. Yalta later became a synonym for FDR's supposed "sellout" to the Soviet Union, with critics asserting that the agreements negotiated there amounted to deliberate treason. In fact, the Yalta Conference mostly confirmed decisions reached earlier, and any unfortunate effects of FDR's actions stemmed from application of those beliefs and behavior patterns, intensified in this case by physical (and perhaps mental) debility, with which he had always operated.

As at the Tehran Conference in November 1943, President Roosevelt assumed the role of mediator between Churchill and Stalin. By treating complex issues as personal matters that he and his two great colleagues could decide, FDR often found himself out of his element, unable to respond with anything more than genial optimism and assurances of mutual esteem. Although he brought a large entourage to Yalta, including his new secretary of state, Edward R. Stettinius, and although the U.S. delegation was well briefed, FDR did not use his advisers in any systematic way, preferring to extemporize and react to British and Soviet proposals.

The conference opened in an atmosphere of impending victory, with Germany toppling into defeat and Japan reeling. For the first time, however, the Allied leaders had to confront directly questions relating to the postwar world. Discussion of the occupation of Germany and reparations, the status of Eastern Europe, the United Nations, and territorial arrangements in the Far East brought to light vast differences in outlook and aspirations among the erstwhile allies. FDR struggled to maintain at least a facade of cooperation, even at the risk of appearing to appease the Soviet Union; but again he obtained amicable relations by glossing over some basic problems and postponing others. When the president, looking exhausted, returned to the United States, he pronounced Yalta a monumental accomplishment, and the public and Congress accepted this judgment. Within a few short months, however, the imprecise, unwarranted assumptions inherent in the Yalta Agreements were proving a source of mistrust and hostility.

Submerged in busywork and the construction of elaborate programs for global peace and prosperity, the State Department was swept along by the rising antagonism toward Russian communism. As a sop to Hull, who was kept away from the summit meetings by explicit presidential order, FDR assigned him to the supervision of State Department planning for American participation in wartime and postwar programs: the United Nations, its Relief and Rehabilitation Administration, the European Advisory Commission, the International Bank for Reconstruction and Development, the International Monetary Fund, and other agencies for international cooperation. This honor proved illusory, since Hull and his cohorts were permitted only to spin gossamer dreams. Meanwhile, war agencies that carried on foreign activities vied with State for power and prestige in foreign affairs. The Bureau of Economic Warfare, Treasury, Agriculture, the Foreign Economic Administration, and the innumerable boards and commissions controlled by the army and navy challenged the department's primacy. This bureaucratic warfare amused FDR, and he ignored the tangle of purposes and the enormous waste it produced.

The patchwork administration of foreign affairs somehow did not prevent the winning of the war, but it functioned at the expense of postponing consideration of vital issues. In this regard the president was depressingly shortsighted and lacking in confidence about his fellow citizens. By awarding his imprimatur to State's utopian proposals on economic and political internationalism, he committed the United States to participation in a vaguely conceived world organization, one presumably with power to maintain peace. Yet he himself always placed U.S. interest ahead of the aims of any supranational agency, and he was prepared to bypass or ignore the United Nations when vital interests were at stake. The international organization he envisioned would be dominated by the great powers—the "four policemen"—who would disarm everyone but themselves, victors and vanquished alike, and proceed to restructure the world according to a model of benevolent paternalism. Statements about the potential effectiveness of the UN were so optimistic, however, that many Americans were persuaded—and it may be that President Roosevelt convinced himself. FDR was fond of saying that he was a realist, that he was determined not to repeat the mistakes of Woodrow Wilson. If so, his was a curious sort of realism, based on two decidedly unrealistic assumptions: that the wartime coalition between the United States, Great Britain, and the Soviet Union reflected their basic interests and thus would continue, and that an economic and political environment for world peace and reconstruction could be created quickly after the war. More likely, though, FDR did not give serious thought to these matters, preferring to hope that some means of dealing with (or ignoring) them would present itself to him before they reached a critical stage.

◇◇◇

A cerebral hemorrhage removed FDR before the defects in his diplomacy became obvious; a cynic would say that his timing once again was brilliant. He left an uncertain legacy. He had followed a cautious, limited policy in foreign affairs and had acted only when sustained by a popular consensus. Following patterns of behavior established in childhood and early adolescence, he responded to events instead of constructing a rational system of ideas and policies. The remarkable achievement of this essentially characterless man was his ability to immerse himself so completely in a particular role that it became *the* FDR and he became that character, faithfully reproducing the character's attributes and methods for the duration of its existence. Unfortunately, such an intensely personal approach to diplomacy relied upon political and dramatic gifts not likely to be duplicated for a long time, if ever.

It is doubly ironic that FDR's search for a solution to the difficulties facing the nation from 1937 to 1945 encouraged the emergence of a new consensus founded on popular enthusiasm, a jumble of stereotypes about other nations, and widespread ignorance about the world. Its dominant element was confidence in the American system. The enormous production rolling out of America's farms and factories, accomplished with comparatively small sacrifice and strain on the nation's political fabric, seemed to demonstrate the superiority of American institutions. Certainly, many Americans believed it did.[7]

These attitudes—especially faith in the transferability of American ideals and institutions and a blind confidence in the future—undergirded U.S. planning with regard to postwar problems. They formed the context within which occurred American responses to the development of a "cold war" with the Soviet Union. In the final weeks before his death, President Roosevelt appears to have attempted to launch a crash program of public education, deflating the optimism generated by administration pronouncements about the new world to ensue after war's end. If that is true, his efforts came too late; and his successor was to find little in FDR's diplomacy that informed him how to deal with the wreckage of war and blighted aspirations.

BIBLIOGRAPHIC NOTE

The documentary residue of Franklin D. Roosevelt's life is enormous. The Roosevelt Library at Hyde Park, New York, contains some ten thousand linear feet of presidential records alone, and the storage vaults

---

7. The shift in popular attitudes regarding America's role in the world is the most striking difference between 1933 and 1945. FDR mirrored this change but, like most of his countrymen, did not fully grasp its causes or its complications. The full effects of the changes in views and the realities of power they represented were obscured by the war and apparent survival of prewar diplomatic alignments; however, outside the normal channels of diplomacy, a floodtide of power and responsibility moved toward the United States.

of the National Archives and the Washington Federal Records Center hold hundreds of thousands of cubic feet of diplomatic-political-military records. Despite (or because of) this huge store of information, would-be biographers and monographers have been unable to find there much of FDR the president or the man. Furthermore, many pieces of the great puzzle of Rooseveltian diplomacy are only now becoming available because of State Department zeal (and the caution of the National Archives and Records Service) in applying regulations on access to diplomatic records. Of great assistance in the interim are the eighty-five volumes of *Foreign Relations of the United States* (Washington, D.C., 1861–) covering FDR's tenure. Edgar B. Nixon, *Franklin D. Roosevelt and Foreign Affairs,* 3 vols. (Cambridge, Mass., 1969), are an important supplement.

This is not to suggest that these obstacles have discouraged scholarly research. In fact, the volume and variety of works on the Great Depression and the Second World War is so immense that it seems to be approaching the state of fragmentation and interpretive chaos that now characterizes the literature on the American Civil War. Soon after FDR's death, Frank Freidel began an ambitious six-volume biography. By 1956 he had completed three volumes, *Franklin D. Roosevelt: The Apprenticeship* (Boston, 1952), *The Ordeal* (Boston, 1954), and *The Triumph* (Boston, 1956). A fourth volume, *Launching the New Deal,* which takes the story through summer 1933, appeared in 1973. Arthur Schlesinger, Jr., like Freidel a friendly critic, has yet to complete a projected four-volume study. The first three volumes are *The Crisis of the Old Order* (Boston, 1957), *The Coming of the New Deal* (Boston, 1958), and *The Politics of Upheaval* (Boston, 1960). The theses of James McGregor Burns's two volumes are contained in their subtitles: *Roosevelt: The Lion and the Fox* (New York, 1956) and *Roosevelt: The Soldier of Freedom* (New York, 1970). For an intriguing "psychohistorical" explanation, see the section on FDR in James Barbour, *Presidential Character* (New York, 1972).

Books by and about the people close to FDR have special value for understanding his personality. Eleanor Roosevelt's *This I Remember* (New York, 1949) is guarded but useful. Christopher P. Lasch, *Eleanor and Franklin* (New York, 1971), portrays FDR as incapable of deep personal intimacy. *The Roosevelts of Hyde Park: An Untold Story* (New York, 1972), by Elliott Roosevelt and James Brough, is a peculiar but informative book. Robert E. Sherwood's *Roosevelt and Hopkins: An Intimate History* (New York, 1948) remains in many ways the best biographical treatment. Also relevant are the memoirs and edited diaries of Frances Perkins, James Farley, Harold Ickes, Henry Morgenthau, Jr., Samuel Rosenman, Elliott Roosevelt, and Henry A. Wallace.

The aridity of Cordell Hull's *Memoirs,* 2 vols. (New York, 1948) offers evidence of the Department of State's isolation. The biography of Hull by

Julius W. Pratt, 2 vols. (New York, 1964) is respectable. See also Sumner Welles, *The Time for Decision* (New York, 1944) and *Seven Decisions That Shaped History* (New York, 1951), the egotistical but deeply perceptive *Memoirs: 1925-1950* (Boston, 1967) by George F. Kennan, and the writings and diaries of career diplomats and cabinet officials such as Adolf A. Berle, Jr., Breckinridge Long, Charles Bohlen, Pierrepont Moffat, William Phillips, Joseph Grew, and Henry L. Stimson.

The standard account on the coming of the Second World War remains William L. Langer and S. Everett Gleason, *The Challenge to Isolation* (New York, 1952) and *The Undeclared War: 1940-1941* (New York, 1953). The works of Herbert Feis, especially *The Road to Pearl Harbor* (Princeton, 1950), *Churchill, Roosevelt, Stalin* (Princeton, 1957), and *The China Tangle* (Princeton, 1953), are indispensable. Robert Divine, *Roosevelt and World War II* (Baltimore, 1969), is a thoughtful discussion of the president's role in foreign affairs. See Gaddis Smith, *American Diplomacy during the Second World War, 1941-1945* (New York, 1965), for an indictment of FDR's personal diplomacy. Postwar planning is treated in Harley Notter, *Postwar Foreign Policy Preparation, 1939-1945* (Washington, D.C., 1949), Robert Divine, *Second Chance: The Triumph of Internationalism in America during World War II* (New York, 1967), and E. F. Penrose, *Economic Planning for the Peace* (Princeton, 1953). Lloyd C. Gardner's *Economic Aspects of New Deal Diplomacy* (Madison, Wisc., 1964) and *Architects of Illusion: Men and Ideas in American Diplomacy, 1941-1950* (Chicago, 1970) offer challenging arguments. Among the critical accounts that emphasize the will to power and America's market imperatives are William Appleman Williams, *The Tragedy of American Diplomacy* (New York, 1962), David L. Green, *The Containment of Latin America* (Chicago, 1971), and the mammoth work by Gabriel Kolko, *The Politics of War: The World and United States Foreign Policy, 1943-1945* (New York, 1968). The most balanced account of Soviet-American problems is John L. Gaddis, *The United States and the Origins of the Cold War* (New York, 1972).

A good bibliography of printed material on FDR is in Burns's *Soldier of Freedom*. John E. Wiltz, *From Isolation to War, 1931-1941* (New York, 1968), is an excellent guide and analysis of the scholarship on foreign affairs. The Roosevelt Library has published *The Era of Franklin D. Roosevelt: A Selected Bibliography of Essays, Dissertations, and Periodical Literature, 1945-1971* (Hyde Park, N.Y., 1973), compiled by William J. Stewart.

National Park Service photograph,
Harry S. Truman Library

HARRY S. TRUMAN

and the Origins of Containment

John Lewis Gaddis

"Complete unbelief. That was first. . . . Then consternation at the thought of that Throttlebottom Truman." The words were those of David Lilienthal, but millions of Americans shared the same thought upon hearing the news of Franklin D. Roosevelt's death on the afternoon of 12 April 1945. At first, Harry S. Truman did seem to resemble Alexander P. Throttlebottom, the eminently forgettable vice-president in George Gershwin's musical *Of Thee I Sing.* The man who had just inherited the White House had been, up to that point, inconspicuous, one reason that Roosevelt, seeking a noncontroversial replacement for Henry Wallace, had chosen Truman as his running mate in 1944. During his brief tenure as vice-president, Truman attracted national attention only twice, by attending the funeral of a bankrupt political boss, Tom Pendergast, and by being photographed playing an upright piano with the sultry movie star Lauren Bacall perched on top.

As events quickly made clear, Truman was no Throttlebottom.

Few men have entered the presidency with less preparation, yet none have filled that position with less hesitation and self-doubt. Truman relished responsibility and thrived on decision making; he bore the burdens of office with a good-humored resiliency that never failed to impress those close to him. If he had second thoughts about the policies he followed, he kept them to himself. From the day he left office until his death almost twenty years later, Truman remained serenely convinced that he had done his best, and that his best had served the country well.

Scholars initially accepted that judgment, especially with reference to foreign affairs, which figured so prominently in the Truman presidency. In a 1962 poll, historians rated Truman a "near great" chief executive, largely on the basis of his decision to implement a policy of containment in dealing with the Communist world. The passing of the cold war and the trauma of Vietnam have altered perspectives, however. Revisionist scholars now argue that the cold war was unnecessary, and that Truman must bear a considerable share of the responsibility for having instigated it. It seems certain that Truman will occupy an important place in the history of United States foreign policy, though how historians will evaluate his role is by no means settled.

◇◇◇

No man approaches power with a completely clean slate; policy makers invariably bring to positions of authority certain principles and practices, based upon previous experience, that influence their behavior. Harry Truman was no exception; indeed his abrupt accession to the presidency may well have reinforced for him the tendency present in all men to seek guidance from the past. Truman's prepresidential career shaped his approach to decision making in several ways: it provided him with a wide range of practical experience while impressing on him a sense of his own limitations; it taught him techniques of leadership in situations of crisis; it gave him familiarity with power without qualms over having sought it; and it furnished him with a knowledge of history from which he derived lessons for dealing with current problems.

Much was made of Truman's inexperience when he entered the White House, and in terms of factual information relating to foreign affairs, this concern was justified; yet Truman was hardly a neophyte when it came to experience in dealing with men and institutions. He had served ten years in the Senate, where his quiet but competent approach, particularly as chairman of the Special Committee to Investigate the National Defense Program, had won him the respect of colleagues on both sides of the aisle. Before his senatorial service, Truman spent twelve years as a county judge in Jackson County, Missouri, a job involving the administration of funds for the maintenance of roads and other facilities. Before entering politics, Truman had already dabbled in banking, farming, oil exploration, zinc and lead mining, and clothes retailing, and he had served as an officer in France during World War I. He would not likely have had such diverse experience if he had been able to attend college; lacking formal training for a particular profession, he had to move from one occupation to another as opportunities arose. In an age when most of the men who shaped United States foreign policy came from relatively narrow backgrounds in business and law, Truman brought to the presidency an unusually broad, if sometimes shallow, range of experience.

At the same time, these experiences gave him a keen sense of his own limitations and painful knowledge of failure. Truman's father had lost thousands of dollars speculating on grain futures, and Truman himself absorbed smaller losses on several of his own business enterprises. In 1922, the clothing store that he and a wartime friend opened in Kansas City went bankrupt. Politics seemed to be the only profession in which Truman did well, and even here his rise to national prominence stemmed more from the support he got from the Pendergast machine than from his own abilities. Persistent success, it has been argued, is intoxicating; it blurs objectivity and fosters an illusion of infallibility. This may be, but Truman's biographers have not had to worry much about the problem.

Military service during World War I taught Truman a great deal about leadership. Previous training in the Missouri National Guard earned him an officer's commission, and in France he commanded an artillery battery. Years later he recalled how he shaped his troops into line: "When I first took command of the battery I called all the sergeants and corporals together. I told them I knew they had been making trouble for the previous commanders. I said 'I didn't come over here to get along with you. You've got to get along with me. And if there are any of you who can't, speak up right now and I'll bust you right back. . . .' We got along." At one point, under German fire, Truman effectively rallied retreating troops by hurling streams of choice Missouri invective at them. The experience of command gave Truman confidence in his ability to lead men. It also reinforced a belief, which he may have inherited from his blunt and feisty parents, that the best way to deal with recalcitrant opponents was to "talk tough."

Despite his proclivity for belligerent rhetoric, however, Truman was a strong believer in the virtues of accommodation. His path to power was paved with compromises. He had to work through the unsavory Pendergast organization to succeed in Kansas City politics. Later, as senator from Missouri, he built an independent political base by winning the support of diverse interest groups, a technique that by its very nature required an ability to reconcile differences. Truman's nomination for the vice-presidency in 1944 was also a compromise, in this case between the liberal and conservative wings of the Democratic party. Conciliation and adjustment, Truman believed, were the lifeblood of politics; although he had principles they did not lead, as they have with other presidents, to inflexible policies.

One principle to which Truman attached particular significance was the importance of keeping one's word: a man who did not carry out his obligations was not to be trusted. It was characteristic of Truman that he did not approve of divorce because "when you make a contract, you should keep it. . . . When I say I'm going to do something, I do it, or bust my insides trying to do it." After the failure of his clothing store, Truman insisted on paying off his creditors, even though this took years and required a considerable financial sacrifice. Loyalty to friends he regarded as a sacred duty; one of the embarrassments of his administration was Truman's refusal to disassociate himself from some of his more disreputable Missouri cronies. Truman judged men by their reliability in keeping agreements, and it was the standard by which he, in turn, wanted to be judged.

As did many of his fellow Americans, Truman thought there was something corrupt about men with an appetite for power. He took pride in the fact that he had not originally wanted to hold any of the offices he subsequently occupied; power had sought him, rather than the other way around. Yet Truman's administrative experience taught him that an executive, to be effective, must not hesitate to use his authority and must jealously guard it from all challenges. The fact that he had not aspired to high political office may have helped Truman rationalize this seeming contradiction; had he actually wanted the presidency he might not have wielded its powers with such self-confidence.

Truman's knowledge of history, the product of extensive reading and a nearly photographic memory, continually astonished those around him; but his approach was a relatively unsophisticated one, as a recent biographer has noted. "He could conceptualize events only by means of the 'great man' idea of history, which he attached to a schoolboy notion that all problems had their parallels and precedents in the past." The fact that Truman drew many lessons from history affected his performance in the White House. Aware that successful presidents had usually been the strong ones, he resolved from the first to be an activist. He understood clearly the distinction between delegating authority and relinquishing responsibility, an important insight he had gained from studying Grover Cleveland's second administration. Knowing how Washington, Lincoln, and other predecessors had been vilified while in office, he was less sensitive to criticism than might have been expected given his inadequate preparation for the presidency. His belief that historical parallels offered reliable guides for dealing with current problems led Truman occasionally to make simplistic comparisons between past and present that did not always serve the nation's best interests.

Truman viewed international relations optimistically; harmony, he believed, was possible, provided there was an organization of nations to sustain and enforce it. World War I convinced him that such a structure was practical and that Woodrow Wilson had found the right formula for it in the League of Nations (a concept that went back to King Henry IV of France, as Truman delighted in pointing out). The failure of the United States to join the league had had tragic results. "I am . . . sure as I can be that this World War is the result of the 1919–20 isolationist attitude," he told the Senate in 1943, "and I am equally sure that another and worse war will follow this one, unless the United Nations and their allies . . . decide to work together for peace as they are working together for victory." Truman labored hard while in Congress to commit the United States to membership in the United Nations; after becoming president he never wavered in his support for the world organization. For most of his life he carried in his wallet a copy of the portion of Tennyson's "Locksley Hall" that predicted a "Parliament of Man, the Federation of the world." "We're going to

have that someday," Truman once commented. "I guess that's
what I've really been working for ever since I first put that poetry
in my pocket."

Shortly after Truman's nomination for vice-president, an old
acquaintance wrote of him, "He is a great man, but he doesn't
know that he is great." In a way, this was true. Throughout his
career Truman had remained unusually humble. His almost osten-
tatious self-deprecation may have reflected a degree of calculation, however, for Truman's reading of history had convinced him
that humility was a prerequisite for greatness. On the eve of his
announcement for the Senate in 1934 he had written a note to
himself reiterating that belief. "Self-discipline with all [great men]
came first. I found that most of the really great ones never thought
they were great." Ten years later, on election night, 1944, Truman
quietly predicted to a friend that Roosevelt would not survive his
term and that he would become president. He worried about the
prospect and thought he would need all the help he could get; yet
he showed surprisingly little doubt regarding his ability to do the
job if the need arose. Confidence, tempered with humility—it was
not a bad attitude to have while waiting for lightning to strike.

◇◇◇

Presidents who enter the White House upon the death of an
incumbent face a peculiar problem. Respect and sentiment tie
them to the policies of their predecessors, yet the exercise of
power requires establishment of a separate identity if authority is
not be be dissipated. Presidents have solved this problem in
various ways; Truman's solution was to embrace the goals Roosevelt had sought but to alter dramatically their implementation.

The new chief executive had no difficulty in committing
himself to carry out Roosevelt's policies because he sincerely
believed in the wisdom of most of what the late president had
done. Truman had been elected to the Senate as a New Deal
supporter and, once there, had rarely deviated from the administration line. An ardent opponent of isolationism, the senator from
Missouri had come out in favor of a postwar collective security
organization even before Roosevelt. Significantly, his first act as
president was to announce that the San Francisco Conference,
due to meet in two weeks to write the United Nations Charter,
would convene on schedule.

Roosevelt's loose operational style appalled Truman, who set great store by administrative efficiency. Bureaucratic jurisdictions overlapped, chains of command were poorly defined, organizational assignments bore little relation to functions performed. FDR himself had been notoriously evasive, as Truman privately complained before becoming vice-president. "He does all the talking, and . . . never talks about anything you want to talk about, so there isn't much you can do." Upon entering the White House the new president sought to establish a reputation for orderliness and decisiveness far removed from the careless habits of his predecessor. Subordinates noticed the change at once. One of them wrote: "When I saw him today I had fourteen problems to take up with him and got through them in less than fifteen minutes with a clear directive on every one of them. You can imagine what a joy it is to work with a man like that." This brisk approach to decision making enabled Truman to establish his own authority without repudiating the substance of Roosevelt's programs. It was also consistent with a lifelong habit: whether rallying frightened troops in France, dealing with recalcitrant politicians in Kansas City, or running for office in seemingly hopeless elections, Truman had always responded to difficult situations by taking the offensive. Now, in the biggest crisis of his life, Truman behaved characteristically by seizing the reins of power with vigor and authority.

The most pressing problem facing Truman was one that would plague him throughout his presidency: the Soviet Union. The new president had come to power at a crucial moment in the evolution of Russian-American relations. Conflicts over postwar objectives were surfacing with alarming frequency as the defeat of Hitler approached. Stalin's chief concern was security from future attack; he sought to achieve this by dominating Eastern Europe while keeping Germany weak. Roosevelt had recognized the validity of many of Stalin's demands, but had found it difficult to satisfy them without sacrificing objectives for which the United States was fighting, notably self-determination and world economic recovery. The Big Three had worked out delicate compromises on several of the issues that divided them at Yalta in February 1945, but these came apart almost at once as each side interpreted vaguely worded accords in line with its own national interests.

Truman knew nothing of these developments when he came into office because Roosevelt had not kept him informed. He quickly sought recommendations from FDR's advisers, most of whom had long favored a firmer policy toward the Soviet Union than the late president had been prepared to implement. Unsure of himself yet eager to appear decisive, Truman accepted their advice to "get tough," a course of action consistent with his own favorite method of handling crises. He was not afraid of the Russians, the new president told W. Averell Harriman, the United States ambassador in Moscow; after all, "the Soviet Union needed us more than we needed them." He would not expect to get 100 percent of what the United States wanted, but "we should be able to get 85 percent." He was going ahead with plans for the San Francisco Conference, and if the Russians disapproved, "they could go to hell."

The president's first opportunity to demonstrate his toughness came on 23 April 1945, when the Soviet foreign minister, V. M. Molotov, stopped off in Washington on his way to San Francisco. Truman lectured the Russian diplomat in a manner not unlike his handling of the unruly troops in Battery D. An agreement had been made at Yalta, he stated, and all that remained was for Stalin to carry it out. When Molotov tried to explain that the Soviet government was following what it considered to be the correct interpretation of the Yalta Agreements, Truman interrupted him. The United States wanted cooperation with Russia, he snapped, but not as a one-way proposition. Known for his usual imperturbability as "Old Ironpants," Molotov emerged from this experience badly shaken. "I gave it to him straight," Truman later bragged. "One-two to the jaw."

Some historians have seen this as the moment the cold war began. Certainly the new president's truculence upset the Russians, who had grown used to the smooth and slippery platitudes of FDR. In fact, though, Truman had no intention of reversing Roosevelt's Russian policy. He had reason to believe he was continuing it. Roosevelt himself had come to see the need for a tougher approach by the time of his death, and the new president's advisers were almost unanimous in urging a firm stand. In his eagerness to appear decisive Truman probably overreacted, as he himself later realized, but he did so in an effort to solidify his own authority, not to wreck chances for postwar accommodation with the USSR.

During this period Truman made other decisions that had the effect of avoiding, rather than encouraging, conflict with the

Soviet Union. He agreed to support Roosevelt's Yalta pledge that the Russians could have three seats in the United Nations General Assembly, even though he himself disapproved of this arrangement. He turned down Winston Churchill's proposal that Allied troops in central Europe remain in the advanced positions they had attained by V-E Day, not withdrawing into previously agreed-upon occupation zones until the Russians became more cooperative. He made no change in the Far Eastern agreement Roosevelt had concluded with Stalin at Yalta whereby the Russians would receive political concessions in return for entering the war against Japan.

By mid-May 1945, Truman had nonetheless begun to fear that the Russians had misunderstood his intentions. The fate of Poland remained unresolved. The San Francisco Conference seemed to be turning into a forum for the airing of differences instead of their resolution. Shortly after V-E Day, overzealous subordinates ordered ships transporting lend-lease supplies to Russia to return to port if the material they carried was not intended for use against Japan. Truman, who had intended a more gradual curtailment of lend-lease, immediately countermanded this order, but not before the Russians had complained bitterly. The incident convinced the president of the extreme anti-Soviet hostility that existed among some Washington officials, and of the need to make a new effort to settle differences with Moscow.

Truman entrusted this delicate responsibility to Roosevelt's favorite unofficial emissary, Harry Hopkins, who went to Moscow late in May. "I told Harry he could use diplomatic language or he could use a baseball bat if he thought that was the proper approach," Truman wrote. Hopkins's sympathetic attitude toward the Russians was no secret; Truman knew very well that his approach would be conciliatory. The Hopkins-Stalin conversations did much to clear the air. They worked out a compromise on Poland that preserved Soviet influence there but allowed the West to save face; Stalin reiterated his promise to enter the war against Japan and helped resolve a stalemate at San Francisco by accepting the American formula on voting in the UN Security Council; and, finally, the Russian leader agreed to meet Truman and Churchill in July at Potsdam, just outside Berlin.

Potsdam was the longest of the wartime summits—two and a half weeks—but it produced the fewest agreements. The Big Three did negotiate a complicated accord on German reparations, but had to refer other controversial issues to the Council of Foreign Ministers, which was to meet at regular intervals after the war. Truman found Potsdam a frustrating experience. "Churchill talks all the time and Stalin just grunts," he complained. "On a number of occasions I felt like blowing the roof off the palace." The president believed that disagreements stemmed from misunderstandings rather than basic conflicts of interest, however. This was to be expected, given language differences and the fact that discussion of so many issues had been postponed until after the war. "If there is complete understanding, there wouldn't be very many difficulties between us," he later commented, "because Russia's interests and ours do not clash, and never have. We have always been friends, and I hope we always will be."

Truman's initial months in office, therefore, offer little evidence to sustain the thesis that the new president deliberately set out to reverse Roosevelt's policy of cooperation with the Russians. Continuity, rather than change, was the keynote as far as the substance of policy was concerned. The difference was style: where Roosevelt had sought to woo Stalin by meeting his demands whenever possible, Truman, like a good poker player, tried to deal from positions of rhetorical, if not actual, strength. The new president's tough talk was designed to facilitate, not impede, negotiations. Any appearance of weakness, he thought, would only encourage the Russians to ask for more.

What Truman failed to take into account was the possibility that the Russians might also be bluffing. In retrospect, it is becoming increasingly obvious that insecurity, not self-confidence, motivated Soviet policy during this period. Severely weakened by years of war and internal upheaval, the Russians badly needed peace and the opportunity to rebuild. Truman's tough rhetoric, together with America's awesome demonstration of the power of the atomic bomb at Hiroshima, may well have reinforced Stalin's conviction that if *he* showed any signs of weakness, all would be lost. Both sides had learned too well that appeasement never pays. Prospects for an amicable resolution of differences suffered accordingly.

◇◇◇

Truman soon realized that it would not be enough simply to carry out Roosevelt's policies. FDR had never formulated his ideas on the postwar relationship between Washington and Moscow with any precision; he had simply assumed that the alliance forged by the existence of common enemies would survive after those enemies had been destroyed. Roosevelt lived just long enough to see that this was not likely to happen but died before he could come up with a plan to meet the new situation. Truman listened carefully to the late president's advisers, but in the end it was he who had to decide what to do. Knowing relatively little about Russia but pressed by the need for action, Truman of necessity fell back upon past experience as a guide. The elements of his program were not always consistent, because lessons drawn from various experiences affected policy in different ways. The net result, though, was to bring about, by early 1946, a determination to make no further concessions to the Russians.

The experience of meeting Stalin at Potsdam did not sour Truman on the possibility of good relations with the Soviet Union; rather, it seems to have encouraged him. In common with most other Americans who dealt with the Russian dictator, Truman found him personally likable, despite his shrewd and tenacious negotiating tactics. Probably any Russian would have seemed gracious after Molotov. There were some tense moments at Potsdam, especially when Stalin refused to consider a pet scheme the president had concocted for the internationalization of strategic waterways; but Truman returned home with a grudging respect for the Soviet leader, in whom he sensed something familiar. "Stalin," he later told Jonathan Daniels, "is as near like Tom Pendergast as any man I know."

What the Kremlin autocrat would have made of this comparison is difficult to say, but Truman drew important conclusions from it. One was that Stalin was a fellow politician, with whom one could make a deal. If he and Stalin could only sit down with each other, the president told Joseph Davies in 1946, they could "get together on a fair basis that would support peace, at least for a trial. But it was impossible to make a deal with Molotov. He was not a 'big man' like Stalin. That was clearly shown at Potsdam. Without Stalin at the table, it would have been impossible to get anywhere with Molotov." Truman liked to say of Kansas City boss Tom Pendergast that, whatever his other faults, he had always kept his word. For a long time the president persisted in the belief that Stalin, had he been able, would have done the same thing; but the Russian leader, Truman regretfully concluded, was not a free agent. "After all," he told C. L. Sulzberger, "[Stalin] is only secretary of the Politburo and has his troubles with the other thirteen members just the way I have my troubles here with my Cabinet and the Congress." The president confided to a whistle-stop audience during the 1948 campaign: "I like old Joe, but Joe is a prisoner of the Politburo. He can't do what he wants to. He makes agreements, and if he could he would keep them; but the people who run the government are very specific in saying that he can't keep them."

Truman's conviction that "you can understand the Russian situation if you understand Jackson County" was perhaps naïve. There is no evidence that Stalin's domestic constituency imposed significant limits on his freedom of action. Truman drew another analogy from his experience in Kansas City politics that was quite revealing. The Russians, he believed, were negotiating from weakness rather than strength. "A dictatorship is the hardest thing in God's world to hold together because it is made up entirely of conspiracies from the inside." This was a perceptive and largely accurate insight into the nature of the Stalinist regime. Because of it, Truman found it easy to accept the key point of George F. Kennan's analysis of Soviet behavior, that internal problems explained Moscow's hostility, not any blueprint for external expansion.

Unfortunately, Truman failed to connect this conclusion and his equally strong conviction that the best way to deal with an opponent was to take the offensive. The possibility that a weak and suspicious adversary might mistake bluffing for belligerence seems to have escaped him. Thus, when Stalin made two tentative efforts to increase Soviet influence in Iran and Turkey in 1946, Truman responded by treating the situations not as defensive probes by the Russians reflecting their own insecurity, but as extremely dangerous threats which, if not contained, would bring on World War III. The U.S. lodged a public protest in the United Nations, Truman sent the fleet to the Mediterranean, and, in the case of the Turkish episode, he actually resolved to go to war if necessary to repel the Russians. Luckily, it was not necessary; Stalin backed down both times. Because threats, not negotiations, had produced results, these incidents reinforced Truman's penchant for the "tough approach" at the expense of his instinct for compromise. They probably also reinforced the Russians' view that Truman, unlike Roosevelt, had no interest in ensuring that the

Soviet Union satisfy what it considered to be its legitimate security needs.

The Iranian crisis also convinced Truman that the Russians could not be trusted to keep their agreements. Stalin had promised to have Soviet troops out of northern Iran (which they had occupied during World War II) by 2 March 1946. His failure to meet this deadline was no small matter. "I held [Stalin] to be a man of his word," Truman noted shortly thereafter. "Troops in Iran after March 2 upset that theory." By 1947, the president had come to believe that the Soviets had not kept any of the commitments they had made during the war. "I have tried my level best to get along with our friends the Russians," he observed, "and I still want to get along with them. But when I make straight out and out agreements with a government, in the name of the United States of America, and not a single one of those agreements is carried out, I have got to use other methods. They understand one language, and that is the language they are going to get from me from this point." There is no doubt that the Russians did have a cavalier attitude about meeting their obligations. In a report to the president in 1946 White House aide Clark Clifford counted some twenty violations of written agreements within the previous four years. Many of these accords were vaguely worded, however, and therefore were susceptible to varying interpretations. Truman's insistence that the Russians meet the same standards of behavior he expected from his personal associates made these discrepancies seem more sinister than they actually were.

Truman did not, interestingly enough, regard ideology as a motive for Soviet expansion. "There's no Socialism in Russia," he wrote in 1945. "It is a hotbed of special privilege." The only example of true communism, he liked to argue, was the Sermon on the Mount. In Truman's view the official ideology of the Soviet state was just a facade for totalitarianism. "Really there is no difference between the government which Mr. Molotov represents and the one the Czar represented—or the one Hitler spoke for." The Soviet Union constituted a threat, therefore, but it was not much different from that posed by Germany and Japan before World War II. Communism, in Truman's opinion, had little to do with it.

Despite his later rhetoric Truman did not—at least in the early days of the cold war—see the international Communist movement as monolithic. Russian imperialism was the real problem; aside from some 1948 campaign oratory there were surprisingly few references in his pre–Korean War speeches to the dangers of world revolution. Truman foresaw the possibility that Communist parties outside Russia's immediate sphere of influence might reject Moscow's leadership and thus was quick to take advantage of Tito's defection in 1948, despite the fact that Yugoslavia remained firmly Communist. He always doubted Moscow's control over China's Communists; one reason Mao Tse-tung's victory upset him so little was that he expected serious difficulties to develop between Moscow and Peking. "I think you will find . . . that the Russians will turn out to be the 'foreign devils' in China," Truman wrote to Arthur Vandenberg in 1949, "and that the situation will help establish a Chinese Government that we can recognize and support."

It has been argued that Truman was insensitive in his dealings with the Russians. To a degree, this was true; but his was an insensitivity derived from inexperience, not deliberate animosity. Despite his own repugnance for the Soviet regime, Truman wanted peace just as badly as Stalin. His perception of Stalin's policy convinced him, though, as it did many other observers at the time, that peace would be safe only if Russian expansion were resisted. The Soviet dictator perceived security *only* in terms of expansion; his probes around his borders, his tough negotiating tactics, his cynical attitude toward agreements he had made seemed almost calculated to drive a man like Truman to the conclusion that "force is the only thing they understand." Nor is it clear in retrospect that Truman was wrong. Stalin's aims do appear to have been limited, but there is no assurance they would have remained so had the West not resisted. The problem Truman faced was how to resist Soviet expansion without at the same time overextending American resources. It was a dilemma much on the mind of the president and his advisers as they began to formulate the policy that came to be known as "containment."

◇◇◇

Harry S. Truman arose before a joint session of Congress on 12 March 1947 to proclaim that "it must be the policy of the United States to support free peoples who are resisting attempted subjugation by armed minorities or by outside pressures." Four months later, George F. Kennan, head of the State Department's

Policy Planning Staff, wrote in the journal *Foreign Affairs* that "the main element of any United States policy toward the Soviet Union must be that of a long-term, patient but firm and vigilant containment of Russian expansive tendencies." Few statements in the history of American diplomacy have produced more confusion. Journalists immediately linked the two, assuming that it was now Washington's policy to oppose communism wherever it appeared. Historians reached similar conclusions, viewing 1947 either as the point at which the United States abandoned isolationism and took up its legitimate responsibilities as a world power, or, alternatively, as the point at which the United States became a world policeman, dispatching men and resources all over the world in a futile attempt to contain a mythical monolith, the international Communist conspiracy.

In fact, neither Truman's speech nor Kennan's article conveyed what their authors intended; both are excellent examples of the obfuscatory potential of imprecise prose. The Truman administration had no global plan for the containment of communism in 1947. Its goal was the considerably less ambitious one of restoring the balance of power in Europe; its choice of means for accomplishing this reflected a keen awareness of the limitations, rather than the omnipotence, of American power.

For American leaders throughout the twentieth century the most important requirement for a congenial international environment has been that Europe not fall under the domination of a single hostile state. Concern over the European balance of power goes back at least to the turn of the century; certainly such considerations influenced Woodrow Wilson's efforts to mediate World War I and his subsequent entry into that struggle. The totalitarian nature of Hitler's regime made Nazi Germany's threat twenty years later seem particularly ominous; it was clearly decisive in persuading Franklin D. Roosevelt that he could not allow the collapse of Great Britain after France fell in 1940. Japan's attack on Pearl Harbor actually thrust the United States into World War II, but the Roosevelt administration had decided a year and a half earlier to risk war in order to prevent the totalitarian domination of all of Europe. Truman, thus, was hardly breaking new ground when he described the world as polarized between democracy and totalitarianism; it can be argued that the American commitment to oppose threats to the balance of power in Europe goes back at least to 1940, and possibly to 1917. What was novel about the Truman Doctrine was not that it marked any fundamental shift in the basic objectives of United States foreign policy, but rather that it indicated the emergence of a new challenge to these objectives in the postwar behavior of the Soviet Union.

Truman and his advisers saw Moscow's threat to the European balance of power as political and economic, not military. Wartime devastation and natural calamities had so disrupted life in Europe that Communist parties in France, Italy, Greece, and elsewhere were thought to have excellent chances of coming to power through coups or even free elections. This prospect seemed dangerous, not because of the general repugnance these men felt for communism, though that certainly existed, but rather because the European Communist parties were, between 1945 and 1948, tools of the Kremlin. Their victory would have placed Europe under the domination of a single hostile power, the very thing Americans had fought World Wars I and II to prevent. United States policy in Europe from 1947 through 1949—the Truman Doctrine, the Marshall Plan, the Vandenberg Resolution, the North Atlantic Treaty, and the Military Assistance Program—can best be understood as an attempt, through political, economic, and, later, military means, to achieve a goal largely psychological in nature: the creation of a state of mind among Europeans conducive to the revival of faith in democratic procedures. As Kennan later put it, "It had been primarily the shadow, rather than the substance, of danger which we, in contemplating a European recovery program, had been concerned to dispel."

The president's advisers did more than he to shape this imaginative and, on the whole, successful policy, but it was Truman who selected these men. Well aware of his own intellectual limitations, Truman never let his ego get in the way of accepting recommendations from experts better informed than he. At the same time, he had enormous respect for the office he occupied; while he was prepared to accord subordinates large areas of responsibility, he insisted that they defer to his ultimate authority by keeping him informed at every stage of the policymaking process and by bringing all final decisions to him. Advisers who did this could expect confidence, a free hand on most issues, and intense personal loyalty.

The careers of Secretary of State George C. Marshall, from 1947 to 1949, and Dean Acheson, who filled that position from 1949 to 1953, illustrate this tendency clearly. Both men carefully kept Truman apprised of what they were doing; in return the president let them formulate foreign policy without White House interference. When Marshall objected to a hastily conceived scheme to send Chief Justice Fred Vinson to Moscow during the final days of the 1948 campaign, Truman immediately vetoed the idea, despite the fact that this required an embarrassing public reversal of policy on the eve of a hard-fought election. Acheson came under intense criticism from right-wing elements during his term of office but Truman doggedly defended him, even though Acheson's resignation might have considerably simplified the task of conducting foreign policy. Marshall and Acheson were both good judges of men; the subordinates they recruited implemented containment with a considerable degree of skill and ingenuity. Truman's wide grant of authority actually made the Department of State, for one of the few times in recent history, the government's chief policy-making agency in the field of foreign affairs. Its performance under this mandate was impressive.

There is no doubt that Truman's choice of advisers limited the range of options brought before him for consideration; but presidents must, in self-defense, restrict the number of counselors to whom they listen. Although the number of viewpoints Truman could consider were therefore limited, he himself was not narrow-minded. The White House staff did not screen options for this president; he generally insisted on hearing alternatives directly from their advocates and on deciding among them himself. Nor did he confuse disagreement with disloyalty; advisers whose recommendations did not meet with presidential approval usually continued to enjoy the chief executive's confidence as long as they met the requirements of deference, decisiveness, and disinterestedness upon which he insisted in his counselors. Comparisons between administrations are difficult to make, but it does seem likely that the relationship Truman established with his advisers provided him with a greater range of alternatives from which to choose than most of his successors have enjoyed.

The basic idea behind containment was a congenial one for Truman: that economic assistance, not military force, was the best way to resist Soviet expansion. "Communism succeeds only when there is weakness, or misery, or despair," he argued. "It cannot succeed in a strong and healthy society." Peace and prosperity went together in Truman's mind; as living standards increased throughout the world, he believed, chances of war would decline.

Like many former New Dealers, Truman was perhaps naïve in his passionate expectation that economic development would cure the world's ills. "I have been dreaming of TVAs in the Euphrates Valley, . . . in the Yangtze Valley and the Danube," he once told David Lilienthal. The president grasped the vital importance of economic recovery in the reconstruction of Europe, and he strongly supported his advisers who advocated this policy. He also played a major role in convincing the American people that it was in their interest to help finance that process.

Truman was keenly aware of the limits of American power, and of the consequent need to distinguish between peripheral and vital interests. "Our resources are not unlimited," he observed in 1947. "We must apply them where they can serve the most effectively to bring production, freedom, and confidence back to the world." Europe had first priority in his mind; he sought to minimize involvement in other troublespots, like China and the Middle East, which seemed less vital to American security. The administration quite deliberately channeled available funds into the European Recovery Program, despite the fact that this required such rigid ceilings on military expenditures by 1948 that the Joint Chiefs of Staff could promise only to defend Great Britain and the Western Hemisphere if war came. The assumption, of course, was that there would be no war, that restoration of the balance of power in Europe would be sufficient to ensure United States security. Confronted with a revived and confident Western Europe, it was believed, Stalin, or, more likely, his successor, would abandon plans for expansion and accept peaceful coexistence with the capitalist world.

Although Truman believed strongly in the virtues of military preparedness, he was equally convinced that the armed forces ought to be the instrument of the nation's foreign policy, not the other way around. Accordingly, he did not hesitate to hold the military to what was left in the national budget after domestic needs and the European Recovery Program had been funded. "The Marshall plan is . . . cheaper than a shooting war would be," he explained. Truman's arbitrary ceilings on arms expenditures during the 1947–50 period stemmed in part from the great significance he attached to balancing the budget; inflation, he feared, would set off a new depression, which was what the Russians wanted. These constraints also reflected a healthy skepticism on Truman's part about exaggerated military estimates. "The air boys are for glamour and the navy as always is the greatest of propaganda machines," he wrote in 1948. "I want a balanced sensible defense for which the country can pay." Secretary of Defense James V. Forrestal, the victim of many of Truman's budget slashes, later commented, "In the person of Harry S. Truman I have seen the most rocklike example of civilian control that the world has ever witnessed."

Despite the sweeping language of the Truman Doctrine and Kennan's containment article, therefore, the actual policies the United States followed between 1947 and 1950 hardly justify description as an all-out effort to contain communism everywhere. Rather Truman and his advisers appear to have been seeking a world in which several centers of power could exist, each exerting a restraining influence on the other. It is difficult, otherwise, to explain the administration's persistent enthusiasm for European unification and, after 1948, Japanese rehabilitation. It seems the only way to account for the almost desperate efforts of Truman and Acheson to keep their options open in dealing with Communist China. Even the administration's steadfast refusal to negotiate with the Russians on substantive issues was a holding tactic. It was never meant to preclude meaningful discussions once the "situations of strength" of which Acheson liked to speak had been established. Speculation about what did not happen is always perilous, but it does seem possible that the policies of Truman, Marshall, and Acheson, had they been allowed to run their course, might have resulted in the evolution of a multipolar world operating on balance of power principles, a world not too different, ironically enough, from what became the apparent objective, twenty years later, of Henry Kissinger and Richard Nixon.

◇◇◇

It did not work out that way. By the end of Truman's administration the United States had moved from implementation of a restrained and cautious policy with limited objectives toward a new and far more sweeping program of action that posited the challenge to United States security as worldwide and made no real distinction between varieties of communism. Containment became globalized; it was at this point that the gap between Washington's commitments and its resources for meeting them began to widen. The reasons for this are many and complex. Certainly Truman's actions alone did not wreck chances for the emergence of the kind of world he wanted to see; the president was, to a large extent, at the mercy of circumstances beyond his control. As Truman would have been the first to admit, however, presidents cannot escape at least partial responsibility for what happens during their term of office. Two characteristics of Truman and his advisers—an inability to see situations from the viewpoint of other countries and a certain casualness about means employed to gain their objectives—contributed to the process by which the United States embarked upon a policy of global containment.

Leaders of great nations often see their own countries as the target of moves by potential adversaries while assuming that their actions could not possibly be interpreted by a rival as hostile. Truman operated in this manner. He consistently stressed the purity of American motives while assuming the worst of the Russians, then puzzled over why Moscow suspected sinister intentions on Washington's part. This tendency was particularly apparent in Truman's attitude toward the international control of atomic energy. The United States, he believed, had made the most generous offer in the history of the world by proposing to turn over control of nuclear weapons to the United Nations. When the Russians failed to view the Baruch Plan in the same light, Truman concluded that they were up to no good, ignoring their understandable reservations about United States retention of sole custody of atomic weapons until the control scheme went into effect. The administration responded in a similar manner during 1947 and 1948 to the creation of the Cominform, the Hungarian and Czechoslovak coups, and the Berlin blockade. It now seems clear, as Kennan pointed out at the time, that these were defensive responses by the Soviets to the unexpected psychological impact of the Truman Doctrine and the Marshall Plan. Truman and his advisers treated them as new provocations and responded by pushing formation of the North Atlantic Treaty Organization and creation of an independent West Germany, moves that stimulated further counter-escalation by the Russians.

In Truman's defense, it ought to be pointed out that Stalin was as prone to this kind of thinking as were Washington officials; he tended to regard every United States action as directed against him. In the case of the Soviet dictator, the problem was compounded by a paranoia so intense that he would not trust even his closest subordinates, much less leaders of the capitalist world. Roosevelt had tried to break through this barrier during the war by doing everything he could to meet Stalin's wishes, but in the end the effort failed; Stalin remained as suspicious as ever. There seems, in retrospect, little Truman could have done to overcome Stalin's paranoia, but he need not have exacerbated it to the extent that he did. A greater concern with how Moscow would interpret American actions might have prevented this.

Truman was also less careful than he ought to have been about the means he employed to gain his objectives; these backfired more than once. Upon the recommendation of his advisers, the president deliberately exaggerated the Soviet threat in his March 1947 address calling for aid to Greece and Turkey and in another appearance before Congress a year later in which he sought to assure final passage of the Marshall Plan, the revival of selective service, and the establishment of universal military training. There were good reasons for making all-out pitches in both of these situations—congressional purse strings were tightly drawn—but the imprecision of Truman's rhetoric made it difficult for Congress or the public to distinguish, as the administration sought to, between Soviet expansionism and international communism. This became painfully obvious with regard to the Far East, where Truman, fearful of impairing support for the European Recovery Program, did nothing to explain why communism was coming to power in China, or how it was that the United States was not resisting that development. The resulting backlash far exceeded in severity anything that would have occurred had Truman been candid about China from the first.

The administration's preoccupation with bipartisanship further encouraged this casualness about means. For men of Truman's generation, who had seen Woodrow Wilson's dream of a league of nations collapse because of partisan bickering, the idea that domestic political differences ought not to extend to foreign policy was close to sacrosanct. Nor were the president and his advisers unsuccessful. On most issues relating to international affairs during this period (China is the major exception), partisan politics did exert little influence; but this consensus, which was supposed to be a means of achieving an enlightened foreign policy, too often became an end in itself. The effect was to

Gib Crockett, Washington Star-News *(24 September 1951), and Harry S. Truman Library*

discourage public discussion of controversial subjects and to cause officials to employ greater resourcefulness in seeking unity at home than in obtaining a reduction of tensions abroad.

Early in September 1949 United States intelligence discovered that the Russians had exploded their first atomic bomb. Truman received this information calmly, for he had never expected the American nuclear monopoly to last indefinitely. Still, the Soviet explosion had come three years earlier than government experts had anticipated. News of it shattered one of the most cherished assumptions of the 1947–49 period—that even if war with Russia came, the physical security of the United States would not be at stake. Shortly after Truman announced that the Russians had the weapon, information leaked out that United States scientists were studying the feasibility of constructing a "super" or hydrogen bomb. Once this happened, Americans quickly fell prey to the illusion that development of a bigger weapon would regain for the United States the advantage it had lost.

In retrospect it seems that this might have been a good time to renew negotiations on international control and other unresolved issues, for the Russians had achieved a rough form of strategic parity, NATO was a fact of life, the Berlin blockade had been settled, and the depression that Soviet economists had been predicting for the United States had not come. Domestic politics, together with the tendency of Truman and his advisers to interpret Russian behavior as invariably offensive, prevented serious consideration of this option. In January 1950, Truman announced that the United States would build a hydrogen bomb. Not for another two decades would Washington officials come to realize that, in the area of nuclear weapons, parity offered greater security than superiority.

The decision to build the hydrogen bomb, in turn, forced reconsideration of the rigid budget ceilings Truman had placed on defense expenditures. Oddly, this reassessment originated in the civilian sector of the government, not the military. Truman's economic advisers had begun to argue that the nation could afford to expand its productive capacity, thus generating increased government revenue, without inflation. These ideas were put forward in support of the president's domestic program, but State Department planners, concerned over the Soviet atomic bomb, quickly seized on them as a justification for increased military spending. The result was NSC-68 (National Security Council memorandum no. 68), the nation's first formal statement of national security policy. This document pictured the Soviet Union as aspiring to world hegemony, refused to rule out the possibility of war, and recommended a much broader, more energetic, and more expensive effort to counter this threat. The question of whether communism motivated Moscow's policy or was the instrument of it was left unclear, but by defining the Soviet challenge as worldwide NSC-68 encouraged the tendency to equate the interests of communism everywhere with those of the Kremlin. Coming at a time when the threat of communism appeared to have increased, and when domestic pressures for more vigorous efforts to contain it had intensified, NSC-68 indicated how a global policy of resisting communism could be implemented without bankrupting the country.

Truman still had not accepted the final recommendations of NSC-68 when the Korean War broke out late in June 1950, but that event could hardly have been better calculated to insure their approval. The administration assumed from the first that the Russians had sanctioned the North Korean attack, a conclusion that recent evidence from Soviet sources tends to support. By suggesting that Soviet ambitions were not confined to Europe or the Middle East, and that Stalin would risk war to attain them, the invasion seemed to confirm, in the most dramatic way, the basic premises of NSC-68. Truman had no difficulty in finding an appropriate historical parallel: "In my generation, this was not the first occasion when the strong had attacked the weak. I recalled some earlier instances: Manchuria, Ethiopia, Austria. I remembered how each time that the democracies failed to act it had encouraged the aggressors to keep going ahead. Communism was acting in Korea just as Hitler, Mussolini, and the Japanese had acted ten, fifteen, and twenty years earlier." After consulting with Acheson, Truman ordered the supreme Allied commander in occupied Japan, General Douglas MacArthur, to assist the South Koreans, first with air and naval forces, then, as the situation became more serious, with ground troops. Simultaneously, the United States convened an emergency session of the United Nations Security Council which condemned the North Korean invasion (the Russian delegate, for reasons still obscure, was absent) and endorsed the effort to repel the attack as a United Nations operation.

Had Truman stopped there it seems likely that the United

States could have resisted aggression in Korea without involving Communist China; but the inability of Truman and his advisers to see events from the opponent's point of view, together with their casual attitude toward means, led Truman to authorize two additional steps that in effect, by the end of 1950, involved the United States in an undeclared war with China. On 27 June Truman announced that the Seventh Fleet was patrolling the Formosa Strait; three months later, General MacArthur received permission to cross the thirty-eighth parallel and "liberate" North Korea.

Republican leaders in Congress had been pressing for a United States guarantee of Formosa's security since Chiang Kai-shek fled to that island late in 1949. Truman had resisted, partly because he considered the Nationalists mainly "grafters and crooks," partly because he and his secretary of state still hoped for a split between Communist China and the Soviet Union and did not want to jeopardize this possibility by adopting a "two China" policy. By sending the fleet to patrol the Formosa Strait two days after the Korean War broke out, Truman and Acheson sought to disarm domestic critics and at the same time reassure Peking that "neutralization" of Formosa was "without prejudice to the political questions affecting that island." The Chinese Communists refused to be reassured. Long suspicious of American motives because of the aid Washington had continued to dole out to the Nationalists (principally to placate Republican critics), Mao Tse-tung and his colleagues interpreted the "neutralization" of Formosa as United States intervention in the Chinese civil war on the side of Chiang Kai-shek. Truman intended so such thing, but in his search for short-term unanimity on the home front, he compromised the administration's long-term goal of playing off the Chinese against the Russians.

Much more damaging was the decision, made in September 1950, to change the objective of the fighting in Korea from defense of the south to "liberation" of the north by allowing General MacArthur to cross the thirty-eighth parallel. This followed MacArthur's brilliant landing at Inchon on 15 September which trapped most of the North Korean army in the south and gave Washington officials the illusion that victory was at hand. Unwilling to halt the momentum built up by a highly successful (and politically outspoken) general, Truman and Acheson authorized the move into North Korea despite the risk of Chinese Communist intervention. In doing so, they acted on two assumptions: that the Chinese would accept assurances that the move was not directed against them, and that MacArthur would follow orders not to deploy his troops in such a manner as to make intervention likely. Neither assumption held. As MacArthur's forces moved north, the Chinese, after warning publicly of their intentions, began infiltrating troops across the Yalu River. MacArthur gave them a tremendous opportunity by foolishly splitting his forces, and late in November the Chinese attacked in full force, bringing about the immediate evacuation of United Nations troops from North Korea. The United States was now involved in a limited war with China. The Truman-Acheson policy of playing Peking off against Moscow lay in ruins.

This was the darkest hour of Truman's presidency, but it was also, in some ways, the finest. The president wisely chose not to respond to the Chinese attack with a counter-escalation of his own which would have meant all-out war with Peking and the probable involvement of the Soviet Union. Instead, he returned to his original objective of driving invading forces from South Korean soil, even though this meant accepting a stalemate on the battlefield. When MacArthur publicly questioned this strategy, Truman relieved him of his command, a move that solidified for years to come the principle of civilian control over the military. At the same time the president authorized his diplomats to begin seeking a negotiated settlement of the war. The armistice took two years to arrange. By the time it was completed Truman was out of office; but it was he who kept the first hot war of the nuclear age limited. For this valuable precedent the world owes him a considerable debt.

By getting into an unnecessary fight with the Chinese Communists, the Truman administration encouraged the view that international communism was a monolith that had to be resisted wherever it appeared. From this it was easy for succeeding administrations to jump to the conclusion that there was no distinction between peripheral and vital interests, that threats to order anywhere endangered American security everywhere. Truman and his counselors never shared this view. Even during the most bitter fighting in Korea they kept their attention focused on Europe, which they believed to be the decisive theater of the cold war. The Far East, for them, was never of more than secondary significance.

The language the Truman administration used failed to reflect the caution its behavior demonstrated in practice. Statements of policy like the Truman Doctrine and NSC-68 are probably necessary; bureaucracies cannot function without broad guidelines establishing operating procedures. Men who draft such statements tend to forget, however, that they will not always be present to control implementation. Sweeping proclamations have a tendency to survive those who proclaim them; successors may not apply them as cautiously as their originators intended. Thus it was that the rhetoric of the Truman administration lived after it; but its restraint was interred in its archives.

◇◇◇

"I have been asked whether I have any regrets about any of the major decisions I had to make as President," Truman wrote in 1960. "I have none. . . . There were many things that had to be done that might have been handled some other way. But considering the information available at the time and the circumstances prevailing when I had to make many of my decisions, I do not see how I could have acted very differently." This is not an unreasonable assessment. Policy makers are at the mercy of their own preconceptions and their perceptions of situations as they occur. Decisions do have to be made; action does have to be taken, often on the basis of limited information. "If you are going to walk the floor and worry yourself to death every time you have to make a decision," Truman observed, "then you are not suited for the job."

It did not take much agonizing to realize that, in the view of the overwhelming majority of informed Americans, the behavior of the Soviet Union after World War II did constitute a threat to the security of the United States. Stalin at no point made clear the limited nature of his objectives; what Americans saw was a progressive escalation of anticapitalist propaganda together with a pattern of action among Communist parties throughout the world too well coordinated to ignore. The Truman administration did not have to trick Congress or the public into initially supporting containment. The problem was rather to bring popular determination to resist the Russians into line with the nation's capability for doing so.

Truman and his advisers did this well. Their goal was to restrict the further expansion of Soviet influence by reinvigorating

European society in the shortest possible time with the minimum possible expenditure of American resources. They succeeded brilliantly, aided by the clumsy brutality with which the Russians cracked down on the Hungarians, Czechs, and Berliners in 1947 and 1948. The initiative in Europe had passed to the West by 1949; containment had worked, without war, inflation, or militarization.

There comes a time, though, when negotiation must replace confrontation if any settlement of differences is to be reached. The president and his counselors failed to make this transition. The difficulty was that continued public and congressional support for containment hinged upon the existence of an obvious threat to American security. Administration officials feared that prolonged discussions with the Russians, even if unproductive, might encourage complacency and a return to isolationism. That could be disastrous, because the whole objective of containment had been to instill confidence in the minds of those vulnerable to Soviet expansionism. The success of postwar American foreign policy had come to depend, in a curious and profoundly tragic way, upon the enduring credibility of the threat it had been designed to contain.

Security is an intangible; only after it has been lost can one estimate with any precision what would have been necessary to maintain it. It now seems probable that the Truman administration missed a promising opportunity to negotiate seriously with the Russians in 1949; after Korea, prospects for a mutual reduction of tensions were much bleaker. It ought to be kept in mind that Truman did not possess the advantage of hindsight; quite understandably he preferred to overestimate American security requirements, even if this helped perpetuate the cold war. Placed in his position, given what he knew at the time, not many responsible men would have acted differently.

BIBLIOGRAPHIC NOTE

Students of Harry S. Truman's foreign policy must, at present, rely chiefly upon printed materials since the pertinent documents at the National Archives and the Harry S. Truman Library are, for the most part, still closed to researchers. Truman's own memoirs, *Year of Decisions* (Garden City, N.Y., 1955) and *Years of Trial and Hope, 1946–1952* (Garden City, N.Y., 1956), provide a basic source, though they should be used with some care. A postpresidential memoir, *Mr. Citizen* (New York, 1960), is also useful. Truman's public statements while in office appear in the *Public Papers of the Presidents: Harry S. Truman, 1945–1953* (Washington, D.C., 1961–66), and there is also some information on Truman's views in the appropriate volumes of the Department of State's series *Foreign Relations of the United States,* which now covers the period through 1947.

Richard S. Kirkendall is writing a biography of Truman; until it appears the best accounts are Margaret Truman, *Harry S. Truman* (New York, 1972), Bert Cochran, *Harry Truman and the Crisis Presidency* (New York, 1973), Jonathan Daniels, *Man of Independence* (Philadelphia, 1950), Alfred Steinberg, *The Man from Missouri* (New York, 1962), Cabell Phillips, *The Truman Presidency* (New York, 1966), and William Hillman, *Mr. President* (New York, 1952), which reprints excerpts from Truman's fragmentary diary. See also two articles by Kirkendall, "Truman's Path to Power," *Social Science* 43 (April 1968), 67–73; and "Harry S. Truman," in Morton Borden, ed., *America's Eleven Greatest Presidents* (Chicago, 1971), pp. 255–88.

Biographies in the series American Secretaries of State and Their Diplomacy, edited by Robert H. Ferrell and Samuel Flagg Bemis, provide useful discussions of the Truman administration's foreign policy; see especially George Curry, *James F. Byrnes* (New York, 1965), Robert H. Ferrell, *George C. Marshall* (New York, 1966), and Gaddis Smith, *Dean Acheson* (New York, 1972). Also of value are Dean Acheson, *Present at the Creation: My Years in the State Department* (New York, 1969), George F. Kennan, *Memoirs,* 2 vols. (Boston, 1967, 1972), *The Journals of David E. Lilienthal,* 5 vols. (New York, 1964–1971), especially volume 2, Walter Millis, ed., *The Forrestal Diaries* (New York, 1951), Arthur H. Vandenberg, Jr., ed., *The Private Papers of Senator Vandenberg* (New York, 1952), James F. Byrnes, *Speaking Frankly* (New York, 1947) and *All in One Lifetime* (New York, 1958), and Charles E. Bohlen, *Witness to History, 1929–1969* (New York, 1973).

Important treatments of special topics include the following: Joseph M. Jones, *The Fifteen Weeks (February 21–June 5, 1947)* (New York, 1955), Warner R. Schilling, Paul Y. Hammond, and Glenn H. Snyder, *Strategy, Politics, and Defense Budgets* (New York, 1962), Alonzo L. Hamby, *Beyond the New Deal: Harry S. Truman and American Liberalism* (New York, 1973), Glenn Paige, *The Korean Decision, June 24–30, 1950* (New York, 1968), John W. Spanier, *The Truman-MacArthur Controversy and the Korean War* (New York, 1965), Barton J. Bernstein, ed., *The Politics and Policies of the Truman Administration* (Chicago, 1970), James David Barbour, *The Presidential Character: Predicting Performance in the White House* (Englewood Cliffs, N.J., 1972), and Richard E. Neustadt, *Presidential Power: The Politics of Leadership* (New York, 1960). A valuable collection of documents is Barton J. Bernstein and Allen J. Matusow, eds., *The Truman Administration: A Documentary History* (New York, 1966). Richard S. Kirkendall, ed., *The Truman Period as a Research Field* (Columbia, Mo., 1974), surveys opportunities for further research.

DEAN
ACHESON

Architect of a
Manageable World Order

Robert H. Ferrell and David McLellan

Throughout the history of the United States, since the beginning
of government under the Constitution, the secretaryship of state
has attracted individuals of intellect as well as action—this in
opposition to the presidency, which has drawn men with the latter
quality alone. Dean Acheson was no exception to this rule.
Indeed, if compared with the other men who have held the first
cabinet post, Acheson stands out as more intellectual, to use a
word popular in our century, than most other secretaries. His was
a special quality of intellect, in which he joined the power of
logical thought with a talent in use of words; he was the author of
eight books including a Pulitzer Prize–winning account of his
secretaryship. The only secretaries of state who approached him in
literary ability were Jefferson, whose writings appeared largely in
the form of discursive letters, together with an occasional state

523

paper or philosophical utterance; and John Hay, whose poetry, so popular in his own time, is now happily forgotten.

To conclude, however, that Acheson was highly effective as secretary of state because he was so gifted with powers of analysis and prose is to venture upon only a portion of the reason for his greatness. A second factor was the president he served, a man of activity, of whom no one could contend that there was inability or unwillingness to make a decision. Acheson could never have worked easily or well with Harry S. Truman's predecessor, and the secretary's brisk judgment of Franklin D. Roosevelt, "admiration without affection," was more than just a personal appraisal. Roosevelt could twist and turn before making up his mind, and was not above or below allowing all sorts of confusion in administrative ranks before a decision at last was reached; not so Truman, who could weigh alternatives and take chances, serene in the belief that he had done his best. Even more fortunately for Acheson, the man of Independence possessed some of the same scholarly inclinations as the cultivated, articulate Washington lawyer. In the newspaper appraisals of Truman after the latter's death in the spring of 1973 one individual who lived in Independence said that he had watched, night after night, as he passed the iron-gated Victorian house, to see the light on in the upstairs study and the profile of the old president reading late into the evening. Acheson understood individuals such as Truman who were familiar with books; in a heartfelt letter to a librarian during the last years of his life he remarked that without books, without the experience of other individuals in other times gained through the printed page, there would have been for him "a sort of partial death—the death of all of me which extends beyond what I can see, hear, taste, or touch, pretty much the whole life of the mind."

The third factor that made Acheson an outstandingly successful secretary of state was of course the times, the dangerous era in which he exercised his power as the nation's leading official in the making of foreign policy. That era demanded greatness, and in cooperation with President Truman, Acheson made his now notable responses. This is not to say that circumstances alone always produce greatness, as a cynic might suppose; but the postwar period called for decisions of participation in affairs around the world, decisions of a sort that had concerned hardly any of the preceding secretaries of state. Acheson responded in ways that; taken together as a foreign policy, surely ensure his place among the memorable leaders of the nation.

◇◇◇

The Middletown experience of Acheson's youth was especially important, perhaps even dominant, in the adult proportions of his life. The future secretary of state was born in that Connecticut town in 1893, the son of the Reverend Edward C. Acheson, the rector of the local Episcopalian church. His family background gave him a sense of identity that was to support him with an almost fatalistic serenity against the attacks later to be launched against him. From his father he acquired a stoic philosophy: "Much in life could not be affected or mitigated, and, hence, must be borne. Borne without complaint, because complaints were a bore and nuisance to others and undermined the serenity essential to endurance." [1] It was, perhaps, easy to practice such stoicism in his secure and privileged place. His status sometimes made Dean Acheson seem a little aloof, a little remote, even a little insensitive to the problems of more ordinary mortals. The feeling of compassion that led him to refuse to turn his back on Alger Hiss did not seem to extend as easily or as deeply to the man in the mass and could even lead to intolerance of those whose approach to problems seemed "sicklied o'er" by the pale cast of idealistic emotion. Still, there is a great deal to be said for a man who believed that the integrity of one's life was his most precious possession.

Academic writers, especially academic historians, are likely to maintain that, whatever the background, the experiences of college are important if not determinative. This was only partly true for Acheson. Yale College would always mean for him a place and time of enjoyment, and he earned only a "gentleman's C" average, presumably so that he would not stand out from the crowd of his fellows, but perhaps also because a C average was not that difficult to obtain. He would not have amounted to much beyond an elegant stockbroker or businessman of sorts had he not passed on from New Haven to Cambridge and attended the greatest law school of his time. At Harvard he came alive, rising

1. Dean Acheson, *Morning and Noon* (Boston, 1965), p. 18.

quickly to the challenge, perhaps in part out of realization that he had not done well at Yale. Among other faculty notables he encountered the still young Felix Frankfurter, who only a decade before had been assisting the U.S. district attorney in New York City, Henry L. Stimson. Already Frankfurter was weaving the web of friendships that would mark him off as one of the master maneuverers of the twentieth century in American politics. Upon seeing the stuff of which his student Acheson was made he arranged for him to clerk for Justice Louis D. Brandeis.

Frankfurter's decision was important to Acheson for two reasons. For one, it placed him under the tutelage of not merely a lawyer of competence but a man who was a Democrat and possessed a social conscience. It is true that Brandeis reinforced in Acheson the incipient strain of elitism; the Supreme Court justice believed that progress and civilization depended very much on the efforts of those few men in every society who have the will and intelligence to resist or overcome the ignorance and folly of the mass. Acheson certainly cultivated a similar outlook, which explains his manifest contempt for those in Congress and the press whom he thought should know better. From Brandeis, however, he also learned an anti–big business philosophy, sympathy for the underdog, and especially concern for the salvation of society.

After clerking for Brandeis it was easy for Acheson to enter a prestigious law firm, Covington and Burling, thereby exploiting his considerable intellectual qualities and his social agilities, becoming well known in the capital, making himself an ideal candidate for high appointive office when the time was right. For twenty years after serving Brandeis, Acheson pursued his law practice with Covington and Burling, a period broken only momentarily by appointment as undersecretary of the treasury in 1933 when the Democrats returned to power. This ill-starred arrangement lasted only a few months, when he got into a contention with President Roosevelt over the administration's monetary policies and with a commendable independence—a sort that was never far from any of his public positions—resigned. His behavior during his years in the Rooseveltian political wilderness, from 1934 to 1941, had a good deal to do with his return to presidential good graces. Roosevelt usually hated the people who quarreled with him. Few individuals were able to move out of the Roosevelt administration and then, years later, move back in again. Paradoxically, Acheson's commitment to New Deal philosophy and programs deepened in his years out of office.

Eventually, with the onset of the Second World War in Europe in 1939, it seemed clear to Acheson and to President Roosevelt that the country would have to help Britain and France, and Acheson joined with other Democrats in private life to speak publicly and otherwise sponsor support of the administration's pro-Allied moves. His help in arranging the destroyers-bases deal of 1940 was so notable that Roosevelt saw advantage in bringing him into the State Department; early in 1941 Acheson became assistant secretary in charge of economic affairs under Secretary Cordell Hull. During the brief secretaryship of Edward R. Stettinius, Jr., in 1944–45, he occupied the lightly regarded but important post of assistant secretary for congressional relations, after which he served as undersecretary for two years for Secretaries Byrnes and Marshall. Resigning in July 1947, he came back to the department as secretary in January 1949 and remained until the Democrats went out of office four years later.

◇◇◇

Acheson's apprenticeship for the high office of secretary during these years was a time when the ideas of intelligent men changed rapidly, and there surely was a change in Acheson. Although his personal fortunes were barely touched by the Great Depression, its social ravages and its aftermath in the form of international lawlessness and aggression made a profound impression. He soon shared the view of Keynes and others that a better way of running the capitalist system would have to be found. As undersecretary he became a strong advocate of the International Monetary Fund and of lower tariffs against those individuals who would have returned to the dog-eat-dog days of the 1920s and 1930s. As the assistant secretary responsible for administering wartime lend-lease he became increasingly aware of the world's parlous economic condition. He frequently found himself opposed to Secretary of the Treasury Henry Morgenthau, Hull, Leo T. Crowley, who headed the Office of Economic Warfare, and even FDR in their attempts to use lend-lease to beat down Britain's imperial preference and economic defenses. His view was that the United States would need Britain's economic strength after the war both as a trading partner and as a force for political stability.

His years of apprenticeship were also a time when the Department of State was having organizational problems, which were compounded by the attitudes of President Roosevelt. FDR possessed a contempt for Hull, distrusted the Foreign Service, and preferred to rely upon the White House staff and a few friends in the department to decide most of the big diplomatic questions. Acheson shared the frustration of other department members at seeing their services treated so disparagingly; but he came to see that the department itself was not working well, for bureaucratic reasons of inertia, incompetence, and irrelevance. During the war the department had expanded from a small group of people, less than a thousand in all, to a vast bureaucracy of more than six thousand persons, only a few of whom were involved in the business of sending and receiving cables pertaining strictly to foreign policy of the old-fashioned prewar political sort. This bureaucracy was capable of good work, but it needed its motor overhauled. The big question that he asked himself when Byrnes offered him the undersecretaryship in 1945 was whether he could do that.

Late in 1944, when Hull resigned, Roosevelt chose the in-effective Stettinius to succeed him. Acheson was offered the post of assistant secretary for congressional relations in the expectation that he too would resign; instead he impudently accepted the post rather than quit, and an appointment that might have seemed a dead end turned out to have an important bearing on his career. It was his responsibility to pilot the United Nations Charter, the Bretton Woods Agreements, and other bills having foreign policy significance through the House and Senate. He came prepared to find dealing with politicians a degrading business, but he actually found it quite exhilarating. In the first place his gentlemanly style won him admission to the inner coterie of the Senate where, over ham sandwiches and bourbon, the important details of the legislative mill were decided. Secondly, he found that it tickled his vanity to be accepted as "one of the boys." Thirdly, since he was not the number-one man in the State Department, he was able to say some pretty harsh things against legislative critics and get away with it. Finally, he made the acquaintance of Harry S. Truman.

When Stettinius was propelled into the United Nations as U.S. representative in the summer of 1945 and replaced by Byrnes, the absence of the peripatetic "Jimmy" at a continuing series of international conferences (Byrnes was out of the country during almost half his tenure as secretary) gave Acheson, who meanwhile had been appointed undersecretary, a chance to get his hands on the administrative machinery. His administrative reordering of the department was an action of major importance. The device by which he brought the floundering bureaucracy into order was a simple one: the ordering of responsibility. He held a conference every morning of the work week during which he personally confronted the department's leading officers and asked for new business and disposition of the old. Everyone knew who was responsible for what, down to the lowliest desk officer. It was merely a matter of people to people, as a later administration described a different diplomacy; but a lot of dead wood had to be eliminated or circumvented, and the principal thing that made it work was Acheson's ability to impart to his immediate subordinates the conviction that what they were doing was important and therefore had to be done to the best of their ability. He detested committee meetings and especially committee decisions, which he believed always dropped to the lowest common denominator. He felt that the principal administrator of any office, bureau, or department needed to hear different opinions, even clashing opinions, but then had to make up his own mind and not take refuge in some group report. He believed most of all in clear lines of authority and responsibility.

During the Byrnes era, however, Acheson was not quite master in his own house, since it was Byrnes's house. This was an awkward arrangement; when Byrnes failed to keep the president informed, Acheson had to explain to Truman what was going on and report Truman's unhappiness to Byrnes. This unnecessary cleavage often put the president on the spot vis-à-vis the administration's critics, and even worse it permitted Senator Arthur H. Vandenberg, John Foster Dulles, and other Republican kibitzers to exert an unhealthy influence on the administration's diplomacy. For example, Truman made unduly hard-line promises to Vandenberg about atomic matters because Byrnes had not informed him of his own initiatives at the Moscow Foreign Ministers Conference of December 1945. Byrnes often undid the work the department had carried out at his own instruction. Perhaps the worst example of this was the fiasco over international atomic control. Before departing for Paris in early 1946 he instructed Acheson to prepare a comprehensive American plan for international control of atomic energy. After months of hard work by a committee led by the then head of the Tennessee Valley Authority David E. Lilienthal and the distinguished physicist J. Robert Oppenheimer, Acheson was able to present a brilliantly conceived plan for an international control system. Instead of adopting it as the basis of U.S. policy, however, Byrnes recommended that Truman appoint Bernard M. Baruch, a stuffed-shirt financier with a winter estate in Byrnes's home state of South Carolina, to head the U.S. delegation to the United Nations meeting on the subject. Baruch and several reactionary associates proceeded to burden the Acheson-Lilienthal Plan with unnecessary provisions for elimination of the veto in the UN Security Council and for all kinds of condign punishment for any state found guilty of cheating. The Soviet Union rejected the Baruch Plan out of hand.

In Byrnes's frequent absences from Washington it fell to Acheson as undersecretary and acting secretary to handle more and more of the day-to-day and month-to-month business of the department. Planning and decisions for the British and French loans, atomic energy, and the United Nations all came his way. At a time when squabbles over ending price control, settling coal and railroad strikes, and keeping harmony within the cabinet hurt the prestige of the administration, he succeeded in running foreign policy on a more efficient basis and in delivering a series of mildly impressive congressional victories—sufficiently impressive for James Reston to write that nothing could be more appealing to President Truman than Acheson's "gift of negotiation and debate. . . . He plugs away, with great powers of definition, for a steady, consistent policy based on the facts . . . and despite the limitations of his job, his intelligence, his knowledge, and capacity of definition are sufficient to be effective if they are not . . . decisive." [2]

Acheson found Roosevelt's successor a congenial leader. There is no need to repeat the many ways in which Truman's character and operating style appealed to him. Suffice to say that while he discovered that it was impossible to work directly with Roosevelt he found Truman's unpretentious, straightforward, and open manner of dealing with subordinates to be entirely accept-

2. "The No. 1. No. 2 Man in Washington," *New York Times*, 25 August 1946.

able. Acheson abhorred secrecy and deviousness in any superior; he could not stand to feel demeaned or used. Truman's personality took this repugnant element out of relations with subordinates. He believed in a strong presidency; he also set great store by administrative efficiency and was prepared to delegate authority without relinquishing responsibility. All these traits were congenial to Acheson's temperament. Seldom have two men from such different social backgrounds found the basis for an enduring partnership. Seldom have men in politics taken a deeper sense of pleasure and joy in a political relationship. It lightened both men's loads and made it possible for both to accept their differences easily and openly.

Acheson's ideas on foreign policy when he became undersecretary in late August 1945 were hardly what his later critics, the revisionists of the 1960s and 1970s, have said they were. He had not been associated with the earlier "tough" line toward the Soviet Union advocated by Averell Harriman and Admiral William D. Leahy that had gotten the president off to a bad start in the conduct of Soviet diplomacy. He arrived in a position to help make policy at a moment when Truman was becoming aware of the extreme anti-Soviet views of some of his advisers and of the need to make a new effort to settle differences with Moscow. As I. F. Stone recognized, Acheson was not identified with these anti-Soviet influences: "He has been pro-De Gaulle, anti-Franco, strongly opposed to the admission of Argentina to the U.N., and friendly to the Soviet Union. . . . Of all the men now in the department, Acheson was by far the best choice for Under Secretary, and it is no small advantage to pick a man who already knows a good deal about the [department's] inner workings." [3] In the minds of men like Adolf A. Berle and Patrick J. Hurley he was if anything identified as neutral on the subject of the Soviet Union and moderate in his whole approach to American interests. His principal preoccupation during his first year in office was with the mounting chaos and despair that threatened so much of the world. His principal lament was that if Americans would only do what had to be done—pass the British and French loans or agree to international control of atomic energy—threats and problems would take care of themselves. At that time he favored a serious

3. "Shakeup in the State Department," Nation 161 (25 August 1945), 171–72.

effort to reach agreement with the Soviet Union on international control of atomic energy as well as one last attempt to negotiate a German settlement before zonal differences sealed the split of Europe indefinitely.

Soon after becoming undersecretary, Acheson confronted evidence that the Soviets were using pressure on Iran and Turkey, which, if successful, would lower confidence in the United Nations and undermine the security of an area of the world strategically important to the West. Hundreds of cables poured into the department from Tehran, Ankara, and Moscow, all stressing the aggressive intentions of the Kremlin. Asked to comment on Soviet purposes in Iran, George F. Kennan—at that time the chargé d'affaires in the Moscow embassy—did not think Soviet leaders would risk war, but believed they were determined "to bring into power in Iran a regime prepared to accede to major immediate Soviet demands. . . . Soviet forces in Iran will serve this scheme by sheer force of intimidation."[4] Acheson agreed. Kennan attributed similar intentions to Soviet pressure on Turkey to give up control of the Bosporus. Whatever the real Soviet intentions, the practical implications of the Iranian and Turkish situations soon changed Acheson's view of the USSR. He advised the Iranian government to bring its case before the United Nations and recommended that the United States "let the USSR know that we are aware of its moves, but leave a graceful way out if it desired to avoid a showdown." In the case of the straits crisis he recommended that Truman send the U.S.S. *Missouri* to Istanbul and that the U.S. go to war if necessary to repel the Russians.[5] For Acheson and the president these episodes were a litmus test of Soviet intentions. Just as Russia had for its objective a security belt in Eastern Europe, so the American leadership believed that the best warranty of American strategic interests lay in a system of formally sovereign and independent states. Roosevelt had mentioned specifically that he regarded a strong and independent Iran as "something of a testing ground for the Atlantic Charter and the good faith of the United Nations."[6] Americans generally believed

---

4. *Foreign Relations of the United States, 1946*, vol. 7 (Washington, D.C., 1969), pp. 362–63.
5. Ibid., p. 347.
6. Gabriel Kolko, *The Politics of War: The World and United States Foreign Policy, 1943–1945* (New York, 1968), p. 309.

that the independence of all countries was a *sine qua non* for a peaceful international order and therefore viewed Soviet moves against Iran and Turkey with particular alarm and foreboding.

Acheson at this time began to use the United Nations to advance American ends, and perhaps this tactic was a mistake. Much of the justification for America's hard-line response to Soviet actions in 1946–47 was that by refusing to evacuate northern Iran and by threatening Turkey the Soviets were demonstrating a disregard for the United Nations. Acheson did not really believe in the United Nations, in frequent sharp contrast to Truman. He was willing to espouse its principles for want of a better justification and later sponsored the Uniting for Peace Resolution[7] which made the United Nations even more responsive to U.S. interests. This attitude, however, embodied the danger of employing the United Nations as a means without being committed to it as an end or endeavoring to make it work. This careful legalism in defense of power politics certainly contributed to the confusion that later reigned in many American minds between actions dictated by national interest and the belief that America was always behaving according to international principles of a higher order.

On the issue of whether American resistance to Soviet moves was blind and unthinking, without comprehension of the Kremlin's limited motives, Acheson's course probably was as good as any alternative. In the preceding essay John Gaddis has written that both Acheson and Truman came to believe that only resistance to Russian expansion would preserve peace. The possibility that Soviet probes might be limited and essentially defensive was not recognized at the time; as Gaddis notes, there was no guarantee that those probes would have continued to be limited if the West did not resist.

It was only a short jump from elaborating policy for the crises over Iran and Turkey to arriving at the conviction that something would have to be done to replace British efforts in Greece. Acheson—who after Byrnes left the department in January 1947

---

7. This was a resolution of the U.N. General Assembly on 3 November 1950 stating that if the Security Council, because of lack of unanimity of the permanent members, fails to exercise its responsibility for peace and security the General Assembly shall consider the matter and make recommendations for collective measures including the use of armed force if necessary.

remained as undersecretary for six months under Byrnes's successor Marshall—was now thinking of the American-Soviet conflict as a duel between two fundamentally incompatible antagonists. "Not since the clash of the Greeks and the Persians, the Romans and Carthage have two such fundamentally opposed civilizations been in the balance," he told a group of skeptical congressmen whom the president and Secretary Marshall had failed to convince of the need for aid to Greece and Turkey. For Acheson it was a typical bravura performance designed to save a bad situation, but he really did believe the situation would become that serious unless the American people and Congress were willing to act. He did not envisage the Truman Doctrine being applied everywhere. He certainly did not believe it could work or should be applied in China where the Communists were slowly gaining the upper hand, and he certainly did not at that time or even as late as January 1950 believe it was necessary or could be made to work in Southeast Asia.

Congress agreed to the Truman Doctrine, not without the usual Vandenberg flourish in favor of the United Nations which Acheson rather hypocritically acceded to. This constant invocation of the United Nations Charter and legalism to cover an American strategy of power not only confused in the American mind the basis on which the U.S. was acting, but also veiled from Acheson and the president the virtue of frankly exploring an alternative approach to the Soviets: an approach of power, of spheres of influence. If they had perceived the existence of that alternative, the U.S. would not so quickly have embarked on the crusade of defeating Soviet machinations wherever they appeared.

In judging American diplomacy for its failure to confront the distinction between its emphasis upon legal and moral principles and its essential practice of power, one cannot be blind to the double standard of all states. Just as the Soviet Union preached Socialist fraternity and practiced repression, so the U.S. can hardly be stigmatized for taking advantage of its corner on the market of international idealism. One of the Department of State's senior officials, Loy W. Henderson, unconsciously expressed this point very well in a memorandum to Acheson in October 1946: "The moral strength imparted by high principles and the conviction that the U.S. is defending not only its own cause but that of all free nations is a tremendous factor in world affairs. . . ." [8]

Acheson remained as undersecretary long enough to see the Marshall Plan proposed, confirming·his long-standing belief that future peace and security depended on the United States doing much more in the economic sphere than had ever been anticipated when Roosevelt, Hull, and Morgenthau were working to weaken the British Empire during the Second World War.

◇◇◇

In analyzing Acheson's statecraft after he became secretary in January 1949, the distinction between the situation as it existed at that time and Acheson's response to it should be kept in mind. The possibility, increasingly discussed today, that Soviet policy was not rooted in self-confidence but in insecurity was not at all apparent then. The Berlin blockade was at its height. Nationalist resistance was crumbling in China. The Communist parties of France and Italy were still working to defeat the Marshall Plan. Most people in Europe as well as in America were convinced that Stalin really meant business. European Communists still hoped that was the case, and influential writers like Jean-Paul Sartre and Hubert Beuve-Mery, the editor of Le Monde, clearly·felt that some form of Marxist regime was preferable to the reign·of capitalism or to another war followed by another occupation and another American liberation.

Very few people thought of Soviet behavior as an expression of weakness; the prevailing mood was one of fear and desperation. In such a case Acheson may not have been so wrong in believing that only a renewal of Western strength could avoid the worst, which might be a Soviet political breakthrough followed by another war, for that is probably what would have happened had Europe succumbed at that time.

Although the Soviet Union was soon to lift its blockade of Berlin, Acheson had already resolved in his mind that there was little if any hope of Russia or America compromising on Germany. The barren results of the Foreign Ministers Conference of that spring in Paris convinced him that discussion would get nowhere.

8. *Foreign Relations, 1946,* vol. 7, p. 242. For the entire memorandum see pp. 240–45.

From then on, he said upon return, these conferences would be like the steam gauge on a boiler. They would indicate the built-up pressure, the gains and losses in position that took place between meetings. He said that the steam gauge's recording of the Paris conference was that the position of the West had risen greatly. Since there was no hope for negotiation, the West should simply ignore the implications for Russia of what it was doing and get ahead with the business of forging its own unity and strength.

Events of that year—the fall of China, the Soviet A-bomb, the seeming lethargy of the Western responses—only added to Acheson's somber view. The Soviet Union was like a force of nature, like a river; it could be dammed up or deflected, but it could not be kept from flowing. Although not unlike Kennan's metaphor about the inevitable tendency of Soviet policy to expand into the basin of world power, Acheson's metaphor had an even more deterministic cast to it. Gaddis Smith has expressed its implications very well: "If, as Acheson believed, the Soviet government was a force of nature propelled entirely by physical laws of expansion, then indeed it would have been foolish to attempt a mutual exploration of American hopes, fears, and attitudes." [9] Acheson took as his basic assumption that the distrust and differences between the USSR and the West were too great to be settled by negotiation. Stalin, of course, acted on the grim assumption that the future would witness a series of frightful clashes before socialism triumphed over capitalism. (Whether Stalin believed it is a moot point.) Under the circumstances Acheson did not believe that negotiations were worthwhile. The Soviets, he declaimed, respected only strength; the West should concentrate on making itself so unified, so strong, so prosperous that the relationship of forces that would emerge would give the Kremlin no choice but to cease and desist from pressure on the West. There would be no need for negotiation. The existing situations of strength would determine the lines of settlement.[10]

This was to be containment with a vengeance; but did it go beyond that? There were position papers prepared for Acheson's negotiations with Foreign Minister Robert Schuman of France and

9. Gaddis Smith, *Dean Acheson* (New York, 1972), p. 101.
10. This might work in Europe where there was a solid base to build on, but Acheson soon discovered that no such base existed in Asia or the Middle East where all was jungle and shifting sand.

Foreign Secretary Ernest Bevin of England that stipulated the withdrawal of Soviet forces from Eastern Europe as the ultimate goal of NATO policy; but neither the British nor the French were ever persuaded to accept that objective, and it seems to have been put forward more as an aspiration than as a practical objective.

Acheson did not believe that a "situations of strength" strategy would increase the likelihood of war; in any case he was convinced that such precautions were necessary if the West was not to remain at the mercy of Soviet threats and pressures. He believed that the men in the Kremlin were realists who would be restrained by the new relationship of power. He does not seem to have appreciated fully the fact that their realism might lead them to greater efforts to increase their situations of strength, or to new and even more dangerous adventures such as unleashing war in Korea. The West, he contended, was not strong enough under any circumstances.

This policy probably was not the most ideal. Although Acheson would have denied that he was imposing a zero-sum game on the Russians, it amounted to that. So long as negotiation from strength was all strength and no negotiation, it was all too likely to be seen as such by the Russians. Acheson was remiss in not tempering his strategic predispositions with some consideration of the possibility that the Kremlin's behavior might be subject to greater restraint and modification than appearances seemed to indicate. This led him to brush aside too readily Kennan's arguments against a rigid commitment to the reunification of Germany on exclusively Western terms, and against too exclusive an imputation to the Kremlin of expansionist intentions in drawing up the famous position paper known as NSC-68 (National Security Council memorandum 68).

Haunted by the seeming weakness and disunity of the West, and prompted by belief in the therapeutic value of action and organization, Acheson as secretary of state determined to bend all his formidable energies and skills to making the North Atlantic area so unified, strong, and prosperous that neither the Europeans nor the Kremlin would have any doubt of Europe's ability to survive. Even before the North Atlantic Treaty had been ratified he was determined to make it more than a guarantee pact. He understood French Premier Henri Queuille's remark that one more occupation would finish France, that America would be liberating a corpse. The Europeans wanted an American commitment.

Acheson had every intention of gaining it for them because he believed it was in America's interest to overcome the divisions of Europe and prevent a repetition of the last war.

By ruling out the need to allow concessions to the Soviet Union, he increased his potential for granting concessions to the Europeans. Since no acceptable compromise on Germany was possible he was free to offer maximum terms for Bonn's adherence to the Western alliance: the unification of Germany on Western terms at some unstated later date. The French were willing to accept this because it did not seem likely that the Kremlin would ever agree to German unification on those terms. This meant that future negotiations with the Soviet Union would be heavily mortgaged and America's room for maneuvering severely restricted by the absolute conditions of Acheson's NATO diplomacy. While it provided the U.S. with maximum support at the time it did not augur well for the future.

Acheson showed real authority in handling the rearmament of Europe, and it was an authority much appreciated at the time. It had its difficulties, but it had its results. As the secretary of state elaborated his European policy he pushed Congress to comply with his requests for military appropriations and authority. Most congressmen preferred to wait and see what the Europeans would contribute to the alliance before action, but Acheson insisted that the United States meet its share of the burden regardless of what the Europeans did or did not do. He then told the Europeans that unless they matched the American effort he could not hope to get the Congress to go along the next time. Painful though the experience was for European statesmen, Acheson's resolution and ability to deliver the goods profoundly impressed them. They were scarcely accustomed to someone who could make the balky congressional cow give such regular milk, and most of them fell all over themselves to accommodate Acheson's requests.

Despite the rigor of Acheson's diplomatic approach and the painful choices with which he frequently confronted European statesmen, the leaders of the European nations essentially liked to do business with him. He was notably free from moralizations and cant. He may have chastised them severely in private for their backsliding, and he put intense pressure on them behind the scenes to settle the nationalist claims of their colonies as quickly as possible, but he did not lecture them or pillory them in public. He always tried to be helpful. He was fertile in innovative expedients and compromises and fortunately able to do much to help them out with public opinion at home. Despite the shock to French relations of Acheson's demand that the Germans be permitted to rearm, it never came to the breaking point. The respect and sympathy between Acheson and Schuman was a remarkable interlude in Franco-American diplomacy.

Running NATO was no easy task. As Robert E. Osgood suggests: "In a multilateral alliance exacting extensive commitments and contributions [collaboration] is bound to be a delicate and exacting task, for the requirements of collaboration do not automatically coincide with the requirements of security. A viable alliance must permit material and political concessions to the requirements of cohesion." Beyond that, agreement on common military plans is difficult because the cost of modern military strategy "affects, and is therefore affected by, strong domestic, economic, and psychological pressures. . . . Then domestic pressures are especially marked where strategy infringes upon public expenditures, individual taxes, notions of fiscal soundness, the conscription of manpower, and the allocation of money. . . ."[11] In order to deal with these problems Acheson had succeeded in getting a system adopted whereby a NATO commission led by the so-called three wise men (Harriman for the U.S., Edwin N. Plowden for Britain, Jean Monnet for France) had been accorded the right to look into each member's finances and make recommendations for the most appropriate and equitable ways to allocate its national resources. This was an unprecedented abridgment of national sovereignty that only Acheson's personal standing and diplomatic skill made possible. It would be another decade before the Common Market achieved a similar authority to intervene in the domestic affairs of the European states. Anyone familiar with the magnitude of the sacrifice that European governments made to the success of NATO strategy during the Acheson years knows that a majority of Europeans were convinced, at least until 1953, that the Soviet Union constituted a mortal danger.

Even before the Korean War he had insisted upon passage by Congress of the Military Assistance Program. Once the war broke out in the Far East he was able to galvanize the NATO allies. He did not do it without some difficulties, for he received much

11. Robert E. Osgood, *NATO: The Entangling Alliance* (Chicago, 1962), pp. 18–19.

criticism from General Charles de Gaulle, then out of office. De Gaulle capitalized on the dissatisfaction of Frenchmen over their country's distinctly second-class place compared with the United States and the United Kingdom. France's sense of being treated as more of an object than a subject of the alliance enabled the difficult Frenchman to mount a campaign that would carry him a few years later to the Elysée Palace. Despite such opposition Acheson went ahead. It is a tribute to his talents of persuasion and improvisation that, especially after 1951, he was able to make steady headway even without the dramatic support of the Berlin blockade or the Korean War. Under his management NATO became more than a military alliance; it enabled the State Department to resolve many tangled and potentially divisive European situations as well as ease their withdrawal from empire by providing them with an attractive alternative in the form of an Atlantic community.

The Lisbon Conference of February 1952 constituted the high-water mark of American NATO diplomacy in Europe. In return for the presence of half a dozen American divisions and equivalent air and naval units on the line in central Europe, the Europeans contributed the equivalent of twenty divisions. Under the aegis of NATO and of the European Defense Community (which the French parliament eventually failed to ratify) the French and British had agreed to end their occupation of West Germany and permit West Germans to rearm. Unfortunately these feats of economic and military collaboration could not be sustained because they rested upon too narrow a base. Although a prodigious diplomat and institution builder, Acheson had a narrow preoccupation with collaboration for purposes of national security that made his edifice vulnerable once the threat that had prompted North Atlantic collaboration began to lose its grim and menacing visage.

◇◇◇

The one area of policy in which much confusion and uncertainty remained during 1949–53 was the Far East. Acheson had participated in the decision, in connection with the Marshall mission to China in 1946, not to permit the U.S. to become involved militarily in the struggles between the Nationalists and the Communists. He became secretary of state three years later when the fall of the Nationalist regime and the flight of Chiang to Formosa were becoming settled facts. Republican critics in and out of Congress had been pressing for a U.S. guarantee of Formosa's security. Despite the ferocity of Republican criticism Acheson refused to extend American protection to Chiang's Formosan regime. Pointing to the already existing Soviet gains at the expense of China he warned that the nation should do nothing toward mainland China that would "deflect from the Russians to ourselves the righteous anger, and wrath, and the hatred of the Chinese people which must develop." Instead of prolonging a futile involvement in the Chinese civil war he envisaged ending the occupation of Japan and restoring Japan, on the model of West Germany, as a counterweight against Communist expansion in Northeast Asia.

As for the future of Southeast Asia, there was great uncertainty in his mind. In his speech to the National Press Club of 12 January 1950, he addressed himself to the issue that would dog Americans for over a quarter of a century: what U.S. policy should be toward those countries whose governments lacked popular support and the means of preventing revolution and Communist take-over. Here ambivalence seemed in order. On the one hand Acheson told Ambassador Philip C. Jessup who was about to undertake a sweeping examination of Asian policy, "You will please take as your assumption that it is the fundamental decision of American policy that the United States does not intend to permit further extension of Communist domination on the continent of Asia or in the Southeast Asia area." On the other hand he told the National Press Club that the day of foreign domination was over in Asia, and the truth was that no outside nation and no outside people were "wise enough and disinterested enough very long to assume the responsibility for another people or to control another people's opportunities." The military security of the countries of Southeast Asia beyond the U.S. military perimeter guarding Japan and the Philippines "lay beyond the realm of any practical relationship" and he preferred, as he said later, "not to speculate" on what the United States "might do in the event of various exigencies in Asia." [12]

There undoubtedly was a dilemma involved in policy toward

12. Dean Acheson, *Present at the Creation* (New York, 1969), p. 356.

Southeast Asia, and Acheson should not be blamed too much for finding himself unable to choose and then dignifying this inability into a policy. A good approach might well have been noninterference, to allow natural forces, particularly Sino-Soviet antagonisms, to run their course. This policy required patience, faith in history, and restraint that the American public did not have; they could not accept such a course.[13] Acheson clung to it as best he could, but by May 1950 he had already sacrificed the principle to expediency by backing the French in Indochina. Then came the shock of Korea.

The attack in Korea could be interpreted in two ways: as demonstrating the prescience of NSC-68, the need to provide more effective military backing against the possibility of Communist aggression in other parts of the globe; or as demonstrating the limits of trying to dam up Soviet power and refusing to continue the search for some basis of negotiation and compromise that would reduce the compulsion on both sides to exploit every weakness possible against the other. Kennan earlier had called for some form of spheres of influence in Northeast Asia, and once again put forth this line of reasoning—to no avail. Acheson chose to view the Korean attack as proof of the wisdom of NSC-68. In a memorandum to Truman before a presidential press conference he wrote, "The attack upon Korea makes it plain beyond all doubt that communism has passed beyond the use of subversion to conquer independent nations and will now use armed invasion and war" —a threat in Asia as well as in Europe. [14]

His support of the president's decision to repel the North Korean invasion was rooted in what men of his generation had felt about the failure of democracies to resist German and Japanese aggression less than a dozen years earlier. It was also rooted in the conviction that if nothing was done it would undermine the confidence and trust of a Europe still uncertain of America's leadership, a belief reflected in Charles E. (Chip) Bohlen's report that when he conveyed word of the American decision to Foreign Minister Schuman the latter's eyes filled with tears. "Thank God," he said, "this will not be a repetition of the past." Europe in general, except for the Communists, applauded the American decision.

13. Smith, *Acheson*, pp. 136–37.
14. Ibid., p. 186.

Less praiseworthy was the alacrity with which Acheson recommended that the Seventh Fleet be put into the Formosa Strait and the relative insouciance with which Communist China's reaction to all this was viewed. In retrospect it appears that the purpose of the policy of hands-off-Formosa was to still the clamor of the China Lobby and also to bury the hatchet between Acheson and Secretary of Defense Louis Johnson in favor of administration harmony; but it is doubtful if Acheson would have so lightly sacrificed his China policy on the altar of domestic harmony had he not been largely insensitive to Communist China's interests in the whole affair—a failing all too quickly confirmed by his approval of the decision to permit General Douglas MacArthur to unify Korea even at the risk of advancing to the Chinese frontier on the Yalu. The carelessness with which he viewed Chinese interests stands in marked contrast to his concern in European policy to avoid provoking the Soviet Union and is principally explainable in terms of a monumental blind spot for what effect America's actions would have on China. Negligence bordering on criminal folly rather than hostility marked the administration's view of China's role during these critical months, as evidenced by Acheson's attempts to reassure Peking in the last desperate weeks of November. Unfortunately, by that time nothing could be done to call off the offensive, and the subsequent disaster must be ranked as one of Acheson's most grievous failures.

Some observers are inclined to rate his management of America's decision to enter the Korean War as the greatest demonstration of his ability to balance the needs of instantaneous reactions with the need to think through the long-range ramifications of those decisions. In retrospect it may well be that his greatest performance came in those desperate days of December 1950 and January 1951 with annihilation facing the United Nations army in Korea, with Prime Minister Clement Attlee and General MacArthur clamoring for evacuation of U.S. forces, and with still others denouncing the administration's countenancing of a Communist Chinese delegation being permitted to present an indictment of the United States before the UN. He steadied the administration, recommended against extending the war to China, and guided America into a winning diplomatic position in the UN debate. This was fully as important a test, both for world peace and for U.S. diplomacy, as the decision to resist aggression six months earlier. It took courage not to give way to the despair and unreason that swept the country and to reduce American goals in Korea to the single goal of holding once again a line at the waist of Korea along the thirty-eighth parallel.

Choosing to fight a limited war was a new experiment in twentieth-century statecraft, but it was the only alternative, given the logic of Acheson's strategy. Unfortunately it was not an experiment for which Americans were temperamentally prepared, and the failure to keep the war limited by bringing in China all but destroyed the administration. Only the greatest courage and responsibility on the part of all involved—Truman, Acheson, Marshall, who by this time was secretary of defense, and General Omar N. Bradley, who was chairman of the Joint Chiefs—kept it from becoming much worse.

The war on the Korean peninsula that might have been ended in October 1950 after the Inchon invasion[15] now dragged on for two more years over issues entirely extraneous to the original matter: namely, the terms for an armistice commission and the repatriation of Chinese prisoners of war. The long-drawn-out statement of these issues in the truce talks only allowed more casualties and was a devastating liability to the Democratic administration's political situation at home.

Events surrounding the Korean War reinforced Acheson's conviction that Communist activities everywhere had to be treated as an extension of Soviet and now, by implication, Chinese expansionism. This was most unfortunate, for it not only led him through his UN spokesman Dean Rusk to brand Peking as a puppet of Russian imperialism with which America could never entertain diplomatic relations, but it also led to abandonment of his previous skepticism about the French role in Indochina.

The disastrous unfolding of events in Korea had locked Acheson into a position on China and Indochina just the opposite of what he had held only a year earlier. He showed far less caution and sensitivity toward Communist China than toward the Soviets. He unwittingly invited disaster, from the trauma of which neither he nor the American people would emerge with a lucid view of the Asian situation. Although he was under heavy political pressure at home to oppose communism more resolutely in Asia

15. In September MacArthur had captured this port in western Korea, near Seoul, outflanking nearly all the North Korean troops in the South.

than had previously been his wont, this alone does not explain the reversal of his position. He had failed to foresee that the crude nature of the situations of strength strategy, which he had begun with such confidence in Europe, could not be extended to Asia where the U.S. was in a far less advantageous situation relative to forces in the area. The result was to freeze policy toward Asia into a rigidly moralistic and anti-Communist position far less favorable to such attitudes than was the case in Europe.

Acheson's thinking did not go anywhere near Senator Robert A. Taft's view that "now that a Communist assault in Southeast Asia is on the horizon it should be clear to our government that the only chance to stop it is by a Chinese Nationalist invasion of the Communist held territory." [16] Acheson was prepared to have America intervene directly in the war in Indochina should Chinese intervention in support of Ho Chi Minh require it. Fortunately, despite the expansionist intentions imputed to Peking, nothing of that sort occurred; but he was no longer willing to accept the distinction between the war in Indochina and the feud with China, and the escalation of aid to the French followed, despite the fact that Acheson knew the French were in a morally false and militarily well-nigh hopeless position.

Admittedly, in some Far Eastern developments Acheson scored well, as in his stand over the dismissal of MacArthur in 1951 and his management later that year of the Japanese Peace Conference that met in San Francisco. His support for Truman's dismissal of MacArthur was dictated by knowledge that Mac-Arthur was not only challenging the president's authority but interfering in a dangerous way with the conduct of policy in the Far East. The decision having been made that it was not in the national interest to prolong or enlarge the Korean War, Mac-Arthur's attempts to do so constituted an intolerable affront to civil authority. The subsequent Senate hearings into the Far Eastern situation permitted Acheson to defend the administration's efforts to keep the war in Asia limited. His success before the senators, and that of Marshall, Bradley, and the Joint Chiefs, was a welcome interlude in the generally difficult implementation of Far Eastern policy.

16. Quoted in Foster Rhea Dulles, *American Policy toward Communist China, 1949–1969* (New York, 1972), p. 124.

In the case of the Japanese Peace Treaty Acheson obtained almost a personal triumph. In a real sense he was the diplomatic father of the treaty, although John Foster Dulles was fond of claiming it and generally it redounded to the credit of the Truman administration. It had been an accident of the Second World War that MacArthur had been in command in the Far East, and his presence in that theater after the war had tended to keep Republican critics away from the administration's policy; a complaint about the Japanese occupation was an implied criticism of a Republican general. Acheson knew as well as anyone that it was highly desirable to maintain this state of affairs, and when the presidential elections of 1948 went against the Republicans he was quick to see the convenience of having another Republican foreign policy expert employed by the administration.

Dulles had attended international conferences since the end of the war and had proved a reliable adviser. At first President Truman, incensed by some of Dulles's campaign utterances, refused to appoint him; but Dulles eventually received appointment as special adviser to the secretary of state, and then special ambassador, to negotiate the Japanese treaty. Even at that time Dulles loved to travel, and his desire was put to good use by a series of trips to the capitals of nations intimately involved in the Japanese Peace Treaty. He secured their approbation in advance. The subsequent peace conference in San Francisco allowed Acheson momentarily to become a popular figure. In a very early televising of an international meeting—television was just "coming in" in those days—he forcefully, by occupying the rostrum, prevented the delegate of a Soviet satellite, Poland, from speaking beyond the allotted five minutes against the treaty; he first declared the delegate's effort to extend his remarks as out of order, and then took the microphone away from him, all visible to television viewers who could applaud this diplomatic victory for the United States. It was not exactly the way Acheson believed in "selling" foreign policy to the American people, but it worked.

In the Far East, then, one might say that there were some bright spots, but generally Acheson's policies did not work well there. He brought to his office a belief that man is capable of avoiding the worst fate in his struggle if he makes the effort to master the forces of human desperation. In Europe he succeeded in putting into effect, within the limits of the possible, the full means of doing this; but the shock of Asian events to American

Out Frisco Way

Buffalo Courier-Express, 1951

expectations proved too powerful, and in the notable case of the Korean War mastery almost succumbed to a loss of control and near disaster.

◇◇◇

In securing adoption of his costly situations of strength strategy Acheson had to pay a fearful personal price. He was not a popular figure at home. His dignified, aristocratic mien was alien to Americans, including most congressmen. He inspired enormous trust and confidence among fellow cabinet members (Secretary of Defense Johnson excepted) and within the department, and he had the respect of the members of the Senate and House committees, which was crucial to passage of so much enabling legislation. His stern and often minatory manner of holding Congress to the logic of containment and alliance building was an abrasive and often scarifying experience, however. As he said to Vandenberg when rejecting the latter's plea that because the North Atlantic Treaty had been passed there was no need for military assistance: "Intangibles do not impress. The Treaty is no substitute for substance." Congressmen and senators, more accustomed to horse trading and compromise, found him a difficult and frustrating figure to deal with. Republicans in particular found his stark and uncompromising positions on the North Atlantic Treaty, on troops to Europe, on Chiang's own responsibility for the fall of China, and on disentangling from the regime on Formosa hard to take. Frequently, if Truman had not intervened with a concession here and there or a little soothing balm, relations would have been even more strained. Of course, among many congressmen and many members of the public the hatred of Acheson reached pathological proportions. Not only was he a symbol of a worldly "Eastern Establishment" but he possessed a gentleman's code that forbade him to turn his back on Alger Hiss or to agree that his associates in the State Department were Communists. So long as he felt he had the genuine support and confidence of Truman, however, he had no intention of resigning. The two men were linked by adversity more closely than ever. Each knew that Senator Joseph R. McCarthy was a scoundrel and neither had any intention of knuckling under to his demagogic attacks.

Perhaps Acheson took some comfort in knowing that his

attackers—McCarthy perhaps excepted—objected far more to his policies than to his personality.[17] Given the source of the animus against him—rooted in the bitterness of Republican isolationists and China Lobby supporters and in the general frustrations connected with foreign affairs—it is doubtful that any other secretary of state would have fared much better. The same hard logic that led him to espouse situations of strength in Europe, which the public had accepted, also led him to oppose extending the war in Asia to include China.

Whatever the future was to reveal about the correctness of his views and the fickleness of much American public opinion during his tenure at the Department of State, his four years as secretary had been rigorous and difficult; the exit of the Democrats in 1953, after twenty years of national power, was a relief. He returned with joy to his Washington law practice, undertook a series of sessions (one weekend every month) at Princeton to tape his recollections together with those of his highest associates, and began to write occasional pieces for the public press and periodicals. The Eisenhower administration clearly was going to be in office for awhile, and Acheson enjoyed the opportunity to be on the outside poking criticisms at the "ins," especially when they were as vulnerable as the businessmen Eisenhower brought into the government.

The absence of the disciplining force of high office led him to espouse unnecessarily harsh and intolerant attitudes toward those individuals with whom he disagreed. He was yet able to distill the philosophy with which he had conducted American diplomacy in a series of distinguished and scholarly books, but his comments upon contemporary affairs sometimes suggested that he was not applying the principles of that philosophy with the same detachment and objectivity. Change meant scrapping the policies and attitudes of the past that were no longer relevant; this Acheson found difficult to accept. Another factor explaining what his critics decried as increasing conservatism, even a hard-line reactionary approach to both domestic and foreign problems, was undoubtedly advancing age. As the twilight years came upon him he

17. Glen H. Stassen, "Individual Preference versus Role Constraint in Policy Making: Senatorial Response to Secretaries Acheson and Dulles," *World Politics* 25 (1972–73), 96–119.

reacted to public issues somewhat in the way his older friend
Truman was reacting. Whatever he said, as whatever Truman said,
was good copy.

As the Republican years stretched on toward the denouement
of 1960 it became clear to Acheson that his own chances of getting
back into government were slight if not nonexistent. The young
faces of the presidential campaign of the latter year meant new
people in the cabinet posts, whoever won; and although President-elect Kennedy carefully consulted Acheson for names for the
cabinet positions the retired secretary of state could be sure that
his own name would not be considered seriously except for some
honorific post he surely would not desire. This fact, too—that he
was permanently out of public office—explains some of the
statements made in his later years after leaving the secretaryship of
state.

During the Democratic administrations of the 1960s his advice
was frequently sought on foreign relations, and he never hesitated
to give it. His advice on Berlin in 1961 (to hang on) was generally
sound. His advice on the Cuban missile crisis (to bomb Russian
missile sites) was fortunately rejected. Here was a perfect example
of a suggestion that was highly inappropriate to the new state of
affairs in the Kremlin. There was need to be firm, but also
conciliatory.

Acheson's early advice to President Lyndon B. Johnson not to
get involved in a land war in Vietnam was sound. He later went
along, probably so as not to lose influence. Had he earlier supported
Undersecretary of State George Ball, he might have halted the drift
into the war. His role as one of the wise men who encouraged
Johnson to reverse himself on Vietnam was highly important. At a
critical moment he staked his reputation as a hawk and a hard liner
against the military and the closed system of the bureaucracy, those
who still wished to pursue that futile war. His opinion helped
Johnson and Secretary of Defense Clark Clifford to reverse the ever
deepening irrationalities of the war.

As Acheson moved into his later seventies he was ever more
enjoying himself, appearing on television, lecturing college and
university audiences, writing for the "op-ed" pages of the *New
York Times*, but his writings, which always were vigorously
interesting, alternated between points of policy, mostly foreign
policy, and memories and invocations of the past. He recalled his
youth in Middletown; *Morning and Noon*, as he aptly had entitled

the first part of his reminiscences, was published in 1965. In *Present at the Creation*, he described the signal acts of his years in the Department of State, when a new foreign policy was produced for post-1945 America. He lived on in Georgetown, close to the scene of national action, but his heart, and usually his physical presence, was at his farm in Sandy Spring in nearby Maryland where he wrote and read. He died there one afternoon in October 1971.

BIBLIOGRAPHIC NOTE

Any account of books relating to Secretary Acheson must begin with the secretary's own eight volumes. The first of these was *A Democrat Looks at His Party* (New York, 1955), an argument for his party's stewardship of the federal government during the years from 1933 to 1953. There followed an analysis resting on Woodrow Wilson's *Congressional Government* (1885) entitled *A Citizen Looks at Congress* (New York, 1956), a distillation of the wisdom of Acheson's years of visits to the Hill. The William L. Clayton lectures at the Fletcher School of Law and Diplomacy, published under the title of *Power and Diplomacy* (Cambridge, Mass., 1958), defined his views about limited war, especially the need for caution during the age of nuclear power. *Sketches from Life* (New York, 1961) offered delightful vignettes of men he had known. Then came *Morning and Noon* (Boston, 1965), the first of what the secretary perhaps envisioned as a two- or three-volume memoir, unfortunately never finished; this book takes his life to 1941 when he entered the State Department. *Present at the Creation* (New York, 1969), a huge account of the department years, was completed at a time when his policies of 1945–53 were coming under sharp criticism from revisionist historians. Acheson was thoroughly aware of this criticism and considered it stupid; shortly before his death he told the *New York Times* reporter Alden Whitman, who (following a quaint procedure recently inaugurated by the *Times*) interviewed him for his obituary, that the revisionists were psychological cases. *Fragments of My Fleece* (New York, 1971) and the posthumous *Grapes from Thorns* (New York, 1972) were collections of essays. In the first of these he offered "these little fragments of my fleece that I have left upon the hedges of life." In the second he remarked that he and his longtime secretary, Miss Barbara Evans, had discovered that "among the thorns of the law and the thistles of politics and diplomacy we found some fruit that had retained its flavor and, in some cases, its tartness." Of secondary accounts there are thus far (1974) only two, the eminently readable and sensible book by Gaddis Smith, *Dean Acheson* (New York, 1972), a volume in the series *American Secretaries of State and*

Their Diplomacy, and *The Shaping of Foreign Policy: The Role of the Secretary of State as Seen by Dean Acheson* (Cleveland, 1969), by Ronald Stupak. See also the articles by David McLellan, "The Role of Political Style: A Study of Dean Acheson," in *Foreign Policy in the Sixties*, edited by Roger Hilsman and Robert C. Good (Baltimore, 1965); "The 'Operational Code' Approach to the Study of Political Leaders: Dean Acheson's Philosophical and Instrumental Beliefs," *Canadian Journal of Political Science* 4 (March 1971), 52–75; and (with Ronald Stupak) "The Statecraft of Dean Acheson," *Worldview* (March 1972), 32–38.

Both authors of this essay have read, reviewed, and/or employed in class most of the revisionist literature on the Acheson-Truman era in American foreign policy. A few among a mountain of books and articles critical of Acheson's diplomacy from the revisionist perspective are Lloyd C. Gardner, *Architects of Illusion: Men and Ideas in American Foreign Policy, 1941–1949* (Chicago, 1970), Joyce and Gabriel Kolko, *The Limits of Power; the World and United States Foreign Policy, 1945–1954* (New York, 1972), Walter LaFeber, *America, Russia and the Cold War, 1945–1971* (New York, 1971), S. E. Ambrose, *The Rise to Globalism: American Foreign Policy, 1938–1970* (Baltimore, 1970). Both authors have essays forthcoming in a new collection entitled *The Truman Period as a Research Field*, edited by Richard S. Kirkendall (Columbia, Mo., 1974), which will examine the literature from both the traditional and revisionist perspectives.

Orren Jack Turner

THE SEARCH FOR MEANING:

GEORGE F. KENNAN

and American Foreign Policy

Thomas G. Paterson

Scholars consider him a first-rate historian, Foreign Service officers rank him as one of their best, presidents and secretaries of state

This essay draws largely upon the Kennan papers at the Princeton University Library; Kennan's two-volume autobiography, *Memoirs, 1925–1950* (Boston, 1967) and *Memoirs, 1950–1963* (Boston, 1972); his prolific published works; official diplomatic correspondence; C. Ben Wright, "George F. Kennan, Scholar and Diplomat: 1926–1946," Ph.D. dissertation, University of Wisconsin, 1972; oral history transcripts at the John F. Kennedy Library and Princeton University; and numerous manuscript collections cited in Thomas G. Paterson, *Soviet-American Confrontation: Postwar Reconstruction and the Origins of the Cold War* (Baltimore, 1973). For an extensive bibliography of Kennan's work and critical commentaries, see Thomas G. Paterson, ed., *Containment and the Cold War* (Reading, Mass., 1973). The author is very grateful to J. Garry Clifford, Holly V. Izard, C. Ben Wright, Walter LaFeber, Thomas G. Smith, Theodore A. Wilson, and Eduard Mark for their helpful suggestions. The Harry S. Truman Library Institute and the University of Connecticut Research Foundation provided travel funds for the author's study of cold war diplomacy; the American Philosophical Society and the Rabinowitz Foundation provided additional financial aid in the preparation of this essay.

have tapped his expertise on the Soviet Union, a generation of
college students has been weaned on his publications and
prescriptions for a "realistic" foreign policy, and literally hundreds
of thousands of Americans and foreigners have become familiar
with his contemporary analyses of international relations. Soviet
leaders went so far as to declare him *persona non grata* in 1952.
Critics of the war in Indochina in the 1960s welcomed him as an
ally, but dissenters from American foreign policy since World War
II identify him as the masterful cold warrior who helped launch
the global containment doctrine. George Frost Kennan has pursued a demanding and varied career as diplomat and intellectual,
often at the center of policy making and public controversy; yet he
claims for himself little influence over events, ideas, or individuals.
The historical record certainly does not substantiate this denial of
influence, but it does reveal, with the help of Kennan's anguished
self-portrayal in his memoirs, an inner tension between the life of
the professional diplomat and the life of the intellectual.

Throughout his career Kennan lived with two competing
aspirations. One was the life of the bureaucrat, the Foreign Service
officer, legalistic and precise, dedicated to a professional creed
and style, enamored with tradition, distant from the winds of
domestic politics, disciplined, moderating the opinions of the
overzealous, and always eager to influence decision makers.
Kennan liked being an "insider," for that role provided a needed
sense of belonging, prestige, and access to power. Yet he never
seemed comfortable in the foreign affairs bureaucracy; he found it
too confining and encumbered, too tied to routine and menial
tasks, too demanding of subservience to assigned missions. More
than once he complained that his superiors, usually depicted as
less able than himself, ignored his talents. He was chagrined that
Foreign Service officers found themselves "tidying up the messes
other people have made, attempting to keep small disasters from
turning into big ones," instead of contributing fresh policy
perspectives. He resented the intrusions of uninformed congressmen and a whimsical public and bemoaned the decline in
stature and power of the Department of State. It seems fair to
conclude that Kennan has felt frustrated because for most of his
career he sought but was denied a role, to use a recent example,
like that assumed by Henry A. Kissinger for President Richard M.
Nixon.

Kennan's other aspiration propelled him toward the life of the intellectual, the scholar playful with ideas, speculative, independent of mind, skeptical and probing, the dedicated teacher, the moralist preaching his convictions, the oracle of reasoned vision, and the artist. This was a life of individualism and loneliness, opposed to the ordinary and routine, always suspicious of pat answers. Whereas the diplomat-bureaucrat attempts to be precise and methodical, the intellectual muses and experiments. Kennan's "irrepressible intellectual brashness," as he described it, found sustenance in the role of the "outsider." Kennan the scholar regretted that he could not interact more with his historical subjects: "They became part of my life. . . . But they were never able to see me, or to react to my interest. I wandered through their lifeless world like a solitary visitor through a wax museum. . . . My concern for them was not matched by any reciprocal concern on their part for me." The life of the intellectual, then, also had drawbacks for Kennan, not the least of which was isolation from the corridors of power and the awful possibility that his ideas would be misinterpreted. Since the 1920s, when he entered the. Foreign Service, Kennan has essentially pursued two careers simultaneously, not finding complete fulfillment in either. Therein lies his self-image as a failure and the differing interpretations others have given to his conception of cold war diplomacy, as well as his alienation from the government he sought so faithfully to serve.

Throughout his life, Kennan nurtured remarkably consistent attitudes and values; as he himself observed, they were quite different from those of the Soviets, whose ideology and government he studied so closely. He has described himself as a "conservative person, a natural-born antiquarian, a firm believer in the need for continuity across the generations in form and ceremony. . . ." Indeed, he looked to the past for models after which to pattern ideas and behavior. Because he witnessed the deterioration of his revered values, he never seemed at home in the twentieth century (or in his own country). Words like honor, responsibility, efficiency, rigor, discipline, steady habits, perseverance, self-restraint, individualism, culture, tradition, decency, courage, cleanliness, order, and humility mark Kennan's reflections on himself and on others—as if he had torn a page from Benjamin Franklin's autobiography. These qualities added up to something he vaguely called "western civilization," rooted in morality, pride in work, competition, individualism, freedom of thought, and "social conservatism." In contrast, Marxism and the Soviet Union prostituted these values through collectivism, fanaticism, denial of individual rights, and a break with tradition. In the early 1930s, Kennan wrote that he "rejected the Communists because of their innate cowardice and intellectual insolence. They had abandoned the ship of Western European civilization like a swarm of rats when they considered it to be sinking, instead of staying on and trying to keep it afloat. . . ." The Communists "had called all their forefathers and most of their contemporaries hopeless fools," and that behavior was a "sacrilege." "I felt," Kennan explained, "that it [communism] must some day be punished as all ignorant presumption and egotism must be punished."

He visited his arrogance and contempt upon Americans as well. He lacked patience with people less bright than himself and held little respect for a political system that permitted the untutored to vote. He chided Americans for their lack of historical perspective, low level of knowledge about the country's problems, and emotionalism. Frequently emotional himself, he could not tolerate it in others, especially when in collective form, in the "masses." He seldom concealed his disdain for those who neither aspired to nor recognized his own quest for the attributes of the ideal diplomat: charming, brilliant, cultured, educated, self-confident, and respected. For much of his life he seemed out of touch with the country he served abroad. He observed and understood foreign countries much better than his own and when in the early 1950s he returned to private life, he had to "re-encounter" America. What he saw there as a drift away from the best in Western civilization repelled him.

Style and method were particularly significant to Kennan. It was crucial *how* one did what he had to do. "Let no one underestimate," he told a Northwestern University audience in 1951, "the importance in this life of the manner in which a thing is done. It is surprising how few acts there are, in individual life, which are not acceptable if they are carried out with sufficient grace and self-assurance, and above all with dignity and good manners. . . ." He believed that in foreign affairs the test for the diplomat was not just purpose, but also conduct. He was easily put off by the style of others, from the often rude, blunt Soviets in the 1930s and 1940s to the long-haired iconoclasts of college campuses in the 1960s. When German troops in 1939 were about to enter Prague, Kennan was "determined that the German army

Drawing by David Levine. Reprinted with permission from the New York Review of Books. *Copyright © 1972 N.Y. Rev. Inc.*

should not have the satisfaction of giving the American Legation a harried appearance," so he shaved "meticulously" before going to the office. Such behavior was impressive, but it also revealed a bureaucrat's obsession with style and routine and a pseudoaristocrat's concern with propriety.

$$\langle\!\langle\!\langle\rangle\!\rangle$$

These traits were evident long before Kennan emerged as a major architect of cold war diplomacy. He was born in 1904 to an Anglo-Saxon family in Milwaukee, Wisconsin. His father was a hard-working lawyer and his mother a self-conscious "aristocrat." By his own admission, young Kennan's life was "comfortable and safe." His family had no quarrel with a society that had rewarded it with a more than adequate income, and Kennan has reflected that his early experience refuted the Marxist image of the blood-sucking capitalist. "I could identify neither with the exploiter nor with the exploited." At age twelve he headed for St. John's Military Academy near Milwaukee. Its strict discipline and spartan environment left little time for frivolous pleasures, and Kennan learned to keep his room neat and orderly and to merge his personal preferences with those of the group. When he graduated in 1921, as if to illustrate that other aspiration, he was designated class poet.

A St. John's administrator advised the somewhat shy Kennan to go to Princeton University, an inclination already stimulated by his reading of F. Scott Fitzgerald's *This Side of Paradise* (1920), which was set in Princeton. He proceeded to flunk part of the entrance examination, but, given another chance, managed to pass the second round of tests. As the last student admitted to Princeton, he was assigned the least desirable room and his demeanor became as gloomy as his accommodations. He was, he later wrote, "an oddball on campus, not eccentric, not ridiculed or disliked, just imperfectly visible to the naked eye." He was a loner, knowing few people, distant from his instructors, always last in line, with no desire to join one of the university's prestigious clubs. Later he recalled that he sought a kind of "martyrdom" in those years, and in 1925 left college "as obscurely as I had entered it."

Not knowing what else to do, Kennan decided to apply to the newly formed Foreign Service. He had liked his limited study of international affairs at Princeton and he had always been impressed with the record of his grandfather's cousin, also bearing the name George Kennan, who had distinguished himself as an expert on Russia. Then, too, Ivy League graduates predominantly staffed the diplomatic corps at that time, so Kennan was following a path well traveled by Princetonians. After a rigorous oral examination conducted by Undersecretary of State Joseph Grew, Kennan was accepted into the Foreign Service School in 1926. He then spent several months in the consul general's office in Geneva, shedding his "introverted" self for that of a man of responsibility in a distinguished profession. He went next to Hamburg as a vice-consul and became absorbed in the intellectual life of that Social Democratic city, attending lectures and musing beside the famed harbor; but apparently stifled by his job, he decided in 1928 to return to the United States to undertake graduate study.

His superiors in the Foreign Service induced him to change his mind by offering him three years of graduate work in Europe, if he would study the Arabic, Chinese, Japanese, or Russian languages. Kennan chose Russian, in part because the elder George Kennan's "tradition" beckoned him and in part because he sensed that the United States would eventually recognize the Soviet Union and need experts. Area specialization was something new for the Foreign Service and Kennan became one of a handful (including Charles Bohlen and Loy Henderson) trained in Russian affairs in the 1920s. Already fluent in German and French, he departed for Estonia to study Russian. He learned fast and was assigned to Riga, Latvia, America's contact with Russia, where travelers to and from Russia were interviewed and Soviet publications collected. From Riga he was sent to the University of Berlin to study Russian history, literature, and language. During the two years there he became annoyed with American "liberals" tolerant of the Soviet experiment, because, as he wrote in 1931, "the present system of Soviet Russia is unalterably opposed to our traditional system, that there can be no possible middle ground or compromise between the two. . . ." It was a pessimistic prediction and adamant conviction, probably encouraged by his contact with anti-Soviet Russian émigrés.

Assigned again to Riga in 1931, now third secretary of the legation, Kennan eagerly threw himself into his work, and from his desk flowed economic reports, analyses of Soviet propaganda, and even an article, "Anton Chekhov and the Bolsheviks." He was less enthusiastic than many Americans about the prospects for Soviet-American commerce, because the Soviets would need American credit, and he advised that diplomatic recognition of the Soviet Union would not be a panacea for facilitating trade. Kennan was not pleased with the imprecision and irresolution of the Roosevelt-Litvinov Agreements of 1933. Later he chided the president for thinking that recognition would somehow curb Germany or Japan. As Kennan recalled, "Never—neither then nor at any later date—did I consider the Soviet Union a fit ally or associate, actual or potential, for this country."

On leave in Washington during the Litvinov-Roosevelt talks, Kennan was introduced to William C. Bullitt, soon to be the first American ambassador to the Soviet Union. They established an immediate rapport and Bullitt, impressed by Kennan's knowledge of the Russian economy and his fluency in the language, added Kennan to his staff. Kennan probably concealed his pessimism about Soviet-American relations from the more optimistic ambassador. The initially cordial Soviets were delighted with the young diplomat because they identified him with the anticzarist elder Kennan and because his mastery of Russian flattered them. The sluggishness of the Soviet bureaucracy exasperated Kennan, but the embassy staff, which included journalist-diplomat Charles W. Thayer and career officers Loy Henderson and Charles Bohlen, exhilarated him. In 1935 Russia entered the terrible period of the purges, and Kennan became an acute and outraged observer, personally attending many of the trials. It was "a sort of liberal education in the horrors of Stalinism." Stalin had eliminated "liberal" forces in favor of a "new gang of young and ruthless party careerists," who had abandoned "modern western civilization" for conspiratorial thinking, secretiveness, cruelty, unscrupulousness, and opportunism.

Kennan had no liking for the "proletariat" or for Marxism. His elitism and conservatism were apparent when he took a short trip to a Black Sea resort area in 1936. He was disgusted with the "simple people's" lack of grace; they made "pig sties" of the hotels and lacked appreciation for the scenery. For Russian Marxism there was intellectual distaste. He rejected its "stony-hearted fanaticism" and its contribution to the liquidation of groups of people like the bourgeoisie because of a rigid application of class distinctions. The Marxist "ideology" was "pseudo-science, replete with artificial heroes and villains. . . ." The new

GEORGE F. KENNAN

561

restrictions on diplomats during the purges exacerbated Kennan's intense disaffection. An aura of suspicion gripped Moscow and Soviet officials tried to isolate foreigners from the Russian people, with some of whom Kennan had built up rewarding relationships.

During the 1930s Soviet-American relations deteriorated over the failure to reach agreement on the payment of World War I debts, the purges, and the meeting of the Comintern Congress of 1935; Bullitt became increasingly disillusioned. Kennan liked the ambassador's sophistication and self-confidence, but found his impatience and contempt for the foreign affairs bureaucracy unbecoming to a diplomat. Yet as Bullitt soured on the Soviet Union and adopted the "hard line" so much appreciated by Kennan, the two grew close in their thinking. Bullitt resigned in 1936. His replacement, Joseph E. Davies, Kennan considered a political hack, ill fitted for the post, lacking in seriousness, looking too much after his "newspaper image." It was an exaggerated assessment, but Kennan chastised Franklin D. Roosevelt more than Davies, for the president was a politician and inadequately hostile to the Soviet Union. Kennan contemplated resigning from the Foreign Service but chose instead to make the best of a bad situation and departed for Washington in 1937.

The "hard liners," members of the Moscow embassy and the Division of Eastern European Affairs in the State Department, shared Kennan's views. This division, under the guidance of career officer Robert F. Kelley, had opposed recognition and seemed an anomaly in the Roosevelt administration. Its hostility was explicable, because, after all, the division had spent the 1920s finding reasons *not* to recognize the Soviet regime. In mid-1937 the division was abolished and its functions distributed to two desks (Russian and Baltic-Polish) in the new Division of European Affairs. Kennan suspected that pro-Soviet attitudes in the "higher reaches" of government governed the decision. Political considerations no doubt had some part in the decision, but Kennan's analysis was far too simple. The reorganization was one of several changes Secretary of State Cordell Hull initiated in 1937 after two years of study; at the same time he merged two divisions into the new Division of American Republics and created the office of counselor.

Despite his disappointment, Kennan accepted the Russian desk post and for about a year (October 1937 to August 1938) talked with businessmen, protested Soviet restrictions on the

Moscow embassy, and watched for violations of the Litvinov-Roosevelt Agreements. It was not a happy time for him—he felt ignored and unappreciated—but his ideas about Soviet-American relations jelled further. In May of 1938 Kennan spoke to a Foreign Service School audience about the wellsprings of Soviet policy. The Russians, he said, had been influenced by "Asiatic hordes" during their long history and were thus conditioned to think of foreigners as enemies. The Asiatic's "acute and abnormal sense of 'face' and dignity" compelled Russian leaders to claim infallibility. Furthermore, the size of the country contributed not to a sense of moderation but rather to "extremism." The Russian character took on the traits of a "typical oriental despotism" and at the same time an "inferiority complex," because the Russians were aware of their own defects. Kennan called for "patience" in American foreign policy: "We must neither expect too much nor despair of getting anything at all." His conclusions were quite deterministic and subjective, but he spoke with amazing assurance. Hostility toward and deep suspicion of the Soviets, as well as the counsel of patience, became the hallmarks of Kennan's thought. Yet Kennan's hostility was often alarmist, contributing not to patience but to urgency and exaggeration.

In mid-1938 Kennan asked to be transferred to the field again and he was assigned to the American legation in Prague. When German troops entered the somber city in March 1939, the legation was shut down and Kennan moved to the embassy in Berlin. He thought there was nothing the Czechs could do but submit to German power; resistance would have been "romantic." He seemed to accept the fall of Czechoslovakia as predestined, because he believed the breakup of the Austro-Hungarian Empire after World War I was a mistake, fragmenting power in the Danube Basin and inviting international squabbles. In Berlin he became bogged down in administrative tasks not to his liking and watched Europe go to war. When Germany invaded Russia in June 1941, Kennan approved lend-lease aid in America's self-interest, but warned against professions of friendship with or moral support for the Soviet Union, which he considered hardly a fit ally. From December 1941 to May 1942, the Germans interned Kennan and about one hundred thirty other Americans. Kennan assumed leadership and maintained discipline, but became bitter toward Washington, believing his government had abandoned the group. He expected the State Department to gain his early release through Lisbon in exchange for Germans and was deeply annoyed when half of his group was ordered to wait for another ship so that some Jewish refugees could be transported to freedom first.

Back in the United States, he rested and thought. He soon identified himself as a moderate between the extreme anti-Soviet and pro-Soviet groups in the United States. In apparent anticipation of considerable Soviet influence in Eastern Europe after the war and in apparent contradiction to his stated views against self-determination for small nations in the area, he opted for the latter in the hope of curbing Soviet expansion. Before the war he demonstrated no such strong opposition to German expansion in that region and argued that small states in fact invited instability. In September 1942, Kennan was assigned to Lisbon as counselor. He did not go willingly. He complained to the State Department that his qualities were being ignored; he was a trained specialist, he had knowledge of ten countries and ten languages, and his departmental ratings were high. Kennan argued against wasting his time "plugging away at administrative jobs." He wanted to be assigned to a German desk or post in economic foreign affairs. Kennan the intellectual, impatient with the bureaucracy, was asserting himself.

In Portugal Kennan handled intelligence operations and negotiations for bases in the Azores. He depicted Antonio Salazar as "one of the most able men in Europe and a man of high moral principle," not mentioning that the dictator supported General Francisco Franco in the Spanish civil war and that he had gained power through the military. For the first time in his career Kennan became a negotiator as well as an observer; yet he felt handicapped because Washington did not keep him properly informed and he had to get much of his information from British officials. With some shock, he received a cable in October of 1943 instructing him to see Salazar to request a naval base, aircraft base, cable system, radar installations, and observation posts in the Azores. Kennan protested that this extensive military request, if granted, would compromise Portuguese neutrality and invite a German declaration of war. He was delighted when the president told him to deal with the matter in his own way, but suddenly he was recalled; he expected to be punished, because, against instructions, he had given Portugal assurances of sovereignty in the colonies before negotiating for the bases.

Shortly after arriving in Washington, he was whisked off to

the Pentagon for a high-level meeting with Secretary of War Henry L. Stimson and the Joint Chiefs of Staff. It was a humilating experience; military officers reprimanded him for not making demands on Salazar. Unceremoniously dismissed, Kennan "slunk away," but while eating lunch alone he grew indignant that he should have been so treated. He resolved, typically, "that if I was to go down, I would go down fighting," and went to the president himself. Roosevelt told him not to worry about the Pentagon people and sent him back to Lisbon, once more to handle the question of bases in his own way. Kennan acquitted himself well in discussions and secured the use of bases important to the war effort. Actually, a new minister had been sent to Lisbon to complete the negotiations and Kennan, wanting nothing to do with him, requested a transfer. He believed that the military establishment had sent the new envoy, because the State Department had become, as he wrote later, a "messenger boy for the Pentagon and accustomed to sneezing whenever the Pentagon caught cold. . . ." The whole affair soured Kennan further on the Roosevelt administration, the growing weakness of the State Department in the making of foreign policy, and the intrusion of the military into diplomacy.

Kennan was sent next as counselor to the European Advisory Commission (EAC) in London, where his disenchantment grew. Before he assumed the post he was admonished to give advice only when asked for it, a reflection on his independent behavior in Portugal and on the low regard with which Washington held the EAC. To aggravate matters further, Kennan became ill with ulcers. The EAC was supposed to draw zones for postwar Germany, but its authority was never well defined and the military seldom explained the zonal boundaries it sought. Again demonstrating his maverick tendencies, Kennan could tolerate no more than a few months (January to April 1944) in such a spineless institution and requested a transfer. He received an unexpected boost: Averell Harriman, ambassador to the Soviet Union, requested Kennan as an adviser and Kennan was appointed counselor of the Moscow embassy. He departed in July 1944 for the land he knew best, whose leaders and foreign policy he liked least.

The years before 1944 were pivotal to the formulation of George F. Kennan's ideas about foreign policy, as well as to his self-perception as a diplomat. In his view, the Soviet Union was aggressive, made so by a fanatical ideology, historical imperatives,

and ruthless leaders. The Soviets' disruptive influence in international relations stemmed largely from internal causes. Seldom did
Kennan consider that the external pressure on Russia from other
nations might have affected Soviet behavior. Furthermore, he held
a mechanistic view of Russian foreign policy, believing it to be
largely constant over time. There was little American diplomats
could do but be patient in the face of Soviet officialdom's
inveterate hostility toward the West. He never conceded that the
West's anticommunism, manifested by the Allied intervention in
Siberia and nonrecognition, as well as the unchecked rise of
Hitler's Germany and the delay in the opening of the Second
Front, may have aroused some of that hostility. This intense
distaste for things Soviet derived not only from Kennan's revulsion
against conspicuously reprehensible Soviet acts, but also from his
own conservatism and fascination with Western Civilization. His
general conclusion was that the United States was too conciliatory
toward Moscow.

In the period before 1944, Kennan's impatience with his own
lack of power and what he believed to be his superiors' ignorance
of his talents emerges clearly. He frequently felt neglected and
stymied; his ideas were rejected, and the tasks assigned him were
routine and uninspiring. He was the bureaucrat who had meritori-
ously learned his job, but felt inhibited and restless. He was an
intellectual who thought analytically, committed his ideas to
paper, and tried to convey them to higher officers, where they
received little attention. Kennan was a gifted man, but as his
colleagues recognized, he was also opinionated, headstrong,
conceited, and sometimes cranky. He could be quite emotional
and subjective, and his assessments of Soviet policy, although
informed by uncommon knowledge, were nevertheless largely
conjecture. In order to illustrate the speculative methods of
Sovietologists, Charles Thayer has recorded a story about a
Kentucky mountaineer asking a neighbor's boy about his parents:

"Where's yer paw?" he asked the boy.
"Gone fishin'."
"How d'ye know?"
"Had his boots on and 'tain't rainin'."
"Where's yer maw?"
"Outhouse."
"How d'ye know?"
"Went out with a Montgomery Ward catalogue and she can't read."
"Where's yer sister?"

"In the hayloft with the hired man."

"How d'ye know?"

"It's after mealtime and there's only one thing she'd rather do than eat."

As he prepared to go again to Moscow, George F. Kennan seemed equally certain about his answers to questions relating to the Soviet Union.

Kennan arrived in Moscow on 1 July 1944 and was soon assigned the rank of minister-counselor; but, typically, he became impatient because his duties were largely administrative, and because Ambassador Harriman, by necessity, talked more frequently with the head of the military mission, General John R. Deane, than with Kennan. He was chagrined, too, that the staff was not interested in listening to his reflections on embassy life in the 1930s. Kennan admired Harriman's efficiency, but he was not a career diplomat and did not hold the Foreign Service in sufficient awe. Still deeply annoyed with the Soviet conduct of isolating foreign diplomats, feeling personally neglected, and dissenting from Roosevelt's wartime diplomacy, Kennan planned to resign.

As Soviet-American conflict over Poland heated up, however, Harriman began to ask his Soviet expert for advice, and Kennan bombarded his chief with "protests, urgings, and appeals." Kennan, "running around with [his] head in the usual clouds of philosophic speculation," became more a political oracle and less an administrator, more an intellectual and less a bureaucrat. From 1944 until April 1946, when Kennan returned to Washington, he drew upon the ideas he had developed in the 1930s to comment pessimistically on prospects for postwar international relations. Harriman himself was reaching for a less conciliatory policy toward Russia. Kennan's advocacy of toughness, so eloquently articulated, probably accelerated the ambassador's conversion. In January 1946 Harriman left Moscow for good, leaving a now more assertive Kennan as chargé d'affaires. Truman administration officials read his thoughtful but alarmist cables to Washington with increasing favor.

During the 1944–46 period Kennan's writings carried several common themes. After the war, he predicted, Russia, yearning to be a great power, would build up militarily and could not be trusted to fulfill agreements. He did not believe the Soviet Union would attack Western Europe, but his cables did not suggest many limitations on Soviet behavior. Indeed, he sketched a picture of the self-confident, aggressive giant, uncompromising, flushed with power, responsible for most of the world's disturbances. In early 1945 he told Harriman that Russia would seek "maximum power and minimum responsibility" in China leading to possible "domination" and "control." Later that year he cabled Washington that "security and aggrandizement" constituted Soviet aims in the Near and Middle East, to be achieved through an "endless, fluid pursuit of power." Soviet tactics would include the support of nationalist groups, political intrigue, subversion, and military intervention. "One of the outstanding characteristics of Soviet foreign policy is its flexible multiformity." Kennan also foresaw problems. Moscow would have difficulty arousing its citizenry to postwar sacrifice. Its postwar empire would prove unmanageable. The question was whether the United States could exploit these handicaps.

Kennan recommended that Washington follow a policy of "political manliness" toward Russia. He shared the growing sentiment in the Truman administration that Russia should be denied postwar economic assistance until it conformed to American interpretations of treaties and proved more cooperative. Believing that Eastern Europe was lost to American influence, Kennan recommended that the United States concentrate its energies in Western Europe, building it up as a counter-sphere of influence, but letting no Soviet action stand without a frank rebuttal. Washington should avoid diplomatic agreements that in any way might suggest American acceptance of Soviet power in Eastern Europe; the United States should not attempt to negotiate the impossible, a rollback of Soviet influence.

Collaboration with Russia in postwar Germany, he thought, was a "pipedream." He looked upon the Potsdam Conference agreements of July 1945 with "unmitigated skepticism and despair," for though they sought to establish quadripartite control, the language was too vague. Russia could not be held to the provisions on reparations, because Moscow would take what it wanted from Germany regardless of an agreement. Dismemberment of Germany, he advised, should be accepted as a fact, and the United States should proceed independently. He feared that centralization, as provided for at Potsdam, would lead to the "communization" of Germany, because Russia would use its zone as a "springboard for a Communist offensive elsewhere in the Reich." The United States should build up the Western zones economically, because the German economy was the backbone of the Western European economy. The Germans, the "strongest people in Europe," were crucial to European reconstruction. A peace settlement of revenge and punishment would only arouse German nationalism and make America's task in Europe more difficult. Kennan strongly disapproved of the Morgenthau Plan, de-Nazification and decartelization programs, as well as the war crimes trials.

◇◇◇

In February 1946, Washington was eager to have an interpretive report on Stalin's election speech and Moscow's reasons for not joining the World Bank—to determine, in short, what made Soviet foreign policy tick. For years Kennan had been preparing himself for just such a request. "The more I thought about this message, the more it seemed to be obvious that this was 'it.'" He was tired of plucking people's sleeves to draw their attention to the Soviet menace. "Here was a case where nothing but the whole truth would do. They had asked for it. Now, by God, they would have it." On 22 February Kennan completed his "long telegram," an eight-thousand-word "elaborate pedagogical effort," which ultimately elevated Kennan to the heralded status of *the* expert on the Soviet Union and *the* intellectual in the Foreign Service.

The telegram began with a discussion of the "basic features" of the Soviet outlook on international relations. Placing heavy emphasis on ideology as the wellspring of Soviet behavior, Kennan pointed out that the Soviet mind was geared to capitalist-socialist conflict. Hostility to the capitalist outside world was not a Russian attitude, but a Communist one, a party line. Yet at the bottom of the Kremlin's "neurotic view of world affairs is traditional and instinctive Russian sense of insecurity." Marxist-Leninist dogma, argued Kennan, was the new vehicle for perpetuating this Russian tradition. The Soviets after the war, he predicted, would use Communist parties as an "underground operating directorate of world communism." Russia would seldom compromise; in fact, its foreign policy would be "negative and destructive in character, designed to tear down sources of strength beyond the reach of

Soviet control." In summary, "we have here a political force committed fanatically to the belief that with US there can be no permanent *modus vivendi,* that it is desirable and necessary that the internal harmony of our society be destroyed, our traditional way of life be destroyed, the international authority of our state be broken, if Soviet power is to be secure." Kennan closed his message with less alarmist language. He believed Russia would not risk a major war because it was too weak. America, furthermore, could counter Soviet expansion by constructive propaganda efforts at home and abroad and by maintaining a healthy and cohesive society in the United States as a model. Kennan seemed to emphasize that Russia was more a "political" than a "military" threat, but his statements could be variously interpreted.

Officials in Washington read the long telegram with relish and excitement, for Kennan seemed to have captured their own moods and fears. He later confessed that the telegram read "exactly like one of those primers put out by alarmed congressional committees or by the Daughters of the American Revolution, designed to arouse the citizenry to the dangers of the Communist conspiracy." Here was a document that was authoritative, convincing, and simple, demonstrating just how intransigent the Soviets were. Kennan's timely message helped persuade the administration to speak out more forcefully against Soviet foreign policy, to "get tough," in popular jargon. It had actually been following a "tough" policy before, but now it was more willing to follow it publicly. Administration figures chose to emphasize the parts of Kennan's message that described an uncompromising, warlike, aggressive, neurotic, and subversive Russia that somehow had to be stopped. Whether Kennan intended to or not, he fed exaggerated fears that an international Communist conspiracy, directed by Moscow, sought to subvert the world.

Kennan's ideas and recommendations in the 1944–46 period contain both merit and shortcomings. Russia *was* too headstrong and blunt, too suspicious and fearful. Ideology held a significant place in the Soviet outlook. Soviet propaganda attacks on the United States were crude and antagonistic. (Unlike many other contemporaries, however, Kennan recognized that the USSR was cautious and not militarily aggressive.) Soviet influence in Eastern Europe did block American influence and there was little the United States could do to change the arrangement of power in that area. Too many agreements were vaguely worded. The

Potsdam accords on Germany probably were wishful, especially given the obstructionism of the French (to whom Kennan gave scant attention). Germany did add significantly to the economy of Western Europe and, given the American perspective, had to be revived.

Yet the historian must conclude that Kennan simplified the complex, ignored contrary evidence, and indulged in a great deal of speculation. He placed too much emphasis on Soviet ideology and in so doing posited a mechanistic view of Soviet foreign policy: that it flowed not from interaction with other nations but from internal imperatives and that it was unchangeable over time. Rarely did he suggest that actions of the non-Communist nations influenced Soviet behavior, an omission glaring in its importance. Kennan relied heavily on *his* sense of what motivated Russia; he became the psychiatrist putting the Russians on the couch. What he found was a country endlessly creating world tension; what he disregarded were the instances of compromise over Poland, Iran, the United Nations, and Germany. He may not have thought the compromises significant, but they were compromises nonetheless.

Nor was communism the smooth-running monolith he depicted. Eastern Europe was not closed to the West before 1947. Soviet influence there was varied, uncertain, and perhaps defensive. There was no master blueprint for empire. Czechoslovakia held free elections in May 1946 and until the coup of 1948 retained a remarkable degree of independence. Hungary conducted elections in the fall of 1945 (the Communists managed to get only 17 percent of the vote) and did not fall to a Communist coup until 1947. Finland, although under the close scrutiny of the Soviets, affirmed its independence. Yugoslavia early squabbled with Russia, and under Josip Tito's independent communism, resisted Soviet subjugation. The exceptions were Poland and Romania, both tightly controlled by Moscow. The point is that Soviet policy was mixed, contrary to Kennan's description (which was not much different from Winston Churchill's account of an "iron curtain"). Tears in the curtain existed. Kennan exaggerated the Soviet presence, making it appear total and much more fearsome than it really was. He of course cautioned the United States to abstain from meddling in Eastern Europe, but his very description encouraged thinking that affirmative action had to be taken there. American diplomats attempted to use the one tool they had in the region: economic aid. They dangled loans before the Eastern

Europeans, alternately extending and withdrawing them, which only aroused Soviet fears of an American intrusion and stimulated further Soviet penetration.

In these early cold war years, Kennan seemed to have little faith in diplomacy itself. Since the Russians could not be trusted, there was no sense in signing agreements with them. Certainly some treaties were violated, but the issues were usually complex. Russia broke its treaty with Iran which required withdrawal of Soviet troops in early 1946, but only because Anglo-American influence in that country bordering Russia had grown through military and economic advisers, as well as oil concessions. Kennan was one of the few American diplomats who recognized that Soviet action there was designed to head off foreign penetration, but he nevertheless seemed to accept the American advances in Iran as a basic good. In most cases, agreements were not broken, but rather interpreted differently by both sides. Too often Kennan discouraged negotiations, and opportunities for accommodation were lost. One might ask, as did critic Henry A. Wallace, whether toughness does not simply beget more toughness.

The issue of a postwar loan to Russia, which Kennan vigorously and successfully opposed, is illustrative. Postwar reconstruction was a primary Russian goal, and as early as 1943 the Soviets inquired about a large American loan. American officials delayed the question until 1945 and then decided to use the loan as a diplomatic weapon *before* negotiations, to gain concessions on Eastern European issues, rather than as a bargaining tool at the conference table. Russia resented the rejection of its request and such overt economic pressure in 1946, especially after it agreed reluctantly to talk about Eastern Europe and a loan in conjunction. In this case, foreign aid was never given the opportunity to reduce tension because the United States, wielding its economic power, refused to negotiate. Kennan helped create that position.

Kennan's long telegram particularly impressed Secretary of the Navy James V. Forrestal. He circulated the message widely in Washington and required military officers to read it. The State Department sent it to American ambassadors, who responded with enthusiasm. Forrestal engineered Kennan's return to Washington and installed him as a lecturer at the National War College. "My reputation was made," Kennan recalled. "My voice now carried." In official Washington he became a recognized philosopher of United States diplomacy; but like most philosophers,

Kennan would suffer under the interpretations and emphases others gave to his ideas.

◇◇◇

From September 1946 to May 1947 Kennan lectured at the National War College to high-ranking military officers, Foreign Service officers, and an occasional cabinet member (including Forrestal). On 24 February Undersecretary of State Dean Acheson asked him to participate in discussions of the Greek crisis, sparked when the British decided to withdraw troops from that country torn by civil war. After the first meeting, during which Kennan endorsed aid to Greece, he participated little. On 6 March he dropped in at the State Department and saw a draft of the president's message, soon to become the "Truman Doctrine" speech of 12 March 1947. Kennan complained about the sweeping language of the address and the seemingly open-ended commitments it implied. He also opposed military aid to Turkey, because he did not believe that country stood in danger of Russian attack. His complaints came too late; the message was delivered to Congress where it sounded a bell of panic at the same time it suggested that the United States would go anywhere on the globe to resist what it perceived to be a Communist thrust.

In late April Secretary of State George C. Marshall arrived in Washington from the frustrating Moscow Conference convinced that the Soviets had little interest in European cooperation. "The patient is sinking," he told a radio audience in reference to economic ills in Western Europe, "while the doctors deliberate." Marshall moved quickly. He called Kennan to his office on 29 April and ordered him to establish the Policy Planning Staff to study the European economic crisis, to make recommendations within two weeks, and to "avoid trivia." A harried Kennan scurried about to find personnel and with commendable speed his new agency produced an important memorandum dated 23 May. Communist activities, it began, were not at the root of Western Europe's problems, but rather the war, which had disrupted European life. American aid, then, should be aimed not at combating communism, but at correcting the economic maladjustment "which makes European society vulnerable to exploitation by any and all totalitarian movements and which Russian communism is now exploiting." In words to appear later in the "Marshall Plan" address by the secretary at Harvard University, Kennan's report suggested strongly that Europe itself initiate a cooperative program. Russia would not be permitted to block the new program and the Eastern European nations would have to accept American conditions before their participation could be allowed.

Kennan's memorandum and one by Undersecretary Will Clayton, which gave a moving account of misery in Western Europe, formed the nucleus for discussion at the decisive high-level meeting of 28 May. Clayton was emphatic that Western Europe did not economically need Eastern Europe, and as his memorandum put it, *"The United States must run this show."* Kennan said, "Play it straight," and they agreed that the plan should be presented in such a way as to let Russia and the Eastern European countries exclude themselves. The conditions would be difficult for Russia to accept: endorsement of multilateral, non-discriminatory trade practices and a reduction of Soviet influence in Eastern Europe. Few conferees thought the Soviet orbit would accept participation. Actually there was little possibility the Soviets would join an American-dominated program essentially aimed at them. Soviet hegemony in Eastern Europe had not been stabilized, and an influx of American dollars and influence could only be read as a challenge. Of course, Congress itself would probably never have funded a program that had Soviet membership, especially after congressmen had been aroused to new heights of anti-Sovietism by the message of the Truman Doctrine. In short, the decision to leave the door open represented diplomatic finesse rather than sincerity. Later, the United States reaped immense propaganda value by claiming that it had offered Marshall Plan aid to Moscow, which rudely had turned down a sincere invitation. Kennan's influence on this question, as well as on the American decision to undertake a major foreign aid program, was significant. His memorandum coherently synthesized ideas and provided core material for Marshall's Harvard address.

Kennan did not see Marshall often—it was not the general's habit to indulge in long conversations or interruptions—but their offices adjoined and the Soviet expert had unusual access to the highest officer in the State Department. Kennan also kept up his "intellectual" relationship with Secretary Forrestal, who was fascinated with a paper Kennan had presented him in January. Forrestal and the State Department gave Kennan permission to submit the paper to the editor of *Foreign Affairs.* Titled "The Sources of Soviet Conduct," the article appeared in the July issue of the journal under the name of Mr. "X." *New York Times* columnist Arthur Krock, who earlier had been shown a copy of the paper in Forrestal's office, soon dispelled the mystery of authorship, and Kennan was propelled to the center of national discussion. Commentators quickly assumed that the "X" article was government policy and Kennan was tagged the father of the containment doctrine. He seemed to provide the theoretical justification for the Truman Doctrine and the Marshall Plan.

The highly respected article repeated many themes expressed in the long telegram, but it emphasized ideology and left vague what the United States should do to combat Soviet expansion. Kennan wrote about the implacable Communist hostility toward the capitalist world, the doctrinaire fanaticism of Stalinist leaders, and the secretiveness, duplicity, suspiciousness, and basic unfriendliness of Soviet conduct. Russia would take its time beating down its foes abroad since Soviet leaders were confident that capitalism would collapse under its own contradictions. Moscow would accept short-run losses to ensure its long-term goal. "In these circumstances," Kennan wrote, "it is clear that the main element of any United States policy toward the Soviet Union must be that of a long-term, patient but firm and vigilant containment of Russian expansive tendencies." "Counterforce" had to be applied to "constantly shifting geographical and political points" in order to "promote tendencies which must eventually find their outlet in either the break-up or the mellowing of Soviet power." Kennan pointed out that Russia had serious internal economic and political weaknesses. In contrast, the United States could stand as a successful model of internal stability before the world.

Although largely responsible for implanting the containment doctrine as the commanding principle of American foreign policy in the cold war, the "X" article was not one of Kennan's best efforts. As he himself later admitted, it was too ambiguous, too imprecise; it failed to deal with Soviet power in Eastern Europe and the difficulties of ruling an empire; and it never defined what the tools of containment were to be. The article's imprecision led to years of debate and to a policy of global intervention as cold warriors borrowed those parts of the "X" article and the Truman Doctrine that fit their conception of the United States as a manager of international stability.

Kennan used words like "force" quite vaguely and the speculative article as a whole was cast in black-and-white, bad guys–good guys terms. He placed no limits, geographical or chronological, on containment, and thereby ignored the resources and will of the United States to undertake such a long-term program. Nor did he consider the constitutional system, especially Congress's role in foreign affairs, which might place some restraints on the continuous fulfillment of containment. Kennan did not distinguish between vital and peripheral areas, and as Walter Lippmann so aptly noted, containment could become a "strategic monstrosity," with the United States supporting a host of client states. Perhaps most importantly, Kennan never spelled out how the United States should implement containment, whether by economic, political, military, or psychological means.

Questionable was his statement that a mechanistic Soviet power "moves inexorably along a prescribed path, like a persistent toy automobile wound up and headed in a given direction, stopping only when it meets with some unanswerable force." Once again, he ignored United States power and expansion as contributing factors to Soviet behavior. Too simply, he applied one interpretive model to Russia and another to the United States. Russia's foreign policy derived from a response to internal needs, not to real or imagined threats from outside; America's foreign policy derived from a response to external challenges. In other papers Kennan had pointed out that both ideology and traditional Russian nationalist ambitions explained Soviet behavior, but in the "X" article the latter element is largely absent. Then, too, ideology can serve a government in several ways: it can be a driving force, but also a rationalization for other motives, a form of communication, a symbol of continuity, or simply an interpretive device to explain a troubled world. Kennan provided no such distinctions, nor did he supply any formula for the solution of issues; he betrayed considerable pessimism about the efficacy of diplomacy.

On numerous later occasions, Kennan claimed that he never meant that the United States should undertake global interventionism or emphasize military means. It is frankly difficult to know what Kennan meant. He did speak frequently of the Soviet Union as a political threat and did argue that Russia would not assault Western Europe. He did oppose the military emphasis in aid to Greece and Turkey and the seeming permanence of American occupation forces in Japan and Germany. He applauded the

Marshall Plan as the best means to fulfill containment. He objected to the development of the H-bomb in 1949–50 and called consistently for tactical military units for limited wars. He questioned the need for a military alliance like NATO, advocating a less formal arrangement, and complained that National Security Council paper 68, which recommended a stronger U.S. effort to meet the threat of Soviet expansion, was too militarily oriented. There is evidence, then, that Kennan did not agree with the Truman administration's movement toward an extensive military buildup.

Yet, at the same time, Kennan conceded a great deal to the military point of view. Forrestal, after all, was his initial patron, widely recognized as one of the most military-minded men in Washington. Kennan could not have been ignorant of the uses to which Forrestal was putting his ideas. Furthermore, it is a truism in international relations that to be effective politically and economically a great power must have a hefty military punch. Kennan himself had frequently spoken of an "adequate military posture." He also endorsed the Rio Pact, the need for some kind of military coalition in Western Europe, and intervention in the Korean War. In the 1947–50 period he wrote publicly on behalf of containment without clarifying what he meant. Indeed, he reprinted the "X" article without alteration in his popular *American Diplomacy, 1900–1950*, published in 1951.

Even if he did not intend or agree with all the means utilized by Truman to administer his cold war policies, however, Kennan seemed to offer a very broad doctrine and essentially to concede the basic notion that an aggressive and uncompromising Russia (and/or communism) was a threat that had to be dealt with through counterforce almost everywhere and at any time. Whether he intended to or not, Kennan helped to establish undiscriminating globalism and interventionism as permanent features of American diplomacy. Kennan the intellectual would henceforth suffer as others, less reflective than himself, used his ideas to support a multitude of interventions and a military establishment of enormous proportions. The father of containment would spend much of the rest of his life attempting to disown his offspring.

〈✕✕〉

After the successful launching of the Marshall Plan, Kennan fixed his attention on three problems: Japan, Germany, and military defense. He believed that Japan was a strategic bastion in the Far East because of its industrial might, and its preservation in non-Communist hands was essential to a balance of power in that area. In early 1948, when Kennan departed for Tokyo for firsthand study, the questions of the duration of the American occupation and a peace treaty were still open. Kennan urged that the Far Eastern Commission largely be bypassed, so that the United States could act unilaterally to help Japan achieve economic rehabilitation, defense, and independence. Kennan questioned land reform, the busting of trusts, reparations shipments, and the purging of Japanese from positions in government, business, and education. These programs should be curbed and a peace treaty should be delayed until Japan was quite able to stand on its own non-Communist feet. New directives encompassing most of Kennan's recommendations and endorsed by the president were sent to Japan in 1949, and to Kennan's surprise, General Douglas MacArthur agreed. He was disappointed in 1949, however, when Secretary of State Acheson moved toward an early peace treaty, and Kennan attributed the outbreak of the Korean War to deep Soviet resentment that treaty negotiations were begun without Russia in 1950 and completed without Soviet signature in 1951.

Occupied Germany presented comparable problems and Kennan recommended similar solutions. He had long opposed a punitive peace. Although American policy contained as many constructive as corrective elements, Kennan wanted decartelization, dismantling, and de-Nazification to cease. With the coming of the Marshall Plan and the recognition that West Germany's rich deposits of coal and iron and industrial potential were vital to Western European recovery, the United States dropped most of the corrective measures in favor of full-scale reconstruction. In March 1949, with the Berlin blockade still operative, Kennan took a short trip to Germany and called for an agreement with the Soviets whereby American troops would gradually withdraw after unification. Secretary Acheson vigorously opposed unification, prompting Kennan to conclude that the United States was locking itself into the endorsement of permanent German division. Actually Kennan himself was partly responsible for this state of affairs; he had said more than once that cooperation with Russia over

Germany was a "pipedream." Acheson was essentially agreeing with Kennan's earlier view.

The disagreement over Germany reflected a growing division between Kennan and Acheson. When he became secretary of state in 1949, Acheson chose to use the Policy Planning Staff infrequently. The issue of military defense sharply widened the differences between the two men. Acheson, always seeking to work from military strength, wanted to enlarge NATO; Kennan thought the alliance unnecessary. Acheson seemed to be preparing for a major war; Kennan did not think Russia would attack Western Europe and advocated mobile tactical units. The secretary set in motion plans to rearm West Germany and to develop the H-bomb; Kennan strongly opposed both because they would close opportunities for accords with the USSR. Finally, during the Korean War, Acheson enlarged American objectives by sending troops across the thirty-eighth parallel, something Kennan had argued against as early as June 1950, fearful as he was of expanding the conflagration through Chinese entry.

Out of tune with the heavy military emphasis and apparent abandonment of diplomacy, and convinced that the secretary had no confidence in his staff, Kennan asked in late September 1949 to be relieved of his duties. He stayed on until August 1950, when he took a position at the Princeton-based Institute for Advanced Study. As an outsider, he seemed obsessed with explaining to others through numerous lectures and publications what he had learned on the inside. He lectured Americans that they were too emotional in their foreign policy views, too easily swayed by simple answers, too susceptible to stampedes of opinion. These themes he eloquently, if too simplistically, expressed in his still-influential book, *American Diplomacy, 1900–1950* (1951). In the midst of McCarthyism he protested strongly against mindless anticommunism and defended fellow Foreign Service officers against the senator's vicious attacks.

The Foreign Service continued to claim his talent. Ironically it was Acheson who called upon him for help. The secretary asked him in May 1951 to speak privately with Soviet Ambassador to the United Nations Jacob Malik about opening truce talks in Korea. The Kennan-Malik discussions were quite fruitful, for they agreed that negotiations should begin. Through such informal diplomacy Kennan spurred formal Korean talks, which began in July. In the fall of 1951 Acheson called again, this time to invite Kennan to become the new ambassador to Russia. Kennan was hesitant; after all, he disagreed with so much that Acheson and Truman were doing. Yet the appointment would represent a culmination of his career in Soviet affairs and he was a bureaucrat at the call of his government, so he dutifully accepted.

It did not take long for Kennan to discover that the appointment lacked meaning. He was not directed to undertake new negotiations nor to reassess policy; indeed, diplomacy was discouraged. He left for Moscow "empty-handed, uninstructed, and uncertain. . . ." His disappointments multiplied. In Moscow, the embassy was bugged, Soviet agents tailed him, and the Kremlin snubbed him. Stuck in the embassy, a "gilded prison," his bitter memories of the 1930s and 1940s revived. Now he argued that much of the Soviet hostility was due to America's overmilitarized foreign policy. He complained to Acheson that "it is not for us to assume that there are no limits to Soviet patience in the face of encirclement by American bases." His superiors did not respond to his analysis and Kennan decided it was time to leave his profession; but before he could, painful events intervened.

In September 1952 Kennan left Moscow for a conference in London. During a brief stop in Berlin, reporters peppered him with routine questions. One query about the relations between the embassy staff and the Russian people elicited an annoyed and terribly undiplomatic reply. Being isolated in Russia, he said, was not unlike his internment at the hands of the Germans in 1941–42. As a result, the Soviet government soon declared him *persona non grata* for comparing the Soviets with the Nazis. Actually he was happy to give up the ambassadorship, although the way he gave it up violated his sense of proper conduct. The appointment of John Foster Dulles as secretary of state reaffirmed Kennan's inclination to break permanently with the Foreign Service. Dulles wanted him out anyway; his stinging critique of containment and his espousal of "liberation" left no doubt about his differences with Kennan. Quietly and sadly Kennan once more left Washington for Princeton.

◇◇◇

Kennan returned to the Institute for Advanced Study and took up his scholarly work. Articles and lectures poured from his typewriter. *Russia Leaves the War* (1956) and *The Decision to*

Intervene (1958), two impressively researched volumes on Soviet-American relations in 1917–20, were widely praised. As a public figure, of course, he could not escape public issues.

After Stalin's death in 1953 and an apparent thaw in the cold war, many prominent European leaders hoped to reduce military weapons and troops in Europe. In 1957, Polish Foreign Minister Adam Rapacki advocated a "nuclear free zone" comprising Poland, Czechoslovakia, and Germany. That same year, Soviet Premier Nikita Khrushchev called for a summit meeting to discuss "ruling war out as a means of dealing with international issues," and British Labour party leaders like Hugh Gaitskell formulated plans for a "disengaged zone" in Central and Eastern Europe. Washington demonstrated little enthusiasm for such ideas, openly rejected the Rapacki Plan, and indeed suggested that the United States might give nuclear weapons to West Germany to counterbalance alleged Soviet military superiority on the Continent.

A number of events stimulated these "disengagement" proposals. Stalin's death and Khrushchev's vehement denunciation of the dictator and espousal of "peaceful coexistence" in 1956 suggested that a less belligerent Soviet foreign policy had developed. Indeed, the peace settlement over Austria in 1955 and the subsequent withdrawal by the United States and Russia from that country seemed encouraging. Other events, however, seemed calculated to heat up the cold war. In 1956, the Soviets crushed the Hungarian revolution and Britain and France attacked Egypt over the Suez Canal controversy. To some observers the failure of the Hungarian uprising indicated that the only way to relieve Soviet pressure on Eastern Europe was the removal of Soviet troops, which a mutual withdrawal of American and British troops from West Germany could accomplish. Yet West Germany had entered NATO in 1955 and continued to expand militarily. The dramatic launching of *Sputnik* in October 1957 convinced disengagement advocates that talks had to begin quickly, before America responded with an accelerated emphasis on missile development and weaponry.

Evidence of the maturation of George F. Kennan's ideas was illustrated in November–December 1957 when he delivered six eloquent, if vague, lectures over BBC radio. Millions in Europe heard the Reith lectures, broadcast from London, and they were widely reprinted. The architect of containment, read the headlines, appeared to be abandoning his creation in favor of "disengagement." He called for a unified, nonaligned Germany, withdrawal of foreign troops from the "heart of the Continent" (Eastern Europe and Germany), and restrictions on the deployment of atomic weapons there. In these lectures, unlike in the "X" article of 1947, Kennan was much less willing to judge Russia. "Their world is not our world." Nor should the United States meddle in the "non-European world." Developing nations should be allowed to grow in their own way; foreign aid, complained Kennan, did more harm than good. Finally, he was critical of strengthening NATO, because in 1957–58 diplomacy rather than a "military fixation" was needed. Implicit in Kennan's speeches was a belief that the United States had overcommitted itself. He had not abandoned the containment of Soviet expansion; rather, he advocated disengagement as a way of "liberating" Eastern Europe and defusing any potential Soviet expansion. The Kennan of 1957, as a comparison of the "X" article and his Reith lectures suggests, had been educated by changes in the Soviet-American confrontation and his realization that unlimited containment stultified diplomacy itself.

A flurry of speeches, serial articles in such opinion magazines as *The New Republic* and *Foreign Affairs*, and heated retorts from Truman and Acheson greeted Kennan's lectures. Opponents of disengagement, like Henry A. Kissinger, asserted that Russia remained a military threat to Western Europe. Therefore, American troops should continue in West Germany as a deterrent; NATO should not be weakened. Others protested that Soviet *political* control of Eastern Europe would not end with the removal of Soviet *military* control. The people of Eastern Europe might attempt to throw off the Communist regimes. Critics predicted the return of Soviet soldiers. The Germans themselves might not accept disengagement and a reduced role in European affairs. Chancellor Konrad Adenauer vocally opposed disengagement and in fact called for more West German military growth. Professor Hans Morgenthau, a German émigré and distinguished political scientist, was equally cautious, suggesting that a united Germany could eventually become a new and threatening German empire and that Russia might prefer a divided Germany, partially restrained by the United States, to a strong one.

Dean Acheson delivered the most stinging and unremitting critique. Correspondent James Reston observed the Kennan-Acheson tussle: "Next to the Lincoln Memorial in moonlight the sight of Mr. Dean G. Acheson blowing his top is without doubt the most impressive view in the capital." Acheson charged that Kennan "has never, in my judgement, grasped the realities of power relationships, but takes a rather mystical attitude toward them." The "realist" appeared to be attacking the "realist." Acheson ridiculed Kennan for his vagueness and imprecision and dismissed disengagement as "new isolationism." The former secretary of state displayed an utter lack of faith in the Soviet Union, which might, he feared, reintroduce troops in Eastern Europe, threaten Western Europe, and sign an anti-American defense pact with the new Germany. Kennan hurled a private barb at Acheson in a letter, commenting that "rarely, if ever, have I seen error so gracefully and respectably clothed. One hates to start plucking at such finery; but I suppose that in one way or another I shall have to do so."

Kennan also received enthusiastic support. British Labour party and German Social Democratic party leaders applauded him. Senator John F. Kennedy wrote Kennan in early 1958 commending his lectures for their "brilliance and stimulation" and reproving Acheson for his "personal criticisms" of Kennan. Walter Lippmann was happy to point out that he had advocated disengagement as early as 1947, when he had criticized the "X" article; a decade later Kennan and Lippmann were struggling as compatriots against cold warriors like Acheson and Kissinger who were reliving the battles of the 1940s and who continued to resist diplomacy in favor of military might. Kennan now trusted in Russian rationality and insisted that despite the risks, disengagement was a viable alternative to a potentially explosive cold war confrontation. The West would not know what Russia thought without at least negotiating. In those days of rigid positions, however, the weight of opinion was against Kennan.

Beginning with the disengagement controversy, Kennan had intermittent contact with John F. Kennedy. While teaching at Yale University in January of 1961, Kennan received a telephone call from the new president and was offered an ambassadorship in either Poland or Yugoslavia. Kennan welcomed the opportunity to serve again, if only to be able to leave the Foreign Service with more honor and propriety than he had in 1952. He accepted the assignment to Belgrade and for two years cultivated contact with Yugoslav officials, gained unusual access to Josip Tito, absorbed the varied culture of the country, and put the embassy staff to work writing a history of Yugoslavia. He noted obvious contrasts between this post and his tour of duty in Russia. Tito was not suspicious and tricky like Stalin. Foreigners were welcome in Yugoslavia and travel was largely unrestricted. Yugoslavia practiced an independent communism, proudly rejecting dictation from Moscow.

What bothered Kennan most was not the Yugoslavian government but his own. In 1961 the Tito-sponsored Belgrade Conference of nonaligned nations triggered vociferous anticommunism in the United States. Congressmen reacted sharply to some anti-American speeches delivered at the conference and began seeking a way to punish Yugoslavia. America's ever-present, undiscriminating, and ritualistic anticommunism flared up again. Kennan blamed the response on Eastern European émigré groups and the American propensity to view world affairs emotionally. Congressmen first disrupted the sale of planes to Tito's government. Then, in 1962, they canceled the "most favored nation" provision in trade relations between the United States and Yugoslavia. It was a vindictive move against a country that had few grievances against the United States and vice versa. Kennan had tried to stop this action by flying to Washington and lobbying with legislators. His failure, and his belief that Foreign Service personnel were minor figures in the American political system, "took the heart out of any further belief in the possible usefulness of a diplomatic career."

Earlier, in 1961, he had asked Kennedy not to endorse the "Captive Nations Resolution" which called for the liberation of peoples living in Communist countries and which Congress mindlessly passed each year. Kennan interpreted it to mean that Washington was committed to the overthrow of the Yugoslavian government, a policy that placed an ambassador in an anomalous position. Kennedy submitted to popular clamor and declared a "Captive Nations Week." This action, combined with the restriction on trade, convinced Kennan that his helplessness as a representative of the United States had been publicly demonstrated to the Yugoslavs. In 1963, without bitterness and with great dignity, Kennan left the diplomatic corps. The Belgrade post was by his own estimation his most rewarding and enjoyable; however, the experience soured him further on the American political process, the intrusions of Congress in foreign affairs, and hysterical anticommunism. Domestic politics, he concluded, was an "intolerable corruption" of diplomacy's "essential integrity."

Yet George F. Kennan felt compelled to go before the Senate Foreign Relations Committee in 1966 to appeal for a gradual withdrawal from Vietnam. Again he acted as the reasoned dissenter trying to persuade public opinion and the Congress—against the president—that the morass in Indochina was an unfortunate consequence of globalism. Interventionists like Dean Rusk, Walt and Eugene Rostow, and Dean Acheson had been justifying the expedition to Vietnam by citing the precedents of anti-Communist containment in the 1940s. Kennan refused to permit himself and his ideas to be used in this way. Under the tutelage of Senator J. William Fulbright, the Foreign Relations Committee was in an early stage of rebellion against the war and was looking for respectable allies. The recognized father of containment was willing to testify. Students and faculties had been protesting and marching, but neither the committee members nor Kennan felt comfortable with their frank and iconoclastic style. Kennan once again thrust himself into the center of a major debate by testifying that the containment doctrine was inapplicable to Indochina.

"I find myself," he remarked, "in many respects sort of a neo-isolationist." By that statement he meant that the United States should be modest and discriminating in its commitments abroad, a view that has gained increasing respect and popularity in the 1970s. He insisted that China was not a military aggressor in Indochina, that a military solution to what was largely an internal political conflict was fantasy, that Vietnam was an area of secondary importance to United States security, and that the war was disrupting American relations with both Japan and Russia. Facile analogies with the 1940s did not face the new realities of the 1960s. Asia was not Europe; China was not Russia. Containment should not be universal. He envisioned Vietnam as an independent Communist country like Yugoslavia; but under vigorous questioning by Senator Frank J. Lausche, ambiguity crept into Kennan's presentation. He said that "if we had been able to do better in Vietnam I would have been delighted, and I would have thought that the effort was warranted. . . ." This note of pragmatism seemed to undercut his appeal to principle. Yet his message was clear: the United States must curb its role as world policeman.

The combination of protest marches, critical analyses by scholars, Communist victories in the hills and cities of Vietnam, and tempered dissent by public figures like George F. Kennan moved both the Lyndon B. Johnson and Richard M. Nixon administrations, however slowly and incompletely, to a de-escalation of military intervention in Indochina.

    In early 1973, a still active and alert Kennan talked frankly during a television interview. "I've been gloomy lately," he commented, because America faced massive problems at home and abroad. He felt the United States should no longer try to be the dominant player on the world stage. Whether or not this was a neo-isolationist attitude (and the term should not be used in a pejorative sense), it meant limited commitments overseas, a reduction in the military establishment, more attention to domestic questions, and a frank realization that Washington had neither the duty nor the capability to establish a world balance of power. Kennan voiced skepticism about President Nixon's dramatically orchestrated trip to Peking in 1972. Kennan was not merely suspicious of Nixon's visions of grandeur as international peacemaker. He also nurtured serious doubt about close relations with the Chinese, a consistent position for him since the 1950s. He always preferred Japan as America's "friend" in Asia and had opposed recognition of the People's Republic of China. His views toward that regime were strikingly similar to his 1940s views on the Soviet Union. In 1964, for example, he depicted China as dominated by "embittered fanatics" wedded to an ideology that encouraged the "ruthless exertion of power." The Chinese were determined to destroy what Americans valued.

    In the 1960s Kennan had begun to comment frequently on domestic issues such as overpopulation and the environment. In the 1973 interview he summarized his views toward America and its diplomacy, pointing out that the United States had no business meddling in other country's affairs until it had straightened out its own. America had become too commercial minded, too dependent upon the automobile. A self-perpetuating technology produced unneeded inventions that "whipsawed" the American people and made them waste their natural resources. A cab ride in New York City, he said, with a cynical cab driver living in an unhappy, polluted city, had brought his thinking into focus. Americans, Kennan implored, needed leadership and inspiration to alleviate their serious environmental disorder. Although his prescriptions derived from a conservative perspective, they were not far removed from more radical views on the importance of preserving individualism, curtailing the machine, respecting the environment, and giving priority to domestic ills. Both recognized that the quality of American life would ultimately determine United States influence in the world.

Having spent many years as a frustrated bureaucrat-diplomat, Kennan had become more accustomed to the life of the analytical intellectual. One of his aspirations had always been in that direction, for impatience with the foreign affairs bureaucracy marked his diplomatic career. He was never the typical obedient functionary. Americans will remember him more for his ideas on Soviet history and diplomacy, containment, disengagement, American emotionalism, the relationship between the political system and foreign policy, and the need for an elite Foreign Service than for his contributions as a diplomat in formulating the Marshall Plan, changing policy toward Germany and Japan, initiating peace talks during the Korean War, or in serving as ambassador to Russia and Yugoslavia. Whether one accepts or rejects his ideas, so eloquently and forcefully expressed since the 1920s, Kennan has persistently demanded that Americans give attention to them and that statesmen confront international problems with energy, integrity, and intelligence. His legacy will, for some time, claim an influential place in discussions of current and future foreign affairs.

BIBLIOGRAPHIC NOTE

Because George F. Kennan was such a prolific author and controversial public figure, the quantity of literature on his career is massive. A lengthy bibliography of Kennan's own articles and books, including his scholarly publications, can be found handily in Thomas G. Paterson, ed., *Containment and the Cold War: American Foreign Policy since 1945* (Reading, Mass., 1973). Kennan's own eloquent two-volume autobiography, *Memoirs, 1925–1950* (Boston, 1967) and *Memoirs, 1950–1963* (Boston, 1972), is indispensable for a surprisingly frank peek into his exciting life.

Although at this time Kennan's private papers are only partially open to scholars, the complete collection is housed at the Princeton University Library. He used many of the documents in the preparation of his memoirs, but many others have not been published. Letters to, from, and about Kennan and his ideas can also be found in other manuscript collections, many of which are cited in Thomas G. Paterson, *Soviet-Ameri-*

can Confrontation (Baltimore, 1973). Oral history transcripts of interviews with Kennan on topics covering the postwar years are open to research at the Princeton University Library (John Foster Dulles Project) and the Kennedy Library. The Department of State's *Foreign Relations of the United States* volumes include Kennan's influential cables from Moscow in the early cold war period and his advice on such programs as the Marshall Plan.

There is yet no full-length biography of George F. Kennan, but Professor C. Ben Wright has begun one based on his Ph.D. dissertation completed at the University of Wisconsin, "George F. Kennan, Scholar and Diplomat: 1926–1946" (1972). Analytical studies of Kennan and his prescriptions for American foreign policy, especially containment, can be found in Paterson, *Containment and the Cold War* (Reading, Mass., 1973). For stimulating interpretations see the following works: Jonathan Knight, "George Frost Kennan and the Study of American Foreign Policy: Some Critical Comments," *Western Political Quarterly* 20 (March 1967), 149–60; Marvin Kalb, "Vital Interests of Mr. Kennan," *New York Times Magazine*, 27 March 1966; Richard Powers, "Kennan against Himself?" Ph.D. dissertation, Claremont Graduate School, 1967; George Kateb, "George F. Kennan: The Heart of a Diplomat," *Commentary* 45 (January 1968), 21–26; Louis Halle, "George F. Kennan and the Common Mind," *Virginia Quarterly Review* 40 (Winter 1969), 46–57; " 'X' Plus 25: Interview with George F. Kennan," *Foreign Policy*, No. 7 (Summer 1972), 5–21; and Alfred Kazin, "Man of State," *New York Review of Books*, 2 November 1972.

Kennan's containment philosophy was spelled out in his famous "X" article, "The Sources of Soviet Conduct," *Foreign Affairs* 25 (July 1947), 566–82. Provocative commentaries include Walter Lippmann, *The Cold War* (New York, 1947); William Appleman Williams, "Irony of Containment," *The Nation* 182 (5 May 1956), 376–79; Lloyd C. Gardner, *Architects of Illusion* (Chicago, 1970), pp. 270–300; and J. William Fulbright, "Reflections: In Thrall to Fear," *The New Yorker* 47 (8 January 1972), 41–62. Kennan's disengagement proposals were published as *Russia, the Atom and the West* (New York, 1958). For debate see Dean Acheson, "The Illusion of Disengagement," *Foreign Affairs* 36 (April 1958), 371–82; and Walter Lippmann, "Mr. Kennan and Reappraisal in Europe," *Atlantic* 201 (April 1958), 33–37. Kennan's belief that the containment doctrine is inapplicable to Asia is well illustrated in his testimony before the Senate Foreign Relations Committee, *Supplemental Foreign Assistance Fiscal Year 1966—Vietnam* (Washington, D.C., 1966). David P. Mozingo, "Containment in Asia Reconsidered," *World Politics* 19 (April 1967), 361–77, is one of the best discussions of this crucial topic.

Kennan's *American Diplomacy, 1900–1950* (Chicago, 1951), an over-simplified survey that finds American foreign policy dominated by mindless moralism and legalism, is revealing about Kennan's self-defined "realism." Interpretive essays include Dwight J. Simpson, "New Trends in Foreign Policy: A Criticism of the 'Kennan Thesis,'" *World Affairs Quarterly* 27 (January 1957), 102–14; and Dexter Perkins, "American Foreign Policy and Its Critics," in Alfred H. Kelly, ed., *American Foreign Policy and American Democracy* (Detroit, 1954), pp. 65–88.

The secondary literature on the history of the cold war is, of course, prodigious. The best overviews, with differing interpretations, are Walter LaFeber, *America, Russia, and the Cold War, 1945–1971* (New York, 1972), Louis Halle, *The Cold War as History* (New York, 1967), Gabriel and Joyce Kolko, *The Limits of Power* (New York, 1972), and Adam Ulam, *Expansion and Coexistence* (New York, 1968).

POWER AND REALITY:

JOHN FOSTER DULLES

and Political Diplomacy

Herbert S. Parmet

John Foster Dulles's critics regarded him as Eisenhower's Rasputin. They understood neither his political mission nor his sophisticated analyses of power relationships and the dynamics of Communist expansionism. Along with much of the electorate, the administration's opponents agreed that he advocated a more aggressive cold war stance than previous secretaries of state. Those who feared the dangerous implications of his public statements thought he viewed the line drawn between East and West as the apocalyptic struggle between good and evil, a fight between thermonuclear powers that pitted capitalism, Christianity, and freedom against atheistic Communist materialism. He was an old Puritan who had insinuated himself into the favor of the well-meaning but naïve and politically inexperienced general who occupied the White House. Little wonder, then, that the president, widely regarded as a man of peace, called Dulles an Old Testament prophet. Indeed, few thought of him as anything other than a foreboding figure,

589

one of considerable intellect and convictions but with the vanity and rigidity of another era.

Even before the Republican convention of 1952, Dulles's position had been well publicized. His statements echoed the cold war militants, particularly those who believed that Truman and his administration had responded inadequately to international communism. Just before the convention battle between the moderates and liberals backing Dwight D. Eisenhower and the conservative supporters of Senator Robert A. Taft, publisher Henry Luce's cold war zeal led him to open the pages of *Life* magazine once more to Dulles's views. The Dulles article was bravely entitled "A Policy of Boldness," and it called for initiatives against Communist expansion. Truman's measures were depicted as mere reactions to Communist aggression, as willingness to "live with it, presumably forever," that condemned to permanent slavery the six hundred million people subjugated by the Soviets since 1945. Clearly, the Dulles prescription was a more vigorous approach.

"It is ironic and wrong," he wrote, "that we who believe in the boundless power of human freedom should so long have accepted a static political role," and "that we who so proudly profess regards for the spiritual should rely on material defenses while the avowed materialists have been waging a winning war with social ideas stirring humanity everywhere." The United States must not accept any "deal" that would confirm Soviet rule over alien people, he wrote. Task forces must be created to develop a "freedom program for each of the captive nations." Rather than meek acceptance of containment, political, economic, and cultural programs must be developed to achieve the liberation of all captive peoples. Although the United States must not resort to military tactics that would encourage bloody uprisings and reprisals, it must strengthen its defenses. Emphasizing his words, Dulles added that the free world must *develop the will and organize the means to retaliate instantly against open aggression by Red armies, so that if it occurred anywhere, we could and would strike back where it hurts by means of our choosing.*

The foreign policy plank of the Republican platform of 1952 confirmed the Dulles influence. Not only would "liberation" be an objective, but certainly the new administration would repudiate those agreements that condemned national groups to eternal "enslavement." That, of course, meant Yalta, where FDR had made concessions to Stalin in 1945. Moreover, the record of the subsequent Republican administration for the following six years was obviously his design rather than the work of the beloved and trusted general-president: McCarthyism not contained but unleashed in the corridors of the State Department building and Chiang Kai-shek unleashed in the Formosa Strait; "massive retaliation" with its implicit threat of substituting nuclear wars for local skirmishes fought by conventional armies; a disingenuous encirclement of Communist-held territory with a chain of mutual security treaties; recognition of the follies of policies that antagonized traditional allies.

It was Nikita Khrushchev who made what was perhaps the most revealing observation about the secretary of state. "I feel very sorry for Dulles," said the Russian leader to Dag Hammarskjöld. "I admire his intelligence, his wide knowledge, his integrity and his courage. Dulles invented brinkmanship but he would never step over the brink." [1] Others, with longer memories, may have recalled a contribution Dulles made to *Life* in 1946. The words he chose to begin a two-party analysis of the postwar outlook were: "No nation's foreign policy can be ascertained merely from what its officials say. More important are the philosophy of its leaders and the actual manifestations of that philosophy in what is done."

◇◇◇

Dwight Eisenhower liked to say that Dulles's life until 1953 had been spent preparing to head the State Department. The president's hyperbole should not detract from the importance of his observation. The selection of Dulles was so obvious, so predestined, that at least once during the preinaugural period the president-elect seemed annoyed that he had no choice but merely to ratify the selection. Perhaps it is no exaggeration to say that at least three other Republican presidential contenders of that era, Arthur Vandenberg, Thomas E. Dewey, and Robert A. Taft, would have chosen Dulles.

If he possessed credentials that surpassed those of anyone else in his party, those qualifications were further enhanced by his

1. David E. Bruce to Dulles, 2 April 1959, Dulles papers, Princeton. Material in this essay from the Dulles papers and the Dulles additional papers is used with the permission of the Princeton University Library and the Dulles Committee.

political standing. Before 1952, however, his reputation required some rehabilitation before he could be acceptable to the party's right wing. At best, the Dulles background as a partisan was not strong. As a Republican foreign policy adviser with the Truman administration, he had been an advocate of bipartisanship; the consequences of the "fall" of China provoked a bitterly partisan denunciation of Democratic culpability. His closeness to Dewey, the man Senator Everett Dirksen condemned so theatrically at the 1952 convention for having twice led the party down the road to defeat, was a considerable liability among the anti-Eisenhower people. A still more serious blemish on Dulles's record was his expression of confidence in behalf of the subsequently convicted Alger Hiss. He lessened such liabilities by waging a strongly conservative campaign during his unsuccessful 1949 fight for the Senate against Herbert Lehman in New York. His connection with the Japanese Peace Treaty and aid in securing that country as an American ally against Far Eastern communism was also helpful, as was the obvious anticommunism, with pronounced spiritual overtones, that he expressed so strongly. His most recent statements, particularly the "Policy of Boldness" article, helped to dispel any remaining doubts about where he stood.

The son of a Presbyterian minister, Dulles was born in 1888 in the far upstate New York community of Watertown. While he was a student at Princeton, fellow undergraduates found it difficult to consider him a congenial companion. Rather withdrawn, somewhat of an elitist, he was a moralizer who lacked the qualities that contribute to personal popularity. Throughout his life, he maintained a prominent association with the National Council of Churches. He stressed spiritual strength and expounded freely on the virtues of Christianity. French Foreign Minister Couve de Murville noted that his own Calvinism enabled him to detect the importance of religion in Dulles's thinking. One astute observer who sat with him at many meetings of both the cabinet and the National Security Council described his demeanor in the following manner: "When it is time for Dulles to speak or make a reply, he does not look at the person he is addressing but fixes his eyes on the ceiling. This creates an unfortunate impression of conscious superiority on his part, as though the people across the table are not as important as the ideas which represent Eternal Truth, and, therefore, must be addressed to the Cosmos."

Nevertheless, it was Dulles who made the Machiavellian

comment to a journalist that the "United States is almost the only country strong enough and powerful enough to be moral," a remark that reveals much about him. As important as piety was to his system of values, as ascetic as his behavior was, he was far too intelligent and sophisticated to ignore realities. "He had the reputation of being a pious man," George F. Kennan wrote, "but I, a fellow Presbyterian, could never discern the signs of it in his administration of the State Department."

Through family tradition, personal experience and study, his diplomatic background was outstanding. His maternal grandfather, John W. Foster, had spent eight months as President Benjamin Harrison's secretary of state. His Uncle "Bertie," Robert Lansing, was more prominent as the most significant of the three men who headed the State Department under Wilson. At the age of thirty, Dulles, trained as a lawyer, went to Paris with the president as counsel to the American commission to negotiate the peace treaty. He also served with the reparations commission and in 1933 was the American representative at the Berlin debt conferences.

The consequences of post–World War I diplomacy did much to mold his thinking. He became convinced that adequacy of power alone had been demonstrably inadequate, that failure to provide for change had created inherent obstacles. Power, Dulles believed, was energy that defied mere containment. Outlets, or safety valves, had to be provided. In his first book, *War, Peace and Change* (1939), he complained that "most political treaties do not seek to create a condition of elasticity, which will be adaptable to changes in the balance of power initially existing. Rather, such treaties tend to perpetuate the results obtainable from possession of an initial command of power." He proceeded to suggest that flexibility rather than rigidity "creates lasting stability." Nowhere had the architects of the "permanent peace" provided for the means to make appropriate modifications. Instead, they tried to maintain the status quo. That misconstrued the nature of power and, therefore, the conditions needed to preserve peace. Careful inspection of the record shows that Dulles had little faith in any single instrument of power; despite the impression he helped to create, he minimized the efficacy of military solutions. All tools were mere elements of power; all had to be used selectively. "Power," he wrote in *War or Peace* in 1950, ". . . includes not merely military power, but economic power and the intangibles, such as moral judgment and world opinion, which determine what men do and the intensity with which they do it."

By the time that book appeared, the cold war had matured beyond its origins. Mao Tse-tung had routed Chiang Kai-shek, the Soviets had secured their sphere of interest in Eastern Europe, and the establishment of both NATO and the Communist Information Bureau (Cominform) helped move the superpowers toward implacable hostility. Despite the rhetoric about the "international Communist threat" and the concomitant evils that he and fellow Americans condemned so freely, the essentials of Dulles's thinking did not change. Communism was, of course, evil. He had no doubts about the inherent advantages of democratic capitalism. Given a choice between the opposing systems, he was certain which would be supported by a Christian sense of values. Still, what becomes fascinating in retrospect, after one recalls the evangelistic tone associated with Dulles as secretary of state, is that he did not, at that stage, permit the current simplistic assumptions to seduce him.

While sharing the common tendency to cite the sequence of events that led to World War II as a justification for existing policy, he did not assume that Stalin was a new Hitler bent on military conquest of the world; Russian expansionism did not follow that course. The Soviets had succeeded with military means in Eastern Europe as a result of successful pursuit of the Germans and lack of competing military forces in the area. More relevant to an understanding of the phenomenon was that communism thrived on internal discontent and decay. Americans had not, in the past, perceived that "misery and despair in Germany was breeding Nazism." To talk, therefore, of the inevitability of a new major war simply failed to account for the changes that had taken place as a result of the recent great war. The defeat of Nazi Germany, the horrors related to that experience, the establishment of the United Nations, the "balance of terror," and abhorrence toward even the thought of a major new conflict made such repetition most unlikely. Frustrating Soviet Communist methods of "fraud, terrorism, and violence" by making "positive and well directed efforts" in fellowship with other free peoples would probably suffice to preserve peace. The Communist threat that did exist was less a result of ideology than their possession of enormous military power. Those expansionist impulses causing such concern were mainly related to traditional Russian aspirations. Overt aggression,

Dulles believed, would probably result from the Kremlin's inability to control the Red Army.

Essential to the Dulles analysis was the conviction that a major war, if it should come, would be "the result of miscalculating." Both world wars that brought American involvement had, he pointed out, come from failure of foreign leaders to understand how we would respond. That the North Korean southward drive across the thirty-eighth parallel had followed the Truman administration's implication that the area lay beyond the American military periphery was the most recent vindication of his belief. Further, the Russians, as he had found at the opening session of the United Nations Conference at San Francisco, respected an uncompromisingly firm position.

He spoke at Princeton in early 1952 and repeated his view of the nature of the cold war. "It is primarily through social ideas that Soviet Communism achieves its victories," he said. "Almost no part of its expansion has been due to the old-fashioned method of open military aggression. The successful weapon has been political warfare, with the main reliance placed on revolutionary slogans which arouse the masses to Soviet-dictated violence." He proceeded to point out that the determination of right and wrong stemmed from "a moral or natural law not made by man . . . and conformity with this law is in the long run indispensable to human welfare." Dulles agreed with Arnold Toynbee in attributing the "crisis of our civilization" to the contradictions of our practices from their Christian context, so that "while Soviet Communism fails to invoke moral principle, we ourselves are not doing much better."

Three years earlier, in a letter to his son Avery, Dulles responded to an inquiry about the inherent qualities of Soviet communism revealing interesting aspects of his thought. "I know you have a contempt for 'expediency,'" the Old Testament prophet wrote to his Jesuit son, "but that is what in fact determines most people's conduct, and when you ask whether as a practical matter communism can be expected to give up violent methods without first becoming converted to a Christian view of the nature of man, my answer is that all history proves that such a development is quite possible." [2]

2. Dulles to Brother Avery Dulles, 3 March 1949, Dulles additional papers, Princeton.

◇◇◇

   If politics may be defined as the art of the possible, to Dulles
expediency was the art of politics. Serving under Eisenhower
brought him together with a fellow practitioner. Their obvious
personal differences did not prevent a remarkably smooth relationship, one so harmonious, in fact, that the virtual absence of
conflict was often interpreted as evidence of Eisenhower's supine
subservience to Dulles, the man who really determined American
foreign policy. In reality, their teamwork was made possible by a
common view of the task. For all Eisenhower's platitudes and
public displays of innocence and for all Dulles's blend of righteousness and bellicosity, they were in basic agreement about the
political requirements of their mission.
   More than has been generally realized, Dulles weighed
domestic political factors and responded accordingly. At the
outset, he was second to no one in appreciating the need for the
Republican party to decimate the traditional Democratic vote as a
means of winning the 1952 election. The old New Deal coalition
was clearly in jeopardy, buffeted by the domestic conservative
reaction of the late 1930s and, more recently, by the consequences
of the wartime alliance. Many Americans, particularly Roman
Catholics, felt repugnance toward friendship with the Soviet
Union. Polish-Americans were alarmed about Russian success in
controlling Eastern Europe after their westward pursuit of the
fleeing Nazis. Even as early as 1944, months before the Yalta
Conference, protests were being voiced about President Roosevelt
giving Stalin too much freedom of action in that area. Jan
Ciechanowski, the Polish wartime ambassador to the United
States, advised Dulles that a Republican return to power would be
hindered severely through failure to appeal to the ethnic Slavic
vote. Dulles never forgot the point. At a luncheon meeting in
Colorado after the 1952 convention, he expounded on how the
forthcoming campaign should emphasize the party's platform
pledge to secure the liberation of the "captive peoples" behind
the iron curtain.
   His display of political consciousness that day impressed his
audience. Eisenhower's subsequent campaign against Adlai Stevenson virtually rivaled Joe McCarthy's contemporary appeal to
the frustration and anger of millions of Americans, especially
Roman Catholic Democrats. Protests about the immorality of the

ideological alliance with McCarthy failed to dissuade Dulles of its political necessity.

With the new administration installed in Washington, Dulles moved decisively to avoid Acheson's pitfalls. Whereas Acheson's "personal relations with Congress were, in the opinion of most observers, abysmal," Dulles worked hard to establish a relationship with the Senate characterized by "complete frankness and honesty." Although Acheson had come before the Foreign Relations Committee only when summoned, the committee's records show forty-eight appearances by Dulles during his six years at the head of the State Department. He always took particular care to journey to Capitol Hill to consult with the senators both before and after important international conferences. He also worked to improve upon Acheson's relations with the press. Most journalists felt that Truman's secretary of state had dealt with them in a high-handed and contemptuous manner. Dulles, understanding the importance of their role, proved far more open and congenial.

Ever conscious of popular support, the secretary tailored every public address to ensure the proper reception. Sophisticated audiences tended to criticize his pious moralizing, but they comprised an insignificant segment of the population; further, they constituted the administration's natural critics. More appropriately, Dulles spoke to the mass audience. He was careful to avoid complex language and even cleansed his speech drafts of foreign words and phrases, particularly those in Latin. He felt they tended to reduce the impact of his message and would make vast segments of his audience doubt his sincerity. So while the nation's intellectuals sneered, Dulles found compensation in the glowing responses from the hinterlands.

More important, perhaps, and puzzling to those who thought they knew Dulles, was his reaction to the whole issue of internal security and Senator McCarthy. One of the ironies of the tumultuous state of American politics during that bitterly partisan stage of the cold war was that he became so closely associated with the dangerously ambitious senator, at least in the eyes of his critics. Having convinced a frightened public that Communist success came from laxity and even treachery in high American circles and having placed the diplomatic corps under suspicion, the anti-Communist crusaders managed to intimidate even those who viewed them with contempt and loathing.

This submission by Dulles to the McCarthy tyranny provided

persuasive evidence of the senator's power. Everytning about
McCarthy's public and personal life was abhorrent to the secretary; a greater contrast between two men could hardly be
possible. Moreover, even conservatives close to the man from
Wisconsin have testified that his notions about communism were
hazy; and, certainly in contrast to Dulles, his emphasis upon
ideology as an internal menace was a gross distortion. For the
secretary, the hunt for domestic subversives held no significance
whatsoever. Further, the McCarthy style and tone reminded Dulles
of Nazi Germany, a point the secretary made to Senator Ralph
Flanders of Vermont as they both heard the senator deliver one of
his harangues. Yet, so thorough was McCarthy's ability to intimidate, so secure was his hold on the public and the Congress,
particularly Republicans, that, to Dulles, any freedom to conduct
the affairs of the State Department meant concessions. Conscious
of his own support for Alger Hiss, the secretary knew that further
suspicions could hinder his conduct of American foreign policy.
Anything that reduced his latitude or detracted from his main
purpose was a nuisance to be eliminated.

As his first concession to what he perceived as the political
realities of 1953, Dulles provided evidence that the new administration had brought changes; after all, the recent election had
been a massive protest against Truman's policies. Therefore, in the
climate of fear that had saturated Washington and the nation, all
suspicions had to be allayed. Even before his own confirmation by
the Senate, Dulles took the discreet step of requesting that his
own loyalty be scrutinized by a full FBI field investigation, a
procedure that became standard for all appointees. Then, shortly
after assuming his office, he addressed an outdoor gathering of
State Department personnel. He called for their "positive loyalty"
to the new administration. Undoubtedly he feared hostility from
Democratic holdovers, but the connotations of the word "loyalty"
during that period were sufficient to send reverberations throughout the staff, including the Foreign Service. Thereafter, as one of
Dulles's close aides has since observed, it was no longer enough to
demonstrate mere "loyalty"; one had to offer "consistent proof of
such fealty."

To dramatize further its reaction against past policies, the new
administration had to purge those who in the public and congressional minds had been made scapegoats for the "permissive"
Truman policies toward international communism. Thus, officials

who had been attacked by what became known as the China Lobby (a pro–Chiang Kai-shek pressure group financed by textile importer Alfred Kohlberg and a coterie of other businessmen and their congressional spokesmen) would have to be sacrificed for the greater cause. Dulles arranged for the departure of the "old China hands," Foreign Service officers John Carter Vincent, John Stewart Service, and John Paton Davies, Jr., whose crimes consisted of having offered perceptive analyses of the situation in China before Chiang's downfall. To further prove that the Eisenhower administration had reversed discredited policies, Dulles also facilitated the retirement of Kremlinologist George F. Kennan, who was far too intimately associated with the policies that the Republicans had promised to reverse by extending hopes of "liberation" for the "captive peoples." What better evidence that the immoral assumptions of "containment" had ended than the purging of the man who had become identified as the main theoretician of that policy!

Also needing correction were suspicions about the lack of security within the department. Dulles, without any illusions about the rationale for such a policy, turned over the problem to Scott McLeod. A former FBI agent and newspaperman, McLeod's mentality and methods invariably brought suspicions that he was one of Joe McCarthy's men. Actually, he had been brought in by Undersecretary of State Donald Lourie on the recommendation of Senator Styles Bridges of New Hampshire. Given a virtually free hand, McLeod went to work with the zeal of a Boy Scout uncovering "enemy agents." Heading a crew of nearly two dozen ex-FBI men, he focused on all the soft spots that had been publicized by McCarthy, particularly on the supposed relationship between homosexuality and security leaks. After three weeks on the job, McLeod publicized his success in removing twenty-one "deviants." His men also patrolled the State Department's corridors, even making after-hours forays into office files that had not been locked. By November, McLeod's mission was justified with the announcement that 306 citizen employees and 178 aliens had been separated from the department for security reasons.

After two youthful agents of Senator McCarthy returned from an inspection tour of overseas libraries operated by the International Information Administration, the agency was accused of harboring on its shelves over thirty thousand volumes by "Communist" authors, including the works of Dulles's cousin, Foster

Rhea Dulles, as well as Arthur Schlesinger, Jr. The State Department promptly announced remedial action. Not only would all such literature be banned in the future, it promised, but also "any publication which continuously publishes Communist propaganda." McCarthy approved, calling it a "good, sensible order." Far from restraining the anti-Communist hysteria of the period, the administration, with Dulles carrying out his part of the mission, succumbed to those political pressures that inevitably fostered fear and insecurity within the government.

Fulfilling certain other promises, however, was not that simple, particularly when they threatened to jeopardize rather than aid the interests of diplomacy. The Republican platform promise to "repudiate all commitments contained in secret understandings such as those of Yalta which aid Communist enslavements" had, of course, been entirely consistent with Dulles's desires to win the votes of Slavic Americans. To make a pitch for votes was one thing, however; to carry out a campaign promise was quite another. The Yalta Conference had confirmed the arrangements made in London in 1944 that gave the West a legal status in Berlin. If this, as well as occupation rights in Vienna, had been given under repudiated treaties, how could such rights be continued? Thoughts about the problems such action would create for the ability of Americans to negotiate in the future rendered an anti-Yalta policy untenable.

Dulles and Eisenhower, therefore, catered to both international and domestic political realities. When the secretary met with the party's congressional leaders on 16 February to present the administration plan, the impossibility of satisfying both needs became obvious. The resolution he unveiled for congressional approval simply condemned diplomacy at the expense of "captive peoples." Rather than denying past obligations, it blamed the Russians for "totalitarian imperialism" that had led to the "subjugation of free peoples." Rather than repudiating the Roosevelt-Truman diplomacy, it blamed Russian deceit. To the Republican party's congressional leaders, that sounded remarkably similar to Democratic explanations for the failures of the wartime conferences. Facing a GOP rebellion over the issue, Dulles appeared before the foreign relations committees of both houses and urged Republicans to forget about the past and to concentrate on the future. He also warned about the international implications of repudiation. Even his critics called Dulles's performance before the House committee the "greatest advocacy of his career," but they were not satisfied. Supported by Senator Taft, the Senate Foreign Relations Committee added an amendment declaring that "the adoption of this resolution does not constitute any determination by Congress as to the validity or invalidity of any provisions of the said agreements or understandings." With Democrats incensed about its implications and siding with the administration on the issue, Eisenhower and Dulles considered dropping efforts to get any resolution through Congress. The simultaneous death of Joseph Stalin salvaged the situation by suddenly rendering the resolution "inopportune." Diplomatically, the timing would be regarded as callous. The change in Soviet leadership demanded cautious assessment.

Still, political exigencies required substantial evidence of departure from past policies. Although neither Dulles nor Eisenhower had international views that differed in substance from Truman-Acheson policies, and although the world appeared remarkably similar to them as it had to the Democrats, rhetoric had to obscure the inevitable continuity.

◇◇◇

The partisan rancor of the past, the blame and bitterness, the charges of incompetence and even treachery, the suspicions of a lack of a "will to win," and the frustrations of an interminable war in Korea left leaders in the Dulles era little choice but to confirm prevailing popular assumptions. However involved the origins of the cold war, however sophisticated Dulles's own view, the options open to American leaders were severely limited. In the process, as close as was the Eisenhower-Dulles association, the secretary was the expendable man, the one exposed to the voters as the cold warrior in contrast to the peace-loving president, and, significantly, the man whose now strident anticommunism was politic in its attractions for the party's conservatives, who were suspicious about Eisenhower's intentions. Just as the president delegated the more sordid political tasks to Vice-President Richard Nixon, so it was in the area of diplomacy. Dulles's role was to placate the right wingers, to convince them that changes had indeed occurred. Therefore, instead of altering previous policies, Dulles's six years were full of strident posturing. With the need to take a hard line in crisis after crisis, to stem the Communist tide that had plagued the Democrats, it became more important to avoid a nuclear showdown than to take bold new initiatives. His own ideas about flexibility vis-à-vis power were severely compromised. In retrospect, considering the political mission and the climate of the nation, there was little room for innovation in foreign affairs.

His tenure, therefore, came and went with essentially the same problems, largely unresolved and often verging on the catastrophic. By definition, his accomplishments were negative. No ground was lost to the enemy and major military conflicts were avoided. More active in his travels than any previous secretary of state, almost constantly flying from capital to capital, Dulles gingerly used his political support to consolidate incipient policies and thereby helped to make his years a sort of plateau of the cold war era. He did succeed in holding the line with a minimum of force. At his death, European recovery and rearmament fulfilled the hopes of its architects, but the division of Germany and the status of Berlin remained as menacing as ever; the Russian hold over the "captive peoples" had been diluted in Poland but reaffirmed with steel and bullets in Hungary, and, in either case, it remained untouched by American policy; a brief war had exacerbated the Middle Eastern muddle over oil, Zionism, Arab nationalism, and Russian intervention satisfying no one and compounding the job of finding a solution; the Korean War had ended and the thirty-eighth parallel was relatively quiet, but American forces were covertly engaged in South Vietnam, sustaining a regime that carried the blessings of Washington more than the support of its own people; recognition of the People's Republic of China was an act that would have meant political suicide and few doubted American readiness to go to war to defend Chiang Kai-shek's right to maintain his garrisons on Formosa, or even the dubious bastions on Quemoy and Matsu; a summit conference had taken place in Geneva and platitudes were expended in behalf of toning down the ever accelerating arms race without a scintilla of substantive progress; the "third world" nations that had just begun to "emerge" at the start of the fifties were providing evidence of nationalistic independence and seemed stubbornly immune to romancing by either Moscow or Washington.

At the outset of his tenure, Dulles delivered a speech that many interpreted as an attempt to regain for the State Department the support Acheson had lost. He chastised those Europeans who "want to go in their separate ways" despite the "deadly serious" threat of encirclement by the Communist bloc. Addressing a national audience via television, he enumerated all the world's trouble spots and detailed the dangers of Communist expansion. "So far as your Government is concerned," he said, "you may be sure that it will not be intimidated, subverted or conquered. Our nation must stand as a solid rock in a storm-tossed world. To all those suffering under Communist slavery, to the timid and intimidated peoples of the world, let us say this: you can count upon us." Only six days later, when the president delivered his State of the Union message, he made headlines by reading from a section written by Dulles. The Seventh Fleet, Eisenhower announced, will "no longer be employed to shield Communist China." Although the act was soon described as the "unleashing of Chiang Kai-shek," it did not in substance alter what had been happening all along in the Formosa Strait.

The presence of the Seventh Fleet no longer deterred the Nationalist forces from striking at the mainland. According to the official Nationalist China news service, raiders had "temporarily occupied" twenty-one cities, three hundred fifty villages, and nine islands during the preceding year. President Truman had actually reversed the policy of guarding against military activities in the area but without the propaganda threat of a wider war. Still, Dulles made his point. Pro-MacArthur and pro-Taft segments of the public and the press rejoiced that the new administration had rejected the "Marshall-Acheson doctrine" by responding vigorously to Russia's challenge. When Dulles reached London shortly afterward, he faced evidence of European dismay at the appearance of growing American belligerence. He assured them that his words presaged no real change.

The Dulles journey marked the start of the administration's efforts to bolster the strength of the Western alliance. Winning ratification of the European Defense Community was the immediate goal. Acheson had given the plan high priority; it would enable the development of a West German army that could be safely— and therefore acceptably—integrated within the European Coal and Steel Community. The Dulles efforts provided a clear example of the continuity of American policy. Since the end of World War II, the United States had spent about thirty billion dollars on Western Europe; it now regarded formation of EDC as vital for the non-Communist world's ability to resist aggression.

Although the plan had been conceived by French political economist Jean Monnet, it had become clear that its main obstacle was the political situation in Paris. A French National Assembly divided almost equally among six different parties and the dependence of Premier René Mayer's government on the anti-EDC nationalist supporters of General Charles de Gaulle dimmed the outlook. Further damaging EDC's prospects was the Soviet "peace offensive" that followed Stalin's death. Prime Minister Georgi Malenkov projected soothing tones from Moscow. His words offered a hopeful world the possibility that Russia's new leadership was looking for a détente with the West. Malenkov stated that there was no dispute that could not "be decided by peaceful means, on the basis of mutual understanding by interested countries." Was the Russian overture genuine, or was it a ploy to sabotage EDC?

Simultaneous developments seemed to indicate a real change. Moscow radio began to glorify the Russian and Anglo-American wartime partnership. Foreign Minister Vyacheslav M. Molotov agreed to cooperate to obtain the release of British citizens being held by the North Koreans. From the Korean War zone came the first significant Communist concession toward relieving the truce deadlock. There was agreement for an immediate discussion to facilitate the exchange of sick and wounded prisoners of war. In Berlin, too, the Russians displayed a more cooperative attitude and relaxed restrictions that had been plaguing the Western sector of the city. Even in the United Nations there was change. The Russians joined the West in support of Dag Hammarskjöld as secretary-general. For Dulles and the American president, all this created a dilemma. Fears of adverse propaganda made it difficult for them to appear insensitive to the "peace offensive." At the same time, its acceptance as heralding a genuine rapprochement threatened to dilute the urgent need to strengthen the Western alliance and complicated the administration's efforts in behalf of continued foreign aid and military spending.

Eisenhower's address to the American Society of Newspaper Editors in April of 1953, an event widely publicized by the United States Information Agency, served as the counter-stroke. The president contrasted the postwar behavior of the Communist countries and the democracies and called for more than words to substantiate Soviet sincerity. In the broader sphere of diplomacy, Eisenhower was executing his function as an advocate of peace,

while Dulles continued to pursue *Realpolitik*. The contrast between the public images of the two men was, of necessity, highly
exaggerated. After all, the state of American public opinion toward
both Russia and the concept of communism and the considerable
influence of the Republican party's right wing made any substantive concessions by the Eisenhower-Dulles team a most hazardous
undertaking.

In reality, the administration's established policy and rhetoric
had combined to make the American position virtually inflexible.
They could not abandon the public advocacy of a unified
Germany governed by free elections, nor could they even appear
to accept the permanence of the captive condition of Eastern
Europe. Abandonment of support for Syngman Rhee and his
Republic of Korea government was equally unthinkable, as was
the reduction of American arms without firm and politically
acceptable agreements with the East. Moreover, at that stage of
the cold war, an administration elected largely through public
belief that it could deal more firmly with communism than had its
predecessors could not suddenly admit that it was possible to deal
with the godless Communists who had, as millions believed,
"violated every treaty." Dulles's mission was the continued mobilization of the "free world" against the immoral enemy.

His determination and abrasive style became evident during
Dulles's subsequent efforts in behalf of EDC. At a session of the
NATO Council in Paris, in a desperate yet calculated effort to force
the issue, he expressed grave apprehensions about "whether
continental Europe can remain a place of safety" despite the
continuing schism between France and the German Federal
Republic. Speaking carefully, he warned that French failure to
ratify EDC "would compel an agonizing reappraisal of basic
United States policy." In other words, there could be an end to
American military support of Western Europe. Whether or not the
subsequent anti-EDC vote in the National Assembly resulted at
least in part from adverse reaction to the secretary's words, the
European community was dead.

The essentials of Dulles's policy survived, however. Creation
of the Western European Union salvaged the early restoration of
West Germany's full sovereignty and won the admission of the
Bonn government as an equal partner. At the suggestion of British
Foreign Secretary Anthony Eden, the Brussels Treaty of 1948, which
had provided for the mutual defense of five nations against a

remilitarized Germany, was revised and expanded. The new organization included Great Britain, which would not have been possible if EDC had been accepted. The administration had achieved its goal after all. Eisenhower's memoirs recall his agreement with Dulles "that the accomplishment of the transformation was a 'near miracle—a shining chapter in history.' "

Quickly, the distinctive characteristics of Dulles's diplomacy had become a stiff military posture and an apparent readiness to go to war if necessary. His "Policy of Boldness" article had pointed to the need to "retaliate instantly . . . by means of our choosing." Additional prominence was given in January 1954 to his statement before the Council on Foreign Relations of the importance to the United States of "a great capacity to retaliate, instantly, by means and at places of our choosing." Subsequent talk about more reliance on "deterrent power, and less dependence on local defensive power," more trust in air power and the efficacy of atomic weapons ("More bang for the buck!") brought the pejorative phrase "massive retaliation" into the speeches of Dulles's critics. While the secretary insisted that deterrence was his objective, those fearful of its implications considered it a dangerous concept. They feared an irresponsible use of atomic weapons and diplomacy that would leave little choice between all-out war or inaction because of the weakness of conventional forces.

In sharp contrast to the continuing depiction of the president as a man of peace, a *Life* article by James Shepley in early 1956 lent more substance to charges that Dulles was a warmonger. Shepley's authorized contribution described the secretary of state as advocating the need to be willing to go "to the brink" if necessary to avoid war. Thus, the author of "massive retaliation" was also a practitioner of "brinkmanship." The rhetoric virtually buried the substance of Dulles's concern with deterrence through the avoidance of miscalculation and ignored the fact that the concept he had expressed was hardly unique. At the same time, "actual manifestations" of the Dulles diplomacy displayed considerable prudence.

Liberating the "captive peoples" was one thing as a political slogan but quite another matter to carry out. Therefore, when the shortage of food and other grievances led to serious uprisings in East Berlin in 1953, there was no overt American response. Even more dramatically, the Hungarian "freedom fighters" of 1956, temporarily in possession of Budapest, found that their frantic

"Don't Be Afraid—I Can Always Pull You Back"

From Herblock's Special for Today *(Simon & Schuster, 1958)*

appeals for American assistance went unanswered. Nor was there aid for the Polish insurgents a few days earlier. Responding to such crises would, of course, have meant sending Western forces behind the iron curtain and a rather brazen provocation of a major conflict. It was pointed out that military force was never planned as the way to effect liberation.

Willingness to go to the brink did not imply lack of restraint. It did emphasize the need to maintain a position of power and guard against any temptation to weaken Western unification. Therefore, Dulles worked to help frustrate any legitimate progress toward disarmament, even when a Russian proposal presented in London in 1955 apparently complied with previous American demands. Dulles fully expected the Russians to continue to maneuver to throw the West off guard and constantly expected attempts by Moscow to promote a sense of euphoria.

Consistent with his thinking, he expressed strong reservations about the wisdom of having the president meet with the Russians in a summit conference in Geneva in 1955. British political pressures following the replacement of Sir Winston Churchill as prime minister by Anthony Eden ultimately led to the meeting. With general elections scheduled in Great Britain that May, it was politically wise for the incumbents to gain popular favor by arranging for a meeting with the Russians. Contrary to public impressions, Eisenhower was skeptical. The president pointed out to Foreign Minister Harold Macmillan, who was exerting pressure on Washington, that he understood why such a conference would be helpful to British conservatives but the more vehemently anti-Communist American public also had to be considered. In the end, Dulles may even have been somewhat less reluctant than the president, who was not ready to provoke the indignation of his party's right wing.

Once the gathering became inevitable, following the signing of the Austrian peace treaty and a meeting of the foreign ministers, Dulles drew up an advisory memorandum for the president. He warned against permitting the Russians to exploit the conference by establishing moral and social equality with the West. "These gains can be minimized," he wrote, "by the President avoiding social meetings where he will be photographed with Bulganin and Khrushchev, etc., while maintaining an austere countenance on occasions where photographing together is inevitable." Further, publicizing that the United States was using the occasion to "push for satellite liberation and liquidation of international communism"[3] could minimize whatever gains the Kremlin hoped to derive from the conference. Indeed, the subsequent conference with its "spirit of Geneva" afterglow did provide both sides with propaganda opportunities, with the American president unveiling his "open skies" inspection proposal, but it made no real progress toward mitigating cold war conflicts.

◇◇◇

If Geneva's value was illusory, it at least marked the high point of Anglo-American cooperation, an issue that underwent considerable stress during the Dulles years. To begin with, his appointment as secretary of state contradicted advice given to the president by Anthony Eden. British sensitivities had been upset by claims that Dulles had reneged on an agreement to permit the Japanese government the choice of dealing with either of the two Chinas. Instead, Premier Shigeru Yoshida was informed that the United States expected them to side with Chiang Kai-shek. When Dulles arrived in London on his first official trip after the unleashing of Chiang, he found the British press denouncing him as a "double-dealer." Personality differences and continued mutual suspicion further strained the relationship between the two outstanding figures of American and British diplomacy. They exacerbated inherent distinctions between the policies of the two governments and complicated the handling of such matters as the Indochinese crisis of 1954, the dilemma over the Formosa Strait, the problem of the offshore islands of Quemoy and Matsu, and, most dramatically, the Suez Canal affair in 1956.

This was more than just Dulles's policy, for the position of the Eisenhower administration necessarily differed from considerations that underlined both British and French needs. In Indochina, the French had been in the throes of a colonial war since 1946; by the spring of 1954, there could be little doubt of the precariousness of their situation. French Union troops, supported largely by American matériel and financial aid, had been backed into a

3. John Foster Dulles, "Secret Paper #4: Estimate of Proscript of Soviet Union Achieving Its Goals," Dulles additional papers, Princeton.

corner—or, more precisely, into the valley that held their garrison at Dien Bien Phu. That Ho Chi Minh's forces were Communist was largely incidental to the French, who were struggling to salvage whatever bargaining hand they could retain at the Geneva Conference that was scheduled to open on 26 April. If they had to relinquish their colonial holdings, which had become a virtual certainty, they nevertheless wanted to retain economic concessions in the area. The British, with a colony to protect at Hong Kong and with continuing diplomatic and economic relations with the People's Republic of China, were in no position to provoke the Peking government. Opposition from the Labourites in Parliament further complicated matters, particularly since Churchill was expected to retire shortly as prime minister.

The Americans could ill afford to tolerate such considerations. Less than one year earlier, the administration had extricated the country from the Korean War. A combination of threatening the possible use of atomic weapons, a warning delivered by Dulles personally to the Indian prime minister obviously for transmission to Chinese ears, and the changed leadership of the Soviet Union after Stalin's death had facilitated an armistice. Acceptance of the Korean division by the American public, drawn along a line that deviated only slightly from the original thirty-eighth parallel boundary, was widely attributed to Eisenhower's personal prestige and its Republican sponsorship. Even then, the party's right wing, particularly William Knowland, then on the verge of becoming the new Senate majority leader upon Taft's death, was clearly unhappy. Further jeopardizing the administration's ability to fulfill its campaign promise of tough anticommunism was the coincidental timing of the Indochina crisis and the opening of Senate hearings that placed the government squarely against Senator McCarthy.

Moreover, neither Eisenhower nor Dulles operated on assumptions that differed from those inherited from Truman and Acheson. A policy statement drawn up by the National Security Council in early 1952 had linked the nation's security needs in that area to American holdings in the Pacific and such resources as natural rubber and tin as well as petroleum and "other strategically important commodities." To Washington, that made the French effort "essential to the security of the free world, not only in the Far East but in the Middle East and in Europe as well." Eisenhower himself cited such interests; at a governors' conference in Seattle in 1953, he warned that if "we lose Indochina" we would also sacrifice the "tin and tungsten that we so greatly value from that area." He also told a news session that the nations in Southeast Asia were like a "row of dominoes" that would collapse in the face of Communist take-overs of adjacent lands.

Nevertheless, Dulles and Eisenhower were in agreement about the inadvisibility of overt, unilateral American military intervention. All along, Dulles had feared the consequences to Indochina of a Korean settlement, which would free the Chinese to send more help to Ho Chi Minh. An administration that had won popular support in large part through faith in its ability to end the war in Korea could hardly commit American troops to another conflict in that part of the world so soon afterward. As Dulles pointed out privately later that spring, the American public had not been "educated" to undertake a war in Indochina. That was substantially confirmed by a Gallup poll that showed 76 percent of Republicans and 70 percent of Democrats opposed to sending troops. Such a move would also undermine the administration's efforts in behalf of its New Look defense policy that minimized the need for the same conventional forces that would have to be used in any such involvement. Helped by an elaborate analysis contributed by General Matthew Ridgway, Eisenhower also understood the persuasive arguments against fighting a land war in that part of the world.

There was little evidence of Senate support for the use of force. When congressional leaders of both parties were given a confidential briefing that informed them about Admiral Arthur Radford's Operation Vulture scheme calling for American air and naval power to aid Dien Bien Phu, there was general agreement that no such action should be undertaken without England and France. There was also substantial understanding that military power was inappropriate for what was basically a conflict over colonialism. Senator John F. Kennedy drew praise from both sides of the aisle when he stated that conviction in a major speech in the Senate.

Eisenhower and Dulles were determined to salvage the situation by strengthening the Western position before the Geneva Conference and by guarding against French temptation to make a hasty and unfavorable settlement. At the same time, Paris had to be handled carefully because ratification of EDC was still being sought. If nothing could be saved, disassociating Washington from the wreckage could minimize at least political losses.

While still in command of NATO forces, Eisenhower had advised the French to "make this a matter between freedom and communism."[4] At a cabinet meeting during the crisis, Dulles acknowledged that many other countries did not regard communism as the most vital issue. "People have to understand," he added, "that there is something better in the world than just giving up to the Commies. It's a long hard road." Vice-President Nixon had already been dispatched on a tour of the Far East to make a series of speeches emphasizing that the conflict was to uphold the cause of "freedom and independence" and the "liberties of the Indo-Chinese peoples." In April of 1954, the vice-president dramatized the administration's stance by expressing the possibility that American land troops might have to be sent to the area. In other words, there should be no miscalculation of American intentions.

Dulles flew to London to meet with Eden. He found the foreign secretary still opposed to any pre-Geneva statement supporting a joint military strike; but two days of talk did end with a joint communiqué that, to Dulles, represented real progress. Both nations agreed to join with the other countries in "an examination of the possibility of establishing" such a coalition "to assure the peace, security and freedom of Southeast Asia and the Western Pacific." He returned home with the assumption that he had obtained the authority to convene a nine-power conference to form such a coalition, but the British ambassador soon informed him that Eden had forbidden participation by a representative of the United Kingdom in a meeting for that purpose. Dulles was angry, convinced that Eden had reneged. Those who knew Dulles well and understood his powers of persuasion guessed he had left London thoroughly convinced that Eden had bought his arguments. Actually, the communiqué had been ambiguous; it had made no definite statement about a coalition, only one that called for an "examination" of such united action as a "possibility." The French, too, opposed "united action." They wanted to end the war, not broaden it. For them, survival on the battlefield long enough for a decent settlement that preserved their economic interests was different from enlarging a war that was already unpopular at home.

Dulles went to Geneva in 1954 prepared to disassociate the

4. Dwight D. Eisenhower, Dulles Oral History Project, Princeton.

United States from any agreement that recognized the right of communism to exist in a part of Vietnam. Not only did he arrange to leave the sessions early by sending a substitute in his place, but the final draft did not carry an American signature. At the same time, the United States helped to install and support the regime of Ngo Dinh Diem with the aid of covert operations directed by CIA operative Colonel Edward Lansdale. As the Pentagon Papers released in 1971 confirmed, belief that the United States–backed regime in Saigon could not win the elections, scheduled for 1956 in accordance with the agreements made at Geneva, led Washington to support President Diem's successful move to cancel the voting. For Eisenhower and Dulles, it was the only possible solution.

Then, to salvage his attempts at containing communism, Dulles arranged a conference in Manila later in 1954 that resulted in the formation of the Southeast Asia Treaty Organization (SEATO). Providing for collective defenses of the area, it fell short of the NATO-type provision for an integrated military command for instant responses to aggression; but its existence, plus Eisenhower's offer to assist the Diem government "in developing and maintaining a strong, viable state, capable of resisting attempted subversion or aggression through military means," provided the justification for the overt intervention undertaken by subsequent administrations.

Anglo-American relations fared no better over Formosa and Suez. Both contributed substantially to weakening the rapport among the Western allies. In the face of Chinese Communist threats against Quemoy and Matsu, Prime Minister Churchill, fearing a new conflict in the Far East, and one that would be fought over insignificant rocks close to the mainland, thought Chiang Kai-shek's garrisons should evacuate the islands. During repeated threats in that area, however, Dulles intentionally avoided telegraphing the American intent to the People's Republic. His Formosa Resolution that was approved by the president and in the Senate by the lopsided vote of eighty-three to three authorized the president "to employ the forces of the United States as he deems necessary for the specific purpose of securing and protecting Formosa and the Pescadores against armed attack, this authority to include the securing and protecting of such related positions and territories of that area now in friendly hands and the taking of such other measures as he judges to be required or appropriate in assuring the defense of Formosa and the Pescadores." Intentionally left ambiguous were the criteria for deciding what kind of attack would constitute a "threat" to Formosa.

To the British, who had recognized the Peking government in 1950, the American attitude toward mainland China was unduly provocative. When Eisenhower met with Prime Minister Harold Macmillan at Bermuda in 1957, in the presence of Dulles, the president mentioned the strong American opposition to giving the People's Republic of China a seat in the United Nations. So great was that pressure, he added, that the successful seating of Peking might force an American walkout. During that conversation it was Dulles who pointed out that, contrary to the president's words, recent public opinion polls indicated that opinion was becoming more flexible on the issue. Macmillan, impatient with Eisenhower's position, retorted that the Americans seemed willing to throw out the UN when it stopped serving their interests.[5]

Even before that Bermuda meeting, the distinctive considerations behind American policy, as interpreted by Eisenhower and implemented by Dulles, had subjected the Atlantic alliance to its most severe blow. As had been the case during the war scare brought on by the 1954 Indochina crisis, Dulles again became the villain in the piece: he was blamed for undermining the British response in the Middle East and creating the crisis there, and it was his arrogance toward President Nasser's ambassador to Washington that prompted Egyptian nationalization of the Suez Canal. The subsequent part played by the United States in ending the rash Anglo-French and Israeli invasion of Egypt to retrieve the canal seemingly vindicated the hostile perceptions of Dulles's influence.

That interpretation simply gave too much credit to the secretary of state. At the same time, it minimized the president's active involvement in the affair. In the Middle East, as in Western Europe and the Far East, the administration's continuation of the containment policy meant drawing a sharp line against Communist expansion. Complicating such a maneuver, of course, was the real problem of nationalism and what was referred to as the "neutralist" attitude of the nonaligned nations. An additional

5. Memorandum of Conversation, 24 March 1957, Dulles papers, Princeton.

element of risk came from Arab-Israeli tensions. Washington
therefore had to navigate a delicate course between Russia's
desires for influence in that area, Arab oil holdings that involved
the interests of American corporations, and Nasser's ambitions;
moreover, the administration had to contend with an electorate
that reflected significant support for Israel. To prop up the region's
anti-Russian proclivities, Dulles inspired what ultimately became
known as the Baghdad Pact. That mutual defense agreement
included Great Britain, Pakistan, and Iran in addition to the
original members, Iraq and Turkey. Unfortunately, it only created
new problems. Egypt feared the pact would make Iraq dominant
and the Soviet Union was thereby challenged to find new ways of
penetrating the Middle East. As the Nasser regime drew closer to
the Russians, the Egyptian position became more ominous and led
to the American agreement to join with the British in helping
Cairo to finance the construction of a dam at Aswan on the Nile
River. Its purpose was to create hydroelectric power and new
arable land for a rapidly increasing population.

Nasser, however, resented Anglo-American provisions that
limited Egyptian expenditures for other major enterprises; the
British, anxious to placate Iraq in order to preserve the security of
two air bases in that country, bore the brunt of the resentment felt
by Egypt's chief Moslem rival toward the deal being prepared for
Nasser. Further, Nasser's actions became increasingly offensive to
Washington. Not only did the Cairo government recognize the
Chinese Communist regime, but Egyptian agents worked throughout the Middle East against rulers in Libya, Lebanon, Jordan, Iraq,
and Saudi Arabia. Congressional anger grew when Nasser purchased additional weapons from the Soviet bloc and considered
accepting a large interest-free loan from Russia. Fears that newly
irrigated lands along the Nile would eventually produce long-
staple cotton in competition with domestic growers fueled the
growing antipathy toward United States financing of the dam.

It was not, then, merely that Egypt's policies had so offended
the Dulles concept of morality that led the secretary to greet
Nasser's ambassador with the information, just when Cairo had
agreed to accept the money, that the loan was no longer available.
More accurately, the positions of both the British and the
Americans had changed. As Eden reports in his memoirs, he and
Foreign Secretary Selwyn Lloyd had already decided that they

HERBERT S. PARMET

"could not go on with a project likely to become increasingly onerous in finance and unsatisfactory in practice."

Eisenhower, not his secretary of state, considered a change in policy essential and led the way to its realization. At a meeting of the National Security Council at Camp David, he expressed doubts about the loan. Dulles also agreed that negotiations over the dam should be terminated. The members of the NSC approved the president's subsequent decision to cancel the offer.[6] This occurred before Dulles met with Nasser's emissary. Therefore, despite notions that became popular, the secretary did not precipitously fling the offer back to the ambassador just because the Egyptian had announced that the Russians were also willing to help. The subsequent nationalization of the Suez Canal, moreover, was a move that Nasser himself later admitted had been under discussion for two years. Considering that monitored telephone calls showed that the Egyptians also knew about the decision on the loan beforehand, there is ample reason to believe that Nasser used or even provoked the incident for his own purpose.

Aware of British and French fears that Nasser had the ability to close the canal at will and thus cut off the flow of oil to Western Europe, Eisenhower and Dulles labored feverishly to prevent or at least to delay any military action. The Israelis were also ready to exploit the situation, because Egyptian *fedayeen* raiders were harassing the tiny nation from Gaza Strip bases. Of particular embarrassment would be the start of a war in the Middle East just before the presidential elections in the United States. Eisenhower, mindful of his cooperation with Eden's domestic political needs when he had agreed to go to Geneva in 1955, informed the prime minister of the folly of impetuous action and said that American public opinion "would be outraged" if there were no efforts to solve the crisis by peaceful means. Dulles then fulfilled his mission by pressing London to delay hasty action. To keep the British and French hopeful, he dangled before them the prospect of American cooperation in the use of force if all other solutions failed. When the diplomatic effort collapsed and a concerted British-French-Israeli invasion began just before the 1956 elections, and without any prior notification to Washington, Eisenhower would have nothing to do with it. Instead, publicly and privately, he worked to

6. Dillon Anderson, Dulles Oral History, Princeton.

stop the invasion. General Andrew Goodpaster, then the president's staff secretary, has confirmed that Dulles merely worked within the parameters established by Eisenhower. By the time the president got the three nations to terminate their thrust just short of their goal (with the help of a threatened Soviet intervention), Dulles was already confined to Walter Reed Hospital for the removal of a cancerous growth.

Ten days after Eisenhower's landslide reelection, Selwyn Lloyd and Sir Harold Caccia, the new British ambassador to Washington, visited Dulles at his bedside.

"Once you started, why didn't you go through with it and get Nasser down?" Dulles asked.

"Foster," replied Lloyd, "why didn't you give us a wink?"

"Oh!" answered Dulles. "I couldn't do anything like *that!*" [7]

◇◇◇

Dulles's diplomacy substantiates the conclusion that his own accomplishments were more noteworthy for holding the line than for new departures. His rhetoric masked the continuation of Truman's policies. Contradicting his own convictions about flexibility and the hope for change within the Communist world, Dulles's policies succumbed to domestic considerations and ignored the deterioration of so-called monolithic international communism. That approach certainly did nothing to relieve tensions. Some of his positions, particularly regarding disarmament, intentionally opposed the kind of rapprochement that was the objective of those American businessmen who wanted economic relations with the Communist world. From those quarters, there was annoyance that he had so little appreciation of the value of trade with the East. Without access to Soviet sources, it is virtually impossible to conclude that greater congeniality would have mitigated the cold war at that stage. Blaming Dulles for its perpetuation simplifies the problems; but one thing seems certain: he mobilized support for the Eisenhower presidency even from among the Republican party's most zealous cold warriors. The importance of that accomplishment should not be underestimated.

7. Herman Finer, *Dulles over Suez* (Chicago, 1964), p. 446; Hugh Thomas, *Suez* (New York, 1966), p. 147.

BIBLIOGRAPHIC NOTE

Much has already been written about the Eisenhower-Dulles era, but future studies of Dulles will follow the availability of his papers now stored at the Dwight D. Eisenhower Library in Abilene, Kansas. Of particular value, especially to those interested in unraveling the intricacies of the Dulles-Eisenhower relationship, will be the extensive files of cables from the secretary to the president. At present, researchers may use papers at the Princeton University Library that offer insights into both Dulles's thought and personal makeup; until more diplomatic material is released, much will continue to depend on the large number of contributions in the Dulles Oral History Project at Princeton. Additionally, both Columbia University and the Dwight D. Eisenhower Library have transcripts of the interviews from the Eisenhower Oral History Project.

For an understanding of Dulles, the student should begin by reading Louis L. Gerson's *John Foster Dulles* (New York, 1968). The book, which is part of the American Secretaries of State series, is without interpretive distinction but written with clarity and offers a useful chronicle. *The Time of Power: A Reappraisal of John Foster Dulles*, by Richard Goold-Adams (London, 1962), remains a worthwhile critique despite the absence of citations. Norman Graebner, *The New Isolationism* (New York, 1956), offers a critical analysis of the administration's earlier diplomacy. Intent on minimizing Dulles as a moralist and upgrading his diplomatic abilities is Michael Guhin's *John Foster Dulles: A Statesman and His Times* (New York, 1972). Two books by contemporary journalists, John R. Beal, *John Foster Dulles*, rev. ed. (New York, 1959), and Roscoe Drummond and Gaston Coblentz, *Duel at the Brink* (Garden City, N.Y., 1960), are limited but cannot be dismissed. A small but annotated sample of Dulles's own views on a variety of issues is available in a book by one of his press secretaries, Andrew H. Berding, *Dulles on Diplomacy* (Princeton, 1965). Eleanor Lansing Dulles has offered a humanizing and poignant account of his final struggle in *John Foster Dulles: The Last Year* (New York, 1963).

Dulles's most accessible writings are two books and several articles: *War, Peace and Change* (New York, 1939) and *War or Peace* (New York, 1950); "A Policy of Boldness," *Life* (19 May 1952) 146–60; "Policy for Security and Peace," *Foreign Affairs* (April 1954), 353–64; and "Challenges and Response in United States Policy," *Foreign Affairs* (October 1957), 25–43.

Many works examine the domestic setting against which Dulles worked. A book that is both a comprehensive view of the administration and a scholarly treatment of the political factors is Herbert S. Parmet, *Eisenhower and the American Crusades* (New York, 1972), from which has been drawn the bulk of the material for this essay. Arthur Larson's *Eisenhower: The President Nobody Knew* (New York, 1968) is a contribution by a White House staff member that does much to alter views of the Eisenhower-Dulles partnership that the president's detractors favored. A highly jaundiced view of Dulles by an insider is Emmet J. Hughes, *The Ordeal of Power* (New York, 1963). Indispensable although tedious and burdened by committee authorship are the two volumes that comprise Dwight D. Eisenhower's *The White House Years* (Garden City, N.Y., 1963, 1965). Fairly sensational at the time of its publication for its use of material provided by the administration was Robert J. Donovan's *Eisenhower: The Inside Story* (New York, 1956). Richard Rovere's *Affairs of State: The Eisenhower Years* (New York, 1956) is a collection of contemporary observations by a liberal journalist. I. F. Stone, *The Haunted Fifties* (New York, 1963), offers more critical and incisive views. Marquis Childs's *Eisenhower: Captive Hero* (New York, 1958) was the first significant evaluation not marred by sentimentality for the general in the White House. Garry Wills, *Nixon Agonistes* (Boston, 1970), is a pungent treatment that says much about Eisenhower and his vice-president. Most useful among the contributions by insiders, despite limited candor, are Sherman Adams, *First-Hand Report* (New York, 1961), and Richard M. Nixon, *Six Crises* (Garden City, N. Y., 1962). Two magazine articles that deserve particular attention are William V. Shannon, "Eisenhower as President," *Commentary* (November 1958), 390–98; and Murray Kempton, "The Underestimation of Dwight D. Eisenhower," *Esquire* (September 1967), 108.

A rapidly growing volume of analyses of the cold war provide useful insights into the Dulles era. Most worthwhile are Walter LaFeber, *America, Russia, and the Cold War, 1945–1966* (New York, 1967), Louis J. Halle, *The Cold War as History* (New York, 1967), Stephen Ambrose, *Rise to Globalism* (Baltimore, 1971), and Seyom Brown, *The Faces of Power* (New York, 1967). Traditional arguments supporting the American role may be found in Walt W. Rostow's *The United States in the World Arena* (New York, 1960) and in his *The Diffusion of Power, 1957–1972* (New York, 1972). More critical views are in Richard J. Barnet, *Intervention and Revolution* (New York, 1968), and Ronald Steel, *Pax Americana* (New York, 1967).

Personal memoirs by foreign and American diplomats help to round out the picture. See, in particular, Sir Anthony Eden, *Full Circle* (London, 1960), Harold Macmillan's *Tides of Fortune* and *Riding the Storm* (New York, 1969, 1971), George F. Kennan, *Memoirs, 1950–1963* (Boston, 1972), and Robert Murphy, *Diplomat among Warriors* (Garden City, N.Y., 1964). Milton S. Eisenhower's *The Wine Is Bitter* (Garden City, N.Y., 1963) is both compassionate and perceptive in viewing conditions relating to Latin America.

THE EDUCATION OF

JOHN F. KENNEDY

John F. Kennedy Library

Robert A. Divine

It was no accident that the cold war reached its height in the administration of John F. Kennedy, the youngest American ever to hold the office of president. Despite his sophistication and graceful style, Kennedy sincerely believed in the cold war shibboleths that men like Dean Acheson and John Foster Dulles had been voicing for a decade and a half. He was convinced that Russia directly threatened the security of the United States (Khrushchev really meant to bury us) and that only a tough, determined American response, grounded in military superiority, could ensure the nation's survival. In the course of his tragically short term in office, Kennedy's attempts to substantiate these beliefs brought the world to the brink of nuclear war and engulfed the United States in the Vietnam quagmire. Yet during his last year in the White House, JFK showed signs that he had learned that arms and will alone were not enough to master world affairs, that the qualities of human understanding and concern for mankind

621

might be equally important. In that sense, the education of John F. Kennedy not only broadened the horizon of one man; it also opened the way for his successors to move beyond the cold war.

◇◇◇

Like all of us, Kennedy was a prisoner of his own past. In spring 1939, while a junior at Harvard, he had undertaken a grand tour of Europe. Through the good offices of his father, Joseph P. Kennedy, then ambassador to England, he had had a chance to observe diplomatic developments in Paris, Berlin, Warsaw, and Leningrad firsthand on the eve of World War II. He returned to the United States after the outbreak of fighting in September and then drew upon his experiences to write an honors thesis in political science entitled "Appeasement at Munich." Though he avoided his father's isolationist belief that Europe was doomed, he condemned England for permitting Hitler to rearm and then to outmaneuver the democracies at Munich. National weakness led to the inevitable surrender of Czechoslovakia to Germany, Kennedy argued, implying that security for any country rested on superior military force and a willingness to use it. With the help of his father and a family friend, Arthur Krock, Kennedy published a revised version of the thesis in the summer of 1940 under the timely title *Why England Slept*. Americans bought forty thousand copies of the slim volume, which offered both a facile explanation of Hitler's astonishing success and this advice to the United States: "We should profit by the lesson of England and make our democracy work. We must make it work right now."

The onset of the cold war served only to sharpen and intensify Kennedy's commitment to a philosophy of force. Winning election to Congress in 1946 on the basis of his attractive personality, fine war record, and family name, he soon criticized the Truman administration for failing to wage the struggle against communism with sufficient vigor. In January 1949, he rose on the floor of the House to condemn the State Department for "losing" China to the Communists repeating the familiar right-wing attack on FDR's Yalta Agreements by charging, "What our young men had saved, our diplomats and our President have frittered away." Kennedy cast votes for the Truman Doctrine and the Marshall Plan, but he had reservations about Point Four and economic aid for development, and when Truman sought to cut back on defense spending in 1949, Kennedy countered by demanding a seventy-group air force and a stepped-up civil defense program. At the same time, he opposed the export of strategic goods to Communist China, calling it "trade in blood." Despite his concern with Asia, he remained European oriented, defending the administration's plan to station troops on the Continent against Republican demands for withdrawal and warning after the outbreak of the Korean War against neglect of NATO, for that could lead to "a major disaster in Western Europe." The lesson of Munich continued to dominate Kennedy's thinking; he joined millions of Americans in transferring the tragic experience with Hitler's Germany to the confrontation with Stalin's Russia.

As cold war attitudes hardened in the 1950s, Kennedy showed few signs of dissatisfaction with the prevailing consensus. He did try to modify Eisenhower's Formosa Strait Resolution in 1954, hoping to avoid a commitment to defend the offshore islands of Quemoy and Matsu, and in 1957 he delivered a stinging indictment of the French refusal to grant independence to the Algerians. Kennedy's record on Vietnam was mixed. He criticized the French conduct of the war against Ho Chi Minh's guerrillas after two trips to Indochina in the early 1950s, but he joined Eisenhower and Dulles in supporting the Diem regime. In a speech in Washington on 1 June 1956, Kennedy, now a senator, declared that Vietnam represented "the cornerstone of the Free World in Southeast Asia, the keystone to the arch, the finger in the dike," and prophesied that if "the Red tide of Communism" flowed into Vietnam, "Burma, Thailand, India, Japan, the Philippines and obviously Laos and Cambodia" would be endangered. His deepest concern, once again, lay with the state of America's defenses. Alarmed by the Soviet *Sputnik* and Russian progress in developing an intercontinental ballistic missile, JFK warned in 1958 that by the early 1960s "the deterrent ratio might well shift to the Soviets so heavily . . . as to open to them a new shortcut to world domination." Kennedy urged Eisenhower to take heroic measures to close the missile gap, reminding him that "our experiences with the illogical decisions of Adolf Hitler" should have taught us the need to be on guard against totalitarian leaders. When Stuart Symington asked if Kennedy were comparing America in the 1950s to Britain in the 1930s, JFK replied, "The Senator is completely correct."

Kennedy was convinced that Eisenhower had let the United States drift dangerously in world affairs and in his campaign for

the presidency he adopted the slogan "Let's get moving again."
Dramatic events in 1960 seemed to confirm Kennedy's diagnosis.
In May, the Russians shot down a U-2 spy plane on the eve of the
Paris Summit Conference and when Eisenhower took full responsibility for the overflight but refused to announce cancellation of
future missions, Khrushchev called off the summit meeting with
an angry tirade that signaled an ominous deepening of the cold
war.

In the next few months, a sense of despair developed in
America as rioting students forced Ike to cancel a planned trip to
Japan, violence and near chaos overtook the newly independent
Congo, and Fidel Castro moved Cuba into the Communist orbit.
Nikita Khrushchev dominated American headlines; he declared
the Monroe Doctrine "dead," accused the United States of
"piracy" when the Russians shot down a second American
reconnaissance plane, and shocked the entire world with his
antics at the United Nations meeting in New York, particularly
when he took off his shoe and thumped it on his desk to express
his contempt for the West. Ignoring the advice of political experts,
Kennedy harped on foreign policy issues to drive home his belief
that the Republicans had failed to preserve America's leadership in
the world. "The harsh facts of the matter are that our security and
leadership are both slipping away from us," Kennedy charged at
the outset of the campaign, claiming that "the balance of world
power is slowly shifting to the Soviet-Red-Chinese bloc."

During the fall campaign against Vice-President Richard
Nixon, Kennedy made two serious foreign policy slips. The first
came during an interview with Chet Huntley, when Kennedy said
that the United States ought to urge Chiang Kai-shek to withdraw
from Quemoy and Matsu, describing the islands as indefensible.
In the second of four televised debates, Nixon jumped on this
remark to accuse Kennedy of advocating a policy of retreat and
withdrawal. Furious at being backed into a corner, Kennedy tried
to clarify his position, but finally he simply let the issue drop when
he realized that he had surrendered the initiative to Nixon, an
even more ardent cold warrior than Kennedy in 1960. Kennedy's
second mistake came on 20 October, when his aides released a
statement on Cuba advocating support of "fighters for freedom"
who were struggling to overthrow Castro's regime. When Nixon,
adroitly shifting to a soft line, accused Kennedy of proposing to
violate American treaty commitments and engage in naked aggres-

sion, JFK again backed away with the limp excuse that his position
had been misunderstood.

At best, foreign policy contributed only marginally to Kennedy's narrow victory in November. Dissatisfaction with declining
American prestige in the world, deepened by the release of secret
USIA public opinion polls taken abroad, undoubtedly won Kennedy many votes, but his inept handling of the offshore island and
Cuban issues probably cost him just as many. More importantly,
Kennedy's actions suggested the dangers of electing so young and
inexperienced a man to the presidency at a time of grave world
crisis. His brash promise of support for the Cuban exiles and his
tactless challenge to Ike's wise policy of ambiguity on Quemoy
and Matsu raised serious questions about his leadership in world
affairs. His rhetoric provoked even greater doubts. His constant
reference to a world divided between freedom and slavery
signaled a determination to escalate the cold war, as did the
repeated call to increase America's military strength. The man who
warned the American people that "the only thing that will deter
Mr. Khrushchev from loosing his hounds of hell on us will be a
strong America" was now president, with the power not only to
get America moving again but also to blow up the entire globe.

◇◇◇

Once in the White House, Kennedy set out to revitalize
American foreign policy. He combed the ranks of the "Eastern
Establishment" to find bright, dynamic men in the universities,
foundations, and Wall Street law firms to replace the businessmen
that Eisenhower had relied upon to lead the nation. Aided by
Robert Lovett, Truman's secretary of defense (and the personifica-
tion of the eastern internationalist elite) who declined a cabinet
position on the grounds of ill health, Kennedy assembled an
apparently brilliant team: Robert McNamara, the whiz kid who
had risen to the presidency of the Ford Motor Company by
applying techniques of systems analysis, as secretary of defense;
McGeorge Bundy, the intelligent and supremely self-confident
dean of the Harvard faculty, as national security adviser; Walt
Rostow, MIT economic historian who had suggested the phrase
"Let's get moving again" and who displayed a tough-minded
approach to the cold war, as Bundy's deputy; and Maxwell Taylor,
the intellectuals' favorite general who had fought a losing war

against the Eisenhower-Dulles massive retaliation policy, as military adviser to the president and later chairman of the Joint Chiefs of Staff. The only lesser light was Secretary of State Dean Rusk, a deliberate, thoughtful man with proven bureaucratic skill, an inclination to defer to the military, and a streak of innate caution that led contemporaries to characterize him as an ideal subordinate without the stuff of command. Kennedy's choice of Rusk seemed a clear sign that he intended to formulate and conduct foreign policy himself.

The "New Frontiersmen" shared one vital quality: they all believed that the world was pliable and that, in the words of David Halberstam, they "could manage and control events, in an intelligent, rational way." They all assumed a tough, pragmatic style, thinking of themselves as "can-do" operators who had the courage, brains, and determination to meet the Soviet challenge and overcome it. Kennedy epitomized this new approach to world problems. He was cool and detached, rising above the moral concerns that inhibited Adlai Stevenson and contemptuous of the softness of so many American liberals. His warm smile and youthful vitality gave him an appealing public image, but reporters who observed him closely noted his aloofness, his refusal to become emotionally involved with either issues or personalities, and quickly dubbed him "Jack the Knife." His sense of irony served him especially well; he could stand back and examine himself critically, aware of his own shortcomings and the very real limits on his power. His wry sense of humor distinguished him from humorless men like Bundy and McNamara and gave him a humility that saved him from their arrogance.

Kennedy's first presidential speeches indicated that he fully intended to live up to his campaign rhetoric. In the inaugural address he and Theodore Sorensen prepared, Kennedy repeated his belief that Russia threatened the very existence of the United States ("Only a few generations have been granted the role of defending freedom in its hour of maximum danger") and reiterated his intention of relying on superior military force ("Only when our arms are sufficient beyond doubt can we be certain beyond doubt that they will never be used"). Ten days later, in his State of the Union address, he painted an even more chilling picture of the world. In each critical area he had examined "the tide of events has been running out. . . . time has not been our

friend," he warned. He identified the Soviet Union and Communist China as the twin dangers facing the Republic, asserting that
neither Communist nation "had yielded its ambitions for world
domination." In words that revealed he was still haunted by
Munich, he declared, "Our task is to convince them that aggression and subversion will not be profitable routes to pursue these
ends."

◇◇◇

The problems facing the new president were enough to
stagger the wisest and most experienced statesman; Kennedy's
belief that he could manage them was yet another sign of
immaturity. In Africa, prompt action by the United Nations, under
the skilled leadership of Secretary-General Dag Hammarskjöld,
had helped restore a measure of order to the explosive Congo,
where the death of Patrice Lumumba had eased fear of a
Communist take-over. The chief threat now came from Moise
Tshombe, leader of the mineral-rich province of Katanga, who
attempted to assert his independence with the backing of European mining interests. Closer to home, Fidel Castro had forced
President Eisenhower to break off diplomatic relations in early
January by insisting that the American embassy staff be reduced
drastically. Kennedy and his advisers feared that Castro and "Che"
Guevara intended to spread their revolution to other Latin
American states; at the very least, Cuba seemed to be a model for
other nations unhappy with the traditional United States hegemony in the Western Hemisphere. In Southeast Asia, the Viet Cong
were waging an increasingly successful guerrilla war against the
Diem regime, whose large American-trained army had been
created to meet an overt invasion from the north, not to fight a
brush-fire war. The situation appeared to be much more critical in
Laos, the tiny country where the Eisenhower administration had
sponsored a right-wing overthrow of neutralist leader Souvanna
Phouma in 1958 only to provoke a Communist counterattack that
threatened to engulf the entire country. In Berlin, tension had
been building since Nikita Khrushchev first announced plans to
sign a separate peace treaty with East Germany in 1958 and thus
undermine Western access rights to the city. The Soviets had
delayed further action after the abortive Paris summit until the

American elections were over; now Kennedy would have to decide how to deal with the Russian insistence that, after sixteen years, the victors of World War II resolve the German problem.

Historians have tended to treat Kennedy's policies toward these crucial issues separately, taking them up one by one and thereby ignoring how they impinged on each other. Yet the only way to understand these crises is to see them as Kennedy did, as interrelated phenomena that came to him intertwined, never permitting time for calm, deliberate judgment. In the first eight months, JFK dealt simultaneously with Cuba, Berlin, and Southeast Asia, and his policies culminated in a major nuclear war scare in the summer of 1961 that served as a precursor to the more famous Cuban missile crisis of the following year.

The hallmark of Kennedy's early behavior in office was a lack of prudence. As a young, bright, but inexperienced president, he tried to deal quickly and pragmatically with these desperately complicated and dangerous issues, hoping to register immediate gains and thus establish his credentials with Nikita Khrushchev. He ignored the advice of moralists, men like Undersecretary of State Chester Bowles, Senate Foreign Relations Committee Chairman J. William Fulbright, and UN Ambassador Adlai Stevenson, who tried to point out the long-run consequences of Kennedy's contemplated actions. Bowles left the State Department in November; Stevenson quicky found himself without any effective influence on administration policy and began to suspect, quite rightly, that he was being used to divert world attention from Kennedy's hard-line actions; Fulbright continued to be consulted, but his advice was disregarded with monotonous regularity. Instead the realists, led by Bundy, Rostow, and McNamara, dominated the administration's inner councils and reinforced Kennedy's own hawkish inclinations. The president and his advisers simply did not have any patience with the long-winded, moralistic objections of the idealists; the world was on fire, and they had to rush to put out the flames.

The acquisition of power gave Kennedy access to information that did not always confirm his prior beliefs. In the first few weeks in office, he and McNamara discovered that the missile gap was an illusion; far from trailing the Soviets in strategic striking power, the United States was opening up an impressive lead. At the time of the inauguration, America had more than one hundred ICBMs, compared with less than fifty for Russia; nearly seventeen hundred long-range bombers to the Soviet Union's one hundred fifty; and eighty Polaris missiles on board five nuclear submarines, while the Russians had none. After studying the figures, the forthright McNamara told reporters on 6 February that there was no missile gap, only to have the White House issue an immediate denial. Two days later, John F. Kennedy informed the press that it was "premature to reach a judgment" on the issue, thus deliberately keeping from the American people the fact that a gap existed in reverse. In the course of the next few months, Kennedy sent three messages to Congress requesting a total increase of six billion dollars in defense spending, a major portion designated for strategic weapons. As a result, by the time of Kennedy's death, the United States had opened up an enormous lead over the Soviet Union in ICBMs and Polaris missiles, creating a dangerous imbalance in the arms race that insured a massive Soviet effort to catch up. The huge nuclear arms buildup of the sixties, which culminated in the ABM, the MIRV, and the SS-9, thus became Kennedy's grimmest legacy.

Kennedy made an equally significant decision in regard to Cuba in his first few weeks in office. Shortly after the election, CIA Director Allen Dulles informed Kennedy of the plan Eisenhower had approved earlier in 1960 to train a group of Cuban exiles in Central America and help them invade Cuba to overthrow the Castro regime. In late January 1961, Kennedy told Dulles to go ahead with the CIA plan, which at that time called for a landing near the Escambray Mountains in south-central Cuba. The plan underwent numerous revisions in the next two months, until finally the landing site was changed to the Bay of Pigs, some eighty miles from the mountains, which were to serve as a sanctuary for the exiles if the invasion failed. Chester Bowles and William Fulbright opposed the scheme; the latter told Kennedy that he had permitted his hatred of Fidel to cloud his judgment. "The Castro regime is a thorn in the flesh," Fulbright said, "but it is not a dagger in the heart." Even Dean Acheson, a superhawk, was appalled, calling it "a wild idea." Kennedy could not forget his campaign promises to help free Cuba and listened instead to the CIA and the Joint Chiefs, who approved the plan without giving it the rigorous analysis it deserved.

Some fourteen hundred brave but misguided exiles splashed ashore on the morning of 17 April. Castro responded decisively; he used his air power to gain control of the skies and sank several support ships. The next day his militiamen quickly overcame the lingering resistance of the survivors and took over one thousand prisoners. Arthur Schlesinger, Jr., sat glumly in the nearly deserted naval air base at Opa-Locka, on the outskirts of Miami, explaining to the leaders of Free Cuba why the United States could not intervene to save their comrades at the Bay of Pigs. Meanwhile, Dean Rusk told the press that the United States was not "intervening in Cuba" and Lem Jones, a New York public relations man, issued press releases in the name of the "Cuban Revolutionary Council" declaring that the "action today was largely of a supply and support effort" and calling upon the Cuban people to rise up in "a coordinated wave of sabotage and rebellion." John Kennedy ruefully admitted that "we will be kicked in the can for the next couple of weeks," but he took the long view, adding, "but that won't affect the main business."

The main business was the cold war with the Soviet Union, and on 19 April Kennedy dispatched a reply to Khrushchev's angry note pledging "all necessary assistance to Castro." The United States, Kennedy informed the Russian leader, had no intention of invading Cuba, but if any foreign power sent troops into the hemisphere, "we will immediately honor our obligations under the inter-American system to protect this hemisphere against external aggression." The events in Cuba, the president explained, simply indicated the growing restiveness of the Cuban people under Castro's dictatorial rule and then concluded, "The great revolution in the history of man, past, present, and future, is the revolution of those determined to be free." Kennedy was equally belligerent in a speech to the American Society of Newspaper Editors on 20 April. He took full responsibility for the fiasco, but at the same time he did not retreat an inch. He repeated his determination to prevent further "communist penetration" in the Western Hemisphere and then stated his personal conclusion from the Bay of Pigs tragedy: "Only the strong, only the industrious, only the determined, only the courageous, only the visionary who determine the real nature of our struggle can possibly survive." The lesson of the Cuban disaster, according to Kennedy, was that harder work, greater sacrifice, and heavier reliance on military force were necessary to win the cold war. In other words, the only thing wrong at the Bay of Pigs was that the United States did not do enough to defeat the Communists.

Kennedy moved quickly to apply this analysis to Indochina.

Laos remained the most crucial spot in the early months of the Kennedy administration as the neutralist forces of Kong-le joined with the Communist Pathet Lao against the American-supported government of Phoumi Nosavan, gaining control of the strategic Plain of Jars in February and beating back a government counterattack in April. Determined to stand firm after the Bay of Pigs, Kennedy ordered CIA advisers in Laos to don American uniforms and called an emergency session of the National Security Council. The Joint Chiefs of Staff opposed a civilian suggestion for a quick airborne strike against the Plain of Jars; remembering Korea, they insisted that if the United States intervened in Laos, it should do so with at least two hundred fifty thousand men and the willingness to use nuclear weapons if China or the Soviet Union entered the conflict. Sobered by this advice, Kennedy began to consider the alternative of diplomatic negotiation to achieve a neutral Laos. At a White House luncheon in May, General Douglas MacArthur reinforced Kennedy's growing doubts by stating bluntly that the U.S. should not "put one American soldier on the continent of Asia—we couldn't win a fight in Asia." (At the same luncheon, the general told the president with evident relish, "All the chickens are coming home to roost and you are living in the coop.") By mid-May, Kennedy had decided against using force and instead sent Averell Harriman to Geneva to work out a diplomatic solution. Harriman helped arrange for a new coalition government under Souvanna Phouma in October, and in July 1962 the United States signed an international agreement at Geneva to guarantee the neutrality of Laos. In succeeding years, both sides violated the terms as the Pathet Lao and the CIA-controlled Laotian army continued to skirmish, but at least Kennedy had avoided full-scale American military involvement in a remote area.

The president's relative softness on Laos undoubtedly contributed to the firmer position he took on South Vietnam. When he assumed office, he had renewed the Eisenhower administration's commitment to the Diem regime, despite growing signs that the people of South Vietnam were more responsive to the National Liberation Front and its Viet Cong guerrillas. A staunch believer in the domino thesis, Kennedy saw Vietnam as far more than just a struggle for one country or even one region. He viewed the violence there as a crucial test of the concept of wars of national liberation which Khrushchev had announced as the new Communist tactic for world control in a January speech. The entire third world, which held the balance of power between the East and the West, was at stake, thereby justifying a major American effort in Vietnam.

The president made his first significant move on 29 April 1961, when he approved recommendations by Walt Rostow to send Vice-President Lyndon Johnson to Saigon and to authorize one hundred additional American military advisers in South Vietnam, thus violating the limits set by the Geneva Agreement of 1954. On 11 May the president adopted revised recommendations of a special task force on Vietnam which included the dispatch of four hundred Special Forces troops (the Green Berets) and the beginning of covert operations against North Vietnam: infiltration, sabotage, commando raids, and even occasional air attacks. The official goal, stated in the highly secret National Security Council memorandum 52, was "to prevent Communist domination of South Vietnam" and "to create in that country a viable and increasingly democratic society." Thus, Kennedy committed the United States to participation in a bloody civil war in the mistaken belief that American vital interests were directly involved.

The president made the decision despite the advice of more experienced world leaders. Not only did General MacArthur warn him against committing American forces on the mainland of Asia, but Charles de Gaulle offered a prophetic view of what that participation would mean. "For you," he told Kennedy on 31 May, "intervention in this region will be an entanglement without end." He went on to cite the French experience in Indochina and said the Americans could not escape the same fate. "I predict to you," de Gaulle declared, "that you will, step by step, be sucked into a bottomless military and political quagmire despite the losses and expenditures that you may squander." Kennedy listened to the old man politely, but the words had no effect. His exposure to world affairs, from Munich on, told him that the only thing that aggressive dictators understood was superior force and the courage to use it. He had failed to stand firm on Cuba and Laos; he felt he must draw the line at Vietnam.

In mid-May, just as Kennedy was making his initial commitment to defend South Vietnam, Khrushchev suggested that the two men hold a summit conference in Vienna in early June. The president, eager to dispel any notions of his softness after the Bay of Pigs, quickly accepted and agreed to an agenda limited to Laos, the issue of nuclear testing, and Berlin. When the two met on 3

June, Khrushchev immediately took the offensive, asserting the Marxist thesis that communism was bound to triumph in the third world and insisting that wars of national liberation were the result of revolutionary nationalism, not Soviet diplomacy. Taken off guard by the ferocity of Khrushchev's attack, Kennedy replied by stating that the responsibility of both superpowers lay in maintaining the existing world balance and avoiding direct confrontations that might lead to nuclear war. Turning from ideological issues, the two leaders discussed Laos and nuclear testing without reaching any agreement and then took up the far more urgent question of Berlin.

Kennedy came well prepared on Germany. In March he had asked Dean Acheson to canvass the European situation and give him recommendations on Berlin. Predictably, Acheson rejected the idea of a negotiated settlement, arguing that the status quo of a divided Germany suited American interests. If the Russians tried to change the situation, the United States should respond with a series of measures, beginning with a new airlift and ranging from the use of conventional forces to a willingness to participate in a nuclear exchange. Acheson did not think such a showdown likely; he saw Berlin as a test of will in which a firm American stance would force the Russians to back down, as they had in 1949. At Vienna, Khrushchev renewed his request for negotiations, and when Kennedy refused to enter into talks once again imposed a six-month deadline, saying he intended to sign a peace treaty with East Germany at that time and turn over Berlin access rights to the Democratic Republic of Germany. Kennedy declared that the United States would insist on asserting its wartime rights in Berlin regardless of such a treaty; Khrushchev replied, "I want peace, but if you want war, that is your problem."

"It is you, and not I, who wants to force a change," Kennedy answered.

On that somber note the talks ended.

Instead of easing the cold war, the Vienna meeting escalated it. Berlin had become a test of will for both sides. Adamantly refusing the negotiations Khrushchev wanted, Kennedy tried to escape from the awful choice of surrender or nuclear war that had always confronted American leaders dealing with an isolated Berlin. He sought a way out by strengthening American conventional forces in Europe, and in a dramatic broadcast to the American people on 25 July he spelled out his program. Denying

Daily Mirror Newspapers Ltd., London

Franklin in The London Daily Mirror

that the city was indefensible ("And so was Bastogne. And so, in fact, was Stalingrad. Any dangerous spot is tenable if men—brave men—will make it so"), Kennedy asked Congress for an additional 3.5 billion dollars in defense funds, authority to increase the armed services by nearly three hundred fifty thousand men, and permission to call up one hundred fifty thousand reservists to active duty. Then he announced plans for a sweeping civil defense program to protect the nation against a nuclear attack. "In the coming months," Kennedy informed the American people, "I hope to let every citizen know what steps he can take without delay to protect his family in case of attack." He thereby touched off a mania for home fallout shelters that brought out the worst rather than the best in the American character (a rush for profits by overnight promoters, the purchase of guns to keep less fortunate neighbors out of a patriot's backyard shelter).

The message to Khrushchev was clear: the United States would fight a nuclear war before giving way on Berlin. The Soviet leader, who had asked only for negotiations to end the abnormal German situation sixteen years after the war's end, took two steps that caught the Kennedy administration completely by surprise. Worried by the steady flow of East German citizens, especially the young and the talented, who fled via Berlin to West Germany on the order of thirty thousand a month, Khrushchev sealed off East Germany by building the Berlin Wall and thus provided a unilateral solution to an urgent problem. The danger of war seemed great, but to his credit, Kennedy acted with restraint, sending Lyndon Johnson to reassure the people of West Berlin and reinforcing the meager garrison with a fifteen-hundred man battle group, yet refusing to challenge the Soviet action as right-wing Americans urged. Khrushchev then dropped the other shoe; on 30 August, he announced that Russia would resume nuclear testing in the atmosphere, breaking the voluntary suspension that had been in effect since 1958. Over the next few weeks, the Soviets exploded over forty nuclear weapons, including one massive hydrogen bomb of nearly sixty megatons, prompting Kennedy's response, "Fucked again."

The Berlin crisis gradually ebbed in the fall of 1961. Kennedy relented on negotiations and allowed Dean Rusk to begin talks with Soviet Foreign Minister Gromyko at the United Nations in mid-September. In October Khrushchev called off his six-month deadline; but the cost was high. Kennedy had raised tensions to a dangerous level by threatening nuclear war over Berlin and had provoked Khrushchev into taking steps that destroyed any chance for a détente in the near future. The world watched in horror as refugees from East Germany died in brave attempts to scale the wall, while everywhere radiation levels increased as the fallout from the Russian tests rained down from the skies.

Kennedy's first eight months in office had been filled with bitter lessons. Setting out to prove that he was tougher than the Communist leaders, he had only demonstrated the futility of such an aggressive approach by the Bay of Pigs, the weapons buildup, his commitment to South Vietnam, and, above all, the dangerous Berlin policy. He mistook action for courage, tough talk for diplomatic strength, realism for wisdom. Yet he had learned that the problems were not so simple nor the solutions so easy. Above all, he now knew the limits of rationality in world affairs. Hugh Sidey commented on one evening during the height of the Berlin crisis when the president and his brother sat up late discussing the ominous situation. "All his days had been spent planning the steps up to and into nuclear war, should it be required of this country," Sidey wrote. "On that night as they talked, there was the eerie realization that war could be the product of a whim, a misunderstanding, a human mistake."

◇◇◇

Vietnam reflected the new urgency Kennedy brought to world problems after the Berlin crisis. His initial commitment of additional advisers and four hundred Green Berets had failed to halt the Viet Cong insurgency. President Diem, who earlier had resisted suggestions that he ask for American combat troops, submitted a formal request for such assistance in late September 1961. Despite CIA reports that 80 to 90 percent of the Viet Cong guerrillas were southerners engaged in a civil war against a repressive regime, Kennedy's advisers, notably Walt Rostow, argued that Hanoi directed the insurgency and that only heroic measures directed against North Vietnam could win the war in the south. Groping for a clearer assessment, Kennedy sent Rostow, acting as White House representative, and Maxwell Taylor, spokesman for the Pentagon viewpoint, on a crucial mission to South Vietnam in early October; significantly, no one of similar stature represented the State Department. After a hurried tour of the country, the two advisers reported to Kennedy that the situation was bad but not hopeless. They recommended increased support for Diem, never questioning his leadership, and the introduction of eight thousand American combat troops disguised as flood relief workers to repair recent ravages of the Mekong River. Taylor, who wrote the report, recognized the dangers involved, but he assured the president that "the risks of backing into a major Asian war by way of SVN are present but are not impressive. . . . NVN is extremely vulnerable to conventional bombing, a weakness which should be exploited diplomatically in convincing Hanoi to lay off SVN."

Kennedy received this naïve report skeptically. "It will be just like Berlin," he told Arthur Schlesinger, Jr. "The troops will march in; the bands will play; the crowds will cheer; and in four days everyone will have forgotten. Then we will be told we have to send in more troops. It's like taking a drink. The effect wears off, and you have to take another." Secretaries Rusk and McNamara, however, endorsed the Taylor-Rostow recommendations, reminding the president of the stakes involved. "The loss of South Viet-Nam would make pointless any further discussion about the importance of Southeast Asia to the free world. . . . The loss of South Viet-Nam to Communism would not only destroy SEATO but would undermine the credibility of American commitments elsewhere." This classic restatement of the domino thesis may have impressed Kennedy, but even more influential was the sober reminder that the loss of Vietnam to the Reds "would stimulate bitter domestic controversies in the United States and would be seized upon by extreme elements to divide the country and harass the Administration. . . ." Kennedy remembered all too well how the fall of China had discredited the Truman administration (after all, he had even participated in a small way in the process) and paved the way for the Republican return to power under Eisenhower in 1952. Vietnam must not become another China; political realities at home made military commitment abroad imperative.

On 13 November 1961, Kennedy approved stepped-up economic assistance for Diem, increased military aid, especially in the form of helicopters to give the South Vietnamese forces mobility in fighting the Viet Cong, and additional American military advisers, but not the combat troops Diem wanted and Rostow, Taylor, and McNamara advocated. Nevertheless, the increased American participation fundamentally changed the character of

the Vietnamese conflict. American prestige was now fully engaged; the distinction between advisers and combat troops
gradually broke down as U.S. officers and soldiers began to take an
active role in the fighting.

◇◇◇

Kennedy faced an equally difficult decision in fall 1961 on the
question of nuclear testing. The United States had suspended all
tests in October 1958 and had entered into negotiations for a test
ban treaty with the Soviets in Geneva. The talks quickly reached a
deadlock on the vital issue of underground tests. It was easy to
detect nuclear explosions in the atmosphere, but scientists had
great difficulty distinguishing small underground tests from earth-
quakes. The United States insisted on frequent on-site inspections
inside the Soviet Union to investigate seismic disturbances reported by "black boxes," clusters of instruments scattered strategically across the world. The Russians finally agreed to a maximum
of three inspections a year, but they also demanded the right to
veto the findings of the international supervisory body, a condition the United States felt it could not accept.

Khrushchev's resumption of atmospheric nuclear testing in
September 1961 put Kennedy on the spot. The president was
already under intense pressure from the Pentagon to resume
testing, despite an impressive American lead in nuclear technology. Kennedy resisted demands for explosions in the atmosphere,
but he announced plans for underground tests on 5 September
saying, "In view of the acts of the Soviet Government, we must
now take those steps which prudent men find essential." The
dramatic news of the Soviet detonations led to increasing public
uneasiness, though the president's science adviser Jerome Wies-
ner assured him that while American tests in the atmosphere
would "certainly contribute to our military strength, they are not
critical or even very important to our over-all military posture." By
the end of the year, however, the president had decided to resume
tests in the atmosphere, and after overcoming the strenuous
objections of British Prime Minister Harold Macmillan (Britain's
Christmas Island was to be the site of the tests), Kennedy
announced his intentions in a nationwide radio and television
appearance on 2 March. He expressed regret for the dangers to
health from fallout, but he felt he could not risk a "relative decline

in our nuclear strength." On 25 April, the first in a series of explosions began in the Pacific.

Kennedy acted for psychological and political reasons. The United States had opened an enormous lead over the Russians in the arms race by 1962; Congress had authorized funds for the building of 1,000 Minuteman solid-fuel ICBMs and 656 Polaris missiles on board 41 nuclear submarines. The Russian resumption of testing was a desperate effort to close the widening American nuclear lead, a lead made doubly dangerous by Kennedy's apparent willingness during the Berlin crisis to risk all-out war. The Soviets were acting out of weakness, not strength; yet the president, trapped by his own excessive reliance on a philosophy of force and fearful of appearing soft when confronted with Khrushchev's belligerence, felt he had to meet the Soviet challenge. Inevitably, American resumption provoked a second series of Russian tests and led Khrushchev to reject a renewed American proposal for a comprehensive test ban treaty.

The ultimate Russian response to America's growing nuclear superiority came in Cuba. Sometime in the first half of 1962, Khrushchev decided to take the dangerous gamble of installing forty-two medium-range ballistic missiles in Cuba. Afterwards, the Russian leader claimed that his sole motive was to defend the Castro regime against an expected American invasion. Others speculated that he wanted to catch the United States off guard in order to impose a favorable settlement in Berlin, while still others thought he strove to reestablish Soviet primacy over China within the Socialist camp. The simplest explanation is that Khrushchev, realizing how far behind the U.S. his nation was falling in nuclear striking power, hoped to redress the strategic balance by placing offensive missiles in Cuba. Even with these weapons in place, the Russians could not overcome the American lead in ICBMs and bombers, but Khrushchev would gain a psychological initiative that he presumably intended to convert into a diplomatic victory.

Whatever his motives, Khrushchev badly miscalculated the impact of his gamble on John F. Kennedy. In early September, Washington had knowledge of an impressive Soviet arms buildup in Cuba, though as yet there was no inkling of the missiles. Republican leaders, hoping to win control of Congress in the November elections, made the Russian action in Cuba a major campaign issue. Richard Nixon, running for governor of California, called for a "quarantine" of Cuba; Senator Barry Goldwater demanded a blockade; Senator Kenneth Keating of New York, relying on often unreliable exile reports, warned that the Russians were bringing in missiles. Kennedy discounted the GOP oratory, but he publicly informed the Russians in September that he would not tolerate introduction of offensive weapons.

On 14 October, an American U-2 flew over the area of Cuba where work on the missile sites had been under way for several weeks; the next day photo-analysts spotted the evidence and on 16 October McGeorge Bundy informed the president. Kennedy immediately made a fateful decision. Instead of confronting the Russians with the evidence of their hostile acts privately, and trying to force them to retreat without fanfare, he decided to say nothing while exploring alternative courses of action with a select group of advisers. For the next six days, the Executive Committee of the National Security Council discussed a wide range of options, including a surprise attack on the missile sites, invasion of Cuba, a blockade of the island, and even a sit-and-wait policy to see what the Russians would do. Surprisingly, no one advocated a diplomatic approach to the Soviets until the president finally consulted Adlai Stevenson, his ambassador to the United Nations. Stevenson proposed a trade: the United States would withdraw its intermediate-range missiles from Italy and Turkey (Kennedy had already ordered their removal the previous summer), as well as evacuate the naval base at Guantánamo Bay, in return for a Soviet pullout from Cuba. The president rejected this suggestion, apparently without any careful reflection. He also rejected, at least temporarily, the hawkish proposals for a bombing strike and invasion, preferring to begin instead with a quarantine of Cuba to prevent the introduction of any more missiles and a virtual ultimatum to force Khrushchev to withdraw those already in Cuba. In effect, Kennedy opted for a nuclear confrontation to force the Soviet leader to back down.

The American people first learned of the missiles in a dramatic presidential television address on Monday, 22 October, only an hour after Secretary of State Rusk had informed the Russian ambassador of American intentions. Kennedy condemned the Soviets for "this sudden, clandestine decision" to effect "a deliberately provocative and unjustified change in the status quo," and he declared that the United States could not accept it "if our courage and commitments are ever to be trusted again by either friend or foe." Then he outlined his plan of action. The navy would enforce a strict quarantine of Cuba, turning back any ship carrying offensive weapons. The United States would bring the Soviet threat to world peace before both the Organization of American States and the United Nations, but the president relied on an implicit nuclear threat to force Khrushchev to remove the missiles already in Cuba. He warned that any nuclear attack on any nation in the Western Hemisphere launched from Cuba would be regarded "as an attack by the Soviet Union on the United States, requiring a full retaliatory response upon the Soviet Union." Kennedy directed his most chilling words to Khrushchev personally, calling on him "to move the world back from the abyss of destruction—by returning to his government's own words that it had no need to station missiles outside its own territory. . . ."

Khrushchev accepted the nuclear challenge, sending Kennedy a message on 23 October in which he refused to honor the quarantine and accused the president of leading mankind "to the abyss of a world missile-nuclear war." For the next few days, the world watched in fascinated horror as the Russian ships approached the U.S. Navy's patrols in the Atlantic while construction continued around the clock on the Cuban missile sites and an American invasion force assembled in Florida. The first break came on 25 October when more than twenty Soviet ships altered course, signifying Russian acquiescence to the blockade. Work on the missile bases intensified, however, and officials in Washington realized that the real showdown had not yet come. On Friday, 26 October, a long, rambling letter from Khrushchev arrived which revealed the Soviet leader's fear of war and contained a possible solution: withdrawal of the missiles in return for an American promise never to invade Cuba. The Russians confirmed this offer through unofficial channels and the president was ready to accept it when a second message from Khrushchev arrived on Saturday morning. Much more formal and unyielding in tone, this note offered a very different way out: the swap of American missile bases in Turkey for those in Cuba. Kennedy, unwilling to back down in public under pressure, refused to consider this bargain, and his military advisers, almost gleefully telling him he had been naïve in relying on limited measures, recommended an air strike on the missile sites within two days, to be followed by a full-scale invasion of Cuba. At this crucial point, the president's brother, Attorney General Robert F. Kennedy, suggested a peaceful alternative. Why not, he asked, ignore the second note and respond instead to Khrushchev's first letter, pledging not to invade Cuba in return for a Soviet withdrawal of the missiles. The president agreed, and late on Saturday sent such a message to Khrushchev. Leaving nothing to chance, the president asked his brother to meet that evening with the Soviet ambassador and make clear, as Bobby Kennedy wrote later, that "we had to have a commitment by tomorrow that those bases would be removed. . . . He should understand that if they did not remove those bases, we would remove them." He then outlined the contents of the note that his brother had just sent to Khrushchev and added that while there was no mention of American missiles in Italy and Turkey, "President Kennedy had been anxious to remove those missiles . . . and it was our judgment that, within a short time after this crisis was over, those missiles would be gone."

The next morning, Khrushchev accepted Kennedy's offer, and the crisis ended. The president promised not to invade Cuba and the Russians dismantled the bases and removed the missiles under American aerial inspection. A few months later, the United States took its missiles out of Italy and Turkey, as President Kennedy quietly lived up to the secret aspect of the missile settlement.

At the time, Kennedy won virtually unanimous praise for his cool and courageous handling of a dangerous situation. The Democrats retained their control of Congress and Kennedy's ratings soared in the Gallup poll. In retrospect, the president's conduct appears to have been unnecessarily provocative. Although he did resist the pressure for a military solution, he failed to explore the possibility of a diplomatic negotiation. Kennedy dismissed Stevenson's suggestion for a *quid pro quo,* yet in the final analysis he made such a swap privately. The tragedy is that his own fear of appearing weak prevented him from approaching the Russians privately and negotiating a solution before threatening the world with a nuclear confrontation. Kennedy handled the crisis with great technical skill, but the doubt remains that he need not have gone to the brink of disaster to achieve his goals.

◇◇◇

The Cuban missile crisis marked a decisive shift in John Kennedy's approach to world problems. During the last year of his life, he displayed a new and far more mature concern for the ultimate question of war or peace in the nuclear age, a concern that culminated in the nuclear test ban treaty and a belated effort to reassess the American role in Vietnam.

The first sign of Kennedy's determination to profit from the missile crisis came the very day that Khrushchev capitulated. In a statement to the press welcoming the news of the Russian withdrawal, the president expressed his "earnest hope" that "the governments of the world can . . . turn their urgent attention to the compelling necessity for ending the arms race and reducing world tensions." Two months later, on 19 December 1962, Khrushchev responded by writing Kennedy his conviction that the "time has come now to put an end once and for all to nuclear tests, to draw a line through such tests." To prove his sincerity in working for "the noble and humane goal of ceasing nuclear weapons tests" the Russian leader agreed to accept three on-site inspections a year to ensure against secret underground explosions. Kennedy cut the American demand for twenty such inspections to seven, but then a deadlock developed as Khrushchev, though Kennedy had unofficially signaled to him a willingness to accept three, returned to the original Soviet refusal to allow any inspections. In a last-ditch effort to break the stalemate, Kennedy joined with British Prime Minister Macmillan in an offer to send senior representatives to Moscow to negotiate directly with Khrushchev. In May, the Soviet leader accepted his proposal (with a noticeable lack of enthusiasm) and the talks were scheduled for late June or early July.

The president decided to inform the American people of his efforts for a test ban treaty in a major speech at American University on 10 June 1963. In eloquent and moving language, Kennedy addressed himself to "the most important topic on earth: world peace." He carefully avoided cold war rhetoric, denying any desire to achieve "a Pax Americana enforced on the world by American weapons of war," and called upon his countrymen "to re-examine our attitude toward the Soviet Union." He spoke admiringly of the Russian people and the huge losses in life and property they had suffered at the hands of Germany in World War II. The United States and Russia, he declared, now had a common interest in halting the arms race and preventing the far greater devastation of a nuclear holocaust. Differences between the two nations were bound to persist, he continued, but "at least we can help make the world safe for diversity. For, in the final analysis, our most basic common link is that we all inhabit this small planet. We all breathe the same air. We all cherish our children's future. And we are all mortal."

It was hard to believe that this was the same man who only two years before had called for an all-out offensive against communism to win the battle of freedom over slavery. Two years of adversity had taught President Kennedy that negotiation and compromise were more vital than military strength and determination in resolving world problems. With a new insight born of the Cuban missile crisis, he told the American people that they must reexamine their attitudes toward the cold war and stop trying to pile up "debating points." "We must deal with the world as it is," he concluded, "and not as it might have been had the history of the last eighteen years been different." Then he announced that the United States and England had agreed on high-level talks in Moscow to seek a test ban treaty and that meanwhile the United States "would not conduct atmospheric tests as long as other states did not do so."

Nikita Khrushchev later told Averell Harriman, the veteran diplomat Kennedy sent to Moscow to conduct the test ban negotiations, that the American University address was "the greatest speech by any American President since Roosevelt." The Russian leader's formal response was more restrained; on 2 July, he offered to negotiate a test ban treaty limited to environments where detection did not require on-site inspection: the atmosphere, outer space, and underwater. Kennedy accepted this proposal for a limited test ban treaty, and in mid-July Harriman arrived in Moscow, along with British diplomat Lord Hailsham. After only ten days, they initialed an agreement that bypassed the earlier deadlock by outlawing all but underground nuclear tests.

In announcing this achievement to the American people, President Kennedy declared that "for the first time in many years, the path of peace may be open." He added that the agreement was only a first step, saying, "No one can be certain what the future will bring." He was wise to admit the limited nature of the treaty. The military leaders accepted the agreement with great reluctance and were persuaded to go along only after Kennedy promised the Joint Chiefs an extensive program of underground nuclear tests and gave them a written commitment to resume tests in the atmosphere "should they be deemed essential to our national security." In testifying to the Senate Foreign Relations Committee, Secretary of Defense McNamara portrayed the treaty as a victory for the United States, asserting that the U.S. had greater experience and proficiency in underground testing to argue that "we can at least retard Soviet progress and thereby prolong the duration of our technological superiority." Undoubtedly this belief that a limited test ban conferred important strategic advantages on the United States was as influential as the idea of a first step in halting the arms race in leading the Senate to ratify the treaty by a sweeping margin of eighty to nineteen. Nevertheless, Kennedy had achieved a goal that Adlai Stevenson had first advocated against overwhelming opposition in 1956. Despite its limitations, the test ban treaty marked the first break in the cold war; it was Kennedy's finest legacy.

In the summer of 1963, Kennedy also seemed to be in the process of changing his mind about Vietnam. The war there had improved following the limited American involvement the president had sanctioned in late 1961. The use of helicopters, the presence of the Green Berets, the adoption of a strategic hamlet policy in the rural areas, above all, the sheer lift in South Vietnamese morale resulting from the infusion of American aid, had set back the Viet Cong. Improvement proved temporary; by early 1963, the guerrillas had regained the initiative in the war and were widening their hold on the countryside. More significantly, Diem created a grave political crisis when he tried to repress the Buddhists in the spring of 1963. On 11 June, a day after the American University speech, an aged monk doused himself with gasoline in Saigon, lit a match, and burned to death before a chanting crowd of Buddhist supporters and the camera of Associated Press reporter Malcolm Browne. The widely published photograph of the self-immolation horrified the American people and forced President Kennedy to question the wisdom of continuing to back the Diem regime.

In the last few months of his life, Kennedy agonized over Vietnam. He sympathized with Averell Harriman and others within the administration who saw the war primarily as a political struggle and who wanted to force Diem into instituting democratic reforms as the only way to win the confidence of the people. He even permitted the State Department to send a famous cable in late August which permitted the new American ambassador, Henry Cabot Lodge, to give South Vietnamese generals the green light in their plans to overthrow the government in Saigon. In a CBS interview with Walter Cronkite on 2 September, Kennedy revealed his belief that only a greater effort by the South Vietnamese could turn the tide. "In the final analysis," he commented, "it is their war. They are the ones who have to win it or lose it. We can help them, we can give them equipment, we can send our men out there as advisers, but they have to win it, the people of Viet Nam, against the Communists."

Yet at the same time, the president allowed the military to continue backing the Diem regime. In an interview with Chet Huntley and David Brinkley on 9 September, he expressed his belief that the loss of South Vietnam would open up all Southeast Asia to the Chinese Communists, revealing that he was still under the grip of the domino thesis. "I think we should stay," he concluded. "We should use our influence in as effective a way as we can, but should not withdraw." Privately, he told aide Kenneth O'Donnell that he planned to negotiate an American withdrawal in the future, but that he could not act until after the 1964 elections, which suggests that the memory of Truman and the fall of China still haunted him. The overthrow and murder of Diem on 1 November probably forced him to reconsider this long-term strategy. The United States, having used its influence to remove Diem, now bore the responsibility of backing his successors; there was no longer any graceful way for Kennedy to withdraw.

Despite the worsening situation in Vietnam, the theme of peace cropped up more and more in Kennedy's speeches in the fall of 1963. On a speaking tour of the West suggested by Majority Leader Mike Mansfield, he drew his warmest response when he spoke about his efforts to end the cold war. In Billings, Montana, the audience came to life when he talked about the confrontations with the Soviet Union over Berlin and Cuba and expressed his heartfelt desire "to lessen the chance of a military collision between these two great nuclear powers which together have the power to kill 300 million people in the short space of a day. . . . That is why I support the test ban treaty, . . . because we have a chance to avoid being burned." He was even more eloquent the next evening in Salt Lake City. Warning against both a return to isolationism and a simplistic, "black and white" approach, he pleaded for "a world of diversity" and expressed the hope that "the world of the future will have room for a diversity of economic systems, political creeds, religious faiths, united by the respect for others, and loyalty to a world order."

The president who spoke these words had undergone a fundamental change in outlook during the thousand days he had been in office. He had taken up his duties believing essentially in a two-dimensional world, one in which overwhelming American power and the willingness to use it would cure all problems. He learned that international affairs were neither so simple nor so malleable. The real world—in which guerrillas in the jungles of Indochina successfully defied the power and technology of the greatest nation on the earth, in which a rival leader would risk nuclear war by placing missiles on the doorsteps of the United States—intruded on Kennedy's rational approach to foreign policy and taught him that there was a third dimension to international affairs whose existence he had not even suspected.

The ultimate tragedy was that John F. Kennedy never had the opportunity to put his hard-won education to work. No one can say what he would have done in Vietnam had he lived; yet it is possible that he could have avoided his successor's escalation of that conflict. Instead, it fell to his bitter rival of 1960, Richard Nixon, to inherit the possibilities for peace that Kennedy had glimpsed and to pursue them to end the long years of hostility toward Communist China, enter into a meaningful arms control agreement with the Soviet Union, and bring about a cease-fire in Vietnam. Perhaps only John Kennedy, with his fondness for the ironies of history, could have fully appreciated this final twist of fate.

BIBLIOGRAPHIC NOTE

The literature on John F. Kennedy's foreign policy divides into early, favorable accounts and more recent critical ones. This essay relies heavily on James MacGregor Burns, *John Kennedy: A Political Profile,* 2nd ed. (New York, 1961), Arthur M. Schlesinger, Jr., *A Thousand Days: John F. Kennedy in the White House* (Boston, 1965), and Theodore C. Sorensen, *Kennedy* (New York, 1965) for information in this study, while rejecting their sympathetic view of the president. This analysis reflects the more skeptical viewpoints expressed by Richard J. Walton in *Cold War and Counterrevolution: The Foreign Policy of John F. Kennedy* (New York, 1972) and Louise Fitzsimons, *The Kennedy Doctrine* (New York, 1972). Other books used include Robert F. Kennedy, *Thirteen Days: A Memoir of the Cuban Missile Crisis* (New York, 1969), Roger Hilsman, *To Move A Nation* (Garden City, N.Y., 1967), David Halberstam, *The Best and the*

Brightest (New York, 1972), the *New York Times* edition of *The Pentagon Papers* (New York, 1971), edited by Neil Sheehan and others, for Kennedy's Vietnam policies, and Hugh Sidey, *John F. Kennedy, President* (New York, 1963), which provides an admirably detached view of Kennedy's years in the White House.

THE CONGRESS AS CLASSROOM:
J. WILLIAM
FULBRIGHT

Courtesy, Senator Fulbright

and the Crisis of American Power

David F. Trask

Congress historically has acted negatively with regard to American foreign relations. The elder Senator Henry Cabot Lodge symbolizes this more notoriously than any other congressional leader. Only a few legislators have ever sought to exercise intellectual influence on foreign affairs; one is the junior senator from Arkansas, J. William Fulbright, Democrat, chairman of the Senate Committee on Foreign Relations. Once, musing on his activities, he said rather wistfully: "I don't exercise direct power, I don't cut people's heads off, politically speaking or symbolically speaking. I don't make people do things." What seemed to Fulbright possibly useful was the educational effect of his commentaries on public issues. "I

Biographical information on this essay is drawn largely from Haynes Johnson and Bernard M. Gwertzman, *Fulbright: The Dissenter* (Garden City, N.Y., 1968), and Tristram Coffin, *Senator Fulbright: Portrait of a Public Philosopher* (New York, 1966).

think these discussions are like any form of education. It's hard to prove, but I think it's there. . . . It seems to me that ideas you advance begin to develop." Perhaps recalling his stormy relations with more than one president, most importantly Lyndon Baines Johnson, he wondered whether his activity had made any great difference. "There are so many prejudices and bitter hatreds and feeling that people have." Despite his self-doubt, it is clear that Fulbright has contributed to the American people's education in the intricacies of international politics, delivering lectures from the Senate during the cold war years, seeking to introduce novel opinions into the public debate of great international questions.

◇◇◇

Fulbright's early experiences prepared him well for the vocation of educator. Born in 1905 to an affluent family who eventually settled near Fayetteville, Arkansas, the seat of the state university, he enjoyed an active, comfortable youth. As an undergraduate at the University of Arkansas he became prominent in intercollegiate sports, particularly football, and student government. These endeavors and a good academic record led to his selection as a Rhodes Scholar in 1925. While at Oxford Fulbright read European history and politics and traveled extensively on the Continent, where international affairs attracted his attention. Returning to Fayetteville in 1929, he planned to help manage his family's multifarious businesses, but on a chance visit to a friend in Washington he met his future wife and decided to attend the George Washington University Law School, from which he graduated second in a class of 135. After a brief apprenticeship in the Antitrust Division of the Department of Justice (he helped argue the famous NRA case, *Schechter* v. *New York*), he returned to George Washington as an instructor in law, his first pedagogical experience. These eventful years ended in 1936 when, at thirty-one, he returned to Arkansas to teach at the university's law school. To others at this time he must have appeared a well-bred and well-educated southern patrician, possibly destined for some public service in the future but hardly for a role as dissenter.

In September 1939, Fulbright became president of the University of Arkansas, an assignment that gave him his first opportunity to comment publicly on international questions. He engendered controversy, particularly when he took the interventionist side in the great debate that preceded American entry into World War II. On one occasion, he planned to say at the University of Missouri that the "weaseling, timid, and fearful policy of the isolationist senators is one of the greatest dangers to our true interests," but his invitation to speak was withdrawn in deference to the anti-interventionist views of Senator Champ Clark. In that same year, 1940, a new governor of Arkansas, Homer M. Adkins, took umbrage at some derogatory remarks about him made by Fulbright's mother, Roberta, who wrote a column in a newspaper owned by the family. "It seems," she had noted, "that the people of Arkansas want a hand-shaking governor instead of one who accomplishes something." In June 1941 the board of trustees of the university, dominated by Adkins's appointees, summarily discharged Fulbright.

This catastrophe marked an important turning point in the life of the young educator. The following year he ran for the House of Representatives as a Democrat from the Third Congressional District. An energetic campaign produced a comfortable victory, and he took his seat in the Seventy-eighth Congress in January 1943. He obtained a place on the House Foreign Affairs Committee, where his activities soon began to attract considerable notice.

A convinced internationalist, Fulbright immediately interested himself in the question of postwar security. During his campaign he had sounded the principal theme he pursued in Congress, that there could be no return to the "so-called good old days of extreme nationalism." The Democratic party "must again catch the spirit of 1918 and 1932 and attack the problems of the world with the same daring and originality that we attacked that peace and that depression."[1] When another freshman member of Congress, Clare Boothe Luce, attacked internationalist views as "globaloney," Fulbright answered that the "narrow, imperialistic policy of grab . . . carries within itself the seeds of its own destruction." He then organized support for a brief statement, known as the Fulbright Resolution, that endorsed a postwar security organization. The House "hereby expresses itself as favoring the creation of appropriate international machinery with power adequate to

---

1. This quotation and most others cited for the years to 1963 are drawn from Karl Meyer, ed., *Fulbright of Arkansas: The Public Positions of a Private Thinker* (Washington, D. C., 1963).

prevent future aggression and to maintain lasting peace, and as
favoring participation by the United States therein." With President Roosevelt's support Fulbright was able to push his resolution
through the House on 21 September 1943 by a vote of 360 to 29.
Together with a similar resolution sponsored by Senator Tom
Connally of Texas, which passed in the Senate, Fulbright's act laid
the foundation for congressional acceptance of the United Nations Charter. His successes encouraged him to run for the Senate
in 1944 against the incumbent Mrs. Hattie Caraway, knowing that
his old adversary, Governor Adkins, would also enter the contest.
Despite allegations that Fulbright was both a draft-dodger and a
visionary he won a runoff election against Adkins by thirty-four
thousand votes. His mother could not resist a parting shot.
"Homer Adkins," she wrote, "has came and went."

Fulbright's first labor in the Senate was to champion the
United Nations. As he would do throughout his career he adduced
historical arguments for this campaign. Looking back to 1919 he
maintained that rapid change had confused the people, leading to
a public reaction against the League of Nations that adversely
affected policy throughout the interwar period. "We made pious
declarations against war . . . and yet did nothing concrete when
Manchuria and Ethiopia were invaded." Americans had miscon-
ceived their role in world politics and had "failed to examine and
agree upon certain basic convictions which are essential to any
policy." The resulting bewilderment led to emotional responses
and to improvisation from day to day; of foreign policy Fulbright
urged that policy stem from clearly articulated principles. Although exhilarated when the Senate accepted the United Nations
Charter, he immediately grasped the sinister portent of the atomic
bomb. The threat of nuclear destruction, Fulbright believed,
strengthened the internationalist case against conventional power
politics. A strain of pessimism—that deepened in later years—
began to appear in his speeches. The discovery of extermination
camps in Germany had provided "an ugly but powerful demonstration of what lies beneath that thin crust of civilization so
laboriously acquired by man." Such thoughts underlay Fulbright's
belief in an international rule of law, enshrined in the charter. The
only alternative was "constantly recurring warfare of rapidly
increasing destructiveness." Binding legal constraints were required because goodwill alone rarely had ensured peace and
order.

In one most important respect Fulbright went beyond the spirit of the charter. He spoke eloquently against the principle of absolute national sovereignty, claiming that it was totally inconsistent with the development of international laws having sufficient force behind them to gain general confidence. His hopes for the UN waned as he realized that conditions necessary to sustain collective security—political and social solidarity among the great powers and the will to enforce charter obligations—had not materialized. The world had attempted, unwisely, "to outrun history, to move in a single leap from world anarchy to world community." Security would come only if people abandoned nationalism, only if people broadened their loyalties, "never forgetting . . . that it is the human individual, and not the state or any other community, in whom ultimate sovereignty is vested." Sponsorship of the Fulbright Scholarships and of other projects for international education derived from the view, expressed regularly, that such programs cultivated "perceptions and perspectives that transcend national boundaries." In 1972 he still maintained that supranationalism, as an alternative to the balance of power, was "not only the course of realism but the only available course of sanity." [2]

Fulbright launched a commentary on Soviet affairs even before the end of the war, recognizing that the future of the UN depended on cooperation among the great powers. To counteract the anti-Bolshevik sentiment that had grown between the wars, he went so far as to claim that "the Russian experiment in socialism is scarcely more radical, under modern conditions, than the Declaration of Independence was in the days of George III." Capitalism, in which he believed, was neither divine nor inviolable, and challenges to it were neither sacrilegious nor treasonable. By May 1946, however, Fulbright had become alarmed by Russian initiatives. His mind went back to the Munich pact of 1938, when Germany had assumed that the United States favored peace at any price. Now the Arkansas senator feared that America's resolve to participate in world politics might decline in the aftermath of war. Complaining about precipitous troop withdrawals from Europe, he

---

2. Fulbright's opposition to nationalism may be traced in later books, such as *Prospects for the West* (Cambridge, Mass., 1963), *Old Myths and New Realities, and Other Commentaries* (New York, 1964), *The Crippled Giant: American Foreign Policy and Its Domestic Consequences* (New York, 1972), p. 177.

wondered aloud, "Are we, or are we not, going to use our influence and play a leading role in foreign affairs?" The United States must show the world that, "while we do not seek war, yet we are willing and able to fight whenever we believe any power threatens the right and opportunity for men to live as free individuals under a government of their own choice." In this statement Senator Fulbright anticipated the Truman Doctrine by nearly a year.

Nothing seemed more important than the reconstruction of Western Europe. Fulbright supported the principal measures of containment developed during the period 1947–49, though he later criticized the broad scope of the Truman Doctrine, maintaining that the country, frightened by Stalin's policies in Eastern Europe, had converted "from Wilson to Machiavelli in the same zealous spirit in which a repentant Communist may become a devout believer in a religion or a repentant hawk may offer himself as a martyr for peace." He even claimed that the UN had failed not simply because of Russia but because Dean Acheson and others had not wanted it to work. At the time, however, he supported the objectives of the Truman administration.

Any reservations he had related to means rather than ends. Fulbright again anticipated evolving administration ideas by proposing a startling change in the political organization of Europe as the best method of curbing Russian ambitions. Standing alone, European nations could not hope to resist Russian pressure. In April 1947, recalling the Continent's ancient unity under the Romans and the Carolingians, he envisioned revival of a parallel system, which he deemed possible because of roughly similar institutions throughout non-Communist Europe. If Germany became a loose grouping of small states and merged into a larger government representing some three hundred million people, German militarism could be controlled and Germans could not dominate the federation. All manner of economic benefits would result, not to mention the political gains. Moscow would oppose this change, but, should France provide leadership, supported by the United States and Britain, a United States of Europe could be built and a new renaissance might occur. Fulbright's Oxford tutors must have been thoroughly proud of this analysis by their old student!

Meanwhile, Fulbright had begun to manifest those maverick qualities that later came to be his most characteristic attributes. In

November 1946, when the Republican party gained control of
Congress, he suggested offhandedly that Truman appoint a leading Republican as secretary of state and then resign, awarding the
presidency to the majority party since there was no vice-president.
This proposal, derived from Fulbright's admiration for the British
pattern of government, would have substituted parliamentary
practice for the presidential system. For this act of lese majesty he
earned the formidable enmity of Truman, who on more than one
occasion referred to him as "that overeducated Arkansasan, you
know, Senator Halfbright." He did not improve his standing in
1949 when he presided over an extensive investigation of the
Reconstruction Finance Corporation and uncovered extensive
corruption in Washington, an issue used to advantage by the
Republicans during the elections of 1950 and 1952.

These setbacks aside, Fulbright finally gained his heart's desire
in 1949: membership on the Senate Foreign Relations Committee;
from this vantage point he observed the era of Senator Joseph R.
McCarthy and President Dwight D. Eisenhower. He stepped
forward as one of the most outspoken critics of the senator from
Wisconsin, a service that won him the respect of civil libertarians
and of many liberals, despite their dislike of his stand on racial
issues. During these years he built an impressive reputation and
acquired seniority, and although he was not as frequently in the
public eye as before, he greatly increased his knowledge of
American foreign policy and his prestige as an authority in the
field.

By 1956 Fulbright discerned a dangerous shift in the balance
of power, to which the United States had not responded.
America's nuclear superiority and ability to distribute foreign aid
had held Russia in check; but now the Soviet Union had become
competitive. What increasingly alarmed Fulbright was the administration's commitment to deterrence, the belief that the maintenance of sufficient power to damage aggressors seriously would
lead such powers to refuse to accept the costs of an attack. Such a
policy would fail because it required a degree of expertise that
could not be expected indefinitely of mankind. Moreover, this
strategy assumed that the Soviet Union was the only likely
instigator of international conflict. A great struggle might start in
the Middle East or even in Southeast Asia, where neither super-
power would necessarily exercise restraint.

The tendency of the country to make an unreasoning defense

of the status quo, just when the world was caught in "a ferment of cataclysmic change," impressed Fulbright at this time; he attributed the policy to the malign influence of John Foster Dulles. He did not yet discern any change in Soviet objectives, but he emphasized the flexibility of Russian policy under Khrushchev. The United States must demonstrate comparable flexibility if it wished to maintain peace and spread freedom in the world. As the nation headed into the 1960s, nothing seemed more wrongheaded than a global crusade in behalf of the established order. Americans, he argued, were "neither omniscient nor omnipotent. . . . We cannot aspire to make the world over in our own image." He favored action, but he opposed "indiscriminate military intervention in response to every provocation and every disorder, regardless of its character and cause." At this time, he was almost alone in raising these questions, considered heretical in the golden age of brinkmanship and containment.

The senator gradually formulated a comprehensive view, historical in nature, of the course of events from 1945 to 1960, and this served as a basis for new proposals. The American response to the revolution in world politics that began after 1945 had come in the form of containment, and this was well and good during the immediate postwar years; but such policies no longer sufficed. The nuclear stalemate, Europe's recovery of economic vigor, development of flexibility in Russia, and stirrings of nationalism in the third world dictated a new approach. In the future, the United States would have to deal not with crude forms of aggression but with "the insidious challenges of psychological penetration, of political subversion, of economic conquest, of the use of foreign aid and trade as political weapons."

Of great concern to Fulbright was the rise of military influence in American policy, convinced as he was that warfare no longer offered a solution to international tensions. He argued that in present circumstances wars, even those ending in total victory, "generate more problems than they solve." Only qualities such as perseverance and sacrifice could further security. In the long run the *character* of Americans rather than magical formulas and prescriptions would decide whether the nation dealt successfully with what he still called the "Communist challenge."

He had long argued that a sound foreign policy rested on moral strength at home; he now sought explanations for the decline not simply in morals but in tastes and values that was shaking the nation. Perhaps, he speculated, this deterioration was unavoidable, given the American past. Preoccupied with growth, the nation had failed to develop a philosophy and culture to support expansion. America now required "qualities that are associated with maturity rather than youth; qualities of wisdom, as well as resourcefulness; persevering determination, as well as righteous indignation; and perhaps most of all, moral courage in the place of adolescent bravado." He admired a sense of mission, but only in proper measure. He did not advocate default on America's international tasks to further essential domestic reforms, but he inveighed against the "globalism" of the Eisenhower years, a pattern that continued in modified form into John F. Kennedy's tenure. As a sound example to follow, he cited Great Britain during the nineteenth century. As director of the European concert, London "led but did not dominate," participating in a system of shared responsibility.

◇◇◇

From the beginning of his congressional career, Fulbright was interested in the perennial question of the relations between the executive and the federal legislature. As early as 1943 he had adopted a moderate position, holding that the president should administer policy, but according to broad guidelines that should emanate from the Senate. Shaping this view was his old complaint about the lack of clear policy and the resulting American tendency to improvise foreign relations. The legislator's responsibility to curb potential executive oppression remained in force, however. A responsible Congress encouraged "a climate in which the genius of individual beings can flourish." He criticized violations of appropriate functions by legislators, most notably in his comments on Senator McCarthy. He had voted for censure of McCarthy in 1954, he claimed, not because of his colleague's character or views, but because of his "official degradation of the power of the Senate, by which he has gravely injured the United States and the Senate." Although the Senate's investigatory role must be safeguarded because this power stood at the heart of the legislative process, Fulbright also argued that a legislator "ought to consider himself a teacher, offering by precept and example a style and method of deliberation that can be imitated by the community at large, as it seeks on its own to know and then to do the

Vadillo in La Prensa, Mexico City

"Mr. Fulbright and the blind giant."

good." The legislator, however, like the teacher, "must be prepared to accept banishment or destruction at the hands of the people because he has aroused their anger in the very act of serving them well."

Fulbright became more and more concerned about executive irresponsibility during the Eisenhower years, but he kept these earlier views. The Senate could not "initiate or force large events, or substitute its judgment for that of the president, without seriously jeopardizing the ability of the nation to act consistently, and also without confusing the image and purpose of this country in the eyes of others." The Senate should confine itself to another, even more important responsibility: to "explain and rationalize the burden which the people bear, to help them to that degree of understanding which will compel their agreement." If this were properly done, a consensus would emerge upon which the president could base his initiatives.

Senator Fulbright spoke with greater confidence and authority as the 1960s began. He possessed the great prestige and not inconsiderable power conferred by his chairmanship of the Senate Committee on Foreign Relations, a post gained in 1959 with the assistance of his old and good friend, Lyndon B. Johnson, then majority leader. Further, he stood apart from the rest of the Senate in his understanding of foreign affairs. With Kennedy, a Democrat, in the White House (and one with whom Fulbright seemed to have in common intellectual if not personal ties), and with a Democratic majority in both the House and Senate, a bold new era of executive-legislative collaboration in foreign affairs seemed about to dawn. It was a safe bet that Fulbright would play a pivotal part in the new diplomatic initiatives of the Kennedy administration. That was not to be, largely because the intellectual differences between the senator from Arkansas and the Bostonian who moved into the White House proved as great as their personal differences. One may assert that a major cause of this falling out was that Fulbright continued to grow intellectually, while Kennedy and his circle of advisers never moved beyond the prevailing wisdom about foreign affairs.

In 1963, Harvard University invited Fulbright to deliver the prestigious Clayton lectures, and in preparation for this pedagogical opportunity he drew together his thoughts about U.S. foreign policy, offering certain broad prescriptions for American diplomacy in accord with his views on the proper role of Congress in foreign affairs. Fulbright began these lectures, which were later published under the title *Prospects for the West,* by recourse to history, as was his wont. During the twentieth century the West had declined in its power relative to other parts of the world. Outside challenges no longer permitted the West to consider its ideas and values as having universal applicability. In addition, the West could not redress its position by resorting to war. Unfortunately, an inveterate tendency toward "baleful nationalism" had prejudiced the West's position. Fulbright's solution to the crisis of the Western world represented a refurbishing of his old dream of a

United States of Europe, which he now expanded into an Atlantic partnership including the United States. However much he desired a world community, it was unattainable. "We must therefore," he continued, "focus our efforts on the more modest goal of building new bonds among those people of the free world who have some feeling of shared values and interests, some feeling of the ability to communicate freely, some feeling of trust and confidence in each other's purposes." He did not approve General de Gaulle's plan for a strictly European organization, based as it was on outworn nationalism and exclusion of the English-speaking nations. Through an Atlantic partnership the West could become a model and a magnet for Asia, Africa, Eastern Europe, and even for the Russians.

Fulbright's analysis reflected a changing appraisal of the Soviet Union. Stalinism had represented a renewal of nationalism and imperialism in the crudest form. Under Khrushchev the Soviet Union still hoped to destroy Western unity, but it now was using sophisticated means. To counteract the Russian challenge the West had to maintain its defenses, but it must make clear that its policy was to counteract Russian imperialism, not ideology. "The Soviet Union, insofar as it renounces expansionist and subversive ambitions, can enjoy a safe and honorable life without threat or danger from the West." As a further measure, the West must strengthen its internal fabric, making itself safe against alien ideologies and an example of social and material well-being. Such a course might encourage moderation in Russia, even a withering away of the idea of a Russianized world.

Fulbright never had manifested more than a qualified optimism about human nature, and the stress of the cold war reinforced his proclivity for an endorsement of human reason that was, at best, ambiguous. Events had shown that "free societies, including our own, have acted foolishly or disastrously as a result of their own shortsightedness and irrationality." This reality might force changes in traditional actions, but Fulbright remained committed to "belief in the moral sanctity of the free mind and the free individual." These views reflected his preoccupation with conservative thinkers such as Alexis de Tocqueville and Walter Lippmann, whom he quoted more frequently than any others in support of his opinions.

Fulbright expanded his views on domestic conditions. Melioration at home determined a nation's success with other nations.

The West would survive if it proved more successful than its enemies in creating "an economic system that provides material abundance, a political system based on justice and freedom and human dignity, and an educational system that cultivates individual excellence and spiritual fulfillment." The United States must further important reforms at home. Postwar prosperity had "benumbed" the American social conscience, diverting attention from pressing domestic problems such as unemployment, deteriorating schools, and urban blight. Progress would not result either from expanding a vulgar consumer culture or pursuing overseas adventures. "If America is to achieve excellence in life and greatness in history," he concluded, "these can only come from the decision of our people to find purpose and direction in their lives, to give shape and coherence to their civilization."

The Clayton lectures represented for Fulbright both an end and a beginning. In them he drew together his earlier experience, when he had struggled with the problems posed by the Russo-American confrontation that followed World War II. If he differed from Acheson and Dulles, he shared the pervasive Europocentrism of those two exponents of containment. Like others at the time he dissented not from the broad views of the cold war entertained in the executive branch but from the tactics of those in power. His more advanced theories (such as his attitude toward national sovereignty) do not seem to have had much if any influence. Fulbright did not ignore the problems of the third world, but he looked at the area in terms of Western interests without undertaking a truly detailed analysis of developments outside the Atlantic region. In 1963 Fulbright had gained the respect of many in the country because of his articulate statements, but he was not considered to be outside the establishment. Very soon, however, he turned to issues that related more to future policy in Latin America and Asia than to the defense of the West, and events during the presidency of Lyndon Johnson forced him to adopt marked changes in his diagnosis of world problems as well as new prescriptions for their cure.

◇◇◇

Fulbright had long been a close associate of Johnson. He had supported the majority leader's presidential candidacy in 1960 and campaigned for him in 1964, praising the programs of domestic reform that became known as the "Great Society." In their days in the Senate, Johnson would proclaim, "Bill's *my* Secretary of State." This mutual admiration society did not endure long beyond the election of 1964. When Fulbright began to adopt a critical stance toward the administration's foreign policies, Johnson attempted to cajole the senator, exposing him to "the treatment," a term journalists used to describe the president's forceful methods of persuading others to support his policies. This method did not sway his old friend from Arkansas. Fulbright's alienation from Johnson during the period 1964–66 paralleled his retreat from the conventional wisdom about American foreign relations at the same time the United States committed itself to war in Southeast Asia. The senator's two important books of this period, *Old Myths and New Realities* (1964) and *The Arrogance of Power* (1966), reveal striking departures from earlier views.

Ironically, he seems to have thought for a time that Johnson would sponsor constructive change. He intended *Old Myths and New Realities* to point the way in foreign relations. The old myth of greatest importance was the view that the Communist world constituted a monolithic conspiracy seeking to overthrow freedom. Adherence to this idea blinded its exponents to great changes in the pattern of world politics as well as to appropriate adjustments. The new reality turned on a sharp change in Russo-American relations, which Fulbright associated with the outcome of the Cuban missile crisis in 1962 and the signing of the limited test ban treaty of 1963. In these situations Moscow had shown restraint, and both sides had implicitly repudiated the idea of achieving total victory. Russia had accepted America's strategic superiority because of indications that it would be exercised responsibly. Some Communist powers posed danger, but others did not. In any event, the real threat remained that of imperialism not ideology. The United States "must deal with the Soviet Union as a great power, quite apart from differences of ideology." Normal relations might not become possible for many years, but thoughtful policies could lessen Russo-American tensions.

It was not clear that the country would take full advantage of these new options. The United States was entrapped by an "excessive moralism, by a tendency to equate means with ends and therefore to attach a mythological sanctity to policies and practices which in themselves have no moral content or value except insofar as they contribute to the achievement of some valid national objective." Fulbright thus confirmed his tendency to identify his own country rather than the Soviet Union as a deterrent to constructive change in international relations. He realized that no dramatic solution could resolve the cold war; it could neither be won nor ended immediately. These notions he labeled the favorite myths of the American Right and the American Left. He drew attention more clearly than in earlier works to the limits rather than the vistas of power. Americans, he urged, should recognize "the realities of a world in which neither good nor evil is absolute and in which those who move events and make history are those who have understood not how much but how little it is within our power to change."

The critical concern was not to end the cold war but to preclude a holocaust. Those nations with nuclear weapons, he noted, were most likely to serve as nuclear targets. Neither of the superpowers needed nuclear arms; they could exist without them. Proliferation of nuclear capability would constitute a "great equalizer" among nations large and small. These realities created Russian and American interest in arms control. The senator was devastatingly critical of calls for general and complete disarmament, labeling such proposals "an exercise in cold war fantasy." They stimulated false hopes and caused disappointments, heightening rather than resolving tensions. More modest initiatives, sustained over time, could lead to constructive change. Cold war encounters might turn to more tolerable rivalries that did not distract mankind from "the creative pursuits of civilized societies."

Fulbright gave increasing attention to places other than Europe, particularly to Latin America where the rise of Fidel Castro in Cuba had created new problems. He believed that Kennedy had overreacted. "We have flattered a noisy but minor demagogue by treating him as if he were a Napoleonic menace." Fulbright opposed unilateral action toward Cuba, arguing that the inter-American system should deal with acts of aggression mounted by Cuba. The Alliance for Progress, an attempt to facilitate peaceful social revolution in Latin America, hopefully would achieve its goals, but he warned that violence was always possible "in countries where feudal oligarchies resist all meaningful change by peaceful means."

Asian problems also came within his purview, especially instability in Southeast Asia. In 1961 he had criticized U.S. policy in Laos, which he thought was unrelated to actual circumstances

there, but had spoken differently of South Vietnam where "qualified success" had rewarded American efforts. Future developments would depend on the Diem regime's capacity for reform.
He placed little faith in paramilitary operations. "The proper
course," he insisted, was "to continue sustaining and supporting
efforts of the Vietnamese army to cope effectively with the foe in
being—tough bands of hit-and-run Communist guerrillas—while
devoting at least as much effort to assisting and guiding the
Vietnamese people in their struggle for dignity and economic
independence." By 1964 second thoughts had come. He opposed
complete American withdrawal and favored supporting the Geneva agreements of 1954 and 1962 which envisioned independent
states free of outside domination, but he argued that this goal did
not require either hostilities between the Indochinese states or an
imposing American presence. Fulbright entertained modest hopes
for the improvement of relations with mainland China. He
dismissed the concept of the "two Chinas," agreeing with those
who proposed that the U.S. consider the option of improving
associations with Peking. He thought that Taipeh and Peking
might someday end the civil war and open up "the possibility
of entirely new patterns of international relations in the Far East."

Fulbright also expanded his early critique of military influences in the making of foreign policy. National security depended
on many elements besides armaments. He lamented the tendency
of civilians to surrender decision making to "highly specialized
technical experts whose experience and knowledge have only very
limited relevance to the complexities of international politics." He
objected to congressional haste in voting huge appropriations for
the Department of Defense, an approach that contrasted with
careful surveillance of expenditures on social programs at home.
The most dangerous consequence of the cold war was its
tendency to force diversion of resources from peaceful to warlike
pursuits. His scathing criticism of the space program reflected
these views. If Russia got to the moon first, but the United States
achieved the objectives of the Great Society, "whose prestige
would be higher, who would then be ahead in the world-wide
struggle for the minds of men?"[3]

3. For a detailed work on the military threat see J. William Fulbright, *The Pentagon
Propaganda Machine* (New York, 1970).

Throughout this analysis, Senator Fulbright continued to rely heavily on historical judgments based on his knowledge of modern history. To him the utility of history lay not in the use of analogy but "in its broad distinctions of the kinds of human effort that are likely to fail; in its empirical distinctions between the desirable and the possible; in its suggestions as to the limits as well as the possibilities of human capacity." He argued that if history contained a lesson it was that "we must be cautious in our prescriptions and modest in our aspirations." Grand designs had led to evil consequences for the Communists, and at times the West had also acted without regard to its limitations. By 1972 he spoke even more pointedly against the use of unsound historical analogies, having in mind reference to the Munich Conference of 1938 and other examples of appeasement to justify unyielding resistance to communism in all situations. Decisions could only be determined by considering existing facts in historical context and not excluding "an active awareness that, whatever our fears of repeating past mistakes, and whatever we think we owe to generations yet unborn, we have a prior obligation to those already born and now alive."

A new theme that would continue in later writings appeared in *Old Myths and New Realities*. Fulbright increasingly felt a need to attain deeper insight into the wellsprings of human behavior, particularly as he grasped the extraordinary solidarity of established attitudes toward policy. This concern drew him to the insights of psychology and even psychoanalysis as possible means for developing capacity to change. "In our quest for world peace," he reasoned, "the *alteration of attitudes* is no less important, perhaps more important, than the resolution of issues." Wars were spawned in the minds of men. To act on the mind was "to act upon the source of conflict and the potential source of redemption and reconciliation." What interested him most was the possibility of "generating a *logical process* in which peoples and statesmen come increasingly to think of war as undesirable and unfeasible." If this process took place, then the world might become capable of the political creativity required to cope with the awful problem of nuclear warfare. These ideas, still inchoate, would play an important role in Fulbright's thought as he headed into the most trying years of his senatorial career, the era of the Vietnamese War.

◇◇◇

In 1964–65 several episodes forced Fulbright to extend his revisionist views into full-blown dissent. In August 1964, he shepherded the Tonkin Gulf Resolution through the Senate, a statement Johnson used as a blank check to pursue the war in Vietnam. Fulbright later regretted his action deeply, claiming that he had been misled as to the facts in the matter. He also considered Johnson's intervention in the Dominican Republic during 1965 an egregious overreaction. Most important was intensification of the Vietnamese War early in 1965, leading to the bombing of North Vietnam and commitment of hundreds of thousands of troops in pursuit of total victory. This activity marked out for the Republic what appeared a quixotic, dangerous course. His reactions to these events appeared in *The Arrogance of Power* (1966), still another book based on speeches delivered in the Senate and elsewhere.[4]

His newfound interest in psychology provided the theme for this volume. Considering the causation of wars, he came to the conclusion that the usual reasons given by historians—to obtain territory, markets, and resources or to defend principles—did not point to roots. Such answers were "explanations or excuses for certain unfathomable drives of human nature," drives he summarized in the term "arrogance of power." Under the compulsion of this drive, nations assumed that "force is the ultimate proof of superiority." The causation of war might "have more to do with pathology than with politics, more to do with irrational pressures of pride and pain than with rational calculations of advantage and profit." Armed with this concept, he proposed to reexamine foreign policy as a "humanist," as one who "weighs human behavior against human *needs*, notes the discrepancy, notes as well the irrational elements in human nature and the limitations these impose, and then tries to find ways, within those limitations, of narrowing the gap between behavior and needs."

Fulbright now viewed the cold war as an outgrowth of total victory in 1945, which had created a vacuum of power in Europe

4. J. William Fulbright, *The Arrogance of Power* (New York, 1966).

and east Asia, filled "quickly and eagerly by Russia and belatedly and reluctantly by America." After twenty years of contention, the condition of the protagonists could be stated clearly. Russia had become a conservative power with a major stake in the status quo, which helped more to explain its course than did its philosophy of world revolution. The United States showed "some signs of that fatal presumption, that overextension of power and mission, which has brought ruin to great nations in the past." Warfare in Vietnam could only accelerate this tendency, which meant that America might become the leader of an international counterrevolution.

According to Fulbright, two strains struggled to dominate American thought: democratic humanism and intolerant puritanism. In troubled times intolerance seemed to control affairs. Given this fact and the danger of nuclear war, radically new attitudes were essential. The world needed no more crusades by high-minded men seeking regeneration. Such endeavors always foundered because of human perversity, because "men are loutish and ungrateful when it comes to improving their souls and more often than not have to be forced into their own salvation." He concluded that the nation required a truly conservative foreign policy, one that would conserve peoples, one that accepted the world "as it is, with all its existing nations and ideologies, with all its existing qualities and shortcomings." The great conservatives, had they been reborn into the twentieth century—men like Burke, Metternich, and Castlereagh—would not have become cold warriors. They would try to deal with the world as it was rather than as they wanted it to be because "they believed in the preservation of indissoluble links between the past and the future, because they profoundly distrusted abstract ideas, and because they did not think themselves or any other man qualified to play God."

Fulbright's idea was reconciliation. The Communist world was no longer monolithic; it was being nationalized and humanized. Remembering that reconciliation posed psychological demands since it required "cultivation of cooperative attitudes and a sense of having practical common objectives," he proposed that the U.S. and Russia eschew great enterprises and instead undertake lesser initiatives, "a great many projects of practical cooperation." The total effect of such measures might alter attitudes. As appropriate activities he mentioned the test ban treaty already accomplished, possible reductions in production of fissionable materials, improved cultural exchanges, arrangements for cooperative space exploration, opening of new consulates, and creation of additional airline connections.

Fulbright remained convinced that strength at home was essential to an effective policy overseas, but he extended analysis of this question to fit his changing views. Nothing troubled him more than the tendency to postpone domestic reform in favor of commitments elsewhere, a frequent cause of national disaster. Sensitive to the charge that he was reverting to the old isolationism, he argued forcefully that he sought not to turn back the clock but to redress the balance between domestic reform and international activism. "Our commitments abroad," he concluded, "are about as permanent as anything can be in human life and . . . the postponement of domestic action until foreign needs subside probably will mean its postponement forever."

For some time Fulbright had been a sharp critic of foreign assistance, commenting frequently on the dangerous consequences of military as opposed to technical or economic aid and maintaining that long-range goals rather than "short-sighted, trivial, and superficial objectives" should guide its distribution. By 1966 he brought this line of thought to maturity. Bilateral aid, he claimed, was operated "as a kind of charity, demeaning to both recipient and donor. In addition, it is becoming a vehicle for deep American involvement in areas and issues which lie beyond our vital interests and our competence." He did not favor eliminating appropriate forms of assistance. He wanted to administer aid as a "community enterprise" on a multilateral basis through institutions such as the UN and the World Bank. In this form economic assistance could foster some redistribution of wealth from the richer to the poorer nations. The aid program in Vietnam had become dangerous because it had fostered "a *state of mind* among American policy-makers under which it was felt that the United States had a proprietary investment in Vietnam—an investment of prestige and money which those responsible were naturally unwilling to see go down the drain."

Fulbright continued his interest in Latin America in *The Arrogance of Power.* He thought American policy contradictory, since Washington supported the Alliance for Progress but also pursued indiscriminate anticommunism. In concrete situations the United States encouraged reactionary governments, a course that played into the hands of the Communists. Having in mind the

intervention in the Dominican Republic, he argued that the country should compete with Communists for influence in reform movements rather than abandon such movements to them. Support for economic development and social justice would counteract communism more effectively than military aid and CIA manipulation. Since Latin America would undoubtedly experience more social revolution, the only question was whether it would adopt Communist or democratic methods. In the short run, perhaps, the best course was to loosen existing bonds with Latin America, remembering that voluntary ties ultimately constituted the closest associations. Let the Latin Americans decide for themselves what relations they wished to maintain and what they wished to discard, and even let them develop arrangements among themselves and with nations outside the hemisphere in which the United States did not participate, a direction that would strengthen pride and mitigate past feelings of indignity and inferiority in relation to the United States.

Almost all of these recommendations were at variance with those of President Johnson—who implicitly represented a prime example of the arrogance of power—but the senator's tendency to root-and-branch dissent came to the surface most clearly in his comments on the Vietnamese War. That struggle was a terrible mistake, if only because the United States could not achieve the end in view with the means at hand. How could Western nations "go into a small undeveloped Asian nation and create stability where there is chaos, the will to fight where there is no tradition of it, and honest government where corruption is almost a way of life?" American policy, motivated by fear of communism, now amounted to what he called the "Asian Doctrine," a commitment comparable to the Monroe Doctrine for Latin America. Johnson's policy envisioned for America a primary role as policeman of the Orient. Unlike earlier commitments of this nature, which were either qualified or exercised cooperatively with other nations, the Asian Doctrine was "unilateral and virtually unlimited in its objectives." The United States was fighting in Vietnam for vague purposes, involving itself on one side of a domestic insurrection. The application of the Asian Doctrine in Vietnam meant not only a commitment to military victory but to long-term engagement: protection of a stable government in Saigon, maintenance of massive power indefinitely in Southeast Asia, and supply of unlimited foreign assistance to create a Vietnamese "great soci-

ety." All these entanglements clearly went beyond America's true national interest. Fulbright detected both domestic and foreign dangers stemming from the Vietnamese adventure. It stood in the way of promising East-West negotiations and prejudiced relations with old friends in Europe. At home it aborted the program of domestic reform launched by Johnson.

He did offer a plan for relieving the crisis in Southeast Asia: neutralization of the region. Any settlement that did not take into account the growing conflict there between the United States and Communist China would be futile. Since neither power could accept defeat, neutralization seemed logical. "In such circumstances," wrote Fulbright, "it is the fact of neutralization rather than the political or ideological complexion of the small countries concerned that has made for stability and peace."

Behind this proposal lay broader views on the revolutionary future of the third world. He did not envision any quick transition to democratic government in Asia, Africa, and Latin America; for most countries a time of troubles would ensue. Americans found it difficult to understand social revolution because their own society was so unrevolutionary. They lacked any "genuine feeling of empathy," even if they thought of their own tradition as revolutionary and as a proper model for others to emulate. Fulbright believed that to relate properly to revolutionary radicalism, the United States must support local nationalism rather than merely oppose communism. Vietnam provided a grisly example of what happened when an anti-Communist policy led the United States to oppose the forces of nationalism.

⟨⟨⟩⟩

To express such views was certain not only to result in exclusion from the inner circles of the Johnson administration but also to engender more public attention than had ever come Fulbright's way. As a leading antiwar spokesman he became a minor folk hero among liberals (and even radicals) despite his proclivity for moderate and at times quite conservative outlooks. He was at the center of the turbulence that overwhelmed the country during the latter years of the 1960s, and his activities then are the services for which he will perhaps be best remembered. As chairman of the Senate Foreign Relations Committee he periodically conducted inquiries associated with the war—to the accom-

paniment of praise from dissenters and often bitter criticism from those who supported the administration's policies. Fulbright's "unthinkable thoughts" continued to mature as the United States finally backed away from its attempt to achieve victory in Vietnam but failed to negotiate an early peace.

The *Crippled Giant*, which appeared in 1972, for the most part extended analyses first presented in 1964–66. Fulbright began with an assumption he had not made before, that nuclear holocaust seemed unlikely because a reasonable balance of power seemed to have developed. In the Nixon-Kissinger foreign policy he saw a shift from ideological crusading to classical power politics. If Henry Kissinger's geopolitics improved on earlier approaches and frequently dictated departures often advocated by Fulbright in the past, the senator nevertheless found fault. A geopolitical approach was both amoral and without substantive purpose. It was also unstable: "Managed with agility, it can hold war off for a time, but war in the end is what it comes to." Once exercised, power could not be allowed to rest. "If you *can* be a bully, then you must be—on pain of being thought a 'pitiful, helpless giant.'" Kissinger's strategy might depict the facts of human experience, but it was unacceptable because of its "utter irrelevance to human needs."

In even more forceful terms than during the 1960s, Fulbright gave witness to his Wilsonian internationalism. The idea of collective security he deemed the one really new thought to develop in the field of international relations during the century. It constituted a critique not only of traditional *Realpolitik* as practiced by the Nixon-Kissinger team but of isolationist thought as well. Recognizing that Metternich and Bismarck had been internationalists of a sort, he insisted that those like himself, who were frequently labeled as neo-isolationists, in fact distinguished between the new and the older variety of internationalism. He and others, he wrote, "welcome the reversion to the old power politics as an improvement on the ideological crusade but regret it in all other respects [retaining] some faith in the validity and viability of the United Nations idea." Looking beyond the Vietnamese War he wondered whether the American people would take advantage of this relative stability to pursue basic changes in the international system. If so, Americans might then shake free of the material and spiritual costs associated with World War II and after. Because the nation had attempted to play a role for which it was unfit—that of international power broker—it had depleted its resources, becoming a crippled giant.

Updating his commentary on Russia, the senator saw further signs of recovery in the balance of power. Giving full credit to Nixon for his successful negotiations in Moscow during May 1972, he saw in this event "the final, belated acceptance by the United States of the postwar balance of power in Europe and in Soviet-American relations." He doubted that the future held much promise unless the country adopted a course that in essentials reverted to Woodrow Wilson's concept of world order. He argued that a corrupted version of this outlook had dominated recent American history, defining Wilson's central premise as the view that "the nation's vital interests are essentially domestic in character, that it is our own democracy that is to be defended, that our proper concern is not with what we can make of the world but what must be done in the world to create conditions under which we will be free to make what we want of ourselves."

As a fundamental guide for the future, Fulbright advocated a much limited foreign policy, not forever and not to the extent of wholesale abandonment of commitments, but long enough "to replenish our depleted resources, renew our neglected society, and restore our endangered democracy." Gone was his earlier preoccupation with grandiose schemes such as a concert of free nations. Changing conditions had reduced the concept of an Atlantic partnership to "little more than a lingering sentimentality." Europe could take care of itself. To those who called him a neo-isolationist for advocating a modest course, Fulbright had harsh words. This charge was "an invention of people who confuse internationalism with an intrusive American interventionism, with a quasi-imperialism."

His views on the latter stages of the Vietnamese War echoed this moderate approach. The policy of Vietnamization, which he considered a disguised extension of the Johnsonian goal of victory, was doomed. Because President Nixon's visit to China pointed toward improved relations with that country, Fulbright felt this development, of and by itself, repudiated the idea that war in Vietnam had to be waged to discredit wars of national liberation. He marveled at the importance attached to the conflict by its defenders. "From the standpoint of American security and interests, the central fact about Indochina is that it does not matter very much who rules in these small and undeveloped lands." He did not favor Communist domination, but such an outcome seemed at least tolerable. He agreed with those experts who believed that a Communist regime in Southeast Asia would erect a more effective barrier to Chinese expansion than a weak non-Communist state, especially since China represented more a political and cultural than a military menace to the region. Given the damage at home wrought by years of struggle abroad, he counseled Americans "to acknowledge and liquidate our mistake and, by that very act, initiate the process of social—and moral—reconstruction of which our country is in so great need."

True to his earlier beliefs, Fulbright remained convinced that an unduly optimistic appraisal of human capacity would lead only to greater difficulties in the future. Man, despite technological accomplishments, remained a "moral primitive." Thought about attaining true human community must begin with "the candid recognition that man's capacity for brotherly love is limited, and so is his capacity for voluntary restraint of his competitive and destructive impulses." Mankind must find means of restraining international lawlessness as it had managed to curb domestic anarchy in order to sustain hopes for the survival of the race. "If that is not the most promising of foundations on which to build," he concluded, "it has at least the solidity of truth."

◇◇◇

Fulbright's thought over the past thirty years contains many elements of continuity. While he has been innovative and flexible in his search for ways of conducting American diplomacy, he has always acted in terms of a moderately pessimistic evaluation of human nature. This fundamental philosophical conviction aligns him against the views of both conservative and liberal thinkers. His recommendations over time have increasingly emphasized caution and restraint. He is a moderate and a realist in the great tradition of the intellectual guides with whom he feels most at home, de Tocqueville and Lippmann. Another sustained commitment has been his rejection of absolute national sovereignty as a principle for organizing international relations. To his mind the system of nation-states is obsolete, and he has always searched for ways of moving the world to supranational modes of organization.

Within this pattern of continuity Fulbright has gone through considerable changes of view, a natural consequence of experiences during an era of profound historical discontinuity. The more important modifications in the realm of policy are related to his growing pessimism. If in his early years there was a strong sense of American power and responsibility, his later commentary stresses partnership with other nations. At the outset he embraced the views of those who advocated containment of Russian expansion, although he advanced as an institutional vehicle the concept of Atlantic partnership. Most recently he has emphasized the need for a sound social and political system at home. In this respect, his views parallel those of the great Progressives of the early twentieth century, including Wilson, who recognized that international involvement might threaten liberal reform. No neo-isolationist, Fulbright believes that the United States must forego the active role it followed during the cold war because of the necessity for overhauling the great tradition of American democracy. Again, overshadowing all else is his strong conviction that foreign policy begins at home, that external success rests on a strong internal polity.

Fulbright has not been a particularly original thinker; his most important function has been to mediate between the intelligentsia and the public. He has synthesized for popular consideration the drift of informed opinion and frequently has served as public advocate for fresh ideas well before the country has been prepared to accept them easily. The validity of his most recent pronouncements will depend primarily on whether he is right in discerning the emergence of a rough new balance of power and whether he is right about the preeminent importance of domestic reform as a basis for continuing successes in foreign affairs.

Fulbright has been a most constructive legislator in the sense of that function that he himself considers so important: as an educator helping to build sound public attitudes toward great questions of policy. He has suffered much in the service of this ideal. No student of his public life can fail to admire his humanity, his sympathy for the lot of ordinary folk despite his patrician proclivities. Fortune cast him in the role of dissenter, not a part that he desired for himself or that came easily. Always a historian, seeking guidance in the study of the changing past, he proved able to explore new learning, especially psychology, when he discerned a need for deeper understanding of human motives at a late point in his career. This capacity marks him as a man of intellectual courage, an appropriate and admirable quality for one who has pursued the vocation of teacher.

BIBLIOGRAPHIC NOTE

The best sources of information for the views of Senator Fulbright are his numerous books and other writings. These include *Prospects for the West* (Cambridge, Mass., 1963), his contribution to *The Elite and the Electorate: Is Government by the People Possible?* (Palo Alto, 1963), *Old Myths and New Realities, and Other Commentaries* (New York, 1964), *The Arrogance of Power* (Cambridge, Mass., 1966), *The Two Americas* (Storrs, Conn., 1966), and *The Crippled Giant: American Foreign Policy and It's Domestic Consequences* (New York, 1972). See also Fulbright's muckraking book, *The Pentagon Propaganda Machine* (New York, 1970). The compilation of Fulbright's public statements by Karl Meyer, *Fulbright of Arkansas: The Public Positions of a Private Thinker* (Washington, D. C., 1963), is informative.

Useful biographical accounts are Tristram Coffin, *Senator Fulbright: Portrait of a Public Philosopher* (New York, 1966), and Haynes Johnson and Bernard M. Gwertzman, *Fulbright: The Dissenter* (Garden City, N.Y., 1968). The characterization of Fulbright in David Halberstam, *The Best and the Brightest* (New York, 1972), is brilliantly done.

The White House

AN AMERICAN METTERNICH:

HENRY A. KISSINGER

and the Global Balance of Power

Michael Roskin

In the late 1960s and early 1970s America suffered a Pearl Harbor in reverse: Vietnam. The former catastrophe had pushed the United States into tremendous overseas involvement; the latter threatened to turn the nation inward. The economy, public opinion, and Congress all pressed for reduction of U.S. commitments abroad. The word "neo-isolationism" was in the air. Coming to the presidency in 1969, Richard M. Nixon recognized the trend toward disengagement, feared it, and contrived to circumvent it. He fervently wished to keep the United States in the international game in a leadership role. The massive U.S. interventionism of the 1940s through the 1960s, however, was no longer possible, so Nixon turned to a body of assumptions that had received little

This essay is based in part on Professor Roskin's doctoral thesis, "Turning Inward: The Effects of Vietnam on U.S. Foreign Policy."

prior attention in American foreign policy: balance of power diplomacy. In practice, balance of power thinking amounted to a radical revision of U.S. foreign policy. The Nixon administration dropped the ideological rhetoric of the cold war and sat down to do business with Moscow and Peking.

This major shift required new concepts, careful planning, and meticulous, even personal, implementation. The traditional executive departments were too large and sprawling to carry out such a program, even if they had been intellectually capable of it. Nixon rather needed a single person who would understand precisely what he was trying to achieve and in whom he could place the highest confidence. It was further important that this agent or alter ego be thoroughly grounded in the principles of international equilibration. A forty-six-year-old Harvard government professor named Henry Alfred Kissinger suited the role admirably.

While Nixon and Kissinger achieved a rare rapport with each other, from the beginning Kissinger served merely as Nixon's personal adviser with no freedom to act on his own. Indeed, Kissinger often described himself as little more than a good and faithful servant to the president, laying out options for his choice and giving advice only when asked. This skirted the question of how often Nixon asked, which was probably quite often. "Frankly, I can't imagine what the government would be like without you," Nixon told Kissinger at the time he decided to stay on and not return to Harvard after two years in the White House. The two men needed each other; their relationship seemed symbiotic. Nixon established the general direction of policy and supplied the power, and Kissinger elaborated the tactics of diplomacy and carried them out, often in highly personal style.[1]

So involved did Kissinger become in the execution of policy, making dozens of flights overseas for delicate negotiations that stunned the world when revealed, that he frequently eclipsed President Nixon in the public's attention. As a celebrity of the 1970s Kissinger had few equals. He stood out both in relation to the colorless, nonintellectual administration in which he served and in relation to his diplomatic predecessors. Of the two dozen

1. The first item on an agenda for future research should be the determination of how much of U.S. foreign policy in the early 1970s was Kissinger's and how much was Nixon's. It may, of course, be impossible to untangle the two.

or so figures in this work, Kissinger is the only Jew, the only one born in Europe, the only divorcé, the only career scholar of international relations, and, most importantly, the only man to have served a president directly with no official position in the State Department, Congress, or the military services. His unique status changed only in 1973, when he was named secretary of state.

◇◇◇

That Kissinger was Jewish, German born, and divorced may have little relevance to his foreign policy thinking. Psychoanalytically oriented writers suggest that Kissinger's birth and boyhood in Fürth (near Nuremberg) scarred his psyche with fear of revolutionary upheavals, causing his conservative, power-oriented viewpoint. Why being a Jewish boy in Nazi Germany should make one a conservative rather than a leftist or Zionist (Kissinger took little interest in Jewish affairs) remains unclear. Further, Kissinger shrugged off his boyhood experiences as "not a key to anything. I was not consciously unhappy. I was not so acutely aware of what was going on." When he was fifteen, in 1938, the family moved to America and settled in upper Manhattan. The only evident remnant of Kissinger's life before 1938 is his German accent, which he has never lost.

Kissinger seems to have harbored no special grudge against Germany; he waited to be drafted in 1943 rather than volunteering earlier. He graduated from George Washington High School in 1941 with a straight A average. Then, intending to become an accountant, he took evening courses at New York City College and worked days in a shaving brush factory. His pursuits were totally conventional.

Army service sharply changed Kissinger's orientation from bourgeois to intellectual. A key figure in this process seems to have been Fritz Kraemer, another German-born immigrant, sixteen years older than Kissinger and a holder of two doctorate degrees. The two men met as privates in the Eighty-fourth Infantry Division, and Kraemer apparently awakened the intellect of his younger friend. "He told me I had a good political mind," Kissinger reflected years later. "It was a thought that had never occurred to me." Kraemer's connections seem also to have produced some choice assignments for Kissinger, including interpreting for a

general, administering a German district in the occupation government, and, after Kissinger left the army as a staff sergeant in 1946,
teaching as a well-paid civilian at an army intelligence school in
Oberammergau.

By this time, however, Kissinger yearned for an intellectual
career and in the fall of 1946 entered Harvard on a New York State
scholarship. Picking up a Phi Beta Kappa key on the way, he
breezed through to a B.A. in government in 1950, an M.A. in 1952,
and a Ph.D. in 1954. His mentor during this period was Professor
William Yandell ("Wild Bill") Elliott, a strongly anti-Communist
scholar of world affairs and an influential Washington adviser in
the Roosevelt and Truman administrations.

In 1949, while still an undergraduate, Kissinger married Ann
Fleischer, also of German-Jewish background. The marriage ended
two children and fifteen years later. Since his 1964 divorce, and
even a little before, Kissinger has enjoyed the company of
numerous attractive women. In the early 1970s he and his dates
were so photographed that he earned the reputation of "swinger."
How much actual swinging he did is uncertain—he often worked
eighteen hours a day—but the pose served him well as a cover to
distract the press from his more serious activities. Once in 1971,
for example, he was spotted in a Paris restaurant with a female
American television producer and got a sly wink from newsmen
who, luckily for Kissinger, failed to unearth the real purpose of his
visit to Paris: ultrasecret negotiations with the North Vietnamese.

Coincidentally, Kissinger's presumed model in international
diplomacy, Austrian Prince Metternich, was an inveterate woman-
izer. Kissinger's relationships with women, however, remained
opaque because he adroitly deflected curiosity by means of his
self-deprecating humor. Explaining his dates with writer Gloria
Steinem, Kissinger announced that she was "not now and has
never been my girl friend. But I am not discouraged. After all, she
did not say that, if nominated she would not accept or, if elected,
she would not serve." Kissinger termed such ploys "humanizing
devices," but left unclear whether they actually served to human-
ize him or merely to convince others that he was human. At any
rate, his female companions turned the portly former academic
into a superstar, which in turn may well have enhanced public
acceptance of his diplomacy.

Kissinger's intellectual foundation was set by the time he
wrote his doctoral dissertation (published in 1957), a highly

regarded analysis of Metternich's and Castlereagh's power-balancing maneuvers after the Napoleonic wars. In current political science language, the dissertation was thoroughly "traditional" in that it used no "variables" or statistics to validate hypotheses. Instead, Kissinger dug into Metternich's and Castlereagh's papers, many in French and German, to paint with grand strokes a picture of balance of power diplomacy in its heyday. Today a political science department might reject such a "wisdom" approach and direct the student to the history department (which might disparage the effort as metahistorical). The work contained at least as much history as political science.

Although it would not satisfy a behavioralist's thirst for empirical verification, Kissinger's approach did distill considerable wisdom that might be of some policy use, which is precisely what Kissinger intended. While his doctoral dissertation dealt with the post-Napoleonic era, the work seems clearly designed as a springboard to twentieth-century problems. The wisdom Kissinger extracted from Metternich's time he applied intact in his best-selling *Nuclear Weapons and Foreign Policy* (1957). He even began both works with the same allusion to Greek mythology: that Nemesis sometimes punishes man by fulfilling his wishes too completely.

Kissinger wrote only one carefully researched and richly documented book, *A World Restored*, a revised and expanded version of his dissertation. His four subsequent books and more than forty articles, aimed at policy thinkers rather than scholars, contained little original research or documentation.[2] These works simply presented Kissinger's views on current strategic and diplomatic problems, supported by little evidence but beautifully (if somewhat turgidly) argued and written.

Kissinger always seemed to find the lessons of his Metternich study closely applicable to the current scene. He argued in his dissertation, for example, that a revolutionary state (in this case France) in a world of status quo powers would feel insecure and would try to alleviate this insecurity by crushing other states. Such a situation of chronic mistrust Kissinger dubbed a "revolutionary"

2. An exception to this might be his 1968 article on Bismarck, which shows a flash of the old depth: "The White Revolutionary: Reflections on Bismarck," *Daedalus* 97 (Summer 1968), 888–924. This study also uses the line, "But the gods sometimes ˹ ˼nish pride by fulfilling man's wishes too completely," p. 890.

world system, the chief cause of which was the revolutionary state's quest for absolute security. "Only absolute security—the neutralization of the opponent," wrote Kissinger in his *World Restored*, "—is considered as sufficient guarantee, and thus the desire of one power for absolute security means absolute insecurity for all the others." Opposed to this is what Kissinger called a "legitimate" world order in which status quo states have no deep fears of their neighbors' intentions and thus neither need nor strive for absolute security. It was a profound and well-expressed insight, and Kissinger repeated it in books and articles from 1955 to 1966. "Absolute security for one power means absolute insecurity for all the others."

Kissinger's writings were repetitive. Many of his arguments published in the 1960s could be found in his dissertation, sometimes word for word. Such behavior is hardly unique to Kissinger; indeed, it is probably typical of most academics. Kissinger, however, could have been a large cut above this; he might have grown intellectually if he had pursued a straight scholarly career; but he was too busy. His repetitive writings were not cheap or dishonest; they appear to be simply the mark of a man in a hurry. Kissinger hoped to influence policy and he seems to have used his many books and articles to build a reputation in policy-making rather than academic circles. Thus, there was an inevitable tendency to rely on his original insight rather than to set aside months for fresh research and reflection.[3]

Kissinger had little time for such an introspective existence. Even as a Harvard graduate student he was immersed in other activities, from running the Harvard International Seminar (which he headed until 1969) to consulting for the army's Operations Research Office and Psychological Strategy Board. Appointed an instructor in government at Harvard in 1954, the thirty-one-year-

---

3. One widely anthologized article can be strongly recommended, both because it is well written and because it contains in a few pages all the main points of Kissinger's four earlier books. "Domestic Structures and Foreign Policy," which first appeared in *Daedalus* (Spring 1966), consists of little more than pasted-together portions of *World Restored* (chapter 1), *Nuclear Weapons* (chapter 3), *Necessity for Choice* (chapter 6), and the 1965 *Troubled Partnership* (chapter 7). It has been reprinted in James N. Rosenau, ed., *International Politics and Foreign Policy* (New York, 1969), Frederick H. Hartmann, ed., *World in Crisis* (New York, 1973), Robert L. Pfaltzgraff, ed., *Politics and the International System* (Philadelphia, 1972), and Henry A. Kissinger, *American Foreign Policy* (New York, 1969).

old Kissinger boldly applied for the vacant managing editorship of *Foreign Affairs*. Although he was turned down, he attracted the attention of Hamilton Fish Armstrong, the quarterly's august editor, who recommended him for an eighteen-month appointment as director of a research program to study methods of dealing with the Soviet Union short of all-out war. From this project came Kissinger's *Nuclear Weapons and Foreign Policy* (1957), which soon became required reading in Washington and in university courses on defense policy.

The basic thesis of the book was not startling; it was, rather, the conventional wisdom of the day, one of many refutations of John Foster Dulles's policy of "massive retaliation" to counter Soviet expansion. Criticism of Dulles's strategy had actually begun in 1954, the year in which he first articulated the policy. By the late 1950s scores of books and articles argued that reliance on nuclear retaliation alone boxed America into the untenable position of having either to ignore minor Communist incursions or make them the potential cause of global war. Massive retaliation left the United States with either/or choices when a spectrum of responses was needed. The argument became more urgent as the decade progressed and the Soviets appeared to have developed warheads and rockets equal or superior to America's. *Nuclear Weapons and Foreign Policy* simply said what many other strategic thinkers were arguing at the time, but said it better than most. Kissinger did not stand apart from the mainstream nor did he lead it. His criticisms had nothing to do with the fundamental assumptions of American foreign policy; he rather criticized methods. He left unexamined the prevailing dogmas that communism was monolithic, expansionist, Kremlin controlled, and responsible for uprisings in the third world. The conventional wisdom of the 1950s, lasting until the late 1960s, saw strategic import in all conflicts; few or none were merely local squabbles. Kissinger accepted this view. With the United States locked into a strategy of "all-out war," he wrote in *Nuclear Weapons*, "the Soviet bloc may then decide, as its nuclear arsenal grows, to absorb the peripheral areas of Eurasia." He lumped the Middle East together with Korea and Indochina as areas where "Soviet and Chinese aggressive moves have occurred." The possibility that Indochina and the Middle East might be scenes of intense, local, nationalistic conflicts rather than Sino-Soviet pincer movements did not occur to Kissinger, just as it did not occur to most Americans.

To block Communist expansion on the Eurasian periphery, Kissinger and others recommended that the United States immediately develop capabilities for fighting limited wars. At this point, however, Kissinger differed somewhat from other critics by urging development of limited nuclear capability as well as conventional capability. Most Dulles critics feared that any use of nuclear weapons would soon escalate into all-out war. They wanted to develop conventional forces to preclude use of nuclear ones. Three years after publication of *Nuclear Weapons* Kissinger dropped his tactical nuclear suggestion and fell into line with the other critics. He shifted in part because the growing Soviet nuclear capability had offset America's former superiority.

Senator John F. Kennedy picked up the debate over strategy, embellished it with urgent rhetoric, and used it effectively in his presidential campaign. He launched the "missile gap" controversy in a 1958 Senate speech, predicting that the "critical years" of Soviet superiority would be 1960 to 1964. Kissinger accepted this view in his *Necessity for Choice* (1960), a book fully as alarmist as a Kennedy speech. Kissinger saw imminent doom for the United States if it did not turn to a flexible response strategy of the sort that Kennedy was advocating. There never had been any missile gap, however, as the Democrats admitted after Kennedy's inauguration; like many others, Kissinger had fallen for Democratic campaign rhetoric. Indeed, American missile strength in the early 1960s so overshadowed Soviet capabilities, some scholars believe, that it prompted Moscow to put missiles in Cuba in 1962 to redress the strategic imbalance. After all, absolute security for one power, in this case the United States, meant absolute insecurity for all the others.

In *Necessity for Choice* Kissinger criticized the Eisenhower administration for reducing the army to a mere fourteen divisions, leaving the United States "in no position to fight a limited war." President Nixon reduced the army from nineteen and two-thirds to thirteen divisions, but by the early 1970s Kissinger and most other defense intellectuals did not protest; the advocates of limited war had had their fingers burned in Vietnam. During the Kennedy presidency their views had been implemented. They got a bigger defense budget, a larger army, a counter-insurgency committee, Green Berets, and Vietnam. They wanted limited war, and they got it. One might almost say, recalling Kissinger's overworked aphorism, that the figure of Nemesis haunted the 1960s, punishing man by fulfilling his wishes too completely.

Kissinger changed a number of his perceptions during the agony of Vietnam, as did America as a whole. He ceased using the words "Soviet" and "Communist" interchangeably. He discarded the monolithic image of communism and stopped referring to the "Sino-Soviet bloc." Kissinger in 1970 was less bellicose and alarmist than he had been in 1960. It is tempting to say that Kissinger the practitioner had turned his back on Kissinger the theorist; that would be an exaggeration, for he preserved the basic framework he had constructed early in his scholarly career, and he took it with him to the White House.

Perhaps the key element of this framework was Kissinger's rather firm belief in a general balance of power approach. Although he conceded that the classic balance of power game was inapplicable to the twentieth century, Kissinger persistently returned to the concepts and phrases of balancing as the only reasonable way to construct a world order. In a 1973 interview, for example, he explained that balance of power was obsolete but that we "must have a certain equilibrium of strength." Kissinger, to be sure, had no fixed formula but rather a general approach that depended as much on the subtleties and sensitivity of the practitioner as on anything else. Power balances do not fall from heaven; the artist-statesman, who must use nuance, ambiguity, and intuition to patiently construct a durable edifice, creates them. One of the greatest errors—to which Americans are particularly prone, according to Kissinger—is to aim directly for peace. A statesman who wishes nothing but peace is at the mercy of any expansionist, revolutionary power willing to risk war. Statesmen who pursue reasonable national interests rather than peace itself may be able to balance and limit their demands. The resulting equilibrium, which Kissinger called a "legitimate" international order, then brings peace as a by-product.

The "revolutionary" world system of the mid-twentieth century was surely due to the destabilizing influence of the Soviet bloc, Kissinger believed. The Kremlin was the revolutionary maverick that felt it must remake the world in its own image to protect itself from hostile outside forces. Kissinger remained untouched by the wave of revisionism that grew in the wake of Vietnam, which posited United States behavior as an important contributor to international tensions. This did not mean that Kissinger presumed permanent Soviet-American hostility. He believed that a firm stance in the face of expansionism can gradually induce revolutionary powers to become legitimate without threatening their existence. The Kremlin could eventually be brought around to play by the rules of a legitimate world order; that is, they would not threaten because they would not feel threatened. The beginning of this process is extraordinarily difficult, Kissinger admitted, because initially a status quo power and a revolutionary power have nothing in common. "Diplomats can still meet but they cannot persuade for they have ceased to speak the same language," he repeated.[4]

To carry out this delicate process, Kissinger firmly believed, bureaucracies are worthless, incapable of policy innovation. He regarded the conventional institutions of United States foreign policy with little more than contempt. He saw a clear incompatibility between "inspiration" and "organization": inspiration brings fresh ideas, but the organization functions only by routinizing old ones. Both may be necessary, but they will not be found in the same place. The State Department might satisfactorily handle daily paper flow, but the American penchant for staffing the higher positions there with businessmen and lawyers produced "pragmatic" compromises between bureaus rather than bold new approaches. For inspiration, Kissinger modestly suggested, outside intellectuals should be recruited, particularly those who understand the historic processes of world politics.

Kissinger's general orientation can be compared to that which George F. Kennan claimed he had in mind in his containment doctrine. Kennan later denied that his 1947 "X" article aimed at a military and ideological standoff between the Soviet Union and the West; it was, rather, to be a flexible tool to teach the Russians international good behavior. Kissinger saw this better than did his postwar predecessors who had turned containment into an ideology. Both Kennan and Kissinger, it should be noted, shared the same "realist" approach to world politics.

In part because of his many books and articles, Kissinger's

---

4. The phrase may not have originated with Kissinger. Raymond Aron said in a 1953 French article, "It takes two to negotiate a settlement; both sides must speak the same language and follow the same principles."

academic and political careers prospered during the 1960s. He became a full professor at Harvard in 1962, and his course on foreign policy was one of the most popular in Cambridge. Kissinger had to miss many classes, though, because of his extensive outside consulting assignments: for the National Security Council in 1961–62, for the Arms Control and Disarmament Agency from 1961 to 1967, and for the State Department from 1965 to 1969. Kissinger attained no position of prominence in the Washington of Kennedy and Johnson, however. In the first place, Kennedy made little use of the National Security Council, preferring instead to conduct policy with the help of former Harvard dean McGeorge Bundy. Bundy monopolized access to President Kennedy and did not much utilize the part-time consulting of Kissinger, who in any case did not like playing second fiddle. On a more philosophical level, Kennedy and Johnson were global crusaders rather than subtle balancers of power. Kissinger's approach was far removed from the "can do" enthusiasm of the Kennedy people and the "shoot from the hip" style of Johnson.

Kissinger had greater success on the Republican side, particularly with Nelson A. Rockefeller, governor of New York and serious contender for the Republican presidential nomination in the 1960s. The two first met as a result of Kissinger's 1954 appointment to the Council on Foreign Relations study project. In 1956, Rockefeller named Kissinger to a Rockefeller Fund study project that resulted in *Necessity for Choice*. At the same time Kissinger started advising Rockefeller on foreign policy matters and then writing speeches for him. Kissinger even had a Telex machine installed in his Harvard office to transmit texts to Albany. The political ties lasted until 1968.

Kissinger's concern with temporal power seemingly marks him as an opportunist, but with two reservations. In the first place, probably all political scientists long for power in the real world; Kissinger was just more obvious and more successful. Everything Kissinger wrote, even his dissertation, related to current policy. This is not necessarily a criticism; indeed, many believe the university should be "relevant" to practical action. Secondly, there is nothing wrong with a scholar wanting to become a practitioner, especially when he is more able in the latter role.

◇◇◇

With his consulting in Washington, it was inevitable that Kissinger become involved in the Vietnam question. In 1965 he visited South Vietnam as a State Department consultant for a firsthand report—a pessimistic one—on how things were going during the year of the major U.S. buildup. In 1967 he helped open contacts between Washington and Hanoi through French acquaintances, journeying to Paris several times to convey messages. The operation, code named "Pennsylvania," stayed secret until 1972 when it surfaced as part of the Pentagon Papers. Until 1969, Kissinger published nothing on the Vietnam War, nor did he even take a conspicuous public stand.

By 1968, however, he was ready to admit that Vietnam had been "a very critical failure of the American philosophy of international relations." He neglected to name himself as a contributor to this philosophy or to find any connection between Vietnam and his earlier enthusiasm for limited war capabilities. By the time Kissinger appeared with an article of his own on Vietnam it was 1969 and his perceptions were banalities: "We fought a military war; our opponents fought a political one." Bernard Fall and Sir Robert G. K. Thompson had touted such conventional wisdom for years; by then it was a shopworn observation in Washington. Kissinger's ideas on the difficulties of getting out, however, were remarkably prescient: Saigon would balk; there would be a scramble for territory before a cease-fire; and a Saigon–Viet Cong coalition could not possibly work.

While admitting that the war had been based on false premises, Kissinger argued that the huge American involvement itself made Vietnam a matter over which the United States must not lose credibility. "Other nations can gear their actions to ours only if they can count on our steadiness," he wrote. Kissinger flatly ruled out a unilateral U.S. withdrawal from Vietnam. On the surface this would appear to be a hawkish position, but Kissinger advocated neither a drive for "victory" nor a policy of indefinite continuation. What he may have had in mind, but did not state publicly, appeared only in private conversations at Harvard in 1968, according to Daniel Ellsberg of Pentagon Papers fame. There, said Ellsberg, Kissinger repeatedly urged a policy of "decent interval," that is, a delay of two to three years between American withdrawal and Communist take-over. This implied that the best the United States could hope for from the Vietnam imbroglio was merely avoiding the appearance of direct defeat.

Kissinger's elaborate concern for appearances, a concern that made him considerably less a thoroughgoing realist than someone like Hans Morgenthau, seems to have matched the views of President-elect Nixon. Nixon, too, wanted United States forces withdrawn, but not in a way that would trigger "neo-isolationism" at home or loss of credibility abroad. A sudden, unilateral American withdrawal and quick Communist take-over could do just that, they feared. An America that believed it had been defeated in war would be divided, rancorous, and unable to play a leading role in world politics. Nixon used these themes repeatedly during his first term.

The newly elected Nixon, who claimed a special interest and expertise in foreign affairs, had followed Kissinger's writings for some years but had met him only once, in 1967, at a social function given by Clare Boothe Luce. In late November 1968 Nixon summoned Kissinger to New York and elicited his views on foreign policy at length. Kissinger had not thought much of Nixon previously, but he emerged from the meetings impressed. Nixon named Kissinger his assistant for national security affairs, and the following January Kissinger moved into a White House office and a $42,000-a-year job.

It soon became apparent that Nixon was using Kissinger as far more than a consultant. Kissinger also became executive secretary of the National Security Council, a body whose fortunes had fluctuated since its establishment in 1947. Eisenhower relied on it heavily, but Kennedy and Johnson preferred to work informally with a few individuals. Nixon upgraded the NSC and used it as the control center for all important foreign policy matters. The reorganizer and master of the NSC's staff was Kissinger. As a result, the Harvard professor soon became far more important than either the secretaries of state or defense.

Kissinger brought together a staff of 46 professional assistants and 105 administrative personnel (more than double the previous administration's) with an annual budget of $2.3 million. The NSC staff commanded compliance from State, the Pentagon, and the Central Intelligence Agency, ordering studies, reports, and options, and then structuring them as Kissinger saw fit. During Nixon's first three years in office, for example, the NSC staff supervised more than one hundred forty National Security Study Memoranda from the traditional departments, sometimes returning them if they were not sufficiently thorough. In 1969 the NSC staff rated studies produced by the State Department only "50 to 70 per cent acceptable."

The State Department's subservient status did little for its employees' morale, which had long been in decline as major foreign policy decisions were increasingly taken over by presidential assistants and the Pentagon. Kissinger and his staff, however, brought this trend to a new high point. An especially stinging remark came in 1971 from Senator Stuart Symington, Democrat of Missouri, who charged that Kissinger rather than William P. Rogers was "the actual architect of our foreign policy" and that Rogers was "laughed at" in Washington. President Nixon called the charge a "cheap shot" at his "oldest and closest" cabinet appointee; nonetheless, the charge was absolutely right, and all official Washington knew it. Even foreign ambassadors often preferred an appointment with Kissinger than with Rogers; they knew where the power lay.

From a functional viewpoint, the swollen (36,600 employees) bureaucracy at State was ill equipped to take foreign policy firmly in hand, considering especially the don't-rock-the-boat caution of career Foreign Service officers and the tendency to staff the top positions with lawyers (such as Rogers), a practice about which Kissinger had written earlier. State retained a certain residual importance in the daily workings of foreign affairs, but not in the actual formulation of policy. The gigantic U.S. overseas involvements after World War II led to specialization: Defense took strategic questions and the disposition of American forces abroad; the CIA did faster and sharper political reporting than State; the Commerce Department played a major role in economic policy; public diplomacy went to the U.S. Information Agency; State tried to play its old role of gentlemen generalist, but the ball slipped from its fingers. Increasingly, presidents turned to small coordinating staffs right in the White House. Kennedy was so exasperated with the State Department's slowness that he formulated most of his own policy in consultation with McGeorge Bundy. Johnson similarly used Walt Rostow, even down to planning bombing targets in North Vietnam. With Kissinger, however, the process probably became irreversible and institutionalized. This by itself was one of Henry Kissinger's major contributions to United States foreign policy.

There was little doubt that Kissinger's NSC staff formulated policies—or, in the special terminology used by President Nixon, "policy options" from which he chose—better than traditional departments. Even if a later president tried to restore decision-making initiative to State, he would still feel compelled to have a coordinator and staff close at hand. Relatively placid times might allow the traditional departments to take over more decisions, precisely because they would then be only routine. Until placid times return—an unlikely event—every future president will want his own Kissinger.

Even more embarrassing for State was the fact that Kissinger was not merely Nixon's idea man but his agent in diplomatic negotiations as well. Important matters were not handled by ambassadors or by the State Department in Washington, but rather by Kissinger personally. He so bypassed the American embassy in Moscow that one diplomat complained, "I have to go to my Soviet counterpart at the ministry to find out what has been going on in these talks." U.S. missions around the world sometimes felt that they served as little more than Kissinger's hotels. This situation was actually a long-term trend. With the development of jet aircraft many of the world's capitals were but a few hours from Washington. It was easier for a president to send his alter ego to discuss exactly what he wanted than to brief a series of State Department people who might not convey precise nuances. Further, Nixon had a penchant for *coups de théâtre,* dramatic international moves that surprised everybody. One man could carry out the groundwork for such moves in reasonable secrecy; a bureaucracy could not. Kissinger became resident philosopher, master planner, and personal executor of the Nixon policy.

To do this Kissinger worked himself and his staff hard. "There can't be another crisis this week," he once quipped. "My schedule is already full." Many of the NSC staff resigned, either under pressure of his demands or over continuation of the Vietnam War, especially at the time of the 1970 United States invasion of Cambodia. By mid-1971 only about a fourth of his twenty-eight original professional-level staffers were still there. Kissinger's treatment of his assistants amused Washington. One story related that he became so angry over a State Department cable that he backed its bearer against a wall and berated him for ten minutes. "I'm not going to clear that cable unless changes are made in it," said Kissinger, "and you can march back down to the state department and tell the secretary. . . ." His victim protested, "But Dr. Kissinger, I work for *you.*"

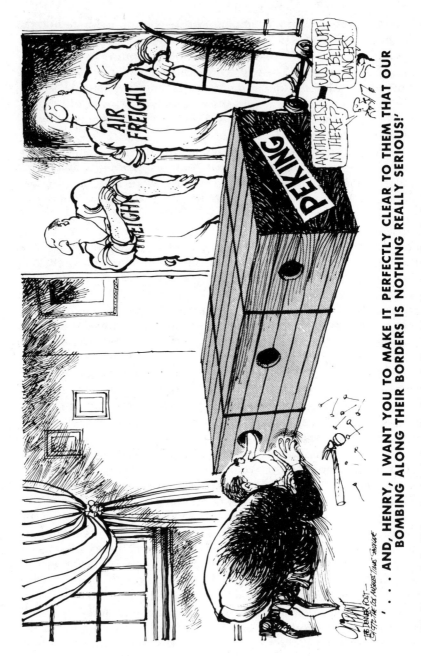

'. . . AND, HENRY, I WANT YOU TO MAKE IT PERFECTLY CLEAR TO THEM THAT OUR BOMBING ALONG THEIR BORDERS IS NOTHING REALLY SERIOUS!'

Editorial cartoon by Pat Oliphant. Copyright the Denver Post. Reprinted with permission of Los Angeles Times Syndicate

Brutal or not, in short order a markedly different United States foreign policy began to emerge from this machine. Twelve days after his inauguration, Nixon instructed Kissinger to put out feelers to Peking through Eastern European contacts. Later in 1969 Kissinger began meeting secretly with North Vietnamese representatives in Paris to try to reach a plausible compromise to cap American disengagement in Vietnam. On the theoretical level, Kissinger and his staff turned out a new and more limited orientation for U.S. policy as a whole. This first surfaced in Nixon's Guam Doctrine of 25 July 1969, and the president elaborated on it in subsequent "state of the world" messages each February.

$$\diamond\!\diamond\!\diamond$$

Major changes were surely due. By 1969 the United States showed signs of war weariness. Even then the Vietnam War, which was to drag on another four years, was the longest in U.S. history (dating it from 1961, as the military does). The public mood was frustrated and snappish. Much of the remaining support for the war had evaporated in the wake of the 1968 *Tet* offensive, which demolished the Johnson administration's claims of progress.

If Johnson had been able to fool the public and Congress about the burdens of the war, he could not fool the economy. Starting with the major U.S. escalation in 1965, the overheated American economy went into an inflationary spiral that developed a life of its own and refused to end with Nixon's wage and price controls. The inflation fueled severe balance of payments deficits and runs on the dollar abroad. By August 1971 Nixon had to do the hitherto unthinkable: devalue the dollar. The move accomplished little, and he had to do it again in February 1973. In total, the dollar lost about one-fifth of its value, even more in relation to German and Japanese currencies. The United States experienced trade deficits for the first time since the 1890s. Large sectors of U.S. industry and labor demanded protectionist trade legislation. America discovered that it no longer had the means to finance major overseas military commitments.

Partly to save money and partly to deflate the biggest single source of discontent, Nixon ended the draft in 1973 and trimmed the armed forces from 3.5 million in 1968 to 2.3 million in 1973. The cuts fell especially hard on ground forces, the army and marines, without which there could be no overseas interventions.

Nixon's biggest problems, however, came as he faced an inflamed, Democrat-controlled Congress that seemed to be looking for excuses to hamstring the executive in foreign policy. Too cowardly to move against the war at the height of the fighting, congressmen tried to make up for lost time by massacring foreign aid, undermining American troop commitment to Europe, limiting presidential war powers, and blocking the bombing of Cambodia. Kissinger emerged as a major irritant to Congress. Shielded by "executive privilege" from direct congressional probing, he appeared as a sort of unreachable secretary of state, neither confirmed by nor answering to the Senate. He claimed he met with members of the Senate Foreign Relations Committee frequently though unofficially, but these meetings appeared to calm the Senåte little or not at all.

Given the factors of public opinion, economic difficulties, shrunken armed forces, and a newly reassertive Capitol Hill, any president in the early 1970s would have had to limit United States engagements abroad. Nixon and Kissinger thus appear as the right men at the right time. Their Democratic predecessors had expanded the postwar interventionism until it met with disaster; Nixon and Kissinger picked up a shipwrecked foreign policy and put it back together, this time with a sense of limits, of the "do-able," that Kennedy and Johnson lacked.

This is not to say that Nixon and Kissinger led an American retreat from world involvement. Indeed, Nixon labeled such a retreat "new isolationism" and sought to avoid it. Instead, he articulated a theme of carefully controlled pullback from Kennedy-style globalism. Speaking to newsmen informally on Guam in 1969, Nixon explained that the United States would provide a nuclear umbrella for its Asian allies in case of direct invasion, but the Asians would have to defend themselves against internal, guerrilla-type attack. The 1970 state of the world report to Congress, written by Kissinger and his staff with no help from the State Department, said that "America cannot—and will not—conceive *all* the plans, design *all* the programs, execute *all* the decisions and undertake *all* the defense of the free nations of the world. We will help where it makes a real difference and is considered in our interest." To sense the change that had occurred in American thinking over the decade, one need only compare this passage with President Kennedy's inaugural promise to "pay any price, bear any burden, meet any hardship, support any friend, oppose any foe to assure the survival and success of liberty."

The mind of America and the external world had both changed over the 1960s; more important than which had changed more, however, is the fact that changes in American orientation enabled its leaders to *perceive* that the external world had altered. The Sino-Soviet dispute had for some time fragmented the Communist world, but it took the anguish of Vietnam to elevate this perception to national policy. In the 1970 state of the world message, Nixon-Kissinger noted that "international communist unity has been shattered." Kissinger helped lay to rest one of his earlier stock themes, the presumed monolithic quality of the Communist bloc.

Indeed, American orientations had changed so much during the Vietnam era that a two-minute televised announcement by President Nixon on 15 July 1971 was greeted with amazement and approval: Nixon would visit Communist China and Kissinger had already been there secretly to work out the details. On 21 February 1972, TV satellite brought back from Peking images of the old Red baiter beaming at his Communist hosts, and the American people loved it.

It may be argued that a new United States–China relationship had been in the making for some time. The Kennedy administration dropped discreet hints in 1963 that things might change between the two countries. Peking reportedly extended initial feelers to the Johnson administration in 1964. By late 1968, China experts tended to agree, the Soviet invasion of Czechoslovakia so disturbed Peking that it reconsidered its hostility to America. Lyndon Johnson, however, busy waging a war against supposed Red Chinese surrogates and encumbered by a frozen-minded secretary of state who insisted that Peking be called by the old Nationalist name of Peiping, was in no position to strike off in new directions had he wished to.

Nixon was free to act with regard to China because he had striven for room to maneuver, with Kissinger's help. He backed up his Guam call for Asian self-reliance by cutting back American forces in Korea, Japan, Okinawa, Thailand, and the Philippines, to say nothing of withdrawing more than half a million U.S. troops from South Vietnam. Additionally, he relaxed trade and travel restrictions to China. Peking slowly reciprocated, and in April 1971 signaled its interest in a new relationship by inviting an American table tennis team to tour China; the breakthrough was dubbed "ping-pong diplomacy."

The evolution of the new China policy clarifies Kissinger's role in the Nixon administration. The basic idea seems not to have originated with him. Nixon came to the White House with such a détente in mind and ordered his assistant to get to work on it, but the execution of the idea was firmly in Kissinger's hands. Kissinger made two trips to Peking to set up the president's visit and another trip in February 1973 to conclude an agreement for each nation to open a "liaison office" (an embassy in all but name) in the other's capital. During that visit, a photograph of Kissinger emerging from a two-hour chat with Mao Tse-tung appeared on the front page of China's, and later the world's, newspapers.

At the same time, Soviet-American relations improved dramatically. This was possibly related to the Sino-American détente; perhaps the balance of power technique had worked with such precision that the specter of a tacit Peking-Washington entente pushed Moscow into new flexibility. Indeed, much happened in Soviet-American relations in 1972. The first part of the strategic arms limitation talks (SALT I) concluded in May with an agreement to limit defensive nuclear weapons. SALT II started with much broader aims in the fall of the same year. A three-day Kissinger visit to Moscow broke deadlocked talks on expanding bilateral trade. In November preliminary talks on a European security conference opened in Helsinki, and the conference itself began in July 1973. At the same time discussions on the mutual reduction of military forces in Eastern and Western Europe began in Vienna. Nixon and Brezhnev exchanged effusive visits in 1972 and 1973.

The cold war logjam was giving way; before attributing this solely to balance of power (or equilibrium of strength, as Kissinger might have it), one must be aware that the *sine qua non* of Soviet-American détente came with Willy Brandt's settlement of the German question in the Moscow Treaty of 12 August 1970. Bonn in effect admitted that German territories lost to Poland and Russia during World War II were gone for good and would never be claimed by Germany. The treaty between the two Germanies of 21 December 1972 further confirmed Bonn's acceptance of the results of the war by recognizing the division of Germany as all but permanent. The rapidity with which Moscow-Washington relations improved at this time suggests that, as far as the Russians were concerned, the cold war had been mostly a geopolitical question of German and Soviet boundaries rather than ideology. The détente in Europe, however, arose as much from Brandt's *Ostpolitik* as from the Soviet need to shift army divisions to the China frontier. The Soviets had considerable incentive for securing their European flank during a period of tension with China. Brandt's *Ostpolitik* gave them this opportunity. The importance of the China factor in Soviet policy toward Western Europe was not clear. The higher one appraises it, the more one turns to balance of power concepts; the lower one appraises it, the more one turns toward ideological, historical, economic, and other factors unrelated to balance of power. Perhaps the best one can say is that Brandt's election as chancellor and the Ussuri River clashes, both events occurring in 1969, were conducive to détente in Europe.

A little-noticed practical consequence of the Nixon-Kissinger policy was the American acceptance of the Soviet and Chinese positions in Europe and Asia, respectively. By supporting Brandt's treaties, Washington accepted division of Germany and implicitly the division of Europe. In coming to terms with Peking, Washington left the Nationalists on Taiwan to "negotiate" their future with the mainland. The only objections to these accommodations came from right wingers who were dismayed at America's "surrender" to communism. There was a grain of truth in such views; America had surrendered—not to communism, but to reality.

◇◇◇

If the rapprochements with the Soviet Union and China were successful, some other Nixon-Kissinger policies were not. Kissinger's most spectacular triumph seemed to be the cease-fire agreement reached with the North Vietnamese and Viet Cong in Paris on 27 January 1973. Kissinger worked on this for four years, making a total of twenty-four trips to Paris, at first secretly but later with crowds of newsmen outside the suburban meeting places.[5] President Nixon called the truce "peace with honor," but critics charged that it brought neither and could have been reached four years earlier. In truth, the Paris agreement had but two operative

---

5. The "official" Paris peace talks that proceeded simultaneously achieved nothing in 174 meetings, except perhaps agreement on the shape of the table.

clauses: the United States pulled out its last few thousand troops from South Vietnam, and the Communists released almost six hundred American prisoners of war. The rest of the document, a vague and complex variation of the 1954 Geneva accords, was inherently unworkable. The agreement left several North Vietnamese divisions in the south, did not delineate which side controlled which areas, and the fighting did not stop. Kissinger returned to Paris in June 1973 to reaffirm with the North Vietnamese the truce's provisions. The firing still did not cease, but the Americans were out, even if Saigon's long-term future was highly uncertain.

Kissinger, who as a professor had harped repeatedly on the impossibility of true negotiations between status quo and revolutionary powers, probably did not really think he had achieved a workable peace in Vietnam. His minimum goal was extrication without humiliation; for this he needed a "decent interval" between U.S. withdrawal and Communist take-over. The 1973 truce provided this interval, but not much else. It delayed both domestic and international reactions to the spectacle of America losing—or at any rate not winning—a war. The eventual fall of Saigon could bring those reactions out into the open with a vengeance. The "new isolationism" that Nixon strenuously sought to avoid was merely held in abeyance, not definitively squelched.

Vietnam had been an albatross around Kissinger's neck, and he clearly wanted to be rid of the miasma so he could move on to the overriding diplomatic questions of the epoch. As he expressed in 1971, "What we are doing now with China is so great, so historic, the word 'Vietnam' will be only a footnote when it is written in history." Kissinger was cognizant, however, of the other possibility. "Vietnam," he told newsmen early in his White House career, "may be one of those tragic issues that destroys everyone who touches it."

While American relations with the Soviet Union and China improved dramatically under Nixon, ties to Western Europe and Japan deteriorated noticeably. Chronic balance of payments deficits and related runs on the dollar gave Europeans and Japanese the impression that America did not have its economic house in order and shirked responsibility by accusing its trading partners of trade discrimination. Washington created further mistrust by dealing with Moscow and Peking over the heads of European and Japanese allies, respectively. Both Western Europe and Tokyo began to go their own ways, a backhanded testament to the efficacy of Nixon's balance of power maneuvers. If enemies did not need to be permanently hostile, allies did not need to be permanently friendly; partners could become rivals.

One clear-cut failure of the Nixon-Kissinger policy came in south Asia. While proclaiming neutrality in the 1971 India-Pakistan war over Bangladesh, word soon leaked out that Nixon had ordered Kissinger to "tilt" the United States in favor of Pakistan, which was in a morally indefensible position for slaughtering Bengalis. Informed observers held that Nixon wished to repay Pakistan for its help in arranging the China visits and to demonstrate to pro-Pakistan Peking that the United States and China had common interests against pro-India Moscow. If so, the move was a gratuitous one that gained America nothing but India's enmity.

$$\diamondsuit\!\!\diamondsuit\!\!\diamondsuit$$

The Kissinger period marked a major change in the thrust of post–World War II United States foreign policy. Kissinger helped end the cold war and make Washington's relations with its erstwhile archenemies, Moscow and Peking, almost normal. In doing so, he may have triggered unpredictable forces in Western Europe and Japan. He tried to reduce Vietnam to a footnote, but it loomed as a large, sad chapter. Probably his longest-lasting contribution, however, lay in helping introduce nonideological balance of power thinking into U.S. foreign policy.

The Kissinger legacy contained a distinct danger, namely, that after Kissinger moved on lesser figures might misuse a balance of power approach. For Kissinger, balance of power was a general attitude, not a fixed formula. Overeager policy makers might someday seize upon it and reduce it to an oversimplified doctrine. One is sobered to recall that a generation of policy makers thought they understood the "realist" lessons of Hans Morgenthau and George Kennan while they had merely picked up the surface toughness of the two thinkers, not their underlying rationality. One of Kissinger's pupils seems to have done just that. "I think it will be a safer world and a better world if we have a strong, healthy United States, Europe, Soviet Union, China, Japan, each balancing the other, not playing one against the other, an even balance," said Richard Nixon in 1971.

Kissinger sensed the problem in his 1968 essay on Bismarck: "Bismarck's less imaginative successors failed even when they strove for 'calculability' or 'reliability.' These qualities seemed more easily attainable by rigid commitments than by the delicate, constantly shifting balancing of Bismarck's policy." Thus the problem of how to institutionalize inspiration faced Kissinger as he became secretary of state in September 1973. The reinvigoration of the moribund State Department bureaucracy was perhaps his greatest challenge. If he failed to impart his individual wisdom to that unreceptive institution, then his comment on Bismarck eventually might serve as Kissinger's own epitaph: "Statesmen who build lastingly transform the personal act of creation into institutions that can be maintained by an average standard of performance. This Bismarck proved incapable of doing."

BIBLIOGRAPHIC NOTE

Kissingerology is a new field, and little has been published on Kissinger himself. One book-length treatment by David Landau, *Kissinger: The Uses of Power* (Boston, 1972), is extremely useful on Kissinger's background, but concentrates excessively on Vietnam as if it were Kissinger's policy rather than Nixon's, and came out before the Paris agreement. Landau adopted the view, current among many critics at the time, that the various Nixon escalations (Cambodia, Laos, mining of North Vietnamese ports, etc.) indicated an obdurate refusal to end American participation. This view is time bound, and the Landau book was dated within a few months of its publication. British journalist Henry Brandon explores the relationship between Nixon and Kissinger in *The Retreat of American Power* (Garden City, N.Y., 1972), which also ends before the Paris accord. A detailed analysis of Kissinger's published works appears in Stephen R. Graubard, *Kissinger: Portrait of a Mind* (New York, 1973).

To understand Kissinger's times, the quarterly *Foreign Policy* (not the stodgy *Foreign Affairs*) is indispensable. It first appeared at the end of 1970 with a generally reformist-critical orientation. Particularly important is number 5 (Winter 1971–72), which contains two helpful articles: "Kissinger's Apparat," by John P. Leacacos, and I. M. Destler, "Can One Man Do?" The radical commentator I. F. Stone cast jaundiced looks at Kissinger in *The New York Review of Books*, 19 October and 2 November 1972.

Although the China breakthrough came as a surprise in 1971, an article in 1969 was oddly prescient and may have paralleled thinking that was going on in the White House. See John Paton Davies, "The U.S. Invented the 'Imbalance of Power,'" *New York Times Magazine*, 7 December 1969. Davies, a former State Department China hand, was purged by Dulles. The article can be read as an exhortation to pursue the course Nixon and Kissinger ultimately did follow.

NOTES ON THE CONTRIBUTORS

Russell D. Buhite, associate professor of history at the University of Oklahoma, studied with Paul Varg at Michigan State University, where he received his Ph.D. in 1965. He has written biographies of two important figures in American-Chinese diplomacy: *Nelson T. Johnson and American Policy toward China, 1925–1941* (East Lansing, Mich., 1968), and *Patrick J. Hurley and American Foreign Policy* (Ithaca, 1973). In addition, Professor Buhite has edited the volume on the Far East in *The Dynamics of World Power: A Documentary History of U.S. Foreign Policy, 1945–1973* (New York, 1973), and is currently writing a book on Soviet-American relations.

James B. Chapin, assistant professor of history at University College, Rutgers University, studied with Walter LaFeber at Cornell, where he received his Ph.D. in 1971. He is now at work on a study of Rhode Island politics from 1776 to 1865 and is revising his doctoral thesis, "Hamilton Fish and American Expansion," for publication.

Cecil B. Currey, professor of history at the University of South Florida, studied with W. Stitt Robinson at the University of Kansas, where he received his Ph.D. in 1964. His publications include *The Road to Revolution: Benjamin Franklin in England, 1765–1775* (New York, 1968) and *Code Number 72: Ben Franklin, Patriot or Spy* (Englewood Cliffs, N.J., 1972).

Charles DeBenedetti, associate professor of history at the University of Toledo, studied with Norman Graebner and J. Leonard Bates at the University of Illinois, where he received his Ph.D. in 1968. He has published a number of articles on American diplomacy and is currently completing a book on the peace movement and American foreign policy during the period 1919–29.

Robert A. Divine, professor of history at the University of Texas, Austin, studied with Ralph Gabriel at Yale University, where he received his Ph.D. in 1954. Among other works, he has published *American Immigration Policy, 1924–1952* (New Haven, 1957), *The Illusion of Neutrality* (Chicago, 1962), *Second Chance: The Triumph of Internationalism in America during World War II* (New York, 1967), and *Roosevelt and World War II* (Baltimore, 1969). He is general editor of the Wiley series on American diplomatic history, and his most recent work is *Foreign Policy and U.S. Presidential Elections, 1940–1960* (New York, 1974).

Robert H. Ferrell, professor of history at Indiana University, studied with Samuel Flagg Bemis at Yale, where he received his Ph.D. in 1951. He has published voluminously on the subject of diplomatic history and has served as editor of the updated American Secretaries of State series (for which he wrote the volumes on Kellogg-Stimson and Marshall). His major works include *Peace in Their Time: The Origins of the Kellogg-Briand Pact* (New Haven, 1952) and *American Diplomacy in the Great Depression* (New Haven, 1957), and he is now working on a volume in the New American Nation series covering the years from 1917 to 1921. Professor Ferrell is a past president of the Society for Historians of American Foreign Relations.

John Lewis Gaddis, associate professor of history at Ohio University, studied with Robert Divine at the University of Texas, where he received his Ph.D. in 1968. He is the author of *The United States and the Origins of the Cold War* (New York, 1972), which received the Bancroft Prize for history. He is currently writing an analysis of Russian-American relations from 1781 to 1973 and is preparing a sequel to his book on the origins of the cold war.

Norman A. Graebner, Edward R. Stettinius Professor of History at the University of Virginia, holds a Ph.D. from the University of Chicago. Among his many works in American history are *Empire on the Pacific* (New York, 1955), *The New Isolationism* (New York, 1956), *Cold War Diplomacy* (Princeton, 1962), and *Ideas and Diplomacy* (New York, 1964); his latest book is *Recent United States History* (New York, 1972). In addition, he has edited a number of important collections of documents and essays in the field of American diplomacy, including *An Uncertain Tradition: American Secretaries of State in the Twentieth Century* (New York, 1961). Professor Graebner is a past president of the Society for Historians of American Foreign Relations.

Ross Gregory, professor of history at Western Michigan University, studied with Robert H. Ferrell at Indiana University, where he received his Ph.D. in 1964. His *Walter Hines Page: Ambassador to the Court of St. James's* (Lexington, Ky., 1970) won the Frederick Jackson Turner Prize; in addition, he has published *The Origins of American Intervention in the First World War* (New York, 1971). Professor Gregory's current project is a study of American life during World War II.

Kenneth J. Hagan, assistant professor of history at the U.S. Naval Academy, studied with Charles S. Campbell at the Claremont Graduate School, where he received his Ph.D. in 1970. He has recently published *American Gunboat Diplomacy and the Old Navy, 1877–1889* (Westport, Conn., 1973), and is compiling a bibliography of nineteenth-century American naval history.

Helen Dodson Kahn resides in Columbus, Ohio; she studied with Walter LaFeber at Cornell, where she received her Ph.D. in 1968. She is now working on a full-length biography of Willard Straight.

William Kamman, professor of history at North Texas State University, studied with Robert H. Ferrell at Indiana University, where he received his Ph.D. in 1962. He has published *A Search for Stability: United States Diplomacy toward Nicaragua, 1925–1933* (South Bend, 1968), and he is writing a multiarchival study of American–Central American relations in the 1930s.

Lawrence S. Kaplan, professor of history at Kent State University, studied with Samuel Flagg Bemis at Yale, where he received his Ph.D. in 1951. He has published extensively on the diplomacy of the early national period, as well as on twentieth-century American foreign policy; his works include *Jefferson and France* (New Haven, 1967) and *Colonies into Nation: American Diplomacy, 1763–1801* (New York, 1972). He is currently at work on a cultural history of American foreign relations.

Lester D. Langley, associate professor of history at the University of Georgia, studied with Charles Stansifer at the University of Kansas, where he received his Ph.D. in 1965. Among other works he has published *The Cuban Policy of the United States* (New York, 1968), and he has edited *The United States, Cuba, and the Cold War* (Lexington, Mass., 1970) and *The United States and Latin America* (Reading, Mass., 1971). Professor Langley is currently at work on a book-length study, *Andrew Jackson and the World.*

Richard D. McKinzie, associate professor of history at the University of Missouri, Kansas City, studied with John Wiltz at Indiana University, where he received his Ph.D. in 1969. A research associate at the Harry S. Truman Library Institute since 1969, Professor McKinzie has written a number of articles on the diplomacy of the Roosevelt-Truman period; he is the author of *The New Deal for Artists* (Princeton, 1973) and (with T. A. Wilson) is working on a study of foreign aid in the Truman administration. In addition, he is a coauthor of a forthcoming textbook of twentieth-century United States history.

David McLellan, professor of political science at Miami University (Ohio), received his Ph.D. from Yale University in 1954. He has written *The Cold War in Transition* (New York, 1966) and coauthored *The Theory and Practice of International Relations* (Englewood Cliffs, N.J., 1970). Professor McLellan is currently preparing a biography of Dean Acheson.

Frank J. Merli, associate professor of history at Queens College of The City University of New York, studied with Robert H. Ferrell at Indiana University, where he received his Ph.D. in 1964. He has written *Great Britain and the Confederate Navy, 1861–1865* (Bloomington, 1970), and is currently preparing a book on nineteenth-century neutrality from 1819 to 1919.

Ian Mugridge, assistant professor of history and assistant vice-president for academic affairs at Simon Fraser University, studied with Alexander DeConde at the University of California, Santa Barbara, where he received his Ph.D. in 1969. He is currently working on an analysis of foreign influences on the making of the U.S. Constitution; in addition, he is editing the American correspondence of Sir Robert Liston and is preparing a monograph on William Randolph Hearst and American foreign policy.

Herbert S. Parmet, associate professor of history at Queensborough Community College of The City University of New York, has written widely about American political history and biography. His published works include *Aaron Burr: Portrait of an Ambitious Man* (New York, 1967) (with Marie B. Hecht), *Never Again: A President Runs for a Third Term* (New York, 1968), and *Eisenhower and the American Crusades* (New York, 1972). Professor Parmet is currently writing a history of the Democratic party since 1945.

Thomas G. Paterson, professor of history at the University of Connecticut, received his Ph.D. in 1968 from the University of California, Berkeley. He is the author of *Soviet-American Confrontation: Postwar Reconstruction and the Origins of the Cold War* (Baltimore, 1973). In addition, he has written a number of articles and edited several important books on recent diplomacy, including *Cold War Critics: Alternatives to American Foreign Policy in the Truman Years* (Chicago, 1971), *The Origins of the Cold War* (Lexington, Mass., 1970), *American Imperialism and Anti-Imperialism* (New York, 1973), and *Containment and the Cold War* (Reading, Mass., 1973). Professor Paterson is currently writing a book on the Truman Doctrine and containment, 1945–75.

David M. Pletcher, professor of history at Indiana University, studied with J. Fred Rippy at the University of Chicago, where he received his Ph.D. in 1946. Among his many publications are *Rails, Mines, and Progress: Seven*

American Promoters in Mexico, 1867–1911 (Ithaca, 1958), *The Awkward Years: American Foreign Relations under Garfield and Arthur* (Columbia, Mo., 1962), and *The Diplomacy of Annexation: Texas, Oregon, and the Mexican War* (Columbia, Mo., 1973).

Michael Roskin, assistant professor of political science at Lycoming College and former Foreign Service officer and newspaperman, studied with Marian Irish at American University, where he received his Ph.D. in 1972. He has published articles on American diplomacy in *Foreign Policy* and *Le Monde Diplomatique.*

Geoffrey S. Smith, associate professor of history at Queen's University, Ontario, studied with Alexander DeConde at the University of California, Santa Barbara, where he received his Ph.D. in 1969. In addition to a number of articles on Latin American history, he has written *To Save a Nation: American Countersubversives, the New Deal, and the Coming of World War II* (New York, 1973). He is currently working on a full-length biography of Charles Wilkes and a study tentatively entitled *The Bifocal Vision in American Foreign Relations: A Study of American Images of Europe and Asia.*

Eugene P. Trani, associate professor of history at Southern Illinois University, studied with Robert H. Ferrell at Indiana University, where he received his Ph.D. in 1966. In addition to a large number of articles, he has published *The Treaty of Portsmouth: An Adventure in American Diplomacy* (Lexington, Ky., 1969), and he is working on a study of Woodrow Wilson and Russia, 1913–21, which has been supported by a NEH Younger Humanist Award. During 1972–73, Professor Trani was a fellow at the Woodrow Wilson International Center for Scholars.

David F. Trask, professor of history and chairman of that department at the State University of New York, Stony Brook, studied with Ernest May at Harvard University, where he received his doctorate in 1958. He has written *The United States in the Supreme War Council: American War Aims and Inter-Allied Strategy, 1917–1918* (Middletown, Conn., 1961), *General Tasker Howard Bliss and the "Sessions of the World," 1919* (Philadelphia, 1966), *Victory without Peace: American Foreign Relations in the Twentieth Century* (New York, 1968), and, most recently, *Captains and Cabinets: Anglo-American Naval Relations, 1917–1918* (Columbia, Mo., 1972). He was a coeditor of *A Bibliography of United States-Latin American Relations since 1810* (Lincoln, Nebr., 1968) and has edited *World War I at Home: Readings on American Life, 1914–1920* (New York, 1970). His current project is a military and naval history of the Spanish-American War.

Gordon H. Warren, assistant professor of history at Central Washington State College, studied with Robert H. Ferrell at Indiana University, where he received his Ph.D. in 1969. He is currently preparing his doctoral thesis on the *Trent* affair for publication and is working on a soon-to-be-published study of American entry into wars, *Firing the First Shot.*

Patrick C. T. White, professor of history at the University of Toronto, did graduate work at Cambridge University and received his doctorate from the University of Minnesota in 1953. A specialist in Canadian and American diplomacy, he is preparing a history of Canadian-American relations from 1815 to 1846. His publications include *A Nation on Trial: America and the War of 1812* (New York, 1965), and he has edited (with an introduction) *Lord Selkirk's Diary, 1803–1804* (Toronto, 1958), *The Critical Years: American Foreign Policy, 1793–1823* (New York, 1970), and (with an introduction) *Conducting the Diplomacy of the New Nation, 1793–1815* (New York, 1971).

Theodore A. Wilson, professor of history at the University of Kansas, studied with Robert H. Ferrell at Indiana University, where he received his Ph.D. in 1966. He has published *The First Summit: Roosevelt and Churchill at Placentia Bay, 1941* (Boston, 1969), which was awarded the Francis Parkman Prize. Professor Wilson has served as senior research associate at the Harry S. Truman Library Institute and has received fellowships from the National Endowment for the Humanities and the Guggenheim Foundation. He is currently completing a study of the origins of foreign aid, 1943–53 (with Richard McKinzie), and preparing a biography of Henry A. Wallace.

INDEX

Aberdeen, earl of, 169–70, 172, 177, 181

Abolitionist movement, 176

Acheson, Dean, 523–52; and Acheson-Lilienthal Plan, 530; and administration of State Department, 529; as assistant secretary, 528; background of, 525–27; as Byrnes's undersecretary, 530; China policy of, 543, 544–45; compared with Dulles, 597; and containment, 511; and Cuban invasion, 629; and disengagement, 581–82; European policy of, 538; Far Eastern policy of, 540–45, 546–48; and German unification, 577–78; and Japanese Peace Treaty, 545–46; and Kennan, 572, 578–79; and Korean War, 517, 542–44; mentioned, 577, 654; and NATO, 538–40; and NSC-68, 537; recommendations on Berlin, 633; relations with Truman, 508, 509, 530–31, 548; and United Nations, 533; unpopularity of, 548–49; and

Vietnam, 550, 584; views of, on Russia, 531–32, 533, 534, 535–38; writings of, 550–51

Acheson-Lilienthal Plan, 530

Adams, Brooks, 308

Adams, Charles Francis, 204–5, 211–12

Adams, Henry, 209, 234, 248, 308

Adams, John, 12–13, 62, 84, 105, 115–16

Adams, John Quincy, 105–33; advocates naval exploration, 138, 140; attitude of, toward partisanship, 110; background of, 105; characteristics of, 107–8, 110; early career of, 106–7; and embargo, 95; as expansionist, 112; and Federalists, 106, 110; and fishing rights, 117; and Florida purchase, 120–21; and Holy Alliance, 114; and intervention in Greece, 129; and Jackson, 119; Latin American policy of, 122–25, 127,130; and Louisiana, 118–21; and military preparedness, 112; and Monroe Doctrine, 20, 127, 128–30;